Old La

14 November 2005

For Francis

Old Labour to New

The Dreams that Inspired, the Battles that Divided

Greg Rosen

Hope you enjoy it
Even if you don't agree with
all of it....
Though I hope you will with much
of it.

Kindest wishes

First published in 2005
Politico's Publishing, an imprint of
Methuen Publishing Limited
11–12 Buckingham Gate
London
SW1E 6LB

10 9 8 7 6 5 4 3 2 1

Designed and typeset by Louise Millar

Printed and bound in Great Britain by St. Edmundsbury Press, Bury St Edmunds, Suffolk

Methuen Publishing Limited Reg. No. 3543167

A CIP catalogue record for this book is available from the British Library.

ISBN 1 84275 045 3

For John Brown and Bernard Crick
who continue to inspire

Acknowledgements

I owe an overwhelming debt of gratitude to all those whose patient support for my historical endeavours have made this book possible. Marie Woolf gave invaluable encouragement and advice throughout, and for their enthusiasm and wise counsel I am also grateful to Lewis Baston; Professor Brian Brivati; Dr John Brown; Jayant Chavda; Professor Sir Bernard Crick; Lord Graham of Edmonton; Jennifer Gerber; Dianne Hayter; Professor George Jones; Phil Larkin; Lord Lea; Patrick Loughran; Professor the Lord Morgan; Rex Osborn; Jonathan Pearce; Kath Raymond; Anne Reisinger; Paul Richards; Lord Sawyer; Matthew Seward; John Schwartz and also to Luke Akehurst; Jessica Asato and Gareth Butler; Jonathan Ashworth; Emily Bearn; Adam Bowen and Alaina McDonald; Beth Breeze; D-J Collins; Clare Cox; Tam Dalyell; Laura Davies; Howard Dawber; the late Henry Drucker; Vicky Fewkes; Mark Glover and Johanna Baxter; Dr Richard Grayson; Melanie Greenall; Professor Peter Hennessy; Sir Ken and Lady Rene Jackson; Stephen Joseph; James Kirkup and Holly Crane; Jemima Kiss; Sara Knockton; Karen Landles; Dr John Lloyd; Dickson Mabon; Una Maclean Mackintosh; Bronwen Maddox; Seema Malhotra; Lord Merlyn-Rees; Andrew Pakes; Rebecca Price; Paul Routledge; Robert Taylor; Anna Turley; David Turner; Tom Watson MP; Sam White; Phillip Whitehead MEP; Mark Dolan; Peter Tavy; Will and Mick Sergeant; James Longworth and Ed Pybus.

My family has been a constant source of inspiration: my parents, Fred and Maria, my brother Alex, and my grandmother, whose historical perspective now stretches to more than ninety-seven years. Penelope has tolerated my historical preoccupations with fortitude, and at some of the most important junctures, including on beautiful Oxleas afternoons, helped me to see the woods for the trees.

For their patience and humour, I am of course grateful to the NSN24 team; to my old Home Office colleagues, Nicky, Helen, Ben, Katrina and the team; and to all my old AEEU comrades to whom I owe so much.

I am grateful to Michael Foot for his kindness in contributing the foreword and for his hospitality over several balmy summer mornings of historical discussion and reflection. Lord Sawyer took time out not only to give me the benefit of his insights into the period of his involvement with the Labour Movement but to let me loose on his collection of particularly difficult to get hold-of books on the Labour Party. Others who took the time to write or discuss their historical recollections and insights, to whom I am profoundly grateful, include: Andrew Adonis; Janet Anderson MP; Rt Hon Lord Archer of Sandwell; Jonathan Ashworth; Lewis Baston; David Bean QC; Rt Hon Margaret Beckett

MP; Rt Hon. Hilary Benn MP; Rt Hon. Tony Benn; Hazel Blears MP; Rt Hon David Blunkett MP; Rt Hon Albert Booth; Professor Brian Brivati; Rt Hon Gordon Brown MP; Dr John Brown; Rt Hon. Nick Brown MP; the late Lord Callaghan; Danny Carrigan; Matt Carter; Jim Cattermole; Alexander Chancellor; Jayant Chavda; David and Clare Clark; Rt Hon. Tom Clark MP; the late Lord Cledwyn of Penrhos; Rt Hon. Anne Clwyd MP; Michael Cockerell; Nicci Collins; Nick Comfort; Mike Craven; Dan Crewe; Professor Sir Bernard Crick; Michael Crick; Tam Dalyell; the later Donald Dewar; Lord Donoughue; Lord Ewing of Kirkford; Rt Hon. Frank Field MP; Rt Hon Michael Foot; Rt Hon Lord Foulkes; Noel Foy, Russell Galbraith, Nicky Gavron; Rt Hon Lord Glenamara; Geoffrey Goodman; Andrew Graham; Rt Hon Lord Graham of Edmonton; Andrew Grice; Nigel Griffiths MP; Joe Haines; Tony Halmos; Dianne Hayter; Rt Hon. Lord Healey; Rt Hon. Patricia Hewitt MP; David Hill; Bob Houston; Joe Irvin; the late Lord Jenkins of Hillhead; Professor Kevin Jefferys; Jack Jones; Professor George Jones; Eric Joyce MP; Peter Kellner; Fraser Kemp MP, Peter Kilfoyle MP; Dave King; Oona King; James Kirkup; Professor Keith Laybourn; Helen Liddell; Roger Liddle; Dr John Lloyd; Rt Hon. Dr. Dickson Mabon; Rt Hon. Ian McCartney MP; Don Macintyre; Andrew MacKinley MP; Lord McNally; Denis MacShane MP; Andy McSmith; Professor David Marquand; Bob Marshall-Andrews MP; Rt Hon. Lord Merlyn-Rees; Rt Hon Bruce Millan; Austin Mitchell MP; Chris Moncrief; Professor the Lord Morgan; Oliver Morgan; Richard Olszewski; Professor Robert Pearce; the late Professor Ben Pimlott; John Rentoul; Rt Hon. Lord Rodgers of Quarry Bank; Paul Routledge; Baroness Smith of Gilmourhill; Professor John Shepherd; Rt Hon Anne Taylor MP; Robert Taylor; Lord Thomson of Monifieth; Charlie Turnock; Bill Weale; Professor Mark Wickham-Jones; Professor Alan Lee Williams; Phil Wilson; Phil Woolas MP; Marie Woolf; Professor Chris Wrigley; and Dr Tony Wright MP.

The process of tracking speeches down was not always simple and I am grateful in particular for the research assistance of Vicky Fewkes, Joe Perry and Erin Sapp; and also to Gina Page; Una Maclean Mackintosh; Professor Brian Brivati; Michael Foot; Lord Rodgers of Quarry Bank; Dr John Lloyd; Lord Sawyer; Ray Collins and his colleagues at the TGWU; John Bird at the National Museum of Labour History; to Audrey Canning and Carole McCallum at the Gallagher Memorial Library, Glasgow Caledonian University; Clare Foges and the staff at the British Library; Westminster City Library; TUC library; House of Commons library, Seeta, Catherine, and everyone else who has been so helpful at the Adam Street library and the Home Office library. For practical assistance I am also indebted to the Rt Hon John Spellar MP, Kate Spicer and the late Lord Chapple of Hoxton.

The necessary process of transcribing speeches was accomplished through the invaluable efforts of a team assembled with the help of Sarah Gillinson and Jessica Asato, whose unstinting efforts made this book possible: Duncan Adam; Matthew Blakely;

Daniel Brett; Kris Brown; Shaun Carroll; Lisa Cunningham; Frances Downey; Gareth Evans; Judith Evans; Hannah Green; Stephen Griffiths; Dan Hancox; Gareth Harrison; Alex Hilton; Abigail Hudson; Mirelle Kaiser; Richard Lomas; Helen McCabe; Glen Mitchell; Emma Musgrave; Rob Newman; Sharon O'Dea; Ketrin Oravecz; Mark Pritchard; David Shaw; Adam Short; Rohan Silva; Luke Smith; Sophie Sutcliffe; Emily Todd; Richard Tooner; Anand Verma; Jane Walker; Chris Wearmouth; Nick Wong; Oliver Wooding; and Patrick Woodman.

Integral to this book has been the fantastic team at Politicos Publishing: Peter Tummons; my editors, successively John Schwartz, Sean Magee, and Alan Gordon Walker, and Emma Musgrave, who all gave generously and patiently of their time and considerable expertise; and Peter Clark who kindly read and commented upon an early draft. Their combined commitment made this book possible.

Unless otherwise credited, all excerpts from speeches included in this volume have been quoted as transcribed either in Hansard (if made in Parliament) or in the official conference reports (if made at Labour Party conference or TUC). For permission to quote from copyright material I am grateful to Matt Carter and Melanie Onn at the Labour Party for permission to reproduce the speeches delivered at Labour Party conferences, which remain (c) the Labour Party. I am also grateful to Chloe and Cressida Wasserman and to Julia McNeal; to Gordon Brown; to the late Lord Callaghan; to Lord Rodgers of Quarry Bank; and to Baroness Smith. Every effort has been made to contact copyright holders. The publishers will be glad to rectify, in future editions, any errors or omissions brought to their notice.

Contents

Foreword

by Michael Foot

It was for a comparatively short period that public speaking was the most important means of political communication: from the last decade of the 19th century when Keir Hardie was making his speeches, until the arrival of radio and television. Democracy was bringing more people into the argument and the public meeting was the place where it was done.

I first heard Ramsay MacDonald when I was at school. I went down to Reading just after the 1924 election when the Tories had done the dirty on Labour with the 'Red Letter'. He made a wonderful and long speech. He had great powers of oratory, though he did not quite convert me then! Emmeline Pankhurst showed what a woman could do from the platform at a time that people didn't think women should be seen on the platform, but the best of the speakers then, particularly at the time of the People's Budget, was Lloyd George, partly because he was Welsh no doubt. Lloyd George, like Nye Bevan, had a wonderful wit which he used on the platform. There were quite a few others who were good at it. The Labour movement was built by them. Ben Tillett I heard the first time I went down to Hyde Park to a big public meeting. I used to go down there when I first came to London in 1935. Tom Mann, though no longer at his peak, I heard too. They had led the dock strikes of the 1890s when the Labour movement was taking over from the Liberals.

Maxton I heard also in the Commons. Like Nye he was good in both but on the platform he was better. Maxton's last speech I heard him make was very moving, he was wishing good luck to the Labour Party even though he had had arguments with it; he was very moved by the Labour victory in 1945. He was a wonderful, witty speaker. Churchill said that too about Maxton. Nye and Jennie had criticisms about him. I don't think he worried so much about whether he would have immediate political victories but he had a real mastery of every audience.

My first Labour conference was at Westminster Central Hall in 1944. It was in London because of the war. That was where Ian Mikardo made his speech on nationalisation. Of the speeches Attlee made in the 1945 election the most powerful was his answer to Churchill's radio broadcast. Nye would make insulting remarks about the way Attlee could 'reduce the atmosphere'; nonetheless what he said was of some importance! The chaps who were really steaming it up in 1945, though, were the people on the left.

The best of the lot was Nye Bevan. Nye never lost his admiration for the way Lloyd George made his speeches. It was partly from Lloyd George that others learned.

Without the people on the platform, the Labour movement wouldn't have been able to develop in the way it did. It was the speakers on the platform who built the Labour movement and inspired it most of all. Many were great debaters too. Bevan was the best. He would say you must go for the strength of the opponent's case, not the weakness. If you go for the weakness you may pick up a few trifles. 'He's a snapper up of trifles,' he used to say rather derogatorily about Herbert Morrison. It's a different thing from winning the actual argument.

I wasn't so much in favour of Nye's most famous speech: the naked into the conference chamber speech. I am quite sure he was absolutely sincere in what he was saying. When he's in a debate he wants to win. I didn't think it was as good as the speech he made in Trafalgar Square, which I also heard, on the Suez crisis. It's one of the few of his properly recorded. I remember coming into the back of that huge great meeting. He says about Eden, 'If that's what he thinks,' and Nye had a stutter, 'then he's too st-st-stupid to be Prime Minister.' We play it in Ebbw Vale when they hold memorial meetings.

Another one was the one Bevan made in the debate with Churchill on devaluation in 1949. Churchill couldn't avoid speaking, he had always tried to avoid Nye, who said, when the Tories want to get rid of you, they'll throw you away like a soiled glove, which is what they did in the end. It saved the Labour Party at that time and justified the Labour government.

Another great occasion was when he introduced the Health Service and the Tories tried to disrupt the whole thing. One of Nye's speeches which made a great impact was the speech he made at the end of the last Labour conference he attended, after we had been defeated at the 1959 election. There was a debate about what we should do about the defeat and whether we should abandon nationalisation in order to accommodate the electorate. Nye spoke then at that conference. I put him number one.

Of my own speeches there is one at the very end of the government in 1979 when we were defeated; we'd only just introduced radio into the Commons, which was pretty good. That speech, the part of it that I think best, is the end of it. At the beginning I was just trying to pay off old Commons scores, I was referring to what that government had done, it was a decent government and what a tragedy it was that it would go because then we would have Thatcher. The first major speech I made as Employment Secretary, in that new Parliament of '74, we hadn't got a full majority. We were wanting to work to get a decent majority. I was putting the case for the government. That was a pretty good speech too.

One of the best speeches I made, I think, was on the social contract at the 1975 party conference. Mervyn Jones said I misquoted Conrad but that's not true! Jack Jones spoke up too. I had very close relations with Jack throughout that government. I would never have had the employment job without him. We were defending decent policies and carrying out the manifesto, working right from the beginning in absolute collaboration with the TUC. The social contract was very different from what the previous government had done. The £6 across the board was a good deal for low-paid workers.

I remember after the referendum on the EEC in 1975, someone asked Tony Benn if he had a message for the British people. He made a witty reply, because he could be very witty, and said: 'It looks as if the British people have sent a message to me.' I was a strong supporter of the referendum. We couldn't have held the Labour Party together without it. I think it was perfectly properly conducted and it did hold the Labour Party together. In the same way now I think we should have a proper debate though I would vote yes this time.

There were quite a number of people then who felt very strongly that we should not cut off our relations with Europe and we needed to take that into account. Some of the people who felt that way were special friends of mine, that is to say John Smith, Harold Lever, Roy Hattersley and Joel Barnett, who had all voted with Roy Jenkins in the rebellion in 1971. If they had left the Labour Party in 1983, there wouldn't have been any Labour Party left at all. We did our best to persuade them to stay. Shirley Williams I pleaded with to stay in 1981; nobody would be asking her to vote against her conscience on Europe. Some of them were being tackled in their constituencies by supporters of Tony Benn, saying that they must make up their minds between supporting the Common Market and staying in the Labour Party.

I went to several of these constituencies and said, 'No that's quite wrong, we're not driving anybody out of this party because he takes a different view on this.' Gerald Kaufman came to me, quite honestly, just before the 1983 election, just when it had been announced, and said that he thought I should resign and hand over the leadership to Denis Healey. I thought, if I resign now, the election has been declared, the whole thing will turn on the argument over whether Tony Benn will be the next leader, and Healey had only just held on as deputy.

Neil Kinnock's speech, 'I warn you not to be poor,' was the best thing at that terrible election of 1983, and his speeches on education were very fine. We were having a very bad time at that election, there is no doubt, with people arguing about what we were going to do about the bomb. His speech about Militant at the 1985 conference I thought was magnificent and absolutely right.

The autocue is destroying the spontaneity of modern speeches. The first person I saw using it in action was Ronald Reagan. He spoke to a joint meeting of the Commons and Lords with this machine. I didn't know what the thing was until I saw it. It has almost become regularly used now by the party leaders. The Tory leaders are doing it:

Iain Duncan Smith, Thatcher. John Smith used it, though he wouldn't have got his position if he had not been one of the very best at putting the Tories on the defensive in the Commons. Some of his speeches are the most memorable of the lot. Tony Blair has used it at party conferences, although he's not reliant on it as he's a very good speaker himself. Blair's speech to the House of Commons when we went to war was impressive. Nobody could make a speech like that and not believe it. He's a very good speaker too. I disagreed with it, because I thought we should have continued with negotiations, but there were no autocues there!

Introduction

It has become a commonplace in some quarters for 1994 to be presented as a kind of 'Year Zero', dividing a distinct and pre-existing 'Old Labour' from 'New Labour'. Partly to blame for this myth-making are the ahistorical handful among those whom the late James Callaghan called 'that splendid army of young recruits to the Labour Party to whom all this is history'.[1] Equally guilty are those critics of 'New Labour' who have sought to reinvent a mythical golden age of Labour politics pre-1994 and claim that Labour has somehow been hijacked and, via the 'abolition' of Clause Four, turned into a different party from that to which they lay proprietorial claim.

Like all governments, Tony Blair's have had unique and distinctive aspects. Nevertheless, between the Labour Party of today and that of a century ago there are elements of profound, often unnoticed and sometimes surprising continuity.

A recurrent theme in many of Blair's speeches has been an acknowledgement of the progressive tradition of Liberals such as David Lloyd George and William Beveridge. This reflected his appreciation of the fact that the twentieth century, partly because of the split between the two non-Conservative parties, was a 'conservative century', with the Conservative Party being in power far longer than the other two parties combined. This book seeks to explain why that split took place. Other splits occurred from within Labour's own ranks. Some of Labour's greatest figures, including Ramsay MacDonald, Philip Snowden, Roy Jenkins and George Brown, now feature in the gallery of those (in the words of the Red Flag) Labour traitors who flinched and cowards who sneered, begging the question of how they became sufficiently revered to cause such damage in the first place and why they should want to break away. Why has Labour so frequently tried to rip itself apart? During the 1930s, the 1950s and the 1980s, the battle for Labour's soul between rival orthodoxies, between rival faiths each with its own high priests, expulsions, denunciations and protestations against 'witch-hunts' were rife. How could one party spawn so many feuding traditions?

Tony Benn famously argues that the Labour Party is about issues, not personalities, but in truth the issues sometimes are the personalities, and the personalities the issues. As Professor Kenneth Morgan has written,

> The British Labour movement has always venerated the collective ideal ... Yet it is one
> of the paradoxes of our culture that a party that came into being as a protest against
> the excesses of individualism can go to extreme lengths to perpetuate the cult of per-

sonality. More than the Conservatives have ever done, Labour draws constant inspiration from the ideas and achievements of key individuals . . . since Labour necessarily arose to represent the poor and inarticulate, its need for charismatic individuals has been all the greater than that of its better-endowed opponents.[2]

The Labour Party is not for nothing known as the people's party: it is about people. Issues become personified, those who can articulate them most effectively become the standard bearers for the causes they espouse: the figureheads for the Bevanites, the Gaitskellites, the Bennites and the Blairites.

It is now over a century since the Labour Party was formed, as Ernest Bevin famously described, out of the bowels of the Trades Union Congress. Though it was not until 1899 that the TUC resolved to create the Labour Party, and 1900 before it had its founding conference, it was the campaigns of Keir Hardie and the socialists of the Independent Labour Party over the previous decade that provided the spark that ignited the TUC tinder. Central to the propaganda battle that rallied people to Labour's red flag were the speeches that articulated a vision of a New Jerusalem, that exposed the hollow failure of Liberal and Conservative promises, that explained to radical working-class men the need to split with Liberalism and form a new party, that pledged women the vote, and that appealed to hearts and to heads. Many of the early Labour orators had the religious fervour of the Methodist lay preachers that they often, in fact, were. Others owed their style to the frequent toe-to-toe confrontations at the factory gates between rival union leaders, some of whom were Marxist, others not.

In the great battles for Labour's soul, the weapon was the word and the word was at its most powerful when wielded by some of the finest orators that politics has known. Whether it be the rapier wit of an Aneurin Bevan or a Robin Cook, or the heavy calibre broadside of an Ernest Bevin, the raw power of the speeches that shaped the Labour Party was often decisive, making and breaking careers in the process. Some speeches, such as Ernest Bevin's 'Dockers' KC' speech in 1920 or Denis Healey's speech to Labour conference in 1945, made reputations. Barbara Castle's 'jam today' speech in 1943 even found her a husband. Others, such as Ernest Bevin's attack on George Lansbury's pacifism in 1935, were destructive, providing, as occurred with the rows between Herbert Morrison and Bevin over nationalisation in 1932 and between Denis Healey and Clive Jenkins over import controls in 1975, the basis for lasting feuds. Some, like John Prescott's speech on One Member One Vote in 1993, helped to swing a vote, or like the speeches on Spain in 1936, led conference to reconsider a decision. Others still, like Hugh Gaitskell's 'fight and fight again' speech in 1960, served to keep the flame of conviction alight in defeat. Ramsay MacDonald's 'left of action' speech in 1921, Hugh Gaitskell's 'why I am a socialist' speech in 1955, Harold Wilson's 'moral crusade' speech in 1962, Michael Foot's 'magician' speech in 1980, Neil Kinnock's 'I warn you' speech in 1983 and Tony Blair's 'tough on crime, tough on the causes of crime' speech in 1993, undoubtedly contributed to their success in the Labour leadership elections that followed.

For those who lived it, Labour's history was profoundly shaped by the speeches[3] that encapsulated the dreams that inspired and framed the battles that divided: over Spain and rearmament in the 1930s, and later over the H-bomb, Europe, public ownership, *In Place of Strife*, Militant and the miners' strike. Some battles were fought against the Tories, others were more fratricidal: the duels between Ramsay MacDonald and James Maxton; between Lansbury, Cripps, Bevin, Morrison and Dalton in the 1930s; between Gaitskellites and Bevanites in the 1950s; and between Jenkinsites, Bennites and others in the 1970s and 1980s. Labour's values, philosophy, political and policy development were often most powerfully articulated, and secured their greatest resonance, through the speeches that shaped them, and it is for this reason that this history of the Labour Party interweaves excerpts from these speeches with the text.[4]

Because speeches are so much of their time, couched in a language designed to appeal to contemporary concerns, they reflect the politics of their time in the raw. They provide, more than anything else in politics, in Queen Elizabeth I's soundbite, a 'window into men's souls'. In the political battles that have riven the Labour Party over the last century, the protagonists have endemically sought to caricature their opponents' arguments. This book seeks to illuminate, to set both sides in context, and to explode some of the myths that have built up along the way.[5] Culminating in Labour's resurgence during the 1990s and rooting the emergence of Tony Blair and of Gordon Brown in historical context, this book is the story of the journey from Old Labour to New.

ONE

The Creation of the Labour
Representation Committee 1888–1900

'The cry of the toiling millions'

James Keir Hardie, arguably more than any other man, was the founder of the Labour Party. Born in 1856, the illegitimate son of a Lanarkshire farm servant, he went down the pit at the age of ten. Having had little schooling, he taught himself to read the works of Carlyle and Ruskin. Becoming a pioneer trade unionist, he was active in the 1880 Lanarkshire miners' strike but gave up the life of a working miner at the age of 23 to become an increasingly forceful journalist in the local Ayrshire press. He was an active Liberal, but his frustration at the failure of Liberal governments to do more to promote the welfare of the working classes became apparent after the local Liberal Association declined to support him as its candidate in the Mid-Lanark by-election of April 1888. Hardie stood instead as a Labour candidate against the Liberal, and during his campaign he called, as in a speech he made at Cambuslang reported in the *Glasgow Herald* of 10 April 1888, for 'men who belonged to the working class' who 'were being poisoned in the pit with foul air . . . being starved in their homes from lack of food . . . to stretch forth their hands and strike a blow for the rights of Labour and not allow themselves to be ridden over roughshod'. In short he was urging the electorate to back the creation of a Labour Party.

Though he polled only 617 votes (the victorious Liberal polled 3,847 and the Tory 2,917), it gave Hardie a new stature as a working-class leader, and gave his call to arms a significance reflected in the formation of a Scottish Labour Party at a conference in Glasgow co-organised by Hardie on 25 August of that year. Hardie became its first secretary. Its programme included: prohibition of liquor traffic; abolition of the House of Lords and all hereditary offices; nationalisation of the land, minerals, railways, waterways and tramways; state banking; free education; free food for children deemed to need it and cumulative income tax on all incomes over £300.

Within a few years, Keir Hardie's reputation had spread across the UK, and it was on the far side of Britain, among the slums of London's East End dockside, that parliamentary opportunity would beckon. West Ham South was a Conservative-held seat but one that had been won by a Liberal back in 1885. It was an area of growing radical ferment. It was at the Bryant and May factory in Bow that Fabian[1] socialist and journalist Annie Besant precipitated the 1888 matchgirls' strike with her magazine article 'White Slavery in London', which had revealed both the appalling pay and terrible working conditions that caused, among other ailments, 'phossy jaw', when the phosphorus for the matches ate away the faces of the girls who made them. The directors of Bryant and May, pillars of the Gladstonian Liberal establishment, sacked the girls suspected of giving Besant the information for her article. To the shock of the company, all 1,400 matchgirls walked out on strike and, with widespread public sympathy for the strikers' cause, the company was to capitulate within a fortnight. The London dockers' strike, sparked in August 1889, for the 'docker's tanner' (minimum sixpence an hour) and minimum four-hour shifts, also enjoyed public support[2] and ultimate success.

West Ham included a large and growing potential Labour vote of dockers, gasworkers and Irishmen,[3] and the local Liberals had split between those who supported a businessman named Hume Webster and those who wanted a more radical candidate.

The radical Liberals and the West Ham Trades Council approached Keir Hardie to see if he would consider becoming a candidate and at the end of February 1890 Hardie visited the constituency for the first time. In March it was announced that Hardie was in the field as a candidate.

Hardie's speeches emphasised a pragmatic determination to batter the Liberals into addressing Labour's concerns. For Hardie, as the *Glasgow Herald* reported in his speech at Cambuslang, 'there was a class who lived on the toil of labour and got more than the labourer did', and 'until this altered the workers would remain in their present position of poverty'.[4] He believed passionately in the power of the working class through the medium of parliamentary democracy to right the wrongs of society. Typical was a speech he made at Canning Town attacking the Liberal Party's failure to support the campaign for a maximum eight-hour day, published in the *Workman's Times* of 31 October 1891:

> If the Liberal Party is prepared to accept our principles we are prepared to work with them. If they are not prepared to accept our principles, the Liberals are no more our friends than the Tories. Take for example the attitude of the National Liberal Federation . . . Mr Sidney Webb endeavoured to obtain leave to move a very mild amendment in favour of an Eight Hours Bill for miners, chemical workers and municipal and all government employees. The chairman of the Federation point blank refused to allow any such amendment to be put to the meeting . . . And those men, the officials of the Liberal Party, who would not even allow the biggest question of the day to be discussed at their conference, come to practical working men and say 'Give us your support, we are your friends.'
>
> They should watch and judge men by what they did and not by what they said. The officials of the Liberals would be driven into taking up the Labour question, and dealing with it as they had been compelled to take up the Irish question, and then, not

before, would they be entitled to the support of the working men of this country . . .

If they did return him it would prove that there was one part of the country where the labour question had taken root and was understood by the workers. What were the cries of the parties compared to their cry? The cry of the toiling millions, the cry of the 1,200 miners done to death every year in the bowels of the earth simply for lack of proper legislation. Men who went to sea in ships sometimes never to come back again. How many lives would be saved if Parliament were based on proper lines, and the representatives were honest working men instead of capitalists, as they now were?

Rivalry continued between Hardie and the prospective official Liberal candidate, Hume Webster, until 25 January 1892, when Webster was sensationally found shot dead in woods near his Croydon estate. The verdict was suicide brought on by the collapse of a deal to buy a South American racehorse. Hardie made the most of his opportunity and in a speech at Plaistow pledged 'to support the Liberal programme in its entirety, but at the same time he would use his best endeavours to call attention to the social questions of the day'. This helped win over the support of most of the local Liberals, who now rallied behind Hardie's candidacy. Attempts by some Liberals to draft in the candidacy of the former Liberal MP for the seat, a Mr Joseph Webster, gathered insufficient support and were ultimately unsuccessful. On polling day, 4 July 1892, the contest was between Hardie and Conservative MP Major Banes. Banes was 'no Rupert of debate' and, having been a fairly inactive MP, proved a fairly inactive campaigner. In the battle between 'the Major and the Miner', as the press dubbed it, Hardie emerged victorious.[5] Hardie's entrance to the Commons in tweed suit, flannel shirt and cloth cap (actually a Sherlock Holmes-style deerstalker) has gone down in political legend. The dockers of West Ham insisted on hiring a wagon to drive him and a team of supporters to Westminster, although the 'brass band' that supposedly accompanied him was, in Hardie's own recollection, a solitary cornet player, albeit one who, playing the Marseillaise, 'did himself proud'. Hardie's first opportunity to make his mark in Parliament, his maiden speech on 10 February 1893, was in proposing an amendment to the Address appealing for justice to the unemployed:

> It is a remarkable fact that the speech of Her Majesty should refer to one section of industrial distress and leave the other altogether unnoticed, and there are some of us who think that if the interests of the landlords were not bound up so closely with the agricultural depression, the reference even to the agricultural labourers would not have appeared in the Queen's Speech . . . [10 per cent of workers were unemployed because of the trade depression] Professor Marshall, who is a Member of the Royal Commission on Labour, stated inferentially the other day that 10 per cent of the population of the country might be reckoned as the surplus population. That is to say, that for 10 per cent of the population no provision is made to enable them to earn for themselves and those dependent upon them the necessaries of life. Well, if that

statement be true, it means that 4,000,000 of the inhabitants of these islands are without visible means of subsistence, not because of any fault on their own part, but because our present land and industrial system denies them the opportunity of working for a living. In London alone it is estimated by those best able to form a judgement that 50,000 men are unemployed. This does not refer to those who are casually employed, and it does not refer to those usually spoken of as loafers and criminals. It refers exclusively to *bona fide* working men who have been thrown out of employment in consequence of bad trade . . .

It was stated in the House yesterday that the laws of this country permitted manufactures to be brought into the country from wherever they could be produced with the greatest cheapness. I admit that is so, and I do not object to its being so; but I submit that if the laws of this country are so framed as to throw men out of employment it is the duty of this House to enable these men to provide themselves with the means of subsistence. Can that be done? Remember that this question not only affects those out-of-work, but also those workers who are in employment. I believe all the horrors of sweating, of low wages, of long hours, and of deaths from starvation, are directly traceable to the large numbers of people who are totally unemployed or only casually employed. The worker in the workshop is fettered by the thought that outside his workshop gates there are thousands eager and willing to step into his shoes should he be dismissed in consequence of any attempt to improve his position . . .

Of remedies on offer, Hardie dismissed emigration:

Emigration sends out of the country the best part of our working classes – the thrifty, prudent, sober and intelligent workers, the very men whom we desire to keep at home . . . It is also said that a turn for the better in trade will absorb the unemployment. But I ask, is it right for this House, representing as it is supposed to do every section of the community, to coldly stand by, waiting for the return of good trade, while men, women and children are literally starving to death? Our present Poor Law system aggravates, but does not enable us to grapple with the evil, and it is not human to expect that the men who are suffering will suffer in silence, waiting for the return of good trade . . . My Amendment has been objected to because it contains no specific proposal for dealing with this evil. Had it done so, it would have been objected to still more, because then I am certain that everyone who wanted to find an excuse for not voting for the Amendment would find it in the proposal it contained. I think the House will agree with me that we have high authority in this House for not disclosing the details of our proposals until we are in a position to give effect to them, which is not quite in my power yet.

Making explicit his opposition to 'Protection . . . it would aggravate every social and industrial evil and divert the minds of the workers from what I believe to be the true solution of this problem,' Hardie went on to suggest several specific measures. Firstly, 'the increase of the minimum wage for labourers to 6d. an hour and, secondly, the enactment of a 48 hours' week for all government employees . . .' and 'the question of keeping contracts for government work at home . . . I submit to the government that it is not consistent with the spirit of the Resolution to go to Bavaria, or anywhere else outside Great Britain, for the supplies of the Post Office . . . Dealing with firms at home they would know whether the terms of the Resolution were enforced.' He went on to suggest that:

> It has been estimated by competent authorities that were the hours of railway servants reduced to eight per day employment would be found for 150,000 additional working men, [and further that] the government might also establish what is known as home colonies on the idle lands . . . I do not refer to the penal and beggar colonies established by some continental countries; I refer to what has been tried at home. Some years ago, at Newcastle, the Board of Guardians made provision for finding employment for the paupers in the workhouse. They were the ordinary class of paupers, belonging to all trades and occupations, and to no special trade or occupations. The Guardians set them to work, first to pull down and rebuild the workhouse, which they did to the satisfaction of all concerned; and afterwards the paupers were set to making their own clothing and everything necessary for carrying on the workhouse. A report was made on the experiment, which stated that in every department it was found that the production was far more than the house needed. 'Everything,' said the Report, 'in the house is made – from an ambulance to a tin plate.' The Guardians also put into cultivation fourteen acres of land in their possession, with such good results that the net profit on the sale of the produce in three years was £338. If the Guardians of Newcastle could do this, is it not reasonable to suppose that every Board of Guardians in Great Britain could do the same in their own locality? There is no lack of vacant land – land capable of producing for the people who are starving; and I submit that this House, as representing the nation, should give these men who are out of work the opportunity of employing themselves through this system of home colonisation. It would prevent the fearful demoralisation which being out of work never fails to bring in its train. One of the most harrowing features connected with the problem of the unemployed is not the poverty or the hardship they have to endure, but the fearful moral degradation that follows in the train of the enforced idleness; and there is no more pitiable spectacle in this world than the man willing to work, who, day after day, vainly 'begs a brother of the earth, to give him leave to toil'.
>
> . . . I observe that a certain section of what are called the London Liberal Members have declared their intention of voting against this Amendment. They are, of course, free so to do; but I promise them a full exchange value for the vote they will give against the Amendment. I would remind the government, too, that what lost them Huddersfield was the absence of the unemployed question from their programme, and the absence of a candidate in sympathy with labour; and unless they desire the experience of Huddersfield to be repeated in the various constituencies where vacancies now exist, they would do well to give heed to a question which is so pressing as the one we are now engaged in discussing. I am sure that if the election addresses and election promises of gentlemen on both sides of the House were examined,

it would be found that during election contests they had plenty of professions of sympathy for the unemployed. I ask of them today that they should translate these professions into practice.

Keir Hardie lost his seat at the election of 1895, but he maintained his momentum. He was the dominant personality at the founding conference of the Independent Labour Party (ILP) in Bradford in January 1893, and was elected its first chairman. Though initially it grew (indeed, the Scottish Labour Party was to merge with it during 1894) its by-election record was disappointing and it was soon, as the Scottish Labour Party had been, riven by disunity and strapped for cash. The ILP lacked substantial trade union support; indeed, few of its leading figures were even trade union members. The historian Henry Pelling contends that its real membership fell from 10,720 in 1895 to 6,084 in 1900.[6]

It was the series of bitterly fought industrial disputes during the late 1890s which transformed the situation, in particular the defeat after a lengthy strike during 1897 of the Amalgamated Society of Engineers[7] and of the Welsh miners during 1898. Hardie's call was for labour unity and he insisted on the central importance of direct and independent labour representation in Parliament. With assistance from an old Lanarkshire ally, Scottish Miners' Federation President Bob Smillie, Hardie secured the support of the Scottish Trades Union Congress (TUC) for his strategy at its third annual conference in April 1899. In September 1899, the British TUC at its Plymouth congress debated a resolution proposed by J. H. Holmes of the Amalgamated Society of Railway Servants[8] and seconded by James Sexton of the Liverpool Dockers. It has been claimed[9] that the resolution was drafted by Keir Hardie and Ramsay MacDonald in the offices of the ILP newspaper, though historians have pointed to the lack of direct evidence to prove this. Whatever the truth, the debate was tense.[10] Support came from Ben Tillett of the Dockers' Union,[11] one of the heroes of the 1889 dockworkers' strike, and from Margaret Bondfield, then the assistant secretary of the Shopworkers' Union.[12] Opposition came from Cotton Spinners' secretary Thomas Ashton who urged the TUC to keep clear of politics and condemned the resolution as a waste of time, but the opposition was defeated by 546,000 votes to 434,000. The resolution called for a special congress of 'all the cooperative, socialistic, trade unions and other working organisations' to cooperate in convening (and sending representatives to) a special congress to 'devise ways and means for securing the return of an increased number of Labour members to the next Parliament'.

A committee was created comprising representatives of the various organisations named in the resolution, including Keir Hardie and Ramsay MacDonald from the ILP, Edward Pease and George Bernard Shaw from the Fabian Society and Will Thorne and W. C. Steadman from the trade unions. This committee convened the congress specified by the resolution, on 27–28 February 1900 in the Memorial Hall, Farringdon Street,

London. It was attended by 129 delegates from the organisations mentioned in the resolution passed at the 1899 TUC, including 65 trade unions (though the largest, the Amalgamated Society of Engineers, had only 85,000 members and 37 of the unions had memberships of fewer than 5,000). The other organisations represented were the ILP, claiming 13,000 members; the Social Democratic Federation (SDF), claiming 9,000 and the Fabian Society with 861. The Co-operative movement failed to take up its invitation to attend. This congress was to be the first conference of the Labour Party (or of the Labour Representation Committee as it initially called itself). A proposal from the tiny Upholsterers' and Waiters' Unions to restrict Labour representation rigidly to members of the working classes was defeated overwhelmingly after speeches by Engineering Union leader George Barnes and Battersea MP and Engineering Union member John Burns. Burns declared that he was 'getting tired of working-class boots, working-class trains, working-class houses and working-class margarine'. The key battle was over whether the new Labour Party was going to be a party of class war, a trade union pressure group on a restricted number of issues or a proper Labour Party. An attempt by the Marxist SDF to make the new Labour Party a party of class war was denounced by James Sexton of the Liverpool Dockers and Frederick Rogers of the Vellum Bookbinders. Rogers argued that, if carried, the SDF resolution 'would place the Labour movement in the position of the boy who cried for the moon. Nothing could be more unfortunate for the conference than to label across its front "class war".' The class war resolution was defeated and it was Keir Hardie's resolution[13] for a Labour Party 'having its own policy, its own whips and acting in all that concerned the welfare of the workers in a manner free and unhampered by entanglements with other parties' that won unanimous support after only a short discussion.[14] Frederick Rogers became Labour's first chairman and Ramsay MacDonald its first secretary.

TWO

The Boer War and Labour's First Election 1899–1901

'The voice of reason is always drowned in the clamour of war'

Ramsay MacDonald was to play a central, some would say *the* central, role in the development of Labour over the next 30 years from a party of protest to a party of government. As Labour's leader over much of that period, his biographer David Marquand argues that 'in a sense true of none of his successors, he not only led it but captured its imagination and seemed to embody its hopes'.[15] Born, like Keir Hardie, in Scotland (in Lossiemouth during 1866), he was said to be the illegitimate son of John MacDonald, a Scottish agricultural worker. Though a socialist and involved with both the Social Democratic Federation and the Fabians from the mid/late 1880s, like Hardie he was originally an active Liberal. He turned to the ILP only in 1894 when he found his parliamentary ambitions thwarted. His prodigious talents as an orator and an organiser ensured his swift rise: within a couple of years he was on the Fabian Society Executive and the ILP National Committee. His speech delivered at the Leicester Temperance Hall in October 1899 on his adoption as ILP parliamentary candidate for Leicester 'may justly be termed Ramsay MacDonald's first statement of his aims and policy as a national political leader':[16]

> . . . this Tory government is none of your old-fashioned Tory governments. It is mainly inspired by one of the greatest demagogues of the century, Mr Joseph Chamberlain,[17] and it has partly to thank his social programme for its present position. Now, that programme was very enticing . . . and the working classes . . . were perfectly entitled to give the Tory social programme a chance . . . And with what result? . . . in not a single case has the hope of the workers who voted Tory been realised. We have had a Rating Act which does not relieve rates, but which does raise land values; we have had a Clergy Relief Act which proceeds on the dictum of Biblical ethics, that to him who hath shall be given and from him who hath not shall be taken away. We have had a Compensation Act which does not compensate and a Housing Act which does not house . . .
>
> And now what of Liberalism? I am not here to curse the great historical Liberal Party. Speaking generally, historical Liberalism is the mortar with which the foundations of our political liberty have been cemented . . . When you think of the Liberal

Party and its work, you imagine a body of men dating from towards the end of last century . . . ever ready to listen to the promptings of progress, ever watchful to do the will of democracy. No idea is further removed than that from the real facts of history. No such body of men ever existed. You will remember the method which Charles the Great adopted for the conversion of the barbarians of Europe to Christianity. He went to them with the holy water of baptism in one hand and the mighty sword of extirpation in the other, and asked them to make their choice. The wise barbarians chose the holy water in preference to the mighty sword. It was by precisely the same method that the Liberal Party has kept democratic . . .

Perhaps if there are two reforms which are claimed by Liberals with more pride than any others they are the ballot and free trade. Now both of these became Liberal measures only after independent candidates were promoted on their behalf, only after the Independent politicians had shown the Liberals that it was simply a question of the mighty sword or the holy water. For 40 years the Liberals opposed the ballot . . .

I do not believe that the Liberal Party will give you anything but the merest shadow of what you expect of it. I do not believe it will face the House of Lords; that it will give you an eight-hours day; that it will tax land values; that it will reform to any great extent our registration law; that it will pursue a democratic foreign policy. I know some of you think I am too sceptical . . .

You must remember two things. The Liberal opposition is not promising you anything now that it did not promise you before the election of 1892, and since then the Liberals were three years in office . . . When elections are to be won, and where the party is in opposition, Newcastle programmes are manufactured and valiant speeches made. But when the party is in power the sinister influences of its rich supporters are paramount. The failure of the last government was not that it had only a majority of 41, but that a majority of the 41 were poor, weak-kneed creatures. In addition, I know that it is the opinion of the best Radicals in the House of Commons that the Liberal Party is becoming more and more mediocre in its powers, and passing more and more completely into the possession of its moneyed men . . .

The worker lives on the slopes of a volcano. It may serve his time; it may overwhelm him. But whilst he is a worker, the rumblings and grumblings of the titanic forces below, over which he has no control and can have no control, keep him in constant dread, if he thinks at all, that a catastrophe is coming . . .

'But,' you may argue, 'you are a socialist, and therefore we cannot support you.' Well what is the socialist remedy? It is simply this: the organisation of labour under public, democratic control, so that a better distribution of labour and of wealth will result . . . But whether the people of Leicester are frightened at socialism or not, they are very proud to make money by it. According to a government return which I have just been examining, you are making £35,711 a year from your water supply, £55,047 from your gas, £1,857 from your electric lighting, £5,435 from your markets; and not a single halfpenny of this £96,000 would you be making unless you were wise enough to be socialists so far as your water, gas, electric lighting and markets are concerned . . . It is too late for you to object to socialism. You are beginning to live in it . . .

I have endeavoured, whilst criticising my opponents, to remove the scat of political enthusiasm from the barren wastes of partisan loyalty, to the generous plains of a human ideal. The task of the twentieth century is to bring peace to dwell within the land, and happiness to rest upon the hearth. In those declining years, in the twilight days of a long and glorious epoch in which this constituency has played such a foremost part, he who detains you as he opens the records that have been written and asks you to dwell in the battles that have been fought, or whose eyes see nought but the next few steps ahead, is not entitled to be ranked amongst the forward spirits of the time. The cause of progress demands that it should be placed under the guardianship of those who are already prophesying of the day of the coming century, of those who foresee the change in its politics: for only those who in their own hearts have a knowledge of the stirrings of the human spirit which are to mould our institutions and determine the course of our industry, can lead us onwards through the times we are facing as we look across the confines of the nineteenth century into the unexplored and, for human possibility, boundless fields of the twentieth.

Within months of its creation, the LRC faced its first big electoral battle, the so-called 'khaki election' of September–October 1900, which led to the re-election of Lord Salisbury's Conservative government with an overwhelming majority. The contest was dominated by the Boer War, an issue that split both the Liberal Party and the infant Labour Party. Hardie, MacDonald and most of the ILP were pro-Boer while many trade unionists and leading Fabians such as George Bernard Shaw were anti-. One of the clearest expressions of the ILP's anti-war position is contained in Keir Hardie's speech to the eighth annual ILP congress in Glasgow during Easter 1901:

Patriotism has been defined as love of one's own country, and Imperialism as love of other people's country . . .

Rulers know . . . it is not merely that war distracts attention from social reform, but it also destroys the desire for such by changing the current of men's thoughts, if not their very nature. The voice of reason is always drowned in the clamour of war . . . A century ago the American war was followed by those of Napoleon, and only ended in Waterloo – 30 years in all. What was the attitude of the nation towards reform during this period? At the outbreak of rebellion in our then American colonies there was a strong radical movement in and out of Parliament. War killed it.

Whilst our troops were fighting for freedom on the Continent, at home the prisons and hulks were being filled, and the gibbet called into play to execute vengeance on men who claimed the right to vote. The victory of Waterloo was followed in four years by the massacre of Peterloo. And what was the condition of the working classes? Children of the most tender age were slaving in factories under the most horrible conditions, and women were toiling in the mines like beasts of burden, whilst men walked the streets in enforced idleness, and woe, want, wretchedness and hunger were in nearly every home . . .

Of fifteen Labour candidates at the 1900 election, only two were elected. One was Hardie, who fought two seats simultaneously, came bottom of the poll at Preston but was elected for one of the two seats at Merthyr, benefiting from the rivalry between the two sitting Liberals. The other was the secretary of the Railwayman's Union, Richard Bell, at Derby. MacDonald went down to defeat at Leicester.

Support for the Labour Representation Committee grew among trade unions following the Law Lords' judgment on the Taff Vale railway strike in 1901, which made unions liable for losses to an employer resulting from their giving support to a strike by its employees. Increasing numbers of trade unions now affiliated. However, with the infant LRC remaining a bare handful of MPs, despite several by-election victories, Labour had little opportunity to make an impact in Parliament. One occasion on which it did was on 23 April 1901, when Hardie delivered the first complete socialist speech in Parliament:

After the discussion to which we have just listened, in which one section of the community has claimed support from the State, and shown that German steamship lines have an advantage over British lines because they are subsidised by the State, I trust the House will listen to the logical outcome of these arguments. I make no apology for bringing the question of socialism before the House of Commons. It has long commanded the attention of the best minds in the country. It is a growing force in the thought of the world, and whether men agree or disagree with it, they have to reckon with it, and may as well begin by understanding it. In the German Empire socialism is the one section of political thought which is making headway, and to an extent which is, I believe, alarming the powers that be. Over fifty socialist members occupy seats in the German Reichstag, between forty and fifty in the Chamber of Deputies in France, and between thirty and forty in the Belgian Parliament. Socialism on the continent therefore is an established and recognised fact so far as its entry into politics is concerned, and if it be argued that while that may be true of the continent it is not true of this country, I reply that the facts and conditions now existing in this country are such as to make it extremely probable that the progress of socialism in this country will be at a more rapid pace than in any other country in Europe . . .

At the bottom of the social scale there is a mass of poverty and misery equal in magnitude to that which obtained one hundred years ago. I submit that the true test of progress is not the accumulation of wealth in the hands of a few, but the elevation of a people as a whole. [Citing the authority of Professor Thorold Rogers, Hardie asserted that] the high standard of comfort reached by the labouring classes at the end of the last century has not brought them that happiness which obtained in England three hundred years ago, when there was no machinery, no large capitalists, no private property in land as we know it today, and when every person had the right to use the land for the purpose of producing food for himself and his family. [This was because, he continued, over the preceding 25 years, any improvements to wages and hours had been massively offset by spiralling rents.] I could quote figures, if that statement is disputed, showing that in all the industrial parts of the country rents during the past twenty years have been going up by leaps and bounds.

I come now to the causes which have forced thinking people of all ranks of society to reconsider their attitude towards socialism. I refer particularly to the great and alarming growth of what are known as trusts and syndicates in connection with industry. We have hitherto been accustomed to regard a trust as a distinctly American product . . .

So long as industry is conducted by individuals competing one with another there is a chance of the article produced being supplied at an approximation to its market value, but competition has been found to be destructive of the interests of the owners and possessors of capital in this as in every other country. Three or four firms which formerly entered one market and competed with each other find it conducive to their interests to combine, thereby creating a monopoly which enables them to charge whatever price they like, and to treat their workpeople in any way that seems good to them . . .

As John Stuart Mill – himself a convert to socialism, despite the fact that as a political economist of the older school he had written against the system before he understood its full meaning and the necessity for it – wrote: 'The social problem of the future we [referring to himself and his wife] consider to be how to unite the greatest liberty of action with a common ownership in the raw material of the globe and an equal participation in all the benefits of combined labour.'

We are rapidly approaching a point when the nation will be called upon to decide between an uncontrolled monopoly, conducted for the benefit and in the interests of its principal shareholders, and a monopoly owned, controlled and manipulated by the State in the interests of the nation as a whole. I do not require to go far afield for arguments to support that part of my statement concerning the danger which the aggregation of wealth in a few hands is bringing upon us. This House and the British nation know to their cost the danger which comes from allowing men to grow rich and permitting them to use their wealth to corrupt the press, to silence the pulpit, to degrade our national life, and to bring reproach and shame upon a great people, in order that a few unscrupulous scoundrels might be able to add to their ill-gotten gains. The war in South Africa is a millionaires' war. Our troubles in China are due to the desire of the capitalists to exploit the people of that country as they would fain exploit the people of South Africa. Much of the jealousy and bad blood existing between this country and France is traceable to the fact that we went to war in Egypt to suppress a popular uprising seeking freedom for the people, in order that the interest of our bondholders might be secured. Socialism, by placing land and the instruments of production in the hands of the community, eliminates only the idle, useless class at both ends of the scale. Half a million of the people of this country benefit by the present system; the remaining millions of toilers and businessmen do not. The pursuit of wealth corrupts the manhood of men. We are called upon at the beginning of the twentieth century to decide the question propounded in the Sermon on the Mount as to whether or not we will worship God or Mammon. The present day is a Mammonworshipping age. Socialism proposes to dethrone the brute-god Mammon and to lift humanity into its place. I beg to submit in this very imperfect fashion the resolution on the Paper, merely premising that the last has not been heard of the socialist movement either in the country or on the floor of this House, but that, just as sure as Radicalism democratised the system of government politically in the last century so will socialism democratise the country industrially during the century upon which we have just entered. I beg to move.

THREE

Breakthrough 1901–06

'The sleeping giant is awakening'

The key issue remained relations with the Liberals. Hardie was always an uncertain supporter of a 'progressive alliance' but he went along with MacDonald's covert negotiation of a secret electoral pact with Liberal chief whip Herbert Gladstone in 1903. As a result, Labour secured a clear run from the Liberals in 30 seats at the forthcoming election and undertook to avoid opposing Liberals where they were fighting the Conservatives. By late 1905 it was clear that an election would soon be at hand. Arthur Balfour's Conservative government was increasingly split over policy at home and in Ireland, and also over tariff reform. Moreover the Parliament had not long to run. Balfour's government resigned in December 1905, gambling that the Liberals would be too split to credibly form an alternative government. They weren't. Far from floundering as Balfour had expected, Sir Henry Campbell-Bannerman formed a government within a week behind which he managed to unite most of the disparate parts of the Liberal Party. Calling a general election for little over a month later, Campbell-Bannerman was rewarded with a strong swing against the Conservatives that produced a higher turnout and a Liberal landslide. The pact proved crucial to the success of 29[18] of Labour's 51 candidates at the 1906 general election: only five of the 29 had faced Liberal opposition. At the first meeting of the newly elected MPs they agreed to call themselves the Labour Party. Hardie was elected chairman by a one-vote majority over former Lancashire Weavers' Union activist David Shackleton, who became vice-chairman.

The general election result was a personal triumph for MacDonald whose organisation and strategy had given Labour a phalanx of almost 30 MPs. MacDonald's influence was also directed to developing Labour's ideas in a gradualist socialist direction. The dominating theme of his books such as *Socialism and Society* (1905) and *Socialism and Government* (1909) was that a form of Social Darwinism ensured that private organisations would get bigger, the state would have to intervene, and that socialism would emerge from the success, not the failure, of capitalism. 'Because of the influence of MacDonald and the Webbs during the First World War,' the historian Keith Laybourn has argued, 'these essentially Fabian views became the defining influence in the socialism the Labour Party espoused after 1918.'[19] To celebrate the great victory of 1906 a mass rally was organised on the Friday evening[20] of the Labour conference in London at the Queen's Hall, Langham Place. The speeches of Labour's leaders gave voice to the hopes and dreams of the assembled crowd and were met with cheers and roars of applause. The official report records that Hardie began:

*The day had been when Labour as a political force was either ignored by the press, or, if referred to by it, was so referred to in terms of contempt. Those days are over. The sleeping giant was awakening, and in days to come, in the very near future, Labour would be the dominant factor in politics, not only potentially, but actually and in fact. The two-party system was breaking up, he believed, and the formation of the Lib-Labs he welcomed: it was their first step towards independence. [The Labour Party was] a party without adjective or qualification. It was no longer necessary to emphasise the fact that they were independent. For all time to come people who spoke, and thought, and wrote of the Labour Party, would think, speak, and write of it as a party separate and distinct from every other party . . . It was said that the Labour Party would find itself unnecessary, and that the new government would be so drastic in its reforms that it would be a waste of money to continue to send gasworkers to the great national gashouse. But if these anticipations turned out to be correct, it would only remain for the government to send up friend Crooks to the House of Lords and send the rest of them home about their business. But it was just possible that the anticipations as to drastic reforms might not be realised, and if they were not, the Labour Party would ask the reason why. They had already had an indication of the difference between promises before the election and performance after. He ventured to say that if the election addresses and speeches of Liberal candidates were to be ransacked, it would be found that not 10 per cent of them won their seats without making more or less definite promises with regard to old age pensions. He knew nothing in politics so utterly degrading as trafficking upon the misery of the aged poor in order to win party successes. A deputation waited upon the Chancellor of the Exchequer upon this very point. Of course he was full of sympathy – he never knew a government which was not; but they had no money! There were pensions for the idle rich, pensions for the well-paid officials of the State, but for the men and women who toiled there were no pensions! He could remember that twelve years ago the same excuse was made by the Conservative government. They were in favour of old age pensions, but they were too poor to afford it! During the eleven years since 1895 the expenditure of the country had increased by close upon 40 millions per year, over 20 millions of which went in wasteful expenditure. The total actual cost of providing a small pension for their aged people had been estimated at from ten to twelve millions per year. The nation could not find that sum in 1895, but since that time it had squandered 300 millions in war, and nobody was a penny the better save the swindling contractors and the rich. It would be the business of the Labour Party to find ways and means to produce the money whereby pensions could be given to their aged fathers and mothers, who had brought up families in credit and respectability, and who had given their lives for their

*Speech transcribed as reported speech.

country in a truer sense than the men who fell on the field of battle. Both that party and the socialists were in agreement on the importance of beginning to reconstruct the lives of the common people. They would seek to restore the land to the people of the country; they would strive to protect subject races from subjugation and from the exploitation to which they had been subjected in the past; they would fight to win political freedom and industrial freedom for men and women; and, knowing the people as he did, he knew that just in proportion as opposition gathered strength against them, so would their hearts and their lives and their strength be more firmly knit together in contending for the emancipation of the classes to which they belonged.

Hardie was followed by a ringing appeal from David Shackleton to the Lib-Labs, and the unions who sponsored them, to join the 'LRC movement'. After Shackleton came Ramsay MacDonald, whose flights of pastoral rhetoric proved as inspirational as ever and retain their flavour even in the reported speech of the official report:

. . . Up to now the Labour Party had always been subordinate in politics. The cottage had had to fight for the palace, and the palace had always been neglecting to legislate in the interests of the cottage. The cottage the previous month said, 'I am going to fight for myself and I am going to work and legislate for myself, because my experience has been that if I don't do it nobody else will do it for me.' For a few fleeting moments, once every five years or so on the average, the great democracy of the country has been the sovereign party in the country. It had been cajoled by Primrose dames; it had been bribed by candidates on both sides who had more money than political intelligence at their command. It had been made drunken with Imperialistic sentiment, which enabled the anti-social classes to exploit the industrial classes more than they had been able to exploit them before. They had been talking too much about the voice of the democracy being the voice of God. At the last election the voice of the democracy was nothing of the kind. The voice of the democracy was the voice of a blind man wandering in the wilderness without guide, without courage, without hope. That had passed away. Last month they had a voice given out from the democracy that at any rate, in some instances, seemed as if it came from the heavens itself. The Labour representatives were there, 29 of them; as their leader had said, a Labour Party without adjective or qualification, and 'Labour' was good enough for them; they were a Labour Party without responsibilities, except to the great toiling masses for whose votes and sympathies they appealed last month; a party that would support no government unless that government was advancing the frontiers of righteousness in this country; a party which would oppose no government that was honestly and genuinely advancing those frontiers. Their opponents told the Labour Party that they were terribly afraid of them. He was not sorry that they were. It was time those people got frightened at somebody, because they were beginning to be like the unjust lawyer, of whom they were told in the Scriptures, that he feared neither God nor anybody else. Their opponents were frightened at them because, they said, they were unpractical people; even the presence of their old friend Shackleton was not good enough for them in that respect. The other parties had ruled the country, the national income of which was now in round figures 1,800 millions; yet these practical people could not solve the unemployed problem, nor answer the question why men and women were 'too old at forty', or how to keep decent, honest, honourable men and women out of the work-house. These 'practical' ruling classes had been blind to over-population and over-crowding in the towns; yet if they would go with him a railway journey to any part of the country, north, east, south or west, he would show them acres upon acres, square mile upon square mile, of land out of cultivation. The other day a few hundred boot and shoe operatives tramped to London. They had holes in the bottom of their boots, and they had to shoe them out of their charity in London. Yet this 'practical govern-ing class' told him that there was no demand for these men's labour as boot and shoe-makers – nevertheless every man was improperly shod! What a strange mystery it was. These men wanted shoes, and they wanted to make shoes, yet this practical governing class could not arrive at an economical solution of the matter, and could not show them how they could go into a boot and shoe factory and make the boots and shoes they required for themselves. It had also been alleged that the Labour Party would split up the democracy, and divide them more than they were divided then ... Let them take two men from the counties of Lancashire and York. The Lancashire workman suffers from precisely the same economic evils as the Yorkshire workman – low wages, high rents, the oppressive power of the landlord, underfed children, unemployment. Every question that affects Yorkshire affects Lancashire. Yet in the old days of these men with the same political and social platforms, half of them in Lancashire sent Tories to represent them in the House of Commons, and the other half, in Yorkshire, sent Liberals to represent them. Thus, when any great social question was before the House in which the Yorkshire and Lancashire men had precisely the same interests, the rep-resentatives of Lancashire went into one lobby, and the representatives of Yorkshire into the other! And so far as political influence and power were concerned, they might have wiped both Yorkshire and Lancashire off the map. The Labour Party had stopped that, and they were going to stop it in the future more effectually even than they did last month.

Another of the successful LRC candidates in the general election of 1906 was the new MP for Blackburn, Philip Snowden: 'a thin-lipped Yorkshireman, whose crippled body and biting invective gave him the delusive air of an English Robespierre'.[21] Snowden was to be one of the defining figures of the pre-1931 Labour Party in the public mind. Born in 1864 to a family of Wesleyan weavers in Keighley, West Yorkshire, he was invalided out of his clerk's job at the Inland Revenue by a back injury,[22] and like Hardie and MacDonald came to Labour via the Liberal Party and the ILP. Indeed, he never lost his commitment to the tenets of nonconformist radicalism: support for free trade, temperance and anti-militarism. Snowden was throughout his Commons career Labour's leading financial expert, serving as Chancellor of the Exchequer in both Labour governments (1924 and 1929–31) before his death in 1937. His biographer Colin Cross is probably not overstating Snowden's influence in arguing that it was Snowden who placed what he called 'sound finance' at the very centre of ILP policy. For Snowden, if the ILP was ever to win public acceptance, it must show itself sound on money. 'The only way in which Snowden's opposition to tariffs differed from that of the Liberals,' writes Cross, 'was his "one leg of the trousers" argument. Free trade, he said, was an essential condition for social justice, but it would not by itself provide social justice. Socialism was required as well.'[23] When Snowden entered Parliament his renown as the 'prophet of the north' had preceded him, and 'his physical appearance added to the fascination – his tapping stick, his pallid features, his glittering eyes, his traplike mouth, long tongue flickering in and out'. Cross calls the occasion of his maiden speech on 12 March 1906, 'one of the great Parliamentary days of all time'. Former Conservative Prime Minister Arthur Balfour had been defeated at the election and was taking his seat for his new constituency. To celebrate the return of the former Prime Minister, the Liberals had put down a motion declaring that 'the people of the United Kingdom have demonstrated their unqualified fidelity to the principles and practice of free trade'.[24] Philip Snowden was the principal Labour speaker. Hansard records that Snowden began by arguing that the election had been about more than the principles of free trade, that people had voted Liberal because of:

> . . . the indignation of the country at the importation of Chinese labour into South Africa', support for Irish Home Rule, financial retrenchment, antagonism to the last Education Bill and 'the expression of a moral indignation amongst the people at the waste and mismanagement which had marked the previous years'. Moreover, though he supported free trade, 'sixty years of free trade had failed to mitigate to any great extent our grave industrial and social evils . . . one-third of our population – which meant nearly 40 per cent of our working-class people' was 'on the verge of hunger, perpetually struggling to keep their bodies and souls together. It was not by the sum total of our iron exports, or tin-plate exports, or by the increase of the Board of Trade Returns that they were going to ensure the happiness and prosperity of the people. They must estimate the result of the application of 60 years of a particular policy, not by the aggregate amount of wealth it had succeeded in creating, but by the extent to which it had diffused happiness and contentment amongst the people. The party with which he was associated, while standing as firmly as the most ardent members of the Cobden Club to the maintenance of our free trade policy, declined to fall down and worship this god.' Moreover, Britain's adherence to free trade had not dissuaded her competitors from imposing tariffs. Meanwhile 'the rich were getting richer and the poor poorer. The Returns of pauperism presented to the House only a week ago showed that under every head of pauperism there had been a continuous increase during the past five or six years.' For Snowden, Joe Chamberlain's critique of the failure of free trade to deliver prosperity for all had a degree of validity. Nevertheless he opposed Chamberlain's alternative: protection. For Snowden, 'Although it was not capable of

dealing as an active force with the distribution of wealth and the social evils and conditions, free trade was a necessary condition. He did not wish it to be understood by the statement he made just now that he denied that any improvement had taken place in the condition of the people. He was prepared to admit that a considerable improvement had taken place, but it was not due to free trade. It must not be forgotten that contemporaneously with the practice of free trade there had been other and active forces at work which were responsible for this improvement in the condition of the working classes of this country. Did free traders forget the Factory Acts, the Co-operative movement, the Municipal Corporations Act, and trade organisation which had done so much for the working classes during the past sixty years? He did not believe that it was historically accurate to attribute the terrible condition of the people in the years previous to the repeal of Corn Laws entirely to protection . . . The people were poor in the days before the repeal of the Corn Laws, but not because the employers could not afford to pay higher wages.' America, he argued, had protection, and yet, while wages had remained stagnant the cost of living had risen substantially. Meanwhile, 'If there were certain classes in Germany whose condition compared favourably with that of the workmen in this country it was not due to protection, but was in spite of protection. It was brought about by the development of the railway system, the better educational system, and other causes. While we in this country stood by free trade, we must recognise that free trade was merely a condition and not an active force.' Snowden demanded 'social reform dealing with such matters as the land question, the railway monopoly, the mining royalty monopoly, and to redress social inequalities by a free use of the power of taxation', particularly of the super-rich. He 'had been hoping that the Liberal Party had learned wisdom during the years they had been wandering in the wilderness. He hoped the government would turn into Acts of Parliament the beautiful sentiments contained in perorations to their speeches when in opposition. The Labour members had been returned expressly to do something to better the lives of the common people. They wanted to put some brightness and joy into the lives of those whose days were a bitter and never-ending struggle to keep body and soul together, and who were ever confronted with the terrible nightmare of extreme poverty in their old age . . .'

FOUR

Ramsay MacDonald Succeeds Keir Hardie 1907–11

'A slap in the face'

Barely a year after Labour's election breakthrough, internal rows surfaced. Labour's 1907 annual conference, held in Belfast amid the cold of January, was dominated by a row over the power of the Labour Party conference to instruct the new Labour MPs. Labour's National Executive substituted a resolution which stated that 'resolutions instructing the parliamentary party as to their action in the House of Commons be taken as the *opinions* of the conference', leaving the 'time and method of giving effect to these instructions' to the MPs in conjunction with the National Executive.

The official conference report records that in his opening speech, Hardie attacked the seventeen resolutions on the agenda 'giving the parliamentary party definite instructions to introduce this and that'. The Labour MPs, he said,

> did not want at the next conference to have it said that they had displayed favouritism in selecting some of these questions and not dealing with others. The conference understood that there was only a limited opportunity for dealing with Private Members' Bills. They were fortunate last session and hoped to be as fortunate again but they might not. They would have to select which of the subjects should be laid before the House of Commons and it was asked that the party in Parliament with the cooperation of the Executive Committee should decide which questions should have priority. There had been a lot of fuss about the party wanting to be boss, to play the part of dictator and all that kind of nonsense, which was most ridiculous. The recommendation lent itself to no such interpretation. The party in Parliament was a composite party. It was composed of the socialist movement and of the trade union movement. There must be some freedom of action, some free play between these two sections. Otherwise they were in for a spill; and nobody wanted a spill at this juncture.

Hardie was attacked by Ben Tillett, the self-educated Dockers' Union leader and labour legend whose victory in the Great London Dock Strike of 1889 had secured the 'docker's tanner'.[25] Tillett's attitude to Labour's MPs can be surmised from the title of a pamphlet he had seen fit to publish in 1906 entitled *Is the Parliamentary Labour Party a Failure?* (it concluded that it was). Indeed, Tillett has been described as 'living in a state of persistent quarrel with the other great figures in the Labour movement',[26] a description he sought on this occasion to live up to, telling the conference that he:

> would not have risen to speak but for the inference that they were not intelligent enough to understand the proposition, which made him feel that their friend Keir Hardie had not the respect for them to which they were entitled . . . Hardie had been unfair to the conference. They did not want any leader to adopt any superior attitude to the conference. He read the resolution to imply an insult to the intelligence of the conference, and he protested against such language as Mr Hardie had used.

Pete Curran of the Gasworkers' Union[27] defended the executive and Hardie protested that they were 'too young as a party to begin to distrust their leaders who were trying to do their best for them in the House of Commons. In spite of their alleged shortcomings they had accomplished a year's work that was creditable to themselves and to the movement.' He was echoed by Flanagan of the Builders' Labourers' Union and by Arthur Henderson.[28] The trouble, declared Henderson, was 'the affiliated organisations who, after getting their resolutions carried, if they do not get them put into the shape of a Bill, were constantly sending letters of protest'.

Baker of the Enginemen said that:

> they found members going to the House of Commons, and not only disregarding the instructions given them, but absolutely voting against the registered wish of the conference. He thought they had a right to be suspicious of actions like those. The Executive Committee would be extremely wise to withdraw this resolution and not challenge the conference to give it a slap in the face.

But it was Baker and Tillett who got the slap in the face: Hardie's resolution was carried by 642,000 votes to 252,000. And in the final minutes of the conference, Hardie pressed home his opportunity. He was infuriated by the criticism he was receiving for his support of the Women's Enfranchisement Bill (recently introduced by a backbench Liberal MP). On one extreme were those like the SDF and Tillett, who had carried a motion that morning, against the Executive's advice, demanding opposition to anything but total and complete enfranchisement of all women. On the other extreme were those who saw Hardie's dedication to the cause of women's suffrage as a diversion from more important issues and resented his friendship with Sylvia Pankhurst, who some thought Hardie's mistress. The Women's Enfranchisement Bill would have given the vote to women on the same (partial) basis that it was at that time held by men and was thought to have a chance of success. In moving the Vote of Thanks at the close of conference Hardie declared that

> twenty-five years ago this year he cut himself adrift from every relationship, political and otherwise, in order to assist in building up a working-class party. He had thought the days of his pioneering were over. Of late he had felt with increasing intensity

the injustice which had been inflicted upon women by the present political laws. The intimation he wanted to make to the conference and friends was that if the motion they had carried that morning was intended to limit the action of the party in the House of Commons he should have seriously to consider whether he could remain a member of the parliamentary party. He said this with a great respect and feeling. The party was largely its own child and he would not sever himself lightly from what had been his life's work. But he could not be untrue to his principles and he would have to do so in order to remove the stigma resting upon their wives, mothers and sisters of being accounted unfit for political citizenship.

Hardie's argument became known to subsequent generations as 'the 1907 formula': the convention that party conferences could not bind the party in Parliament. As Hardie's biographer Kenneth Morgan has written: 'Labour leaders from Ramsay MacDonald to Harold Wilson continued to treat conference decisions, often the product of unrealistic euphoria conceived in the heady atmosphere of delegates assembled for an annual safety valve of oratory, as statements of opinion, but not mandates.'[29]

Keir Hardie's time as leader in 1906–08 was not a great success. He did not enjoy the compromises of leadership and Ramsay MacDonald made far more impact in Parliament. During 1906 the Liberals, significantly influenced by Labour pressure, had passed a Trade Disputes Act setting aside the Taff Vale judgment, a Workmen's Compensation Act, and an Act enabling local councils to provide free school meals to deprived children. But 1907 saw rising unemployment and Labour enjoyed little success in securing further legislative reforms from the Liberal government. Hardie's health also suffered and he retired as party leader with some relief at the start of 1908.

Despite pressure from MacDonald and others, the able trade unionist David Shackleton refused to stand, so Hardie was succeeded by Arthur Henderson. Though Henderson was a popular trade unionist and Wesleyan lay preacher, neither he nor his successor George Barnes, the Dundee-born former Engineering Union leader and Glasgow MP who led Labour during both the 1910 elections, proved inspiring or successful leaders. Henderson's lack of socialist zeal and closeness to the Liberals frustrated the ILP radicals. Barnes's lack of political judgement provoked unnecessary clashes between not only Labour and Liberals, but between himself and other Labour MPs, whom he openly accused of 'slackness' and 'timidity' in his draft report to the 1911 conference.

Against this background MacDonald's star continued to rise, and in 1911 he became leader. Despite his growing parliamentary reputation, for much of the time MacDonald's role had been confined to the parliamentary fringe. As his biographer David Marquand has written, 'he could put a Labour gloss on Liberal proposals and introduce socialist arguments into the struggle between the two capitalist parties, but he could not decide what proposals were to be made or determine the framework within which the struggle was to be conducted'.[30] An exception to this, which enabled him to play a far more commanding role, was the 1908 Right to Work Bill, initially drawn up in 1907 by MacDonald and Isaac Mitchell, the secretary of the General Federation of Trade Unions. It was clumsily drafted, resembling more a manifesto than a conventional Bill, and got no further than a first reading. Nevertheless it was, as Marquand recognised, 'a landmark in labour history'. Unemployment brought poverty and destitution which in turn helped explain why, according to government admission, coroners had blamed the deaths of 49 Londoners during 1906 on starvation.[31] The Bill sought to make local authorities responsible for finding work for the unemployed and for providing maintenance if no work could be found. When unemployment reached 4 per cent national funding would automatically come into play to finance local job-creation schemes, entailing both 'a deliberate national effort to tackle the trade cycle' and the introduction into British law of 'the revolutionary principle that work was a right'.[32] In 1908, a sympathetic Liberal MP, Philip Whitwell Wilson, was successful in the ballot for private members' bills and reintroduced it. Its bitterest opponents included John Burns. During the 1880s Burns had been the greatest working-class orator in London, star speaker of the Social Democratic Federation and, along with Tom Mann and Ben Tillett, a leader of the great London Dock Strike of 1889. Elected MP for Battersea at the 1892 general election, he was never enthusiastic for Keir Hardie's vision of an independent Labour Party, although he had attended the Farringdon Street conference that had founded the Labour Representation Committee in 1900. Since 1905 he had been president of the Local Government Board in the Liberal Cabinet, and his failure to tackle the blight of unemployment drove the Labour MPs from frustration to anger. Burns denounced the Bill as a 'delusion and a snare' that would discourage the workers from actively seeking work and destroy the trade unions and friendly societies. Though it was defeated by 267 votes to 118 after the second reading debate, MacDonald's speech on 13 March 1908, seconding it on behalf of the Labour Party, was 'the most effective he had yet made in the House of Commons'.[33] Hansard records that he began boldly:

> The Labour Party stood for the right to work; they had nothing to withdraw from that and no modification to make. [MacDonald argued that if modern industry required a level of unemployment of some 10 per cent] not because the men unemployed were inferior in character to the men employed, but because of the very nature of the organisation of their industry they must have that margin. [Was there not] a logical, fair, and humane corollary that the burden of unemployment should not be placed upon the backs of those weak men? If it was necessary for society that a section should be without work, was it not the duty of society to take care that that section should not be trodden down to destruction? [He attacked the idea that unemployment was] a most blessed experience sent from heaven to discipline them and make them better men

41

than they were before [and the argument that action would be too costly:] Supposing they compelled a compositor to give two or three hours a day, while work was being found for him, to teaching a typographical class in St Bride's Institute. Supposing they thus got a *quid pro quo* . . . they were making an admirable bargain . . . It was all very well for the House to say it provided for the poverty-stricken. It did, that was admitted. It provided for them when they got to the gutter. It provided for the poverty-stricken when they entered the sombre gates of the workhouse. The Labour Party had come into existence to help the poverty-stricken while they were still capable of working. It was all very well to talk about the cost. The cost would not be more than on 'Dreadnought' per annum. The House must not forget, when dealing with economic problems, that its coin was not always gold and silver. It was often of a human quality; and, if they were going to allow a human mass to fester in their midst, they were reducing the vitality of their women and demoralising their men; and from such sources they were creating a poisoned centre which would lower their national vitality. That was the coin in which they were going to pay for this chronic state of unemployment. Pounds, shillings and pence were too often before the eyes of sections of the House. The human character of the nation was too frequently put aside without adequate consideration . . .

They did not want relief work. That was a fallacy. They did not want to put a spade in a man's hand and tell him to go and dig a hole. That was no good. If it ended there, it was no good, but if it subserved something else, of course it was good. They wanted training work . . .

He felt perfectly certain that the government was altogether underestimating the tremendous interest that was being taken by the working men of the country in this question. They were thoroughly ashamed of the spectacle of a workman out of employment, trudging about the streets, ragged and fringed, going down to his own destruction. They believed that the people of the country would support them in asking that the House should lend every energy it had, and use every power at its disposal, to remove that stain and that disgrace from our Christianity and our civilisation.

FIVE

George Lansbury and the Fight for Women's Suffrage 1910–12

'A message of hope for millions of women'

Not all Labour MPs were impressed with MacDonald's leadership. A notable dissident was George Lansbury, who had become MP for Bow and Poplar in December 1910, at the age of 51. Lansbury had been secretary of the Bow and Bromley Liberals in the late 1880s, before disillusion and involvement in the Gasworkers' and General Labourers' Union took him on a journey via the Social Democratic Federation to the ILP and election to Poplar council and the London County Council. He was a Christian socialist, a convinced pacifist and a teetotaller (the last conviction in part a reaction to his parents' alcoholism). Deeply idealistic, he resented what he saw as the moral compromises that under MacDonald's leadership the Parliamentary Labour Party was making with the Liberal government. During 1911 Lansbury led a small group of Labour MPs, including Philip Snowden and Will Thorne, who opposed the contributory principle of the Liberal government's National Insurance proposals and campaigned unsuccessfully for a non-contributory scheme and the state provision of a national health service. MacDonald led the bulk of Labour MPs in support of the Liberal proposals on the basis that while they may not have been perfect, they were nevertheless a step in the right direction and the best that could be secured at that time given the reluctance of many Liberal MPs to support anything more radical. Crucially, MacDonald, unlike Lansbury, was not prepared to risk bringing down the Liberal government and letting the Conservatives in. Lansbury wrote in the *Labour Leader*:

> There is a great danger that if the government once imagine in the Labour Party that they may count on 42 safe votes, under all conditions and circumstances, they will see us to Heaven or Hades before they will trouble about the unemployed, the destitute and the women's question. I am not content that the next two or three years should be devoted to Constitutional Reform, plus Welsh Disestablishment. The condition-of-the-people question is of greater importance than any other reform.[34]

The other major issue on which Lansbury came to clash with the Labour leadership was that of votes for women, of which, with Hardie and Snowden, he became perhaps the most vociferous parliamentary advocate. The problem for Lansbury was not that most other Labour MPs did not support it too. It was that they did not share Lansbury's preparedness to bring down the Liberal government over its failure to deliver reform on the issue. The deep split on the issue within the ranks of Liberal MPs, with the Liberal Prime Minister among those against, meant that on a free vote there was not a majority for it in the House of Commons.

On the second reading of the Women's Enfranchisement Bill on 5 May 1911 (which proposed the enfranchisement of women who independently occupied property) Lansbury intervened decisively to counter the traditional arguments used to deny women the parliamentary vote. He began by attacking the idea that:

> The vote only represents the power behind it, and that it must in the last resource rest on physical force. I want the House to realise that that argument might be perfectly sound and true when the nation fought as it used to fight centuries ago. But at the present moment it is, I think, rather out of date to say that the growing mass of men and women in this country who have the votes would be capable of fighting, even if they were called upon to fight . . . I venture to say that the women who manipulate the machinery in the cotton fields of Lancashire could just as easily manipulate the machinery either of a 'Dreadnought', a submarine or a maxim gun . . .' [It was 40 years since Parliament had first voted on votes for women] and we say that women have knocked at that door long enough. [The same arguments were being deployed against votes for women as had been deployed against extending the franchise to working men: that they didn't want the vote and that they were uneducated and that they would all vote Liberal] and that the Monarchy and goodness knows what would be pulled down. I have lived long enough to know that there are Conservative working men, and when the men were enfranchised instead of voting all one way they voted in different kinds of ways on the different kinds of questions. Therefore, there is no reason to imagine, as the hon. gentleman does imagine, that if the women got the vote that all of them would come together in one mass. There is nothing in the argument about civil war, if the ultimate of it is not that the women are going to organise definitely against the men . . .
>
> It is said that woman has nothing to complain of, that men have guarded her interests, looked after her, and managed affairs for her. The streets of this end of London reek with conditions which show that at any rate some men have not dealt very decently with a large number of women. In the East End of London the same kind of horror exists, mainly because of the helplessness of the women, and because they have had no part or lot in definitely framing the conditions of life under which they have to live. The Divorce Laws are, in my judgement, the most iniquitous that it is possible to make women live under. Then there is the question of the children. A barbarous thing has happened, not a century ago, but under the law of the land today. A woman is deserted by her husband, and her children are taken care of by the Board of Guardians, who have given her notice that they have taken over the custody of the children, and are going to send them to Canada or anywhere they please. I say that a

woman who bears children ought at least to have some right in owning them. But at present that is not the case.

It is said to be all right to give women the vote for municipal affairs, because they can administer. That, I think, is rather an absurd argument. Surely if women are capable of administering laws, they ought to be able to advise the community as to the kind of laws they shall administer. What is the record of women in this respect? I speak with some knowledge on the subject, having served on local authorities for many years. Take the Royal Commission, to which reference was made yesterday. Who were the most brilliant members of that committee? Who were the two people who took the greatest part in building up both the Majority and the Minority Reports? The two persons who were most industrious and gave the most help on that Commission were Helen Bosanquet and Beatrice Webb. But these two women are ruled out from having a vote as to whether their propositions shall be carried through . . .

If you refuse to earnestly carry this Bill today, if you refuse the Session to pass this Bill, we are going to have all the old, hideous riot, noise and disorder. Yes, you are bound to have it. Men fought in that way. Women are outside your constitution. You keep them outside. You are putting them under laws that they have had no part or lot in framing. They are rebels against that condition of things. For my part I glory in the magnificent fight that they have put up on behalf of themselves and their sex. If this House can settle the riot and disorder in Ireland by the grant of Home Rule, next year you are going to settle the disturbances there, not by dragooning, not by refusing to give justice, but by giving it . . .

However, although the Women's Enfranchisement Bill passed its Commons second reading, Asquith refused to provide further government time for it to progress, promising instead a new manhood Suffrage Bill (extending votes to all men) with a free vote to convert it into a Universal Suffrage Bill. Lansbury feared, correctly, that they would lose the free vote and end up supporting Asquith's new Bill unamended in order to secure votes for all working-class men and to avoid turning out the Liberal government. Meanwhile the cause of women's suffrage would have got nowhere.

On 25 June 1912, against a background of increasing numbers of gaoled suffragettes going on hunger strike and being force-fed in Holloway Prison, Home Office Under-Secretary Ellis Griffiths joked in the Commons to the laughter of other MPs that one suffragette who had attempted to throw herself from an upper prison floor had not intended suicide, 'or she would have chosen a higher drop'. Asquith added that any of the suffragettes could go free from prison if they would only renounce militancy (some had been gaoled for violent acts such as arson and stone throwing). Lansbury's anger boiled over, causing one of Parliament's most heated scenes:

You know that they cannot! It is perfectly disgraceful that the Prime Minister of England should make such a statement. [White and shaking with rage, Lansbury left his seat and with the Commons in uproar strode across the chamber to confront

Asquith directly:]

You are beneath contempt; you call yourselves gentlemen and you forcibly feed and murder women in this fashion! You ought to be driven out of office. It is perfectly disgraceful. Talk about protesting! It is the most disgraceful thing that ever happened in the history of England! You will go down in history as the man who tortured innocent women. That is what you will go down in history as.

[Returning to his seat below the gangway, Lansbury initially refused to follow the Speaker's instruction to leave the chamber] while this contemptible thing is being done . . . murdering, torturing and driving women mad, and telling them they can walk out . . . You may talk about principle and fight in Ulster. You ought to be driven out of public life. You do not know what principle is. You should honour them for standing up for their womenhood. I say for the Prime Minister to say that they could walk out is beneath contempt . . .[35]

Within months, Lansbury had decided that his position within the Parliamentary Labour Party was untenable. Refusing to be bound by the Labour whip to support a manhood Suffrage Bill unamended to include votes for women, Lansbury resigned his parliamentary seat and fought a by-election on the issue. The contest was between Lansbury, fighting as an 'Independent (Women's Suffrage and Socialist)', and a Scottish Conservative accountant from Harrow. Pro- and anti-women's suffrage campaigners poured into the constituency to help each campaign. By more than seven hundred votes, Lansbury was defeated, not to return to the Commons until 1922. Ironically there were actually three women voters on the parliamentary register. Two were absent on polling day. One voted: for Lansbury's Conservative anti-suffrage opponent, despite a personal visit from Mrs Pankhurst. But though Lansbury lost the battle, he helped win the war, turning the screw ever tighter on the reluctant Liberal government to concede a democratic franchise.[36]

SIX

Labour at War 1914–17

'It was Germany, the greatest opponent of international arbitration, that brought about the war, and where were Mr Snowden and the others when these things ought to have been pointed out?'

The next few years were dominated by the First World War, which broke out in August 1914. Labour had expected its Social Democratic comrades in Germany and other countries to mobilise against the war they feared, to vote against the money to wage it in their parliaments and to take strike action in the munitions factories. But the prospect of international anti-war solidarity among the workers proved a mirage. Most Labour supporters agreed with Ramsay MacDonald's criticisms of the Liberal government's 'secret diplomacy', but following the German invasion of Belgium, they felt overtaken by events. The German workers did not prevent the invasion of Belgium: they filled the army that was doing the invading. On the Sunday the crowds in Trafalgar Square had gathered to demonstrate against war and on the Monday and Tuesday they massed in favour. They wanted, in the words of Fabian and novelist H. G. Wells, 'to be done forever with this drilling, trampling foolery at the heart of Europe'.[37] And the war would be over by Christmas. Only a few ILP stalwarts supported MacDonald's continued criticism of the government.[38] Within days MacDonald had resigned as leader, being succeeded by Arthur Henderson.

By 1915 Labour had agreed to join a Liberal-led coalition government, Arthur Henderson becoming Labour's first Cabinet minister. In December 1916 Lloyd George ousted Asquith as Prime Minister and formed a new coalition government. Lloyd George pledged that there would be wartime food rationing (food prices had risen by nearly 80 per cent since war had begun) and state control of the mines and shipping, winning round several key Labour figures who had been sceptical of Labour's participation in the previous coalition. These included the Lancashire-born Gas and General Workers' Union president and Manchester MP J. R. Clynes and the railwaymen's leader and Derby MP Jimmy Thomas, widely acknowledged as 'rapidly becoming the most powerful personality in the trade unions'.[39] When Lloyd George formed his new coalition government, Arthur Henderson joined the five-man War Cabinet, while John Hodge of the Steel Smelters' Union became Minister of Labour and former Labour leader George Barnes became Minister of Pensions.

The decision to participate so fully created a memorable clash at the next Labour Party conference at Manchester in January 1917. Manny Shinwell, then a young member of the ILP and later to serve in several Labour Cabinets, recollected,

> the party conference was held . . . within six weeks of the government changes and many delegates were worried about the inferences of close liaison with the Liberals. The conference president, George Wardle, sought to warn the delegates at the outset that criticism of the parliamentary party's cooperation would merely be sources of moral injury. 'After the election of 1910,' he reminded conference, 'an American critic prophesied that the Labour Party would eventually fail through absorption or through internal dissensions, and considered the latter more likely. Is this to be its fate?' Many delegates thought that it was.

Philip Snowden summoned up all his venom to unleash a ferocious attack on Henderson and Thomas, accusing them of betraying the independence of the Labour Party:

> Was conscription one of the great causes Labour wanted to promote? Was industrial slavery under the Munitions Act one of the great causes Labour wished to promote? Was the suppression of civil liberty and the right of public meeting a cause in which they were interested? The fact of the matter was that the freedom of action of the Labour members in the government had been shackled during those eighteen months, and the action of the party had been hindered and hampered. They were called disloyal when they criticised or opposed legislation introduced by the government and for which Labour members were responsible . . . [In contrast, argued Snowden, the Irish Nationalists had remained independent and served] the interests of their own people far better than if bound to the feet and legs of men who were strong enough to drag them in the opposite direction to that which they wish to go.

Snowden agitated for the repeal of the Conscription Act despite Labour conference having voted against such action, and he was accused by Gilmour of the Miners' Federation of contempt for a cardinal trade union principle: loyalty to democratically agreed majority decisions. Instead Snowden was 'going out of his way to write articles in the capitalist press when trade unionists were fighting a life and death struggle . . . There was no loyalty in that. If there was to be loyalty from the trade unions there would have be loyalty from everybody.' Tom Shaw[40] of the Textile Workers was more florid: he was not concerned as to whether Mr Henderson was:

> a kind of semi-idiot without brains, without will, and without initiative, or as to whether Mr Snowden was a God-gifted intellectual who could perceive in the first moment everything that was best for the movement, but he was concerned about the principles he imbibed 20 years ago and the results of which he wished to see. In all this discussing at conference there had been a remarkable type of individual in evidence, an individual with only one lobe to his brain and only one eye capable of seeing every fault of the Allies and absolutely blind to the faults of the other side.

In the international movement the two resolutions which were always passed with acclamation were in favour of reduction of armaments and international arbitration. When this struggle came along what was the position of affairs? It was Germany, the greatest opponent of international arbitration, that brought about the war, and where were Mr Snowden and the others when these things ought to have been pointed out? They were silent. They had done everything to hinder an advance of the principles they all held dear. The answer as to what the Labour movement wanted at the beginning of the war was given by the workers when they voluntarily enlisted to fight for a cause they thought was the cause of freedom. Labour was not Mr Snowden, nor Mr Henderson, nor Mr Gilmour, nor himself, it was the men who paid the piper all the time. The Labour Party was composed of the men and women in the mines and the workshops. Those people had decided, and approved that decision, that they believed the war to be a just war. The question he asked himself was: Was it a good thing for Labour men to go into the Cabinet or was it not? What were other nations doing? In Germany universal military and industrial conscription had been introduced with the consent of the socialist party. Only nineteen votes were cast against it, and the social-ist party was the largest individual party in the State. There was a people united to fight. To fight what? To fight the lads who had gone from this and other countries and were fighting in defence of the principles that socialist congresses, national and international, had laid down for the last quarter of a century. He was not a Jingo. He detested the man who said his country ought to be defended right or wrong. The only thing that was worth defending was the right. He detested the man who believed in his country right or wrong, but the miserable person who believed that his country was always wrong and tried to make it always wrong was the subject of his special detesta-tion. He did not know how they were going to get a better state of things for the lads who had gone to fight and for those whom they ought to consider first and foremost than by a concentrated effort on the part of every party. Did anyone doubt that the withdrawal of the party would have a bad effect? Did anyone doubt the fact that their withdrawal would stop peace coming as soon as it might? [Snowden lost the vote by 1,849,000 votes to 307,000.]

SEVEN

Electoral Defeat and Victory for the Dockers 1918–20

'Dockers' KC'

The 'Coupon Election' of December 1918 gave Labour only 57 seats. Henderson, MacDonald and Snowden were all defeated; the last two undoubtedly suffered for the anti-war stance that they had taken. Henderson had resigned from Lloyd George's War Cabinet and as leader of the Parliamentary Labour Party in October 1917 after his War Cabinet colleagues sought to block his involvement in a proposed international socialist conference at Stockholm. This conference was to include workers' organisations of the belligerent countries who would discuss potential peace terms which they could then force upon their respective governments.

In the absence of more suitable candidates, Henderson was succeeded in the War Cabinet by George Barnes and as Labour's leader by Willie Adamson. Adamson was a devout and heavily built Baptist who had co-founded the Dunfermline Temperance Society, was to serve as Scottish Secretary in both the 1924 and 1929–31 Labour governments and retained a bristling chestnut moustache into his later years. Widely trusted and industrious though he was, Adamson was a poor debater and illness contributed to absences from Parliament during much of 1919 and 1920. Manny Shinwell recalled him as 'a dour and phlegmatic Scottish miners' leader very much out of his depth in the Commons'.[41]

While Labour's performance in Parliament was disappointing, outside Parliament, one of the next generation of Labour's leaders was coming into his own. When Ben Tillett's Dockers' Union failed to persuade the employers to accept its pay claim, Ernest Bevin, its little-known Assistant General Secretary, feared that his union would be manoeuvred into a debilitating strike that it would be too weak to win. He persuaded his union colleagues to agree instead to a government-sponsored Court of Inquiry (made possible under the new provisions of the 1919 Industrial Courts Act) to arbitrate the dispute. Bevin's mother had died when he was eight. He had never even known who his father was. He had been brought up by his half-sister and her railwayman husband in a small cottage by the Exeter–Barnstaple railway line, working as a farm labourer on leaving school at eleven. But he believed that the dockers' case was sufficiently strong for him to present it to the inquiry and win through against potentially the most eminent barristers in the land. And he was right. His eleven-hour speech, delivered over three days, earned him the epithet 'Dockers' KC' from the *Daily Herald*. Even the Northcliffe-owned *Daily Mail* called his performance 'masterly'.

Bevin began:

> The court will appreciate that this is an unusual environment for me to be in and also that the proceedings are very novel for the whole Labour movement of this country. We have agreed as transport workers to submit our claims to the test of public inquiry, first because we are convinced of the justice of our claim, and secondly because we have no objection to the whole question of the standard of life being open for public inquiry. We hope it will serve not only to obtain what our men desire but to influence public opinion to a higher conception of what that standard of life ought to be.[42]

He went on to argue that dockers' wages had been inadequate for years and that although some increase had been secured in monetary terms it had only been with the greatest difficulty:

> It is true and we say it with pride that, by sheer weight of organisation we have effected improvements, but never yet can I remember a single concession ever handed out to the workmen willingly . . .The dockers have had one of the highest death rates in this country, due to their irregular life and the horrible slum conditions. Men were injured and it was a common thing for the bullying foreman to say: 'Throw him in the wing and get on with the work . . .' If the men dared to protest . . . it was 'To the office and get your money and clear out.' And then they might stand on the stones for weeks . . . as an example to other people for obedience.[43]

He explained that the Great War had reduced wages in real terms: that while dockers had secured a 104 per cent increase in wages, the cost of living had increased by 134 per cent. Meanwhile 'the shipowners pocketed £350,000'. He then torpedoed the employers' central claim that they could not afford to pay a higher wage by putting before the court ample evidence of the considerable profits made by employers. He even cited the admission of Conservative Cabinet minister and future leader Andrew Bonar Law that in the previous year he had made a profit of 47 per cent on his shipping shares, after the excess profits tax had been paid. Bevin continued:

> I find that the Admiralty Arbitration Board to fix the rates for requisitioning ships were all shipowners with one exception . . . They were trusted to fix the rates which they still charge the State . . . and their rates were accepted, with the result that at the end of the war, they have added millions to their profits, while our men are worse off than in 1914.

He concluded with an emotional appeal that held the courtroom silent and produced several minutes of sustained applause as he sat down:

The claim covers practically all classes of dock work. I challenge counsel to show that a family can exist in physical efficiency on less than I have indicated. I say that if the captains of industry cannot organise their concerns so as to give labour a living wage then they should resign from their captaincy. If you refuse our claim then I suggest you must adopt an alternative. You must go to the Prime Minister. You must go to the Minister of Education and tell him to close down our schools and teach us nothing. We must get back then to the purely fodder basis. For it is no use to give us knowledge if we are not to be given the possibility of using it, to give us a sense of the beautiful without allowing us ever to have a chance to obtain the enjoyment of it. Education creates aspirations and a love of the beautiful. Are we to be denied the wherewithal to secure these things? It is a false policy. Better to let us live in the dark if our claims are not to be met.[44]

Over the following days Bevin tore apart the shipowners' expert witnesses. To demonstrate the inadequacy of the shipowners' 'model budget' Bevin and his secretary Mae Forcey bought exactly the amount of food allowed for in the model budget at a street market in Canning Town, cooked and divided it on to five plates to simulate the portions that the average docker's family would receive, and the next morning placed the plates in front of the court. 'I ask the court,' said Bevin, 'to examine the dinner which Counsel for the Employers considers adequate to sustain the strength of a docker hauling seventy-one tons of wheat a day on his back.' The employers then put A. L. Bowley, the Professor of Statistics at the University of London and author of their 'model budget', into the witness box. Bowley argued that if the budget were spent properly then sufficient 'calorific value' of food could be purchased. Bevin was incensed.

Francis Williams, later editor of the *Daily Herald*, wrote a memorable account of what followed:

Next day Bevin produced a 'ration' of bacon bought according to the model budget and divided onto five plates. 'Would the Professor with his vast knowledge of calorific values, he asked, consider one of these plates sufficient for a docker – a docker, not a scientist.' Bowley replied tartly that the docker did not eat bacon and nothing else. He might prefer fish. Next day Bevin produced a new set of plates, this time with the model budget's worth of fish. 'Is this what the Professor regards as adequate?' he asked. Bowley replied that the children could be given bread and margarine instead and later added that the mother could buy flour and bake them a cake – to which Bevin responded: 'But what about fat?' Flour for a cake was no use without fat. How much fat, he asked the Professor, was required to a pound of flour to make a cake? Bowley admitted ignorance. Bevin told him it needed three ounces of fat to a pound of flour for a cake mixture. 'It does not matter much where you put the fat so long as you get the children to eat it,' replied Bowley. 'No,' said Bevin, 'but you see if you didn't put it in the cake the children wouldn't eat the cake.'[45]

Eventually Bevin pulled out the menu from the Savoy Hotel restaurant:

This is a menu which an ordinary shipowner, whom we are asking for a living wage, would go to the Savoy to have today at 7/-. You allow for five persons 40/- a week for food, and that is 7/- for one person for one lunch. What is the calorific value of that when he has eaten it? As a scientist have you entered into a careful diagnosis of what the rich live on compared with the poor; have you worked out a budget for them? Do you live on 40/- worth of food? You have never carried 5cwt bags on your back for eight hours continuously? – No.[46]

Bevin later told Francis Williams: 'People thought all that business with the plates was just a clever stunt. It wasn't. Those fellows quote statistics but they forget about human beings. I had to make 'em remember they were dealing with human lives – it's terribly easy to forget that when you're sitting in a court or on a government commission.'[47] The court found in favour of the dockers on virtually every count. Though Bevin didn't immediately secure the de-casualisation of dock labour (that had to wait until he himself became Minister of Labour 20 years later) he did secure a 44-hour week and a national minimum rate of 16s. per day. He had also successfully demonstrated an effective alternative to strike action in securing better conditions for British workers.

EIGHT

MacDonald and Clydeside
Set the Tone 1921–22

'A left of action, and not of talk'

Willie Adamson was replaced as Labour's leader in February 1921 by his deputy of 1918–21, J. R. Clynes, a far more effective speaker and an organiser of ability but nevertheless not someone in the same league as Ramsay MacDonald. MacDonald's defeat in 1918 and his narrow failure to secure victory at the East Woolwich by-election in March 1921 had occurred in the face of appalling attacks by both his opponents and the press: 'The most notable instance of this hostility was the occasion when *John Bull* editor Horatio Bottomley published MacDonald's birth certificate. This revealed that MacDonald was illegitimate, being registered as James MacDonald Ramsay after his father. Bottomley claimed that MacDonald was both an imposter and a traitor, and as such should be taken to the Tower of London and shot at dawn.'[48] These defeats served to create much sympathy for him and he was gladly accepted as candidate for Aberavon. He easily won the seat in the election of November 1922, when Labour secured four and a quarter million votes and 142 Commons seats. Clynes was renominated as leader but Manny Shinwell, the new MP for Linlithgow, nominated MacDonald, who defeated Clynes by 61 to 56. Many of those who supported MacDonald were younger MPs. They had been greatly impressed when at the June 1921 Labour conference he had spoken out ostensibly on behalf of the Labour left. The occasion was in a debate on a resolution of support for the miners, then suffering terribly from a prolonged lock-out in the wake of 'Black Friday' and the collapse of the 'Triple Alliance' with the railwaymen and transport workers. MacDonald paid tribute to the miners:

> in their capacity to sacrifice, in . . . one of the most inspiring fights . . . Labour had to be warned against mere talk on occasions like this. The left was not composed of irresponsible men who spoke of grand things knowing that it would never have the responsibility of carrying them into effect. The left was composed of men who faced reality, and who, when they were up against a mountain, honestly said that they were up against a mountain. The left were men who were constantly living in the real world, and who did not sit down by their firesides and imagine an unreal world in order to make fine-sounding speeches and tickle the attention and the imagination and the

minds of the great mass of the people . . . look to your tactics; Labour, do not be mis-led by mere words; Labour, do not put to the left mere talkers; remember that the left is the left of action and not of talk; remember that the left is a left of reality and not of imagination; remember that the left is a left of responsibility and not of irresponsi-bility. They were going on with the whole of the Labour movement in its manifold aspects united together in one spirit to attain one goal. It may have its ups and downs but, as was said by Gibbon of the Roman Empire, it lost many battles but it never lost a war. They might lose battles but they would never lose the war. They might be worsted now and again and might have to adopt new weapons, but their path was onward, onward, onward all the time . . .

The 1922 election, precipitated by the break-up of Lloyd George's coalition govern-ment, more than doubled Labour's MPs: from 61 to 142. On Clydeside it was said that Glasgow blazed red. Ten of the city's fifteen constituencies had elected socialist MPs including James Maxton and John Wheatley. The Conservative Prime Minister Andrew Bonar Law had only narrowly escaped defeat at Glasgow Central. Gordon Brown, biog-rapher of James Maxton, perhaps the most famous of the 'Red Clydesiders' and perhaps the most charismatic socialist orator of his generation, evocatively described the scene when on 20 November 1922 eighteen of the new Scottish Labour MPs left on the 10.45 p.m. mail train from Glasgow's St Enoch's Station:

> In their ears rang the words of Psalm 124, sung by the massive and triumphant crowd around:
>
> > 'Now Israel may say and that truly
> > If that the Lord had not our cause maintained
> > If that the Lord had not our right sustained
> > When cruel men against us furiously
> > Rose up in wrath to make of us their prey.'

Not sentiments widely heard in Bolshevik Russia, and the declaration issued earlier in the day owed more to the Bible than to Bolshevism, more to the traditions of the Scottish Covenanters than those of Soviet Communism . . . Two huge Red Flags glowed brilliant in the gleams of arc lamps above the station, as from the steps James Houston conducted the William Morris choir and the crowd sang *The Red Flag*, the *International* and *Jerusalem* . . . The crowd in their thousands joined in . . . some say 40,000, others 80,000, others still 120,000. They filled the station square and over-flowed into Argyle Street and its side-streets.

Maxton, 'swarthy, lantern jawed and intense with a huge lank forelock (definitely not for tugging) – not only preached the revolution but, as one commentator remarked at the time, looked it'. Though only 37 when he went to Westminster, he had been first a teacher, then the Glasgow organiser for the ILP and a member of the local education authority. 'From a truck he addressed possibly the most enthusiastic audience he had ever faced . . . "People talk about the atmosphere of the House of Commons getting the better of the Labour men," he said, "they will see the atmosphere of the Clyde getting the better of the House of Commons."'[49]

Maxton made his maiden speech on 8 December 1922, playing the Commons 'as he might have played a half-hostile crowd in his stump orator days, provoking interjections he could then handle on his own terms'[50] and gaining great prominence in the national press, not least for the implicit threat contained in his closing words:

> . . . at the end of June of this year we were feeding in the city of Glasgow 10,000 necessitous children of unemployed men. They were only a fraction of the necessitous children, and the Prime Minister knows that as well as I do. Every one of those cases, before public feeding could be allowed, had been carefully investigated by paid investigators of the Glasgow Education Authority. They had to go through the eye of a needle before they got the three meals a day which they required to maintain them in mere physical fitness to be educated. They were being fed on the last day of June, and by an administrative act of the last government, of which the late Minister of Labour was a Member, on 1 July every one of those 10,000 children was reduced to starvation. That has continued almost up to the present day. Out of the 10,000 only 1,000 have been put back on to the scale for feeding, and as to the rest the parents are told to go to the parish council. They were told that only after three months' delay, and the children have starved in the meantime.
>
> We who come from the Glasgow district to this House have had many lectures on etiquette, on how to conduct themselves, from right hon. and hon. gentlemen on the other side of the House and on this side. There is Dr. Macnamara. I mean the right hon. Member for North-East Camberwell, but it does not matter one damn.
>
> *The Chairman:* That is not proper language to use.
>
> *Mr Maxton:* I apologise, and withdraw the word. I will know in time what is the proper vocabulary for use in this House. We have had many lectures on etiquette, manners and conduct from right hon. gentlemen in all parts of the House, and from the Press of this city, addressed particularly to those of us who come from the west of Scotland. We admit frankly that perhaps on the nicer points of good form we have different ideas from hon. Members on the other side of the House. Our dialect is somewhat different also, and perhaps our mode of dressing is slightly different. But we think it is the very worst form, the very worst taste, that it shows very bad breeding, to kick a man who is in the gutter, or to withdraw a crust from a starving child. That is the Glasgow idea of conduct and breeding. Is it the idea of the right hon. gentlemen and hon. gentlemen on the other side? If they believe that in private life it is a cowardly thing to bully a child or to kick a dog, the good form of private life should be carried into the public duties of this Chamber.

[Unemployment relief money was too little to live on, argued Maxton, and of course expired after a year. Neither would he accept that] the receiving of public money by an unemployed man has a deteriorating effect on the character of that man . . . any more than I believe that the receiving of unearned income by hon. Members opposite has any deteriorating effect on their character. They are what they are for an entirely different reason . . . Whatever hon. Members on the other side may believe, we believe in the West of Scotland that our working classes are as good, as capable, and as hard working and energetic men and women as are to be found anywhere in this wide world . . .

I am going back to my constituency, to 37,000 people, men, women and children, mostly on the verge of starvation, and I have to tell them that the new government of this country is going to do for them exactly the same as the last government did – nothing of any account, apart from by attempting to produce in this country cheaper than in any other country in the world. That is to say, our people are going to be enabled to get the means of life by going down to the starvation level of wages.

That is a poor look out for the people of this country for the next three years, and I will not go back to my constituents in the West of Scotland – I have not consulted them, but I think I can speak for all the Members for the West of Scotland in this matter – we will not go back to our people, and tell them that they are to starve in peace and quietness. We will not do so. It would not be right. I am as great a constitutionalist as any Member on that Front Bench or this Front Bench, but there is a point where constitutionalists have to give way before human necessity. I tell the working-class people of the West of Scotland that this House has nothing to give them. They will have to depend upon themselves and win through to security and comfort by their own efforts. I am quite certain that the working class of the West of Scotland will devise ways and means of making themselves felt in that direction . . .

NINE

Opposition and Government 1922–24

'The inevitability of gradualness'

The 1922 election saw Labour become His Majesty's Official Opposition. For the first time it had overtaken the combined Liberals in terms of its share of votes cast. Labour had come a long way since 1900. One aspect of its transformation was the adoption of a new constitution by the party conference of 1918. This new constitution provided for individual membership of the Labour Party, enabling Labour's growth into a proper national political party. Previously individual Labour membership had been through trade unions or affiliated socialist societies. The new constitution was written largely by Arthur Henderson and Sidney Webb. Webb, a precise-minded lower-middle-class London civil servant, had been one of the key driving forces in the Fabian Society since its creation in 1884 as a progressive socialist society aiming to permeate the existing political parties with its ideas. But he had come to recognise the limitations of the original Fabian strategy. He began to realise, as the *Daily Herald* editor observed, that

> however strong the case for socialism put up by the Fabians and however much support they might be able to secure for individual items in their social reform programme from some members of the older parties, neither Liberals nor Conservatives were going to let themselves be argued into abandoning the positions of economic power and privilege which they regarded as theirs by right. If socialism was to come it must come through the securing of political power by a socialist party. And the one party able and willing to become socialist was the Labour Party.[51]

The new constitution that he and Henderson drafted gave Labour an explicit socialist commitment defined in terms of public ownership. This was the famous Clause Four: 'to secure for the producers by hand or by brain the full fruits of their industry and the most equitable distribution thereof that may be possible upon the basis of the common ownership of the means of production and the best obtainable system of popular administration and control of each industry and service'. Having served as the Fabians' representative on Labour's National Executive for many years, it fell to Webb to deliver the President's Address to Labour's annual conference on 26 June 1923, at the Queen's Hall, London. He used the opportunity to predict the inevitability of Labour's continued rise to power and set out his vision of a socialist future for Britain:

. . . First let me insist on what our opponents habitually ignore, and indeed, what they seem intellectually incapable of understanding, namely the inevitable gradualness of our scheme of change. The very fact that socialists have both principle and a programme appears to confuse nearly all their critics. If we state our principles, we are told, 'That is not practicable.' When we recite our programme the objection is, 'That is not socialism.' But why, because we are idealists, should we be supposed to be idiots? For the Labour Party, it must be plain, socialism is rooted in political democracy; which necessarily compels us to recognise that every step towards our goal is dependent on gaining the assent and support of at least a numerical majority of the whole people. Thus, even if we aimed at revolutionising everything at once, we should necessarily be compelled to make each particular change only at the time, and to the extent, and in the manner in which ten or fifteen million electors, in all sorts of conditions, of all sorts of temperaments, from Land's End to the Orkneys, could be brought to consent to it . . .

But the Labour Party, when in due course it comes to be entrusted with power, will naturally not even want to do everything at once. Surely, it must be abundantly manifest to any instructed person that, whilst it would be easy to draft proclamations of universal change, or even enact laws in a single sitting purporting to give a new Heaven and a new Earth, the result, the next morning, would be no change at all, unless indeed, the advent of widespread confusion. I remember Mr Bernard Shaw saying, a whole generation ago, 'Don't forget that, whilst you may nationalise the railways in one afternoon, it will take a long time to transform all the third-class carriages and all the first-class carriages into second-class carriages.' Once we face the necessity of putting our principles first into bills, to be fought through committee clause by clause; and then into the appropriate administrative machinery for carrying them into execution from one end of the kingdom to the other – and this is what the Labour Party has done with its socialism – the inevitability of gradualness cannot fail to be appreciated. This translation of socialism into practicable projects to be adopted one after another is just the task in which we have been engaged for a whole generation, with the result that, on every side, fragments of our proposals have already been put successfully into operation by Town and County Councils, and the national government itself, and have now become accepted as commonplaces by the average man. The whole nation has been imbibing socialism without realising it! It is now time for the subconscious to rise into consciousness . . .

Today, I make bold to say, what the world needs is not less government but more. This need for a perpetually increasing cooperation in social functions, in place of individualistic anarchy, springs inevitably from the ever-growing complexity of the social life of crowded populations, in which this very cooperation is the condition under which alone individual liberty can be maximised. We enjoy actually greater freedom on the highways because there is a Rule of the Road, than we should if everyone drove as the whim of the moment dictated . . .

What we had always to insist on is that government should, at all points, be effectively democratised; that it should be, wherever practicable, entrusted to the local representatives of the community rather than to the necessarily centralised departments at Whitehall; that in every branch the widest possible sphere should be assigned to the voluntarily associated Consumers' Co-operative Movement, which, be it remembered, is, to the socialist, an integral part of socialism itself; and that everywhere the necessary supervision and control to be exercised in Parliament and the central government should be supplemented by a steadily increasing participation in management by the vocational organisations of all grades of workers concerned . . .

We must always remember that the founder of British socialism was not Karl Marx but Robert Owen, and that Robert Owen preached not 'class war' but the ancient doctrine of human brotherhood – the hope, the faith, the living fact of human fellowship – a faith and a hope reaffirmed in the words of that other great British socialist – William Morris – in *The Dream of John Ball*. 'Forsooth, brothers, fellowship is heaven, and lack of fellowship is hell; fellowship is life, and lack of fellowship is death; and the deeds that ye do upon the earth, it is for fellowship's sake that ye do them; and the life that is in it, that shall live on and on for ever, and each one of you part of it, while many a man's life upon the earth from the earth shall wane.'

The next election came sooner than expected, in December 1923. Stanley Baldwin had replaced the ailing Andrew Bonar Law as Conservative Prime Minister in May. Within months he had decided to call an election to secure a mandate for tariff protection. The election, fought largely on tariffs versus free trade, saw the Conservatives remain the largest party with 258 seats (and 38.1 per cent of the vote) but lose their overall majority and saw gains both for Labour (who secured 30.5 per cent of the vote and 191 MPs) and the Asquith-led reunited Liberal Party (who secured 29.6 per cent of the vote and 159 MPs). Although, contrary to Webb's prediction, Labour's vote failed to increase considerably on 1922, Labour had now definitively pushed the Liberals into third place. When predictably he failed to defeat a vote of no confidence in the new Parliament, Baldwin resigned the premiership. Labour's leader, Ramsay MacDonald, seized the opportunity to prove that Labour could govern and on 22 January 1924 he became Labour's first Prime Minister. Unusually he decided to be his own Foreign Secretary. His Cabinet included Philip Snowden as Chancellor of the Exchequer, Sidney Webb at Trade, and Arthur Henderson at the Home Office. Clynes became Lord Privy Seal and deputy Leader of the House. Margaret Bondfield, the first woman to become a British government minister, became Parliamentary Secretary at the Minister of Labour (under Tom Shaw). One of his most successful ministers was to be 'Red Clydesider' John Wheatley, a largely self-educated ex-miner and ex-publican who on Glasgow Council had devised and popularised slum clearance schemes and in 1923 had established his own weekly newspaper. 'Well-dressed and rotund, with thick glasses, Wheatley looked more like a successful capitalist than a crusading socialist but it was Wheatley, more than anyone else, who had helped shift Glasgow's Catholics towards Labour.'[52] Some wanted the new

Labour government to produce a comprehensive socialist programme in the King's Speech and challenge the Liberals to combine with the Conservatives to vote it down. MacDonald, Henderson and the parliamentary leaders agreed on a different course: to try and carry through a moderate programme of domestic social reform and international cooperation, accepting necessary compromises with the Liberals. In doing so they hoped to demonstrate Labour's capacity to govern responsibly and so earn the support of the greater proportion of the electorate in future elections that would be necessary to secure a majority government and a more solid democratic mandate. MacDonald set out his approach on 8 January 1924 in a speech at Labour's Albert Hall victory rally:

> We are on the threshold of government. We may be called upon within the next few days to take upon our shoulders the responsibilities of office. We shall do it . . .
>
> Why will we take office? Because we are to shirk no responsibility that comes to us in the course of the evolution of our movement. There are risks, certainly, risks on every side – risks behind, before us, to the right of us, and to the left of us. Ah, but there is more than risks, there is a call. We have built our final habitations away on the horizon. We are a party of idealists. We are a party that away in the dreamland of imagination dwells in the social organisation fairer and more perfect than any organisation that mankind has ever known. That is true, but we are not going to jump there. We are going to walk there. We are upon a pilgrimage, we are on a journey. One step is enough for me. One step. Yes, on one condition – that it leads to a next step. If we shirked our responsibilities now we ourselves would be inflicting upon ourselves the defeat that our enemies could not inflict upon us. So we accept our responsibilities.

TEN

Division in Defeat 1924–28

'If socialism was at the end of the way one might have no great objection to the contents of this programme'

It was less than a year before the first Labour government itself lost a Commons confidence vote. Its achievements were limited but nevertheless tangible. It abolished the gap between periods of benefit under the unemployment insurance scheme, it raised unemployment benefit rates, children's allowances and adult education grants, it improved pension conditions, it reversed the education cuts of the previous governments and progressed public works schemes including the construction of forty new secondary schools. Perhaps most notably, John Wheatley's Housing Act gave subsidies to local authorities to build rental houses.

The occasion of its defeat was a vote of censure over the 'Campbell Case'. This was the sequence of events in which the threat of prosecution for sedition of J. R. Campbell, a decorated war hero and acting editor of the Communist *Workers' Weekly*, was first made by the Labour government and then clumsily withdrawn. The *Workers' Weekly* had published an open letter to British soldiers calling on them not to allow themselves to be used against striking workers. An election was called for 29 October 1924 and even though Labour's vote rose by over one million, the Conservatives' vote went up by far more and they were returned with a substantial overall majority. The reason was a slightly higher turnout and the collapse of the Liberals' vote by a third. Labour, reduced to 151 seats on their highest share of the vote so far (33 per cent) was again His Majesty's Official Opposition. The Liberals, reduced to 17.6 per cent of the vote and a mere 40 seats, were never to recover.

Just as the occasion of its defeat was linked to Labour's real and perceived relations with the Communists, so was the campaign itself, overshadowed as it was by controversy over the proposed trade loan that the Labour government had been planning to extend to Russia and the 'Zinoviev letter' affair. This was a fake letter allegedly signed by Comintern President Zinoviev and instructing the British Communist Party on the revolutionary action it should take in the wake of the signing of the trade deal. The text of it was plastered all over the *Daily Mail* accompanied by screaming headlines announcing 'Civil War Plot by Socialists' three days before polling day. Published alongside it was a draft note written by Foreign Office officials for Ramsay MacDonald (and amended, but not initialled, by him) that the Prime Minister was to have sent to the Russian Ambassador were the Zinoviev letter to have turned out to be authentic. This, the Foreign Office officials had seen fit to send to the press without checking with MacDonald or indeed anyone in the Labour government, the implication being that Foreign Office officials were accepting the letter as genuine, and that Labour had done nothing about it, possibly as part of a deliberate design to deceive the British people. It was 'an act of such treachery and bad faith that everyone would have expected our socialist ministers immediately to reply by expelling every Bolshevik in Britain', declared the *Daily Mail* on 27 October. It made the proposed trade loan look naïve in the extreme and Labour candidates, confronted with the issue on the hustings, did not know what to say.

Though the letter itself was almost certainly a fake, aspects of it were plausible and throughout the 1920s there was a running battle within the trade unions between Communist and democratic socialist forces for power and influence. This battle spilled over into Labour conference where, having been banned from affiliating to the Labour Party directly, the Communist Party still sought to secure influence by other means. Harry Pollitt, for example (from 1929-56 the General Secretary of the Communist Party of Great Britain) was able to speak in favour of Communist affiliation at the Labour Party conference of 1922 as an accredited delegate of the Boilermakers' Union. Year after year motions to allow the affiliation of the Communist Party were overwhelmingly defeated by votes on conference floor (for example by 4,115,000 to 224,000 at the 1921 conference). Eventually, Labour's National Executive proposed at the 1925 Labour conference in Liverpool to exclude Communists from individual Labour Party membership and to urge affiliated trade unions to appeal to their members not to send Communist delegates to Labour Party conferences. A vigorous debate ensued, with Harry Pollitt moving the rejection of the ban on individual membership:

> ... nothing that the conference could do could prevent the rise of Communism in this or in any other country. Where they had a Labour Party constituted in the same way as the British Labour Party, it was perfectly obvious that no barrier was strong enough to keep them out, for, if they could not get in by one way they could by another ... [And he attacked MacDonald personally]: If the movement and the Labour Party was wide enough to include in its ranks those who could go to the Isle of Wight with Lord Inchcape, or to Balmoral, then it ought to be wide enough to include the others.

Ernest Bevin, now the General Secretary of the 300,000-strong Transport and General Workers' Union (into which the dockers had merged), hit back:

> having had experience of the agitation carried on within his own union, he felt that the Communists could not conscientiously reconcile the Communist basis with the basis of evolutionary democracy that the Labour Party represented. He was tired of

tactics. Working-class men in this country wanted people to be straight with them. Dialectics, moving for position – and if he might say to the party, being too anxious to manoeuvre even for votes – would not in the end mean triumph for the political Labour Party or the trade union movement . . . if a man said, 'I am diametrically opposed to you,' it was not fair for him to come along and suggest that he should be brought into their counsels and help direct their affairs. In regard to his own union, they had gone though a crucifixion of this very nature.

MacDonald concluded the debate by citing a statement by the Communist Third International:

Therefore, the workers are prepared, not for an easy parliamentary victory, but for victory by a heavy civil war. Now they could not run those two things together. It is not that we want to have an easy, quiet, obedient conference. As Mr Bevin assured you, he and I have a little bit of a row occasionally. Why not? Provided we are in the same spirit, holding the same view. Bevin, with his experience; I with mine. I say to Bevin, and Bevin says to me, both of us in the common interests that we hold: 'Look here, my dear friend, I do not think you are in the right.' Is not that for the good of everyone? Of course it is. But if Bevin and I were poles asunder in our philosophy, and in our outlook, Bevin ought to go his way and I ought to go my way, and I hope I should have enough common sense to shake hands with him and say, 'You are quite right to do so.' That is my position. I say if I were a Communist I would not ask you to have me inside: I would say to you: 'You believe you are right; I am convinced you are wrong; I am going to make a party that will be an antagonistic party to you. I am going to try and set up a rival party, and God defend the right when the crash comes!' Instead of that, they get Maryhill and Richmond to move, and we have that miraculous discovery that when Maryhill wants to say two and two make five, Richmond also says it in exactly the same language. These machine-made resolutions and amendments are scattered broadcast, in order to enable some delegates to say: 'Look how we have spread those feelings. There are actually 30 local Labour parties out of six hundred that have all said the same thing!' . . . Division on certain policies held by men with the same spirit, certainly within the same movement; but with different philosophies, different outlooks; no, that can only hamper each in trying to move in step. No, let them go out and remain out, let them propagate their opinions honestly outside, and I say again, 'God defend the side that is right!' I believe we are right, and I support the Executive proposals.

With the next general election approaching, 1928 saw Labour embroiled in an increasingly bitter battle over the manifesto. Maxton, John Wheatley and their allies on 'Red Clydeside' dominated the ILP (still then an independent but dwindling socialist grouping affiliated to the Labour Party) and had secured support at the ILP conferences for a radical programme entitled *Socialism in Our Time*. MacDonald had dismissed it as 'flashy futilities' likely to so frighten the electorate from voting Labour as to postpone socialism indefinitely. Its key planks included a 'living wage', nationalisation of banking and credit, the reorganisation of the trade union movement to facilitate 'workers' control', 'working-class resistance to all wars' and opposition to any rearmament. Following the collapse of the 1926 General Strike and the repressive Trade Union Act 1927, negotiations between a group of large employers led by Sir Alfred Mond of ICI and the TUC General Council (chaired by Ben Turner) produced during 1928 proposals for greater industrial partnership and consultation and a recommendation in favour of trade union recognition by employers. In June 1928, Maxton issued a joint counterblast to this with miners' leader A. J. Cook which became known as the 'Cook–Maxton Manifesto'. It denounced 'class collaboration' and demanded 'unceasing war against capitalism'. Some felt that the ILP was becoming increasingly a party within a party.

Labour's leadership had drafted a quite different programme for the forthcoming election entitled *Labour and the Nation*. 'The style was unmistakably Tawney's: the conception as unmistakably Macdonald's.' It consisted of

> a high-minded if sometimes prosy, statement of the moral case for gradualist socialism, heavily flavoured with the scientific optimism of the day . . . the Labour Party was portrayed as a movement of all classes, ranged against a small minority of property owners, and socialism as the creed, not only of the working class, but of all 'practical men and women' who wished to apply the resources of science to bring within the reach of all the conditions of a dignified and civilised existence. 'Without haste but without rest,' land, coal, power, transport and life insurance were to be transferred to public ownership. Taxation would be 'scientifically adjusted' to the ability to pay; arms expenditure would be cut down; and the social services would be extended . . . With a brave flourish [it] denounced the 'placid assumption that, in the twentieth century, the recurrence of involuntary idleness is still to be regarded, like tempests and earthquakes, as an act of God'. It then proceeded to demonstrate that, in practice, its authors had no other assumption to put in its place.[53]

Labour's 1928 conference was dominated by a three-day debate on *Labour and the Nation*. This was, in effect, a gladiatorial battle between the contrasting visions of MacDonald and Maxton. It was a triumph for MacDonald, who introduced and replied to the main debate on the first day as well as dealing with most of the detailed amendments later in the week.

> MacDonald's critics on 'Red Clydeside' played into his hands. Just as he talked gradualism, but lacked a strategy for the transition period he presupposed, so they talked class war, but lacked a strategy for the crisis they appeared to welcome. Thus demands for an expansionist monetary policy quickly turned into demands for the nationalisation of the banks, and demands for nationalisation of the banks turned into demands for a revolutionary confrontation, for which no one was prepared and in which only a minority wished to be engaged.[54]

The debate was opened by MacDonald, for whom:

... this manifesto, this programme, is not merely something for May 1929, but something for the years to come – full, not only of one programme, but pregnant with programme after programme after programme ... [It included specifics, like the demand for a minimum wage, and a grander, yet somehow ill-defined, vision:] Under the present system there must always be masses in poverty. If you try to reform the present system by merely making distribution better, giving each one more than he has before you satisfy each individual on the basis of private and personal property, your national income will not be sufficient. But when you devise the method of pooling, when you devise the method of putting your share of a penny and your neighbour's share of a penny together, so that the whole of your share comes to thousands and thousands and millions of pounds per annum, then each one of you can enjoy, by the operation of this socialist idea, not the privilege of possessing your penny, but the privilege of possessing everybody else's penny without in any way taking advantage of him. That, again, is one of the great fundamentals of this programme ...

For James Maxton, the issue was clearly in part a matter of his failure to trust the leadership not to sell out the aspirations of the rank and file, a recurring theme in Labour's history.

... This is not a programme ... What you are doing here ... is giving a free hand to the next Labour government to define any programme it pleases providing it is not outside the scope of the sixty-five Articles ... I have got the works of all the socialists of the world to help me to make socialist speeches. What I want is somebody to guide me as to what my practical duty is as a Labour Member of Parliament on a given issue ... When the Labour government was in office, Mr Snowden dealt with the question of old-age pensions. They were 10s. a week at 70, and we kept them at 10s. a week at 70 – the Labour government. What the Labour government did was to alter the disqualification – not to abolish it, but to alter it. The matter was discussed in the parliamentary party, and a majority was given for that view. Those who were in the minority had no mandate or guidance of a definite nature from the rank and file of the movement to buttress them up in demanding something more, because all the resolutions of the past were not realities, they were mere flashy futilities as compared with the practical work in the House ...

London Labour Party Secretary and ex-Mayor of Hackney Herbert Morrison attacked Maxton's attempt to micro-manage:

... if you tried in a conference of one thousand people to lay down the detailed action which the Labour government has got to take, this conference would make a profound mistake. I have known in an exceptional case a local Trades Council do something which would be much easier; to control its Labour Councillors by going through the agenda of the Local Council and telling the Councillors what they had to do at the next meeting; and I have known these poor fellows having to decide something on the spur of the moment, and not knowing what to do because they had to wait for the next meeting of the Trades Council. How much worse it would be for this conference now to try and determine in detail what the next Labour government is going to do . . .

Maxton's main supporter was John Wheatley, who claimed that:

With the exception of the land – the moderate control in an advisory capacity, but to a large extent in practice, the control of the Bank of England – the rationalisation of services like mines and railways, which in this country are almost derelict – leave these out for the moment and look over the other 60 items and say whether they are not to a very large extent simply amendments of the health, industrial, educational, factory, and other legislation that has been placed in principle upon the Statute Book by the Liberal Party during the past 25 or 30 years . . . Is it for that you climbed the stairs? . . . Is it for that you formed your Parliamentary Labour Party? . . . If socialism was at the end of the way one might have no great objection to the contents of this programme. We might go to our people and say: 'We find it necessary that you should go through the wilderness for forty years, but at the end of the forty years you are to enter into a land flowing with milk and honey.' . . . If the goal was socialism it would be all right, but the goal is still capitalism, and all these measures are merely to salve the wounds, to bandage the feet of the people who have to travel that painful ruthless journey to that bitter end . . .

He demanded:

the first session of the Labour government . . . pass an Act of Parliament entitling it to take complete control of the administration of wealth in this country, and I want them from that common pool which they have taken from private enterprise to fix not only a minimum wage, but a maximum wage for the people of this country. You go on to talk about the aged man. What are you going to do for the aged man? I would pension him with full pay, and I would find the money for it in the pockets of the rich, and a Labour government that was not afraid would take that course, and a conference of working men, if they knew their own position and had some conception of their place in society, would definitely instruct the Labour government to use the power that you are putting into their hands to take the fixing of wages and prices from the hands of individuals in this country and place it in the hands of the community, in the hands of a Labour government . . .

Labour's deputy leader J. R. Clynes took to the rostrum to dismiss the idea that:

you can establish socialism by resolution, and that by introducing a Bill in Parliament to acquire the wealth of the nation and distribute it as you like is the way to solve all your ills [and to attack John Wheatley's charge that the programme was essentially Liberal]. The principle of the enforcement of international labour standards; the transference to public ownership of the coal, transport, power and life assurance industries; the transference of land to public ownership; the provision of an adequate supply of houses at rents within the means of the workers; the establishment of homes for the aged, and the prevention of profiteering in land and building material; the creation of a democratic system of education, adequately financed, free from the taint of class distinction and organised as a continuous whole from the nursery school to the university . . . If it be true that the Liberals would accept these doctrines I cannot understand the violent condemnation of this programme in the Liberal press and on Liberal platforms . . . Our difficulty appears to be this, that in spite of spelling the word 'socialism' precisely in the same way as our critics, they insist on declaring that they mean something different from us . . . let Mr Maxton come down from the clouds . . .

Former dockers' leader Ben Tillett also backed MacDonald, telling the story of:

. . . a very intelligent woman, a wife with five children and a decent sort of husband. We had spoken at one of our meetings of the right of the mother to an ample cupboard, an ample wardrobe, and ample domestic comforts, with a right to see that her children were medically attended, their eyes, their ears, their teeth, and that they should be properly fed, and that the woman should have such a competence that she should be, as it were, not merely the mother of her children, but the queen of her home. She repeated that and asked: 'Is that socialism?' I said, 'It is.' 'Well,' she said, 'I am a socialist, but what am I to do? Shall I refuse my maternal and wifely duties because my old man only brings me thirty bob a week?' (*laughter*) . . . I say this to Maxton, I hope he still keeps young, I hope the poetry still keeps in him, I hope his soul keeps young, as I hope mine does, but I know, as that woman knew, there are realities to be faced . . .

In the end, support for Maxton and Wheatley was so minimal that *Labour and the Nation* was adopted without a formal vote.

ELEVEN

The Tragedy of the Second MacDonald Government 1929–31

'I detest class politics and want to end them in national unity'

A portent of the next general election was the landslide victory by 24-year-old miner's daughter Jennie Lee in a by-election at North Lanark following the death of its elderly Conservative MP, Col. Sir Alexander Sprot, of a heart attack in the House of Commons lobby. A fervent socialist, she was not yet even old enough to vote. Her maiden speech, delivered on 25 April 1929 during the heat of the budget debate, made quite an impact: 'Her striking good looks, extreme youth and fiery reputation fascinated an almost entirely male house . . . her gestures were dramatic, imported from the soapbox and borrowed from Maxton: the drumming fingers, the arms suddenly outflung, the toss of her head as she threw back her hair and then the theatrical discarding of her speech notes.'[55] Moreover, it broke with convention in being a full-frontal assault on the incumbent Conservative government in general, and Chancellor of the Exchequer Winston Churchill in particular. She concluded:

> Before unemployment, before poverty, before any of these questions become for this House more than a matter of fooling and buffoonery, the government of this country will have to be changed . . . I hope and believe that the Chancellor of the Exchequer, in putting before this House the Budget statement that he has, has made it absolutely certain that, when the election comes, all honest, honourable citizens of this country will rise in revolt and hound from office this government which has so misused its opportunities and its power.

And they did. The May 1929 general election saw Labour gain over 130 new seats to emerge for the first time as the largest party, though with only 288 MPs, it lacked an overall majority. Labour also secured its largest share of the vote yet, 37.1 per cent, marginally less than the Conservatives' 38.2 per cent.

Despite a vigorous campaign pledging to 'conquer unemployment', the Liberal Party, led since 1926 by Lloyd George, secured a mere 59 seats on 23.4 per cent of the vote, less than in 1923. After the betrayal of radicalism that had characterised the final years of Lloyd George's 1918–22 government, and the fratricidal feuds that had torn apart the Liberal Party for more than a decade, attractive though the Liberal programme sounded not enough voters were prepared to trust the Liberal Party to implement it.

MacDonald's final election speech was broadcast from the BBC's Newcastle Station on 28 May 1929; 'the resonant voice, a little tired maybe, with its spice of Scottish brogue, was probably heard by the greatest number of electors ever addressed by a party leader in a single speech'.[56] MacDonald's central charge was that Lloyd George's pledges on unemployment were not worth the paper on which they were not necessarily written:

> Sir John Simon,[57] who addressed you last night on his behalf, said that he agreed that in his own experience his leader was so unreliable that what he did at one time was no sure indication of what he would do at another. Those are the exact words used as recently as 11 December 1926, and they have a very direct and serious bearing on the value of a pledge when a pledge is being considered.

The main focus of his speech, and to the prescient a harbinger of things to come, was his aspiration to a government of national unity beyond class:

> We are charged with terrible sins, some of which, however, are really so silly that they need hardly be mentioned on the assumption that you take them seriously. One of these is that we are an unconstitutional party. That from a party which stirred up rebellion in Ireland and mutiny in the British Army, which challenged by armed forces a decision which they themselves accepted later on after conditions have become humiliating – that, my friends, seems to be rather barefaced.
>
> Another charge is that we are a class party because the party was created for the purpose of bringing the life experience of the great mass of our people to guide political and economic policy. Against us our opponents say that they stand for national unity and suchlike. You cannot talk of national unity unless that unity embraces all classes and functions which give services to the whole varied life of the community. I cannot understand how it is that intelligent and honest people can continue to think that Labour is merely a class party. If I had time tonight, and if it were profitable, I could prove to you not only the contrary, but I could turn the tables upon our Conservative antagonists and show that on their minds, on the composition of their party, on their funds, on their appeals, and their achievements class and sectional interests are deeply stamped. One of the great reasons why I belong to the Labour Party and hold the socialist views of what a wise and just social structure is, is because I detest class politics and want to end them in real national unity. In bringing that about we have to consider the claims of the great mass of our people, who, on account of their poverty, cannot adequately protect themselves. What has national unity meant to them? A change in a machine can make them outcasts; a change in fashion can make them paupers.

MacDonald formed a minority government, relying on Liberal abstentions to avoid defeat. His governmental team in 1929 was similar to 1924, although Wheatley was excluded. Snowden was again Chancellor, Henderson this time became Foreign Secretary and Clynes became Home Secretary. Snowden's talented young Scots protégé Willie Graham became President of the Board of Trade and set to work to achieve an international 'tariff truce'. Health Minister Arthur Greenwood, a Leeds-born ex-teacher, Workers' Education Authority (WEA) lecturer and former secretary of the Labour Party's research department, launched a Bill to progress slum clearance. The aristocratic ex-Liberal MP Charles Trevelyan became Education Minister and introduced a bill to raise the school leaving age to fifteen. Herbert Morrison became Transport Minister and produced a Road Traffic Bill to reorganise the road passenger transport industry. In addition, the Widows and Old Age Pensions Act and Unemployment Insurance Act were amended and improved.

The greatest challenge facing the 1929 Labour government was unemployment. It had been rising under the Conservatives and had reached 1,163,000 when Labour took office. It rose more steeply still as the ripples from the Wall Street Crash spread around the world. Manny Shinwell, a Clydesider who served as a junior minister throughout the government, remembered acerbically:

> The appointment of Margaret Bondfield as Minister of Labour [and Britain's first woman in Cabinet] was in reality an appointment to a Ministry of Unemployment: her job was to organise the welfare of the unemployed rather than to devise ideas for creating work. That task was in the hands of three ministers: J. H. Thomas, Lord Privy Seal; George Lansbury, First Commissioner of Works; and Sir Oswald Mosley, Chancellor of the Duchy of Lancaster. All three posts were sufficiently light or vague to enable these three men to devote all their time to the major problem of finding work for the masses. Thomas, with his inevitable ebullient vanity, served the government ill by taking every opportunity to promise publicly that the total of unemployed would be rapidly reduced. Lansbury was too parochial for a big task, seeking trivial palliatives like his Lido in Hyde Park ... Mosley offered grandiose ideas for roads and so on which would have been prohibitively costly to put in hand.[58]

Mosley, an aristocratic ex-Tory MP who had rapidly swung to the left, produced with Lansbury and junior Scottish Office minister Tom Johnston a famous 'Memorandum' to Cabinet in early 1930. It proposed import controls possibly through tariffs which were anathema to free-traders like Snowden and an expansion of domestic purchasing power to increase demand. On its rejection, Mosley resigned from the government (to be replaced by Clement Attlee), and on 28 May 1930 he launched an aggressive attack on the government in what has been acknowledged to be 'one of the most powerful resignation speeches of recent times'.[59] He did not deny:

> that world conditions have been vastly aggravated since the arrival in power of the present government, and that no one can suggest that the government are responsible for those conditions. [But, he argued,] the more serious the situation the greater the

necessity for action by the government . . . [He dismissed] both laissez-faire and Protection [as] utterly irrelevant to the modern world . . . [Instead he advocated] large constructive works schemes . . . slum clearance . . . land drainage . . . a £100,000,000 programme of the Unemployment Grants Committee . . . concentrated into three years, and £100,000,000 road programme should be concentrated into the same period . . . [The government's failure to act he blamed partly on the Civil Service:] The Ministry of Transport would not [expand the roads programme]. I think they properly would not do it until they had settled in principle with the Treasury whether they could go ahead to that limit of money, if they were permitted to do it . . .

We have to face up to this fact, that if men are to be employed on any large scale that employment has to be paid for either by the State or by local authorities. There is a tremendous struggle, an incessant struggle, going on in every government department to put every penny they can off the taxpayer and on to the ratepayer. What holds up these plans for months is the struggle for these pennies, these minor details. What does it matter? What is the use of shifting the burden from the taxpayer to the ratepayer? What is the use of lifting the burden from the right shoulder to the left? It is the same man who has to carry it . . .

To break this gridlock he advocated raising a loan:

Why is it so right and proper and desirable that capital should go overseas to equip factories to compete against us, to build roads and railways in the Argentine or in Timbuctoo, to provide employment for people in those countries while it is supposed to shake the whole basis of our financial strength if anyone dares to suggest the raising of money by the government of this country to provide employment for the people of this country? . . . the situation which faces us is, of course, very serious . . . I feel this from the depths of my being, that the days of muddling through are over, that this time we cannot muddle through.

This nation has to be mobilised and rallied for a tremendous effort, and who can do that except the government of the day? If that effort is not made we may soon come to a crisis, to a real crisis. I do not fear that so much, for this reason, that in a crisis this nation is always at its best. This people knows how to handle a crisis, it cools their heads and steels their nerves. What I fear much more than a sudden crisis is a long, slow, crumbling through the years until we sink to the level of a Spain, a gradual paralysis beneath which all the vigour and energy of this country will succumb . . . If the situation is to be overcome, if the great powers of this country are to be rallied and mobilised for a great national effort, then the government and Parliament must give a lead. I beg the government tonight to give the vital forces of this country the chance that they await. I beg the Parliament to give that lead.

Labour's 1930 annual conference in Llandudno some four months later would open the day after the loss of the British airship R101, which had crashed near Beauvais at the beginning of its first flight to India. Most of its passengers and crew were killed. Among the dead was the father of Britain's airship programme, Lord Thomson, a Labour-supporting ex-general who had become Secretary of State for Air in both MacDonald's Cabinets, the Prime Minister's golfing partner and probably his closest friend in politics. Two days after the crash, on 7 October 1930, MacDonald had to address conference. Unemployment was now past two million and rising and MacDonald's growing number of critics were looking to challenge the government. Looking 'drawn and haggard' he paid tribute to the dead. After this, 'he paused; straightened himself up; and having created an atmosphere in which criticism must have seemed tantamount to blasphemy, he launched into a passionate and uncompromising defence of the government and its record . . . politically, as well as rhetorically, it was a tour de force'.[60]

. . . The Air Service, by the death of Lord Thomson, has lost a great and conspicuous servant. Those of us who are human in our hearts – love for fellows, love for beauty, love for lightsomeness – have lost a companion like unto ourselves, whose place will never be filled . . .

But, as I said, we are still alive, and we must do our work, and, however hard it is to pass from these thoughts to the thoughts that are more appropriate to the work of this morning, I shall try my best to do it, and if you find traces of an unsuccessful effort I hope you will understand the reason why that is so . . .

We have had just over twelve months in office as a government. We have had criticisms from inside and outside. But I want to say to you in one sentence, in one challenging sentence, that the government has fulfilled the confidence that you reposed in it at the last election (cheers). I have no apologies – none whatever. I am not one of those who, standing aside, imagine that pettifogging criticism is either helpful or illuminating. Not at all. The plough, my friends, is in the furrow, and the place for you and me is in the furrow dragging the plough (cheers). We have not fulfilled all our pledges – no. Did you expect us to do so? Our pledges are the pledges of men and women who are socialists, our pledges are the pledges of men and women who know that this system of society cannot and will not work smoothly, and that the great task of statesmen of vision is to transform that system of society from the 'is' until it has become the 'is to be'; and in the course of that transformation, rightly or wrongly, my creed, and, I think, the creed of the great majority, if not all of my colleagues, has been evolution – evolution applied in precisely the same way as the scientific medical man, the scientific healer, applies his knowledge and his art to the frail and the ailing body. He does not prescribe straightaway the final food, the final exercise, the final standard of life, but being a knowing man, a man with an eye, a man not only with scientific knowledge but psychological knowledge, a man who knows how to lead gently and truly as well as to feed accurately, knowing his problem, knowing that it is not a problem of mathematics, not a problem of material things only, but a problem of mental and psychological things, works out a great policy and goes on with it from stage to stage. The men who remain out may say: 'You have not got your journey's end,' but the men who remain in say 'No, we have not, but we are going to get there' (cheers) . . .

My temptation this morning, my friends, is to take up the whole time – there is so much to say. Take traffic, take coal, take a thousand and one things. Widows' pensions, not finished yet – no, not at all. Old-age pensions, coordination of insurance – not finished yet. My friends, if there is one fault that perhaps one gets really more credit for confessing to than another, it is this, that in respect to all those reconstructions of social fabrics a little slowness contributes to accuracy and permanence far more than the blaring 'hustle, and, when it is done, turn round and see if it is going to stand'. That is not our method. Our method is this. You have got your experts scattered from John O'Groats to Land's End, you have got your officials who understand your purpose. There is not one single and permanent contribution that is going to be made to social reconstruction that has not to be considered again and again and again. They are not simple problems, and I would far rather come to you, my friends, at the end of twelve months or two years, and say 'The schemes have not yet been produced,' provided, after I have done that, the scheme that is going to be produced will bear the wear and tear of examination and of time.

But the chief thing this morning, I understand, that our thoughts were to be concentrated upon was unemployment. There are a variety of picturesque and somewhat familiar slogans about it. What is it they say? 'Get on or – (*A voice:* 'Get out.') Yes, that is it (*laughter*). 'Get on or get out.' We will get on, and in the getting on, if my experience of the last few weeks means anything at all, it will be somebody else who will get out (*laughter*). We are joined in a conference; what have we got to hide? I detest the ordinary claptrap of party politics. They are not after my heart, and I hope they never will be. If we have a case for unemployment, I do not care who gets the papers – not at all. I will give them to the Tories, I will give them to the Liberals, I will give them to the new party that is being formed – I am not sure exactly what its position is, or what its parentage, or what its registration, or what its baptism – (*laughter*) – but if it would appear, I would give our papers to it, because the more that we get of honest examination the better will be the schemes and proposals that will emerge from the study . . .

[The unemployment problem faced by the government was] of a totally different nature from that we faced at the last general election [he believed].

First of all, a very large contribution to the situation is absolutely international. No nation working alone can cure it . . . an 'international policy' [was needed, and President of the Board of Trade Willie Graham had gone to Geneva to propose a tariff truce] . . .

We are blamed that we have not raised loans. It is not money so much we are short of; it is work. Work has not been stopped for want of money. The great trouble is – and we have spent any amount of time pushing it on – first of all, you approve of a scheme in principal; then that scheme has got to be worked out; then you approve the scheme for operation; and then you discover – say, at the end of August a scheme was approved, not in principle only, but ready for work – the machinery to get it into work is slow and cumbrous that at any given moment you have approved of twice the value of work that is actually in operation then. That is one of the great troubles we have had. That is being speeded up now; the actual work in hand is steadily overtaking the work that has been approved of. But you do not get up one morning, either at Churt or at Downing Street, and half between sleeping and waking wave a wand, and lo and behold, somebody on a flying carpet comes down with a scheme of how to build a road between Liverpool and Manchester. It is done differently, and it well that it should be so.

Another thing is this. We must, in all our work, maintain the responsibilities of Local Authorities and get their cooperation. And then, do remember that much of what we call relief work is, first of all, only drawing on future normal demands – a very important consideration – and those of you who are in Public Authorities know it. Secondly, it is not as a matter of fact contributing to the solution of the unemployed problem. It is a provision of temporary work, very often at high cost, for men who do not want it, but want to get into permanent occupation. Now, our position today is this. Our main and trunk road programme is as complete as it can be. Perhaps the newspaper that is so much interested in conferences will ask its informant whether that statement is true or not. Country and unclassified roads, and the narrow and weak bridges, must be dealt with in bits and sections. You cannot knock out of action 20 bridges that cross the same stream at the same time. You cannot in an unclassified narrow road, just wide enough to allow two vehicles to pass each other when there is no obstruction, put ten miles of that road out of action at the same time. You have to study the road map, and in the constructing and reconditioning of our country roads we have to take a section which is easily circumvented without serious loss of rural traffic in the mean time. Therefore you cannot run £40 million schemes of country roads and bridges at the same time; you have got to run your maximum, but your maximum is fairly circumscribed by the hour-to-hour and day-to-day needs of the countryside through which the roads run . . .

The outsider complains about our taxes. Our taxes are high; nobody knows that better than the Prime Minister . . . Why are the taxes high! Because we are paying other people's debts. Mr Churchill tried for years to scrape here and scrape there and scrape elsewhere; he was like a Chinaman I once came across in the Never-Never Land, who was sifting the dust of the desert to see if he could get a grain of gold, and he got enough just to keep him going. Mr Churchill produced his budgets in that way, but by 1929 he had come to the end of the sifting of the desert sand, and a discovery of an odd grain of gold like a balance in the Unemployment Fund, the National Health Fund, or a balance in the Sinking Fund. They had all come to an end, they had all been scraped clean. His last washings did not display a single glitter of dust worth lifting – it was rubbish. Mr Snowden has had to face that, and the very men who created the necessity turn round upon my poor friend and say, 'What a wicked, extravagant, incompetent financier you are; you are actually finding money to pay the debts that we left behind. Get out!' (*laughter*). We shall see about that . . .

It is not the Labour government that is on trial; it is capitalism that is being tried. We told you in those days that the time would come when finance would be more powerful than industry. That day has come . . .

So, my friends, we are not on trial; it is the system under which we live. It has broken down, not only in this little island. It has broken down in Europe, in Asia, in

America; it has broken down everywhere, and it was bound to break down. And the cure, the new path, the new idea is organisation – organisation which will protect life, not property; but protect property in proper relation to life; organisation which will see to it that when science discovers and inventors invent, the class that will be crushed down by reason of knowledge, shall not be the working class, but the loafing class. That is the policy which we are going to pursue slowly, steadily, persistently, with knowledge and our minds working upon a plan. And I appeal to you, my friends, today, with all that is going on outside – I appeal to you to go back on to your social-ist faith. Do not mix that up with pettifogging patching, either of a Poor Law kind or of Relief Work kind. Construction, ideas, architecture, building line upon line, stone upon stone, storey upon storey: it will not be your happiness, and it will certainly not be mine, to see that fabric finished. It will not be your happiness, and it will certainly not be mine, to see that every stone laid in sincerity has been well laid. But I think it will be your happiness, as it is mine, to go on convinced that the great foundations are being well laid, that the ennobling plan is being conceived, and that by skilled crafts-men, confident in each other's goodwill and sincerity, the temple will rise and rise and rise until at last it is complete, and the genius of humanity will find within it an appro-priate resting place (*loud cheers*).

Winston Churchill once dubbed MacDonald the 'boneless wonder' for the lack of solid content underpinning the rhetorical body of his speeches: this was a classic of the genre, and to modern eyes lays bare the tragedy of a government unable to surmount the obstructionism of the civil servants on whose advice and procedures it had become wholly dependent. Yet as MacNeill Weir put it some years later, 'The tumultuous applause that followed the great peroration showed that MacDonald had retained his power as a spellbinder ... He had completely turned the tables on his opponents.'[61] James Maxton, perhaps chief among MacDonald's opponents, moved on behalf of the ILP what was in effect a motion of censure on the government, but he was clearly on the back foot:

*... The Prime Minister, in his very great speech – he said 'very great speech' because he knew the circumstances of personal feeling under which the Prime Minister was delivering it, he could see the deliberate wrench that he made with his own personali-ty when he pulled himself away from the personal thing that was filling his mind on to the work of the conference. It was a great speech, and it finished with a peroration, which he (Mr Maxton), who sometimes also perorated, regarded with admiration and not a little envy ...

Mr Thomas stated last year at the conference that they would be judged by the electors on the impression they made on the unemployment figures. It was true they were told that 'world causes' had come in to affect the situation during the last twelve months, but had not world causes been an element in their considerations as socialists since the beginning of their movement? ...

The amendment laid it down that the great fundamental purpose of their

*Transcribed as reported speech.

movement was to secure a decent and a full life for the working classes, and that government policy should have driven right at that end from the very beginning – to raise the standard of life of the whole of the people. There had been criticism on more than one occasion. He hoped the government were not seriously going to put it forward as an excuse that some of them had not got down into the furrow with the plough. Well, he challenged the Prime Minister. He (Mr Maxton) put his hand to the plough 25 years ago, and he had never taken it off; and he had always been in the dirtiest furrows . . .

Since 1918, it was true, they had spent £700,000,000 on unemployment allowance, and £4,000,000,000 in the same period in war debt interest . . . If the present circumstances could not permit of them proceeding along the lines of socialist construction, then they must tell the country freely, fairly, and squarely that they could not do the things that they knew must be done to solve the problem, and ask the workers to give them a mandate that would furnish them with the necessary power to proceed.

MacDonald replied briefly before returning to London to meet the bodies of the victims of the crash. His speech – almost wholly insubstantial, but rhetorically brilliant – began with mockery and concluded by putting the boot in:

. . . My old comrade, Maxton – friendly, but just a little bit troubled, a very good comrade but a little bit restive, still with his hand on the plough, but a little bit doubtful as to whether he or the majority of his colleagues ought to set the line of the furrow – (*laughter*) – as wishful to be with us as ever he has been, but not quite sure whether he is goalkeeper, half-back, or captain of the team. (*A voice:* 'Or linesman.' *Another voice:* 'Or referee.') No, I am quite sure Maxton could never be a linesman or a referee; he must have more intimate association with the ball – and he and I are a little bit in dispute occasionally whether he shall kick it with his feet or knock it with his head. Our disagreements will always be of the very same friendly and sympathetic character which I hope both of us have displayed this morning after disagreeing with each other. But that is really the problem. Maxton said, and said quite truly, he surveys the field but he does not see the ripened harvest. I say no, he does not. (*Mr Maxton:* 'I do not even see the seed.') He says he does not even see the seed. No, perhaps he does not, but the seed is there all the same, and the seed is sprouting all the same, and it is sheer folly for any of us, either for propaganda or any other purpose, to go on and say that during the last fifteen or sixteen months there have been no beginnings of reorganisation which are the seed of the complicated systematic socialism. It is there, and just between Keir Hardie's day and ours, anyone who just stands aside for a minute and looks back is bound to see progress of an organic kind – not of a superficial kind. So I say the work we are doing today will enable people to look back a few years from now and say: 'The harvest that we are now reaping comes from the seed that the Labour government in 1929-30 sowed so abundantly in the fields of its day.' That is all I can ask for and that is all I do ask for. Socialism is not a thing of dogma, socialism is not a thing of colour. That never has been the socialism of the ILP. That was an issue which Keir Hardie and the rest of us fought and fought and fought again . . .

... I have gone into the House of Commons again and again, and I have found the back benches putting questions to the front benches with a blazing eye and wild violence which put to shame all the ardour, all the criticism, that came legitimately upon us from the opposition. I say that is not helping the party. That is not helping us on to victory; that is not helping socialism; that is not making us more amenable to the legitimate pressure that you ought to bring to bear upon us ...

When the vote was announced Maxton and the ILP had been decisively defeated. MacDonald's authority within the party had been reinforced and his leading critics began to consider alternative political vehicles. In February 1931 five Labour, one Conservative and one Liberal MP would join Oswald Mosley in forming the short-lived New Party.[62]

That same month, Education Minister Sir Charles Trevelyan, a baronet and former Liberal MP, had resigned from Cabinet in protest at MacDonald's failure to back the Education Bill raising the school leaving age with sufficient vigour and at Snowden's push for economies to meet the challenge of the economic crisis. At a meeting of the Parliamentary Labour Party following his resignation Trevelyan declared:

I am utterly dissatisfied with the main strategy of the leaders of the party ... I never expected a complete breakthrough to socialism in this Parliament. But I did expect it to prepare the way for a government which in spirit and vigour made such a contrast with the Tories and Liberals that we should be sure of conclusive victory next time ... If ever there was a chance of presenting the socialist alternative it is today ... But all we have got is a declaration of economy from the Chancellor of the Exchequer ... It implies a faith, a faith that reduction of expenditure is the way to salvation ... You must bear all the implications of your new religion when you join a church. No comrades. It is not good enough for a socialist party to meet this crisis with economy. The very root of our faith is that prosperity comes from the high spending power of the people ...[63]

Though MacDonald was effective in fending off his government's critics, he failed to conquer unemployment. Snowden opposed tariffs (which Thomas favoured) and also rejected any other measures which might jeopardise Britain's adherence to the Gold Standard and commitment to balanced budgets. As unemployment rose so, inevitably, did the costs of providing unemployment benefit. A committee of inquiry set up in March 1931 under ex-Prudential chairman Sir George May to review the situation painted a picture so bleak when it reported on 30 July that it triggered a further run on British banks, inciting the Bank of England to seek further emergency loans from abroad to safeguard Britain's adherence to the Gold Standard exchange rate. Conditions attached to these loans required Britain to balance its budget and appeared therefore to require 'economies'.

The political pressure was also rising. Since 1929, MacDonald's government had relied on the Liberals not to combine with the Conservatives to vote them out. The Liberals, fearing the election of a Conservative government that would introduce tariffs, had played ball. Lloyd George knew, however, that for the Liberals to have a long-term future they needed electoral reform, and to get it they had to offer Labour something that Labour needed in exchange: a pact that guaranteed the government's survival for longer. But his proposed deal, involving a two-year pact in exchange for the Alternative Vote[64] aroused implacable opposition from anti-Labour Liberal MPs led by Sir John Simon, who opened secret talks with the Conservatives about an electoral pact.

At a meeting of Liberal MPs on 24 March 1931, seventeen voted against Lloyd George's proposal to negotiate a deal with the Labour government. On 26 May, Simon spoke out in the Commons against the Labour government's proposed land tax of a penny in the pound on capital values, a cause which Lloyd George had very publicly espoused before the 1914-18 war and a month later, accompanied by two other Liberal MPs, including a former Chief Whip, Sir John Simon resigned from his party. Others followed, and by October Simon's new Liberal National Party comprised two-dozen ex-Liberal MPs. Had Parliament reassembled after the summer recess, it is likely that the Conservatives, emboldened by their new breakaway Liberal allies, would have tried to eject MacDonald's minority government.

In the event they never got the chance. MacDonald saw the writing on the wall. On 24 August 1931, having failed to secure agreement from his Cabinet to cuts in unemployment benefit, MacDonald offered the resignation of his government to the King. To the surprise and shock of his colleagues, he agreed to remain in office as Prime Minister of a new 'National' coalition government that would include both Conservatives and Liberals to resolve the crisis and save Britain's adherence to the Gold Standard. On MacDonald's invitation, Snowden, Thomas and Lord Sankey (the Lord Chancellor) agreed to serve in the new government.[65] Ironically, one of the first actions of the new government,[66] following further runs on the pound and an inability to secure further overseas credit, was to suspend the very Gold Standard which Snowden and the City of London had declared inviolate. This was just days after having carried through a Budget imposing the cuts at which the Labour government had balked, and which had been supposedly necessary to maintain Britain's adherence to the Gold Standard. On 25 August MacDonald made a broadcast pledge that the National government had been formed only to deal with the crisis, would be dissolved immediately after and that 'the election which will follow will not be fought by the government'.[67] Within weeks he would eat his words because the Conservatives now insisted on calling an election. MacDonald, his relations soured with most of his former Labour colleagues, now agreed to lead the National government into it. It was a bitter campaign.

TWELVE

Labour Swings Left
in Defeat 1931–32

*'Socialism in deed as well as in words . . . so the fortress
of capitalism will begin to crack and crumble'*

The election of 27 October 1931 was called by MacDonald on 5 October, the first day of Labour's annual conference at Scarborough. Labour braced itself for losses. The heady optimism of past years was gone. A new pessimism was evident in the speech of Sir Stafford Cripps, son of Lord Parmoor and nephew of Beatrice Webb. Parmoor was an ex-Tory MP who had served in both Ramsay MacDonald's Labour Cabinets. Sir Stafford himself was a brilliant and somewhat high-minded Wykehamist barrister who had served briefly as Solicitor General 1930–31, having joined the Labour Party a bare two years before. Proposing a resolution pledging to reverse the unemployment benefit cuts, Cripps declared: 'It is not now a question of "the inevitability of gradualness". The one thing that is not inevitable now is gradualness.' The disastrous election results seemed to confirm his words. Now led by Arthur Henderson, with Clynes and Willie Graham as joint deputies, Labour were reduced to a mere 52 MPs. Of these, half a dozen were Clydeside ILP members led by Maxton who, increasingly frustrated by the Labour Party, were soon formally to disaffiliate. Of the former Labour Cabinet members who had remained loyal to Labour, only Lansbury retained his seat. Henderson and all the others were defeated. MacDonald's National government had a majority of five hundred. With Labour's leader Arthur Henderson[68] now out of Parliament, Lansbury became acting leader of the Parliamentary Labour Party. Henderson's defeated deputies, Clynes and Graham,[69] were replaced by Clement Attlee, a modest, somewhat suburban-mannered public school-educated barrister with an obsession for cricket and *The Times* crossword.[70]

At Labour's October 1932 annual conference in Leicester the mood was caught by Sir Charles Trevelyan's resolution committing a future Labour government to 'immediately' promulgating 'definite socialist legislation' on which the government, with or without a majority, would 'stand or fall':

> we must have socialism in deed as well as in words . . . I look back on the parliamentary history of our country and I see how rarely the leaders of any new Parliament have used their opportunity. Probably the only Parliament that took its enemy by the throat in the

first month was the Long Parliament, and that was the greatest and most successful in its early days of any of our Parliaments. Let us make no mistake when our chance comes again . . . our leaders . . . must not fritter away those first months when our enthusiasm is at its height and when our opponents are staggered by our success. Let us lay down in some such resolution as this the unshakable mandate that they are to introduce at once, before attempting remedial measures of any other kind, great socialist measures, or some general measure empowering them to nationalise the key industries of the country. Have we not been taught our lesson? We look back on the wasted chances of the last Labour government when the MacDonald spirit decreed that we should try the cautious least, instead of anything like a big challenge. We have got rid of MacDonald now, and is it not good that here in the De Montfort Hall in Leicester we should lay down a policy of action that if he had been on the platform still, would have shocked him to the marrow of his timid soul? If in the first month of a new Labour government it lays down a mighty challenge, a new era will thereby begin. Let us be frank about it. The people are not certain about the Labour Party now, and they have got to get back their confidence; we have to make them confident. One hundred years ago a Whig government surprised a numbed and sceptical England by producing the Reform Bill. It was a brave challenge to the ruling aristocracy. So when the world knows by our action what they do not know yet, that there is a Labour government that stakes all on socialism; when they really know that, then while there may mocking laughter of mixed horror and dread in the country houses and drawing-rooms, and in the capitalist press, there will be the stirring of a new hope in the dead mining villages. There will be a rising among our people much greater than the rising for the Reform Bill of 1832, as our case transcends in vital human value the beginnings of modern democracy. And don't we all of us here believe that, as the depths begin to heave, so the fortress of capitalism will begin to crack and tumble.

'I have just had the biggest success of conference', Trevelyan wrote to his wife, 'I swept the assembly completely. Uncle Arthur [Henderson] simply wasn't listened to in asking for postponement. I got a unanimous vote, but what was more important, I moved them to their depths.'[71] It was the sort of response that Tony Benn was to evoke after Labour's election defeats half a century later. Clement Attlee spoke in support of Trevelyan:

> I think the events of last year have shown that no further progress can be made in seeking to get crumbs from the rich man's table. I think in the present condition of the world we are bound in duty to whom we represent to tell them quite clearly that they cannot get socialism without tears, that whenever we try to do anything we will be opposed by every vested interest, financial, political, and social, and I think we have got to face the fact that even if we are returned with a majority, we shall have another crisis at once, and that we have got to have a thought-out plan to deal with that crisis; that we have got to put first things first, and that we have not got to wait until our mandate has been exhausted and frittered away, but, as Sir Charles Trevelyan says, we have got to strike whilst the iron is hot.

Labour's leader Arthur Henderson tried to caution against binding the hands of the next Labour government, but struggled even to get heard. He resigned soon afterwards, to be replaced by Labour's de facto Commons leader George Lansbury. Perhaps, had he not also been swept out of Parliament by the election of 1931, Labour's next leader might have been Trevelyan. Like Lansbury, his left-wing revivalism suited a party shocked by apparent betrayal and reeling from defeat. With an impassioned denunciation of the cuts imposed by MacDonald's new National government, Trevelyan defined the battle as he saw it:

> . . . this government with that great bank of rich men behind them in the House of Commons has chosen to lay down a class challenge. It has chosen to say to the Durham and Bradford people: 'You have had your children educated in secondary schools for a genera-tion, but that is now at an end. You shall go down to the level of those backward Authorities who know how to keep the working people in their places.' Now I say that means class war . . . Even as he is, MacDonald ought to have known better. I say this to you – some of you who want to ban him for the future from the Labour Party – well, cannot you trust that he will not come back to you; that he will stay in the drawing rooms where he now resorts? . . .
>
> We ought to make it perfectly clear that our response to this is free secondary edu-cation at once for all – the moment we get the chance . . . the millions which will be required for that shall be made available from the super-tax payers whose present meanness and unpatriotic selfishness is denying the sons and daughters of humble homes – who are, in many cases, cleverer than their own – what they obtain at Eton, Winchester, and Marlborough for the dullest of their own favoured progeny.

The most divisive debate of the 1932 Labour conference was over the issue of Labour's plans to nationalise and reorganise transport. Former Transport Minister Herbert Morrison proposed on behalf of Labour's National Executive that a National Transport Board should be appointed by the minister 'on appropriate grounds of ability':

> The workers must not be made the victims of incompetence in socialised undertakings as they are made the victims of incompetence in the cotton industry and other indus-tries today. We ought, therefore, to say unhesitatingly that real ability – not the tech-nician only, nor the expert – that real business ability, of which the Labour movement has its share, shall be the test of appointment to boards of this kind . . .
>
> I beg of this conference not to snatch at the shadow of control but to take the substance . . . Once you concede to any industry the right of representation, your board will be run by interests, thinking of their interests with sectional minds, scratching each other's backs . . . A man should be there as a competent individual, not as a representative of a trade union . . .

Harold Clay and Ernest Bevin of the TGWU tried to amend his proposals so that some board members 'should be appointed by the minister only after consultation with the trade unions engaged in the industry'. 'This report provides for an efficient bureaucracy being placed in control with no effective check upon it,' argued Clay. 'You have a public corporation now in the BBC. What effective control have you there?' Moreover, as Clay pointed out, although Morrison was right to argue that socialists needed to be competent, the 'independence' of public appointments meant that there would be no guarantee that the 'experts' appointed would be socialists. Indeed, many of those appointed to run the nationalised corporations post-1945 would indeed be the same 'great and the good' that had run them so badly pre-nationalisation:

> The report itself pays no regard to the statutory limitations that are imposed upon either municipal or national ownership. It pays no regard to the fact that municipal ownerships have largely been under the control of non-socialists and anti-socialists, and yet public ownership today in all the services it has handled can hold its own with the best of private enterprise. In the amendment we are seeking to humanise the machinery that the report visualises, and we believe we can do that without loss of efficiency. We have no room for inefficiency in industry, because our people are the people who suffer; but we believe we can bring from the trade union and Labour side an element into industrial management that has been absent in the past, and it is due to the absence of that element that industry is in many cases in the position it is today . . .

Ex-minister Emanuel Shinwell agreed:

> . . . My friend Mr Morrison says – and I can understand that he must have had painful experience in this connection – that when you seek to appoint appropriate persons on boards of management, commissions, and the like, serious difficulties arise. Let me tell you a secret. I will tell you how we appoint members of commissions . . .
>
> Imagine Mr Morrison, or someone else, as Minister of Transport, charged with the responsibility of appointing persons of proved ability requisite for the task in view. What happens? He asks his chief civil servant to prepare a list, and his chief civil servant goes to the financial 'Who's Who' or the industrial 'Who's Who'. Mr Morrison says that was done in the Mines Department. Yes, but it was also done in the Transport Department; and indeed there is no other method of selection. You have to look around and to rely to a considerable extent on the advice rendered by your civil servant. There is no minister, not even Mr Morrison himself, who is capable of displaying the necessary ability to nose around and find the appropriate man without seeking advice in that direction. You have to ask someone to do it. Then there is canvassing . . .

Though this was debated, on both sides, as a question of high principle. The real trouble, according to Hugh Dalton, was that Morrison, when Minister of Transport in 1929–31 had not, in Bevin's view, sufficiently consulted Bevin, or sufficiently followed his advice on the appointment of Traffic Commissioners.[72] Morrison was forced to withdraw his transport plan in order to avoid defeat. As Bevin's biographer Francis Williams points out, 'This particular controversy is important not only because it brought forward in concrete form the question of the status and responsibilities of the trade unions in a socialised society regarding the nationalised industries which still [in 1952] await satisfactory solution but because it continued to colour Bevin's and Morrison's relationships long after the immediate dispute was settled.'[73]

THIRTEEN

In the Shadow of Totalitarianism
1933–34

'The maximum of socialism in the minimum of time'

Labour's 1933 conference in Hastings took place against the background of Hitler's assumption of power in Germany. The challenge of totalitarianism and its cult of 'men of action' loomed large in the mind of Stafford Cripps, who proposed that any future Labour government should abolish the House of Lords, take to itself emergency powers, and govern by decrees that would be confirmed in the House of Commons at its leisure:

> . . . Arthur Greenwood in his speech said that our purpose was to get the maximum of socialism in the minimum of time. With that I think we are all agreed. The question then arises, how are we to do this thing? In the light of the experience in Europe in recent years, are we satisfied ourselves first of all that we can do it by democratic methods, and are we prepared to satisfy the electorate, especially the younger portion of the electorate who were so disastrously led astray in Germany by the temptations of Fascism and Communism, that using constitutional and democratic methods we are capable of bringing about the transformation which it is our express desire to bring about? I think anybody who looks round this country at the present time must realise that the conviction of the effectiveness of social democracy is one which has got to be rammed home if we are going to keep with us all the keener elements in our movement . . .

Cripps demanded:

> immediate abolition of the House of Lords . . . [and] the immediate passing of an Emergency Powers Act . . . There is now on the Statute Book the Emergency Powers Act of 1921, and I have never heard anyone raise a cry for its removal. It is only designed to deal with the workers; it can only deal with industrial strikes. What we want are similar powers to deal with the financial strikers. Emergency powers have no relation to dictatorships whatsoever. Emergency powers are powers granted by Parliament for an extremely short space of time – seven days under the present Act – to do things which are urgently necessary to preserve the government and the stability of the country. Those orders when made have to be brought back to Parliament for confirmation within seven days; if not they fall. There is nothing of dictatorship in that, and it is something which is essential if we are going to face a problem of the magnitude that we believe this problem to be . . .

Manny Shinwell spoke against Cripps in the debate, arguing that:

to precipitate, immediately a Labour government with a majority is formed, a constitutional crisis, would be a mistake. We have ever so much to do. It is true, of course, that you cannot achieve your socialist state so long as you have anti-democratic noodles in the House of Lords, but our people will ask for something, will expect something, will expect social changes and progress, and I believe there are many things we can do even while the House of Lords is in the offing, and there are many things we ought to do for tactical reasons before we enter into the decisive conflict with the House of Lords . . .

He later reflected: 'Such proposals at a time when Hitler was adopting similar measures were, of course, extremely ill-judged. Strangely, [Cripps] found allies in Attlee . . . but general objections, of which Bevin's was the most formidable, got Cripps's amendment shelved for a year.' Bevin's objection was simple:

. . . I know something about emergency powers. The first Labour government rushed down to Windsor to get them signed in order to operate on me, and I have a vivid recollection of it, and we were only striking to restore a cut – not a very serious crime. I do not like emergency powers, not even when they are operated by my friends . . . [Moreover, he did] not believe the British people will follow us if we put it around in the way that is suggested. I believe we should put forward proposals which are intended to deal with unemployment, which are intended to deal with the social conditions of the people – because, after all, the people of this country might defend the House of Lords on a question of Home Rule, or some political question, but we can unite our people on bread and butter . . . We should work out our programme, go forward with it, and, if we find resistance, call for support to overcome the resistance, but not create the resistance as an excuse for not going forward with our own measures.

Brilliant and talented a barrister as Cripps was, 'he has no political judgement at all', agonised his former ministerial colleague Hugh Dalton in his diary. 'He over-simplifies everything into "the capitalists" and "the workers". An adolescent Marxian miasma!'[74] Though Cripps was defeated, as Shinwell recalled, 'Cripps's dictatorial and revolutionary words received far more publicity than the general opposition of the conference which they engendered.'[75]

Though 1933 had seen the rise to power of Hitler and his rhetoric of militarism, conflict and conquest, many Labour activists were slow to grasp the reality of the potential military threat. The preoccupation of Labour's October 1933 annual conference was not with foreign fascist aggression, but with the perceived risk of British aggression, led by the National government, against Russia. It was this that underpinned a resolution proposed by Charles Trevelyan and passed by acclamation committing the Labour movement to sabotaging war by means of a general strike in the UK which it was hoped would be emulated by workers in other prospectively combatant countries. Trevelyan spoke powerfully:

> ... The League of Nations is worked by feeble and sceptical governments like our own, or by governments that openly deride our world peace, like Italy and Germany. If our government would not use the League of Nations to try to check Japan, have we any belief at all that it would itself be checked if it embroiled itself with other nations? ... Our government ... are capable of finding causes for war with Russia or any other country in the next few years. When a sudden crisis comes we must not be unprepared ... Do not we all know by the confession of the rulers themselves that it was the organised workers that stopped open war with Russia a few years ago ... that because of the workers, they could make nothing but gestures? ... the rulers must know that if war comes they will fight with a divided nation. They can make their bourgeois war themselves, but they will make it without the workers ... let it be known that the greatest democratic working class in the world is determined that war shall not be ...

Trevelyan's speech was supported by Labour's parliamentary candidate in Coventry, Philip Noel-Baker, the Quaker son of the former Liberal MP for East Finsbury, who had worked for the League of Nations and believed in it absolutely:

> ... The next war is not inevitable if the British people want to stop it. If I have one difference with the authors of the resolution it is that I regret they did not base it on the Kellogg Pact and the Covenant of the League of Nations ...
>
> We know, because we have had in office a socialist Foreign Minister, that the League of Nations can be made to work, and if Sir John Simon, who voiced a government decision, has thrown the Covenant to the winds in a Far Eastern dispute, we have seen that by so doing he has unloosed the forces of lawless violence throughout the world, and we know that if a socialist Foreign Minister came back to office he would again be able to use the League of Nations.

Noel-Baker would subsequently play a leading role in the creation of the United Nations and during 1947–50 would serve in Cabinet, where Attlee was bitingly to describe his contributions as 'talkative but not illuminating'.[76]

It fell to Hugh Dalton to flag up the threat from Hitler in his brief speech on behalf of Labour's National Executive. An Old Etonian, Fabian intellectual and junior foreign office minister 1929–31, Dalton had developed a passionate hatred for Germans while serving on the Western Front during the Great War. He knew the conference was in no mood for a wrangle and with Arthur Henderson scheduled to speak next as President of the World Disarmament conference the Executive wanted to give in gracefully and promptly. Dalton's reference to the threat from Hitler was an early indicator of the determination of some of those who would come to occupy leading positions within the Labour Party to steer it towards a more realistic foreign policy in the future:

My only criticism of the drafting would be that the resolution does not carry us perhaps quite far enough, that it does not commit us to the economic and financial boycott of any war-mongering State – Hitler, or any other person who may disturb the
peace and murder the workers of the world . . .

Though Labour was united in seeking to avoid a war with fellow Soviet workers, it
was divided in its attitude to working with the Communists against fascism. Many of
Labour's leading figures had been supportive of the professed ideals of the original
Russian revolution and admired the apparent successes of economic collectivism.
However the behaviour of the British Communists had been little different from the
Communists in Weimar Germany who had bitterly attacked Labour's sister party, the
Social Democrats, whom they dubbed 'social fascists', and had materially weakened the
opposition to Nazism, making it impossible to form a stable democratic government of
the centre and left. The Communists had in effect united with the anti-democratic parties of the right to destroy German democracy. They had believed that it was necessary to
destroy 'bourgeois' democracy for capitalism to implode and a situation propitious to
Communist revolution to develop. In doing so they contributed directly to Hitler's rise
to power. Too late they, and Moscow, realised the magnitude of their misjudgement.
Instructions from Moscow changed and Communist parties across Europe swung round
to call for a United Front against Fascism. The Joint National Council of Labour issued
a blunt statement in response: 'If the British working class hesitate now between majority and minority rule and toy with the idea of Dictatorship, Fascist or Communist, they
will go down to servitude such as they have never suffered.'[77] A TUC statement declared:

> There are some who deny that freedom can exist in a capitalist society. They regard it
> as a bourgeois institution of no real value to the people. It is not to disregard the dis-
> abilities of a wages system under capitalist control of industry, to point out that in
> Great Britain an individual normally possesses certain liberties that are worth pre-
> serving. The State has not yet the authority to shoot citizens without trial. Nor do peo-
> ple disappear at the hands of a secret police; nor is criticism of the government a crime
> . . . Against the tyranny of governments and a return to economic servitude the insti-
> tutions of free citizenship and the organisations of democracy are our strongest safe-
> guards . . . The freedom and independence of the unions would not be worth a day's
> purchase if these safeguards were destroyed.[78]

At the 1933 Labour conference, the opposition of Labour's National Executive
(NEC) to the United Front approach was unsuccessfully but determinedly challenged on
several occasions, on three occasions being defeated by powerful speeches from Herbert
Morrison. First he urged Labour members to assist with the creation of United Front
organisations:

This debate indicates a certain amount of confusion of thought as to the various classes of organisations with which we are dealing. I make no complaint about that, for confusion about these organisations is to be understood and excused. There is no keeping track of them; they come and they go and, like burglars, when they are found out they sail up under a new name . . . Our friends come here and say these organisations are innocent, but the leaders of the Communist International are not so gentle in their observations and are far more frank, open and honest in their declarations than some of the defenders of these organisations have been this morning. Let us go to fountain head, Mr Stalin. He laid it down in *Die Internationale* of 1932 that 'the United Front tactics were set up by Lenin in order to make it easier for the millions of workers in capitalist countries who are infected by the prejudices of Social Democratic opportunism to come over to Communism'. No obscurity about that; perfectly honest, perfectly frank. The honesty of the Russians is like a breath of fresh air compared with the confusion among some of their friends in this country who get mixed up with these organisations which have the perfectly clear purpose of having contact with the Labour Party in order to win our members over to Communism. We are expected to be mugs enough to make it easier for them to do it. Let me go to someone else, Mr Kuusinen of Moscow, who says quite frankly: 'We must create a whole solar system of organisations and smaller committees around the Communist Party, so to speak, smaller organisations working actually under the influence of our party (not under mechanical leadership).'

There is no evasion, no dishonesty, in that, and if the British Communists and their friends get muddle-headed and lead themselves up the garden, that is all right, but there is no reason why they should lead us up the garden . . .

A later attempt suffered the same fate after Morrison pointed out that:

we should have been in a difficulty in fighting fascist dictatorship by associating with the Communists, because they themselves believe in a form of dictatorship, and a united front upon such a platform would have presented certain difficulties . . . we condemn dictatorship as such, whether that dictatorship is of the left or of the right, and the conference must face up to that issue. We cannot hunt with the hounds and run with the hare. If we are opposed to dictatorship we must be open about it and say so . . .

Determined advocates of a United Front included Ellen Wilkinson, who had campaigned in Germany for the Social Democrats in 1932 and was later to become a supporter, close friend and possibly a lover of Morrison. She joined the fray in a further debate that same conference:

Today many of the German leaders are sitting in concentration camps very largely as a result of the deep divisions in the working class of Germany. Let us say quite frankly that both sides are equally to blame . . . If democracy is going to win through this crisis, democracy must have teeth and claws; democracy cannot afford to have divisions in its own ranks. The time has come for the big organisation in the Labour movement to take the first step forward in healing the breach . . . If you just sit there and say we will not have anything to do with the Communists or with the ILP or with anything that does not just keep on our tramway lines, I say the rank and file, whom we represent, will not listen . . .

It was Morrison again who replied for Labour's National Executive, to devastating effect:

> . . . It is true that part of the German problem was the deep division in the working-class forces, as Miss Wilkinson has said, but surely, with her reading of working-class history in Germany, she should know that that division was not created by the Social Democratic Party; it was not created by the German socialist trade unions; it was created, and it was deliberately created and maintained by the Communist International . . .
>
> Trotsky himself has criticised the Communist International for its handling of the situation, and Trotsky is right and Miss Wilkinson is wrong. Miss Wilkinson said that democracy must fight, and must fight with tooth and claws. Well, we shall play our part. Miss Wilkinson said that the Executive should have acted with more energy and drive . . . But may I put it to Miss Wilkinson, with the greatest respect, that if the official organisation of the party could do with a bit more energy and drive, she, instead of running straight over and starting an unofficial organisation in association with people whom she knows she ought not, in loyalty to the party, to associate with, instead of criticising the Executive for lack of energy and drive, would be better occupied by concentrating her undoubted energy and drive on the forward work of the party. Now, it is impossible to unite with people who are not really willing to unite with us, and, moreover, there is no point in uniting with people who, in numbers and in capacity, if I may say so, are a negligible quantity. What is there to unite with, compared with the weight of the great trade union movement and the Local Labour Parties? We are a United Front, and I ask you to stand by the Executive in maintaining the united front which we have got.

Despite the opposition from Labour's leadership, the agitation by the Communists and ginger groups such as the Socialist League[79] for a United Front against fascism increased through 1934. In July 1934 a United Front was established between socialists and Communists in France, and Spain followed suit in September. But in Britain, where the Communist Party was far smaller, the Labour leadership was antipathetic to what it saw as being more about promoting division within Labour rather than unity outside it. It therefore proposed to revise its list of banned Communist 'front' organisations and take disciplinary powers to deal with Labour members who took part in United Front campaigns organised under the auspices of such organisations. At Labour's conference in October 1934 the leadership's proposals were challenged by Aneurin Bevan, a brilliant and largely self-educated young Welsh ex-miner who had been MP for Ebbw Vale since 1929 and had become increasingly close to Cripps and the Socialist League. Condemning the 'insipidity' of Labour's NEC, who he demanded do more to protest against fascism,

Bevan asked, ' . . . Where is the Executive going to stop? Are they going to expel Mr Lansbury and Major Attlee and Mr Wall for associating with Communist members on the Council for Civil Liberties? . . . ' His star had been rising through his passionate speeches during the Commons debates on the Special Areas and on unemployment pay. And he believed Morrison and Bevin to be utterly wrong in their opposition to a United Front; born in 1897 (Bevin was born in 1881 and Morrison in 1888), Bevan lacked their bitter memories of fighting the Communists in the 1920s. Bevin was incensed:

> . . . It is rather curious that there is a section of this movement who are always telling us we do not go fast enough, who claim a liberty in their own conduct almost amounting to licence, and who forget that the trade unions in this conference when they formed this party took a step that entitles the party itself to recognise their responsibility to these great organised bodies. We said in effect we will divorce ourselves from utilising any influence or collaborating with any political party and we said: 'We entrust our political destiny to the hands of the Labour Party.' If organised labour in the trade union sense has trusted its destiny to this party, this party has no right to allow an individual member to flirt with that responsibility. When you go into opposition we go into opposition, and when you are in a crisis we do not run away. We may not be spectacular, we may not posturise, we may not be publicity mongers, but at least in a crisis we stand four-square with the Labour Party . . .
>
> They have said, 'Gloves off!' As far as I am concerned with them, it is gloves off! . . . A previous speaker said that the Communist Party was an insignificant party. It would not have been if we had not kept down this intrigue. And if you do not keep down the Communists, you cannot keep down the fascists. It is not good criticising our friends on the Continent when they failed at the critical moment to maintain discipline as we propose to do now. That is where they went wrong and they got eaten out and undermined; and when they had to take action, half of their members were in one party and the other half were in the other party. Bevan tells us we did not do right on the Unemployment Act. Did he do right when he got up in the House of Commons and tried to let the fascists in, and supported everybody going to the Courts of Referees to the detriment of the trade union movement?
>
> *Aneurin Bevan:* On a point of order, I want to ask for the protection of the chair. I challenge Ernest Bevin to make a public statement with me on any public platform in Great Britain.
>
> *A delegate:* This is a public platform.
>
> *Ernest Bevin:* Apparently my namesake – spelled differently – can get on this platform and denounce the National Council of Labour, he can denounce the Labour Party Executive, and he is so thin-skinned that he cannot take his own medicine back again. No, in this conference, Aneurin Bevan, you are not going to get the flattery of the gossip columns that you get in London. You are not going to get flattery, you are going to get facts. I am stating the case – that when the trade unions had fought their damnedest to try and deal with this unemployed problem, had carried

more responsibility than any other body in the country, that was the moment when in the House of Commons this 'loyalty' was displaced . . .

The clash between Bevan and Bevin was so heated that Bevan appealed to the chair for protection. 'Yet another private war amongst future Cabinet colleagues had broken out,'[80] reflected future Cabinet colleague Manny Shinwell ruefully. Shinwell had himself spoken in the debate:

I know from my experience that much of the confusion that exists in the minds of the rank and file is due to the innuendoes and insinuations of men like Aneurin Bevan . . . It is very often the case that instead of the rank and file criticising the Executive, the criticism comes from the people who go down to address the rank and file on behalf of the party. That creates embarrassment and confusion and gives rise to discussions such as we have had this afternoon. There are some people who are constantly attacking us. They say we are weak and insipid, and sometimes they take us to be traitors. When we reply to them they squeal about personalities, forgetting they are insulting us all the while. It is not good enough. If they are to be permitted to say things about us, personal things, over and over again, vile things about character and integrity, about people being 'on the make' and the rest of it, they ought not to squeal when they get a little of their own medicine paid back to them . . .

FOURTEEN

The Left in Retreat 1934–36

'When the revolution comes it will not be won by fierce countenances and menacing voices'

Labour's 1934 conference in Southport saw the adoption of *For Socialism and Peace*, setting out Labour's aims and values. This was in effect the successor document to the MacDonald-era *Labour and the Nation*. It rejected the idea that an incoming Labour government should take emergency powers in order to force through legislation and to protect itself from subversion by capitalists and as such explicitly repudiated the approach of Stafford Cripps and the Socialist League. In consequence, the Socialist League put down no fewer than 75 amendments to the draft, many of which were so drastic as to change its approach completely.

The main debate centred on an amendment moved by Cripps and William Mellor of the Socialist League. They branded *For Socialism and Peace* too vague and demanded the insertion of five key pledges to make it more specific. The pledges, somewhat vague themselves, were:

I.   — To make Parliament effective.

II. — To secure at once for the government economic power sufficient to enable it to proceed unhampered with the socialist reorganisation of our industrial and social systems.

III. — To change the whole basis of production and distribution so that productive power may be used to satisfy the needs of the people in accordance with a planned economy.

IV. — To pursue a foreign policy designed to secure world peace.

V.   — To put into operation measures to relieve some of the worst hardships brought upon the workers by capitalism.

Their arguments were spectacularly demolished by a barnstorming speech from Herbert Morrison:

> ... Mr Mellor has accused the Executive of using general phrases. I listened very carefully to the speech of Mr Mellor, and it was full of general phrases. The only difference between his general phrases and our general phrases is that ours are somewhat more specific. He has a fiercer countenance and a more menacing voice, but, if I am not

mistaken, when the revolution comes, it will be not be won by fierce countenances and menacing voices. He complains that the Executive have not reproduced the original paragraph in the constitution of the party about the workers by hand and by brain having the whole fruits of their industry. Neither has he. The Socialist League amendments do not reproduce it. Why did not Mr Mellor and his colleagues reproduce it out of the party constitution? It was there, it was handy, and all they had to do was to cut it out and get the paste and stick it on. So he is as bad as we are.

But take this talk of general phrases. As my friend Dalton says, we have but a skeleton in italics. Look at these italics, *'to make Parliament effective'*. Was there ever a more general phrase in the history of mankind than that? Yesterday the Executive brought up a quite definitive statement to conference, and it was passed. Now we are asked to be fobbed off with a phrase, 'to make Parliament effective'. We are then told in the second italic head – I speak in Mr Mellor's journalistic jargon – *'to secure at once for the government economic power sufficient to enable it to proceed unhampered with the socialist reorganisation of our industrial and social system'*. What is this power sufficient to proceed unhampered? Oh! simple Mellor. Oh! unreal revolution! Oh! how he still lives in the petty bourgeois outlook of his early Communist days. How are we to get the means to proceed unhampered? This is all we have to do: socialise the Bank of England, socialise the Joint Stock Bank and the main financial institutions. Foster the State ownership of the land, and then, kind friends, the trick is done. Really, I would be ashamed to bring up such a mild Liberal programme as that to enable you to proceed unhampered.

Then, proceed to the next general phrase – *'to change the whole basis of production and distribution'* – and, mind you, before I go on to the other ones, Mr Mellor was going to seize these three items – seize them directly. You know Mr Mellor has come out of the Communist Party, but the theories persist, and he still has some of its false ideas. (*A voice:* 'No.') You know we had to sit up here and listen to Mr Mellor calling this Executive a gang of Liberals. I am saying what I think and I believe it. The phrase then goes on: *'to change the whole basis of production and distribution so that productive power may be used to satisfy the need of the people in accordance with a planned economy'*. We can all agree to that platitude.

Then the fifth phrase: *'to put into operation the measures to relieve some of the worst hardships brought upon the workers by capitalism'*. That is a perfectly general phrase. I cannot agree with Mr Mellor that that substitution is any more definite than our submission in 'Labour's Aims'. Who is going to say that the Liberal Party would accept this declaration of ours: 'There is no halfway house between a society based on private ownership in the primary means of production, with the profit of the few as the measure of success, and a society where public ownership of those means enables the resources of the nation to be deliberately planned for attaining the maximum of general wellbeing.' It is monstrous to suggest that that is a Liberal declaration . . . It is all very well for Mr Mellor to say that he believes in socialising, and not in public corporations. He will still have to find the instrument of management under socialisation . . .

I am getting a little weary of people who sneer at the job I did. I do not say that the London Passenger Transport Board Bill is socialism, but I say that that Bill was definitely socialistic in character . . . On the back of the Bill was not only my own name as Minister of Transport, but, if I remember rightly, the name of the Solicitor General was there as well, who is now the Chairman of the Socialist League, and I wish publicly to pay my tribute to the great help and assistance I received from Sir Stafford Cripps, particularly in drafting the original compensation clause that it contained . . . I will not play the game of being one thing when I am a minister, and another thing when I come into opposition . . . [The Socialist League was decisively defeated in the vote that followed.]

Meanwhile, the idea that world war could be averted by a general strike was finally killed off by the trade unions, and Ernie Bevin's TGWU in particular. Discussing the issue at the TGWU Executive immediately after the 1933 Labour conference at Hastings, Bevin asked:

Who and what is there to strike? Trade unionism has been destroyed in Italy and Germany; practically speaking it does not exist in France; it is extremely weak in the USA . . . while there is no possibility of a general strike against the Russian government in the event of war. What is left? Great Britain, Sweden, Denmark and Holland; virtu-ally, these are the only countries in which strong trade union organisations exist. Ought we, in the light of these facts, to go on talking glibly, misleading the people and our-selves as to what we could do with a general strike weapon in the event of a world war?[81]

On 28 February 1934 the National Joint Council of Labour (Labour Party National Executive, Parliamentary Labour Party and TUC General Council) met at Transport House to discuss taking forward the resolutions agreed at the 1933 conference. The same day the Austrian trade unions were brutally suppressed by armed force. The document drawn up in the light of the discussions of that day, *War and Peace*, and approved by a fur-ther meeting of the three committees in June 1934 and later by the TUC and Labour con-ferences, stated that 'there might be circumstances under which the government of Great Britain might have to use its military and naval forces in support of the League in restraining an aggressor nation' and affirmed 'the duty to take part in collective action against a peace-breaker'. On 1 October 1935 at Labour's conference in Brighton came one of the longest debates ever heard at a Labour Party conference, and one of its most bitter clashes. With fascist Italy's invasion of Abyssinia clearly imminent, Hugh Dalton moved the resolution for Labour's National Executive. It called upon the conference to pledge its support for the government and 'in cooperation with other nations represent-ed at the Council and Assembly of the League to use all the necessary measures provided by the Covenant to prevent Italy's unjust and rapacious attack upon the territory of a fellow member of the League'.

Dalton said:

. . . We stand for the collective peace system, for strong collective action in defence of peace against any aggressor . . . on March 11 of this year: 'What would we have done,' said a speaker from the Labour front bench, 'as regards the Sino-Japanese dispute? As I understand it, when we signed the covenant of the League of Nations we honestly meant to keep it. It was our duty in cooperation with the other nations, who were equally bound, to do our utmost immediately that aggression became apparent to take every possible step to stop the aggression, in the first place, no doubt, by recalling the Ambassador, and if that failed, by economic pressure. If that failed, then in cooperation with other nations equally bound to take action, by armaments if necessary' (*interruption*) . . . So spoke Sir Stafford Cripps. And I agree with every word of that.

The immediate question for us to decide today is: do we stand firm in this crisis for the policy to which we have so often pledged ourselves, or shall we turn tail and run away, repudiate our obligations under the covenant of the League and signal 'All clear' to Mussolini in his barbarous and long-premeditated assault upon Abyssinia? Do we stand firm, or shall we run away? . . .

I wish to say one word on sanctions. The *Daily Mail* tells you that sanctions mean war. It is not necessarily so. On the other hand, the scrapping of sanctions as a reserve force behind international law certainly means war, and war soon, and war in a far more terrible form than even a war between Italy and Abyssinia – a war with more people coming in and more serious people than either Abyssinia or even Italy. A threat of sanctions may be enough to prevent war. If not, the actual use of sanctions, economic and financial, without any military or naval action, may be sufficient to re-establish peace even if Mussolini breaks it.

If not – face all the facts – it is hard even now to believe it, but if Mussolini be so lunatic as to resist the united League of Nations by force, then so be it. He will order the firing of the first shot, and he will take the consequences of that order.

But again face realities. Mussolini has led Italy into a desperate position, financially and economically very weak, her foreign credits all exhausted . . . And in naval terms, an Italian army in East Africa, with its lines of communication passing through a narrow ditch in the Egyptian sands, which it used to be said any two men unseen could block, which could be blocked in more ways than one with the greatest ease, her communications passing through this little ditch, an Italy without an ally in the world and without command of the sea at either end of that little ditch – well, I will not develop this line of thought. I will leave it to you . . .

Are we going to play the part of a great comrade among the nations, or are we going to slink impotently away into the shadows; impotent by our own choice; unfaithful to our solemn pledges; not a comrade but a Judas among the nations; deservedly left, as we should be, without a friend in the world; preparing, through our own dishonour, our own sure downfall at no distant date?

Stafford Cripps had resigned from Labour's National Executive on the eve of the conference and spoke against Dalton from the floor of conference, claiming the resolution risked committing Labour to supporting a:

'capitalist and imperialist war' and that sanctions may entail war. [The League of Nations,] with three major powers outside, has become nothing but the tool of the satiated imperialist powers. If we feel a desperate urge to do something at all costs in the present situation, we must fall back on the attempt to use working-class sanctions . . .

It was 'an eloquent speech against capitalism, imperialism and all that imperialism stands for', declared John Marchbank of the National Union of Railwaymen, speaking in support of the resolution, but 'said nothing with regard to the real issues at stake'. Marchbank also pointed out that from the foundation of the League of Nations, British support for the League Covenant and the enforcement of sanctions always carried with it the possibility of the use of armed force and war, quoting Lansbury speaking at the time of Japan's invasion of China two years previously: 'Some people may think that Great Britain signed the Covenant of the League and did not mean it. I think we did mean it. If we did not mean that we were going to use these means of stopping or preventing war, I do not know why we signed the Covenant.' George Lansbury, Labour's leader, was profoundly unhappy with the resolution. As his nephew by marriage G. D. H. Cole observed, Lansbury 'saw the drift to war, hated the rising forces of dictatorship and violence in Europe, but was inhibited by his personal pacifism and his abhorrence of war and warlike gestures under all conditions from believing wholeheartedly in a collective security resting on armed force or in any sort of rearmament directed against the threats of Nazi aggression'.[82] Declared Lansbury:

> . . . I am in a very difficult position today. Often – and only the Executive and my colleagues know how often – I have disagreed with their policy, and because I was a member of the Executive, and lately because of my other position, I have remained silent during the whole of the conference . . . I agree with the position of those of my friends who think that it is quite intolerable that you should have a man speaking as leader who disagrees fundamentally on an issue of this kind . . .
>
> I believe that force never has and never will bring permanent peace and permanent goodwill in the world . . . One Whose life I revere and Who, I believe, is the greatest Figure in history, has put it on record: 'Those who take the sword shall perish by the sword.' . . . I personally cannot see the difference between mass murder organised by the League of Nations, or mass murder organised between individual nations; to me it is exactly the same . . .
>
> I believe that the first nation that will put into practice practical Christianity, doing to others as you would be done unto, that that nation would lead the world away from war and absolutely to peace . . . I know that you will say to me: 'Say that to Mussolini, or say that to Hitler.' If I had had power during this period I would have gone and faced these men at Geneva and I would have let the world know what it was I was proposing to do . . . during the last war the youth, the early manhood of my division, was slaughtered most terribly, and now I see the whole world rushing to

perdition . . . If mine was the only voice in this conference, I would say in the name of the faith I hold, the belief I have that God intended us to live peaceably and quietly with one another, if some people do not allow us to do so, I am ready to stand as the early Christians did, and say, 'This is our faith, this is where we stand, and, if necessary, this is where we will die.'

Lansbury's words 'produced a wave of highly emotional sympathy', recalled Shinwell, 'but the Lansbury line was not practical politics in 1935. It was left to Bevin to point this out, and he did with all the considerable brutality at his command':

> . . . I think the movement ought to understand the Trades Union Congress position. Let me remind the delegates that, when George Lansbury says what he has said today in the conference, it is rather late to say it, and I hope this conference will not be influenced by either sentiment or personal attachment. I hope you will carry no resolution of an emergency character telling a man with a conscience like Lansbury what he ought to do. If he finds that he ought to take a certain course, then his conscience should direct him as to the course he should take. It is placing the Executive and the movement in an absolutely wrong position to be taking your conscience round from body to body asking to be told what you ought to do with it. There is one quotation from the Scriptures which George Lansbury has quoted today which I think he ought to apply to himself – 'do unto others'. I have had to sit in conference with the leader and come to decisions, and I am a democrat and I feel we have been betrayed . . .
>
> . . . if ever you have seen pacifism ineffective it was in China, the greatest pacifist nation in the world, having nothing to defend itself with, and being unable to stop Japan marching in. The coloured races of the world have been pacifist, they had nothing to defend themselves with, and we marched in . . .
>
> . . . the people who oppose this resolution ought to have had the courage of their convictions and tabled a resolution at this conference to the effect that we should withdraw from the League of Nations. You can not be in and out at the same time, not if you are honest, and that is the only thing that makes me question the honesty of some of them . . .
>
> Every one of us on the General Council of the TUC feel that we have been let down. We have had enough of it during the last ten or twelve years as trade union leaders – a very stiff time. I want to say to our friends who have joined us in this political movement, that our predecessors formed this party. It was not Keir Hardie who formed it, it grew out of the bowels of the Trades Union Congress. It was a struggle for status and equality, for Labour representation leading ultimately to power, and none of us have ever 'ratted'. Whether we have won or lost, we have taken our corner. We have never bothered much about whether we had place or power. Very few of us aspired to leadership . . .
>
> They say he who takes the sword shall perish by the sword. The man who has taken the sword is Mussolini, and because Mussolini has taken the sword we stand by the Scriptural doctrine and say that he shall perish by economic sanctions. I honestly

believe in this movement. I have shown you its history from the beginning, how its policy has been built up, how we have accepted responsibility, and pledged ourselves to the League, and I ask you to give tomorrow an almost unanimous vote, leaving it to those who cannot accept the policy of this great conference to take their own course.

Even had it not been already, after Bevin's attack, Lansbury's position was clearly untenable. 'Bevin's surgery had been cruel, but it was effective as a cure. In a matter of an hour he had saved the Labour Party, moving towards a mild renaissance, from a repetition of the disastrous situation of 1931, when the leader had one policy and his lieutenants another, with the rank and file bewildered and disillusioned.'[83] Bevin himself is reported to have told those who reproached him afterwards for his brutality: 'Lansbury has been going about dressed in saint's clothes for years waiting for martyrdom: I set fire to the faggots.'[84] Most of the trade unions agreed with Labour's National Executive and Cripps was overwhelmingly defeated by 102,000 votes to 2,168,000. Lansbury had wanted to resign for some time and did so a few days later, on 8 October.

Barely two weeks after Lansbury's resignation as Labour leader, the National government called a general election. Lansbury's deputy, Clement Attlee, took over as caretaker leader. Held on 14 November 1935, the election saw Labour regain some hundred seats to secure 154 MPs. This was a handful more than in 1924 and fewer than in 1929, but Labour had secured its highest ever share of the vote, 37.9 per cent. Having secured a mere 20 seats and 6.5 per cent of the vote, Liberal hopes of maintaining any substantial role as a 'third force' evaporated. The overwhelmingly Conservative 'National' government, now led by Stanley Baldwin who had succeeded the ailing Ramsay MacDonald as Prime Minister in June 1935, had won 432 seats. MacDonald himself was defeated by Manny Shinwell at Seaham, his constituency since 1929, leaving J. H. Thomas the only survivor among the Labour Cabinet seceders of 1931 in a 'National Labour Party' reduced to eight MPs. MacDonald returned briefly to the Commons in 1936 as MP for the Scottish Universities, but his time at the heart of politics was over. He died in November 1937.

After the election, the Parliamentary Labour Party held a proper election for its leader. The candidates were the caretaker leader Clement Attlee, Herbert Morrison and Arthur Greenwood. Morrison and Greenwood were respectively Ministers of Transport and Health in the 1929-31 Labour Cabinet. Morrison had been the favourite to succeed Lansbury for several years and had led Labour to victory in the London County Council elections of March 1934. For the *News Chronicle*, the 1935 election campaign was 'dominated by one man – Herbert Morrison'.[85] Arthur Greenwood was respected, able and favoured by trade unionists such as Bevin who distrusted Morrison, but his growing drink problem was already widely known among MPs. Hugh Dalton, Morrison's campaign manager, described the choice to MPs as being between 'a nonentity, a drunk and

Herbert'.[86] Morrison had the support of most of Labour's 'intellectuals', including Philip Noel-Baker, Beatrice Webb, Stafford Cripps from the left and journalists such as *New Statesman* editor Kingsley Martin.

Attlee had the quiet loyalty of most of the MPs, in particular the mining MPs such as Tom Williams and David Grenfell, with whom he had worked in Parliament during the difficult years following 1931. In the event the votes split on the first ballot 58 for Attlee, 44 for Morrison and 33 for Greenwood. On the second ballot, held on 3 December, virtually all of Greenwood's supporters backed Attlee, giving him 88 votes to Morrison's 48. Attlee was confirmed as leader. A furious Morrison declined the nomination for deputy, leaving it to Greenwood. He told MPs he would instead concentrate on his role as leader of the London County Council, leaving many MPs feeling snubbed. It was a blunder that made it all the more difficult for Morrison to supplant Attlee in years to come.

One of the other MPs elected at the 1935 election (for Jarrow) was the diminutive Ellen Wilkinson, dubbed 'Red Ellen' for her politics and her flame-red hair. Born in 1891, the daughter of Manchester textile workers, she had joined the ILP aged sixteen. After a history degree at Manchester University, where she was Secretary of the University Fabians, she had become a women's suffrage campaigner, an organiser for the Shopworkers' Union, a Manchester City Councillor and from 1924-31 the MP for Middlesbrough East. The desperate plight of Jarrow, blighted by unemployment, poverty, slum housing and enforced malnutrition, was ignored by the government. Their *laissez-faire* attitude was epitomised by Walter Runciman, President of the Board of Trade in the National government and formerly a member of Asquith's Liberal Cabinet: 'Jarrow,' he said, 'must work out its own salvation.'[87] The Jarrow Crusade was a protest of desperation, of two hundred men carrying a petition to Westminster from the people of Jarrow calling for the government to 'realise the urgent need for providing work for the town' and to 'actively assist the resuscitation of industry'. Setting out on 5 October 1936 they marched all the way from Jarrow to Parliament to present their petition, arriving at the end of the month. Ellen Wilkinson marched with them for much of the way, speaking nightly at public meetings along the route. Labour's National Executive feared that some of those involved in organising the march were Communists seeking to discredit the parliamentary road to socialism Labour trod and to incite people to direct action. They therefore declined to give the march official support. On 8 October, Ellen Wilkinson rushed up to Edinburgh to appeal to Labour's annual conference for a change of mind:

> Here we have malnutrition reports, Jarrow with an infant mortality of 114 and the rest of the country 57 . . . What is the use of us coming here and stating facts that are known to every single one of you in your ordinary work? What we ought to be discussing is what we are going to do about it . . .
>
> Mrs Gould of the Executive says: 'We will have another report.' Have we not had

enough reports? Is there a pore in the body of an unemployed man that has not been card-indexed? What are you going to do? . . .

You cannot expect men trapped in these distressed areas to stay there and starve because it is not convenient to have them coming to London. What has the National Council done? It has disapproved of it. What has gone out from our General Council? Letters to the local areas in fact saying, in the politest language, 'Do not help these men.' We have had to appeal to the Local Authorities. Why? Because some of these marchers might be Communists. I hope when Sir Walter Citrine gets to the pearly gates, St Peter will be able to assure him there is no Communist inside. It is no use really criticising the party. This party is bone of our bone and flesh of our flesh. But here I tell the Executive that they are missing the most marvellous opportunity in a generation. You have no conception of the depth of indignation there is, far outside our party ranks – people whom you would never get in the ordinary way inside our party ranks. If you had seen that march from Jarrow you would have realised that it was a great folk movement with everybody there. What propaganda speech in your life was equal to that vast object lesson of what had been done in that town which has been murdered in the interests of the Stock Exchange and of rationalisation . . .

Let us look at things in a bigger way. This is bigger than a political party; it is a national danger and a national scandal. I appeal to the National Executive even now, at this late hour, to come forward, to head this national movement, to head this march, to do the generous thing and say to these men when they come to London, 'Comrades, we are with you. We will see you through. We will take you to Parliament and force the issue there and nothing shall be done in Parliament until your wrongs are righted.' If you do that, we can have a revival.

FIFTEEN

Spain and Civil War 1936–37

'I hope then that the Labour Party will have some other policy to offer than their sympathy accompanied by bandages and cigarettes'

The spectre of war with fascism became all too real in 1936. Early that year, Hitler had sent his army into the 'de-militarized zone' of the Rhineland and Mussolini had secured victory in Abyssinia. On 18 July Spanish General Francisco Franco led a fascist rebellion against the democratically elected socialist Spanish government, precipitating a civil war. Most of the Spanish army had deserted to Franco, taking with them their weapons. The Republic desperately needed arms with which to rebuild an army and defend itself. Nevertheless, Labour's leadership supported the British government's policy of non-intervention, supposedly an internationally agreed policy under which neither arms nor assistance were to be given to either side. Its justification was that it was seen as the only realistic way to stop Italy and Germany actively and decisively intervening in support of Franco. Were they to do this the only way to prevent a swift and overwhelming Franco victory was thought to be direct and equivalent intervention by Britain, France and the USSR on the other side, which would mean world war. Unstated was Hugh Dalton's fear that so great was the risk of war with Hitler and so inadequate the preparedness of Britain's defences that Britain could ill afford to send arms to Spain that it needed itself. Moreover, Labour's leadership, with good reason, thought it unlikely that a Conservative-dominated British government would want to ally itself in any way with anti-clerical socialist governments abroad, feeling that the government was, in many respects, more sympathetic to Franco. As Michael Foot has written, 'if some Tories regarded Franco as a gallant Christian gentleman, why should they not soon detect the same saintly qualities in Hitler and Mussolini'.[88] Ironically, while most Labour supporters of 'non-intervention' did so on the understanding that it was the preferred policy of France's socialist government, the main reason for French adherence to it was the insistence of Stanley Baldwin and his Foreign Secretary Sir Anthony Eden in London. Britain's National government did not want to get embroiled in a war against both Hitler and Mussolini on behalf of a socialist/communist Spanish government supported by the Soviet Union. Thus the diary of Baldwin's private secretary records the Prime Minister telling Eden 'that on no account, French or other, was he bring us into the fight on the side of the Russians'.[89]

The widespread belief within the Labour movement that the policy of universal 'non-intervention' was proving a fiction would precipitate the greatest battle at Labour's conference of October 1936. The debate itself was opened by Labour's new deputy leader, Arthur Greenwood, whose supporters included Ernest Bevin and Clement Attlee. Greenwood began by uncomfortably setting out the reasons behind the Executive's support for non-intervention:

> ... I admit and have said in public, and have written that I regard this policy of non-intervention as a very, very bad second best. I regard it as establishing a new precedent, that rebels should be treated on equal terms with governments ... But remember this, it was a situation created by the weakness of governments, and especially of our own government during the past five years. Had Japan been kept in her place four years ago, Mussolini would never have taken his troops to Abyssinia. Had Mussolini not been able to come back to Europe as the founder of a new empire, Hitler would never have dared to snap his fingers at the international agreements he had signed. If these things had not happened, the rebellion in Spain would not have happened, and we are facing now a very critical situation in the history of Europe, due to this onward and unchallenged march of dictatorship across the world ... [Though he expressed] very grave doubts as to the effectiveness of the agreement, [he feared the alternative,] free trade in arms to both sides ... I have to remind you that this country and certain others have legislation which requires government approval before arms can be exported, and I am going to put this point to you. Suppose you get free trade in arms, which side in the struggle is going to get the most? Do you suppose a machine-gun is going from this country with this government's approval? ... I can assure you – you know it in your hearts yourselves – that if there is to be freedom to send arms into Spain, Germany and Italy will send 50 guns and 50 aeroplanes for every one that goes from other countries. (*A voice:* 'No.') ...
>
> There are people who are prepared to take action which might lead to war, and let me remind some of them that they were the people who were against the policy adopted at our conference last year ... Do the ordinary people of any country want war? They do not ... Is this conference prepared to have the battle between dictatorship and democracy fought over the bleeding body of Spain? ... Is anybody in this conference prepared to suggest action which, if it were taken, might mean that a lighted match was dropped into the powder barrel? ... we have to look at the spectacle of Spain today, torn by civil war, the cockpit of a possible European war, out of which we could not keep, and we have to think of the possible consequences of that ...

But when challenged from the floor, Greenwood admitted that the Spanish government had told him 'they want – what we should want in the same circumstances. They want arms.' After that, the emotion in the hall boiled over with a series of powerful pleas, as Sir Charles Trevelyan put it, that 'all the socialist countries and the democratic countries of the world should put their heads together to see if this thing cannot be stopped. They have not tried . . . When the last great war that is looming comes, and when Japan and Germany crash in to try to destroy Soviet Russia, I hope, then, that the Labour Party will have some other policy to offer than their sympathy accompanied by bandages and cigarettes.'

Christopher Addison, a respected ex-Liberal minister who ended up in both MacDonald and Attlee's Cabinets pointed out that:

this non-intervention business is being conducted and was devised, so far as its oper-ations are concerned, at the Foreign Office, by the same men who practised the Abyssinian duplicity on this country twelve months ago. [For him there was no choice between] intervention and plunging Europe into war. The alternative was and is for us to demand that the British government takes a lead at Geneva . . .

It was Bevan who plunged the knife into the heart of Greenwood's arguments .

. . . Every newspaper office in London is full of information about arms pouring in through Lisbon. Del Vayo has made statements at Geneva and laid a document before the League to the effect that arms are pouring into the rebels and that now the rebels are superior in the air. Everybody in the world knows about the rebels getting arms – except the National Council of Labour . . .

We have had a dreadful picture painted to us of what would be the consequences if free trade in arms took place. Will conference consider for a moment the conse-quences that will occur in Europe if the present situation is allowed to work out to its logical conclusion? Is it not obvious to everyone that if the arms continue to pour into the rebels in Spain, our Spanish comrades will be slaughtered by hundreds of thou-sands? Has Mr Bevin and the National Council considered the fate of the Blum gov-ernment if a fascist government is established in Spain? How long will French democ-racy stand against fascism in Germany, fascism in Italy, fascism in Spain, and fascism in Portugal? How long will French democracy stand if the French fascists attempt a coup d'etat against the French Popular Front government, and are supplied with arms by friends in Spain? [Bevan feared a domino effect:] If the Popular Front French gov-ernment is destroyed and democracy in France is destroyed, then the Franco-Soviet Pact will soon be denounced, and democracy in Europe will soon be in ruins.

Philip Noel-Baker agreed and urged Britain to lift the arms embargo, unilaterally if it had to:

I believe in non-intervention, the mutual respect of different regimes in different States . . . But in this dispute there has never been non-intervention, from the first day onwards. When Mussolini's aircraft made forced landings on French soil, we had the absolute proof that he was intervening with the armed forces of the Crown to support the rebels, and that he had plotted with them beforehand to do so . . .

Clement Attlee's summing up was weak, a plea that:

... when we go to the Foreign Office and we say 'this agreement is being broken' they say: 'What are your facts?' ... it is no good for you or me or any of us to say: 'I am persuaded of these facts because the newspapers say so, or this or that person says so.' You have to prove them ... We are demanding action by the government at once to take steps to have these serious charges investigated ...

Morrison did not speak: unusually he disagreed with the Executive's policy. The debate was impassioned and Greenwood's resolution was carried by 1,836,000 votes to 519,000.

Two days later, the conference heard from two fraternal delegates from Spain. One was Señor de Asua, who spoke in French, Philip Noel-Baker translating. He set out the evidence of the supply of arms by the fascist powers to Franco of which the non-interventionists had said in the debate two days previously that there was no proof. 'The very quietness of the reproach struck like a dagger,' recalled Michael Foot.[90] Denouncing the Non-Intervention Pact as a 'monstrosity' and citing evidence of its breach by the fascist powers, he highlighted the atrocities of Franco:

Already, not in the firing line but in the peaceful towns, 47 Deputies of the Popular Front – 35 socialists – have been shot by the rebels. In the places they occupy, every man with a trade union card, every member of the socialist party, is taken out and shot, and often their women and children with them ... [In conclusion he pleaded:] We ask you to help us to remove the obstacles that now are stopping us from getting arms. We do not ask your country your vote of Monday last to change ... we are fighting with sticks and knives against tanks and aircraft and guns, and it revolts the conscience of the world that that should be true ...

The other speaker was Señora Isabel de Palencia, 'a proud Amazon straight from the Spanish battlefields, speaking perfect Scottish and recalling her own Scottish childhood when she had walked the streets of Edinburgh'.

Since I arrived yesterday morning it has seemed to me that I am living in a dream [she began]. A nightmare is what the last two months have been to all Spanish women. [She made an unforgettable speech of calculated passion],[91] [ending with a plea:] if you wish this atrocious war to end soon, come and help us as you have been asked, whenever you can. Think of the difference in the price of lives of two months to one year. Think of the precious gift that is being wasted, of the lives of our own youth. Do not tarry. Now that you know the truth. Now that you know what the situation is in Spain. Come and help us ... Scotsmen, you ken noo!

When she had finished the conference rose and sang the 'Red Flag' while she stood motionless and erect giving the clenched fist salute. The speeches profoundly moved the delegates and, as G. D. H. Cole recalled: 'simply swept away the pretence that the Non-Intervention Pact was not proved to have been broken'.[92] In the lunch break that followed, the National Council of Labour held an impromptu discussion of the situation and agreed to send Attlee and Greenwood at once to London to see the acting Prime Minister Neville Chamberlain and demand that the allegations of breaches of the pact be immediately investigated. On Friday, having returned to Edinburgh, Attlee moved a new resolution demanding that if proof of violations of the Non-Intervention Agreement were to be found, the British and French governments should restore the right to buy arms to the Spanish Republic. It was carried unanimously.

On 7 October the Soviet Union alleged violations of the Non-Intervention Agreement and two weeks later announced that it would be sending aid to the Republic. On 29 October Labour announced in the House of Commons the formal withdrawal of its support for non-intervention. Twelve months later, at Labour's 1937 conference a resolution proposed by Charles Trevelyan demanding greater pressure on the British government to abandon its continued support for 'non-intervention' would be carried unanimously.

SIXTEEN

Facing the Dictators 1936–39

'The Labour Party conference has always opposed unilateral disarmament, and now I find it difficult in logic to believe that this conference can support unilateral non-rearmament in a world where all others are increasing their armaments'

In July 1936 Hugh Dalton, supported by fellow shadow Cabinet members A. V. Alexander and Bertie Lees-Smith, had tried and failed to persuade the Parliamentary Labour Party to refrain from voting against the annual government defence estimates: 'What possible answer,' asked Dalton, 'had we got in the country to the accusation that we wanted arms for Spain but no arms for our own country?'[93] Attlee, Morrison and others had argued that procedurally to vote against an increase in the defence budget was not a vote against rearmament but was a vote against the government in whose overall foreign policies they had no confidence. In parallel with Labour's shift in policy over Spain came a shift in policy over rearmament. At Labour's conference in October 1936 Hugh Dalton moved an opaque resolution on behalf of Labour's National Executive declaring that 'the armed strength of the countries loyal to the League of Nations must be conditioned by the armed strength of the potential aggressors'. Although other speakers for Labour's National Executive, including Attlee, made clear that 'there is no suggestion here that we shall support the government's rearmament policy', Dalton made the most of the opportunity, using his speech to open the door to a future Labour government rearming Britain:

> ... Since 1931 the international sky has gone black. In 1931, when Arthur Henderson was Foreign Secretary, we thought we saw light in the sky. We thought we saw the first gleams of a coming sunrise. We thought we saw the promise of the dawn of a new era of brotherhood and cooperation between nations. The world was moving forward hopefully under British leadership towards disarmament by international agreement, towards the peaceful removal of the political and economic causes of war, and towards the creation of a stronger League of Nations, a more fruitful League of Nations, which should be an instrument of peace and plenty and security and goodwill. I add, facing the facts of 1931, this country was secure. In 1931 there was no external armed menace which we feared. In 1931 British armaments, relatively to the armaments of other countries at that time, were adequate for all purposes, and an all-round reduction of

armaments everywhere seemed to be within our reach. We were planning towards it. That was five years ago. Today it is a different world which we inhabit. The high hopes of 1931 have all been dashed. Today there is talk of war and fear of war in every land, fear of war in the hearts of millions of mothers of the citizens of the future. Armaments have increased and are increasing; they have not diminished, they have not been regulated. The League of Nations has grown weaker not stronger. International law and treaties have in these five years been broken shamelessly and without penalty by Japan, by Italy, by Germany, in China, in Abyssinia, in Germany itself, in the Rhineland and now in Spain. Treaty breaking becomes a daily fascist habit, and we sit by and pass resolutions of regret. How long shall we go on like that? I add, five years ago Britain was secure in the military, naval and air sense. Today British security has gone. Collective security has not been organised and our insular security has vanished with the growth of air forces on the Continent of Europe within a few hours' flight from our shores. That is the situation, and in this most dreadful situation, which is quite new since Labour left office and this crowd came in, for this most dreadful situation those who have held office during these five years have a responsibility which they cannot escape either now or in the eyes of history hereafter. They will go down in history as a body of men . . . who failed to do their duty, who broke their election pledges, who nearly killed the League of Nations (though we may yet be able to revive it) and by their ineptitude destroyed our security and exposed our country to new and deadly perils . . .

Now I wish to speak very frankly about German rearmament. For this is the central brutal fact in Europe. Anybody who discusses the present situation without taking account of it is not facing the facts. Never before in history in years of peace has any nation piled up in so short a time so formidable a mass of instruments of war. There is a delusion that before Hitler came to power Germany was disarmed. That is a delusion. Even before Hitler came, Germany was very far from being unarmed. In 1930 according to official statistics Germany's expenditure on armaments stood at 50 per cent of her pre-war level, which was not low; but since Hitler came to power in March 1933, German armament expenditure has broken all records. According to Mr Francis Williams, the Financial Editor of the *Daily Herald* . . . the German armament expenditure for the first three years of the Nazi regime was more than double the total British armament expenditure for the eleven years from 1924 to 1935, and was more than the total British effective expenditure on armaments – that is, leaving out pension charges – for the sixteen years since 1920.

. . . I say to you that I cannot exclude from my own mind among the many dreadful possibilities which today surround us – I cannot exclude the possibility of a direct attack upon this country, which is more vulnerable to air attack than any other great country in the world.

I quote some words spoken in an after-dinner speech at the Nuremburg Party Rally in 1935 to the delegates from foreign branches of the League of German Girls by Herr Hitler himself. This is what he said to those young ladies: 'If I were going to attack an opponent I should act quite differently from Mussolini.' This speech was made when

Mussolini was in negotiation with the League with regard to Abyssinia. He goes on: 'I should not negotiate for months beforehand, and make lengthy preparations, but, as I have always done throughout my life, I should suddenly, like a flash of lightning in the night, hurl myself upon the enemy.' Those are not reassuring words for any of the neighbours of Germany. I draw this conclusion from what I have just said. In planning collective security by which this party stands, it is just as necessary for us to inquire who would come to our help if we were attacked as to whose help we would go if they were attacked. But that is not all . . .

The Labour Party conference has always opposed unilateral disarmament, and I find it difficult in logic to believe that the Labour Party conference can support unilateral non-rearmament in a world where all are increasing their armaments . . . a Labour government, if it came into power tomorrow, and was faced, as it would be, with the present world situation, that such a government, pending an international agreement to reduce and limit armaments – and such a government would strive its utmost to negotiate such an agreement – pending that, a Labour government would be compelled to provide an increase in British armaments . . .

But . . . it is profoundly important that British armaments at whatever level they must be built, would be built under a Labour government on a planned system of collective security . . . The purpose of armaments is to make sure that aggression, if it is attempted, shall not succeed, and better still, to change the mind of the would-be aggressor, and to make him, in spite of his inclinations, a peace-keeper against his will . . .

I believe the time has passed for vague humbugging phrases. I believe the time has come for the greatest degree of clarity, precision and courage which we collectively can command. The time has come when we must say to the fascist states acting now for the first time in collusion together, for Germany and Italy have now for the first time linked arms: 'There is a limit; so far and no farther. Henceforth, law must be observed; treaties must not be broken; aggression must not be committed.' We must also say: 'Come in and join us, and if you have grievances, say what they are; say it in a reasonable tone of voice, and we will reply to you in the same tone.' We must get rid of the fog of mushy generalities and come down to a clear-cut policy, and until we do that, we shall never clear out this gang of incompetents who are misgoverning this country. Unless we do that the people will not turn to us, and they will be right in not turning to us . . .

Ernest Bevin added, presciently:

If I am asked to face the question of arming this country, I am prepared to face it . . . Which is the first institution that victorious fascism wipes out? It is the trade union movement . . . I regret that there appears to be this desire in every line of the resolution to put in something to make clear that we do not agree with the National government. Does that not go without saying? Would not one paragraph have done it? Then it could have gone on with a very clear statement of what we intended to do. If ever there was a time when, whether it is popular or unpopular, we have got to tell people the truth, it is now and we must do it fearlessly . . . The international movement are wondering what we are going to do in Britain. Czechoslovakia, one of the most glorious little democratic countries, hedged in all round, is in danger of being sacrificed tomorrow. They are our trade union brothers. They want to know what the British are going to do. You cannot save Czechoslovakia with speeches. We are not in office but I want to drive this government to defend democracy against its will, if I can . . . I want to say this to Mussolini and Hitler: 'If you are banking on being able to attack in the East or the West, and you are going to rely on that at the critical moment, you are taking us too cheaply' . . . I believe that if this great movement says to Hitler: 'If you are going to rely on force and the forcing of your system . . . we will stand four-square to it' it is the best thing that can be done for peace.

In July 1937, Dalton and his allies tried again to persuade the Parliamentary Labour Party to refrain from voting against the annual government defence estimates. This time, with the support of most of the trade union MPs at a full meeting of the Parliamentary Labour Party, they triumphed. Attlee accepted the new approach and thereafter the overwhelming majority of Labour MPs voted in support of rearmament.

The Bournemouth Labour conference of October 1937 heard a passionate debate over the acceptance of Labour's new report on *International Policy and Defence*. While the report itself was not exactly a model of clarity, the conference debate, as Bevin's biographer Alan Bullock has written, 'made clear what the resolution left unsaid, that acceptance of the report meant the abandonment of opposition to rearmament'.[94] George Lansbury, the veteran pacifist and former Labour leader, had just returned from a peace pilgrimage to Hitler and Mussolini and appealed to the conference to support unilateral disarmament as an example to the world:

> Nobody will settle the internal affairs of Germany but the German people, no one can settle the internal affairs of Spain but the Spanish people . . . I gave up the leadership of the Labour Party because I know it is impossible to cast out war by war, or to establish peace by brute force, whether the war is a collective war or a national war.

But beyond fellow pacifists such as Lord Ponsonby, an ex-Liberal who had briefly been Labour's leader in the Lords, Lansbury received little support. Lansbury's arguments were torn apart by veteran miners' MP Gordon MacDonald:

> The difference between Mr Lansbury and us is that he believes that for Britain to disarm now would strike the imagination of the peoples of the world in such a way that they would very soon follow and disarm too. He believes that fascist Italy and Nazi Germany would not take advantage of a disarmed Britain. He has more confidence in Hitler and Mussolini than we have. He visited Mussolini. Mussolini told Mr Lansbury that he was sending his men to Spain because of his own religious fervour. 'It is because of my religion, Mr Lansbury,' says Mussolini, 'that I am sending these men to Spain.' He might have the same idea that it was necessary for the sake of his 'religion'

109

to send them to Britain too . . .

Lansbury was attacked by Derby MP Philip Noel-Baker:

A League of Nations without sanctions [meant that] aggressors have had nothing to fear but resolutions. What are the results? The long, cumulative martyrdom of Manchuria, which still goes on; the squalid degradation of Mussolini's triumph over black men whom he burned and bombed; the 80,000 corpses that rotted without a grave in the green hell of the Gran Chaco; the fearful holocausts in Spain; a major war in China in which the oldest and most pacific civilisation in the world may be destroyed . . . That is the result of Mr Lansbury's policy. It is cause and effect. Italy attacked disarmed Abyssinia and disarmed Spain, and Japan attacked disarmed China, because there was no collective security to make them safe . . .

Richard Crossman, a 29-year-old Wykehamist Oxford City Councillor and don who during the 1960s would be a senior Labour Cabinet minister, added:

. . . You have in Germany today the greatest concentration of political unity and economic power which the world has ever seen, a concentration which has only one purpose, one significance, and one meaning, and that is the prosecution of a successful war; any responsible party in this country, when considering its foreign policy, must consider that fact above all else . . . we have to consider . . . how best we can negotiate . . . some agreement in Europe today. Mr Lansbury says the best way is to disarm, but when Mr Lansbury negotiated with Hitler he carried his British passport. If he had been a Social Democrat without a British passport, and without armament power behind him, he might have had a very different result from his visit to Germany . . . We are faced with an opponent who, at the first sign of cowardice, takes another bit. I believe negotiations for universal pacification are futile unless England, France and Russia are armed, resolute, and believe in themselves . . .

In March 1937 Ernest Bevin had told the executive council of the TGWU,

From the day Hitler came to power, I have felt that the democratic countries would have to face war . . . We have been handicapped by the very sincere pacifists in our party who believe that the danger can be met by resolutions and prayers and turning the other cheek. While I appreciate the sincerity, I cannot understand anybody who refuses to face the facts in relation to the happenings in China, in Abyssinia, in Spain, all virtually disarmed countries. I cannot see any way of stopping Hitler and the other dictators except by force.[95]

Bevin's powerful speech (backed by an equally powerful block vote) carried the day for the rearmers:

. . . The first movement that will be wrecked with the coming of fascism is ours. We have had thousands of resolutions, but we cannot stop fascism by resolutions. We cannot stop it by a few dockers holding up a ship. There is no public opinion we can appeal to in the fascist states. To whom can we offer anything? With whom can we settle? I do not believe that the transfer of colonial territory – a little strip here or there – settles the matter at all . . .

We have had, perforce, with the facts of the world staring us in the face, with our movement wiped out in Germany and Italy, with the thought of the heroic dead in Austria, with our comrades perishing in the concentration camps, we have had to say: 'Notwithstanding all your wickedness, here is the hand of friendship if you will have it, but if you are going to reply to the hand of friendship with a bomb on our movement, we are not going to leave ourselves defenceless for you to do it.'

Despite a passionate plea from Aneurin Bevan against trusting the National government to use its armed forces against the fascist powers rather than against the British workers ('we are not going to put a sword in the hands of our enemies that may be used to cut off our own heads') which won the biggest ovation of the week, the final vote gave victory to the rearmers by 2,169,000 to 262,000.

SEVENTEEN

Facing Down the Appeasers 1939–40

'In the name of God, go!'

When Hitler launched his invasion of Poland on Friday 1 September 1939, Parliament remained in special session over the weekend. Clement Attlee was convalescing from a bungled prostate gland operation so Arthur Greenwood, as deputy, was in charge of the Parliamentary Labour Party. In response to an approach from Prime Minister Neville Chamberlain, Greenwood consulted with Attlee who agreed with him that Labour should not join a coalition government if Chamberlain remained Prime Minister. They simply did not trust him. The general feeling of Labour MPs was that Chamberlain was hoping to discover a way to avoid war, despite the Anglo-Polish Treaty which stipulated that each country was to assist the other 'at once' in the event of invasion. On the Saturday evening, 2 September, Chamberlain made a statement to the Commons which fell far short of honouring Britain's treaty obligations to Poland. In the debate that followed, 'Labour was virtually unanimous for a declaration of war,' remembered Manny Shinwell, 'while the government remained indecisive.'[96] Leo Amery, a former Tory Cabinet minister, famously spurred Labour on, shouting across the floor, 'Speak for England!' Greenwood did so in a restrained but splendid speech that destroyed for ever any lingering beliefs from the past that the Labour Party was unpatriotic:

> *Arthur Greenwood:* This is indeed a grave moment. I believe the whole House is perturbed by the right hon. gentleman's statement. There is a growing feeling, I believe, in all quarters of the House that this incessant strain must end sooner or later – and, in a sense, the sooner the better. But if we are to march, I hope we shall march in complete unity, and march with France.
>
> *Mr McGovern:* You people do not intend to march – not one of you.
>
> *Mr Greenwood:* I am speaking under very difficult circumstances with no opportunity to think about what I should say; and I speak what is in my heart at this moment. I am gravely disturbed. An act of aggression took place 38 hours ago. The moment that act of aggression took place one of the most important treaties of modern times automatically came into operation. There may be reasons why instant action was not taken. I am not prepared to say – and I have tried to play a straight game – I am not prepared to say what I would have done had I been one of those sitting on those benches. That delay might have been justifiable, but there are many of us on all sides of this House who view with the gravest concern the fact that hours went by and news

came in of bombing operations, and news today of an intensification of it, and I wonder how long we are prepared to vacillate at a time when Britain and all that Britain stands for, and human civilisation, are in peril. We must march with the French. I hope these words of mine may go further. I do not believe that the French dare at this juncture go, or would dream at this juncture of going back on the sacred oaths that they have taken. It is not for me to rouse any kind of suspicion – and I would never dream of doing so at this time, but if, as the right hon. gentleman has told us, deeply though I regret it, we must wait upon our Allies, I should have preferred the Prime Minister to have been able to say tonight definitely, 'It is either peace or war.'

Tomorrow we meet at twelve. I hope the Prime Minister then – we, he must be in a position to make some further statement – [*Hon. members:* 'Definite'] – And I must put this point to him. Every minute's delay now means the loss of life, imperilling our national interests –

Mr Boothby: Honour.

Mr Greenwood: Let me finish my sentence. I was about to say imperilling the very foundations of our national honour, and I hope, therefore, that tomorrow morning, however hard it may be to the right hon. gentleman – and no one would care to be in his shoes tonight – we shall know the mind of the British government, and that there shall be no more devices for dragging out what has been dragged out too long. The moment we look like weakening, at that moment dictatorship knows we are beaten. We are not beaten. We shall not be beaten. We cannot be beaten; but delay is dangerous, and I hope the Prime Minister – it is very difficult to press him too hard at this stage – will be able to tell us when the House meets at noon tomorrow what the final decision is, and whether then our promises are in process of fulfilment, for in my mind there can be no escape now from the dilemma into which we have been placed. I cannot see Herr Hitler, in honesty, making any deal which he will not be prepared to betray. Therefore, thinking very hurriedly in these few moments, I believe that the die is cast, and we want to know in time.

The next morning the British Ambassador in Berlin delivered an ultimatum to the German Foreign Minister. Two hours later it had expired and Britain was at war with Germany.

Despite the declaration of war, Britain did little to save Poland from Hitler's *Blitzkrieg* and after Poland's defeat several months of so-called 'phoney war' set in as the Germans turned their forces around and prepared for offensive action in the west. Concern grew among Labour MPs that Chamberlain's government was not maximising the opportunity to prepare itself for Hitler's inevitable onslaught: 'the government lumbered along. Its internal organisation was not adequate or sufficiently intensive for the purpose of war,' recalled Herbert Morrison, 'the organisation of labour for war production was quite unsatisfactory . . . when the whole nation ought to be hard at work it really was disgraceful that there was still an army of unemployed.'[97] Emotions were crystallised by the German invasion of Norway and Denmark on 9 April 1940. The Franco-British attempt to intervene in Norway was, as Herbert Morrison later wrote, 'badly planned, inadequately equipped and hopelessly small'.[98] The failure of the Norwegian campaign and the Allied withdrawal led Labour to precipitate what was effectively a vote of censure on the government, following a vigorous two-day debate over 7 and 8 May 1940. Morrison, in a historic speech, laid down the gauntlet to Chamberlain, who had continued to cling to office. Morrison's speech began with an attack on the failures in Norway:

> The Prime Minister has stressed quite rightly, and we all agree with him, the brilliant success of the evacuation operations, but quite frankly, having regard to the interests of this country and the world, I would sooner be able to boast of the success of landing operations than the success of evacuation operations, brilliantly as they were conducted. When war is being conducted, and particularly a war of this kind, against such an enemy, whose methods and tactics and whose little as well as big tricks we really ought to be familiar with now – we have had a long experience of Herr Hitler in peace and we have had now a number of months' experience of Herr Hitler in war – I really begin to wonder how much experience of him we are to have, how near we are to get to disaster before ministers will try to understand the psychology of this man . . .
>
> It seems to me that there must have been a weakness in British diplomacy, at any rate before the war started in Norway, in the Scandinavian countries. I am very doubtful whether the Foreign Office has the right standards and instincts in selecting diplomatists for service abroad. Diplomacy under modern conditions is a totally different job. It is not enough to have nice gentlemen with cultured manners and who are good mixers with the upper classes in the country . . .
>
> The fact is that before the war and during the war, we have felt that the whole spirit, tempo and temperament of at least some ministers have been wrong, inadequate and unsuitable. I am bound to refer, in particular, to the Prime Minister, the Chancellor of the Exchequer and the Secretary of State for Air. I cannot forget that in relation to the conduct of British foreign policy between 1931 and 1939, they were consistently and persistently wrong. I regard them as being, perhaps more than any other three men, responsible for the fact that we are involved in a war which the wise collective organisation of peace could have prevented, and just as they lacked courage, initiative, imagination, psychological understanding, liveliness and self-respect in the conduct of foreign policy, so I feel that the absence of those qualities has manifested itself in the actual conduct of the war. I have the genuine apprehension that if these men remain in office, we run grave risk of losing this war. That would be a fatal and a terrible thing for this country and, indeed, for the future of the human race. We are fighting for our lives. Humanity is struggling for its freedom. The issues of the war are too great for us to risk losing it by keeping in office men who have been there for a long time and have not shown themselves too well fitted for the task. There is much more than politics involved in this discussion. There is the war and all its consequences. Because we feel, in view of the gravity of the events which we are debating, that the House has a duty and

that every Member has a responsibility to record his particular judgement upon them, we feel we must divide the House at the end of our debate today.

His speech so stung Chamberlain that the Prime Minister immediately jumped up and cried: 'I say this to my friends in the House – and I have friends in the House . . . I accept the challenge . . . we shall see who is with us and who is against us, and I call on my friends to support us in the lobby tonight.' From his own back benches came a reply from Leo Amery, former member of Baldwin's Cabinet and impassioned anti-appeaser, who ended by quoting Cromwell's famous words of dismissal to the Long Parliament: 'You have sat here too long for any good you have been doing. Depart, I say, and let us have done with you. In the name of God, go!' Another who attacked Chamberlain was Conservative MP and admiral Sir Roger Keyes, who attended the Commons in the uniform of admiral of the fleet. Britain's previous war leader, Lloyd George, intervened later in the debate after much persuasion by Morrison to recall Chamberlain's appeal for sacrifice: 'I say solemnly, that the Prime Minister should give an example of sacrifice, because there is nothing that can contribute more to victory in this war than that he should sacrifice the seals of office.' When the vote came, Chamberlain's friends deserted him. Hugh Dalton recalled: 'When I went into our lobby it seemed to be full of young Conservatives in uniform – khaki, Navy blue and Air Force blue all intermingled. How many of these young men, I wondered, were giving the last parliamentary vote that they would ever give – for their country and against their Whips? Keyes was there, in the midst of them, saying in a loud voice "they wouldn't let me lead an expedition into Trondheim [Norway], so I'm leading an expedition into this lobby instead."'[99] Forty-three of the National government's MPs voted with Labour and a further 70 abstained. Two days later Hitler invaded Belgium, the Netherlands and Luxembourg and on 11 May Chamberlain resigned, having tried and failed once again to persuade Labour to join a coalition government which he himself would lead. It was Winston Churchill who succeeded him as Prime Minister and formed immediately a new coalition government in which both Attlee and Greenwood sat in the five-man War Cabinet. Other Labour ministers included Morrison as Minister of Supply, Ernest Bevin as Minister of Labour and National Service, Hugh Dalton as Minister of Economic Warfare, Co-operative Party MP A. V. Alexander as First Lord of the Admiralty and Sir William Jowitt as Solicitor General. Bevin was to join the War Cabinet in October 1940 and Morrison in November 1942, having become Home Secretary in October 1940. With only five MPs not counting themselves as government supporters (Maxton, three other ILP Clydesiders and the single Communist), Attlee and Churchill agreed that first Bertie Lees-Smith and after his death in 1942 Fred Pethick-Lawrence, both veteran Labour ex-ministers, would perform the formal duties of leader of the opposition, even though both were actually wholeheartedly government supporters. Labour as a whole continued to sit on the opposition benches and the opposition front bench was filled by leading non-ministers of both parties.

EIGHTEEN

The Voice of the People's War 1942–43

'If honourable members opposite think we are going through this in order to keep their Malayan swamps, they are making a mistake'

Although Churchill's leadership of the coalition government saw Britain safely through the fall of France and the Battle of Britain, the turning of the tide proved more problematic. Early success in North Africa, where General Wavell had overwhelmingly defeated numerically superior Italian forces in Abyssinia and Libya, had proved illusory. Britain had been defeated in Greece and Crete, and been forced back into Egypt by combined German and Italian forces under the command of General Erwin Rommel. On 21 June 1942, Rommel had captured the great fortress of Tobruk. In the Far East, following Japan's attack on Pearl Harbor, Japanese forces seemed able to inflict defeat after defeat upon the British, who had surrendered the supposedly impregnable fortress of Singapore in February. On 2 July 1942 Chamberlainite Tory MP Sir John Wardlaw-Milne put down a motion of 'no confidence in the central direction of the war'. This produced, recalled the then editor of the *Evening Standard*, what was, 'next to the Norway debate – the most critical parliamentary occasion of the war'.[100] Though most Labour MPs were loyally to vote with the government, eight (whom Attlee swiftly 'carpeted') were among the 25 MPs who voted against Churchill after the debate. The speech of Wardlaw-Milne himself collapsed amid parliamentary incredulity when he called for the Duke of Gloucester to be appointed Commander-in-Chief of the British Army. The authentic voice of censure that day was that of Aneurin Bevan. Churchill, he said:

> wins debate after debate and loses battle after battle. The country is beginning to say that he fights debates like a war and the war like a debate. [Bevan criticised] the main strategy of the war . . . second, the wrong weapons have been produced; and third, those weapons are being managed by men who are not trained in the use of them and who have not studied the use of modern weapons. [Britain had failed to respond adequately to '*Blitzkrieg*' tactics and he blamed the Prime Minister:] No one was more Maginot-minded that the Prime Minister himself. I have read all his speeches very carefully, and I say that no one has thought of this war in terms of the last war more than the Prime Minister himself . . . the Prime Minister had not penetrated to the heart of the methods that were being used by the Germans or were going to be used in this war. It is that primary misconception of the war which has been responsible for the

wrong strategy of the government, and, the strategy being wrong, the wrong weapons were produced. The chief evidence of that is the case of the dive-bomber. The second chief evidence of that is the complete failure to equip the British Army with transport planes . . .

For the last five or six years I have heard the Prime Minister making eloquent speeches about the German military preparations. His reputation to this day rests upon those speeches. The affectionate regard the country still has for him arises out of gratitude because he warned the country at that time. But he warned the country about them quantitatively; the qualitative position he left aside. He gave us the figures, but there was no insight behind the figures. He has been in charge of this war really for three years. He must have known the nature of the weapons that the Germans were making. Dive-bombers were not a secret. The Czechs knew of them and had prepared to resist them. Czech military strategy was based upon the use of the dive-bomber . . .

The Prime Minister must realise that in this country there is a taunt, on everyone's lips, that if Rommel had been in the British Army, he would still have been a sergeant. Is that not so? It is a taunt right through the Army. There is a man in the British Army – and this shows how we are using our trained men – who flung 150,000 men across the Ebro in Spain, Michael Dunbar. He is at present a sergeant in an armoured brigade in this country. He was chief of staff in Spain; he won the battle of the Ebro, and he is a sergeant in the British Army. The fact of the matter is that the British Army is ridden by class prejudice. You have got to change it, and you will have to change it. If the House of Commons has not the guts to make the government change it, events will . . . It is events which are criticising the government. All that we are doing is giving them a voice, inadequately perhaps, but we are trying to do it . . .

If this debate resulted in causing demoralization in the country in the slightest degree, I would have preferred to cut my tongue out . . . This country can fight. If the government think that there is any dismay in the country, they are wrong; there is anger in the country. This is a proud and brave race, and it is feeling humiliated. It cannot stand the holding out of Sebastopol for months and the collapse of Tobruk in 26 hours . . .

Let us get rid of this defeatist complex. This nation can win; but it must be properly led, it must be properly inspired, and it must have confidence in its military leadership. Give us that, and we can win the war, in a fashion which will surprise Hitler, and at the same time hearten our friends.

For Bevan's biographer, 'it was on this day that Bevan stepped into his place as a debater of the first order, the only living rival to Churchill in the parliamentary art'.[101]

It was only a few months later that the tide did turn. Since then, Bevan had been keeping up a relentless critique of Churchill's coalition government for its failure to open a second front to divert the Germans from their renewed offensives in Russia. During October 1942, at El Alamein in Egypt, Montgomery's newly reinforced Eighth Army won a historic victory. Over the following months the British were able to drive Rommel's

German and Italian forces out of Egypt and Libya, chasing them all the way back to Tunisia. In early November, Anglo-American forces had launched Operation Torch, the amphibious invasion of French North Africa. Hailed as the second front for which Bevan had noisily been calling and Churchill's government had quietly been preparing, it entailed the swift occupation of Morocco and Algeria and would by early 1943 have facilitated a pincer movement against the Axis forces who by then were bottled up in Tunisia. When the Commons met to debate the situation on 12 November 1942, Bevan was attacked as a 'fireside fusilier' by backbench Conservatives. 'Never in his belligerent parliamentary career was [Bevan] more nearly on the ropes,' but he could not resist a counter-attack, one which gave voice to the hopes of a great many Labour activists and as Michael Foot later wrote, 'roused the Tories to a higher pitch of fury than ever before':[102]

> . . . If we are to conduct our offensive now with effect, there is one thing we must do and that is put before the people of Europe some clear conception of where we are going. You can shorten this war very much if you can widen the breach now made in the whole Nazi conception. The occupation of all France not only strains the policing difficulties of Germany, but at the same time proves that the whole German conception of reorganising the world was fundamentally false. Germany expected to govern conquered countries through satraps, puppets and quislings. The whole of that conception has failed. The Germans now have to hold down with their own arms what they have won. That is an ideological breach more significant than is the additional strain upon their military resources. Therefore, we have in Europe a political and psychological opportunity such as we have not had since the war began, but we can exploit it only if we can show the ordinary men and women of Europe that if they fight and take risks and it may be die, they will do it for something rather better than they have had in the past.
>
> What have we done recently? We have guaranteed the Spanish Empire. We have guaranteed the Portuguese Empire. We have guaranteed the Dutch Empire. At the Mansion House the other day, the Prime Minister guaranteed the British Empire. What we have we hold [*interruption*]. Hon. members dare not say that in the Rhondda Valley or on the Clyde, the British Army are not fighting for the old world. If hon. members opposite think we are going through this in order to keep their Malayan swamps, they are making a mistake. We can see the Conservatives crawling out of their holes now. In 1940 and 1941 they would not have dared to say these things. It was a different story then. We hear made by some members of the government, well-meaning and smooth-tongued decoys, agreeable speeches, in ambiguous terms, about a new world, but the authentic voice of the Conservative Party was Lord Croft [*interruption*]. Is the authentic voice the Prime Minister? [*interruption*]. The Prime Minister said at the Mansion House the other day that he had not become the King's First Minister in order to liquidate the British Empire [*interruption*]. But have hon. members heard the speeches delivered by the American Vice-President? How does the Prime Minister's statement square with the Atlantic Charter? How is the guarantee to all

these ramshackle empires to be reconciled with what we have led the people of this country to expect? Will Czechoslovakians, Frenchmen, Belgians and Russians lose their lives and go through the horrors through which they are now going in order to establish the suzerainty of the British Empire? I say that if we are to arouse Europe, we have to put before the people of the world a better ideal than that . . .

NINETEEN

Planning the People's Peace – Beveridge and Full Employment 1942–44

'Do not speak to this great people in "ifs" and "buts"'

It was the Beveridge Report on Social Insurance, published in December 1942, that was to crystallise 'what we all hoped for from the post-war years' as James Callaghan,[103] later Labour's fourth Prime Minister, put it. Writing in his memoir, *Time and Chance*, he recalled:

> Those who are too young to recall pre-war days and who grew up to think of the welfare state as part of the natural order can hardly understand the enthusiasm which greeted these proposals. They were no less than a charter of human rights. They meant that the quality of life in post-war Britain could, if we chose, be entirely different from that before the war. They meant greater equality, they meant that the worst evils of poverty and old age would be swept away. They were achievable and practicable. I bought my own personal copy and carried it with me in my kit bag as a missionary would carry the gospel. The test of where a man stood on the Beveridge Report was the benchmark of whether he was friend or foe.[104]

The three-day debate over Sir William Beveridge's plan 'to provide social security from want in adversity', led to the largest parliamentary rebellion of the entire war, when with only two exceptions all Labour MPs not actually in the government voted for a stronger endorsement of the report. Churchill had been keen to avoid a division and it had originally been agreed that the debate should take place on a motion supported by all three parties. However Churchill's decision to appoint Sir John Anderson to chair the Cabinet committee on the proposals and to open the debate for the government proved a disastrous miscalculation. Anderson was a former civil servant and Governor of Bengal turned National MP who was then Lord President of the Council and would become Chancellor of the Exchequer in September of that year, serving until the 1945 general election.

James Griffiths was a respected Welsh Labour MP and former anthracite miner who as Attlee's Minister for National Insurance was later to take responsibility for implementing much of Beveridge. Griffiths recalled that Anderson

> was known as a man who counted every penny twice and so was the worst possible choice as chairman of the government's committee on post-war reconstruction. His

speech in the debate was so full of 'ifs' and 'buts' that it caused obvious embarrassment to his colleagues on the government benches and infuriated ours. To add to our misgivings another civil servant turned minister, Sir James Grigg, Secretary of State for War, refused to allow a summary of the Beveridge plan to be circulated to the forces on the grounds that to do so would have 'conveyed the impression that the scheme was settled government policy, whereas in fact no decision of any kind had been taken'. The speech by Anderson and the veto by Grigg confirmed our fears that the reactionaries within the government carried the day.[105]

Their fears were not groundless: as Michael Foot has written, 'unbeknown to the outside world, Churchill had in January and February circulated two memoranda to his Cabinet colleagues stating that he would not seek to implement Beveridge during the war or even make any firm promises about the post-war period'.[106] At a meeting of Labour MPs during the second day of the debate it was decided, despite impassioned appeals by Ernest Bevin and Herbert Morrison (who ironically was probably the most enthusiastic supporter of Beveridge's plan in Cabinet but whose hands were tied by collective governmental responsibility), to table a motion expressing dissatisfaction with the government's attitude to the Beveridge Plan and calling for its early implementation. It was also resolved to carry the motion to a division. It was James Griffiths who was given the task of moving Labour's amendment and on 18 February 1943 he did so in 'a rousing speech, frequently cheered by the Labour Party':[107]

> . . . Our people have memories of what happened at the end of the last war, memories of the period of depression, memories of the unemployment, frustration, poverty and distress into which large masses of our people were thrown. In public, and much more in private, at the fireside, men and women are asking: 'After this, what? After victory, what? A return to the old days, a return to those years in which never less than 1,000,000, and sometimes 2,000,000, and at one time 3,000,000 of our people, were allowed to rust on the streets, unwanted in this country?' There is a deep determination among the mass of the people that we must build up a Britain in which, if there is want which we can prevent, we shall collectively prevent that want and give our people a real opportunity in life.
>
> In addition to being a symbol, this plan of Sir William Beveridge's has become a test, a test of the sincerity of our professions and our promises. I believe it is going to be much more . . . Under democracy we have secured for the people of this country religious liberty and political liberty, and I believe that the great task that awaits democracy in the next generation is to add to that religious and political liberty the liberty without which they can become meaningless, and that is economic liberty and economic freedom . . .
>
> It is not only the working class who dreads insecurity. Members on the other side – I have heard it during this debate – sometimes refer to the middle class as if we on this side had no relationship with them – not always but sometimes. If there is one section

of the community which now, in consequence of the war, feels a sense of insecurity for the future, it is the middle class. One of the remarkable and significant things about the Beveridge Plan is the wide and cordial acceptance given to it by the middle class. I say that this is a test. We have said there is no going back, Ministers have said there is to be planning forward. Believe me, if we are to be believed in the country, we must start that job today. It is deeds, not words, which will count from today onwards . . .

Let me say a word about the plan. The plan has, among others, these three great merits: first, it is comprehensive. It brings within the range of social insurance practically every citizen in this country. It brings them all in instead of dividing the country into sections and saying that one section shall be brought in and another left out. The second great merit is that it provides security from want in adversity by guaranteeing a minimum subsistence income, whatever the cause and however long the period. Lest there be here or in the country any idea that Sir William Beveridge is proposing that people shall be given such a standard of life that they will be tempted to become malingerers, I would point out that what he proposes is a subsistence income, an income upon which people can subsist, and by the instrument of insurance he provides that the subsistence income shall be related to need and based upon standards which he outlines in his report. He ends the anomalies by which the benefit which people get in adversity depends not, as now, upon the need the adversity creates, but upon how the adversity arose. The plan proposes that a minimum subsistence income shall be provided for people in adversity, whatever may be the cause and however long the period. The third great merit of the plan is that it consolidates our social insurance and allied services into a single scheme under the direction of a single ministry and with unified administration . . .

I suggest that the question which we ought to ask ourselves is not whether we can afford the plan, but whether we can afford to face the post-war period without it . . . We have called our youths to the Services . . . We have called for sacrifices, and . . . I hope we shall remember that we owe these people a debt that we must honour and that we shall begin to honour that debt today . . .

Despite a speech by Herbert Morrison seeking to gain support for the government, 119 MPs voted in the opposition lobby, including Arthur Greenwood, who had while serving in Cabinet originally commissioned Beveridge's report.

Discontent at the wartime coalition government's failure sufficiently to commit to the Beveridge plan spilled over at the Labour Party annual conference in London during June 1943. An amendment criticising the coalition government's 'timidity' was moved by Sydney Silverman, the MP for Nelson and Colne. Silverman was in turn attacked by acting TGWU chief Arthur Deakin for endorsing disloyalty to those Labour MPs, like Deakin's mentor Ernest Bevin, who were constrained by government responsibility: 'The party in opposition must recognise clearly and unmistakably that they have a responsibility to those of our colleagues in the government. The party cannot act one way in opposition and in another way in the government.'

One of the delegates to speak in support of Silverman and against Deakin was 32-year-old Barbara Betts.[108] Her message was simple:

> Here is the first attempt to translate into concrete terms the generalities with which we have been nauseated about the brave new world ever since this war began. 'Jam yesterday, and jam tomorrow, but never jam today.' That is what the government is trying to say to the people of this country. But we want some proof that there is going to be jam today . . .

For Labour there was a tremendous sense of hope, but also of fear: fear that the power to change Britain would once again elude them. Despite being in government, albeit as part of a coalition, Labour's power to influence policy was still limited and there appeared no certainty at that time of a majority Labour government after the war to ensure that the hopes for 'a land fit for heroes' were not betrayed once again as they had been by the Liberal/Conservative Lloyd George coalition post-1918. The sense of frustration was powerfully captured by Aneurin Bevan's famous story about his pursuit of power, related to the Commons during a debate on 15 December 1943:

> . . . I have spent now more than a quarter of a century of my life in public affairs, and as I grow older I become more and more pessimistic. I started – if this House will forgive me this personal note – my career in public affairs in a small colliery town in South Wales. When I was quite a young boy my father took me down the street and showed me one or two portly and complacent-looking gentlemen standing at the shop doors, and, pointing to one, he said, 'Very important man. That's Councillor Jackson. He's a very important man in this town.' I said, 'What's the council?' 'Oh, that's the place that governs the affairs of this town,' said my father. 'Very important place indeed, and they are very powerful men.' When I got older I said to myself, 'The place to get to is the council. That's where the power is.' So I worked very hard, and, in association with my fellows, when I was about 20 years of age, I got on to the council. I discovered when I got there that the power had been there, but it had just gone. So I made some inquiries, being an earnest student of social affairs, and I learned that the power had slipped down to the county council. That was where it was, and where it had gone to. So I worked very hard again, and I got there – and it had gone from there too. So I followed it, and sure enough I found that it had been here, but I just saw its coat tails round the corner.
>
> The ordinary man in Great Britain has been spending his life for the last couple of generations in this will-o'-the-wisp pursuit of power, trying to get his hands on the levers of big policy and trying to find out where it is, and how it was that his life was shaped for him by somebody else. We were conceived by our institutions and representative democracy that the House of Commons itself was that instrument, and that seat of power; but these debates, and especially the speech of my right hon. friend yesterday, convinced me that the House of Commons is becoming almost irrelevant . . . He was not telling us the decisions at which the government had arrived; he was

preventing us from finding out what the decisions were. Judged from that point of view, it was an extremely successful speech, but it leaves the House of Commons entirely in a position of not knowing at all what decisions have been made on our behalf. It means that I have now got to start out on my journey once more. I have got to set out on a global journey to find out where this power has gone to, and by the time I have circumnavigated the globe and established communication with Mars, I shall have lost it again. This is an extremely serious matter. All we can do is to deduce what the government propose to do from what the government have already done. That is all that is left to us.

To make the Beveridge plan a reality, it would be necessary to tackle the potential burden of unemployment. Merlyn Rees, later a Labour MP and Home Secretary, was then a 23-year-old RAF squadron leader. He recalls:

> In the twenties and thirties the main sources of our concern in the party were peace, war and unemployment. Little progress was made and the country turned from us. Little did we know that war would change the basis of all discussion and bring electoral victory. The first signs of change were during the war itself. I only wish that many comrades who stuck to the last of democratic socialism in the twenties and thirties were alive to see the changes that took place.[109]

The great day was 21 June 1944, just a few weeks after D-Day, when Ernest Bevin announced to the House of Commons that the government was accepting in a new White Paper on Employment 'as one of their primary aims and responsibilities the maintenance of a high and stable level of employment after the war'

> ... if we take the period from the seventies right up to the outbreak of this war, we have only had really full employment under three conditions – the making of armaments for impending war, during war, or on the discovery of more gold fields and the expansion of credit ... But ... [government] measures [were] to minimise the effect of unemployment, not a recognition that unemployment was and is a social disease, which must be eradicated from our social life. The State's job up to this date has been to deal with the after-effects of the disease, and not to take active measures itself to promote and maintain economic health. This motion is an assertion that, while there will still be difficulties to contend with, and the social services must continue to play their part, the first consideration must be the way to remove the cause. Having tried relief in all its forms, we now propose to diagnose, and we hope to cure.
>
> The government welcome the fact that Parliament is – I hope irrespective of party, and with widespread agreement – at last facing this problem as a fundamental issue. We are, indeed, grappling with the problem which is uppermost in the minds of those who are defending the country today, at home, overseas, and in those bitter fights across the Channel. With my right hon. friend the Prime Minister, I had an opportunity of visiting one of our ports and seeing the men, of the 50th Division among others, going aboard ship – gallant men, brave men with no complaint. They were going off to face this terrific battle, with great hearts and great courage. The one

question they put to me when I went through their ranks was, 'Ernie, when we have done this job for you, are we going back to the dole?'

Mr Pickthorn (Cambridge University): For you?

Mr Bevin: Yes, it was put to me in that way, because they knew me personally. They were members of my own union, and I think the sense in which the word 'Ernie' was used can be understood. Both the Prime Minister and I answered, 'No, you are not.' That answer of 'No' to those brave men, going aboard those ships to fight, was an answer which, I hope, will be supported by the House, and I hope that policy will be directed towards making that answer a fact, not only for them but for future generations . . . I am convinced that although of course governments may change and, I hope, will change – I should not like this job for ever – any party which faces the people of this country at a general election and refuses to accept the principle of full employment, will not be returned to this House . . .

The proposals would act irrespective of whether industry will, for ever, be privately or publicly owned. Some say that all benefits of enterprise arise from private industry, and some say they arise from public ownership. Well, I have seen a bit of both. I have seen enterprise absent from public ownership and I have seen enterprise completely absent from private ownership. Therefore, the question of how you can give effect to decisions as to who will own industry, is not prejudiced by this White Paper . . .

The main purpose of the White Paper, and the motion, is to declare war on unemployment, and to indicate how our resources should be harnessed for that purpose . . . There cannot be long periods of unemployment without malnutrition and a weakening of physique; and then what did we get? During that period just over a week in every year for every man and woman in industry was lost owing to sickness. That is a terrific loss . . .

The coming of the State into the arena, full-blooded, as is now proposed, must mean the writing of a new code of conduct for industry, a new set of rules in our economic life, which must be respected and respond to the will of Parliament, if the problem is to be solved . . .

TWENTY

Winning the Peace 1944–45

'Labour will fight for power'

By 1944, Labour was preparing in earnest for the challenge of building the New Jerusalem after the war. Although Labour's 1944 policy document *Economic Controls, Public Ownership and Full Employment* reaffirmed the principle of public ownership that had been central to Labour's programme since at least 1937 and proposed taking control of the Bank of England, it lacked specific commitments to nationalise particular industries. At Labour's annual conference in December 1944, a resolution calling for 'the transfer to public ownership of the land, large-scale building, heavy industry and all forms of banking, transport and fuel and power', was moved by Labour's new parliamentary candidate for Reading Ian Mikardo, the then nationally unknown Portsmouth-born son of an immigrant Jewish tailor. Attacking the failure of the Executive's resolution:

> ... to mention public ownership in any part [he insisted that assurances from] three distinguished members of the Executive [that public ownership was] implied in the Executive resolutions and the policy pamphlets [were not enough.] There are over 30 million electors in this country and they do not all read all the statements of our Executive. What they do read, and what will be quoted at us at the election, is the Executive's resolution, and when they read that our rank and file comrades, to whom socialism still means a great deal, will be appalled and disappointed at its unsocialist character. The ordinary man in the street cares nothing about mere verbiage. He talks politics in simple phrases. Some of our leaders have been talking so long about the economics of the transition to socialism that they have come to think too much about the transition and not enough about the socialism.
>
> We seem to be losing the capacity that the old socialist pioneers had for putting over their socialism in simple and uncompromising terms which every man and woman can understand ... I wonder sometimes whether they would not sigh with regret for the days when our movement could talk to the common man in the language he understood and express the sentiments in which he believed.
>
> Let us make no mistake about the fact that the average man is sceptical about party programmes and election platforms. He has been soured by 25 years of Tory tricks. To the Conservative Party an election platform is like the platform of a trolley bus – they use it to get in, but once they have got in, like the bus passenger, they do not

stay on the platform. By contrast, we have got to show the people that we mean what we say and say what we mean . . .

Despite the pleas of Manny Shinwell and Philip Noel-Baker, speaking from the platform on behalf of Labour's NEC, Mikardo's resolution won considerable support from conference floor including from Mikardo's Portsmouth-born near-contemporary, 32-year-old James Callaghan, the newly adopted parliamentary candidate for Cardiff South and later a Labour Prime Minister. It was carried so overwhelmingly on a show of hands that no card vote was called for. 'Mikardo was euphoric, Herbert Morrison less so. He put a hand on Mikardo's shoulder: "Young man, you did very well this morning. That was a very good speech you made – but you do realise, don't you, that you've lost us the general election."'[110] Fortunately, he had not: while Mikardo would become the backbench MP for Reading, Morrison would be the man in Labour's new government charged with pushing forward the nationalisation programme. The impact of Mikardo's resolution can be overstated. Labour never did in fact nationalise land or building and Morrison, Bevin and the miners would have ensured that the next Labour government would undoubtedly have nationalised fuel, power and transport. But as Herbert Morrison's biographers have pointed out, 'the resolution gave an added impetus to nationalisation, if any were needed and made it much more difficult to retreat from nationalisation commitments (as Morrison found to his cost when trying to compromise over iron and steel in 1947)'.[111]

Churchill wrote to Clement Attlee in May 1945, on the eve of Labour's annual conference in Blackpool, offering to continue the coalition government until the defeat of Japan. Churchill knew that with the development of America's atomic bomb, the war against Japan was unlikely to last beyond the autumn. To Attlee and others, the proposal implied continued coalition for a year or more. Labour's leaders were split on the issue. Bevin, Dalton and Attlee were sympathetic to Churchill's proposal. Neither Attlee nor Dalton thought Labour likely to win a majority in an immediate election. Herbert Morrison favoured continued coalition until the new electoral register was ready in October but no longer than that. Manny Shinwell, Nye Bevan and Labour's Chief Whip Will Whiteley were among those who believed Labour had nothing to fear from an early election. Labour's conference overwhelmingly rejected a motion that the coalition be continued until the defeat of Japan. Its mood was best captured by Ellen Wilkinson:

> We are all agreed now that after the First World War a tragic mistake was made. The democratic political leaders of the Weimar Republic who had replaced the Kaiser's government were treated as though they were themselves war criminals, which is in sharp contrast to the way the Chamberlain government treated the Nazis. The terrible fact is that the British and French governments gave more concessions to Hitler in the first months of his power than would have sufficed to have kept in office a democratic government in those early days.

The danger of having a government in this country run by the upper social crust is that quite naturally it tends to think that the corresponding upper crust in Germany are the 'right people'. From the British point of view, apart from any party considerations, those upper crust people in Germany – or for that matter, in Greece or Italy – are the wrong people . . .

The Labour Party's policy is straightforward. We want not only millions of houses, jobs for all and social security, but also educational opportunity for all, and a real state Health Service. We know how these are to be got. They must be based on and paid for by the only means by which they can be – for there are no hidden reserves of wealth from which these things can be paid for – by a highly efficient industry and properly planned agriculture which will make possible a steady advance in the standard of living. We are prepared to adopt the means, consistent with democracy, that are necessary to achieve our aims.

Labour's opponents are trying to serve two masters – Big Business and the popular electorate; they regard Big Business as the dominant partner. Already we can see which way the wind is blowing. The Conservative report just issued says they want full employment, but they will not tolerate any interference with private enterprise. They say they want to build plenty of houses, but they are not prepared to take drastic action to deal with the landlords who own the land on which the houses must be built and who have power to hold the whole country to ransom . . .

In the coming election the Labour Party will fight, and fight for power. We are not interested in talk of coalitions and arrangements, we fight for power: power for those who fought and worked and bled, power for the workers in the widest sense, for those who work with hand or brain, for the inventors and the technicians, yes, and for the managers too who do not want to see the fine work they have done in planning for the public interest thrown back into the scramble for private profit . . . we believe that in this programme which we are putting forward lies the one hope of building in Britain, this beloved island of ours, the type of civilisation which we so passionately desire.

'The cheering which followed Ellen Wilkinson, the conference chairman, when she said forcefully but quietly, "Labour will fight – and fight for power," was as great as anything ever experienced in the history of the Labour movement,' wrote Manny Shinwell. 'It was inspired by the scent of victory rather than any evidence of practical probability. But it impressed even the solemn-faced leaders on the platform. They were having greatness thrust upon them.'[112] Before the conference ended, news arrived that Churchill had called a general election. Parliament would be dissolved on 15 June. Polling day would be 5 July.

Many of those who would vote for the first time in that general election of 1945 were the young men and women who had fought and won the war. Some of them were also candidates, and appeared at Labour conference, straight from the battlefront, in their full military uniform. Maurice Edelman, then war correspondent on *Picture Post* and from 1945–75 a Coventry Labour MP, described the scene:

Instead of all the white-haired, bald-headed pacifists of the past, there was a new breed of Labour supporter. The young Labour officer at one time would have seemed like a contradiction in terms, but here suddenly you had very striking, good-looking young men . . . coming to the rostrum one after the other – speaking as servicemen who had fought for their country and who had a vision of a new Britain after the war which would be based on socialist principles.[113]

Their mood was captured by a scholarship boy from Bradford Grammar School who after Balliol, Oxford had ended up beach-master at the Anzio landings: Labour's 27-year-old candidate in Conservative-held Pudsey and Otley, Major Denis Winston[114] Healey. In a dramatic speech, containing more than a hint of his Marxist past, Healey 'powerfully denounced the corrupt kings and decadent pre-war societies of southern and south-eastern Europe',[115] recalled Hugh Dalton:

. . . the socialist revolution has already begun in Europe and is already firmly established in many countries in eastern and southern Europe. The crucial principle of our foreign policy should be to protect, assist, encourage and aid in every way that socialist revolution wherever it appears.

The Labour Party must be extremely alert and vigilant in judging its friends and enemies in Europe. It is quite easy for a person like myself who has spent the last three years in Europe to tell who are our friends and who are our enemies. The upper classes in every country are selfish, depraved, dissolute and decadent. These upper classes in every country look to the British Army and the British people to protect them against the just wrath of the people who have been fighting underground against them for the past four years. We must see that that does not happen. There is very great danger, unless we are very careful, that we shall find ourselves running with the Red Flag in front of the armoured cars of Tory imperialism and counter-revolution, very much as in the early days of the motor car a man ran with a red flag in front of the first automobiles . . .

Healey recalled:

When I returned to my seat, my neighbour, George Thomas, later Speaker of the House of Commons and Lord Tonypandy, congratulated me with the words: 'Denis, you have the most wonderful gift of vituperation!' It was that speech which led Hugh Dalton, Philip Noel-Baker, and Harold Laski, representing Right, Centre and Left of the Party, to ask me if I would apply for the job of International Secretary of the Labour Party after my defeat in the general election, which they took for granted.[116]

Healey got the job and 40 years later he would be shadow Foreign Secretary.

Another sign of the new mood was the sight of Aneurin Bevan's first address to conference on behalf of the 'platform'. For most of his political career, he had been the rebel. In 1944 he had been elected on to Labour's National Executive Committee and at Labour's 1945 conference he found himself in the unfamiliar position of replying to the debate on full employment on behalf of Labour's NEC. Within a few months he would find himself not only in government but in Cabinet:

> If orthodox and conventional means of finance were effective, we would not have the situation which now exists in the mining industry. We started off this war with a state of affairs where mining wages had been so reduced that the miners were 83 steps down the ladder of industrial wages; so you had low wages. Mining profits had gone up as a result of labour legislation in 1930. So you had an industrial situation which private enterprise has always claimed to be the condition for the financing of the industry in which that situation exists: low wages, high profits.
>
> Nevertheless, what is the situation? The situation is that £200,000,000 to £300,000,000 of new capital is required to make the mining industry modern and well equipped. In other words, orthodox methods of finance have completely broken down in that basic industry, and it is necessary for us, especially for those associated with the mining industry, to tell the country quite clearly that it is no use fiddling about with this mining problem in Great Britain, you can say 'Goodbye' to every scheme of industrial expansion that we are considering. Therefore we say it is not nearly enough to make finance available to the mining industry; it is not nearly enough to think in terms of mining reorganisation, because you have a state of affairs where the mine-owners are unable to attract finance into the industry where finance is holding back, Therefore the country must be told, quite plainly, 'You can have coal without coal owners, but you cannot have coal without coal-miners . . .'
>
> At the moment politics overhang the mining industry to such an extent that capital will not find its way into it, even if the Conservatives get a majority, because all the while there will be overhanging the industry the intense desire of the miners to get that industry nationalised. Therefore we say that the nationalisation of the mining industry is a prerequisite for assembling conditions of productivity in which finance can be found . . .
>
> I remember some friends and I went out to the European coalfields in 1927. We went to Silesia, and there found a new pit being sunk in a very rich coalfield. We had come from Great Britain where, by every test that was to be applied, our industry was becoming derelict. Bank charges were mounting up in South Wales and Durham to a terrific height, but those overdrafts were no use for the capitalist equipment of the industry because they were all on short call. The Prudential Assurance Company which was denying capital to the British coal industry was sinking pits in Poland. In other words, the investment market of Great Britain has always known more about the investment possibilities of darkest Africa than of Dowlais, Jarrow and Glasgow. We therefore take the view that the establishment of an Investment Board is an essential part of the apparatus of the modern state.
>
> Now our enemies have admitted that orthodox and conventional means of finance have broken down. The *Daily Herald* yesterday announced the formation of a Finance Corporation for Industry with a capital of £25,000,000 and borrowing powers of another £100,000,000: that is £125,000,000 are going to be made available – for what?

For industries unable to attract finance by the normal means. The chairman is going to be Lord Hyndley, a 61-year-old Director of the Bank of England and of several big steel and colliery companies. It is a remarkable situation that here you have a man involved in the two heavy industries which are at the moment technically obsolescent, and he is made the chairman of the new organisation to provide finance. In between the wars these gentlemen have been carrying on a totally opposite policy; they have been making one blade of grass grow where two grew before. It is unreasonable to expect from these people any intelligent and enlightened approach to this problem . . .

Only a society on the verge of bankruptcy could produce the situation that we have in this nation at the moment, and had before the war. This island is almost made of coal and surrounded by fish. Only an organising genius could produce a shortage of coal and fish in Great Britain at the same time. It therefore is for us – as John Wilmot said, quite properly – a question of where power is going to lie. There is no absence of knowledge, there is no lack of wisdom, as to what to do in Great Britain. What is lacking is that the power lies in the wrong hands and the will to do it is not there . . .

It is in no pure party spirit that we are going into this election. We know that in us, and in us alone, lies the economic salvation of this country . . . we are the voice of the British people; we are the natural custodians of the interests of those young men and women in the Services abroad. We are the builders. We have been the dreamers, we have been the sufferers; we are the builders, and we enter this campaign at the general election, not merely to get rid of the Tory majority – that will not be enough for our task. It will not be merely sufficient to get a parliamentary majority. We want the complete political extinction of the Tory Party, and 25 years of Labour government.

TWENTY-ONE

Attlee Forms a Government 1945–46

'We are the masters now'

Despite the close working relationship Labour had enjoyed with the Conservatives during Churchill's wartime coalition, the campaign itself was bitterly fought. Labour's successful participation in the coalition had rebuilt its credibility as a potential party of government, a credibility that had been shattered by the implosion of MacDonald's government in 1931. Despite Churchill's huge personal popularity as a war leader, an overwhelming number of servicemen and women did not want to go back to civilian life under a Conservative government pursuing the sort of policies that the Chamberlain and Baldwin governments had espoused during the 1930s. They wanted better, a People's Peace to follow the People's War. Labour's charge that people couldn't trust the Tories struck a chord: voters wanted the Beveridge Report implemented and they remembered the lukewarm reaction to it from Conservatives.

As the campaign progressed, the Conservative leaders began to realise that Labour posed a greater challenge than in the past and decided to raise the stakes. In a broadcast on 4 June 1945 Churchill warned the nation: 'I declare to you that no socialist system can be established without a political police. They would have to fall back on some sort of Gestapo, no doubt very humanely administered in the first instance.' For Denis Healey: 'Winston Churchill threw away his potential advantages by accusing Labour of wanting to introduce a Gestapo in Britain; he was handicapped by his obvious inability to understand the men and women he had led in war. For example, in one broadcast he addressed the British people as, "you, who are listening to me in your cottages".'[117] Shinwell recalled:

> In the public mind a possible candidate for the role of a British Himmler might be the man responsible to Parliament for the police forces during most of the war: Herbert Morrison, the Home Secretary. The vision of the man known to millions of Londoners and blitzed provincial towns as 'Our 'Erbert' strutting around in jackboots was too much for the electorate. The Churchill warning became a subject for mirth . . . in those few seconds of a foolish outburst [Churchill] undid much of the honour he had attained as the nation's champion.[118]

Attlee's reply, broadcast the following evening, on polling day, was moderate and measured and was said to have swung many votes Labour's way:

When I listened to the Prime Minister's speech last night, in which he gave such a travesty of the policy of the Labour Party, I realised at once what was his object. He wanted the electors to understand how great was the difference between Winston Churchill, the great leader in war of a united nation, and Mr Churchill, the party leader of the Conservatives. He feared lest those who had accepted his leadership in war might be tempted out of gratitude to follow him further. I thank him for having disillusioned them so thoroughly. The voice we heard last night was that of Mr Churchill, but the mind was that of Lord Beaverbrook.

I am also addressing you tonight on the wireless for the first time for five years as a party leader. But before turning to the issues that divide parties, I would like to pay my tribute to my colleagues in the late government, of all parties or of none, with whom I have had the privilege of serving under a great leader in war, the Prime Minister. No political differences will efface the memory of our comradeship in this tremendous adventure, of the anxieties shared, of the tasks undertaken together and of the spirit of friendly cooperation in a great cause which prevailed. I know well the contribution made by one and all to the achievement of victory . . .

It was, however, inevitable that when an approach was made to the long-term policy in relation to the economic organisation of the country, there would be a divergence of view on the principles to be applied, which necessitated an appeal to the country . . .

We have fought a great war for democracy. It is of the essence of the democratic system that the people should, from time to time, have the opportunity of deciding by what persons and on what principles they should be governed. In the USA, for instance, there must be an election of a president, war or no war, every four years . . . I am sorry that the Prime Minister, who after all owed his position as Prime Minister to the Labour Party, should have accused us of putting party before country. His proposal to carry on for another year would have meant a Conservative majority in the House during the crucial period of reconstruction . . .

It is here on domestic policy that we get the main clash between parties. The Prime Minister spent a lot of time painting you a lurid picture of what would happen under a Labour government in pursuit of what he called a 'Continental conception'. He has forgotten that socialist theory was developed in Britain long before Karl Marx, by Robert Owen. He has forgotten that Australia and New Zealand, whose peoples have played so great a part in the war, and the Scandinavian countries had had socialist governments for years, to the great benefits of their peoples, with none of these dreadful consequences. There are no countries in the world more free and democratic. When he talks of the danger of a secret police and all the rest of it, he forgets that these things were actually experienced in this country only under the Tory government of Lord Liverpool, in the years of repression when the British people who had saved Europe from Napoleon were suffering deep distress. He has forgotten many things, including, when he talks of the danger of Labour mismanaging finance, his own disastrous record at the Exchequer over the Gold Standard.

I shall not waste time on this theoretical stuff which is merely a second-hand version of the academic views of an Austrian – Professor Friedrich August von Hayek – who is very popular just now with the Conservative Party. Any system can be reduced to absurdity by this kind of theoretical reasoning, just as German professors showed theoretically that British democracy must be beaten by German dictatorship. It was not.

Instead Attlee offered a vision of a better Britain through planning and controls:

The late government wisely and firmly by strict control maintained prices fairly steadily. The Labour Party is determined not to countenance inflation . . . Similarly, if controls were removed from rents, the present shortage would mean that the community would pay an immense toll to the landlords . . . It is obvious to all that building materials and labour must be employed on providing for the urgently needed houses, schools and factories and not on luxury buildings and non-essentials . . . We need a prosperous agriculture. We need well-planned, well-built cities with parks and playing fields, homes and schools, factories and shops in their right relationship. We do not want our beautiful country spoilt by haphazard development dictated only by hope of gain. Enough damage has already been done in the past. Therefore we must control the use of the land and have power to acquire what the nation or the local council need, paying a fair price, but not an extravagant ransom extorted on account of the needs of the community . . .

The Prime Minister made much play last night with the rights of the individual and the danger of people being ordered about by officials. I entirely agree that people should have the greatest freedom compatible with the freedom of others. There was a time when employers were free to work little children for sixteen hours a day. I remember when employers were free to employ sweated women workers on finishing trousers at a penny halfpenny a pair. There was a time when people were free to neglect sanitation so that thousands died of preventable diseases. For years every attempt to remedy these crying evils was blocked by the same plea of freedom for the individual. It was in fact freedom for the rich and slavery for the poor. Make no mistake, it has only been through the power of the state, given to it by Parliament, that the general public has been protected against the greed of ruthless profit makers and property owners.

No one supposes that all the industries of this country can or should be socialised forthwith, but there are certain great basic industries which from their nature are ripe for conversion into public services . . . Labour's policy is to transform the whole business of providing fuel, power and light into a public service . . . Those who cry out against state control are generally the loudest in demanding subsidies, tariffs, and other state aids for themselves. It is Labour's policy to stimulate industry and especially to help our export trade, but that help will only be given on condition that industry and trade are efficient . . .

The Conservative Party remains as always a class party. In 23 years in the House of Commons I cannot recall more than half a dozen from the ranks of wage earners. It represents today, as in the past, the forces of property and privilege. The Labour Party is, in fact, the one party which most nearly reflects in its representation and

composition all the main streams which flow into the great river of our national life
. . . We have to plan the broad lines of our national life so that all may have the duty
and the opportunity of rendering service to the nation, everyone in his or her sphere,
and that all may help to create and share in an increasing material prosperity free from
the fear of want. We want to preserve and enhance the beauty of our country to make
it a place where men and women may live finely and happily, free to worship God in
their own way, free to speak their minds, free citizens of a great country.

The 1945 election saw Labour win almost twelve million votes, nearly 48 per cent
of the total vote share and the largest number any single party had secured in British
political history. The Conservatives secured just short of ten million votes (39.8 per cent)
and the Liberals 2.25 million (9 per cent). Among the Conservative MPs defeated were
thirteen ministers. When the new House of Commons assembled, on the red benches of
the House of Lords as the Commons chamber had been bombed, there were 393 Labour
MPs, only 213 Conservatives and only 12 Liberals. The Labour MPs broke the rules by
singing the 'Red Flag'. 'Some did not know the words and some, judging by the rendering, the tune,' Herbert Morrison recalled ruefully.[119] According to Morrison, Manny
Shinwell was virtually alone among Labour's leading figures in having predicted victory.
Despite a Gallup opinion poll in June having given Labour 45 per cent, the Conservatives
32 per cent and the Liberals 15 per cent, the fact, never mind the scale, of Labour's election victory, remained a shock to many. Major Christopher Mayhew had served in the
wartime Special Operations Executive and was then the newly elected Labour MP for
South Norfolk. He recalled: 'I doubt if anyone dreamed we would win like that. I shall
never forget those Forces' votes being tipped out of their tins. They were all for me. Really
almost every one for me. It was astounding.'[120] Some sought to replace Attlee at the
moment of triumph with Morrison, but their attempt came to nothing. When the results
were announced, after a three-week delay following polling day to enable the Forces'
votes to come in from overseas, Churchill resigned and Attlee formed the first majority
Labour government. Ernest Bevin became Foreign Secretary, Hugh Dalton the
Chancellor of the Exchequer, Sir Stafford Cripps the President of the Board of Trade, ex-
coalition Education Minister Chuter Ede became Home Secretary, and Herbert Morrison
became Leader of the House of Commons and coordinator of the legislative programme.
Arthur Greenwood, in Cabinet as Lord Privy Seal, was to supervise the social services; Jim
Griffiths as Minister for National Insurance outside Cabinet was to drive through the
implementation of Beveridge's report; Aneurin Bevan in Cabinet as Minister of Health
was to create a National Health Service and drive forward the government's house-building and slum-clearance programmes; Manny Shinwell, in Cabinet as Minister of Fuel and
Power, was to nationalise coal, electricity and gas; and Ellen Wilkinson, in Cabinet as
Education Minister, was to secure universal free education for all up to the age of fifteen.

Others in Cabinet included the respected Co-operative Party MP A. V. Alexander at the Admiralty; Viscount Stansgate (the father of Tony Benn) at the Air Ministry; and Attlee's old friends Tom Williams, a Welsh ex-miner who became Agriculture Minister and Jack Lawson, a former Durham miner, at the War Office. George Isaacs, an experienced trade unionist, became Minister of Labour and the veteran ex-Liberal Christopher Addison had a formal Cabinet role at the Dominions Office and an informal role as Attlee's mentor. The King's Speech promised the nationalisation of the coal industry, civil aviation and the Bank of England; repeal of the 1927 anti-trade union laws; more social security, a food production drive, more housing and a National Health Service.

It fell to one of Labour's newly elected young MPs, Major John Freeman, to make the first speech of the new Parliament, his maiden speech, on 16 August 1945. Thirty-year-old Freeman was a barrister's son, who, after Westminster School, Oxford and several years pre-war as an advertising consultant, had seen wartime service from 1940–45 in North Africa, Italy and north-west Europe. He had joined Labour in 1933 and had just been elected the first ever Labour MP for Watford. 'It was a faultless act which I shall always remember,' recalled Hugh Dalton, the new Chancellor of the Exchequer, who listened to Freeman's speech from his seat on the government front bench. 'In the uniform of a Major in the Rifle Brigade, wearing several ribbons, very erect and astonishingly handsome, seeming, as was appropriate, ever so slightly nervous, but speaking in a very clear and pleasant voice,'[121] Freeman's final words captured the passionate optimism of the Labour benches: 'Today may rightly be regarded as "D-Day" in the Battle of the New Britain.'

'Later, on that memorable afternoon,' recalled Dalton, 'Attlee took Freeman with him to the Smoke Room and introduced him to Churchill. Looking on this young soldier, the old man wept.'[122]

Attlee's new government was distinguished not only by the enthusiasm of the massed benches of young, new MPs, but also that of James Maxton of the ILP. Already consumed with stomach cancer and with barely six months to live, Maxton returned once more to the Commons to speak against a Tory motion of censure on 5 December 1945 and offer the new Labour government his blessing:

> On this occasion we feel we can support the government without any qualms of conscience or with any great intellectual labour in advance . . . The government . . . are making as good a shape of things, man for man, as any government ever did . . . I want the Labour government to succeed in doing things for the people of this country that have never been done before. If they fail, the curses of hundreds of thousands of men who have laboured and sacrificed to put them there will rest upon their heads, and rightly so. But, should that day come, the power will not shift from that side of the House to this, but to an even more fundamental party. I think that even the right hon. gentleman the leader of the opposition is with me there.

One of the totemic battles of the 1945 Parliament was over the repeal of the 1927 Trades Disputes Act. This was an Act that had been introduced amid great controversy in the wake of the 1926 General Strike to undermine the political levy and restrict trade union rights to picket. The winding-up speech for the government on the final Third Reading Debate on 2 April 1946 was given by Attorney-General Sir Hartley Shawcross, a clever young barrister (and Labour activist since his teens) who had played a central role as the British prosecuting counsel at the Nuremburg War Crimes trials and had become Labour MP for St Helens in 1945. Shawcross was a particularly 'well-breeched champion of the sans-culottes',[123] as one contemporary observed. Overly conscious of his good brains and good looks, he was nicknamed 'Sir Peacock' by Hugh Dalton. Churchill had challenged Labour to make repeal of this Act an election issue. Labour had done so and had of course also won the election. Shawcross taunted the Tories in his peroration: 'We are the masters at the moment, and not only at the moment but for a long time to come,' and was soon misquoted in the press as having, 'in an exultant voice told the House that "we are the masters now"'. It was a misquotation that would continue to dog him for the rest of his life.[124] Shawcross began:

> The plain fact is that this Bill is long overdue. It has been a permanent part of the Labour programme ever since 1927. At every election since that date the repeal of this Bill has been one of the things for which Labour candidates stood. The right hon. gentleman the Member for Woodford, in winding up the debate on the 1927 Bill, threw out a challenge to the Labour Party as to what would happen if they were unwise enough, in his view, to make this an issue at an election. We accepted the challenge and made it an issue, and we accepted the challenge he threw out later on, in the early part of last year, when he invited us to submit this matter to the verdict of the people, and said that that verdict would govern the way this matter was dealt with in Parliament. I know that that phrase has been referred to many times in the course of this debate, but I do not know what those words mean unless they mean what they say. I realise that the right hon. member for Woodford is such a master of the English language that he has put himself very much in the position of Humpty-Dumpty in *Alice*. There are other respects, incidentally, in which he resembles Humpty-Dumpty. Humpty-Dumpty had a great fall – *'When I use a word,'* said Humpty-Dumpty – and this must be what hon. members are saying about the words that the right hon. gentleman the member for Woodford used in that letter when he said this matter should be submitted to the verdict of the people – *'It means what I intended it to mean, and neither more nor less.' 'But,' said Alice, 'the question is whether you can make a word mean different things.' 'Not so,' said Humpty-Dumpty, 'the question is which is to be the master. That's all.'*
>
> We are the masters at the moment, and not only at the moment, but for a very long time to come, and as hon. members opposite are not prepared to implement the pledge which was given by their leader in regard to this matter at the general election, we are going to implement it for them. The people, having been asked for their verdict,

and having given their verdict on this matter, are going to have their verdict put into effect by the representatives of the people on this side of the House, and this wretched Act – because that is all it is – this bastard product of narrow legalism – (*interruption*) – I am using the word that was so well used by the right hon. gentleman member for Horsham [Earl Winterton]; I felt that I could not choose a more proper expression. This bastard product of narrow legalism and craven politics is now going to be swept for ever from the law of this country.

TWENTY-TWO

A Rocky Road to the New Jerusalem
1946–48

*'If we try to reap rewards we have not yet earned
we shall cause chaos and confusion'*

Radical and substantial as many of the great reforms of the Attlee government were, one issue it manifestly failed to address was that of equal pay for women. It was not that Labour did not support it in principle. It was that other issues were given greater priority. Moreover, it was an issue that not only cut across the Labour movement as a whole but also split the small group of women Labour MPs. For Jennie Lee, by now married to Nye Bevan, the real issue was class. She believed, her biographer Patricia Hollis has written, 'that you advanced working-class women by advancing their class. That you helped them by helping their men . . . [through securing] not equal pay for the working woman but a better deal for the married woman's family.' Other Labour women MPs such as Barbara Castle, Eireen White and Edith Summerskill disagreed. Jennie Lee once told Barbara Castle, 'we cannot ask for equal pay when miners' wages are so low'. 'In that case,' said Barbara, 'we will wait for ever.'[125] Eireen White, future MP for Flint, NEC member and minister, was not prepared to wait for ever. On 28 May 1947 she moved a resolution at Labour's annual conference in Margate demanding that the government and local authorities immediately implement equal pay for women in the services under their control:

> This is not just one reform among many others which must take its turn with other reforms . . . If you take women's work and refuse to pay women the rate for the job it is sheer dishonesty. We have waited with increasing interest for some announcement by the government. We have not had any announcement, but only rumours, and the rumours are that the government intends to let the women down. Let us see what they put forward, according to rumour, as the reason for merely 'accepting the principle' and do not proceed to the action which follows upon it may fairly be called unprincipled persons. It is said that they cannot afford it - in other words, they cannot afford to be honest. Is that a position for the British government to be in? . . .
>
> If we really could not afford to pay the rate for the job would not sound finance suggest that we should change the rate to something we could afford and pay that something for the job, whether done by men or women? . . .

Forty years ago there was a great progressive party in this country called the Liberal Party. That party destroyed itself, and will never recover, because of the humbug and hypocrisy with which it treated the question of votes for women. That, and the mishandling of the Irish situation, did for them . . . Would it not be a tragedy if this progressive party of ours, in the full flood of its achievements were to go down the drain in the same way because of its mishandling of the economic enfranchisement of women? . . .

I want to make a suggestion. I do not want it to be thought I am so unreasonable that, knowing what the situation of the country is at the present time, I am pressing this claim. What I want is that the government should give us a post-dated cheque – a very different thing from an ante-dated cheque, the date indicating when this necessary and long-delayed reform will be brought about. Then we should know when the time was coming. I believe that the government is waiting to see how the cat jumps. Make it a tiger-cat, and make it jump until this is secured.

She was opposed by Labour's National Executive, who argued that though they supported the principle of equal pay, matters of cost and practicability meant that they could not support a pledge to take such action 'immediately'. The economic condition of the country meant that other areas for action had to be prioritised. They asked her to withdraw the resolution. She refused. Conference voted. She won. Nevertheless, the issue of equal pay would remain unresolved for decades to come, as would the issue of the death penalty, which a growing swathe of the Labour Party wished to abolish. In February 1948 former solicitor Sydney Silverman, Labour MP for Nelson and Colne from 1935 until his death in 1968, managed in a free vote to amend the government's Criminal Justice Bill to include the suspension of capital punishment for murder for five years. But the House of Lords favoured the death penalty and struck out Silverman's amendment. This led Home Secretary Chuter Ede, fearing the complete loss of his Bill in the Lords, which until 1949 retained a delaying power of two years, to resort to the whips to block Silverman from reinserting his amendment when the Criminal Justice Bill returned to the Commons on 14 April of that year. Though Silverman tried again, citing the risk of miscarriages of justice and the lack of substantive evidence of a deterrent effect, and only narrowly lost the vote, the power of the Lords meant that capital punishment would not be abolished for another two decades.

Part of the reason for the government's caution on issues such as equal pay, which potentially involved substantial expenditure, was that after six years of war, Britain's economy had by 1945 been gravely weakened. The UK had become the largest debtor nation in the world. With exports at only 40 per cent of their pre-war level, they would need to rise by 175 per cent to enable Britain to pay its way. But the merchant navy was only two-thirds of its pre-war size, factories and housing had been extensively bomb-damaged, the coal industry and railways were badly run down and earnings from 'invisibles', such as insurance and overseas investment, had halved. A worldwide grain shortage in 1946 caused by the combination of the ravages of war and poor harvests led to virtual famine in parts of central Europe, including the British occupied zone of Germany. To alleviate it the government had been forced to introduce bread rationing in Britain, something that had been avoided during the war.

By the end of 1946 a lot of progress had been made: exports, for example, were 111 per cent above the level of 1938, investment was high and so was employment. On 1 January 1947 coal mines were nationalised, but soon the dream would turn into a nightmare. Within weeks the longest and coldest winter of the twentieth century froze the sea off Margate and left most of Britain so snow-bound that the inadequate coal stocks could not actually be moved. The resulting power shortages cut the national newspapers to four pages and threw two million people out of work. The Conservatives coined the slogan 'Shiver with Shinwell[126] and starve with Strachey'.[127]

Meanwhile there were still 1,500,000 men in the armed forces, costing huge sums to pay, feed and support. British overseas aid was going not only to countries like Germany but also to Greece and Turkey, where the risk of Soviet subversion was ever present. Britain simply could not afford its overseas commitments and had to make clear to America that it was withdrawing its support from Greece and Turkey. Faced with the probable alternative of Greece and Turkey succumbing to Soviet influence, America agreed that spring to step into the breach: Britain had called into being the so-called Truman Doctrine.

The strain began to tell on the government. Herbert Morrison had a severe thrombosis during late February and was out of action for the next two months. There was even speculation that he might need to be retired. In a powerful speech at Labour's 1947 annual conference in Margate on 28 May he confronted the country's difficulties and in doing so announced that he was back to form. His words explain the central thrust of the government's thinking at that time. He began by emphasising his solidarity with:

> . . . the so-called middle class [who had] for some time past, been experiencing a painful and difficult reduction in their living standards . . . Many of this great middle class voted for us two years ago, and it is important . . . that we should retain their support. But whether the middle classes did or not vote for the government, if they stand the strain today, with no undue grousing but with patience and understanding, then they are our partners in the great social enterprise on which we have embarked. I would say to them: ours is far more than a sectional policy; it represents the long-term interest of all the constructive elements in the community – yours included. It will in due time offer to every worker, by hand or brain, to every useful member of every so-called class in the community, opportunities of service, of achievement, of personal satisfaction, and of joyful cooperative work, such as we have never known before.
>
> [Morrison then took to the offensive:] Just one word, in rather a different vein,

141

about another group: the drones. It is a blot on our national life that there should be, in this crisis of production, a fair number of 'useless mouths' and still worse, people engaged in activities which are a hindrance to the national effort or, in some instances, defiantly anti-social. We have no hands and brains to waste, and no resources to fritter away on those who don't contribute to our national effort. Let us point the finger of public scorn at such parasites who make themselves comfortable at the expense of the community.

[Turning to offer] good counsel to . . . my fellow trade unionists of the rank and file so well represented in this great conference [he continued:] Well, the first danger is to rest a bit on our oars . . . At the end of that is decline and bankruptcy. We've got to turn out the goods – or bust. In Britain today the battle for socialism is the battle for production. Anything that delays or lessens production is a blow in the face for the organised workers and their cause. Today any avoidable strike – whether caused by employers or workers – is sabotage. And an unofficial strike is sabotage with violence to the body of the Labour movement itself.

The second danger is to snatch at our objectives too fast . . . It's a silly thing to do to start adding to the comforts and luxuries of your house before you've got the roof on and made it watertight. Higher wages and lower hours before the goods are there to be bought – that's far worse than useless. They give no more real income and, by inflation and financial strain, they may wreck the whole structure we are trying to build. A reasonable sense of urgency is all right, but if we try to reap rewards we have not yet earned we shall cause chaos and confusion in which our own people will be the worst sufferers. Believe me, there's little or no more to be got towards a better standard of living by squeezing the incomes of the rich. The Chancellor of the Exchequer has had a good look round! From now on what we get in social benefits and higher wages we shall, broadly speaking, have to earn by higher production – more effort, better management, better tools. We cannot live indefinitely on overdrafts without heading into an economic and financial smash. And that would damage the workers and smash the Labour Party . . .

TWENTY-THREE

In the Shadow of Stalin 1946–49

'Stabbed in the back'

Labour's domestic travails occurred against the backdrop of an increasingly difficult relationship with the Soviet Union. In 1945 Ernest Bevin had hoped that left could talk to left: that as a fellow socialist government, Britain's Labour government would be able to work constructively with the Soviet Union in a way that the Conservatives had been unable to. To his intense frustration, Stalin's paranoid determination to crush democracy and cement his sphere of influence in Eastern Europe meant that Britain soon faced what Churchill described in March 1946 as 'an iron curtain' stretching across Europe from Stettin to Trieste. It is unlikely that Bevin gave up hope of a proper peaceful settlement in Europe until 1947. However, in November 1946 Dick Crossman and 52 other Labour MPs sponsored an amendment to the King's Speech accusing Bevin of being too anti-Soviet and pro-American. Bevin was not in the Commons for the debate, he was in New York negotiating a loan to keep Britain's bread ration from being cut and was told later that day over the phone by his junior minister, Hector McNeil. Bevin's 'Corsican concept of public business' meant that he neither forgave nor forgot.[128] At Labour's 1947 annual conference six months later, Bevin used his main speech to attack those who had stabbed him in the back. He was shaking with rage.

'It brought the house down,' recalled Douglas Jay, then the newly elected Labour MP for Battersea and 20 years later to serve alongside Crossman in Cabinet: 'Near me were sitting some of the guilty men who had supported the rebel amendment – for instance Benn Levy and Geoffrey Bing. They looked at each other in impotent fury as wave after wave of applause surged round the crowded hall':[129]

> . . . There is a reference in this resolution to capitalist America – being subservient to capitalist America. Not one fact was brought out on the platform to show in what way we have been subservient. We have had to borrow, and we did not like borrowing, but on the borrowing we made an open agreement which was reported to Parliament, with all its obligations. May I say – I think I am entitled to say this now – but I have no feeling about it – that when I was in the United States there was a rebellion so called against me in the House of Commons. What was I doing? Not discussing foreign policy at all. I received telegrams from the Cabinet that the Minister of Food wanted 120,000 tons of grains and 700,000 tons of another cereal, and would I do my best

with the American government to get the allocation. I did it, and I think the Minister of Food will agree that I did not make a bad job of it in the end. It tided over a very difficult period. Mr Dalton was cabling me to try to do something about this German zone, and the amount of dollars he would have to find under an old Treasury agreement . . . And because I was doing that, on the very day I was trying to get the agreement with the Americans to prevent the bread ration going down, on that very day I was stabbed in the back.

I am emphasising this because those concerned never went to the government to find out what it was they were asking me to do, and I do say that if you are to expect loyalty from ministers, the ministers – however much they may make mistakes – have a right to expect loyalty in return. I grew up in the trade union, you see, and I have never been used to this kind of thing . . .

The naïveté (or dishonesty) of Bevin's pro-Soviet critics was illustrated by the tragic consequences of the Communist coup in Czechoslovakia during February 1948. Following 1945 most countries within the Soviet sphere of influence in Europe had been governed nominally by multi-party coalitions. But Stalin was determined to bring their governments under direct Communist control and from the spring 1947, the non-Communist parties were ruthlessly purged: Bela Kovacs, Secretary General of the Hungarian Smallholders Party, arrested on 26 February 1947 and never seen again; Nikola Petkov, leader of the Bulgarian Agrarian Union, arrested in June 1947 and executed three months later; Juliau Maniu, leader of the Rumanian National Peasant Party, arrested in July 1947 at the age of 74 and condemned to solitary confinement for life; Stansilaw Mikolajczyk, Polish Peasant Party leader and coalition Deputy Prime Minister, forced to flee impending arrest and execution in October 1947. The Communists took control of most of the social democratic parties from within. Denis Healey, then Labour's International Secretary, recalls visiting the decisive congress of the Czech Social Democrats in November 1947:

> When I landed at the airport in Prague I was told that the government had called a strike to protest against the conduct of the non-Communists – a typical example of the role of trade unions under Communism. The Social Democrats were under heavy pressure to accept fusion with the Communists, whose leader, Gottwald, was Prime Minister; the Communists had been a powerful party even before the war, and Russia's popularity as the liberator of Prague (thanks to an agreement with the Allies), had made them (with 38 per cent of the vote) by far the largest party in the 1946 election. The Social Democratic leader, Fierlinger, had been Ambassador to Moscow and was universally regarded as a Soviet stooge. To the amazement of all outside observers, the Social Democratic Party Congress rejected Fierlinger in favour of the centrist, Lausmann and went on to defeat a motion for fusion by an overwhelming majority. I shall never forget the wolfish snarl with which Fierlinger, white as a sheet, received the announcement of the votes.[130]

By February 1948, having failed to take control over the Social Democrats from within, and fearing the expected outcome of the impending elections of May 1948, the Communists, who had been packing the police with their members, had many of their opponents arrested and began a full-scale purge. Within weeks the non-Communist Foreign Minister Jan Masaryk was mysteriously found dead, alleged to have hurled himself from a high window. When the elections came, the electorate was confronted by lists of candidates approved by the Communists on a 'take it or leave it' basis. Speaking in Grimsby on 6 March 1948 Herbert Morrison denounced them:

> . . . We have seen the Communist-controlled government in Czechoslovakia use the trade unions for its own revolutionary and dictatorial ends. It must be a unique thing in history for ministers to call a general strike. Yet this was done for the purpose of using industrial power to destroy parliamentary debate . . .
>
> 'There is no danger,' says Mr Gottwald, 'in giving arms to the people in a truly democratic state.' The short answer to that is that there is no need. The truth is that if you expel all who are not Communists or their tools from the police, and arm the rest with rifles; if you organise and arm a party militia; if you parade them through the streets; if you give them red armbands and order them to take possession of government departments; if you, for no reason of industrial dispute but as a mere gesture of blackmail, call a general strike; if you commandeer, or suppress, or censor news and newspapers and order the expulsion of individual journalists from their union; if you threaten foreign correspondents and curtail the sale of British and American newspapers; if you censor your radio, deny proper access to the microphone, and are too nervous of the truth to allow the BBC near it; if you, in true Nazi style, go in for terrorist 'purges', and start tampering with your schools, your universities, your Civil Service, your local authorities, and even your Boy Scouts, your sport and your music; if you arrest your political opponents and raid their offices; if you coerce your President into excluding fair representation of political parties in your 'coalition' government; if you force parliamentary representatives to sign a declaration of agreement with you and your ideas; and if, while you're doing all this, you make sure Parliament is not sitting, don't tell the British people that you are 'truly democratic'.
>
> Nothing could have shown the people of this country and of the rest of democratic Europe more clearly the dangers of Communist trickery. There can be no mistaking the lesson for the trade unions and all voluntary associations of free men to be read in the hidden preparations and ruthless use of Communist Action Committees. Let socialist simpletons who urge cooperation with Communists take warning. Czechoslovakia today proves that the Communists are enemies to parliamentary or any other kind of democracy, that they will stoop to any depth of blackmail or violence in their attempt to seize power.

Within months the Soviet authorities would impose a blockade of Western-controlled West Berlin, forcing the Western powers to resort to the famous Berlin airlift to keep the city from starving. The Berlin blockade not only helped cement Europe into East and West, it raised the temperature of the new 'cold war' sufficiently to enable Bevin to persuade the USA to commit itself formally to collective security, the ideal for which Labour had fought for so long. It was enshrined in the second clause of the North Atlantic Treaty, signed on 4 April 1949: 'An armed attack against one or more of them in Europe or America shall be considered an attack against them all.' It was this that became the enduring foundation of NATO: deterrence of world war through a system of collective security.

TWENTY-FOUR

Bevan the Builder 1947–50

'What is Toryism except organised spivvery?
So far as I am concerned they are lower than vermin'

Meanwhile the Labour government continued to build the New Jerusalem in England's green and pleasant land. Master builder was Nye Bevan, who as Minister of Health was additionally responsible for housing. Bevan sought to maximise both quantity and quality of new houses. He insisted that new house building should be permanent rather than temporary, that it should be for council houses for rent rather than private houses for sale and that the new council houses should be larger and with better amenities than in the past. 'At this moment, and for a few years to come, we are going to be judged by the number of houses that we build,' he told Labour's 1947 annual conference. 'In ten years' time we shall be judged by the kind of houses that we build and where we are building them, and I am not going to be panicked into doing a bad job.' In 1950 he told the Commons, 'If I go down in history for nothing else, I will go down at least as a barrier between the beauty of Great Britain and the speculative builder who has done so much to destroy it.'[131] His achievement was considerable. By 1950, taking into account repairs to existing bomb-damaged homes to make them habitable again, two and a half million people had been housed. By 1951 Bevan had built one million new houses. Harold Macmillan, responsible for the housing programme of the 1951–55 Conservative government, would later boast that he had built more houses than Bevan. This was true, but Macmillan's houses were 'smaller, cheaper, meaner'[132] and many were concrete flats: the road to Ronan Point had begun. Moreover, it was Bevan who had had to operate in the post-war climate of material shortage and economic stringency. Macmillan was able to harness the house-building industry that Bevan had rebuilt.

The achievement for which Bevan is most remembered, however, is not his success in securing the construction of council houses with two bathrooms rather than one, but the creation of the National Health Service. 'Most heartening of all for many of us,' recalled Barbara Castle,

> was Nye Bevan's success in bringing the National Health Service not only into being, but into people's hearts. In doing so he showed uncharacteristic patience and consummate skill. The medical profession resisted the whole idea stubbornly. Tory MPs

trooped into the division lobby to vote against it. There had been talk during the wartime coalition of setting up a health service of some sort, but Nye's comprehensive, centrally coordinated service, financed out of taxation and free at the point of use, was more than the Tories had bargained for. They openly yearned for a return to flag days and a mishmash of voluntary and municipal hospitals. To the very end GPs declared that they would not join the new service. The difficulties seemed insurmountable.[133]

Bevan had quite a battle on his hands, and, using Parliament as his weapon, he fought to win. On 9 February 1948 Bevan threw down the gauntlet to his opponents, tabling a motion welcoming the creation of the NHS. His speech, wrote one who heard it, was 'one of the most coruscating he had ever delivered . . . Danton himself could not have done better.'[134] He began with an attack on his critics in the British Medical Association (BMA):

. . . So much misrepresentation has been engaged in by the BMA that the doctors who have voted or are voting in the plebiscite are doing so under a complete misapprehension of what the National Health Service is . . .

From the very beginning, this small body of politically poisoned people have decided to fight the Health Act itself . . . I have before me a letter written to the *Scotsman*:

'Parliament, through the National Health Service Act – "State Medical Service Act", would have been a more descriptive designation – has vested certain totalitarian powers in the Minister of Health. The Minister has not been slow in revealing these powers in his scheme of things to come. Stripped of the goodwill of his practice, subjected to "negative" direction, denied the right of appeal to a court of law against dismissal from service and salaried from Whitehall – such is to be the lot of the physician of the socialist future. In brigand-like fashion this would-be Fuehrer points an economic pistol at the doctor's head and blandly exclaims "Yours is a free choice – to enter the service or not to enter it."'

I have quoted from one of the more modest of the letters, because I am not anxious to raise the temperature just now . . .

It has been suggested that one of the reasons why the medical profession are so stirred up at the moment is because of personal deficiencies of my own. I am very conscious of these. They are very great. Absence of introspection was never regarded as part of a Celtic equipment; therefore I am very conscious of my limitations. But it can hardly be suggested that the conflict between the British Medical Association and the minster of the day is a consequence of any deficiencies that I possess, because we have never been able yet to appoint a Minister of Health with whom the BMA agreed. My distinguished fellow countryman had quite a little difficulty with them. He was a Liberal, and they found him an anathema. Then there was Mr Ernest Brown who was a Liberal National, whatever that may mean, representing a Scottish constituency. They found him abominable. As for Mr Willink, a Conservative representing an English constituency, they found him intolerable.

I am a Welshman, a socialist representing a Welsh constituency, and they find me even more impossible. Yet we are to assume that one of the reasons why the doctors are taking up this attitude is because of unreasonableness on my part. It is a quality which I appear to share with every Minister of Health whom the British Medical Association have met. If I may be allowed to make a facetious transgression, they remind me of a famous argument between Chesterton and Belloc. They were arguing about the cause of drunkenness, and they decided to apply the principles of pure logic. They met one night and they drank nothing but whisky and water, and they got drunk. They met the third night and drank nothing but gin and water, and again they got drunk. They decided that as the constant factor was water it was obviously responsible – a conclusion which was probably most agreeable to Bacchic circles . . .

We are not now dealing with a body which is seeking to bring about the modification of principles in what they consider to be the legitimate interest of the members of the medical profession. We are dealing with a body organising wholesale resistance to the implementation of an Act of Parliament.

[Moreover, he continued, the BMA had already rejected the Act before they knew what was going to be in it:] In fact the whole thing begins to look more like a squalid political conspiracy than the representations of an honoured and learned profession and, I say this deliberately, when the bulk of the doctors in the country learn the extent to which their interests have been misrepresented by some of their spokesmen, they will turn on those spokesmen . . .

Consider the long record of concessions we have made . . . We have also conceded that general practitioners and specialists can have private patients . . . I would warn hon. members opposite that it is not only the British working class, the lower income groups, which stands to benefit by a free health service . . . Consider that social class which is called the 'middle class'. Their entrance into the scheme, and their having a free doctor and a free hospital service, is emancipation for many of them . . . I know of middle-class families who are mortgaging their future and their children's future because of heavy surgeons' bills and doctors' bills . . .

We desire to know from the opposition whether they support . . . the BMA organising resistance on 5 July, because I would warn them that the beginning of that road might look very pleasant but the end would be exceedingly unpleasant, not only for us but for members opposite. (*An hon. member:* 'Is that a threat?') It must be clear to everyone that if there is one thing we must assert, it is the sovereignty of Parliament over any section of the community. We have not yet made the BMA House into another revising chamber. We have never accepted the position that this House can be dictated to by any section of the community.

We do concur in the right of any section of the community to try to persuade the House of Commons to change its mind. That is perfectly sound. The position we are taking up is that the BMA have exceeded their just constitutional limitations, and that the best thing they can do now is to put on record their opinion that while they may disagree with the Act in this or that particular, or in general if they wish, nevertheless, they will loyally accept the decision of Parliament and continue to agitate for such revisions as they think proper. That is the right position for any section of the community to take up.

At the end of the debate, the Conservatives voted against the creation of the NHS and were defeated by 337 votes to 178.

On Monday 5 July 1948 the NHS was born. The night before, Clement Attlee had paid tribute in a radio broadcast to all political parties for the contributions that they had made to the development of Britain's social services. Bevan had seen Attlee's prepared text and felt the Prime Minister's generosity to be excessive: he believed that the Conservative contribution to the development of social services had been essentially negative. Speaking to a rally of seven thousand Labour supporters at Belle Vue in Manchester that same Sunday Bevan let fly at his critics, launching an onslaught that would dominate the front-page headlines on 5 July and for the rest of the week.

He declared that the Conservatives would have built mansions and hotels rather than decent houses for the poor:[135]

In 1945 and 1946, we were attacked on our housing policy by every spiv in the country – for what is Toryism except organised spivvery? They wanted to turn the spivs loose. [He recalled how] in early life I had to live on the earnings of an elder sister, [and was told to emigrate,] that is why no amount of cajolery can eradicate from my heart a deep burning hatred for the Tory Party that inflicted those experiences on me. So far as I am concerned they are lower than vermin. They condemned millions of first-class people to semi-starvation. I warn young men and women: don't listen to the seduction of Lord Woolton. He is a very good salesman. If you are selling shoddy stuff you have to be a good salesman. The Tories are pouring out money in propaganda of all sorts and are hoping by this organised, sustained mass suggestion to eradicate all memory of what we went through. But I warn you, they have not changed – if they have, they are slightly worse than they were.

The next morning Bevan awoke to the NHS's first day and to a media firestorm. 'Mr Bevan's "burning hatred". Attack on Tory "vermin"' was *The Times* headline. Others were similar. And it got worse: that night (Monday) someone daubed 'VERMIN VILLA – HOME OF A LOUD-MOUTHED RAT' on Bevan's house in huge black letters. The media maelstrom continued: 'THE MAN WHO HATES 8,093,858 PEOPLE' was the headline in the *Sunday Dispatch* a full week later. Attlee was not pleased. Other colleagues were furious. It was a propaganda gift to the Conservatives: the Young Conservatives even formed a 'Vermin Club' complete with rodent badges. Churchill dubbed him the Minister of Disease, 'for is not morbid hatred a form of mental disease . . . and indeed a highly infectious form? Indeed I can think of no better step to signalise the inauguration of the National Health Service than that a person who so obviously needs psychiatric attention should be among the first of its patients . . .' Bevan tried to dismiss it all. He was not so much a politician as 'a projectile discharged from the Welsh valleys' he told a dinner given in his honour by Monmouthshire County Council. When that failed to work he confronted it, and Churchill, head on. At the Durham miners' gala, to a crowd of fifty thousand, Bevan declared:

> When I speak of Tories, I mean the small bodies of people who, whenever they have the chance, have manipulated the political influence of the country for the benefit of the privileged few . . . In 1926, when Churchill was Chancellor of the Exchequer . . . the infant mortality rate was 70 in a thousand. In 1946 it was 43, last year it was better than that again and for the first half of this year it was better still. In 1926 2,092 mothers died in childbirth. In 1946, 1,205 died. Now who ought to be Minister of Disease? I am keeping the mothers and children alive but he half-starved them to death. He has the impudence to call me Minister of Disease when every vital statistic by which the health and progress of the population can be measured is infinitely better now under the provision of a common miner than it was under the supervision of an aristocrat. I know if you took the vital statistics of the aristocrats they were as well off then as now. He looked after them all right. I am not concerned about that. I am concerned about our own people . . . It is a queer definition of a gentleman, one who is prepared to forget and forgive the wrongs done to other people. I am prepared to forget and forgive the wrongs that were done to me. I am not prepared to forget and forgive the wrongs done to my people. We need 20 years of power to transfer the citadels of capitalism from the hands of a few people to the control of the nation. Only after 20 years can we afford to be polite. Then maybe I won't have enough energy to be rude, but while we have the energy, let us be rude to the right people.[136]

TWENTY-FIVE

Devaluation and Consolidation 1948–49

'The language of priorities is the religion of socialism'

The first few years from 1945 saw a frenzy of parliamentary activity as the Labour government strove to pass its legislative programme. As the next election campaign approached, the priority, Morrison believed, should be the 'consolidation' of the new Labour Britain rather than further upheaval. In particular he was concerned to ensure that the nationalised industries would be demonstrably better run under public ownership than they had been pre-nationalisation, otherwise he feared that the Conservatives would make political capital out of an anti-nationalisation backlash and on winning an election unpick the achievements for which Labour had striven so hard. He set out his thinking in a famous speech to Labour's annual conference at Scarborough on 7 May 1948. The first, legislative, stage had finished:

> There is no virtue in passing Acts of Parliament and in setting up new organisations except to enable the people to create more wealth and more happiness under the powers and with the resources that have been given. A time comes, as we know, in war when headlong advance must be followed by detailed consolidation, and by exploiting the territory that has been gained. That is the stage which we are now reaching, and if we go on always stretching our hands out for more and not making good the gains we have claimed, only disaster can follow. The test must now be the test of results. We have swept away the Charity and Poor Law State and established the Social Security State, but the Social Security State cannot endure unless it is also a State of Social Responsibility.
>
> Vast cheques have been drawn on our future natural resources in the confidence that the inspiration and incentive of these advances will lead to the increase of national production, which is essential if the cheques that have been drawn are to be met . . . Don't let us think that we can meet this bill as a whole simply by squeezing the capitalists further, or by any short cut other than producing more both to sell abroad and for our own needs . . .
>
> We have started a peaceful revolution and while we can be proud of what has been done we must remember that we cannot sit down on a revolution any more than we can sit down on bayonets. We are getting to that very perilous stage in which previous revolutions have sometimes foundered, when the ideals set out in words in the programme have been given the force of law, and the framework has been set up to carry them out.

At that stage comes the test whether the ideals and purposes which were enshrined in legislation are to become a living reality, or whether human imperfections will convert the dream of the reformers into just another piece of bureaucratic routine . . .

Socialism has always aimed at an abundance of goods and services, but past socialists have sometimes been so preoccupied with the immense problems of securing a *fair distribution* that they have not tackled in detail the equally immense problem of securing *full production*. Now that we have got so far in the direction of fair shares . . . we must really get down more vigorously to the problem of producing plenty. We, after all, are the party of the producers, the consumers, the useful people. We are not content just to go on measuring out fair shares of scarcity . . .

In my early days socialists used to say – I wouldn't be surprised if I did! – that capitalism had solved the problem of production and socialism would solve the problem of distribution. The first part of the slogan was too innocent, for capitalism has not solved the problem of production. During the last 20 years, and especially since the war, one investigation and inquest after another has demonstrated an alarming degree of incompetence, lack of human understanding, waste and lack of enterprise in some of our industries. Well-informed visitors from America and elsewhere, who are far from critical of private enterprise, have been appalled to see how many of our works had been allowed to fall behind in their buildings, their equipment and their standards of management as compared with the best plants in this and other countries . . .

There is another thing we have to tackle and that is making social democracy less of a mere platform word and more of a living reality. Ballot-box democracy, where people go and vote – if they can be bothered – every few years and do nothing much in between, is out of date. We must have an active democracy in this country and we must whip up our citizens to their responsibilities just as we canvass them in elections or just as the air-raid wardens did in the war . . .

The individual today counts not less, the individual counts more, and the individual will count more and more as our socialist programme goes forward. Too many of our so-called democratic institutions are little better than shams which are run by small minorities in the name of large bodies of citizens who take not the least practical interest . . . Let British Labour and socialism give the lead. And the watchwords are – boldness, courage, honesty and plenty of good British common sense.

Labour's annual conference in June 1949 was expected to be, and was, the last before the next general election. Over the preceding months the NEC had been working to produce a draft manifesto to present to it and had seen monthly wrangles between Bevan and Morrison over the commitments to further nationalisation, and principally over the issue of nationalising industrial assurance – Bevan (supported by Jim Griffiths) was in favour and Morrison, who worried about turning the Prudential's agents into doorstep canvassers for the Conservatives, was against. Cripps and Dalton both agreed with Morrison. After one meeting Bevan remarked to Michael Foot, then a newly elected fellow member of Labour's NEC:

'It is a form of torture unknown to the ancients, to be compelled on the last Wednesday of every month to convert the leaders of the Labour Party afresh to the most elementary principles of the party; to be compelled to fight every inch of the way to recapture territory occupied by Beveridge. Now I can sympathise with S-S-Sisyphus and his bl-bl-bloody boulder.' But in these NEC discussions, Bevan markedly failed to support calls from the Keep Left Group for the nationalisation of shipbuilding, aircraft construction, machine tools, parts of the motor industry and the high street banks.[137] And on industrial assurance, after discussions with Co-operative Insurance union representatives who sided with Morrison, a compromise was eventually reached: mutualisation.

Indeed, the great debate at Labour's annual conference on the draft manifesto, *Labour Believes in Britain*, on 8 June 1949, showed most of all the common ground between Morrison and Bevan, who both spoke on the debate on behalf of the National Executive. Though Morrison believed the priority should be the consolidation and improvement of industries already nationalised while Bevan thought there were a number of industries that could yet benefit from nationalisation, both men explicitly believed in making a success of public industry within a mixed economy. Both received warm applause from the hall. Bevan's speech, containing a memorable rebuke to the speech of the utopian Christian socialist, former Liberal MP and Common Wealth Party founder Sir Richard Acland, 'showed a virility which goes ill with the notion of a government on its knees before its enemies', wrote Bevan's biographer Michael Foot:[138]

> ... We are vitally concerned with that private sector. We are as much concerned about making it efficient as we are the public sector, because unless the private sector is efficient it will drag the economy down. Therefore we have given our attention to setting the private sector free. We have taken Mr Churchill's advice! We are pointing out to the nation that part of the private sector is suffering grievously from exploitation by some other part of the private sector. For instance, British private enterprise has got itself absolutely tangled and frustrated by monopolies, cartels, trusts, price-rings and all kinds of things that prevent the robust spirit of private enterprise properly expressing itself. Therefore we have decided that it is necessary for us to come to its rescue ... It is of no advantage at all to a socialist that private enterprise should be languishing ...
>
> So we are going to make an attack on all those restrictions that prevent private enterprise from playing its proper part. That is the reason why we have set up a Monopolies and Restrictive Practices Commission, and three candidates for liberty are already appearing before it ...
>
> Then, in order to stimulate private enterprise to do its job, we are taking power to compete with it. If there is something wrong with an industry, it ought not to be necessary for us to take the whole of it over. It might even not be necessary to take any of it over. It might be wise in particular circumstances for the community to start up in business itself, to show how it ought to be done ... we are not going to pump public

money indefinitely into a State enterprise in order to keep it alive. We are simply going to set it up and then let it compete with the others, and by that means we shall stimulate the others, because, after all, they claim that competition is the spirit of life of them. At the same time we shall have checks and tests and costs of our own with which to find out how they are behaving . . .

This morning . . . Dick Acland almost reproached us for the absence of what he described as a religious or spiritual approach to our problems. I sometimes suspect people when they speak of religious and spiritual approaches in too abstract terms. We are told that somehow or another the vision is lacking . . . When Acland speaks in that way, when he almost rebukes us for appearing to be materialistic, I would point out that in someway or another the conceptions of religious dedication must find concrete expression, and I say that never in the history of mankind have the best religious ideas found more concrete expression than they have in the programmes that we are carrying out. 'Suffer little children to come unto Me' is not now something which is said only from the pulpit. We have woven it into the warp and woof of our national life and we have made the claims of the children come first.

What is national planning but an insistence that human beings shall make ethical choices on a national scale? Planning means that you ask yourself the question: Which comes first? What is the most important? Every attempt to choose between alternative courses of conduct is a moral choice. Therefore those who say that we are materialistic, that we have no sense of comprehensive design, are failing to fit what we are doing into our central purpose. The language of priorities is the religion of socialism. We have accepted over the last four years that the first claims upon the national product shall be decided nationally and they have been those of the women, the children and the old people. What is that except using economic planning in order to serve a moral purpose?

Therefore I say that this great movement, so far from having to go down with its head bowed, as though it had its eyes fixed on the mud, should, on the contrary, raise its head high and look at the stars . . .

The spring and summer of 1949 saw the doubling of Britain's dollar trade deficit and growing speculative pressure on the pound. Recession in the USA had meant less demand for UK exports. UK gold reserves were draining rapidly. With Sir Stafford Cripps taken ill to a Swiss sanatorium, Treasury minister Douglas Jay, Minister for Fuel and Power Hugh Gaitskell and President of the Board of Trade Harold Wilson were made responsible for economic policy in his absence. Jay and Gaitskell concluded that a devaluation of the pound was inevitable and that they ought to grasp the nettle now rather than later. Together they convinced Attlee and Morrison, after which they convinced Cabinet. A reluctant Cripps gave his assent to the *fait accompli* from Zurich.

The decision was announced on 18 September and the Conservatives launched a savage onslaught on the government and on Cripps in particular for his past denials that devaluation could be on the cards. Parliament was recalled and Cripps gave a strong defence of the government's position, despite his own reservations. But it was Bevan's defence of devaluation on 29 September, replying for the government to a speech from Churchill the previous day, that was the most powerful and was regarded as being one of his greatest parliamentary performances. For Michael Foot the debate was the greatest of the 1945 Parliament.[139] It was, writes biographer John Campbell, a *tour de force* of destructive debating which 'left Labour MPs wondering why they had kept their heaviest artillery under wraps, confined to health and housing matters, for so long'. A readers' poll of the *Sunday Pictorial* the following week showed Bevan to be far and away the most popular choice for Prime Minister, beating Attlee, Morrison and Cripps.[140]

Bevan: We on this side of the House welcome cordially the full-throated abandonment of the speech of the leader of the opposition because it provides us with an opportunity of making a full reply. Foreigners have been very much puzzled over the last four years by one peculiar phenomenon of British public life.

They could not understand at all how it came about that His Majesty's government did not lose one single parliamentary seat in a by-election and yet they could read in the national newspapers of this country statements by the right hon. gentleman purporting to show that the British people were undernourished, were fatigued and were almost down and out. They could not understand how it came about that a government which was supposed to have brought the people to such a sorry pass nevertheless could not lose a parliamentary seat. Therefore, I welcome this opportunity of pricking the bloated bladder of lies with the poniard of truth.

Mr Churchill (Woodford): I think, Mr Speaker, that the other day you gave a ruling that the word 'lie' was no more to be used about statements made in this House than was the word 'liar'. I endeavoured to limit my own actions by your ruling.

Mr Speaker: It is perfectly true, but I thought the right hon. gentleman was making a quotation. I did not think he was applying the word 'lie' to anything said by the right hon. gentleman the Member for Woodford [Mr Churchill].

Mr Bevan: No, I was referring to the almost Goebbelesque system of mass suggestion which has been evolved in the course of the last four years to try and persuade the British people that they were far worse off than they really were . . .

Therefore, I say at once that I welcome the opportunity of confronting the right hon. gentleman with the facts. He is known as a very great stylist, and one reads his prose with delight. A reason why he moves gracefully across the pages is because he carries a light weight of fact. He sub-edits history, and if there is any disagreeable fact, overboard it goes. This has always been characteristic of the right hon. gentleman, and it has had a most unfortunate effect on the party opposite because now they have begun to think in phrases as well.

The first fact with which I wish to confront the right hon. gentleman is that the last favourable balance of payment enjoyed by this country was in 1935. It is an extraordinary thing –1935. In other words, we inherited a bankrupt nation . . . Since then we have had a war. In those years the average number of unemployed in Great Britain was two million . . .

We had already brought the nation back to a more favourable situation than that in which it was left in 1945 ...

... The right hon. Member for Woodford trailed his coat yesterday. He invited us to have a historical review. I am astonished that he should do so. It has been suggested, I think by the hon. Member for East Aberdeen [Mr Boothby], that the most constructive suggestion he could make was to urge an early general election and a return of a Tory government in Britain. Why on earth should he want to prophesy what might result from a Tory government when history has the record for him? Why read the crystal when he can read the book? We are furnished with all the facts that are necessary.

[Churchill] yesterday told us that he had no regrets whatsoever for his performance in 1925 – the restoration of the Gold Standard. In fact, he defended it yesterday ... The right hon. gentleman yesterday suggested that throughout his career he had been a friend of the British working man. He suggested to us that he and the Conservative Party would be the most effective defenders of the social services. I am a miner. I was brought up as a miner in a mining family in a mining area and a steel area. The right hon. gentleman's name was execrated. It is not always wise to try to revive these old memories, I know, but the right hon. gentleman himself provoked it yesterday ...

In between the war years this nation was under the guidance of the right hon. gentleman and hon. gentlemen opposite. They were the people who were mainly responsible for shaping policy ... [for introducing] the unemployment regulations which produced such a flood of protests from all over the country that there were stormy parliamentary scenes ... Those are the people the right hon. gentleman [Churchill] would ask the country to send back. You see, sir, they are the same ones. The right hon. gentleman thinks that he is the leader of the Conservative Party. He is not. He is their decoy. There is a little disturbance going on at the moment inside the Conservative Party as to whether the right hon. gentleman is a liability or an asset. It is a very considerable disturbance. The rumbles have reached us. Now, he of all men ought not to be caught, because he has had great experience. He ought to know that the Conservative Party have always tried to find a false face. They have always tried to find people who have endeared themselves to their fellow countrymen, in order to bring the Conservative Party back once more into power.

The right hon. gentleman should know what they did with the right hon. David Lloyd George. He should remember what they did with J. Ramsay MacDonald. If he capitalises the reputation he still has in the affections of the British people to get them, the Conservative Party, once more back to power, he will not be in office long himself. They will fling him aside like a soiled glove. When the right hon. gentleman tells the House of Commons about his accomplishments as a minister, does he not remember that, although he was himself one of the most brilliant parliamentarians of the day, a crowd of mediocrities kept him out of office for nine years, and that when eventually, in the war years, it became necessary to have a leader from that side of the House – because it had to be from that side of the House – with unrivalled gifts of speech and of evoking courage, it was the Labour Party that virtually made him Prime Minister?

I do beg and pray the right hon. gentleman to realise that. It was one of the most vivid of my parliamentary experiences to see those two great parliamentarians, two great men, Lloyd George and the right hon. gentleman – sitting in the House of Commons, with unsurpassed gifts, kept out of office by a crowd of people who were doing nothing but undermining the industrial fabric of Great Britain . . .

But those are the people he would lead back. There they are. Those are the guilty men – all of them. They are the ones that he, day after day, was indicting in the House of Commons. Does he think the nation would be grateful to him if he could persuade the nation to put that lot of bankrupt intelligences back into office again? The right hon. gentleman has a great historical sense. Surely he must realise what history would say about it if he succeeded in doing that. Even his great services during the war would not compensate for such a calamity . . .

'I almost believed at that moment that Winston was going to abstain on his own amendment,' wrote J. P. W. Mallalieu in *Tribune*:

No one who heard it and saw it – no one in the packed galleries, no member of the house, not Winston, nor the Guilty Men, nor the Chaplain leaning intently behind the Bar – no one will ever forget it. It hauled down Winston's election flag and trampled on it . . . And as for his followers, his confederates, his masters, or whatever they might rightly be called in the Tory Party, Bevan not merely pressed their noses in the brimstone but hurled them over the abyss into the everlasting bonfire.[141]

TWENTY-SIX

The Price of Disunity 1950–51

*'It is not enough always to be looking
for Communists under the bed'*

The general election of 23 February 1950, recalled Manny Shinwell, was 'a subdued and rather colourless affair'.[142] At a national level it was essentially a battle between Labour and the Conservatives. With the death of James Maxton in 1946, the ILP, even on Clydeside, was a party of the past, while any pretensions the Liberals had had to a national role had been crushed by their devastating results in 1945. Polling day saw both main parties increase their votes. Labour received 13.2 million votes (46 per cent) and the Conservatives 12.5 million (43.5 per cent) on an 84 per cent turnout, the second highest of the twentieth century (the highest was in February 1910). Labour's manifesto included a further 'shopping list' of industries to nationalise, including sugar, insurance, cement and water supplies. The Conservatives are said to have benefited from the redrawing of constituency boundaries in 1948, from their more efficient garnering of postal votes and from suburban middle-class resentment at restrictions and rationing. Churchill's theme was 'set the people free', and Attlee's 'fair shares for all'. 'The complaint was not so much that shares were unfair but that they were too small,' reflected Hugh Dalton ruefully.[143] While Labour's vote remained solid in its working-class citadels, there was a higher than average swing to the Conservatives in the suburbia and commuterland of London and the south east.

Labour's overall majority was cut to just six by substantial Conservative gains (the Liberals were reduced to just nine MPs on some 9 per cent of the vote). Though Labour's losses had been expected, they had not been anticipated on this scale. Labour had successfully implemented every major pledge in its manifesto and had not lost a single by-election. Moreover, though opinion polls had indicated that the Conservatives had been ahead of Labour since early 1947, few yet gave them much credence.

It was agreed in Cabinet on 25 February 1950 that Labour's small majority meant that controversial manifesto commitments on nationalisation would have to be put on hold. Then, for several months after the election, the government carried on much as before. The Cabinet was little changed, at least among the heavyweights. New faces included Jim Griffiths as Colonial Secretary, Patrick Gordon Walker at Commonwealth

Relations and Hector McNeil, promoted to Scottish Secretary. Manny Shinwell returned to Cabinet as Defence Secretary, having since October 1947 been outside Cabinet as Secretary of State for War.

Four months after the 1950 election, however, the landscape changed. Communist North Korea, supplied and supported by the Soviet Union and Communist China, invaded non-Communist South Korea. The invasion was condemned by the United Nations and an American-led United Nations force was swiftly deployed to stem the Communist tide. UN intervention was only possible because the USSR had walked out of the UN Security Council meeting and had therefore been unable to follow its usual tactic of deploying its veto, while China's seat was still occupied by the old Nationalist government, even though they now controlled no more than Taiwan. The recent Russo-Chinese treaty and the Soviet explosion of an atomic bomb in 1949 highlighted 'the fact that the peace which had come in 1945 was a very tender plant indeed', recalled Herbert Morrison; a third world war was thought to be 'possible, even imminent'.[144] Britain sent forces to Korea too, and raised both the arms budget and conscription from eighteen months to two years. During the autumn a £3.6 billion three-year rearmament programme was agreed. The strain on Britain's economy was increased by the soaring price of imports, up by 40 per cent in twelve months, due to the extensive stockpiling of raw materials by the USA.

When Ernest Bevin rose on 5 October 1950 to answer his critics at Labour's annual conference in Margate, he had literally just returned from the United Nations in New York. Bevin now had serious angina of his heart, had lost weight and looked a shadow of his former self. Many of those present realised that they might be seeing him at his last Labour conference. The great debate on collective security and rearmament was sparked by criticism of Bevin from left-wing MPs and future 'Bevanites'. Ian Mikardo, who told conference that, 'We have knuckled under too easily to other people, for example in Western Germany where we let the Americans get away with re-establishing big business. We are entitled to be equal partners with any other nation in the world in the shaping of international relations . . . ' and Emrys Hughes (Keir Hardie's son-in-law) who attacked Britain's involvement in the UN force in Korea: 'In the old days the Roman historian said: "They made a wilderness and called it peace." Today they have made a hell upon earth in Korea and they call it collective security.'

Bevin's speech in reply to the debate, wrote his biographer Allan Bullock,

> had the unmistakable ring of sincerity if only because Bevin no longer had the force to do more than say, without artifice, what he believed and had argued passionately to convince the party of for more than five years . . . the argument about the character of a Labour government's foreign policy was to be renewed, but the card vote showed more convincingly than anything else could – by 4.8 million votes to 800,000 – that in his generation he had won it . . .[145]

... With the support of every member of the Cabinet, I tried from the day I took office until 1947 to be friends with Russia. There is not a speaker who has been on that platform this morning and urged the adoption of this resolution who would stand more insults, more abuse and put up with more than I have put up with from Molotov and Vyshinsky. But I have looked beyond Molotov and Vyshinsky; I have looked for peace, and I have thought 'I will carry on whatever they say.' I have discussed these problems with Joseph Stalin in Moscow. I offered, on behalf of the government, a 50 years Treaty of Peace. I asked why a little country like Turkey should, for five years, be subjected to a war of nerves. Is Turkey going to attack Russia? Why has she been compelled to stand all the cost of mobilisation all this time? She cannot afford it. She is a poor country. And yet every now and again the threats go out and she is put on edge. But the Turk shows a stiff upper lip. She is a great, old and resistant nation and she is determined to preserve her independence.

And I ask, why the continual conflict with Greece? It is all moonshine, you know – this attack on Greece. It is strategic, my friends, and why do you not recognise that it is strategic? Whenever there is a favourable opportunity, Soviet Russia makes this attack on Greece. She has been kept in a state of civil war all this time ...

You have been talking about doing what you can for the nations of the Middle East, to help them on their feet. My friend Creech Jones, who unfortunately lost his seat at the general election, carried through, as Colonial Secretary, a scheme which is far bigger than the TVA scheme in America. It taps the resources of Lake Victoria, and when it is completed will bring its water down through Egypt ... Work in Tanganyika and many other places which I have not time to enumerate this morning is being attended to . . . We are in those countries not to exploit the natives but to bring them to self-government, leading them along the road that India has gone, leading them along the road to freedom, giving to them universities and education, fitting them out for a standard of life which will enable them to govern themselves ...

On the question of seeking terms with Russia, I say that Russia can sit down at the table with us tomorrow and we will forget the past. But I ask for your support in this: we have a right to be treated as honest people. We may have a different point of view. A sage once said if we all agreed we would all be sane and then it would be a mad world. If we have a different point of view, the purpose of these discussions is to try to reconcile it with others. But I want to enter this caveat ... To be quite frank, I do not like this prospect of five people assuming that every little country can be handled and bandied about because we are five big ones. Therefore I give preference to dealing with a thing through the United Nations where everybody can have his say big or little ...

In Germany we were very near war over the Berlin blockade. An incident one way or the other might have been like a match. Yet, without one word to us, notwithstanding our legal rights (and it is now admitted that it was proper for us to be there under the terms of the surrender) two-and-a-half million people were suddenly cut off from their food. I have not heard of a left-wing fellow traveller get on that rostrum and condemn the effort to starve two-and-a-half million people. I find myself condemned for trying to organise or help to organise the greatest transport venture in the world

161

and for feeding those people and probably contributing to a measure for freedom which history will record in one of its headlines when the time comes . . .

Now then, Korea. If you had been in the government this summer and you had been faced with the Korean situation, what would you have done? . . . Here was a State created by the United Nations, guaranteed by the United Nations commission there. If anything was wrong with it, it could be raised at the Security Council in discussion and put right. But that is not what happened. What happened was that there was a deliberate organisation for aggression; because the tanks the North Koreans used were not made in Korea, they were sent there. It was intended to wipe out South Korea in a few moments and then present the United Nations with a *fait accompli* . . .

I said in the House of Commons in the last debate that I feared the possibility of two struggles going on at one time. And it nearly came off. One would be in Germany, the other in the Far East. Why has East Germany had created for it a force of 100,000 police who are not police, since they have light arms, armoured cars, tanks and can expand to a quarter of a million almost in a night? Could you sit down and believe they were honest and sincere when they created a force like that right on your doorstep? . . .

The figures of the tremendous military power of Russia have been given to you by Shinwell this morning. It is a standing menace to the whole of Europe. They have more troops, more tanks, more guns, than the whole of the rest of Europe put together. Why do they need them, and why do they need them at peace meetings, when they are adding to the tremendous armaments every week? . . .

Europe has been bled twice in a fight for freedom. We are in a very vulnerable spot . . . Do you think we like it? . . . Is there any minister who likes going down to the House of Commons to ask for £3,600 million for war? The man who would do that for fun would go to hell for pleasure . . . Is there any delegate in this conference who would go back to his constituents and say we are doing wrong in paying the proper insurance premium now for our security? We blamed the Conservatives for knowing Hitler was on the march and not making adequate preparation. We blamed the Conservatives because they would not go in for collective security . . . We are in office now and shall we refuse to do what we called upon others to do which would have prevented the 1939 war if they had only done it?

No, this is not for war, it is for peace, the most priceless thing in this world. I do not think the government or the executive can allow without challenge those who come up in support of this resolution to claim that they have a monopoly of the love of peace.

The question is how can you get it, how can you preserve it? Can you lay down your arms and be safe? China had no arms and Japan walked in. Abyssinia had no arms and Mussolini walked in. Poland, Hungary, Rumania, Bulgaria after the war were ill-equipped. Czechoslovakia had no arms and a *coup d'état* was carried out one evening and their liberty was gone. Inside that iron curtain now stretching from the Baltic to the Black Sea there is no freedom. Do you want that to be extended? Would you sit down and let it be extended? I could not. I could not be a member of a party that decided that was their policy, and I do not believe you could either . . .

With that I think I have said enough for you to see that the policy which we have been following, which we shall continue to follow, is to make the United Nations a living reality. It must not fail again. If some say they will not go with us, we must still carry on with those who will. We must not let it break down . . . A few failures by the aggressor will mean, as it must inevitably mean, the triumph of peace over the sadistic desire for war and destruction.

By 1951 it was clear that Bevin's career as Foreign Secretary was at an end. Seventy years old in March, in April he would be dead: that Attlee was considering a successor was an open secret. Names being considered included Attorney General Sir Hartley Shawcross, Colonial Secretary Jim Griffiths (favoured by Dalton and Bevin), Herbert Morrison and Nye Bevan.

Bevan had already been passed over for one of the other top jobs. On 19 October 1950 Sir Stafford Cripps, like Bevin on the point of death, had been sent on doctor's orders to a Swiss sanatorium. He had resigned from Cabinet and Parliament and had been replaced as Chancellor by Hugh Gaitskell, promoted from outside Cabinet, a 45-year-old Wykehamist protégé of Hugh Dalton. Bevan felt slighted at having been passed over for a more junior colleague. He was also still unhappy about cuts to his house-building programme that had been enforced by Cabinet as part of the post-devaluation cuts in public expenditure during late 1949. In the context of rising NHS costs, Bevan had battled against pressure from Chancellor Stafford Cripps, supported by Herbert Morrison, to impose charges for prescriptions, dentures and spectacles in the NHS. If socialism was about priorities, Bevan wanted to put butter before guns, and believed that if cuts were necessary they should come from the defence budget rather than from health and housing.

Worse was to come. On 17 January 1951 Attlee had reshuffled his Cabinet and effectively sidelined Bevan with a move from the Ministry of Health to replace the dependable but unflamboyant George Isaacs as Minister of Labour, who was in turn moved out of Cabinet to run the Ministry of Pensions. Bevan was now less well placed to defend his beloved NHS against the depredations of the rearmament programme. On 25 January 1951, under American pressure, Cabinet agreed to increase the rearmament programme by over £1 billion, to £4.7 billion for 1951–54. This was double the planned pre-Korea level of expenditure. Bevan feared that this was more than the economy could bear and risked even greater cuts in welfare provision. Nevertheless, despite support from the 35-year-old President of the Board of Trade Harold Wilson, he was overruled by the powerful combination of Attlee, Dalton, Morrison and Gaitskell.

Bevan had accepted both NATO and Britain's possession of the atomic bomb. He was not against rearmament and he fully supported the need to stand up to Communist aggression. His position was sophisticated and was set out commandingly on 15 February 1951, in his first speech as Minister of Labour, replying to a Churchillian vote of censure on the government. For 25-year-old Tony Benn, who had just succeeded Stafford Cripps as MP for Bristol South-East, Bevan's speech was 'brilliant . . . it cut Churchill particularly into little pieces by scorn and laughter . . . For us it was a shot in the arm. It gave Nye his big chance to enunciate policy on the grandest scale and . . . immeasurably strengthened his claim to the leadership of the parliamentary Party and to the next premiership.'[146] Hugh Gaitskell, in the midst of battles with Bevan, conceded that,

> Nye gave one of the most brilliant performances I have ever heard him give. It was also all in good taste, good humoured, interesting and glittering with striking phraseology . . . What a tragedy that a man with such a wonderful talent as an orator and such an interesting mind and fertile imagination should be such a difficult team worker, and some would say even worse – a thoroughly unreliable and disloyal colleague. Will he grow out of this? Will he take on the true qualities that are necessary for leadership? Who can say. Time alone will show.[147]

For Roy Jenkins, later the very model of a modern Gaitskellite, Bevan's speech was 'exceptionally powerful . . . wholly commanding the House with its range and passion'.[148] For Bevan's biographer Michael Foot, it was 'the authentic voice of an independent British foreign policy suited to the time'.[149] Perhaps it was the speech of a man who had reason to hope that he could be about to become Britain's Foreign Secretary. He began on matters of 'departmental significance', criticising restrictive practices in industry:

> I deplore them on both sides – on both sides. There is as much Ludditism amongst employers today as there is amongst workers . . . I do hope that organised labour in the country will realise the very serious times through which the country is passing. There have been a number of unofficial strikes recently, and some more are threatened. There is in this country at the moment plenty of conciliation machinery that can be used; it is ready; it is available all the time . . . It very often happens that some of these disputes occur because modern managements have not realised that in the absence of the whip of unemployment, common sense must be applied more frequently.
>
> May I say in passing that it is not enough always to look for Communists under the bed. That can be an awfully lazy habit. I remember when I was connected with the coal mining industry; whenever there was an explosion there was an inquiry, and the inquiry used to be directed wearisomely to the cause of ignition. We always used to say, 'Look for the cause of the gas.' There are lots of people going about trying to ignite inflammable material, but we must ask ourselves: Why is the material so inflammable? It very often happens that many of these disputes would never occur if they had not been festered and fostered by personal relationships which could quite easily be, if I may use the term, anodyned . . .
>
> [Then he turned to] the size of the Armed Forces, which fell below expectations because of the manpower position . . . it has been found necessary to make a decision that the 'blanket' shall be removed from agriculture . . .
>
> I am convinced . . . that the only kind of political system which is consistent with a modern artisan population is political representative democracy . . .

The curious thing is that the Soviet Union has won its victories in those agrarian parts of the world where poverty is her chief ally. She has not won them, and she will not win them, in modern industrial communities. Therefore, we on this side of the House say that we must put ourselves in the position of armed preparedness, not to tempt her into seeking an easy victory, but, on the basis of that armed strength, to realise that the earliest opportunity must be taken to bring about not appeasement but the pacification of the tensions of the world . . .

If there is one thing of which the Russian people are aware it is the existence of the atom bomb. Therefore, if there is fear of the atom bomb, it is mutual fear, and out of mutual fear, mutual sense may be born. Therefore we ourselves consider – we have always considered on this side of the House – that every opportunity must be eagerly sought in order to try to bring about an alleviation of international tension. But there was little evidence of that on the opposite side of the House . . .

Furthermore, may I remind the right hon. gentleman that if we turn over the complicated machinery of modern industry to war preparation too quickly, or try to do it too quickly, we shall do so in a campaign of hate, in a campaign of hysteria, which may make it very difficult to control that machine when it has been created . . .

[Whereas Attlee had sought the friendship of India and Pakistan, Churchill] would have still faced that situation with early-nineteenth-century conceptions. We think that things happening in Asia at the present time are not only the consequences of malignant plottings by the Soviet Union. Do not let us get it wrong. It is certain, of course, that the Soviet Union are doing their very best to work these things up, but the events taking place in Asia at the present time are under the influence of historical compulsions which do not have their seat in the Kremlin at all. We shall deal with them.

That is the reason we do beg that we shall not have all these jeers about the rearmament that we are putting under way. We shall carry it out; we shall fulfil our obligations to our friends and allies, and at the same time we shall try to prevent such an exacerbation of the world atmosphere as makes it impossible for the nations to come together in peace and harmony and give mankind another breathing space.

When on 9 March Bevin was finally replaced as Foreign Secretary, despite Bevan's great speech, it was not by Bevan but by Herbert Morrison. During March 1951 the temperature in Cabinet rose as the battle over guns and butter intensified. At a Health Service Cabinet Committee meeting of 15 March, Chancellor Hugh Gaitskell advocated a ceiling on health expenditure at existing levels and the imposition of charges for dentures and spectacles. For Gaitskell it became a matter of principle that the government could not have a purely open-ended commitment to expenditure, even on the NHS. Gaitskell, moreover, was not alone in believing that many opponents of the rearmament programme were naïvely underestimating the Soviet threat and risked repeating the approach taken during the 1930s when Labour condemned Nazi aggression but opposed giving the British government sufficient arms to defend against it. The following week Bevan and Harold Wilson denounced the proposals at full Cabinet, arguing that raw material shortages would make it impossible to spend the additional planned defence budget while the imposition of NHS charges would be to breach a fundamental matter of principle, making the NHS no longer free at the point of use. During early April both Bevan and Wilson made it clear in Cabinet that if the government introduced the charges they would feel compelled to resign. Their protests went unheeded and on 10 April Gaitskell announced the charges in his Budget speech. On 22 April Bevan resigned, to be followed the next day, the day of Bevan's resignation speech to the Commons, by Harold Wilson and John Freeman, now a junior minister at Supply.

Tony Benn witnessed the scene:

> With the sunlight pouring through the windows opposite the Chamber was suffused in a warm glow of light. Jennie Lee came in at about ten past three and sat, flushed and nervous, on the very back bench, below the gangway. At ten past three Nye walked in briskly and jauntily and went straight to his seat three rows back. He looked pale and kept shifting his position and rubbing his hands . . . [Bevan's] rising was greeted with a few 'hear, hears'. Not many. The government front bench looked sicker and sicker as the speech went on and the violence of the attack intensified. Jennie Lee behind him sat forward and became more and more flushed. Every now and again he pushed back the lock of his iron-grey hair. He swung on his feet, facing this way and that and his outstretched arm sawed the air:[150]

> It has for some time been obvious to the members of the government and especially to the ministers concerned in the production departments that raw materials, machine tools and components are not forthcoming in sufficient quantity even for the earlier programme and that, therefore, the figures in the Budget for arms expenditure are based upon assumptions already invalidated. I want to make that quite clear to the House of Commons; the figures of expenditure on arms were already known to the Chancellor of the Exchequer to be unrealisable. The supply departments have made it quite clear on several occasions that this is the case and, therefore, I begged over and over again that we should not put figures in the Budget on account of defence expenditure which would not be realised, and if they tried to be realised would have the result of inflating prices in this country and all over the world.

> . . . The lurchings of the American economy, the extravagant and unpredictable behaviour of the production machine, the failure on the part of the American government to inject the arms programme into the economy slowly enough, have already caused a vast inflation of prices all over the world, have disturbed the economy of the western world to such an extent that if it goes on more damage will be done by this unrestrained behaviour than by the behaviour of the nation the arms are intended to restrain.

> This is a very important matter for Great Britain. We are entirely dependent upon other parts of the world for most of our raw materials. The President of the Board of Trade and the Minister of Supply in two recent statements to the House of Commons have called the attention of the House to the shortage of absolutely essential raw materials . . .

I say therefore with the full solemnity of the seriousness of what I am saying, that the £4,700 million arms programme is already dead. It cannot be achieved without irreparable damage to the economy of Great Britain and the world, and that therefore the arms programme contained in the Chancellor of the Exchequer's Budget is already invalidated and the figures based on the arms programme ought to be revised . . .

This great nation has a message for the world which is distinct from that of America or that of the Soviet Union. Ever since 1945 we have been engaged in this country in the most remarkable piece of social reconstruction the world has ever seen. By the end of 1950 we had, as I said in my letter to the Prime Minister, assumed the moral leadership of the world [*interruption*]. It is no use hon. members opposite sneering, because when they come to the end of the road it will not be a sneer which will be on their faces. There is only one hope for mankind, and that hope still remains in this little island. It is from here that we tell the world where to go and how to go there, but we must not follow behind the anarchy of American competitive capitalism which is unable to restrain itself at all, as is seen in the stockpiling that is now going on, and which denies the economy of Great Britain even the means of carrying on our civil production. That is the first part of what I wanted to say . . .

May I be permitted, in passing, now that I enjoy comparative freedom, to give a word of advice to my colleagues in the government? Take economic planning away from the Treasury. They know nothing about it. The great difficulty with the Treasury is that they think they move men about when they move pieces of paper about. It is what I have described over and over again as 'whistle-blowing' planning. It has been perfectly obvious on several occasions that there are too many economists advising the Treasury, and now we have the added misfortune of having an economist in the Chancellor of the Exchequer himself . . .

I now come to the National Health Service side of the matter . . . The Chancellor of the Exchequer is putting a financial ceiling on the Health Service. With rising prices the Health Service is squeezed between that artificial figure and rising prices. What is to be squeezed out next year? Is it the upper half? When that has been squeezed out and the same principle holds good, what do you squeeze out the year after? Prescriptions? Hospital charges? Where do you stop? I have been accused of having agreed to a charge on prescriptions. That shows the danger of compromise. Because if it is pleaded against me that I agreed to the modification of the Health Service, then what will be pleaded against my right hon. friends next year, and indeed what answer will they have if the vandals opposite come in? What answer? The Health Service will be like Lavinia – all the limbs cut off and eventually her tongue cut out, too . . .

Why has the cut been made? He cannot say, with an overall surplus of over £220 million and a conventional surplus of £39 million, that he had to have the £13 million. That is the arithmetic of Bedlam. He cannot say that his arithmetic is so precise that he must have the £13 million, when last year the Treasury were £247 million out . . . There is no justification in the arithmetic, there is less justification in the economics, and I beg my right hon. and hon. friends to change their minds about it . . .

Tony Benn observed:

> Gaitskell showed clearly the contempt he felt. Dalton looked like death once warmed up and now cooled down. The fact is that though there was substance in what he said Nye overplayed his hand. His jokes were in bad taste. I felt slightly sick. He sat down, the hum of conversation started and the exodus began. Nye stayed put for a few moments. He rose to go, and Emrys Hughes shook his hand as he passed the front bench. It has to be said that Nye has written the Tory Party's best pamphlet yet. I predict it will be on the streets in a week.[151]

For Bevan, his resignation speech was a political disaster, at least in the immediate sense, alienating most of the Parliamentary Labour Party with its bitter invective against Gaitskell. 'He would leave Britain confronting a perilous world, armed only with false teeth,' declared the *Daily Sketch*. In hindsight however, it is broadly accepted that on the central issue Bevan was right and Gaitskell was wrong; indeed the Conservative government post-1951 abandoned much of the rearmament programme, and as the historian Ben Pimlott has observed, it was particularly insensitive for a fledgling Chancellor, facing opposition from a senior colleague, 'to refuse to treat health service expenditure any different from food subsidies'.[152]

TWENTY-SEVEN

'Bevanite' Battles 1951–52

'We cannot solve our problems merely by passing self-gratifying resolutions'

After Bevan's resignation the Labour Party polarised between those who supported his stand and those who supported the leadership. Bevan became the figurehead for the left-wing caucus around the Keep Left Group and *Tribune* newspaper, giving them a weight and prominence that they had not enjoyed since the 1930s. Dick Crossman, one of the Keep Left Group, recalled: 'When Nye Bevan and Harold Wilson and John Freeman resigned, we had the "Keep Left" Group as a going, highly organised, concern. We simply put the "Keep Left" Group at the disposal of the three great cuckoos who had arrived in our nest. It was rather a cosy nest before, now there were the great big cuckoos in it. So we became Bevanites overnight, having been "Keep Lefters" before.'[153] The Bevanites campaigned through the pages of *Tribune*, through the newspaper columns of their supporters and by means of 'Brains Trusts' that they organised up and down the country. At Labour's 1951 conference in Scarborough thousands of votes in the constituency section of Labour's NEC swung to the 'Bevanite' candidates at the expense of the 'loyalists' like Hugh Dalton and Herbert Morrison. Manny Shinwell was unseated completely.

Labour's 1951 conference had been intended to provide a springboard for the election campaign that followed. Attlee had felt that to struggle on with a majority of six was not the best way to run a government and had called an election for 25 October 1951. Drafted by Dalton, Bevan, Mikardo and Labour's General Secretary, Morgan Phillips, Labour's manifesto included suggestions for dividend limitation, a capital levy, and, instead of a nationalisation 'shopping list', a vague pledge to take over industries that were 'failing the nation'. Ironically, although Labour again secured more votes, 13.95 million (48.8 per cent) as compared to 13.7 million (48 per cent), than the Conservatives, the uneven distribution of votes around the country meant that this time the Conservatives secured more seats, 321 compared to 295. The Liberal vote collapsed to 730,000 (2.5 per cent), largely due to the party's failure to stand candidates in most seats (it stood only 109 candidates). Of six Liberal MPs elected, only one, Jo Grimond, won an election in which a Conservative candidate had taken part. The broadcast of their leader notably attacked only Labour, and in the absence of Liberal candidates in many marginal Conservative versus Labour battleground seats, many former Liberal voters now voted Conservative.

With Labour now in opposition, factional infighting worsened. On 5 March 1952 an amendment put forward by Bevan and his supporters condemning the rearmament programme gained the support of 57 MPs against the Labour leadership line. Hugh Dalton described Labour's annual conference in October 1952 as being 'the worst Labour Party conference, for bad temper and general hatred, since 1926 . . . it was very cold and wet, and windy at Morecambe . . . We haven't had so strong hatreds since 1931 – and then one section left the party, but now everyone is staying on.'[154] 'During some debates at Morecambe,' recalled Battersea MP and future Labour Cabinet minister Douglas Jay,

> an apparently organised claque of extremists yelled from the gallery in a chorus of combined hysteria and hatred such as I had never encountered before and found acutely distressing, even alarming. The hatred had a totalitarian ring. I had never before, not being a football enthusiast, seen human beings transformed in the mass into screaming fanatics; and as I listened in the worst moments, I reflected that presumably this was the type of frenzy which Hitler and Goebbels excited . . .[155]

The pattern for the week was set up as early as the Monday afternoon of the conference when usually, as the seasoned gladiator Michael Foot put it, 'the gladiators are still content to polish their lances and daggers'. At a debate on a resolution calling for direct industrial action to bring down the Conservative government, an approach which the TUC had rejected as long ago as the General Strike, more than two decades before, Transport Workers' boss Arthur Deakin and Miners' Union leader Sir William Lawther were heckled and howled as they spoke against the motion. Lawther had been typically blunt:

> Shut your gob for a minute, will you? If your wisdom was commensurate with your clamour you would be wise. I want to say to Small Heath, just as kindly as they have said to us, that the miners will not take instructions from either Small Heaths or Big Heaths, that we shall determine our own action, and please remember that we might be fighting when a lot of you are running in the other direction . . . this conference has no right whatever to lay down a mandate as to how the unions in any given situation will act. Not only have you no mandate, but even if you had one we would not accept it. Our instructions are given in the right form by the members themselves.

Deakin later described those who tried to shout him down as the 'howling dervishes'.[156] Significantly, although Deakin and Lawther won the vote, the 1,728,000 votes the resolution received as compared to their 3,986,000 was far higher than would have been expected a few years before for a motion so completely opposed by Labour's leaders.

Building on the previous year's success, in the NEC elections at Labour's 1952 conference the Bevanites took six out of the seven constituency seats, knocking off both Hugh Dalton and Herbert Morrison. Dalton blamed 'half vague emotion, half Mikardo's cunning organisation'.[157] The successful candidates were Bevan, Barbara Castle, Tom Driberg, Harold Wilson, Ian Mikardo, Dick Crossman and Jim Griffiths, the sole non-Bevanite to survive. In addition to Dalton and Morrison they had beaten Hugh Gaitskell, James Callaghan and Manny Shinwell. While some of the Bevanites were clearly as substantial figures as those they had beaten, others were more questionable assets to the party. Denis Healey recalled acidly, 'Tom Driberg [later Lord Bradwell] was elected year after year by the constituency parties, largely on the strength of articles he wrote for *Reynolds News* during the war, when he was a member of the Communist or Commonwealth Parties, although he . . . gave the information he gained on the Executive both to MI5 and to the Russians.'[158] Morrison's opportunity to reply to the conference hall, to those who had rejected him, came on the afternoon of 30 September. At a debate on Labour's new policy platform, *Facing the Facts*, which turned into a battle over whether Labour should commit to greater nationalisation, ex-TGWU official and future Labour deputy leader George Brown was moved to tell the conference:

> It may or may not interest the conference – it certainly will not surprise them – if I tell them that it seems to me this conference is rapidly going mad . . . We have always believed that public ownership had its place where the circumstances of the case made that the only way of being able to effect the changes we want . . . [he declared, but,] neither in the case of coal, nor in the case of steel (unless it has been denationalised in the meantime), nor in the case of food production is the 'old agony' of public owner-ship relevant at all. We are beginning to learn, I hope, that public ownership merely provides the means of getting on with the job . . .

Herbert Morrison rose to reply to the debate for Labour's outgoing NEC, and was received with thunderous applause, much of it from the leadership-loyal trade union del-egations who, having their own section of representatives on Labour's NEC, had had no opportunity to vote in the constituency section. Stating his opposition to a 'shopping list' of industries to nationalise, he:

> would sooner say to the country, 'Here is a list of circumstances in which it is right that we should give consideration to the transfer of industries from private to public ownership or for the State to enter into competition with private industry.' [He con-cluded:] None of us has come here merely to gratify his emotions. We have to impress the country, our country, including that 25 per cent of the working class – and there may be more – who are still voting Tory. We have to convince these people. It is no good merely hating them, because that will only make them worse. It is far better to talk nicely to them, even in Beckenham. We have to convince them that we know what we are talking about and that we are ready to face unwelcome, as well as welcome, facts; that we are responsible and that our first duty is to our country and our people, and also to the world. We cannot solve our problems merely by passing self-gratifying resolutions.

171

Dick Crossman, one of the new Bevanite members of the NEC, conceded that Morrison 'received an ovation for what I thought was a really impressive performance. Indeed he really did achieve victory out of defeat.'[159]

Morrison's dignity in defeat was thought by some to be too dignified. The loyal chiefs of the big unions, Arthur Deakin of the Transport and General Workers' Union, Will Lawther of the Miners, Tom Williamson of the General and Municipal Workers' Union and Lincoln Evans of the Steelworkers, were furious at what they regarded as subversive activities by the Bevanites, blaming them for losing Labour the election and letting the Conservatives back into government. Arthur Deakin was that year's Fraternal Delegate to Labour conference from the TUC and used his speech to make his views on the Bevanites clear. There was, wrote Dalton in his diary, 'a frightful row with continuous booing from both sides'.[160] He began by attacking:

> industrial action for political purposes. We are conscious of the calamity which would overwhelm this movement if the organised trade union movement acted with reckless irresponsibility towards the form of government of which we in this country are so proud. The people who are now advocating industrial action for political purposes are the people who applied unofficial action for the purpose of seeking to coerce our own Labour government ...
>
> There are few people, today, who believe that the difference in policy on rearmament is the real issue within this party. What most people are thinking is – that there is a great struggle for leadership going on ...
>
> My suggestion is that such misunderstandings can only be disposed of by a complete abandonment on the part of this dissident element within our midst of the tactics they have so recently been employing. Let them get rid of their whips; dismiss their business managers and conform to the party constitution. Let them cease the vicious attacks they have launched upon those with whom they disagree, abandon their vituperation, and the carping criticism which appears regularly in the *Tribune* (*interruptions*).

Afterwards, delegates 'stepped out for lunch as if over cascades of molten lava', recalled Michael Foot.[161]

The man who most overtly took up Deakin's call to arms was not Morrison but Labour's former Chancellor Hugh Gaitskell who, following Morecombe, 'decided that the time had come for him to speak out'. He did so the following weekend, on 5 October 1952, to an audience of 450 in an old theatre in Stalybridge 'in a speech which he discussed only with Solly Pearce [editor of the *Leeds Weekly Citizen*] when he drafted it in the offices of the *Leeds Weekly Citizen*', recalled fellow Leeds MP Denis Healey. 'It ... won him the succession to Attlee; it persuaded Arthur Deakin, Bevin's successor as head of the Transport and General Workers' Union and the other powerful union leaders that Gaitskell was the man to back.'[162] It also infuriated the left. For Michael Foot, 'the

Stalybridge speech was a scandalous one . . . almost McCarthyite in tone . . . It was the speech of a loser who had been beaten by the votes of the conference and who tried to pretend that the votes had in some way been improperly weighted, which was not the case at all.'[163]

> The defeat of Herbert Morrison for the National Executive is not only an act of gross political ingratitude, but a piece of blind stupidity which, until it is put right must gravely weaken the party. Members of the National Executive know well that he has been all along the principal architect of efficient organisation and realistic policy. The loss of his services in this policy-making year is a heavy if not a crippling blow . . .
>
> A most disturbing feature of the conference was the number of resolutions and speeches which were Communist inspired, based not even on the *Tribune* so much as on the *Daily Worker*. There is no doubt that Mrs Braddock was quite right when she warned us some weeks ago in the *Daily Herald* that the Communist Party had now adopted a new tactic of infiltration into the Labour Party. I was told by some observers that about one sixth of the constituency party delegates appeared to be Communists or Communist inspired. This figure may well be too high. But if it should be one tenth or even one twentieth it is a most shocking state of affairs to which the National Executive should give immediate attention.
>
> Fortunately, apart from the elections to the Executive, the conference came down firmly on the side of sanity and responsibility. The issues of foreign policy and defence are now settled. All the silly nonsense about withdrawing troops from Korea, breaking away from the Atlantic Alliance, and going back on what the Labour government stood for has been blown away. We are definitely opposed as a party to unilateral cuts in our defence programme, though we favour periodic re-examination with our allies, as was indeed proposed by the Labour government at Ottawa. Loyal members of the party must now accept all these decisions, including the new members of the National Executive.
>
> I believe that many constituency party delegates who came to the conference pre-pared to vote Bevanite were impressed by the strength of the anti-Bevanite case which they had never heard properly presented before. The reason for this is twofold – first that the Bevanites have largely controlled the left-wing press. Through the *Tribune*, the *New Statesman*, *Reynolds* and even the *Sunday Pictorial* (until recently), they have been able to pour out a stream of grossly misleading propaganda with poisonous innuen-does and malicious attacks on Attlee, Morrison and the rest of us.
>
> The second reason is that in the hope that all this would die down, in the belief that we ought to confine ourselves to attacking the Tories and because of a distaste for public rows inside the party, we endured it for the most part in silence. But it is now clear to me and to others from what we saw at Morecambe that we were wrong to let all this go on without reply. The constituency parties have heard only a very distorted side of the case, have been seriously misled and in consequence are now unwittingly endangering the very thing they care about most: a Labour victory at the next election. We who stood loyally by the Labour government and its policies must now repair the

damage. We must speak out plainly and fearlessly, answering the slanders and standing up always for a responsible, honest and realistic policy both in home and foreign
affairs.

Let no one say that in exercising the right of reply to Bevanites we are endangering
the unity of the party. For there will be no unity on the terms dictated by *Tribune*.
Indeed its very existence so long as its pages are devoted to so much vitriolic abuse of
the party leaders is an invitation to disloyalty and disunity. It is time to end the
attempt at mob rule by a group of frustrated journalists and restore the authority and
leadership of the solid sound sensible majority of the movement. If we don't or can't
do this we shall not persuade and shall not deserve to persuade our fellow citizens to
entrust us once again with the government of the country.

Although Attlee did not speak out publicly as Gaitskell had done his private view is
clear from a letter he wrote to his brother Tom on 5 October: 'There had been a considerable infiltration of near Communists into the constituency delegations. I fancy that in
weak constituencies the crypto-com volunteers go and pay his expenses. There was quite
an organised claque.'[164] Following Gaitskell's Stalybridge speech Attlee decided that the
temperature was now so high that at a meeting of the PLP at the beginning of the new
parliamentary session he personally moved a resolution banning all unofficial groups
within the party, a resolution which was approved by 188 votes to 51. On 11 November
1952 Bevan unsuccessfully challenged Morrison to a contested election for Labour's
deputy leadership (held unopposed by Morrison since Arthur Greenwood's retirement
from the post in 1945). Morrison proved secure with the votes of 194 MPs, but the fact
that 82 MPs voted for Bevan was highly significant in the context of the expected battle
to succeed the almost septuagenarian Attlee as leader. Bevan also stood in the shadow
Cabinet elections and was elected, twelfth out of twelve. For eighteen months the
Bevanites went relatively quiet, though splits would soon resurface over the issue of further nationalisation and on the contentious issue of German rearmament which
Labour's leadership supported (while the Bevanites and the ever Germano-sceptic Hugh
Dalton opposed) as a necessary means of buttressing NATO against the Soviet threat.

TWENTY-EIGHT

The Torch Passes 1953–55

'Why I am a socialist'

While Hugh Gaitskell was clearly a champion of Labour's right wing, he also saw himself as a radical. Education policy was an area where Labour's 1945–51 government had made great strides forward. It had carried through a huge school-building and teacher-training programme to enshrine universal free education up to the age of fifteen on the basis of the tripartite model of schools: grammar, technical and modern. But dissatisfaction was growing with the tripartite model and the inflexibility of the eleven-plus examination on which it was based. Few technical schools had been created and the secondary moderns, to which most children were condemned by the eleven-plus, were often profoundly inadequate. Additionally, Labour seemed to be tempering its commitment to raising the school leaving age to sixteen. And then there was the age-old question of private schools. Having had direct experience of it himself, at Winchester, Gaitskell was convinced that the existence of a separate privileged system of private education was a fundamental barrier to a truly classless society in Britain. James Griffiths, who served as Gaitskell's deputy leader during 1956–59, remembered 'how strongly he urged the view that one of the first priorities should be the integration of the public schools into the state national system'.[165] Gaitskell spoke on this issue, and against the position of Labour's NEC at the party's 1953 conference at Margate:

> If we believe in genuine equality of opportunity, we really cannot go on with a system of education under which the parents of wealthy children are able to buy what they and most people believe to be a better education for their children. I am not attacking the public schools; I was at one of them, and one of the best of them. I am not attacking the parents who send their children there, because it is the natural thing to do to try and do the best for your children. But I do say that the system is wrong and must be changed.
>
> How are we to do it? There are, of course, those who say 'Abolish them immediately.' I can see the difficulties there . . . They are good schools, and I do not think it is a good plan to abolish them. I think also that we do not want to get ourselves in the position of being blamed as people who are always closing down things. What we want to do is to throw doors open, not to close them. At the same time there is no reason to go to the opposite extreme and dig our heads in the sand and do nothing at all about them, and that is really what 'Challenge to Britain' implies.

I must admit that at one time I myself took the view that the best thing was to go on improving the ordinary schools until nobody would bother to send their children to public schools. However, I have come to the conclusion that that really will not do. It may be 50 years before you really achieve that object, and even at the end of it the snob value of the public schools may still remain, and that being so, I suggest we must look for an alternative. I am not an expert in these things, but it seems to me that we might consider treating the public schools as we have treated the universities. More and more they are coming to be places where clever children go because they are clever, and not because their parents are wealthy. Surely, we can consider doing the same thing in the case of the public schools. I am not for one moment suggesting that merely throwing open three or four or five per cent free places does anything, because it does not. I do say that if we could manage to offer, say, half the places at public schools free as a start, we could proceed from that and gradually abolish fee-paying altogether. I know the Executive will say that is not consistent with the principle of the comprehensive school, you are creaming off the best people. That is an argument one might expect from those who want to abolish the public schools, but if we are going to keep them, if we are going to have some kind of segregation, it should be segregation based on brains and not on wealth.

I do appeal to the Executive . . . to think again about it, to bring into consultation this time more of the people who really know about education, and to produce for us proposals which really do implement our principle of equality of opportunity, which after all lies at the heart of our socialist faith.

Though he won the support of TGWU boss Arthur Deakin, Gaitskell clashed directly with Jennie Lee:

. . . Hugh Gaitskell has alarmed me even more than the Executive have . . . If I were a Tory I would be delighted by any proposals that were made for segregating the best of our children to learn Latin verse, the right kind of accent and clothes to wear, and how to wear them, while at the same time apparently the less gifted children have got to go into the pits, on the railways, and do all the harder work of society.

I would like to see our party put all its enthusiasm and skill into comprehensive schools. The privileged class educates together the backward and the bright, the academic and the sporting types. My vision of the future is that we should give all our children the same social environment and not segregate them . . .

The maximum compromise that a socialist should be asked for is to let people send their children to private schools if they wish to do so, but we should concentrate on building up our own state-aided schools. Instead of that we are going to do something the Tories do not do, we are going to maintain standards in the private schools, have them licensed and examined . . .

Gaitskell's arguments were also rejected by fellow Leeds MP Alice Bacon, an exteacher and early advocate of comprehensive schools who nevertheless 'had a personal devotion to Gaitskell', recalls Denis Healey, 'which went far beyond politics'.[166] She replied to Gaitskell on behalf of the NEC. The last Labour government had raised the school leaving age, she began, but there was more to do to tackle:

insanitary school buildings, over-crowding [and a] great shortage of teachers . . . One of the greatest faults in our education system is the inequality of opportunity. It is not only a question of the privileged and the unprivileged according to money. The privileged children are not only those whose parents can afford to buy a privileged education, there is privilege within the state system itself. There is a great amount of luck regarding the education of our children, luck which to some extent is dependent upon where the child lives. For instance, a child who lives in Merioneth has eight times the chance of going to a grammar school as the child who lives in Gateshead, because in Merioneth they have got sufficient grammar school places for 64 per cent of the children, whereas in Gateshead they have only got sufficient places for 8 per cent. Sometimes luck is according to sex. For instance, the girls in Preston have twice as good a chance of getting to a grammar school as the boys in that same town, whereas in Oxford the boys have twice the chance. We really must get rid of this game of chance in our educational system.

There is also the game of chance in regard to the examination at eleven. Geography and any other kind of luck ought not to determine the child's opportunity. We know every child cannot attain the same standard, but we do believe that all can be given the opportunity to make the best of their natural abilities. It is not the prerogative of the clever child alone to have a good education; the average child and the weak child have the right to as much education as the clever child. It is as good to spend more money to get smaller classes in our primary schools to eliminate backwardness in reading as it is to spend it at the other end of the scale.

. . . We have been criticised because there is no mention of raising the school leaving age to sixteen. We want to raise the school leaving age to sixteen as soon as possible, but we would be burying our heads in the sand if we thought we could do that within the lifetime of the next Labour government . . .

[Turning to private education she said:] If we wanted to close all the public schools in the country we would have to pass an Act making it an offence to pay for any form of education, and that would lead to a black market in private tutors and lead to a privileged market in private tutors and lead to a privileged section of the community sending their children abroad (cries of 'No'). Let me remind conference that when we brought in the National Health Service it was not found possible by the government to close down the nursing homes at the same time. I would ask you, therefore, to reject the Edinburgh North resolution which asks for the Labour government to take over immediately all the public and private schools.

Hugh Gaitskell put forward a suggestion that we should integrate the public schools into our national system of education. He would make it a condition of their being kept open that a certain percentage, say 50 per cent or 60 per cent of the children in them would be, as it were, scholarship children from the county schools. The

177

National Executive considered this and we do not like the idea for various reasons. First of all, we should have to have some kind of selection. Secondly, can you really go to your local authorities and suggest to them that they spend £300, £400 or £500 a year on the education of selected children while you have got conditions such as we have got in the primary schools today?

There are some minor public schools only managing to keep open because local authorities are sending scholarship children to them, and why should we provide public money to bolster up a system with which we disagree? Therefore, we propose that local authorities should not any longer send children to public boarding schools. With respect to the public day schools there may be something in what Hugh Gaitskell said in trying eventually to take over and integrate some of the day schools into our school system.

Conference would be making a great mistake in thinking that the problem of the public and the private schools was the burning educational topic in our homes today. Mr and Mrs Brown, the ordinary parents of this country, do not feel aggrieved because their Tommy goes to a council school while little Lord Pontalduke goes to Eton, but what does grieve them is that Jimmy Jones over the road has a scholarship to a grammar school while their Tommy has to stay in the modern school . . .

Winston Churchill retired on 5 April 1955, handing on the premiership to his Foreign Secretary, Anthony Eden, who took office on the following day. A 'give-away' Budget followed almost immediately on 19 April, cutting sixpence off income tax, and Eden called a general election for 26 May. Labour pledged to review the length of national service and to renationalise road transport, iron and steel, all just denationalised by the Conservatives. The Conservatives boasted that they had built 300,000 houses a year, ended food rationing and created a more affluent society in which numbers of private cars rose by one third and television licensees from just over one million to 4.5 million. Labour, claimed the Conservatives, might reintroduce food rationing. Labour bitterly denied this and poured scorn on 'Tory talk of a property-owning democracy', but to no avail: this time Labour was defeated definitively. On a reduced poll the Conservatives secured 13.3 million votes to Labour's 12.4 million (49.7 per cent to 46.4 per cent). The Liberals, although dented by the defection to Labour of their former deputy leader Megan Lloyd George, retained 722,000 votes and six MPs. This gave the Conservative government an overall majority of 59. The 1955 election was the first in which television had played a really important role, and the contrast between the septuagenarian Attlee and the glamorous and comparatively youthful Conservative Prime Minister Anthony Eden, every inch the matinee idol, could not have been more stark. Hugh Dalton was one of many who believed that the time had come for Labour's younger generation to take over and launched what he modestly called 'Operation Avalanche', publishing a letter calling for the retirement of all the older generation of the shadow Cabinet, including himself. Chuter Ede in particular was furious at being 'bounced' by Dalton, but he, Manny Shinwell, Glenvil Hall and Attlee's loyal Chief Whip Will Whiteley all followed Dalton into retirement on the backbenches. Attlee still did not retire and Morrison, five years younger than Attlee and until now heir apparent, was now 67. With a solid Conservative working majority an election could be five years away. Morrison's erstwhile supporters began anxiously to ask themselves whether he would be up to leading Labour to victory at the age of 72 and then forming a government. Moreover, Morrison was losing his sureness of touch at the despatch box.

On 31 October 1955 Morrison's rambling Commons performance, 'almost inconceivably bad'[167] according to Hugh Dalton, opening a censure debate on the government's autumn emergency Budget, earned him media brickbats. 'He has taken a sudden dive out of the running for the succession,' from which it would be 'impossible' to recover, wrote the *Sunday Times* of 6 November.

Hugh Gaitskell had for many years been one of Herbert Morrison's strongest supporters. During 1952 he, along with fellow front benchers Alf Robens and Richard Stokes, had actually suggested to Attlee that he stand aside for Morrison, a proposal to which Attlee had apparently acceded and then reneged. The younger lions in the Parliamentary Labour Party had not known Morrison in his prime and some, particularly the young Fabian intellectuals such as Roy Jenkins, Tony Crosland and Woodrow Wyatt, preferred Gaitskell's youthful radicalism to Morrison's rhetoric of 'consolidation'. By 1955, Gaitskell's support had grown across the party. He had trounced Bevan for the party treasurership at the 1954 conference by more than two million votes and came equal top in the shadow Cabinet elections at the beginning of the parliamentary session.

At Labour's 1955 conference Herbert Morrison attacked left-wing activists who gave 'the impression that the Labour Party is a party without a policy and without a philosophy . . . [and tried to] divide the conference into socialists and non-socialists'. In his own speech to the same conference, Gaitskell took up the baton, departing from his notes to speak off the cuff and from the heart, declaring himself a socialist 'in warmer fashion than the Bevanite propaganda had prepared people's minds for', wrote Dalton.[168] Gaitskell was 'emotional and completely personal, removing rank and file worries that he might be a "desiccated calculating machine"', and receiving the greatest ovation of the conference:[169]

> I would like to tell you, if I may, why I am a socialist and have been for some 30 years.
> I became a socialist quite candidly not so much because I was a passionate advocate of
> public ownership but because at a very early age I came to hate and loathe social injustice, because I disliked the class structure of our society, because I could not tolerate
> the indefensible differences of status and income which disfigure our society. I hated
> the insecurity that affected such a large part of our community while others led lives

of security and comfort. I became a socialist because I hated poverty and squalor.

We in the Labour movement can be proud of what we have done in these 50 years to remedy these ills, but do not let us make the mistake of supposing that all is over. I want to see – and I am a socialist because I want to see – a society of equal men and women. As was said in a very fine sermon last Sunday, it may be that men are not equal in all respects but they are all equally men. I want to see a society in which the rewards correspond to some generally accepted criterion of merit. Pay people more if they do harder, more dangerous, and even more responsible work; pay people more if they have larger families. But the rewards should not be, as they still are, dependent upon the accident of whether you happen to be born of wealthy parents or not. I want to see our socialist society because, as Jim Griffiths said, I want to see everybody have an opportunity to develop his or her personality to the full. I am a socialist because I want to see fellowship, or if you prefer it, fraternity, that kind of relationship, not easy to describe though we know what it means, existing in our country more and more. And I want to see all this achieved by democracy, by our democratic processes which we have won in this country. I want to see them achieved without in any way departing from the liberties we cherish. I want to see all this not only in our country but over the world as a whole.

These to me are the socialist ideals. Nationalisation, as Jim said the other day, to me at any rate is a means and not an end in itself. It is a vital means, but it is only one of the means by which we can achieve these objects. It is in that spirit that we should look at this. If you look at the party constitution, just in case anybody wants to remember what it actually says, you will find among the seven objects this one: 'To secure for the workers by hand or brain the full fruits of their industry and the most equitable distribution thereof that may be possible upon the basis of the common ownership of the means of production,' and so on. The first part of that sentence is the object itself and the common ownership of the means of production is the means.

I hope that nobody is going to accuse me of betraying anything. I know that that is said; it is said in one of these resolutions, but I cannot feel that there is any betrayal if we think hard about our faith. I believe our faith is strong enough to bear thinking about. I would say that it would be a betrayal if we on this platform, whom you have elected to guide the party, were deliberately to confuse the issue, to mislead you, to hide from you the difficulties and problems that we face. If we were to do that, that would be a betrayal of trust. We do not intend to do it. We say let the clear fresh wind of hard and fearless thinking blow though our minds and hearts. It is in this spirit that we believe that this inquiry must be conducted and it is in that spirit that we commend to the conference these resolutions (*loud and prolonged applause*).

The left were livid, some walking out of the hall. Bevan was seen 'red faced and furious at the back of the hall muttering "sheer demagogy, sheer demagogy"'.[170] Many of Morrison's erstwhile supporters were now looking to Gaitskell as the surest bet not only to beat Bevan for the leadership, but also, being 20 years younger than Morrison, to keep

Bevan out for the longer term. Patrick Gordon Walker, a fellow shadow Cabinet member and ex-Morrison PPS, confided to his diary what must have been the private thoughts of many of Morrison's protégés: 'I have decided to back Gaitskell . . . I dearly love Herbert . . . But I have gradually changed my mind . . . We cannot miss the chance to kill Bevan. If Herbert has the leadership, Bevan will be able to challenge in three or four years. That would be fatal for us electorally. Morrison is undoubtedly failing both mentally and physically. He still has deep knowledge of the movement which Gaitskell lacks. But . . . in Parliament, his performances of late have been horrible.'[171] In the leadership ballot when it finally came, following Attlee's eventual retirement that December, Hugh Gaitskell, an MP for a bare ten years, became the youngest party leader of the century, winning with an overall majority of 157 MPs on the first ballot. Bevan had secured the votes of 70 MPs and Morrison, acting leader during the contest itself, a mere 40. Gaitskell invited Morrison to continue as his deputy, but Morrison knew in his heart that it was the end politically. On 2 February 1956 James Griffiths defeated Nye Bevan in the contest to succeed him and was elected Labour's new deputy leader by 141 votes to 111.

TWENTY-NINE

Suez 1956–57

*'The law of the jungle has been invoked by the
British government and the Russians are following suit'*

While foreign and defence policy had provided so much of the ammunition for the growing feud between Labour's right and left, beginning in 1956 it was also to provide the arena for the development of a shared sense of purpose between their two great gladiators, Hugh Gaitskell and Aneurin Bevan. The catalyst was the Suez crisis. 'The speeches of Gaitskell and Bevan throughout the crisis – the combination of Gaitskell's relentless, passionate marshalling of the whole legal and moral case against the government's expedition to Suez and Bevan's sardonic and reflective commentary upon it – complemented one another,' wrote Michael Foot in his biography of Bevan, 'and constitute together the most brilliant display of opposition in recent parliamentary history.'[172]

The Suez crisis was precipitated by Colonel Abdel Nasser, who had appointed himself Egypt's Prime Minister in 1954. A pan-Arab nationalist, he denounced the alliances of other Arab states with the West and sought to unite them against Israel. In 1955 Nasser began to purchase Soviet arms; Britain and the USA nevertheless continued to try and offer him a stake in alliance with the West, financing the construction of the Aswan hydroelectric dam. However, when Egypt recognised Communist China and announced that it had consulted Moscow on alternative and potentially cheaper financing for the Aswan dam, the USA and UK cancelled their loan offer. A few days later, on 22 July 1956, informed by the Soviet Ambassador that no firm offer had been made to build the dam, Nasser suddenly found himself without funds. Days later he announced that he had solved his problem by seizing control of the Suez Canal. British politicians and public were incensed. *The Times* was mistaken in its smug prediction that the Egyptians would be unable to work the canal. Within days the Cabinet's Egypt subcommittee had decided that force would be necessary to bring down Nasser and secure a pro-Western Egyptian government who would hand back the canal. The French government was in agreement: they were enraged at Nasser's declaration of support for Algerian rebels at war with France. Israel was another ally, angered by Nasser's blockade of Eilat, Israel's port on the Gulf of Aquaba, by Nasser's prohibition of Israeli shipping from using the Suez Canal, and by Egyptian-backed terrorist attacks.

US President Eisenhower, sensitised to his impending re-election in November, made clear his opposition to the use of force. US Secretary of State John Foster Dulles favoured persuading Nasser to accept that the canal be run by an international users' consortium. Gaitskell and Bevan agreed and wanted Britain to work with America at the UN to secure a solution. Eden, however, chose to disregard US concerns: he planned to present them with a *fait accompli*. Together with France and Israel, Eden hatched a clandestine plan under which Israel would invade the Sinai to provide a pretext for an Anglo-French 'peace-making' force to occupy the canal zone.

On 29 October the plan was set in motion by an Israeli offensive against Egyptian military positions in the Sinai Desert. An Anglo-French carrier force had already began sailing towards Egypt from Malta two days previously. On 30 October an Anglo-French ultimatum was delivered demanding that both Egypt and Israel withdraw their forces ten miles from either side of the canal, but, as Conservative minister Anthony Nutting later admitted, 'The thing was quite ridiculous, because when we issued our ultimatum . . . the Israelis still had another forty or fifty miles to go to get to the canal and the Egyptians were still in contact with the Israelis on the Eastern side of the canal.'[173] As expected, Nasser rejected the ultimatum and on 31 October Anglo-French bombers destroyed the Egyptian air force, comprising some 260 Soviet-supplied aircraft, on the ground. Nasser thereupon withdrew his forces from Sinai to more central positions and within 48 hours Nasser had sunk 47 blockships in the canal, scotching the pretext for Anglo-French intervention to keep open the canal. Nasser also cut the oil pipeline to Syria, a crucial British fuel source.

On 1 November Eden told the Commons, 'The first and urgent task is to separate these combatants and to stabilise the position . . . police action there must be to separate the belligerents.' The following day the UN General Assembly passed a resolution calling for all parties involved in hostilities, including Britain and France, to agree an immediate cease-fire and halt the movement of military forces into the area. This Eden refused to accept. Anglo-French military action was necessary to station troops 'between the combatants', he insisted to the Commons on 3 November, until and unless a UN peace-keeping force was constituted to take over. Gaitskell attacked Eden in the Commons for undermining the UN and called for Conservative MPs to depose him.

On Sunday 4 November Nye Bevan addressed a crowd of thirty thousand in Trafalgar Square. Highlighting Eden's claim to have acted to preserve free passage of the canal, and the fact that Nasser's immediate reaction had been to sink blockships, Bevan declared:

> If Sir Anthony is sincere in what he says – and he may be – then he is too s-s-s-stupid to be Prime Minister. He is either a knave or a fool, and in either capacity we don't want him. The government has besmirched the name of Britain, they have offended against every sense of decency . . .[174] I am not saying that the United States is blameless.

I have been spending the last five years blaming them for a number of things. I am not saying – and let us get this right – that because Eden is wrong, Nasser is right. I am not saying that the Israelis did not have the utmost provocation. What we are saying is, that it is not possible to create peace in the Middle East by jeopardising the peace of the world . . . We are stronger than Egypt but there are other countries stronger than us. Are we prepared to accept for ourselves the logic we are applying to Egypt? If nations more powerful than ourselves accept this anarchistic attitude and launch bombs on London, what answer have we got?[175]

Not everyone agreed. British public opinion was largely behind Anglo-French action in standing up to Nasser, and so were some Labour figures, particularly of the older generation, such as both Herbert Morrison and Manny Shinwell. 'We have managed to give the impression that the party is anti-British, and pro-every foreign country, which is an unfair exaggeration. Sometimes the British are wrong, and it is necessary to say so with intelligent and constructive criticism expressed in sorrow, not with pleasure,' wrote Morrison.[176] Troops in the invasion fleet were incensed when Hugh Gaitskell's broadcast calling for Eden to resign was relayed to them over the ships' tannoys as they prepared to land on hostile shores and possibly to die for their country.

But British public opinion didn't know the truth: they had been denied knowledge of the secret conspiracy and were unaware of the precarious nature of the enterprise. Conservative ministers Edward Boyle and Anthony Nutting could see the iceberg ahead and told Eden that they were going to resign. Eden's press secretary William Clark resigned after having refused Eden's instruction to brief the press that Nutting was 'terribly under the influence of his American mistress and anyway was not quite himself nowadays',[177] describing his Prime Minister to psephologist David Butler as 'a criminal lunatic'.[178] Clark was speeded on his way, it is said, by a flying prime ministerial inkpot.[179] Eden himself, assisted by prodigious quantities of amphetamines, tried to carry on. But it couldn't carry on. Britain's policy was in a mess, and while Eden had been creating his mess, as many as thirty thousand people were dying, crushed by the troops, tanks and bombers of the Soviet Union, sent into Budapest to remove the reformist regime of Imre Nagy. Nagy had announced Hungary's neutrality and appealed for United Nations intervention, but the West had not responded. 'Port Said fell to the British and French troops on the same day as Budapest fell to the Red Army', recalled Denis Healey, 'I asked Eden if he had exchanged congratulations with Bulganin. While I was driving to a protest meeting in York against Suez, I heard on the car radio that last broken appeal from Hungary for help from the West. I had to pull into the side of the road until I had stopped weeping.'[180]

'We had world opinion overwhelmingly against us, Commonwealth opinion, American opinion – our own allies wanted us to stop,'[181] recalled Edward Boyle. Eden's government also faced Soviet threats to launch missiles against London and send 'volunteers' to Egypt unless the fighting stopped, a run on the pound, a consequent drain of UK gold reserves and threats from an irate American administration to block support from the International Monetary Fund. During November the UK lost some 15 per cent of its total gold and dollar reserves. Eden's Chancellor, Harold Macmillan, now swung from hawk to dove: Eden had lost his most crucial Cabinet ally. Moreover, by the time British ground troops actually arrived in Egypt at dawn on 6 November, after a six-day voyage from Malta, Egyptian and Israeli forces were no longer fighting or on the canal. That same day, 6 November, the day of the US presidential election, Eden had to telephone the French Prime Minister, Guy Mollet, to inform him of the Cabinet's decision to announce a cease-fire from midnight. The French government was furious at being let down by their ally, but knowing that to continue fighting alone was impossible, reluctantly agreed. The Anglo-French were still 75 miles from Suez. In the Commons debate that afternoon, Hugh Gaitskell gave what is widely acknowledged to be his most masterly speech of the crisis, calling for an immediate cease-fire and a reversal of government policy. 'This was on all counts one of the two most powerful speeches I heard in my thirty years in Parliament,' recalled Douglas Jay, 'It was one of those very rare speeches which left its hearers of all kinds with the conviction that the government's policy simply could not be continued.'[182] And the plaudits came not just from self-styled young 'Gaitskellites': 'Bevan was also impressed, as who could not be,' wrote Michael Foot, 'by the revelation of the iron in Gaitskell's character; somehow what formerly looked like obduracy was transformed into shining courage'.[183]

... The Prime Minister, in his broadcast on Saturday night, said for the first time that it was the intention of Her Majesty's government to make the Israeli forces go back within their own territory, and that was repeated yesterday by the Foreign Secretary in this House. I wish to ask a number of questions about that important statement ... Why, if this was our view last Tuesday, did we not merely refrain from mentioning it at the Security Council but refuse to accept the original resolution before the Security Council, which called upon the Israeli forces to withdraw within their own territory?

If we had done that ... we could then have gone on to propose that there should immediately be set up a United Nations force to see that it was carried out.

We could, indeed, with our hands clean, have offered to take part in that United Nations force. All that would have made sense; all that would have been acting, not on our own, but on behalf of the United Nations; all that would have been genuinely a police action and not aggression. Alas, that was not what happened ...

Why, if, indeed, the object of continuing hostilities in the Canal Zone is to drive back or force back the Israeli troops, are we attacking Egypt? What conceivable justification can there be, if one says that one intends to bring about a withdrawal of a force, which has undoubtedly invaded another country, for attacking the country, which has been invaded ...

What are we accomplishing by continuing with this war at the gigantic cost of destroying our reputation in the world by three times defying resolutions carried by large majorities in the United Nations?

So far as oil supplies are concerned, we have lost heavily and, above all – in my opinion perhaps the worst consequence of all – we have split the British Commonwealth. Now, on top of this, in these last 24 hours – less – there is the Russian threat of intervention.

[Turning to Hungary, he said:] Yesterday in this House there were some bitter exchanges about the part which our adventure in Egypt has played in this matter . . . I would not claim that what the Russians did was wholly determined by our action . . . But . . . if, by that intervention in Egypt and all that it implied, in any way whatever we tilted the balance or influenced the Russians to suppress the Hungarian national revolt, nothing can excuse it. I know that hon. members are with me when I say that this Hungarian revolt was the most hopeful, encouraging and heart-raising event since 1945. But if in any way we destroyed it, we are profoundly guilty . . .

I wish to make it absolutely clear that we on these benches cannot for one moment accept the hypocritical, indeed the odious, claim that Soviet Russia, which has invaded and suppressed Hungary, has any moral right in the Middle East to talk about withstanding aggression. What has happened? The truth of the matter is that the law of the jungle has been invoked by the British government and the Russians are following suit (*Hon. members:* 'Oh'). But the jungle is a dangerous place and we are beginning to realise that there are much more dangerous animals wandering about than Great Britain or France.

In his broadcast the Prime Minister said that we went in to stop the forest fire from spreading. Mr Speaker that fire is spreading with appalling rapidity. It has spread to Hungary (*Hon. members:* 'Nonsense'). Our spark was sufficient, perhaps, to cause the Russian invasion of Hungary. It is spreading through the Middle East. Do hon. members realise the gravity of the situation? Do they realise why the Prime Minister and the Foreign Secretary are not here? It is because those right hon. gentlemen realise it. They understand. This forest fire may engulf all of us and destroy our civilisation unless action is taken quickly . . .

We must – I make this appeal hon. gentlemen – somehow or other stand together with our allies, with the vast majority of the United Nations, and with the free nations of the world, and lend all our moral authority in dealing with the Hungarian question.

Only one thing can achieve this object and that is to go back to the principles which we abandoned last week, to call off the fighting in Egypt, to obey at last and this late moment, the cease-fire resolution of the United Nations, to withdraw our forces as soon as possible, give up taking the law into our own hands and to give our full support for the new international police force without quibble or conditions. Let us go back into line with our friends and allies, and save our reputation and the peace of the world.

On 23 November 1956 Eden left Britain to recuperate at James Bond author Ian Fleming's Goldeneye retreat in Jamaica. He had had a breakdown from which his political career would never recover. Denis Healey was told 'by an official friend of mine, who saw him regularly during the crisis that [Eden] would respond to a question simply by gibbering'.[184] On 3 December, with Eden still in Jamaica, the Conservative Foreign Secretary Selwyn Lloyd announced to the Commons the unconditional withdrawal of British troops from Egypt. Despite all the obvious evidence to the contrary, the Conservatives still denied collusion between Britain, France and Israel. Nye Bevan, whom Gaitskell had appointed shadow Foreign Secretary the previous month, spoke in the debate that followed: 'in his speech on 5 December – regarded by many who heard it as the greatest of his life – Bevan welded the scattered indictment into a single glittering synthesis; the wit merged with the wisdom and the wisdom with the wit, like two edges to the same sword'.[185]

The reasons Eden had given for making war had kept changing over time, Bevan began:

On 30 October, the Prime Minister said that the purpose was, first, 'to seek to separate the combatants'; second, 'to remove the risk to free passage through the canal'. The speech we have heard today is the first speech in which that subject has been dropped. Every other statement made on this matter since the beginning has always contained a reference to the future of the canal as one of Her Majesty's government's objectives, in fact, as an object of war, to coerce Egypt . . . One does not fire in order merely to have a cease-fire. One would have thought that the cease-fire was consequent upon having fired in the first place. It could have been accomplished without starting. The other objective set out on 30 October was 'to reduce the risk . . . to those voyaging through the canal' [*Official Report*, 30 October 1956, Vol. 558, c. 1347].

We have heard from the right hon. and learned gentleman today a statement which I am quite certain all the world will read with astonishment. He has said that when we landed in Port Said there was already every reason to believe that both Egypt and Israel had agreed to cease fire.

The Minister of Defence (Mr Anthony Head) indicated dissent.

Mr Bevan: The Minister shakes his head. If he will recollect what his right hon. and learned friend said, it was that there was still a doubt about the Israeli reply. Are we really now telling this country and the world that all these calamitous consequences have been brought down upon us merely because of a doubt? That is what he said.

Surely, there was no need. We had, of course, done the bombing, but our ships were still going through the Mediterranean. We had not arrived at Port Said. The exertions of the United Nations had already gone far enough to be able to secure from Israel and Egypt a promise to cease fire, and all that remained to be cleared up was an ambiguity about the Israeli reply. In these conditions, and against the background of these events, the invasion of Egypt still continued. In the history of nations, there is no example of such frivolity . . .

As to the objective of removing the risk to free passage through the canal, I must confess that I have been astonished at this also. We sent an ultimatum to Egypt by which we told her that unless she agreed to our landing in Ismailia, Suez and Port Said, we should make war upon her . . . Is our information from Egypt so bad that we did not know that an ultimatum of that sort was bound to consolidate [Nasser's] position in Egypt and in the whole Arab world? . . .

Did we really believe that Nasser was going to wait for us to arrive? He did what anybody would have thought he would do, and if the government did not think he would do it, on that account alone they ought to resign. He sank ships in the canal, the wicked man. What did hon. gentleman opposite expect him to do? The result is that, in fact, the first objective realised was the opposite to the one we set out to achieve; the canal was blocked, and is still blocked . . .

On 1 November, we were told the reason was 'to stop hostilities' and 'prevent a resumption of them' [*Official Report*, 1 November 1956, Vol. 558. c. 1653].

But hostilities had already been practically stopped. On 3 November, our objectives became much more ambitious – 'to deal with all the outstanding problems in the Middle East' – [*Official Report*, 3 November 1956, Vol. 558, c. 1867].

In the famous book *Madame Bovary* there is a story of a woman who goes from one sin to another, a long story of moral decline. In this case, our ambitions soar the farther away we are from realising them. Our objective was, 'to deal with all the outstanding problems in the Middle East'.

After having outraged our friends, after having insulted the United States, after having affronted all our friends in the Commonwealth, after having driven the whole of the Arab world into one solid phalanx, at least for the moment, behind Nasser, we were then going to deal with all the outstanding problems in the Middle East . . .

The next objective of which we were told was to ensure that the Israeli forces withdrew from Egyptian territory. That, I understand, is what we were there for. We went into Egyptian territory in order to establish our moral right to make the Israelis clear out of Egyptian territory. That is a remarkable war aim, is it not? In order that we might get Israel out, we went in. To establish our case before the eyes of the world, Israel being the wicked invader, we, of course, being the nice friend of Egypt, went to protect her from the Israelis, but unfortunately, we had to bomb the Egyptians first.

On 6 November, the Prime Minister said: 'The action we took has been an essential condition for . . . a United Nations force to come into the Canal Zone itself' [*Official Report*, 6 November 1956, Vol. 559, c. 80].

That is one of the most remarkable claims of all, and it is one of the main claims made by right hon. and hon. members opposite. It is, of course, exactly the same claim which might have been made, if they had thought about it in time, by Mussolini and Hitler, that they made war on the world in order to call the United Nations into being. If it were possible for bacteria to argue with each other, they would be able to say that of course their chief justification was the advancement of medical science.

As *The Times* has pointed out, the arrival of the United Nations Force could not be regarded as a war aim by the government; it called it, 'an inadvertence'. That is not my description; it is *The Times*. It was a by-product of the action both of Her Majesty's government and of the United Nations itself . . .

[Bevan then turned to the accusation of 'collusion':] If collusion can be established, the whole fabric of the government's case falls to the ground, and they know this . . . It is believed in the United States and it is believed by large numbers of people in Great Britain that we were well aware that Israel was going to make the attack on Egypt. In fact, very few of the activities at the beginning of October are credible except upon the assumption that the French and British governments knew that something was going to happen in Egypt.

Indeed, the right hon. and learned gentleman has not been frank with the House. We have asked him over and over again. He has said, 'Ah, we did not conspire with France and Israel.' We never said that the government might have conspired. What we said was that they might have known about it. The right hon. and learned gentleman gave the House the impression that at no time had he ever warned Israel against attacking Egypt . . .

The fact is that all these long telephone conversations and conferences between M. Guy Mollet, M. Pineau and the Prime Minister are intelligible only on the assumption that something was being cooked up. All that was left to do, as far as we knew from the facts at that time, was to pick up negotiations at Geneva about the future of the canal, as had been arranged by the United Nations. But all the time there was this coming and going between ourselves and the French government.

Did the French know? It is believed in France that the French knew about the Israeli intention. If the French knew, did they tell the British government? We would like to know. Did M. Guy Mollet, on the 16 October, tell the British Prime Minister that he expected that there was to be an attack on Egypt? Every circumstantial fact that we know points to that conclusion. For instance, Mr Ben Gurion, the Israeli Prime Minister, had already made it clear in the Knesset on several occasions that Israel regarded Egypt as the real enemy, not Jordan. Therefore, a warning not to attack Jordan was not relevant. At the same time, many Israelis were saying that at last Israel had got a reliable friend.

What happened? Did Marianne take John Bull to an unknown rendezvous? Did Marianne say to John Bull that there was a forest fire going to start, and did John Bull then say, 'We ought to put it out,' but Marianne said, 'No, let us warm our hands by it. It is a nice fire'? Did Marianne deceive John Bull or seduce him?

Now, of course, we come to the ultimate end. It is at the end of all these discussions that the war aim of the government now becomes known. Of course, we knew it all the time. We knew where they would land. After this long voyaging, getting almost wrecked several times, they have come to safe harbour. It was a red peril all the time. It was Russia all the time. It was not to save the canal. The hon. member who interjected has been deceived all the time. It was not the canal, it was the red peril which they had unmasked. The government suspected it before, said the right hon. and learned gentleman, about the arms to Egypt . . . I think that the Russians ought not to have done it and I will say further that I think that Nasser ought not to have invited them.

189

It seems to me – and here I probably shall carry hon. members opposite with me – that Nasser has not been behaving in the spirit of the Bandung Conference which he joined, because what he did was not to try to reduce the temperature of the cold war: what he did was to exploit it for Egyptian purposes. Therefore, Nasser's hands are not clean by any means. I have said this before. I said it in Trafalgar Square. We must not believe that because the Prime Minister is wrong Nasser is right. That is not the view on this side of the House.

What has deeply offended us is that such wrongs as Nasser has done, and such faults as he has, have been covered by the bigger blunders of the British government. That is what vexes us. We are satisfied that the arts of diplomacy would have brought Nasser to where we wanted to get him, which was to agree about the free passage of ships through the canal, on the civilised ground that a riparian nation has got no absolute rights over a great waterway like the canal. That is a principle which has been accepted by India and by America and by most other nations. We have never taken the position that in the exercise of sovereign rights Egypt has the right to inflict a mortal wound upon the commerce of the world.

Mr Osborne: Will not the right hon. gentleman agree that six years of patient negotiation had not caused Nasser to allow the passage of Israeli ships?

Mr Bevan: Do not let the hon. members now bring to the forefront of the argument the fact that Egypt had not been allowing Israeli ships to go through the canal. If they thought so much of the seriousness of that, why did they not even invite Israel to the conference? It is not good enough to bring these things forward all the time as though they were the main objectives. Of course, we take the view that Egypt should permit the ships of all nations to pass through the canal . . .

It has been clear to us, and it is now becoming clear to the nation, that for many months past hon. members opposite have been harbouring designs of this sort. One of the reasons why we could not get a civilised solution of the Cyprus problem was that the government were harbouring designs to use Cyprus in the Middle East, unilaterally or in conjunction with France . . . We have had all these murders and all this terror, we have had all this unfriendship over Cyprus between ourselves and Greece, and we have been held up to derision in all the world merely because we contemplated using Cyprus as a base for going it alone in the Middle East. And we did go it alone. Look at the result. Was it not obvious to hon. members opposite that Great Britain could not possibly engage in a major military adventure without involving our NATO allies? . . .

Even if we had occupied Egypt by armed force we could not have secured the freedom of passage through the canal. It is clear that there is such xenophobia, that there is such passion, that there is such bitter feeling against Western imperialism – rightly or wrongly: I am not arguing the merits at the moment – among millions of people that they are not prepared to keep the arteries of European commerce alive and intact if they themselves want to cut them. We could not keep ships going through the canal. The canal is too easily sabotaged, if Egypt wants to sabotage it. Why on earth did we imagine that the objectives could be realised in that way in the middle of the twentieth century? . . .

Exactly the same thing is true of the Russians in Hungary. The Russians in Hungary are attempting to achieve civil, social and political objectives by tanks and guns, and the Hungarian people are demonstrating that it cannot be done.

The social furniture of modern society is so complicated and fragile that it cannot support the jackboot. We cannot run the processes of modern society by attempting to impose our will upon nations by armed force. If we have not learned that we have learned nothing. Therefore, from our point of view here, whatever may have been the morality of the government's action – and about that there is not doubt – there is no doubt about its imbecility. There is not the slightest shadow of doubt that we have attempted to use methods which were bound to destroy the objectives we had, and, of course, that is what we have discovered . . . How on earth do hon. members opposite imagine that hundreds of miles of pipeline can be kept open if the Arabs do not want it to be kept open? It is not enough to say that there are large numbers of Arabs who want the pipeline to be kept open because they live by it . . . I beg hon. members to turn their backs on this most ugly chapter and realise that if we are to live in the world and are to be regarded as a decent nation, decent citizens in the world, we have to act up to different standards than the one that we have been following in the last few weeks . . .

Chuter Ede, Attlee's former Home Secretary, called Bevan's speech 'for all who heard it the greatest parliamentary utterance to which they have listened', while for former Liberal deputy leader Megan Lloyd George it 'brought Violet Bonham Carter [Asquith's daughter] and me together in almost glowing unity in the gallery'. For the *Daily Mirror* it anointed Bevan as Britain's next Foreign Secretary.[186] Tony Benn recorded it in his diary as being 'the best speech I've heard from anyone. It was cool, calm and deadly.'[187] Though the Conservatives whipped their backbenchers to win the vote, their self-confidence began to desert them. Though Eden returned from Goldeneye on 14 December, his health did not return with him. On 9 January he tendered his resignation to the Queen, and the magic circle of senior Conservatives anointed Harold Macmillan as his successor.

THIRTY

Battling the Bomb 1957–58

'Naked into the conference chamber'

Under Clement Attlee's leadership, Labour had previously framed a compromise policy under which they supported making and possessing the H-bomb, but opposed actually testing it. The decision of Macmillan's new Conservative government in March 1957 to announce a series of tests on Christmas Island put Labour somewhat on the spot. The tests risked considerable health hazards and environmental damage, yet without them it would be difficult to be sure that the British H-bomb actually worked, potentially undermining its deterrent capability. The shadow Cabinet agreed to respond with a call for a temporary suspension of the tests while appealing to other countries to cancel theirs. Gaitskell confided to a friend, 'The H-bomb is an almost impossible subject for us . . . It is impossible to reach a real logical conclusion without splitting the party. So I am afraid we just have to go on with compromises . . . It is perfectly clear that the party much prefers this . . . to . . . a resumption of the trouble of a few years ago.'[188] But Gaitskell's hopes for unity were doomed, the instrument of their defenestration being one Frank Cousins, the new boss of Ernest Bevin's old TGWU.

That autumn, at Labour's annual conference in Brighton, Cousins would call from the conference platform for the unilateral nuclear disarmament in which he so fervently believed, despite being constrained by his union delegation from casting the block vote against the union's own non-unilateralist policy. 'The Big Fella', as he was known to many of his officials, 'dropped on an unsuspecting trade union movement like the H-bomb he so vehemently decried,' recalled John Grant, later an Employment Minister.[189] Cousins had been catapulted into office in May 1956 by the unexpected deaths in quick succession of Arthur Deakin and fellow Gaitskellite Jock Tiffin, who succeeded Deakin for only a few brief months. Tiffin was already terminally ill when he took office. Cousins was a self-proclaimed radical, opposed to wage restraint, industrial cooperation and nuclear weapons. It was two years before Cousins could change his own union's policy so that he could use the T&G as a battering ram for unilateral nuclear disarmament, and even then he did not actually secure an explicit endorsement of the unilateralist policy he desired.[190] Nevertheless, even in 1957, his rhetoric was as uncompromising as his convictions:

This country, if no other will do it, ought to take the moral lead . . . how can we be told that we would not use it, and at the same time we must have it in case we have to tell other people we would use it? . . . We must say that this nation, of all nations, great or small, however we may like to think of ourselves, does not approve of the maintenance and manufacture, either by ourselves or anyone else, of this idiot's weapon. There is no compromise with evil.

Other voices for unilateralism included future Cabinet minister Judith Hart, who insisted:

I have yet to find any evidence which is being produced to this Labour movement that a clear-cut decision to renounce the hydrogen bomb would do any damage to this party at the general election . . . I want to say . . . that if this party this morning does not renounce the hydrogen bomb we are being far more wicked than any member of the Tory Party, because there is not one of us in this conference hall, there is not one person on the platform or in the galleries who does not firmly believe that the hydro-gen bomb is an evil thing . . . I would appeal to you, no matter what arguments of com-plicated diplomacy are produced by Aneurin Bevan, to vote for the right thing to do.

The unilateralists spoke with passionate conviction, but their case was demolished by Bevan, who had visited the Crimea during September 1957 and was told by Khrushchev that British renunciation of the H-bomb would make no difference to the USSR. He began:

. . . There is no member of the Executive in favour of the hydrogen bomb. To state the argument as though we are divided among people who support the hydrogen bomb and those who are against the hydrogen bomb is completely to falsify the argument . . . for heaven's sake do not get into a false antithesis. [Bevan advocated an interna-tional nuclear test ban, declaring that] if there is a socialist government in Great Britain, Britain will take the initiative in suspending all tests. [A test ban, he argued, would be verifiable], although nations may say things other nations will not believe that they are doing what they are saying . . . But we would be believed if we decided to suspend the tests because that fact could be found out.

It has been said this morning, quite rightly, that the suspension of the tests would itself mean, so long as they were suspended, that we would not be able to go on making nuclear weapons. That is all right, isn't it? Nothing wrong with that, is there? It meets both points, doesn't it? What we would then be hoping for, very much hoping for, is that in the climate of opinion created by that fact it would be possible for the other countries to follow our example and by the relaxation of tension that would be then produced we could proceed to further stages of disarmament.

One of the greatest difficulties about the talks in the past has been that they have attempted to put too much in the package deal which other nations would not accept . . . if you try to go too far you will get nowhere, but if you do take practical action on a limited area of agreement, when that has been accomplished further action may become possible . . .

I saw in the newspapers the other day that some of my actions could be explained only on the basis that I was anxious to become Foreign Secretary. I am bound to say that is a pretty bitter one to say to me. If I thought for one simple moment that that consideration prevented the intelligent appreciation of this problem, I would take unilateral action myself, now. Is it necessary to recall to those who said 'Hear, hear' that I myself threw up office a few years ago? And I will not take office under any circumstances to do anything that I do not believe I should do.

But if you carry this resolution and follow out all its implications and do not run away from it you will send a British Foreign Secretary, whoever he may be, naked into the conference chamber. Able to preach sermons, of course; he could make good sermons. But action of that sort is not necessarily the way in which you take the menace of this bomb from the world. It might be that action of that sort will still be there available to us if our other actions fail. It is something you can always do. You can always, if the influence you have upon your allies and upon your opponents is not yielding any fruits, take unilateral action of that sort. (*A cry of* 'Do it now.') 'Do it now,' you say. This is the answer I give from the platform. Do it now at a Labour Party conference? You cannot do it now. It is not in your hands to do it. All you can do is pass a resolution. What you are saying is what was said by our friend from Hampstead, that a British Foreign Secretary gets up in the United Nations, without consultation – mark this; this is a responsible attitude! – without telling any members of the Commonwealth, without connecting with them, that the British Labour movement decides unilaterally that this country contracts out of all its commitments and obligations entered into with other countries and members of the Commonwealth – without consultation at all. And you call that statesmanship? I call it an emotional spasm.

Comrades, if that it what you mean, you ought to have said it, but you have not said it. It has not been said in the resolution at all. It has been brought out in the debate. It has not been carefully considered. It has all been considered merely as a byproduct of an argument about the hydrogen bombs.

If we contracted out, if we produced this diplomatic shambles it would not necessarily follow that this country would be safer from the hydrogen bomb. (*Cries of* 'Nehru has no bomb.') No. Nehru has no bomb, but he has got all the other weapons he wants. Nehru has no bomb, but ask Nehru to disband the whole of his police forces in relation to Pakistan and see what Nehru will tell you.

The main difficulty we are in here is that in this way we shall precipitate a difficult situation with the nations that are now associated with us in a variety of treaties and alliances, most of which I do not like – I would like to substitute for them other treaties more sensible and more civilised and not chaos and a shamble. If any socialist Foreign Secretary is to have a chance he must be permitted to substitute good policies for bad policies. Do not disarm him diplomatically, intellectually, and in every other way before he has a chance to turn round.

This country could be destroyed merely as an incident of a war between Russia and the USA. It is not necessary for any bombs to drop on us. If war broke out between the USA and the Soviet Union, this country would be poisoned with the rest of mankind. What we have, therefore, to consider is how far the policies we are considering this morning can exert an influence and leverage over the policies of the USA and of the Soviet Union.

I do seriously believe in the rejection of the bomb. But that is not the issue. That is what I am telling you . . . Are we thinking merely in terms of stronger and stronger resolutions accompanied by no action at all? If I may be permitted to strike a facetious note, it is like the comedian in the music hall who told his wife he was going to give her a bicycle. 'But,' she said, 'you promised me that the week before and the week before last.' He said, 'I'm a man of my word. I will promise it you next week too.' It is no use here, because we have passed a resolution, to pass a stronger one when the weaker one itself has not been started . . .

Clem Attlee pointed out in the House of Commons that greater than the danger of the existence of these deadly weapons is the problem of anticipation. You have already had articles written in the newspapers by soldiers. You had an article the other day in the *Telegraph* in which a soldier pointed out that the decision to use this bomb will never be a decision taken by parliaments; it will not even be a decision taken by an individual man who, acting upon some report of some of his spies, maybe by telephone tapping, will have been made to fear that the other chap is going to drop his bomb. (*A cry of* 'Do not give it to him.') We do not give it to him. He has got it. And we are not speaking about our bomb, we are speaking about their bomb.

A Voice: Give an example.

Mr Bevan: All right. We are endeavouring to. I am endeavouring to face you with the fact that the most important feature of this problem is not what we are going to do in this country, because that lies within our control. What we have to discuss is what is the consequence of the action upon other nations with far more deadly weapons than we have. I do beg and pray the conference to reconsider its mood on this matter, and to try and provide us with a workable policy, with a policy which in the consequence I believe will be more effective in getting rid of the bomb than resolution 24 if it is carried.

In fact I would say this; I would make this statement. I have thought about this very anxiously. I knew this morning that I was going to make a speech that would offend and even hurt many of my friends. Of course. But do you think I am afraid? I shall say what I believe, and I will give the guidance, and I do not care what happens. But I will tell you this, that in my opinion, in carrying out resolution 24, with all the implications I have pointed out, you will do more to precipitate incidents that might easily lead to a third world war – (*Cries of* 'Rubbish,' 'Oh,' and 'Shame'). Just listen. Just consider for a moment all the little nations running one here and one there, one running to Russia the other to the USA, all once more clustering under the castle wall, this castle wall, or the other castle wall, because in that situation before anything else would have happened the world would have been polarised between the Soviet Union on one side and the USA on the other. It is against that deadly dangerous negative polarisation that we have been fighting for years. We want to have the opportunity of interposing between those two giants modifying, moderating, and mitigating influences . . .

I am convinced, profoundly convinced, that nothing would give more anxiety to many people who do not share our political beliefs than if the British nation disengaged itself from its obligations and prevented itself from influencing the course of international affairs. I know that you are deeply convinced that the action that you suggest is the most effective way of influencing international affairs. I am deeply convinced that you are wrong. It is therefore not a question of who is in favour of the hydrogen bomb and who is against the hydrogen bomb, but a question of what is the most effective way of getting the damn thing destroyed . . .

The Bevanites were furious with their hero. In the adjournment afterwards Crossman 'told him that he wouldn't want me to say it was one of his best speeches but it was one of his greatest performances . . . when Barbara [Castle] and Ian [Mikardo] attacked him immediately afterwards he did not concede to them in any way'.[191] 'Bevan had rubbed the nose of conference in its own impotence,' wrote his biographer John Campbell; 'Their own Nye had dismissed the righteous aspirations of the left as so much hot air.'[192] His speech helped ensure the unilateralists' overwhelming defeat, by 5,836,000 votes to 781,000. It was 'Bevan into Bevin', observed the *Daily Telegraph* the following day. But Bevan had never actually been a unilateralist. He had not criticised the decision of the Attlee government, in which he had served, to manufacture the atomic bomb. He opposed a strategy which relied on the first use, or indeed the early use, of nuclear weapons in a crisis. And he sought a situation where agreement with the Soviet Union would be possible to achieve multilateral disarmament of nuclear weapons. He was, argues his biographer John Campbell, 'an orthodox multilateralist'.[193]

The unilateralists were not slow to regroup. In January 1958, Cannon Collins of St Paul's Cathedral and Bertrand Russell were to found the Campaign for Nuclear Disarmament. Initially 'a movement of eggheads for eggheads',[194] as the historian and supporter A. J. P. Taylor characterised it, it was swiftly to grow in strength. Its hallmark became the annual march from Aldermaston to Trafalgar Square. 'Heading the marches was always Michael Foot,' recalled Barbara Castle, 'accompanied by his shaggy white bitch Vanessa, of doubtful lineage but delightful temperament. I once told Michael I was reporting him to the RSPCA for making the dog walk eleven miles each day on hard tarmac, but he pooh-poohed the idea as he would pooh-pooh anything with which he disagreed, asserting that the dog revelled in every mile.'[195]

THIRTY-ONE

The Cost of Compromise 1956–58

'Between socialism and the betrayal of socialism'

Second only to defence as an area of potential controversy during 1956–57 was the question of public ownership. To examine the issue properly, a policy committee on nationalisation had been established by Labour's 1956 conference. Chaired by deputy leader James Griffiths, its members included Harold Wilson. Its report, *Industry and Society*, was as Gaitskell's official biographer has pointed out, 'precisely the kind of intellectually inglorious but politically convenient compromise of which Gaitskell was later supposedly incapable'.[196] Accepted unanimously by Labour's NEC, it pledged to renationalise steel and road haulage and 'to extend public ownership in any industry or part of industry which, after thorough enquiry, is found to be seriously failing the nation', but through government share purchasing instead of wholesale nationalisation. *Industry and Society*, jointly endorsed as it was by both Hugh Gaitskell and Aneurin Bevan, was the first specific and clearly conceived party statement on public ownership since the 1940s.

Despite best efforts, it soon became clear that it would not secure a universal welcome at party conference. The ageing Herbert Morrison, by now well past his prime, felt that the new policy implied criticism of Labour's previous approach to nationalisation which of course he himself had framed. Moreover, with the approach of the annual conference and the NEC elections, Barbara Castle and Ian Mikardo, both left-wing NEC members, discovered that the policy which they had approved was in fact a betrayal of socialism by the right-wing leadership. Gaitskell was furious, telling Dick Crossman: 'If they can't stand by a document which, like *Industry and Society*, they have helped to draft on the NEC, he wouldn't trust them in a Cabinet.'[197]

At the 1957 party conference, Jim Campbell of the National Union of Railwaymen (NUR) proposed a resolution rejecting *Industry and Society* and calling instead for a 'shopping list' of industries to be nationalised by the next Labour government: 'Why has nationalisation, almost overnight, become a dirty word? . . . Inject into the document the rich red blood of socialist objective and swing the electorate solidly behind you,' he demanded. Herbert Morrison urged the approach he himself had wanted in the early 1950s, not a shopping list, which he opposed, but an agreed set of criteria for nationalisation on which a Labour government would then be free to act. *Industry and Society* was 'trying to please so many wings of the movement that it will have no wings to fly with itself', and he opposed it. Jennie Lee announced that in agreeing with her old adversary Herbert Morrison 'I am beginning to feel like Alice in Wonderland.' Ian Mikardo's then secretary Jo Richardson[198] spoke for a resolution proposed by Hornsey Constituency Labour Party demanding a 'shopping list' but continued: 'You know, we are not perhaps so concerned about having an actual list. What we are afraid of is that when the next Labour government gets into power it will not even go shopping.' It was fundamentally a question of trust and the old fear of leadership betrayal. Arthur Woodburn, who had been Attlee's Secretary of State for Scotland during 1947–50, confronted it head-on:

> I am sorry to see that there is such a lack of confidence in the people that you have just elected as your leaders, that you should think they are going to betray the socialist promise whenever they get into power and that we must mark down every comma and see that they are bound, tied hand and foot in the programme that they are going to carry out. I think you must have confidence in your leaders.
>
> . . . the issue today is not between socialism and the betrayal of socialism; what we are discussing today is the best way to make progress. It is nonsense to say that the only way to progress is by nationalisation. Plenty of Tory governments have nationalised things. That does not mean to say that they were all socialists . . .
>
> If anybody here believes that we are going to abolish all the capitalists within the next 20 years he is purely romantic. We have to get rid of the bitter memories that make us sacrifice progress in order to have a kick at the capitalists. Anybody who is a historical socialist, as opposed to a Utopian socialist, realises that the capitalist system has made great progress for the human race and that socialism must be built on the basis of capitalism. Are you going to scrap all your mechanised industries? Let us be practical. It is ten years since we nationalised the railways and no government has yet been able to give the railways the capital necessary to re-equip and modernise the railways . . . Nationalisation is not a thing you can just do by making declarations in the House of Commons . . .

Fortunately for Labour's leadership, one key figure whose trust they had on this issue was TGWU chief Frank Cousins, whom Bevan had persuaded not to support Campbell:

> we are supporting [*Industry and Society*] because we do not think it is put there as the alternative to nationalisation. We think it is put there as a means by which we can get control of industries where it is not easy immediately to take over in the old-fashioned sense . . .

The young MP for Birmingham Stechford, Roy Jenkins, agreed:

> . . . if the conditions were the same as in 1945 we should all be glad to go back. If the coal industry were still under private ownership we should not dream of buying shares in it . . . Conference will be deluding itself if it thinks that there are candidates for nationalisation today which choose themselves in the way our 1945 candidates did.

Then we had a series of industries clearly defined, basic, mostly inefficient and with the overwhelming majority of the employees in those industries wanting a change to public ownership . . . there are different circumstances today. There is a case for the general extension of public ownership and public property, but it is a different case from that which existed so powerfully in relation to coalmining and other industries. Now there are those who accept the fact that we must have a different approach – the approach by firms, if you like – but who would like, as in the Hornsey resolution, to commit the Executive to take over into full public ownership a very large number, per-haps the majority, of these 512 firms in the period of the next Labour government . . . How are you going to do it? They would presumably be responsible to the President of the Board of Trade. The Minister of Fuel and Power already has enough difficulty in controlling three nationalised industries. How the President of the Board of Trade in a future Labour government is going to effectively to control a majority of the 512 I do not know. And if you have full ownership of a vast number of these firms without effective control over their policy you will be in a very serious position. You will be blamed for everything which goes wrong in those industries. You will, in effect, have responsibility without effective power, and I cannot think of a better way in which to lose the next election but one . . .

I do not regard this document as being in any sense a retreat from socialism . . . What I am interested in is how much public ownership we get under the next Labour government. We shall get a great deal more [public ownership under the next Labour government] by accepting this document than by throwing it back. You have to win the next election before you get any public ownership at all . . .

Having failed to secure the support of any other big union, the NUR's resolution would be defeated by 5,309,000 votes to 1,276,000. Hornsey's suffered a similar fate.

For much of 1958 an election was expected in the autumn. In consequence, there was a tendency for the party to close ranks and unite behind its leader. By the time delegates arrived at Labour's annual conference in Scarborough at the end of September, it was clear that the election was now more likely to be in 1959. Nevertheless, disputes remained at a minimum. The main area over which controversy did arise was education. The National Executive Committee had prepared a policy paper, *Learning to Live*, and it was introduced to the conference with a speech from deputy leader Jim Griffiths. It set out six priorities for the next Labour government, the first five of which were to be achieved within five years: the reduction of maximum class sizes to 30, the closure of slum schools, better provision for handicapped children, the closure of 'all-age' schools, raising the school leaving age to sixteen, and the abolition of the eleven-plus and in consequence the reorganisation of schools on a comprehensive principle. 'The most important single reform we could now make in our education system is to reduce the size of classes,' Griffiths began. He highlighted that facts that one third of primary-school children were at that time taught in classes larger than 40 and two-thirds of children in secondary schools taught in classes larger than 30. He then tackled the more controversial issue of the eleven-plus. The eleven-plus, he declared, was iniquitous, and the tripartite system impossible to operate without it. However, he went on to emphasise his concern to address two key fears among

> all persons, headmasters and teachers . . . the first is the fear that in the new reorganised secondary education the standards that have been attained and the traditions that have been built up by the grammar schools may be lost. The second fear, both of some parents and of some teachers, is that in the reorganised secondary system we are about to create the gifted child may lose the opportunity it now gets through the grammar school . . . I accept the challenge that in the new system we must preserve the standards and indeed improve them. We must maintain the traditions. I believe we can maintain the traditions and improve the standards in the new system which we propose to create and make those standards and traditions available to many more than the tiny proportion of children who get them now. I would say to parents: I do not believe you need fear. Your gifted boy or girl will not lose his or her chance. If you think otherwise come with me to some of the new schools, see the wide variety of choices open to the gifted child . . . We recognise that there must be a full chance and a full challenge to the gifted child, and we must strive to provide it. I believe we can, but we will provide it not only for the gifted child who gets it now, but for the thousands of gifted children who are denied it in our country.

It was a vision rooted in the conception of comprehensives sketched out in a conversation between two shadow Cabinet heavyweights, Patrick Gordon Walker and George Brown, back in November 1954 and recorded in the former's diary: 'many people, [Brown] said, are looking for a policy to distinguish us from the Tories. He suggested a big education programme – grammar school education for all, as good as the public schools, free. I agree.'[199] *Learning to Live* failed, however, to address the issue of the public schools, raised so powerfully from the conference floor by Hugh Gaitskell back in 1953, with anything more profound than the suggestion that they be considered by a Royal Commission. This, felt many delegates, was a serious flaw, and led to an amendment proposing the abolition of fee paying and the integration of formerly fee-paying schools into general local authority provision. The amendment was moved by Workington MP Fred Peart, who was to serve in Cabinet throughout the Wilson and Callaghan governments 1964–70 and 1974–79, but never at the Department for Education:

> Jim Griffiths . . . said we should not dodge the main issues, and we should bear in mind the rights of parents. I accept that. But honestly, the rights of parents also concern the provision of opportunities throughout our system. In that sense 'liberty' is a positive word and that has always been our socialist approach. What liberty has the ordinary citizen to send his child to our Etons, our Harrows and our Haileyburys? His right in the main is determined by geography and the size of his purse . . .

I would remind the Executive that conference two years ago passed a policy document *Towards Equality* . . . On page six the document says this:

'Scarcely less important then the division within the State system is the division between the State schools as a whole and fee-paying independent or public schools.'

Then it goes on to say:

'These schools' effect is to heighten social barriers, to stimulate class consciousness and to foster social snobbery.'

The document then declares:

'But one conclusion can be stated: a classless society and our present pattern of education cannot be reconciled. We can have one or the other, but we cannot have both at the same time.'

We declared our faith and our policy two years ago; you and the Executive approved this. That is why I want to see in *Learning to Live* an approach in relation to the independent schools in the spirit of *Towards Equality* . . .

We tried, in the period 1945 to 1951, to change the economics of society which inspire social and class distinctions. But I believe sincerely that in education we only scratched the surface. The 1944 Act, after all, was a compromise measure. Apart from a few bold experiments like the London Labour authority's comprehensive plan, our system is still riddled with class prejudice and social snobbery. It is all very well Jim [Griffiths] saying that there are only a few children concerned with this. There are more than a quarter of a million of them. There are certainly 50 to 60 public schools which exert great influence, which contrasts in industry and politics where the upper and middle classes of this country buy social privilege, and where they gain influence in key positions in our society. For these children there are no crowded classes, there is no shortage of teachers. Not for them are circulars 242 and 24 and the economy measures. These elite in our society are always insulated from Tory economy measures. But they have a worse influence; their influence permeates the whole of the private sector where parents, seeking to buy educational privilege, waste their money by sending their sons and daughters to small inferior prep and day schools. Our large cities, we all know, are cluttered with inferior snob schools which, I believe, corrupt our democratic values. I say quite sincerely, speaking as a parent, that it is criminal to segregate our children. I condemn racial segregation, I condemn apartheid in South Africa, and I condemn social segregation in England.

I was inspired in my youth by men like that grand old man of British politics and the British Labour movement, who is still living, and who served in the working party, Professor Tawney. He wrote a book on equality. Professor Tawney said that no nation can call itself civilised unless its children attend the same schools. I believe fundamentally in that . . .

Like many of you, I came back from the service in 1945 sincerely thinking we had turned our backs on the past and that our children would be able to live more freely in an egalitarian society where democracy was something practised as well as preached. I am afraid we misjudged the situation . . .

There is certainly argument about the remedy ... about whether or not we should advocate a Fleming solution, or what is called the democratisation of public schools ... Tony Crosland, in his very fine book *The Future of Socialism*, said that we must do something. Even Dick Crossman said so too ... [and] Hugh Gaitskell, our leader, at Margate in 1953 ... said ... 'Something must be done.'

The Trades Union Congress declared that something must be done during the war. I ask my trade union friends to support this resolution and to reaffirm what they did at the Trades Union Congress during the war ... If education is good enough for the dull son of a rich man, it is good enough for the brilliant son of a poor man. I believe that Britain, faced with a scientific revolution, must match its education system to meet the possibilities of that new scientific age ...

The debate that followed included a speech from Michael Stewart, Wilson's future Foreign Secretary who questioned the workability of the Peart plan:

Ask yourselves how many of your own constituency Labour parties want to send their children to boarding schools.

Renee Short, later a left-wing MP and member of Labour's NEC hit back:

We shall be told that it is going to be very difficult; that they will start private tuition and new schools if we take over Eton, Winchester and the rest. But is the next Labour Minister of education going to be a mouse and say 'No, I can't deal with this?'

She was echoed by Manny Shinwell and by TGWU boss Frank Cousins, who pointed out that:

we are facing the real issue that this country's economic, international, political and industrial affairs are in the hands of a privileged group who pass privilege on from place to place.

Stockton MP George Chetwynd argued that the Peart plan was a distraction from the real issue, namely improving education for the vast majority of children, particularly those of Labour voters, who did not attend private schools:

if we diffuse our efforts we will be defeated. There is a saying that the Battle of Waterloo was won on the playing fields of Eton. I say to the conference seriously today that we should not willingly go forward to meet our Waterloo in a sham battle on the classrooms of Eton.

But 35-year-old Robert Sheldon, from 1974–79 a senior Labour Treasury Minister, supported Peart:

To say ... that the private sector will wither away is as much, if not more, of a fallacy than to say that the state economy in Soviet Russia will also wither away. It will increase year by year in spite of the comprehensive schools, rather more because of them, because these comprehensive schools gather up all the forces of education together save one . . .

Twenty-eight-year-old former Fabian staffer and future minister Gerald Kaufman suggested a 'third way':

> Fee-paying public schools do not prevent those without money from attending the state grammar schools, but if the child wants a university education the only place you can go to is the university, and all the universities require the payment of fees . . . For eight years now we have been spending our time abandoning socialism in a vain attempt to get the middle-class vote. A progressive measure of this sort would be advancing socialism and, incidentally, gaining middle-class support. Socialism with a dividend is not something which worries me . . .
>
> It is easier for a public school child to get into university than it is for a child educated at a State grammar school. There are, first of all, the scholarships which are tied between the public schools and the universities. Mr Gaitskell could tell you, as could other people, about the links between Winchester and New College, Oxford. There are in addition other links with smaller schools. The one-eyed pseudo public school which I was unfortunate enough to attend has its own link with Oxford . . . There is in Oxford, too, the qualification of Latin, which is required and which automatically excludes quite a number of children . . . The Labour Party proposes the sort of solution which the Liberal Party might well consider, but which frankly nauseates me – the idea of a Royal Commission, the excuse of any government to do nothing at all.

Kaufman went on to propose that:

> Universities should be free to all and maintenance grants should be provided in addition; [and] that throughout the country the standards of entrance to the universities should be the same to all. I would like the National Executive Committee to consider the question of a national entrance examination which would be for all the universities of the country . . .

But although the TGWU was backing Peart, the NEC would not accept the amendment and the conference chair, Tom Driberg, refused to accept a proposal from Gaitskellite NEC member Eireen White to 'refer back' the section of *Learning to Live* dealing with private schools. The block votes split, Peart's amendment was narrowly defeated and private schools were saved.

THIRTY-TWO

Hola Camp and Clause Four 1959

'It is no use waving the banners of a bygone age'

Despite Labour's relative moderation on many issues in the late 1950s, its radical edge remained as sharp as ever, never more so than on the issue of decolonisation and African liberation, which to many Labour activists summed up the profound moral, as well as philosophical, dividing lines between the parties. The Conservatives had yet to acknowledge the 'wind of change' blowing through the empire, and their continuing attempts to prop it up prompted impassioned exchanges and invited the most bitter animosity. The Bevanite Labour MP Barbara Castle had since February 1958 been sending reports of alleged brutality in camps holding Mau Mau guerrillas in Kenya to the Colonial Secretary Alan Lennox-Boyd. Lennox-Boyd had insisted that the complaints were 'misleading and inaccurate'. In February 1959 Labour had tabled a Commons motion demanding an independent inquiry, but the government had rejected it. In March news filtered through of the cover-up of the deaths of eleven detainees in Hola camp who had been beaten to death. The Kenyan government's report on the deaths in Hola camp came out in May but the British government blocked a parliamentary debate on the issue for weeks afterwards. Eventually, just before the Commons rose for the summer recess, Labour managed to insist. At 10.30 p.m. on 27 July 1959, the debate began. The Conservative ministers sought to play down what they claimed to be an 'unfortunate . . . error of judgement'.

As the historian Tim Bale has observed, 'Castle had been building a reputation for combining emotional force with equally devastating forensic skill,'[200] a reputation she sealed with a speech delivered to a packed Commons chamber at 12.30 a.m. Her speech destroyed the reputation of Lennox-Boyd. Had a general election not been in the offing, Macmillan would have accepted his offer of resignation. The Conservative MP for Leicester South-East, John Peel, had referred to the camp inmates as 'sub-humans'. Castle blazed red:

> To hear hon. members opposite speak of it one would imagine it was an unfortunate minor incident . . . We are discussing in all seriousness the future of the British Commonwealth. I ask hon. members opposite this: if in any prison in Britain twelve men had been beaten to death, would anyone on the benches opposite have said, 'Keep a sense of perspective about this, in view of the fine record of the Prison

Administration'? Of course not. Public opinion in this country would not have permitted anyone to do so. The speeches to which we have listened tonight are a reflection of the very basis of the problem we face in our remaining Colonial Territories. Quite instinctively, sincerely and genuinely, without being aware of it, hon. members opposite do not believe that an African life is as important as a white man's life.

If it had been eleven European prisoners who had been beaten to death, what would the hon. members opposite have said? Would they have said no heads need roll except the head of the man lowest on the ladder? Would they have said these were in any case criminals, so it did not matter? The hon. Member for Blackpool, South (Sir R. Robinson) himself became party to this argument. He asked us to remember that, after all, these were desperate, hard-core Mau Mau murderers. He gave us an example of a Mau Mau detainee who confessed to 35 murders.

The men whose fate we are discussing tonight are men who have not confessed. That is why they are dead. Simply because they had not confessed, simply because their guilt had not been established, they have been subjected to the Cowan Plan of being taken forcibly to a work site and put in such a situation that death inevitably resulted.

It is Enoch Powell's speech, directly after Castle's, that is more remembered. But as Powell's biographer Andrew Roth has written, Lennox-Boyd when he replied to the debate paid tribute to Powell's speech as the most powerful partly because he 'was naturally reluctant to give the accolade to his most formidable Labour opponent Barbara Castle, who had been at her slashing best'.[201] 'I felt proud,' wrote Castle in her memoir, 'when David Wood, the political correspondent of *The Times*, reported my speech with the words: "She gives no quarter, nor does she ask any." I would like this to be my epitaph.'[202]

But profound as were the consequences of the Hola camp controversy in many ways,[203] its impact on the outcome of the general election held on 8 October 1959 was minimal. Conservative Prime Minister Harold Macmillan told the electorate that they had never had it so good. Labour's campaign was better organised than at previous elections and party workers more enthusiastic. But it was to no avail. Labour's share of the vote fell by 2.6 per cent on the previous general election and the Conservatives gained 21 additional seats. Labour's particular failure was among the young: they secured the support of only 10 per cent of middle-class 18–24-year-olds while the Conservatives secured the support of 35 per cent of working-class voters of equivalent age. Though Labour support increased in Scotland and in industrial Lancashire, it fell back in the more prosperous Midlands and south. Thirty per cent of manual workers had voted Conservative.[204] The Liberal vote at the election remained low, at a mere 6 per cent. But the fact that Tory unpopularity during 1958 had put the Liberals on as much as 19 per cent in the Gallup opinion poll, rather than turning voters to Labour, gave many of Labour's leaders cause for concern.

The result came as a shock [wrote shadow Home Secretary and Gaitskell confidant

Patrick Gordon Walker in his diary]. I have no doubt that the things that hurt us most were nationalisation, the trade unions and local Labour councils . . . On the Sunday after the election Gaitskell called some of us together. Jay, Jenkins, Bowden [Chief Whip], Crosland, John Harris of *Forward* and myself. We all came to the conclusion that by some means or other we must drop nationalisation. This has been settled by the vote of the people. Jay wanted to change the name of the party – or to incorporate 'Radical' in it. I said that it was significant that the new estates did not vote as solidly as the pre-war estates . . . The general feeling was that we should call a brief and early conference in December and that Hugh should make a key-note speech dropping nationalisation.[205]

Gaitskell feared that the compromise approach he had previously pursued, for example through the deliberate ambiguity over nationalisation of *Industry and Society* in 1957, had bought party unity at the price of electoral defeat. 'If there is one thing that the 1959 general election result shows, it is surely that unity is not enough,' he wrote later.[206] Douglas Jay published a famous article in the Gaitskellite weekly *Forward* which called publicly for a change to the Labour Party's name and the abandonment of further nationalisation. It caused a furore and Gordon Walker, who had written a similar article, toned his down in consequence.

For the Gaitskellites it was about, as Roy Jenkins characterised it, forcing the Labour Party to face and make a fundamental choice between being 'a party of power' or simply a 'party of protest'.[207] 'The party simply had to have an argument,' believed Crosland, 'and come out at the end of the day on one side or the other.'[208] Their opponents denied the inevitability of such a choice, arguing that the Labour Party needed to be about both and that the real issue was what kind of party Labour was to be. Geoffrey Goodman, then a journalist on the *News Chronicle*, remembers attending a private lunch at the St Ermin's Hotel in July 1958 at which Gaitskell and Jay talked about turning Labour into a 'left-of-centre radical party', while Harold Wilson, who was also present, disassociated himself, 'partly by silence and partly by an open difference of opinion'.[209]

On 28 November 1959 the Labour Party conference opened under the grey skies of rain-drenched Blackpool. The three main speeches of the conference were deliberately uncoordinated and the first two were highly competitive. The first was from the heroine of Hola camp, Barbara Castle, that year's Labour Party chair, who opened conference with what fellow Bevanite Michael Foot has called 'the most telling chairman's address ever delivered at a party conference'.[210] It was, Dick Crossman recorded in his diary, 'a brilliant doctrinal speech' attacking the affluent society, contrasting for Labour's left with Hugh Gaitskell's 'complacent acceptance of it'.[211]

Last year we met in the bright hope of victory. This year we meet in the shadow of electoral defeat. Despite a good programme, better organisation than we have ever had and brilliant leadership by Hugh Gaitskell, we lost . . . [What were the lessons of defeat? Conceding that] It would be absurd to suggest that nothing needs changing in our policy, constitution, organisation, or anything else, [she attacked the idea] that we have so much to un-learn that we must go back to school and re-write the alphabet . . . [Advocates of change] tell us that we have become the victims of our own success. And of course to a certain extent it is true. We all of us know of electors who voted Tory this time because they had become more prosperous, yet they came from a class that owed its chance in life to us. Democratic politics is full of similar ironies. And we are told, quite rightly, that we mustn't moan about it. We can't expect to reap an endless harvest from our past victories. We don't want to spend our time reminding young voters of the grim old days – they wouldn't listen to us anyway, even if we did. The real question is: what conclusion do we draw from our own achievements? Do we say that, because the poverty and unemployment which we came into existence to fight have been largely conquered, the ideas which inspired us no longer apply?

This is, indeed, one of the arguments being offered to us. We are told that we have succeeded so well in reforming capitalism that we have made it, not only civilised, but indestructible. Our best bet, therefore, we are told, is to accept it almost completely in its present modified form, to abandon the attempt to take over any more industries and to use public ownership merely to ensure that the community gets a cut of the capitalist cake. Such a policy, it is urged, would enable us to concentrate on social reforms and the sort of moral issues which will rally the radicals. Thus by uniting all progressive forces we should sweep back into power.

Let us by all means examine this argument carefully, for only in that way shall we find where it would lead. And in my view it would lead us slap-bang into a fallacy. That fallacy is the belief that you can separate moral issues from economic ones. We are not prigs in the Labour Party; of course we believe that people should have a good time, but we also believe deeply and enduringly in the good life. And we have spent 50 years of political life proving to the people of this country that economic and social morality go hand in hand . . .

The morality of a society is not created in a vacuum: it springs from the way it organises its economic life and distributes its rewards. Today we live in a society in which the bonds of common interest have been deliberately loosened by government policy. The highest virtue lies in looking after Number One and the greatest merit is being strong enough to do it. The victory of such a philosophy at the last election was signalised by an unprecedented boom on the stock exchange. There was a rush to climb on to the bandwagon of profits by all who knew that, if they merely relied on hard work or skill to ensure their future, they would be left behind. Keeping up with the Clores has become a national necessity. Can we be surprised that 'wild-cat' strikes flourish in such an atmosphere? We can't expect Jack to work to a code which his masters have just spent millions of pounds defeating at the polls. Economic might has become social right and the Devil has taken the communal interest.

In such a society the social reformer is battling hopelessly against the tide. For it is above all a commercialised society in which the customer is bombarded every day with

207

advertisements persuading him that his highest happiness lies in acquiring more and more immediate satisfactions and consumer goods. And so he is conditioned to feel that anything that stands between him and those satisfactions is his enemy. The communal services, which add quality, beauty and vision to our national life, become the residuary legatees of a consumer spending boom. Today we are making more TV aerials than houses to put them on. Millions of pounds are spent encouraging our children to eat more sweets per head than any children in the world – while government starves the schools' dental service. The *British Dental Journal* warned us the other day: 'By the time the new government quits office, hundreds of thousands more children will have left school with diseased and permanently mutilated mouths.' We complain about juvenile delinquency – and then diddle probation officers out of £30,000 of back pay. Our social and professional services are increasingly taking a back place. The beauty of our cities is being wrecked by the speculative building boom. But who is going to care about these things in a society whose values are dictated by the profit motive and in which the hidden persuaders have become the Fourth Estate? It is chasing fantasies to imagine that we can win elections on moral issues in a democracy built on such amoral foundations. Nor can we get very far in our fight for equality. As long as our economy depends on large accumulations of private capital, it needs inequality to make it work. This is the only way it can be financed and no amount of tinkering with taxation can alter it; indeed, if it did, the system would break down! And when we try to attack these inequalities through the social services we find that the wage-earners they are designed to help have become their enemy because they have to carry the main burden of financing them through PAYE. The only way to attack inequality is at the source. Radicalism without socialism is an also-ran.

The objection to the reformist argument, therefore, is a practical one: it just won't win votes. In a materialist society, the Tories can always beat us in an appeal to selfishness. Worse still, in a private enterprise society, they have overwhelming superiority in the means to put that appeal across, as we found in the last election. Next time we can be sure that the Conservative Party and their industrial allies will be willing to spend three or four times as much in trying to defeat us. A long time ago Professor Tawney warned us that democracy is unstable as a political system as long as economic power remains irresponsible. Now his words are taking on a new urgency. Today, the elector can be brainwashed at his TV set by the big money boys before ever he listens to a political argument. No wonder the Tories are pressing for commercial radio!

This then is the real challenge to us: the dilemma we can't escape. Either we must convince the people of this country that they – and not a few private interests – should control their economic lives or we shall shrink into an impotent appendage of the windfall state. And this is the real case for public ownership. We don't want to take over industries merely in order to make them more efficient, but to make them responsible to us all. And I believe that one of the reasons why the idea of public ownership alienated people in the last election is that we have not yet presented the real case for it. To say, for instance, that the State should acquire shares in private industry on the strict understanding that it exercises no control over it is like legalising the

Burglars' Union on condition that we share the swag. Nor are the existing nationalised industries exactly a model of public accountability. They are not really accountable to their workers, to the consumers or even to Parliament. And until they are, they are not socialist.

But, these arguments apart, why should we be frightened at this moment of all moments about public ownership? It isn't as though Britain's economic problems had been magically solved by the Conservative victory. On the contrary, we read every day about some new muddle in our unplanned economy. After only a few months of a return to expansionist policies Britain is already running into a shortage of vital raw materials like bricks and steel. Nor are there any signs that our manufacturing industries are expanding investment on the scale we need. As the Federation of British Industries points out in its latest survey: 'The point has not yet been reached at which there is a widespread planning of new capacity.' Or take the transport chaos. What could be more typical of a Tory 'boom' than the pouring out of private cars on to roads as yet unbuilt and into cities which are completely unprepared to take them? And this is done at the very moment when the public transport system, which was prevented from making itself more efficient by the government's investment cuts of 1958, is being compelled to raise its fares . . .

No, comrades, it simply won't wash to say that nationalisation is fusty and out-of-date. What are the typical symbols of this modern age? Russia's nationalised sputnik now circulating round the moon tracked at every stage by Britain's publicly owned radar telescope at Jodrell Bank. The Hovercraft – the most revolutionary development in transport – sponsored by the National Research Development Corporation which you and I own. Nimrod, the giant atom-smasher now being built next door to Harwell – another product of national enterprise. Contrast these leaps into the new world with the fumbling inadequacies of our machine tool industry whose total failure to meet our needs has just been exposed in an official report the government dare not let us see. The man in the street simply does not know what is being achieved by public enterprise because no one takes full-page advertisements to tell him.

Of course this does not mean that we want to nationalise everything from atomic energy to pin-table saloons. But it does mean that the community must control, inspire and finance new industrial developments as it is already doing in so many fields . . .

Comrades, we have received a setback in this election; perhaps even a shock. But I have faith in the resilience and adaptability of our movement . . . I believe the young people are eager and waiting for a call: a call to public service; a call to idealism; a call to comradeship between all peoples at home and in other lands. Let us be big enough to give them that call: to show them that a prosperous Britain need not be a selfish one; that a planned Britain need not be bureaucratic; that the pursuit of principles need not lead to bigotry and intolerance, but to greater freedom of expression and a creative variety of thought . . .

It was then the turn of Hugh Gaitskell to open the general debate. His speech, written with the assistance of Anthony Crosland, 'fairly and squarely put the cat amongst the pigeons, [as one commentator observed] of whom there were many as self-confident as those heavy birds which fly in your face in London parks'.[212] 'I agreed with most of it,' wrote Tony Benn, but 'it was constructed in quite the wrong way', confronting the party rather than leading them. Gaitskell began:

> it is not the purpose of this debate to reach final conclusions . . . The Executive is putting forward no proposals. So this afternoon I speak for myself alone.
>
> Since the election I have received many letters . . . all concerned with why we lost the election and what we should do now . . . Some blamed not the Labour Party but the electorate – 'those illiterate women and ignorant men', as one man put it. This reminds me of Oscar Wilde's remark, 'The play was a great success but the audience was a failure.'

One factor, he acknowledged, was that the Conservatives outspent Labour on their propaganda machine. Gaitskell rejected, however, the charges that Labour had been either insufficiently idealistic, or had made too many uncosted promises: it was right, he believed, to prioritise social spending over 'reducing taxes on the rich'. He also defended Tony Benn's television election broadcasts:

> Some say they were too smooth, too slick, too polished. But had they been rough, clumsy and dull we would have heard much more about it . . .
>
> Why then . . . did we lose? . . . the stark fact is that this is the third successive general election we have lost and the fourth in which we have lost seats.
>
> [This was an] almost unprecedented . . . adverse trend. [Its causes were firstly the] changing character of the labour force, [firstly] from heavy physical work towards machine maintenance, distribution and staff jobs; [secondly] the absence of serious unemployment or even the fear of it; [thirdly] the improvements to life afforded by the welfare state and the conveniences of the affluent society such as televisions and refrigerators.
>
> Again and again, especially talking to candidates in the Midlands and the south, I have heard the same story of the relatively prosperous younger married couples who, having moved from older houses in solid Labour areas to new attractive housing estates, usually built by Labour councils, then lost their Labour loyalty and voted Conservative. And, indeed, it is hard otherwise to explain the fact that in England we did not win a single seat where there is a new town and that we gained much less than we expected in those constituencies where huge new housing estates had been built.
>
> [What should Labour do? Gaitskell firmly rejected the idea] that perhaps we should be content to remain in permanent opposition until somehow in 20 or 30 years' time the country comes to its senses and condescends to elect us to power. It is our job to get back into power as quickly as possible so that we may do the things in which we believe for our country and the world. [He explicitly rejected a pact with the Liberals:] No one knows how far the Liberals take votes from us or the Tories – whether it is to our advantage or disadvantage for Liberal candidates to intervene. [He dismissed changing Labour's name.] I have had several letters to this effect from

people who are alarmed by the snobbery of some of the new suburban voters. We should toss this out of the window too. Our name is one which evokes the loyalty of many millions of British people. And I doubt if the snobs would be much influenced if we did change it. The proposal that the Labour Party should break with the unions [came from] not a friendly quarter [and he rejected that too:] I have always looked upon the [Labour–trade union link] as one of our greatest strengths.

Instead he wanted:

not . . . looser ties but . . . better coordination of our activities . . .

We should put more stress on the issues which especially appeal to younger people. I believe these include the cause of colonial freedom; the protection of the individual against ham-handed and arrogant bureaucracy; resistance to the squalid commercialism which threatens to despoil our countryside and disfigure our cities; a dislike of bumbledom in all forms; a greater concern for sport and the arts.

It is sometimes said that we appeal too much on behalf of the underdog. True, the underdogs are fewer than they used to be, and consequently they bring us fewer votes. But I cannot accept that we should cease to appeal on their behalf. To me that would be a betrayal of socialist principles. And I believe too that young people still respond more to idealism that to purely materialistic and selfish causes . . .

We should welcome and encourage newcomers . . . Above all our object must be to broaden our base, to be in touch always with ordinary people, to avoid becoming small cliques of isolated doctrine-ridden fanatics, out of touch with the main stream of social life in our time. We should be missionaries, not monks, a mass party not a conspiratorial group. [Labour's electoral appeal was also undermined by] the unpopularity of certain Labour local councils [and] nationalisation [because] some of the existing nationalised industries are unpopular. This unpopularity is very largely due to circumstances which have nothing to do with nationalisation. London buses are overcrowded and slow – not because the Transport Commission is inefficient but because of the state of London traffic and the way the Tory government have neglected it all these years. The backward conditions of the railways are not really the result of bad management but inadequate investment in the past which has left behind a gigantic problem of modernisation. Coal costs more not because the Coal Board or the miners have done badly but because in the post-war world we have to pay miners a decent wage to induce them to work in the pits. But all these things are blamed on nationalisation . . . we must face the fact that nationalisation as such will not be positively popular until *all* these industries are clearly seen to be performing at least as well as the best firms in the private sector . . .

Gaitskell also blamed the distortion of Labour's 'moderate, practical proposals' by Labour's opponents so that:

Voters were induced to think that we intended to nationalise any and every private firm, however efficiently it might be operating . . .

Some suggest that we should accept for all time the present frontiers between the public and private sectors. We cannot do that. It would imply that everything works so perfectly in the private sector that we shall never want to intervene. But things are far from perfect in the private sector. One industry after another today is begging for government financial help. Recently there have been critical reports by independent investigators – on the machine tool, shipbuilding, shipping and other industries. I am not saying that we shall want to nationalise all these industries, but I do mean that we can't conceivably commit ourselves to the view that no future Labour government will ever want to do anything about them . . .

At the same time I disagree equally with the other extreme view that nationalisation or even public ownership is the be all and end all, the ultimate first principle and aim of socialism. I believe that this view arises from a complete confusion about the fundamental meaning of socialism and, in particular, a misunderstanding about ends and means.

So I want now to set out what I at any rate regard as the basic first principles of British democratic socialism . . .

So I say, first, we express what G. D. H. Cole once called 'a broad, human movement on behalf of the bottom dog' – on behalf of all those who are oppressed or in need or hardship . . . Secondly, we believe in social justice, in an equitable distribution of wealth and income. We do not demand exact equality. But we do demand that the differences should be related not to the accident of birth and inheritance but on how much of effort, skill and creative energy we each contribute to the common good. Thirdly, we believe in a 'classless society' – a society without the snobbery, the privilege, the restrictive social barriers which are still far too prevalent in Britain today. Fourthly, we believe in the fundamental equality of races and of all peoples, and in the building of an international order which will enable them to live together in peace. We detest equally the arrogant postures of white supremacy and the exercise of unbridled power by large nations over small ones. Suez, Hungary, Hola are words of infamy to us. For we believe quite simply in the brotherhood of man.

Fifthly, British socialism has always contained an essential element of personal idealism – the belief that the pursuit of material satisfaction by itself without spiritual values is empty and barren and that our relations with one another should be based not on ruthless self-regarding rivalry but on fellowship and cooperation. It is hard to convey this idea in plain language. But we can, surely, agree that without it our socialism would be poorer.

Sixthly, we believe that the public interest must come before private interest. We are not opposed to individuals seeking to do the best they can for themselves and their families. But we insist that the pursuit of private gain should not take precedence over the public good. The idea of public planning in the interests of the whole community both for economic and social reasons is certainly a basic principle of socialism.

Finally, we believe that these things must be achieved with and through freedom and democratic self-government. We intend to maintain this for ourselves and, so far as lies within our power, to help others enjoy it too.

These I believe constitute the essential first principles of our democratic socialism. Everything else – nationalisation, controls, our particular policies on housing or education or old-age pensions – constitute only the means to realising the principles in practice . . . we hold that in order to plan and control the working of the economy, to . . . use Mr Bevan's words, we need to control 'the commanding heights of economic power' . . . But here again the public sector is a means not an end . . .

As I have already said I am against starting on a new election programme now. But I do think that we should . . . try to express in the most simple and comprehensive fashion what we stand for in the world today. The only official document which embodies such an attempt is the party constitution, written over 40 years ago. It seems to me that this needs to be brought up to date. For instance, can we really be satisfied today with a statement of fundamentals which make no mention at all of colonial freedom, race relations, disarmament, full employment or planning? The only specific reference to our objectives at home is the well-known phrase: 'To secure for the workers by hand or by brain the full fruits of their industry and the most equitable distribution thereof that may be possible, upon the basis of the common ownership of the means of production, distribution, and exchange . . .'

Standing as it does on its own, this cannot possibly be regarded as adequate. It lays us open to continual misrepresentation. It implies that common ownership is an end, whereas in fact it is a means. It implies that the only precise object we have is nationalisation, whereas in fact we have many other socialist objectives. It implies that we propose to nationalise everything, but do we? Everything? – the whole of light industry, the whole of agriculture, all the shops – every little pub or garage? Of course not . . . had we better not say so instead of going out of our way to court misrepresentation? . . .

I am sure that the Webbs and Arthur Henderson, who largely drafted this constitution, would have been amazed and horrified had they thought that their words were to be treated as sacrosanct 40 years later in utterly changed conditions. Let us remember that we are a party of the future, not of the past; that we must appeal to the young as well as the old – young people who have very little reverence for the past. It is no use waving the banners of a bygone age. The first need now, in the words of one who has already been quoted today, that great socialist teacher R. H. Tawney, 'is to treat sanctified formulae with judicious irreverence and to start by deciding what precisely is the end view'.

I hope, then, that the Executive will during the next few months try to work out and state the fundamental principles of British democratic socialism as we see and as we feel it today, in 1959, not 1918, and I hope that in due course another conference will endorse what they propose. I hope that the Executive in doing this work will tilt the balance to the future rather than the past, so that what is decided will be and will seem relevant in 1970 – even, if you like, in 1980; after that we can have another look at it again . . .

I ask myself what most [Labour supporters] want of us now? . . . What they want us to do now first of all is to go on fighting for the things we fought for in the election, and they are dead right. We have got to go on fighting for a square deal for the old people, for the widows, the disabled and the sick; we have got to go on fighting for a real proper superannuation plan which will abolish poverty in old age, not the sham thing the Tories put up, which merely distributes the burden more unfairly than before. We have to go on pressing for the abolition of the eleven-plus; for more, not fewer council houses; for councils to take over the older rented houses and modernise them. We have to go on pressing for freedom and self-government for the colonies, and an end to the repulsive policies of racial discrimination. We have to go on fighting for an end to nuclear tests, for all-out disarmament and a real effort to stop the hideous danger of the spread of nuclear weapons from one country to another ... Our defeat, comrades, must not be a depressive or a sedative, but a supreme challenge, a challenge to keep up the spirit of the attack again and again and again, until we win ... (*prolonged applause*).

After Gaitskell's speech, the floodgates burst. Former Putney candidate Dick Taverne, an ardent young Gaitskellite and future minister, compared Labour Party meetings to the:

atmosphere of a latterday fundamentalist society, in which people are more concerned to affirm their orthodoxy and chastise heretics than increase the number of followers.

Michael Foot, who had just lost Plymouth Devonport, praised Castle's speech and claimed that:

Many of the ends Hugh Gaitskell described at the end of his speech are in such general terms that the Tories could agree with them, too ... in the months ahead we are bound to have arguments about policy ... in order to win an election we have to change the mood of the people in this country, to open their eyes to what an evil and disgraceful and rotten it is ...

TGWU boss Frank Cousins, whose union's 1959 biennial delegate conference had repudiated the painstakingly crafted compromise on nationalisation of *Industry and Society*, weighed in to declare that:

whilst we can have nationalisation without socialism, we cannot have socialism without nationalisation ... Let us give over pretending we have to get half a million Tory people to change their allegiance to us at voting time. There are five million or six million people who are socialists in embryo waiting for us to go out and harness them to the power machine we want to drive, and the sooner we get on with that job the better for all of us ...

I was a bit disturbed by Hugh's reference that [Clause Four] is likely to be revised to make a different reference to our attitude towards public ownership, I would suggest, with the greatest respect to our leader, that no way – Douglas Jay's or any other way – is going to change that one.

Cousins and Foot 'roused the conference to a fury of opposition', recalled Taverne, a fury only tempered by 'the best speech of all at that conference, from Denis Healey . . . by far the best and toughest speech from him that I have ever heard'.[213] Healey himself recalls having gone to Blackpool 'with no intention of speaking since there was to be no debate on foreign policy – the only subject on which I had ever addressed our conference till then. The frightening refusal of so many delegates to face the reality of our defeat finally forced me to my feet':[214]

> . . . We who are here at this conference do not represent the average voter. Let us face it. We represent the average party worker who slaved away so hard and so enthusiastically for a Labour victory six weeks ago. Hugh Gaitskell was absolutely right when he said yesterday that what gets cheers at this conference does not necessarily get votes at elections. If it did we would have won Devonport. [The seat at which Michael Foot had just been defeated.]
>
> There are far too many people who have spoken from this rostrum in these last two days who seem to think it is all right to do without votes. Some have even said so. It is better to lose elections, they say, than to win them so long as we know we are fighting on the socialist policy; and they seem to face with equanimity the idea of staying in opposition, an opposition that gets smaller and smaller, at every election. If they want to luxuriate complacently in moral righteousness in opposition they can do it, but who is going to pay the price for their complacency?
>
> You can take the view that it is better to give up half a loaf if you cannot get the whole loaf, but the point is that it is not we who are giving up the half loaf; it is the people whom we are trying to help in the country and in the world. They are the people who suffer if we lose elections.
>
> In Britain it is the unemployed and old-age pensioners, and outside Britain there are thousands and millions of people in Asia and Africa who desperately need a Labour government in this country to help them. If you take the view that it is all right to stay in opposition as long as your socialist heart is pure, you will be 'All right, Jack'. You will have your TV set, your motor car and your summer holidays on the Continent and still keep your socialist soul intact. The people who pay the price for your sense of moral satisfaction are the Africans, hundreds of thousands, millions of them being slowly forced into racial slavery; the Indians and the Indonesians dying of starvation. If you are prepared for them to pay the price of your sense of moral superiority, all right. But do not come to this conference and say that because of that you are better socialists than those who want to get a Labour government in Britain.
>
> We are not just a debating society. We are not just a socialist Sunday school. We are a great movement that wants to help real people living on this earth at the present time. We shall never be able to help them unless we get power . . .

It was Aneurin Bevan, 'witty, scintillating, positive, conciliatory',[215] who, the day after Gaitskell's great speech on Clause Four, made the concluding speech of the 1959 conference. Earlier that same month he had succeeded Jim Griffiths as Labour's deputy leader in an unopposed election. For Michael Foot, 'it was the classic Bevan speech, shaped to secure an immediate end and yet elevating the party debate to the realm of political philosophy . . . [and] amongst the three or four greatest he ever delivered'.[216] Geoffrey Goodman, then a journalist on the *Daily Herald*, recalls it as 'one of the greatest speeches that I ever heard – perhaps the greatest in terms of ideological content, vision, perception and quality of oratory'.[217] Gaitskell's allies such as Healey have acknowledged that Bevan 'rescued Hugh from disaster at the winter conference in Blackpool which followed our defeat in the 1959 election. His speech on this occasion was a masterpiece of virtuoso rhetoric . . . devoted solely to establishing his personal solidarity with the man who had been his victorious rival for so long.'[218]

> . . . I used to be taught as a boy, not at university but even in the board school, one of Euclid's deductions: if two things are equal to a third thing, they are equal to each other. Yesterday Barbara quoted from a speech which I made some years ago, and she said that I believed that socialism in the context of modern society meant the conquest of the commanding heights of the economy. Hugh Gaitskell quoted the same thing. So Barbara and Hugh quoted me. If Euclid's deduction is correct they are both equal to me and therefore must be equal to each other.
>
> So we have a kind of trinity – I am not going to lay myself open to a charge of blasphemy by trying to describe our different roles. I am not certain in which capacity I am speaking, whether as the father, the son or the holy ghost. But you will have seen that, despite the attempts which are made to exploit differences of opinion, so as to inflict mortal wounds upon the party, those differences are not of a character that should divide this movement permanently. That is not to say that there are not differences. Of course there are! Hugh Gaitskell and Barbara Castle and myself would not be doing a service to this movement if we did not make our individual contributions to its variety, but making the contributions to its variety and to its diversity without mortally injuring its unity.
>
> One of the reasons why we have got into trouble in the last few weeks, I think, was because one or two people rushed too early into print in order to try and alter in their minds the programme we put before the country at the last election. That was a mistake tactically, it was a mistake psychologically, and it was a profound error philosophically. You cannot really go before the country with a programme and tell the country that you thought the programme was good for the country, and immediately the country rejected it, say you would like to alter it. It won't work; it is not right. It is almost like saying you put before the country a false prospectus. The programme we put before the country we believed in. We are very sorry that the electorate rejected it. We think the electorate is going to be sorry for having rejected it. In the course of time, as the years go by, and as circumstances change and the issues are altered, we may find it necessary to change some part of the programme; that will not be because we thought the programme was wrong, but just because we think it might be readjusted to changing conditions. You know, comrades, to change programmes is not an

admission of error, otherwise all history would be a series of confessionals . . .

Hugh said – and I think he was right – that from the information we can get, a lot of people said that one of the reasons why they did not vote for us was because they did not believe in nationalisation. I think it is correct that they did say this; but what does it amount to when they have said it? Are we really now to believe that the reasons that people give for their actions are the cause of their actions? Such a naïve belief in the rational conduct of human beings would wipe out the whole of modern psychology. Of course many of them said they did not like nationalisation, and therefore they did not vote for us. Is it suggested that because of that we should drop it? . . .

What does it prove? If it is said that we lost the election because of our belief in public ownership, then 12,250,000 people voted for us because they believed in public ownership. It is not a bad start-off, is it? Now you may say: 'Ah, but they did not vote for you because they believed in public ownership.' Well, you cannot have it both ways, can you? Or even suppose you were allowed to have it both ways, then you must conclude that 12,250,000 people did vote for us despite their distaste for public ownership. That is the biggest single vote ever given for public ownership in any country in the whole world. Then why the hell this defeatism? Why all this talk that we have actually gone back? Of course, it is true that in the present-day affluent society a very large number of people are not discontented as they were, and because we are a party that stands for the redress of discontent and the wrongs caused by discontent, the absence of so much discontent has reduced our popularity. But you know, comrades, I have been in this movement now for many years. I was in this movement in between the war years when there were two million unemployed, and still the Tories got a majority . . .

The fact is – and that is accepted, and derive your lessons from it – that a very considerable number of young men and women in the course of the last five or ten years have had their material conditions improved and their status has been raised in consequence and their discontents have been reduced, so that temporarily their personalities are satisfied with the framework in which they live. They are not conscious of frustration or of limitation as formerly they were, in exactly the same way as even before the war large numbers of workers were not sufficiently conscious of frustration and of limitation, even on unemployment benefit, to vote against the Tories.

What is the lesson for us? It is that we must enlarge and expand those personalities, so that they can become again conscious of limitation and constriction. The problem is one of education, not of surrender! This so-called affluent society is an ugly society still. It is a vulgar society. It is a meretricious society. It is a society in which priorities have gone all wrong. I once said – and I do not want to quote myself too frequently – that the language of priorities was the religion of socialism, and there is nothing wrong with that statement either, but you can only get your priorities right if you have the power to put them right, and the argument, comrades, is about power in society. If we managed to get a majority in Great Britain by the clever exploitation of contemporary psychology, and we did not get the commanding heights of the economy in our power, then we did not get the priorities right . . .

Therefore I agree with Barbara, I agree with Hugh and I agree with myself, that the chief argument for us is not how we can change our policy so as to make it attractive to the electorate. That is not the purpose of this conference. The purpose is to try, having decided what our policy should be, to put it as attractively as possible to the population; not to adjust our policy opportunistically to the contemporary mood, but to cling to our policy and alter its presentation in order to win the suffrage of the population . . .

I would also like to remind our comrades of another thing . . . modern capitalism has not succeeded; it has failed . . . We are asked in 1959 to believe that if we are only patient, if we only work hard, we will double the standard of living in 25 years. That is the same rate of progress as before the war. Within all the techniques of modern production, with automation, with electronics, with all the new industrial techniques, the capitalists of Great Britain can promise us exactly the same rate of progress as before the war.

The challenge which is going to take place in the next ten years is not going to come from Harold Macmillan . . . The challenge is going to come from Russia . . . [and] from those nations who, however wrong they may be – and I think they are wrong in many fundamental respects – nevertheless are at long last being able to reap the material fruits of economic planning and of public ownership. That is where the challenge is coming from, and I want to meet it, because I am not a Communist, I am a social democrat. I believe that it is possible for a modern intelligent community to organise its economic life rationally, with decent orders of priority, and it is not necessary to resort to dictatorship in order to do it. I believe that it is possible. That is why I am a socialist. If I did not believe that, I would be a Communist; I would not be a capitalist! I believe that this country of ours and this movement of ours, despite our setbacks, nevertheless is being looked upon by the rest of the world as the custodian of democratic representative government. But, comrades, if we are going to be its custodian, we must at the same time realise what the job is. The job is that we must try and organise our economic life intelligently and rationally in accordance with some order of priorities and a representative government; but we must not abandon our main case . . . that in modern complex society it is impossible to get rational order by leaving things to private economic adventure. Therefore I am a socialist. I believe in public ownership. But I agreed with Hugh Gaitskell yesterday: I do not believe in a monolithic society. I do not believe that public ownership should reach down into every piece of economic activity, because that would be asking for a monolithic society. In fact, it would be asking for something that does not even exist in China or Russia. But what I do insist upon is this, and as a movement we must insist upon it. We will never be able to get the economic resources of this nation fully exploited unless we have a planned economy in which the nation itself can determine its own priorities . . .

Frank Pakenham[219] made a speech here yesterday in which he said that his beliefs were derived from his religion. I do not claim to be a very religious man; I never have. But I must remind Frank Pakenham that Christ drove the moneychangers from the Temple. He did not open the doors wide for them to enter. He drove them away. If we go on to apply the principles of Christianity to contemporary British society, they have been done elsewhere rather better than they have been done here. I think there is something evil, something abominable, something disgraceful in a country that can turn its back on Hola, that can turn its back on old-age pensioners, that can starve the health service, and reap £1,500 million from the stock exchange boom immediately after the election is over.

What are we going to say, comrades? Are we going to accept the defeat? Are we going to say to India, where socialism has been adopted as the official policy despite all the difficulties facing the Indian community, that the British Labour movement has dropped socialism here? What are we going to say to the rest of the world? Are we going to send a message from this great Labour movement, which is the father and mother of modern democracy and modern socialism, that we in Blackpool in 1959 have turned our backs on our principles because of a temporary unpopularity in a temporarily affluent society? . . .

I was rather depressed at what Denis Healey said. I have a lot of respect for him; but you know, Denis, you are not going to be able to help the Africans if the levers of power are left in the hands of their enemies in Britain. You cannot do it! Nor can you inject the principles of ethical socialism into an economy based upon private greed. You cannot do it! . . .

I have enough faith in my fellow creatures in Great Britain to believe that when they have got over the delirium of the television, when they realise that their new homes that they have been put into are mortgaged to the hilt, when they realise that the money lender has been elevated to the highest position in the land, when they realise that the refinements to which they should look are not there, that it is a vulgar society of which no decent person could be proud, when they realise all those things, when the years go by and they see the challenge of modern society not being met by the Tories who can consolidate their political powers only on the basis on national mediocrity, who are unable to exploit the resources of their scientists because they are prevented by the greed of their capitalism from doing so, when they realise that the flower of our youth goes abroad today because they are not being given opportunities of using their skill and their knowledge properly at home, when they realise that all the tides of history are flowing in our direction, that we are not beaten, that we represent the future: then, when we say it and mean it, then we shall lead our people to where they deserve to be led (*loud and continual applause*).

It was to be virtually Bevan's last major speech. Six months later he was dead of cancer.

THIRTY-THREE

Gaitskell's Battles 1959–61

*'There are some of us . . . who will fight and fight
and fight again to save the party we love'*

Gaitskell left Britain for a visit to the USA and the West Indies on 30 December 1959 and while he was away the noise of battle increased. Michael Foot, no longer an MP but seen as speaking for many on the left who were, told the eight million viewers of BBC's 'Panorama' that he personally intended to oust Gaitskell.[220] Symptomatic of the attitude of the left was the pamphlet *Anatomy of a Sacred Cow*. Written by Tito-ist Labour MP Konni Zilliacus it was published by CND in July 1960 and explicitly linked Labour's debates over domestic policy with the growing H-bomb controversy, claiming that Gaitskell was 'so far to the right as to make him almost indistinguishable from a Liberal in home affairs and a Tory in foreign policy'.[221]

The Clause Four row rumbled on, generating a great deal more heat and far less light than Gaitskell had hoped. Although intimates of Gaitskell's so-called Hampstead Set believed that radical reforms were necessary, other Gaitskellites[222] from the traditional trade union right wing of the party were less convinced that this had been the best ground on which to pick a fight:

'I didn't think it really mattered a damn, one way or the other,' recalled George Brown,

> but the proposal to amend Clause Four at once aroused all the hostility of those who were really opposed to Gaitskell on defence and all the other matters on which a practical approach to the problems of government contrasted with a doctrinaire approach. The ostensible dispute over Clause Four ended up almost in a farce. I thought I saw a way of patching up the differences over Clause Four. I wrote an addition to the traditional Clause Four which I likened to adding the New Testament to the Old Testament. But no amendment was put formally to the party and so none was ever written into the party's constitution. Instead the NEC presented its statement to the next conference [which] was accepted as 'a valuable expression of the aims of the Labour Party in the second half of the twentieth century'.[223]

Even the Gaitskellite arditi acknowledged that the master plan had backfired, as some, including Tony Crosland, had always feared. As Dick Taverne, one of the most enthusiastic young Gaitskellites, acknowledged in his memoir, Gaitskell 'was soon forced to realise that he had no hope of carrying the National Executive of the party. While his strategic analysis had to my mind been impeccable, it was now shown that his tactics had been misguided. You should not raise issues as fundamental as Clause Four if you cannot win.'[224] Gaitskell's position was made more difficult by the death on 6 July 1960 of Bevan, his recent ally, and the incapacitation of Labour's General Secretary Morgan Phillips by a serious stroke that August.

The debate that Gaitskell had sparked over Labour's aims and values formally concluded with the presentation of the NEC statement to Labour's 1960 annual conference in Scarborough. It was debated in conjunction with *Labour in the Sixties*, written largely by Morgan Phillips, the young head of the Labour Party research department, Peter Shore and Dick Crossman, which urged that Labour prioritise increasing its appeal to white-collar workers, women and young voters. With Phillips incapacitated, another member of Labour's NEC had to be found to introduce it at conference. Dick Crossman wanted to do it but he was already speaking on pensions. It therefore fell to Ray Gunter, Labour MP, Transport and Salaried Staffs' Association (TSSA) president, and former Welsh railway clerk, who made a moving speech on Phillips' behalf. Many thought that it was this speech that secured Gunter's place in the next Labour Cabinet.[225] Its rhetoric of 'scientific revolution' presaged Harold Wilson's famous speech as leader three years later in which he harnessed the rhetoric of 'white heat' to substitute the notion of modernisation for the divisive debate over nationalisation.

... The phenomenon of the last decade has been the scientific revolution. Its pace and its extent are beyond anything the world has ever known before. New discoveries and new inventions today produce social and industrial upheavals in five or ten years that hitherto have taken 50 or 100 years to work out. The almost incredible performance of our scientists and technicians makes it physically possible for the first time in history – and this is the significance of the sixties – for mankind, if it will do so, to find the means to be fed properly. There can be universal literacy. We can give a decent standard of living to everyone. Our own standard of living can rise beyond the dreams of the founding fathers of our party . . .

As a result you have at the present time the tremendous car sales. You have refrigerators, washing machines, and millions of motor cars pouring on to the roads; and at that very point you cannot afford to raise the school leaving age, improve the lot of your old-age pensioners or build the hospitals the nation needs . . . if the blessings of the scientific age are not going to be distributed properly, if socialist principles are not to be applied in this revolution, then I believe there may be a deeper tragedy than even the fall of socialist power. There is a possibility at the present time or in the next decade that if the unleashed powers of our scientists are not controlled, if socialist principles are not applied to them, then democracy itself is in very great danger, because the free institutions of free men, the parliamentary institutions we boast of, will be held of little importance if the right of determination of the economic power is in the hands of a few faceless ones. If it is to be kept in the hands of the financiers and the industrialists in their small circles, I believe that our institutions may become mere historic monuments and the real power will be outside them . . . Therefore for socialists, the scientific revolution [he argued] requires both greater planning and the extension of public ownership, though not solely in terms of public corporations . . . because different means and ways will have to be adopted in the new setting of the technical revolution . . .

Gunter's sentiments caught the mood of the conference. He was echoed by Anthony Crosland, who also felt that:

if we are going to criticise the public corporation, then we must have something to put in its place, and at the moment we have not got that. The National Executive has the job of finding it, preferably by next year. [He continued:] Almost everybody here would agree that nationalisation is not the same as socialism. It is not the be all and end all. On the other hand, everybody here would agree that we want more public ownership. What we disagree about is how much and how quickly.

But the calls for unity fell on deaf ears. The nationalisation debate was now linked irrevocably in the minds of the left with another: the H-bomb controversy. During the summer of 1959 Gaitskell, Bevan and shadow Defence Secretary George Brown had sought to unite Labour around the concept of a non-proliferation treaty, under which Britain would get rid of its nuclear weapons if all other countries excepting the two superpowers were to agree neither to make nor acquire them. CND however were campaigning hard for unilateral disarmament. 'Week after week one heard that yet another MP or constituency party or trade union branch had joined their cause,' recalled shadow Education Minister Michael Stewart:[226] 'I felt as if I were participating in a play then running in London, in which one character after another turned into a rhinoceros, to the despair of the dwindling minority of humans.' Stewart was one of many Labour MPs who believed that 'as CND gained ground in the party, so the party lost ground in the country'.[227] CND's most powerful supporter was TGWU leader Frank Cousins, who had 'put himself out on a limb and is now being pressed by the nuclear disarmers to stay out on it', mourned Dick Crossman in his diary,

Michael Foot came out in this week's *Tribune* for a fight to the death and for the campaign to go on through the election . . . anything which is accepted by the establishment becomes unacceptable to the opposition inside the Labour Party . . . they used to think the non-nuclear club an excellent idea when put forward by Bertie Russell and Nehru. But the moment we adopt it, they feel it has been corrupted because they don't trust us. What they are looking for is an undefiled cause with undefiled leaders.[228]

On 9 July 1959 Frank Cousins succeeded in getting the TGWU biennial conference to agree a resolution rejecting the non-proliferation treaty and condemning nuclear weapons, though it implied rather than explicitly stated the unilateralist case.[229] 'I have never believed,' declared Cousins in the concluding speech of the debate, 'that the most important thing in our times was to elect a Labour government. The most important thing is to elect a Labour government determined to carry out a socialist policy.'[230] In a speech at Workington on 11 July, Gaitskell told Cousins that:

> the problems of international relations will not be solved by slogans, however loudly declaimed, or by effervescent emotion, however genuine . . . our party decisions on these matters are not dictated by one man, whether he be the leader of the party . . . or the General Secretary of the Transport and General Workers' Union.[231]

After the election, the conflict intensified. At a meeting with Gaitskell, Tony Crosland and Roy Jenkins at Jenkins's flat on 12 May 1960, Patrick Gordon Walker 'began to fear that Gaitskell . . . almost wants to destroy himself . . . he . . . wants to take up absolute and categorical positions that will alienate all but a handful . . . Gaitskell was not prepared to "fudge" principles. He had always stood personally for a clear defence policy, for NATO and for our share in nuclear defence.'[232] Crosland, Gordon Walker and Jenkins believed that it was important to work closely with Alf Robens and George Brown and feared that Gaitskell's 'insistence on extreme and provocative clarity' would undermine Brown's attempt to build a consensus position that would isolate the pacifists.

Although the issue was narrowly about nuclear weapons, the wider issue was of Britain's commitment to NATO and the Western Alliance. For ex-miner Roy Mason,[233] then the MP for Barnsley and still in his early thirties,

> unilateralism was not only misguided but positively dangerous, because it would inevitably undermine NATO and make a Soviet attack more rather than less likely . . . After the Berlin blockade of 1949 and the savage suppression of the Hungarian uprising in 1956, nobody but a blinkered fool could possibly doubt the militaristic nature of Soviet Communism; but some on the left managed it somehow . . . who saw the NATO alliance as a capitalist and militarist conspiracy, people who were wilfully blind to the aggressive nature of Soviet communism and whose hatred of the Americans went beyond all reason . . . in their eagerness to defy party policy and undermine the leadership of Hugh Gaitskell, they were going a fair way to making Labour unelectable.[234]

The year 1960 was, as the now septuagenarian MP Manny Shinwell observed,

> the nadir of Gaitskell's fortunes. Gaitskell's first strategy, the pre-1959 compromises to secure party unity and through it electoral victory, had papered over the ideological cracks but failed to make Labour electable. His new strategy, the attempt to make the party confront its demons and embrace electability, had ripped the paper off the cracks in full public view. And the cracks were now getting wider. Having raised Clause Four as an issue, Gaitskell had failed to persuade the party to tackle it. He had also waved a red flag to the more bullish of the left. The TUC was in the throes of its own

internecine strife. At the Trades Union Congress complete bewilderment was ingeniously achieved when the Congress approved not only the Labour defence statement but also a resolution of the Transport Workers disapproving of it.[235]

On Sunday 2 October, CND paraded outside the hotel where the NEC was meeting at the beginning of Labour's annual conference in Scarborough shouting 'Ban the Bomb! Gaitskell must go!' The parade was led by Cannon Collins, Ian Mikardo and John Horner of the Fire Brigades Union. 'It almost drowned our proceedings,' recalled Tony Benn, 'and introduced an element of mob violence into our affairs'.[236] Frank Cousins had triumphed at the TUC only a few weeks previously and with several key unions recently captured for unilateralism, the expectation was that he would repeat his success at Scarborough. October 4 heard a bitterly anxious speeches from several MPs, including veteran Durham ex-miner Bill Blyton, and shadow ministers Chris Mayhew[237] and Reg Prentice,[238] against a motion to force them to obey conference decisions on pain of expulsion. Prentice asked:

> what is the position of an MP who has campaigned on a position of multilateral disarmament, and who has said that he does not believe in unilateral disarmament, in relation to the people who sent him to the House of Commons to represent them? Can I go down to East Ham tonight and say, 'Everything I said on this subject at the general election I now reverse, not because I want to reverse it, not because my constituents want to reverse it, but because I have to obey the dictates of the party conference.' . . .
> We say we are a party of democratic socialism. The word 'democratic' is a word we use, and we should consider carefully what it means. I believe that it means the belief in a democratically elected Parliament as the sovereign body of this country. I believe that we strike at that belief if we say that members are just puppets of a party machine . . .

It was a portent of the future. Though the motion was defeated, Reg Prentice was to be deselected during the 1970s by local activists who argued that he was not sufficiently representing the views of party conference and local activists. The great defence debate came on Wednesday 5 October. Sam Watson of the Mineworkers put the case for the NEC. TGWU boss Frank Cousins hit back:

> I want it to be understood by every one of you that we regard ourselves as the real patriots in our organisation, who can say to the people that this is an attempt to make you an expendable base for America . . . Let us say that if two mad groups in the world want to have a go at each other, we want no part of either of them . . .

Keith Dickinson of Liverpool Walton, Ayrshire MP Emrys Hughes and *Tribune* editor Michael Foot agreed.[239] Foot declared:

> . . . We supply the Americans with nuclear bases and missile sites . . . from which a counter-attack or an attack would be made on the Soviet Union if a war came, [in

which case] this country would be utterly obliterated . . . I say that we are taking these enormous risks without any fair exchange . . . it is not true that you can only have effective influence if you have an H-bomb of your own, or supply bases to your allies . . . India, Indonesia, Yugoslavia, Egypt and Ghana – not an H-bomb or a nuclear base among them. Who says they have not got influence? . . .

Other delegates disagreed. Staffordshire County Councillor and GP Dr Katherine Rogers asked:

Do you really consider that if we unilaterally disarm and America and Russia press the button and start a nuclear war we shall escape from the holocaust? . . . Did Norway escape in the last war because she was neutral? No! . . . Now I am a socialist, but I am also British and I happen to like our British way of life and I am prepared to die for it . . . Do not forget, comrades, if we lived under the Russian Cossack boot there would be no Labour Party conference . . .

Former deputy leader Jim Griffiths reminded the conference:

By temperament, by upbringing, I was a pacifist. Circumstances compelled me to change, and I remember the time when I changed [during the 1930s] . . . for the problem of how to prevent aggression and war, pacifism is not enough. Friends, we failed to stop aggression in the thirties. We sacrificed Abyssinia. We killed the League, which was our greatest hope. Non-intervention did not save the Spanish Democrats from being crucified. And appeasement did not prevent, but led to, the Second World War . . .

Denis Healey was the most forthright of all:

. . . The unilateralists are saying, and they have been saying to us for a long time, that we have got to give a lead. The question I ask you is: if we give a lead, who is going to follow? . . .

What really surprises me is that there are a lot of very, very good trade unionists in this hall who support unilateral military disarmament; I have not heard one of them support unilateral industrial disarmament. I was very interested in Ted Hill, who made a good speech this morning. I rather like the picture of him walking into negotiation with the employers armed with nothing but 'the purity of his intentions'!

I ask you to face this question: the reason Ernest Bevin was a great Foreign Secretary was that he was a great trade unionist and he applied to foreign affairs the lessons he had learned in his union life; and unless we do, we are not getting anywhere. Is there anybody in this hall who really thinks it is so much easier to deal with Mr Khrushchev than with the Chairman of the London Transport Executive? The plain fact is, you know, that Mr Khrushchev is not the George Lansbury type. You remember at the press conference he held after the Summit collapse in Paris he boasted that when he was a boy he use to kill cats by swinging them round by the tail and breaking their heads open against a wall. He said this. The plain fact is that Khrushchev is probably the best Russian Prime Minister we have, but he is not a man who is going to

225

respond to a lead for unilateral disarmament. Hugh Gaitskell, Nye Bevan and I asked him this question last year when we saw him in Moscow and he replied: 'We do not want our grandchildren to call us fools.' Do you want your grandchildren to call you fools? The plain fact is that the Russians – Khrushchev has said so in public – do not believe in unilateral nuclear disarmament; they believe in multilateral nuclear disarmament, like the Labour Party has up to this moment.

There is no country in the West that would follow a lead for unilateral nuclear disarmament. Our friends all over the world are watching us, appalled at the idea that we might decide to leave the Western Alliance and starve ourselves of our defences. As Noel-Baker says, the policy the Executive is putting forward has the support of the whole of the socialist International. The Social Democratic Party of Germany is 100 per cent for our policy and it may win the election next year – and I did not like the way, when it was mentioned yesterday by a comrade on this rostrum, there was a sneer ran round the hall. The man responsible for defence in the German Social Democratic Party is sitting on that platform now – Fritz Erler. He spent seven years in Hitler's concentration camps. When I see the man in this hall who has made the same sacrifice to defend freedom and socialism I will be prepared to listen to his sneers but I shall not heed them . . .

Gaitskell gave the final speech in the debate. He began speaking just before 3 p.m., white-faced with tension and heat, dressed in a dark three-piece suit with a small sprig of heather in his left lapel. He had not finished drafting his speech until four that morning. It was, thought Tony Benn, a 'magnificent defence of multilateralism that captured the conference'.[240]

. . . Strangely enough, Mr Chairman, a most powerful, vivid argument for our point of view was put forward this morning by none other than Ian Mikardo. You will remember his simile, his example, of the two men and one with the pistol, and you will remember what he said was: 'You would never use nuclear weapons because to do so would involve blowing out your own brains.' Yes, that is true – provided the power of the other chap to retaliate exists; but without it, no! . . . That is the value of deterrence . . .

Mr Khrushchev himself has repeatedly advocated the value of deterrence so far as Russia is concerned. And when you speak of threatening to use nuclear weapons, he is not averse to threatening from time to time. I do not complain. But if this theory applies to Russia, if he believes that the possibility of retaliation deters the United States or the West from attacking the Soviet Union, why should we not apply the theory the other way round? That is the case – the overwhelming case – for the West retaining nuclear weapons so long as the Russians have them.

But if you were to go to the countries in the alliance, in NATO, and say to them: 'Please give up your nuclear weapons,' we all know quite well that they would refuse to do it. In my view, they would be right so to refuse. Thus the logic of the unilateralists' position is clear. You cannot escape it. If you are a unilateralist on principle, you are driven in to becoming a neutralist; you are driven to becoming one of those who wish us to withdraw from NATO. I do not know whether the union concerned – the Amalgamated Engineering Union – appreciates this . . . if they are unilateralists in principle, and therefore opposed to us, then either they mean that they will follow the cowardly, hypocritical course saying: 'We do not want nuclear bombs, but for God's sake, Americans, protect us,' or they are saying that we should get out of NATO . . .

What is the case against neutralism? What is the case against our withdrawal from NATO – our going it alone? It is surely simply this: NATO was created because the nations of Western Europe and ourselves and the United States felt themselves threatened. I think they were right to feel threatened. I think the behaviour of the Soviet Union under Stalin was quite sufficient to justify an attempt at creating a unity in the West. I have not forgotten – because they were some of the worst years through which we lived – the awful period of the thirties. I remember very well the longing we had then for the democracies of the West to stand at the time with the Soviet Union against Hitler's Germany. And I say this to you: if you could have created that alliance, if, above all, the United States of America had been in it, I do not believe we should ever have had a Second World War . . .

I know there are people who say they would like to see the Americans out. They were glad enough to see them in 1942! Of course, the break-up of the alliance will leave the individual countries of Western Europe exposed to any threat or pressure from the Soviet Union.

I know that you can say: 'Well that is all right; Khrushchev does not mean any harm.' Let me tell you what I think about Russia's policy. I do not believe that the policy of the Soviet Union is incautious. I do not believe that Mr Khrushchev has any intention of deliberately starting an aggressive war in present circumstances. I do not believe any country has the intention of doing this. But I do believe that if you give them the opportunity of advancing the cause they believe in without cost or serious risk to themselves, they will not reject the opportunity. I ask you, bearing in mind all these things, and reflecting on the events of recent years – what they did in Hungary, even their attempt to influence affairs in the Congo outside the United Nations – to say that it would not be wise for us to take the risk . . .

Either the difference between the policy statement and the Transport and General Workers' resolution is a minor one or it is not. If it is almost negligible, as some of my colleagues believe . . . how can one explain the determined opposition of the General Secretary of the union to the policy statement?

I am sure we can expect a great union of this kind to have regard to the need for unity in the party, and if there are minor points of difference I cannot see the justification either for the resolution or for the opposition to the policy statement.

Perhaps you will say they are not minor, that they are major differences. All right. I have given you the arguments, and if that is the case, of course we ask for the rejection of the resolution.

There is one other possibility to which I must make reference, because I have read so much about it – that the issue here is not really defence at all but the leadership of this party. Let me repeat what Manny Shinwell said. The place to decide the leadership of this party is not here but in the parliamentary party. I would not wish for one day to remain a leader who had lost the confidence of his colleagues in Parliament. It is perfectly reasonable to try to get rid of somebody, to try to get rid of a man you do not agree with, who you think perhaps is not a good leader. But there are ways of doing this. What would be wrong, in my opinion, and would not be forgiven, is if, in order to get rid of a man, you supported a policy in which you did not wholeheartedly believe, a policy which, as far as the resolution is concerned, is not clear.

Before you take the vote on this momentous occasion, allow me a last word. Frank Cousins has said this is not the end of the problem. I agree with him. It is not the end of the problem because Labour Members of Parliament will have to consider what they do in the House of Commons. What do you expect of them? You know how they voted in June overwhelmingly for the policy statement. It is not in dispute that the vast majority of Labour Members of Parliament are utterly opposed to unilateralism and neutralism. So what do you expect them to do? Change their minds overnight? To go back on the pledges they gave to the people who elected them from their constituencies? And supposing they did do that. Supposing all of us, like well-behaved sheep, were to follow the policies of unilateralism and neutralism, what kind of an impression would that make upon the British people? You do not seem to be clear in your minds about it, but I will tell you this. I do not believe that the Labour Members of Parliament are prepared to act as time servers. I do not believe they will do this, and I will tell you why – because they are men of conscience and honour. People of the so-called right and so-called centre have every justification for having a conscience, as well as people of the so-called left. I do not think they will do this because they are honest men, loyal men, steadfast men, experienced men, with a lifetime of service to the Labour movement.

There are other people too, not in Parliament, in the party who share our convictions. What sort of people do you think they are? What sort of people do you think we are? Do you think we can simply accept a decision of this kind? Do you think that we can become overnight the pacifists, unilateralists and fellow travellers that other people are? How wrong can you be? As wrong as you are about the attitude of the British people.

In a few minutes the conference will make its decision. Most of the votes, I know, are predetermined and we have been told what is likely to happen. We know how it comes about. I sometimes think, frankly, that the system we have, by which great unions decide their policy before even their conferences can consider the Executive recommendation, is not really a very wise one or a good one. Perhaps in a calmer moment this situation could be looked at.

I say this to you: we may lose the vote today and the result may deal this party a grave blow. It may not be possible to prevent it, but I think there are many of us who will not accept that this blow need be mortal, who will not believe that such an end is inevitable. There are some of us, Mr Chairman, who will fight and fight and fight again to save the party we love. We will fight and fight and fight again to bring back sanity and honesty and dignity, so that our party with its great past may retain its glory and its greatness.

It is in that spirit that I ask delegates who are still free to decide how they vote, to support what I believe to be a realistic policy on defence, which yet could so easily have united the great party of ours, and to reject what I regard as the suicidal path of unilateral disarmament which will leave our country defenceless and alone.

'Gaitskell sat down sweating profusely as the hall exploded into two-thirds of sustained cheering and applause and one-third booing or silence.'[241] One of those who remained seated was Harold Wilson. 'There were few hard-faced cynics in the press seats that day. It was a heroic effort and widely recognised as such,' recalled John Grant of the *Express*.[242] Much of the hall sang 'For he's a jolly good fellow' and then the result of the vote was announced. Although the unilateralist resolutions had been carried, the margin was very narrow: Gaitskell's defeat was chiefly due to the block votes of the TGWU and the AEU. The constituency delegates, not all of whom would have been 'mandated' in advance, actually voted two-to-one against unilateralism.

> I was enormously exhilarated and encouraged by it [recalled Patrick Gordon Walker]. It was clear that we were going to be defeated, that the motion on unilateral nuclear disarmament was going to be carried. Gaitskell made such a fine and tremendous speech that people were visibly being won over during the course of the speech, and the majority against us was much less, substantially less, than everybody including us had expected. I was in my room in my hotel within half an hour after the end of that conference. There was a spontaneous gathering of 20, 30, 40 people, mostly Members of Parliament, planning how we could fight back.[243] We decided to set up an organisation . . . the purpose would be to coordinate action instead of dissipating our forces. There was very strong feeling in favour of this – and of getting rid of Harold Wilson.[244]

The fight-back was swift to begin, partly because preparations had been laid over the previous six months by those who believed it necessary to stiffen Gaitskell's resolve over Clause Four reform. The Campaign for Democratic Socialism (CDS) launched its manifesto on 18 October at a press conference at Caxton Hall, Westminster. It called uncompromisingly to 'resist and reverse the present disastrous trend towards unilateralism and neutralism', in both the unions and the constituency parties. CDS was a grass-roots campaigning organisation, consciously intended as a counterweight to the \tory for Socialism group, to CND and to *Tribune*, which at the time enjoyed the masthead: 'the Paper that leads the fight against the H-bomb'. It was run by three young Gaitskellites: Dick Taverne, Denis Howell and Bill Rodgers. Howell had briefly been a Birmingham MP. Rodgers had recently stepped down as General Secretary of the Fabian Society. 'Dick, don't you realise?' Gaitskell asked Crossman that day, 'This issue of collective security versus neutralism is the greatest issue of our time and I am faced by a dangerous, malicious, underground conspiracy.'[245]

While some such as Crossman were unhappy at Gaitskell's swipe at 'pacifists, unilateralists and fellow travellers', others endorsed it. Engineering Union leader Bill Carron publicly declared that of the 52 members of his executive, twelve were members of the Communist Party and another six to eight were fellow travellers.[246] Indeed, one of the unilateralist speakers in the conference debate had been one Keith Dickinson, later unmasked as 'in charge of administration and security' for Militant, a founder of the newspaper and one of the five key Militant figures expelled from the Labour Party in February 1983.[247]

Over the next year, with the support of key union figures such as Fred Hayday of the General and Municipal Workers, Bill Carron, John Boyd and Jim Conway of the Engineers and Bill Webber of the white-collar TSSA transport union, CDS would succeed in turning the tide against unilateralism. Labour's 1961 conference would see three of the big six unions,[248] and a quarter of the union vote, change sides and the unilateralists decisively defeated, despite the continued support of Frank Cousins' TGWU. The unilateralists had also lost the votes of the Communist-controlled Electrical Trades Union, which had been temporarily disaffiliated from the Labour Party because, as the then Labour MP Woodrow Wyatt pungently observed, 'its leaders' fraudulent practices in cooking the votes had at last been officially recognised'.[249]

The reaction of the left manifested itself most prominently in a direct challenge to Gaitskell himself. Following the Scarborough conference, Labour MP Stephen Swingler claimed Gaitskell was 'unfit to do the job' and that 60 MPs would support an anti-Gaitskell candidate to challenge for the leadership.[250] Barbara Castle and Tom Driberg, both of whom supported unilateral nuclear disarmament, said that Gaitskell must go if he insisted on trying to reverse the conference decisions. Left-wingers including both Castle and Frank Cousins tried to persuade Harold Wilson to challenge Gaitskell directly, but Wilson feared the consequences of such a direct confrontation: 'the little spherical thing [Wilson] kept twirling around in dismay', was Crossman's unhappy description of one of several attempts by former Bevanites to persuade Wilson to stand. Eventually Tony Greenwood, left-leaning MP and pro-CND son of Labour's former deputy leader Arthur Greenwood, announced he would throw his hat in the ring, at which point Harold Wilson decided to beat him to it, and persuaded Greenwood to withdraw in his favour. 'Gaitskell was a man of passion and commitment, or – as his enemies saw it – intransigence and dogmatism,' wrote Wilson's biographer Ben Pimlott. 'Wilson now cultivated an impression of cool, calm, even weary, rationality, with a plain man's willingness to compromise.'[251] The Gaitskellites saw Wilsonian compromise as both unprincipled and politically mistaken: 'To pretend that compromise is always possible,' wrote Roy Jenkins in the *Daily Telegraph*, 'and that policy statements can mean both everything and nothing is a certain recipe for the continued erosion of the Labour vote.'[252]

Wilson's position on unilateralism was in reality little removed from Gaitskell's, resembling, indeed, Bevan's preference for butter over guns while retaining decent clothes for the conference chamber: 'Whereas our wives are pacifists really,' Wilson had told Crossman in 1958, 'you and I, Dick, are both economic opponents of nuclear weapons.'[253]

The Gaitskellites were livid, and never forgave Wilson for what they saw as rank opportunism. 'We thought Wilson behaved appallingly,' recalled Roy Jenkins. 'He had betrayed Bevan (by taking his shadow Cabinet seat in 1955 when Bevan had resigned over German rearmament), and now he was betraying Gaitskell by standing against him when he was most vulnerable. It was discreditable: he simply put his head down and tried to benefit from the clash in the party.'[254] And it was not just the Gaitskellite elite who felt strongly. Wilson's papers include a letter from Fred Williams and colleagues at Hammersmith Bus Garage: 'what a dirty, treacherous, back-stabbing bastard we think you are. You sit on the fence to see which way the cat jumps, and then you stab Hugh in the back.'[255]

On 3 November 1960 Wilson was defeated by 81 votes to 166. Gaitskell's victory was substantial, yet so, clearly, was Wilson's core base. Labour's deputy leadership, vacant since Bevan's death in July 1960, was filled by George Brown, who defeated the more left-wing Mancunian MP Fred Lee, a former Metro-Vickers AEU shop steward, by 146 votes to 83 after a second ballot on 10 November (the first ballot had given Brown 118 votes to 73 for Lee and 55 votes to James Callaghan).

THIRTY-FOUR

Winds of Change 1960–62

*'The test of a civilised country is how it behaves to all
its citizens of different race, religion and colour'*

James Callaghan, the 'third man' in the deputy leadership campaign of 1960, was destined to become one of only three people in the twentieth century[256] to have held the three
so-called 'Great Offices of State' (Home Office, Foreign Office and Chancellor of the
Exchequer). He would also become Labour's fourth Prime Minister. Appointed a junior
minister by Attlee (1947–50 at Transport and 1950–51 at the Admiralty), he made a
strong impression on the Commons. 'Crisp and confident' as a backbencher, 'he was
apparently fluent without the use of visible notes', and 'useful to the whips in difficult
debates', according to his biographer Kenneth Morgan. As a minister he was 'bouncy and
energetic, manifestly ambitious yet also courteous in debate'.[257] His great achievement, as
he would proudly relate for years afterwards, was to champion the introduction of 'cat's-
eyes' on Britain's highways, in the teeth of opposition from civil servants who insisted
that they would cause more accidents by encouraging motorists to drive down the centre
of the road. Callaghan was also in the 'middle of the road' politically: leadership-loyal,
pro-NATO and anti-CND, but nevertheless prepared to rebel if he believed the party leadership to be wrong, as he did in 1948 when as a junior minister he defied the government
line to vote against capital punishment. In Parliament he was sociable and affable, building a popularity among MPs that would secure him election to the shadow Cabinet every
year from 1951. He was also a capable television performer, which raised his profile outside Parliament: over the two-year period preceding April 1954, Callaghan appeared on
Britain's single television channel more often than any other politician.[258]

It was Hugh Gaitskell, whom he had backed vigorously for leader, who gave
Callaghan his chance to shine, appointing him shadow Colonial Affairs Secretary in
December 1956. Decolonisation, especially in Africa, was arguably the only central polit-
ical issue of the time on which the Labour Party was both passionate and united.

Before the 1959 election Callaghan had unsuccessfully appealed to TGWU boss
Frank Cousins, who shared his passionate anti-racist commitment, not to allow his
determination to commit Labour to unilateral disarmament to prevent the election of a
Labour government: 'If the Tories are returned, they will do a carve up on South African

lines with Welensky [leader of the Rhodesian whites]. I know the main lines that such an agreement (or more realistically such a betrayal) would take,' wrote Callaghan. 'Frank, we can't let them down! We should lose the whole continent of Africa to racialism of a vicious character on both sides. The H-bomb is not the only thing that matters!'[259]

In developing his stature, Callaghan's time as colonial spokesman was crucial to Gaitskell's decision to appoint him shadow Chancellor in December 1961 and to his eventual rise to the leadership. The massacre in March 1960 of 70 peaceful demonstrators by South African police at Sharpeville brought the horrors of apartheid into sharp focus and at Labour's 1960 conference Callaghan was at the forefront of those expressing 'repugnance of a country which has deliberately turned its back on democracy . . . detestation of a country which has turned itself into a police state . . . unwillingness to tolerate the actions of a government which at a time when the rest of the countries in Africa are bringing African people into the franchise is deliberately excluding them'. For his advocacy of democratic rights and self-determination in both South Africa and the remaining British colonies, Callaghan won great praise from Dr David Pitt, 'one of the party's greatest natural orators', and, but for the racist swing against him at the 1970 general election, very nearly Britain's first black MP.[260] For Callaghan:

> For fifteen years the cry of all of us for Africa has been freedom – freedom to make your own mistakes and live your own life. Now, with the independence of Nigeria, 75 per cent of the people of Africa are free. Only the debris of colonialism remains to be swept up. But free for what? What sort of lives are they going to live? Although the cry for the last fifteen years has been for freedom, the cry for the next decade must be for national unity so that they move and work together, and must be for cooperation among themselves, backed by the immense technical resources of the West.

The battle for freedom in Africa was partly an issue of Britain's disengagement from empire, but also it was a matter of the attitude Britain took towards other countries, less willing to concede independence. Labour's 1961 conference, the first to be properly televised, was dominated by Jennie Lee's impassioned denunciation of the refusal of the Conservative government to condemn Portuguese colonial atrocities in Angola. Jennie Lee was, with Bevan's death the previous year, the widowed queen of the conference. Her speeches

> coloured and inflected that wonderful Scottish voice; its soprano top note gave her projection, its underlying mezzo pitch stopped her sounding shrill. She spoke in chords. Other platform speakers would naturally lift and drop, lighten and darken their voice within a sentence; Jennie did it within a single word . . . Tom Driberg thought she had a better feel for the mood of conference than anyone he knew . . . Her tears lay just behind her voice and conference rose with her:[261]

. . . Supposing there were no other issues separating us from the Tory Party, the manner of how we treat racial problems, how we deal with the new Africa and Asia and India should lead us all to work to get rid of this government at the earliest possible moment. I am not going over the detailed votes that have shamed us at the United Nations; the fact that in this year, in February, March, April, May and June, while news was coming out about Angola and of unthinkable atrocities, we were shamed by the British votes which were, directly or indirectly, being cast on the side of Salazar . . .

We talk about our oldest ally, Portugal. I was sent to America before America came into the war. I had a job to do. I went to Portugal, like all the other people travelling in war conditions, soldiers without uniform, and I can remember how our oldest ally behaved during the Battle of Britain. When we gathered in Estoril there were British agents, German agents, all on the way to America to various jobs, and at the great central table in the main hotel, at the moment of our greatest danger, there were the backs of plump German officers, wearing civilian clothes, sitting at the central table, while British personnel were in the corner. Why? Because Portugal had backed Hitler to win. On my return journey there were British personnel sitting at the important central table and the Germans on the side. I did not bring America into the war all on my own. But when we get all this nonsense talked about our oldest ally, I must remind you of precisely what its record was. It was precisely the same as the record of Franco. And the British Tory attitude to Salazar is the same as its attitude to Franco.

When I think of what is going on in Angola at the present time I do not want to believe it. It took me a long time to accept the fact that in our generation 7 million men, women and children could be put into gas chambers. I did not believe it, and I find it hard to believe that men, women and children have been hunted through the burning grass in Angola as if they were animals. But we know it is true. We have to believe it, although there is darkness, a lack of information, and it is many weeks since we have had accurate news of what the up-to-date situation is.

When I heard in February that in the capital of Angola desperate Africans had attacked their gaols and police stations, do you know what I felt? I thought of our own not so far distant past. It is not much more than a hundred years ago since the Chartists were marching over the mountains in Wales to Newport, hungry, desperate men, with arms a mere caricature of arms, going out to be slaughtered. It is not so long before that when the people of west Scotland, driven to desperation by poverty and oppression, came out under the banner, 'Liberty or Death'. There again they were men with no money and no formal education, marching in desperation against impossible odds.

I was looking at a passage I have heard Nye talk about many times, and I think it is the essence of all this. Not much more than a hundred years ago, in our country a rich and privileged Englishman, Charles Greville, visited Tyburn Gaol. He recorded his impressions in his diary, and he wrote that he found incomprehensible the attitude of some small boys who had been sentenced to be hanged. He goes on to say, 'Never did I see boys cry so much.' Why mention that? The important word is 'incomprehensible'. He was closer to the horses' stable and dogs' kennels than those waifs, those children of London who were being hanged for minor thefts.

Do not let us be patronising towards Africa and talk about this benevolent British spirit. They stand now where we stood not so long ago. We have to think in terms, in that month of February, of Africans gathered outside the gaols in Angola, pleading for those inside, their leaders, to be brought to trial. They did not know what was happening to them. Were they being tortured? They knew that others had disappeared, not singly but hundreds at a time. If you had been standing outside that gaol, how would you have felt if it had been your leaders you loved and who had borne the brunt of the battle for you? Would you have skulked away, or fought for it? . . .

Instead of going down into darkness and the deepening of the cold war, instead of these emergent nations standing away from us, looking at Britain and seeing only the strange, distorted figures of Lord Home and the rest, let them see that there is a great, powerful Labour movement that cares intensely and at its great annual conference has pledged itself, with all its heart and all its energy and all its powers, to stand in every possible way by their side in order to shorten their misery and increase the pace of their progress towards complete freedom and emancipation.

In parallel with the battles over decolonisation abroad, Labour also fought the Conservative government's decision to introduce immigration controls at home. A race riot in Notting Hill during 1958 had precipitated a minor revival in fascist activity[262] and led to calls for immigration controls, which the Conservative government agreed to introduce in a Commonwealth Immigration Bill in 1961. Hugh Gaitskell opposed it 'with passion and vigour', recalled Roy Jenkins. 'He saw it as the beginning of a racialist road along which he would not take a single step.'[263] He highlighted the ridiculousness of the debate being undertaken in the absence of any net migration figures, which Conservative ministers insisted were difficult to calculate, and demanded that the government fight racism and not appease it. His impassioned Commons speech in unequivocal opposition to the Bill on 16 November 1961 won praise from *The Times* to *Tribune*.[264]

Gaitskell began by attacking the argument of the Tory MP for Louth, that:

we cannot afford to allow the open door to the Commonwealth because we must think of all the people who might come in, because 'we are better off than they are [and] they will come in their floods to enjoy the higher living standards which we have here'. The Home Secretary went one better. He talked about a quarter of the globe being able to come in. I wonder if the Home Secretary and the hon. Member for Louth realise that the situation they describe so vividly existed in 1900, in 1910, in 1920, in 1930 and in 1940. But the arguments were not used then . . . [and] in all those years – 1910, 1920, 1930 – although they could have come they did not . . .

[Gaitskell dismissed the question:] Are you prepared to say that under no conditions will you ever wish to close this door? . . . [as] unreal and irrelevant: the question is not whether if 50 million Indians came here we should be able to maintain the open door; the question now is whether this Bill should be passed into law or not. [Most immigrants, Gaitskell insisted, came not to live off 'public assistance' but to work and not to push local workers out of jobs but to fill vacancies], the movement of immigration is closely related to the movement of unfilled vacancies. If we were to run into a recession, we should find the immigration drying up extremely quickly.

Confronting the arguments that immigrants were diseased ('The hon. Member for Louth once spoke about leprosy') and bred crime ('One hon. member this afternoon spoke in vivid terms about the murders and rapes and everything else in these communities'), Gaitskell quoted statements from Conservative ministers rejecting both charges:

> What then is the reason for the Bill? The immigrants are healthy, law-abiding, and are at work. They are helping us. Why then do the government wish to keep them out? We all know the answer. It is because they are coloured and because in consequence of this there is fear of racial disorder and friction. This is the real question. Why do we have so much hypocrisy about it? Why do we not face up to the matter? . . . with the Irish out all pretence has gone. It is a plain anti-Commonwealth measure in theory and it is a plain anti-colour measure in practice.

In Britain there was a labour shortage:

> Today one can see notices up in the Tube stations about the booking offices closed because they have nobody to service them [but in the Caribbean Commonwealth there was over 20 per cent heavy unemployment]. They are still our colonies. We are responsible for them, and they think of themselves, as anybody who has been there knows, as British people. Oh, yes, they do. It is rather moving. I found when I was there they look on us as the Mother Country in a very real sense – (*An hon. member:* 'As they have a right to') – as they have a right to – because of their history, as has been said this afternoon and before, a history of British merchants collecting their ancestors from Africa as slaves and taking them over there and treating them in a way I think none of us would approve of . . . Let us not overlook the possibility that if we do this thing Castroism may spread . . . It is worth adding that the two countries which will be most affected by this measure, Jamaica and India, do not at present impose any restrictions on immigrants from the United Kingdom . . .

For Gaitskell, the Commonwealth was:

> A multi-racial society and . . . the whole future of the world will probably depend on whether people of different colours can live in harmony with each other . . . this measure as now put forward strikes at the very root of this principle.
>
> It is no part of our case to pretend that any amount of immigration of people of different colour and social customs and language does not present problems, though I urge that we should beware of exaggerations here. Do the government deal with it by seeking to combat social evils, by building more houses, by enforcing laws against overcrowding, by using every educational means at their disposal to create tolerance and mutual understanding, and by emphasising to our own people the value of these immigrants and setting their face firmly against all forms of racial intolerance and

discrimination? That is what we believe, and that is what I hope the government believe, but it is not what is implied in the Bill. Indeed, there is no shred of evidence that the government have even seriously tried to go along this course and make a proper inquiry into the nature of this problem. They have yielded to the crudest clamour, 'Keep them out.'

It may be said that this is the wish of the nation, though I would beware of oversimplifying questions in Gallup polls when all the implications are not explained to those who are answering. But, even if this were the case, I do not believe it to be our duty merely to follow what we are convinced are wrong and dangerous views. Even the government, to their credit, resisted in one particular sphere this kind of situation when they refused the reintroduction of flogging. It was very greatly to their credit, but equally I could have wished that their courage had extended a little further.

It has been said that the test of a civilised country is how it treats its Jews. I would extend that and say the test of a civilised country is how it behaves to all its citizens of different race, religion and colour. By that test this Bill fails, and that is fundamentally why we deplore it. Of course, there are some people who would be glad. I have no doubt that there will be some fascists who will claim that as the first victory they have ever won. I am sure that the Nationalists in South Africa will be rubbing their hands and saying, 'You see, even the British are beginning to learn at last.'

I beg the government now, at this last minute, to drop this miserable, shameful, shabby Bill . . .

Though the Conservatives refused to heed his plea, and the Bill passed into law, Labour activists were reminded that there were issues that mattered beyond nuclear disarmament on which they could agree with their leader. Embattled though he might have felt on other issues, Gaitskell's courage on this issue earned him the genuine respect of Labour's idealist left, playing a crucial role in rebuilding the unity that Labour sorely needed.

THIRTY-FIVE

Labour and the Common Market 1961–63

'It means the end of a thousand years of history'

The year 1962 was the one in which Gaitskell reunited his feuding party. The battle against the Conservatives' Commonwealth Immigration Control Bill had provided crucial common ground between the factions, and it was Gaitskell's Commonwealth ideal which also underpinned the battle through which the new unity would be finally consummated: the battle over whether to back entry into the new European Common Market. During the 1940s and 1950s both Labour and Conservative governments had stood aside from continental efforts at building what was to become the European Union. Eurosceptics argued that Britain, as a world power, had more to lose than to gain from pooling sovereignty in the European 'project'. Pro-Europeans sometimes ascribed darker motives: 'There were many like Eden, Attlee and Douglas Jay who instinctively felt it was dangerous to consort with foreigners,' recalled the then Labour MP Woodrow Wyatt:

> Not long after the war I attended at Koenigsinter a conference run by an Anglo-German friendship society . . . For our meals we sat on benches in front of long wooden tables. One morning at breakfast I found myself sitting opposite Douglas Jay. He had a large number of brown envelopes scattered around his place. Out of one of them he took Shredded Wheat, out of another Grapenuts, out of another Cornflakes and so on. Seeing my interest he said, 'Can't trust these foreigners with breakfast. Always take mine with me when I go abroad.' It was not a complete surprise to me when some years afterwards he announced his vehement opposition to Britain joining the Common Market.[265]

The attitude of both Labour and Conservatives in government had been firstly that the EEC wouldn't happen, secondly, that if it did happen, it wouldn't work, and thirdly, that if it did work, Britain didn't want to be part of it. When the 1957 Treaty of Rome created the Common Market, or European Economic Community, or 'the Six',[266] the UK's Conservative government not only stood aside but set up a rival European free trade Area (EFTA)[267] which unlike the EEC did not involve a formal pooling of sovereignty. In so far as it was intended to rival the EEC it was a failure: the trend in Britain's overseas trade was with 'the Six', and in the aftermath of Suez and the economic weakness it exposed, Macmillan's Conservative government began to rethink. On 22 July 1961 the Conservative Cabinet belatedly decided to apply to join the Common Market. While George Brown and John Strachey[268] wanted Britain to support joining the Common

Market, the majority of the shadow Cabinet, including Harold Wilson, James Callaghan, Denis Healey, Michael Stewart and Patrick Gordon Walker, was against. Gaitskell's younger supporters were also split. While Douglas Jay was ardently anti-EEC, Roy Jenkins was equally passionately in favour, and had become chair of the Labour Common Market Committee.

Gaitskell himself had made a major statement on the issue in a party political broadcast on 8 May 1962 where he said:

> You still hear some people speaking as though we could decide whether the Common Market existed or not. Now this, of course, is quite untrue . . . what we have to ask ourselves, looking ahead, is whether . . . we would be better outside it, or . . . inside it . . . To go in on good terms would, I believe, be the best solution . . . Not to go in would be a pity, but it would not be a catastrophe. To go in on bad terms which really meant the end of the Commonwealth would be a step which I think we would regret all our lives and for which history would not forgive us.[269]

Most pro-Marketeers concluded, fairly, that he was not opposed to entry in principle. Indeed, Gaitskell wrote to his friend and protégé Roy Jenkins that same day asking him to 'get rid of any idea that I am deliberately building up a position in which, whatever the terms, we should be opposed to them'.[270]

The uncompromising tone of Gaitskell's speech at Labour's annual conference that October thus came as a shock to his pro-European supporters. The night before Fred Hayday of the General and Municipal Workers' Union, arguably the most powerfully pro-EEC union in the TUC, had said to CDS organiser Bill Rodgers: 'It will be all right, I've just spoken to Hugh. There will be nothing we can't endorse.' But for the pro-Europeans it was not all right. Gaitskell's speech, delivered at 10 a.m. on Wednesday 3 October 1962, in the overheated hall of Brighton ice rink, was 'of tremendous force and power', and while not formally closing the door on the possibility of negotiations with the Common Market was, recalled George Brown, 'emotionally totally opposed to Britain's having any involvement with the continent of Europe'.[271] Its tone and content owed a great deal to Peter Shore, later to be one of Britain's most prominent advocates of withdrawal from the EEC, who as the then Head of Research at Labour Party headquarters bore considerable responsibility for drafting the speech. But it was abundantly clear to the conference that Gaitskell meant what he said:

> . . . There are certain ways in which we should not decide this issue. It is not a matter to be settled by attractive pictures of nice old German gentlemen drinking beer on the one hand or, on the other, by race or national hatred stimulated by the past. It should not be decided because on the one hand we like Italian girls, or on the other, we think we have been fleeced in Italian hotels . . . I say this to start with, because I do not think the level of argument in the press has been all that high so far . . .

Are we forced to go into Europe? The answer to that is, No. Would we necessarily, inevitably, be economically stronger if we go in, and weaker if we stay out? My answer to that is also, No . . . Britain's entry into a Customs Union – such as the Economic Community of Europe – has a double effect. The barriers go down between us and the six countries of Europe. But they go up between us and the Commonwealth [which Gaitskell believed still to be an important market. For Gaitskell] our faults lie not in our markets or the tariffs against us but in Conservative economic failures and their 'stop, go, stop' economic cycle. [The economic effects of joining were therefore] no more than evenly balanced.

[Turning to 'the political aspects' he welcomed] the idealism implicit in the desire of European people in Germany and France and Italy and the Low Countries to join together, to get rid of the old enmities . . . the European Economic Community has come to stay. We are not passing judgement on that; it is not our affair. It may well be that political union will follow. It would be the height of folly to deny that therefore in the centre of Western Europe there will in all probability develop a new powerful combination, which may be a single state, and it would, of course, be absurd to question the immense impact that this can have upon world affairs. Nor would I for one moment question the force of the argument so frequently put that it would be better, since this thing has come to stay, that we should go in now and influence it in the best way . . .

But we would be foolish to deny, not recognise and indeed sympathise with the desire of those who created the Economic Community for political federation. That is what they mean, that is what they are after when they admit freely that under the present constitution of the EEC the Assembly has no powers except the very far-reaching, overriding one, which they are most unlikely to use, of dismissing the Commission by a two-thirds majority. When it is pointed out that the Commission is a body which has powers but is not responsible or under anybody's control, what is the answer? The answer they give is: 'That is why we should set up a Federal Assembly with powers over them . . .

What does federation mean? It means that powers are taken from national governments and handed over to federal governments and to federal parliaments. It means – I repeat it – that if we go into this we are no more than a state (as it were) in the United States of Europe, such as Texas and California. They are remarkably friendly examples, you do not find every state as rich or having such good weather as those two! But I could take others: it would be the same as in Australia, where you have Western Australia, for example, and New South Wales. We should be like them. This is what it means; it does mean the end of Britain as an independent nation state . . . It means the end of a thousand years of history. You may say, 'Let it end,' but, my goodness, it is a decision that needs a little care and thought. And it does mean the end of the Commonwealth. How can one really seriously suppose that if the mother country, the centre of the Commonwealth, is a province of Europe (which is what federation means) it could continue to exist as the mother country of a series of independent nations? It is sheer nonsense . . .

That brings me to the terms . . . we laid down last year at this conference, we laid down in the House of Commons what became five conditions . . . We said: 'If these terms are agreed, if our demands are met, right, we go in. But if they are rejected, no, we stay out.' . . .

Let me very briefly go though them. Take our condition that the countries of EFTA – the rest of Western Europe – must have their reasonable interests safeguarded . . . those who want to come in as full members should be allowed to come in as full members and those who, for special reasons, want to come in as associate members should come in as associate members . . .

I come to the second condition: that we should be free to plan our economy . . . There are, I must frankly tell you, many unsound arguments used in this matter. There is far more public ownership in Italy and France today than there is in Britain, and more central planning, at any rate in France . . .

There was thirdly agriculture. We had a system of planned production through guaranteed prices and production grants which . . . cannot continue to exist if we go into the Common Market . . .

Fourth, there is . . . the right to maintain as at present our own independent foreign policy . . . We need to lay down, if we go into the Common Market, that there is no commitment whatsoever by going in which involves any political institutional change of any kind. The right of veto in this matter is imperative and must be maintained. We must be free to decide whether or not we want any further political development . . . I do not believe the British people now, at this stage, are prepared to accept a supranational system, majority decisions being taken against them, either in a Council of Ministers or a Federal Parliament, on the vital issues of foreign policy.

Then there is the Commonwealth . . . I am the last person in the world to belittle what we might call the old Commonwealth. When people say, 'What did we get out of New Zealand; what did we get out of Australia; what did we get out of Canada?', I remember that they came to our aid in two world wars. We, at least, do not intend to forget Vimy Ridge and Gallipoli . . .

Where would our influence be in the world without the Commonwealth? It would be very much less. And I believe with all my heart, that the existence of this remarkable multi-racial institution, of independent nations, stretching across five continents, covering every race, is something that is potentially of immense value to the world . . .

Then there is the argument: 'But what if the Six refuse?' The question implies, of course, a discussion to enter whatever the conditions. But we are not forced to enter . . . If we are obliged to say: 'Well, we cannot accept these terms,' to suspend the talks for the moment, we are not going to face economic disaster . . . I repeat again my demand: if when the final terms are known, this party – the major opposition party, the alternative government of the country – comes to the conclusion that these terms are not good enough, if it is our conviction that we should not enter the Common Market on these terms, so that there is a clear clash of opinion between the two major political groupings in the country, then the only right and proper and democratic thing is to let the people decide the issue . . .

We do not close the door. Our conditions can still be met; they are not impossible; they are not unreasonable. I profoundly hope that they can be met . . . We must reject the terms so far negotiated, for they are quite inadequate for the government's pledges. But no final decision can be taken until we know the final terms, and when that moment comes we shall judge it in the light of the conditions that we have laid down.

While he spoke nobody coughed, stirred or smoked. Sweat was running off his nose by the time he had finished. His collar was soaking wet. 'As a political performance it was his finest hour,' was the verdict of his biographer Brian Brivati: 'He had mastered his private capacity for emotion and moulded it into a political weapon.'[272] 'All the same,' wrote Hugo Young, 'the speech wasn't intellectual so much as intensely, manipulatively emotional. For more than an hour, it plucked the mystic chords of memory. Gaitskell seemed so anxious to propitiate the past that he felt obliged to deny any real urgency about the future . . . It was full of passionate doubt, but almost totally devoid of prophetic insight.'[273]

In the hall the ovation was unparalleled. For an anti-Marketeer such as Douglas Jay it was inspirational: 'It was unique amongst all the political speeches I ever heard; not merely the finest, but in a class apart.'[274] 'Charlie, all the wrong people are clapping,' whispered Gaitskell's wife to her husband's parliamentary colleague Charlie Pannell.[275] The pro-Europeans were outraged.

'I went back to the hotel in an absolutely raging temper,' recalled Gaitskell's deputy, George Brown.

> Sam Watson, Gerry Reynolds and Sidney Jacobson, who was the political editor of the *Daily Mirror*, joined me in my room. I remember flinging my glasses across the room and breaking them, so that I was in the position of having to make a new winding-up speech from notes that I couldn't even read. My wife was so scared of all the noise that was going on in our room that she decided to go down to lunch, and promptly fell down the staircase.[276]

Harold Wilson, who had foreshadowed Gaitskell's stance in his opening chairman's address, declared that Gaitskell's 'historic speech' should be printed and sent to every party member. Frank Cousins was so inspired by Gaitskell's speech that he announced that his union would pay for a print run of a million. In the debate that followed, one of Gaitskell's ablest young lieutenants, Roy Jenkins, attacked the defeatism of the anti-Europeans:

> I cannot understand the defeatism of those who think that once in we should be in a perpetual minority of one . . . [and warned] against the danger that by taking up too rigid an attitude now we might in a few months' time find ourselves more pro-Commonwealth interests than the Commonwealth itself . . . [Jenkins concluded with an assault on] Imperial Preference. Do not let us treat it as the heart and centre of the Commonwealth. After all, it is only a 30-year-old trading device, and there is nothing

about its origin to make it particularly sacred to socialists. It is, in fact, a Chamberlain family invention, thought up by Joseph Chamberlain, propagandised by Austen Chamberlain, introduced by Neville Chamberlain at Ottawa in 1932 and opposed by the Labour Party at that time. And of course, when the old Commonwealth came to our help at Gallipoli and Vimy Ridge, it did it without Imperial Preference. The Commonwealth, I believe, is something more important and of far tougher fibre than Imperial Preference.

Denis Healey disagreed, claiming that:

There is a growing fear and hostility in the Conservative Party to the new Commonwealth because coloured men are now going into what they regard as a white-man's club . . . for the Tories the decision to enter Europe is the culmination of a process which started at Suez. The Europeanism of the Conservative Party is nothing but imperialism with an inferiority complex . . .

George Brown, now Labour's deputy leader, wound up the debate for the National Executive, delicately remaining loyal to both his leader and his pro-European convictions. Like Jenkins he could see that the idea of an alternative Commonwealth trading bloc was a mirage, but like Jenkins he also assumed that Britain would be able to lead Europe in the direction it wanted, an idea that cannot have been attractive to French President De Gaulle:

. . . The Common Market, as Hugh Gaitskell said, is no panacea. Equally, staying out does not mean Easy Street either . . .

Can we go in? . . . we can. And we *should* go in, as the document says, if we can get the conditions for it . . .

First, there are some economic advantages. Hugh Gaitskell puts it at 50-50 . . . I frankly put it higher than he does. But nobody will claim that it is more than marginally so.

The second reason is the influence that we should exert if we were able to go in. Do not let our colleagues forget – and a number of those coming to the rostrum seemed to me to forget – that it is not a case of us going in by ourselves. The Norwegians and the Danish people are talking about going in with us – as are the Irish . . .

That leaves one last question, the crucial one. On what terms? Here in the document, we set them out under the heading 'The essential conditions'. We do not believe that these terms are extravagant or unattainable. We believe that these terms are not only necessary for us; they are the terms that the Six could grant without harm to themselves . . . If we have a government prepared to argue for them, not as supplicants needing aid, not as a nation from economic weakness, but as a strong and powerful nation with something to bring, *they can be got* . . .

But we are more likely to get it done, I submit, if we sound as though we are contributing than if we sound and look as if we are sniffing down our noses at the very mention of our Continental partners in Europe . . .

We are, and we want to be – and I am sure that every socialist wants this – able and willing to play our part in the world; not as one little island, not as a member of a group of little islands, not even as a member of a tight group of our own choosing, but in a bigger and outward-looking European Community . . .

Mr Gaitskell said this morning that the very pro-Common Market people must accept that on present terms we cannot go in, and I am sure they do accept it – reluctantly, but loyally. The very anti-Common Market people I think must also respond. They must, in their turn, accept that we cannot make our final decision now . . .

In the event French President De Gaulle doubted the real depth of Britain's commitment to Europe and believed the UK to be too irrevocably wedded to its American alliance to be a comfortable and constructive EEC bedfellow. In consequence he vetoed the UK's application to join in January 1963.

THIRTY-SIX

White Heat and New Britain 1962–64

'They cling to privilege and power for the few,
shutting the gates on the many'

At Labour's 1961 conference the Gaitskellite fightback had paid off and unilateralism was decisively defeated, as was an attempt by Frank Cousins to insert a stronger commitment to nationalisation into the party programme. Gaitskell had been determined to shift Wilson from his post as shadow Chancellor, and now felt strong enough to do so, although with Wilson topping the 1961 shadow Cabinet poll it was difficult to demote him. Hence it was that Gaitskell shifted Wilson sideways, appointing him shadow Foreign Secretary. A staunch Atlanticist and Bevin protégé, Christopher Mayhew, was appointed Wilson's deputy: 'I want you to keep an eye on Harold,' Gaitskell told him.[277]

His anti-Common Market speech at Labour's 1962 conference saw Gaitskell reach the peak of his popularity, both within the party, and also in the country where for the first and last time he managed over 50 per cent approval ratings in the Gallup opinion poll for four consecutive months. His anti-European stance also helped bring him into political alliance with Harold Wilson, whose turn it was, as that year's conference chair, to make the opening address: 'With loving and careful hostility, Harold Wilson took Harold Macmillan apart, piece by piece.'[278]

> The cameras which take in this vast assembly encompass doctors, dockers, parsons, professors and plumbers, nuclear scientists and engineers, railwaymen, works managers, miners, weavers, teachers, technicians, workers by hand and brain, those who form what Herbert Morrison once called the 'useful' people of the country, those whose work and skill create the wealth, the economic and the social capital of this nation.
>
> It is true we cannot boast of any delegates representing some of the parasitic growths of Tory freedom – the Amalgamated Society of Share Pushers and Company Promoters is not an affiliated organisation, nor have constituency Labour parties thought fit to send us representatives of the property speculators, take-over bidders, dividend strippers or bond washers. They will no doubt be more than adequately represented at Llandudno next week – if not in the glare of the television lights, certainly in the penumbral anonymity which shrouds the Tory Party's wealthy paymasters . . .
>
> We meet this year on the threshold of victory. Month by month evidence has

mounted of the total collapse in support for our Tory opponents. The challenge to us is still represented by the fact that too much of that dissatisfaction has found its way into the blind alley of Liberalism, not enough of it yet into positive support for the Labour Party.

This fact is a measure of the task which faces us. For . . . this party is a moral crusade or it is nothing. That is why we have rejected timorous and defeatist proposals for a Lib–Lab alliance. We are not going to sail into power under any flags of convenience.

We seek the privilege of serving this country as its government on one basis only: to seek a majority on a socialist mandate . . . The socialist movement came into being because nineteenth-century Liberalism aimed only at political and religious freedom: the economic freedom which we demand cannot be achieved within the confines of Liberal or any other non-socialist philosophy.

And if we believe in freedom we cannot contain that demand to these islands alone. The 40 Labour MPs who, with me, this year went to Berlin on the invitation of the SPD condemned the denial of freedom in the building of that prison wall. We condemn no less the blot on Western civilisation for which so-called white men are responsible in Mississippi this week.

Fifteen years ago Britain had the moral leadership of the world . . . but today? On the Congo, where danger threatens an entire content, our voice is muted and strangled by the obedience a Tory government owes to Tanganyika Concessions Limited and Union Minière. In disarmament, in the war against world poverty, above all in the condemnation of racial oppression by Portugal and South Africa, Britain turns aside from the task of leadership. In the United Nations, in vote after vote, we are found siding with the colonialist powers, the racialists, the oppressors, instead of helping and leading those new nations who are slowly emerging from the darkness of centuries into the light.

I do not intend to anticipate Wednesday's debate on the Common Market . . . but . . . we are not, whatever the terms, going to join any rich man's club if it means turning our backs on the rest of the world.

Wilson then turned to Harold Macmillan's call in a Prime Ministerial broadcast two days before for British industry:

To concentrate more . . . on the complicated, sophisticated, specialised goods. Not just the things which almost anybody can learn to make . . . [Wilson derided] those sophisticated products of the Tory affluent society, the one-armed bandit and Blue Streak . . . Where are the men to design these complicated, sophisticated specialised goods? I will tell you where they are. One of them, the man whose inventiveness produced the means of guiding American astronauts from outer space back to safety, has been signing on at his local labour exchange. Still more are in so-called defence . . . Many more are working on the production of new variants of Brand X to produce a new punch line for the advertising men . . .

We have had this Prime Minister for five and a half years – but it seems longer. Just after he was democratically elected by the Marquess of Salisbury, he went on television to tell us his vision for Britain's greatness. He attacked those who deprecated Britain's role in the world. 'This is a great country and do not let us be ashamed to say so . . . Britain has been great, is great, and will stay great.' That was Mr Macmillan in 1957.

We recall the Tory Party conference two years ago, the mighty Wurlitzer heralding his arrival with 'There'll always be an England'; his glowing account of what our influences could, and, please God, will be in this second Elizabethan Age. That was two years ago. Now he tells us that we are nothing without Europe . . .

And now we look nervously over our shoulder to see what an 86-year-old Chancellor says about us on German television, reading between the lines to see what he thinks of us. I should like to see us develop our latent economic strength so that they will be worrying about what we think of them. This country is getting a little tired of being pushed around.

We have said that when the final terms are known, if they are unacceptable to the Labour Party representing a great section of the country, the issue must be submitted to the highest court of all – the electorate. For the issue is not only one of economic or foreign policy: we have pointed out the constitutional implications. We shall have, after seven hundred years, a written constitution – and one not written by us. We sign a treaty whose fulfilment means binding the hands of this and every future Parliament . . .

Labour will fight the election, when it comes, pledged to restore economic purpose and social justice; economic purpose to enable Britain not to follow but to lead Europe, the mobilisation of our economic resources for greater production and more socially necessary production; a return to social justice in a society where today the paraplegic ex-miner is denied a Ministry of Health invacar while the Chancellor subsidises thousands of expense account cars for the surtax payers. For Labour stands, not only for Britain, but for the least privileged of its citizens . . .

'When delegates dispersed,' wrote Wilson's biographer Ben Pimlott, 'they were not quite sure whether it had been Gaitskell's conference or Wilson's.'[279] In that year's NEC elections, Wilson topped the poll, as he had done in the shadow Cabinet elections the previous year. On 30 October 1962 Wilson announced that he was challenging George Brown for the deputy leadership. For his supporters, Brown was a charismatic figure who, recalled Denis Howell, 'had one of the best brains I have ever encountered in politics, untrained but precise and decisive'.[280] Nevertheless, he was perceived to be vulnerable. Partly this was the consequence of a growing awareness among MPs of his drink problem and partly it was the unpopularity of his trenchant advocacy of British membership of the Common Market. This was an issue which now divided Brown from Gaitskell, who backed Brown in the contest but nevertheless was now on the same side of the European debate as Wilson. Wilson's challenge was serious and the whips initially feared Brown's defeat. In the event Brown defeated Wilson by 133 votes to 103. Brown was safe, but the strength of Wilson's vote, 20 more than he had secured against Gaitskell in 1960, foreshadowed things to come.

Within weeks of Labour's 1962 conference Gaitskell was showing signs of increasing weariness and in mid-December he went into hospital for tests. A month later, on 18 January 1963, he was dead: struck down by lupus erythematosus, 'Red Wolf', a rare disease of the tissues impossible permanently to cure and almost as hard to diagnose.

The left of the party immediately rallied behind Harold Wilson's campaign for the leadership. The Gaitskellites, meanwhile, were wracked by grief and indecision. They were largely united in their determination to stop Wilson, but unable to agree on a single alternative candidate to support. 'Where Gaitskell was straight, Wilson was tricky; where Gaitskell had vision, Wilson was the super-tactician. But looking back,' Bill Rodgers would later write, 'I now think that, like a child confronted by a step-parent, I felt a resentment towards Wilson simply because he took Gaitskell's place.'[281] Patrick Gordon Walker and shadow Home Secretary Frank Soskice were mentioned as anti-Wilson candidates by some, but the clear choice soon became between George Brown and James Callaghan.[282] It was a choice that left the centre and right of the Labour Party heavily split. Brown's trenchant pro-Europeanism attracted Roy Jenkins but put off others like Douglas Jay, whose son had just married Callaghan's daughter. James Callaghan acknowledged that Brown 'exceeded us all in his darting imagination, his demonic energy and his persuasive power'.[283] Callaghan stood partly out of ambition (didn't they all?) and partly out of a conviction that Brown's erratic and sometimes violent bouts of drunkenness meant that the centre and right of the party needed an alternative candidate. 'Like the immortal Jemima,' recalled Healey, who supported Callaghan, 'when [Brown] was good he was very, very good, but when he was bad he was horrid.'[284] Chris Mayhew agreed: 'I'm not going to vote for a crook or a drunk so I'll vote for Jim.'[285] Alf Robens, who would otherwise almost certainly have been the favoured anti-Wilson candidate, and would probably have won,[286] had ruled himself out of the race by quitting Parliament in 1960 for the Chairmanship of the National Coal Board.

As the campaign progressed, Brown was 'in a mood of despondency and despair', writes his biographer, 'genuinely grief-stricken, and nowhere as prepared for the electoral battle as was Wilson, whose machine was clicking smoothly into place'.[287] When the votes had been counted, Wilson, whose campaign was efficiently managed by Dudley MP Colonel George Wigg, secured 115 votes on the first ballot, to Brown's 88 and Callaghan's 41. Callaghan withdrew, leaving Wilson with victory if he managed to pick up more than eight of Callaghan's supporters. On 14 February Wilson was elected Labour's new leader, by 144 votes to Brown's 103.

For all Gaitskell's strengths and abilities as a Labour leader, Wilson in his first phase as leader of the opposition seems more successfully to have been able to capture the

WHITE HEAT AND NEW BRITAIN 1962-64

imagination of the voters. Wilson's Gallup poll approval rating was over 56 per cent from July 1963 until the 1964 election, peaking at 67 per cent in November 1963. Gaitskell had only once achieved greater than 56 per cent approval rating (57 per cent in October 1961) and had to be content with ratings in the mid-forties for most of his career as Labour leader. Partly this was down to luck, or what Harold Macmillan called 'events, dear boy': by the time that Wilson became Labour's leader, the shine had somewhat scuffed off the Conservative's ball. By 1963 Harold Macmillan's government was tarnished by the Profumo affair, the rebuff of its application to join the European Common Market by De Gaulle and the failure of 'stop-go' economic policies. 'Wilson caught the mood of the British people,' recalled James Callaghan, 'and even elicited a hearing from industry and commerce, the readier to listen because they had become impatient with successive balance of payments crises in the Tory years of 1955, 1957 and 1961.'[288] And the theme with which Wilson was to catch that mood, building on the foundations laid by *Labour in the Sixties*, was science. Wilson's authorised biographer has argued that Wilson's 'greatest contribution to the unity of the party and its electoral prospects was to transfer its main thrust from the scorched earth of nationalisation and Clause Four to the brave new world of science and technology'.[289]

It was at Labour's annual conference in Scarborough on 2 October 1963 that Wilson set out his vision for the New Britain. He 'had been up until half-past three in the morning and later told me he was so tired when he started that it was quite a pleasure to wake himself up by speaking', recalled Dick Crossman. 'He spoke beautifully, completely collectedly, carrying the whole conference with him . . . he had provided the revision of socialism and its application to modern times which Gaitskell and Crosland had tried and completely failed to do':[290]

> . . . It is, of course, a cliché that we are living at a time of such rapid scientific change . . . We are living perhaps in a more rapid revolution that some of us realise . . . It is no good trying to comfort ourselves with the thought that automation need not happen here . . . there is no room for Luddites in the socialist party. If we try to abstract from the automative age, the only result will be that Britain will become a stagnant backwater, pitied and condemned by the rest of the world. The danger, as things are, is that an unregulated private enterprise economy in this country will promote just enough automation to create serious unemployment but not enough to create a breakthrough in the production barrier . . .
>
> Now I come to what we must do . . . First, we must produce more scientists. Secondly, having produced them we must be a great deal more successful in keeping them in this country. Thirdly, having trained them and kept them here, we must make more intelligent use of them when they are trained than we do with those we have got. Fourthly, we must organise British industry so that it applies the results of scientific research more purposively to our national production effort . . . our aim must be at the

earliest possible moment to provide facilities for higher education for at least 10 per cent of our young people, instead of the 5 per cent at which the Tories are tepidly aiming . . . Relevant, also, to these problems are our plans for a university of the air . . .

Again we must relate our scientific planning to the problems of the war on world poverty. In a system of society beset by the delirium of advertising and the careless drive to produce new and different variants of existing consumer goods and services, there is no thought being given to the research that is needed to find the means of increasing food production for those millions in Asia and Africa who are living on the poverty line and below the poverty line . . .

In all our plans for the future, we are redefining and we are restating our socialism in terms of the scientific revolution. But that revolution cannot become a reality unless we are prepared to make far-reaching changes in economic and social attitudes which permeate our whole system of society.

The Britain that is going to be forged in the white heat of this revolution will be no place for restrictive practices or for outdated methods on either side of industry. We shall need a totally new attitude to the problems of apprenticeship, of training and retraining for skill. If there is one thing where the traditional philosophy of capitalism breaks down it is in training for apprenticeship, because quite frankly it does not pay any individual firm, unless it is very altruistic or quixotic or far-sighted, to train apprentices if it knows at the end of the period of training they will be snapped up by some unscrupulous firm that makes no contribution to apprenticeship training. That is what economists mean when they talk about the difference between marginal private cost and net social cost . . .

For the commanding heights of British industry to be controlled today by men whose only claim is their aristocratic connections or the power of inherited wealth or speculative finance is as irrelevant to the twentieth century as would be the continued purchase of commissions in the armed forces by lordly amateurs. At the very time that even the MCC has abolished the distinction between amateurs and professionals, in science and industry we are content to remain a nation of Gentlemen in a world of Players . . .

Wilson had made 'the best platform speech of his career', wrote John Cole, then of the *Guardian*. Bernard Ingham, then a young *Guardian* reporter, was 'visibly moved'. Alan Watkins had to restrain Charles Douglas-Home from applauding.[291] Wilson had 'presented a vision of a new Britain and in doing so redefined socialism', enthused the *New Statesman*.[292]

Wilson's vision of a brave new white-hot world 'was politically expedient, distracting attention from issues that were best ignored and offering a future to which it seemed the Tories did not aspire', wrote Philip Ziegler in his authorised life of Wilson. 'It does not follow from this, however, that Wilson saw it as being no more than a political device. On the contrary, he believed every word he said and preached his doctrine with a messianic zeal that could have left only the most cynical in any doubt of his sincerity.'[293]

Ten days after Wilson's Scarborough speech, Prime Minister Harold Macmillan was scheduled to address his assembled party faithful at the Conservative conference in Blackpool. He never did. Instead, it was announced that he was in hospital with prostate trouble and that he had decided to step down as leader. The Conservative Party at that time had no democratic system for electing its leader: 'soundings' were taken among senior figures and a new leader and Prime Minister 'emerged'. His name was Alec Douglas-Home. Formerly known by his courtesy title of Lord Dunglas, during the late 1930s he had been PPS to Neville Chamberlain. In 1963 he was, as the 14th Earl of Home, Britain's Foreign Secretary. Making use of the change in the law secured by the young Tony Benn, who on the death of his father, Lord Stansgate, had himself been catapulted protestingly into the Lords, the 14th Earl disclaimed his peerage and was found a safe Conservative seat in the Commons.

Wilson was not slow to adapt to the new political landscape and moved swiftly to contrast his own meritocratic appeal with the aristocratic Douglas-Home. On 3 December Tony Benn went to see him with an idea: 'I suggested that he anticipate our election manifesto with one major keynote speech in which he outlines the programme of a Labour government. This must have a specific name like the "New Britain" programme – an idea Caroline[294] had suggested – comparable to Kennedy's "New Frontier" . . . People who support and work with Wilson would become New Britons.' On 17 December Benn had a further meeting with Wilson to discuss the 'New Britain campaign': Wilson 'is delighted with it and I can see that I am firmly entrenched as his speech writer . . . Dick [Crossman], Peter [Shore], Tommy [Balogh], and I are the inner circle and round us will be the phrase-makers, like Ted Willis, James Cameron and Hugh Cudlipp.'[295] Wilson gave the first speech on Sunday 19 January 1964 at Birmingham Town Hall:

> We are living in the jet age but we are governed by an Edwardian establishment mentality. Over the British people lies the chill frost of Tory leadership. They freeze initiative and petrify imagination. They cling to privilege and power for the few, shutting the gates on the many. Tory society is a closed society, in which birth and wealth have priority, in which the master-and-servant, landlord-and-tenant mentality is predominant. The Tories have proved that they are incapable of mobilising Britain to take full advantage of the scientific breakthrough. Their approach and methods are 50 years out of date.
>
> Labour wants to mobilise the entire nation in the nation's business. It wants to create government of the whole people by the whole people. Labour will replace the closed, exclusive society by an open society in which all have an opportunity to work and serve, in which brains will take precedence over blue blood, and craftsmanship will be more important than caste . . .
>
> This is what 1964 can mean . . . A chance to sweep away the grouse-moor

conception of Tory leadership and refit Britain with a new image, a new confidence ... Socialism, as I understand it, means applying a sense of purpose to our national life: economic purpose, social purpose, and moral purpose ... If you fly the Atlantic in a jet, you want to be sure the pilot knows his job, that he's been trained for it. If you're in hospital, you feel more confident if you know that the surgeon has given his life-time to fitting himself for his work. Pilot or surgeon: it matters not who his father was, or what school he went to, or who his friends are. Yet in government and in business we are still too often content to accept social qualifications rather than technical abil-ity as the criterion ...

The pioneers of our movement were levellers, centuries ago, but they believed in levelling up, not in levelling down. When, for example, they said that security was a privilege of wealth, they were not seized by an envious passion for destruction. Instead, they resolved to transform this private security into a social security and make it not the privilege of a few but the right of every citizen ...

Conservative policy throughout these past years ... has denied and eroded this principle ... More than two million old people today are forced to submit themselves to a means test in order to obtain the minimum living standard provided by National Assistance. We have put forward, and our conference has endorsed, a plan for ending this scandal. In the long run, our system of graded benefits and graded pensions will ensure half-pay in retirement, in sickness and old age, to the average paid worker, and rather more than half-pay at somewhat reduced contributions to those whose earnings are at the lower end of the scale. As for the urgent problems of existing pensioners, one of our first acts will be to introduce what we call the 'income guarantee' ... [to] lift the vast majority of those two million who are now forced to accept the means test well above the level of National Assistance.

So the extent of need, not the size of personal wealth, will be the passport to social security. There will be no incantations about 'never having it so good' until we have dealt with the pockets of real poverty in this country ...

In 1961 *The Times* had predicted that Labour would need two or three elections to wipe out the Tory parliamentary majority. They were wrong, though Labour's victory in 1964 was nevertheless very narrow. The Conservative vote slumped 6 per cent on 1959 to 43.4 per cent. Labour received barely more than 200,000 extra votes, 12,205,814 as compared to 12,001,396, but it gave them 61 new seats (they lost five) and the necessary overall parliamentary majority of four. The Liberals failed to capitalise significantly on their 25 per cent showing in the opinion polls following their victory in the Orpington by-election of March 1962: they secured 11 per cent of the vote (three million votes) in the actual election and increased their seats from seven to nine. The election saw big swings to Labour in Scotland, north-west England, Greater London and most of the big cities.

Election day itself saw not only a Labour victory and the end of 'thirteen wasted years' of Conservative rule but the removal of Khrushchev from power in Moscow and the detonation of China's first atomic bomb. The anti-Tory swing was smallest in the West Midlands, and it was here that Labour suffered its own bombshell: the defeat at Smethwick of one of its highest-profile figures, shadow Foreign Secretary Patrick Gordon Walker, by a Conservative on a 7.2 per cent swing. It was no ordinary defeat. The Conservative candidate was said to have achieved his victory by way of a racist campaign that had seen Smethwick daubed with slogans proclaiming, 'If you want a nigger for your neighbour, vote Labour.' Wilson was determined not to bow to racism, and appointed Gordon Walker his Foreign Secretary despite his lack of a parliamentary seat.[296]

His other Cabinet appointments included James Callaghan as Chancellor, George Brown as First Secretary of State at the new Department for Economic Affairs, Sir Frank Soskice at the Home Office, Denis Healey at Defence, Michael Stewart at Education, Dick Crossman at Housing and Local Government, Barbara Castle at Overseas Development, Tony Greenwood at Colonies, Ray Gunter at Labour and Douglas Jay at the Board of Trade. James Callaghan's mentor Douglas Houghton had an overall co-ordinating role in Cabinet for the non-Cabinet ministries of Health and Pensions. TGWU boss Frank Cousins was persuaded to come into the Cabinet to run the new Ministry of Technology. Another innovation was the appointment for the first time of a Secretary of State for Wales, a position Wilson filled with Labour's veteran former deputy leader James Griffiths. It was a talented Cabinet, yet a curiously divided one: nearly half had been to Oxford and of the other half, most had not been to university at all.

In his first speech as Prime Minister, on 3 November 1964, Wilson sought to exact revenge for the defeat of Labour's Foreign Secretary. He began with some general knock-about at the expense of the aristocratic Conservative leader and Old Etonian Sir Alec Douglas-Home:

> Hon. gentlemen opposite may find something unusual and strange about this govern-ment. For one thing, there are no relatives of mine in the government. There are none of my wife's relatives in the government. Nor have I any intention whatsoever of appointing any relatives or in-laws either to the government or to offices of profit or power in the State. If I may put it this way, the day of the dynasties and the era of nepo-tism is over. Secondly, there is no one in the government who was at school with me or, indeed, at any time attended any of the schools I went to – and I wonder what would have been said if half the Cabinet had consisted of schoolmates of mine from the past.

And then Wilson directly challenged the Conservative leader to disown the new Conservative MP for Smethwick, Peter Griffiths.

> When foreign affairs are debated my right hon. friend the Foreign Secretary will not, I am sorry to say, be taking part in the debate (*laughter*). I am surprised that hon. gentleman opposite should laugh at that, because the reasons why he will not be taking part – making allowance for the freedom of electors to make their choice and

the freedom of political parties to seek to influence that choice – will leave a lasting brand of shame on the Conservative Party, not excluding its leader, because in a television broadcast the right hon. gentleman was induced – not readily, I admit, but nevertheless induced – without qualification to condemn the use of racist appeals to win votes. He refused to dissociate himself from the utterly squalid campaign of the Smethwick Conservatives.

He cannot be happy about this outcome, and there are sitting alongside and behind him hon. and right hon. gentlemen who, in the Midlands and elsewhere, acquitted themselves on this issue with courage and honour. I hope that the right hon. gentlemen will now make his position clear about this. Perhaps he remembers the phrase 'straight talk' which was used not long ago. Is he proud of his hon. friend the Member for Smethwick [Mr Peter Griffiths]? Does he now intend to take him to his bosom? Will the Conservative Whip be extended to him, because if he does accept him as a colleague he will make this clear: he will betray the principles which not only his party but the nation have hitherto had the right to proclaim. And if he does not, if he takes what I think is the right course, and what, I am sure, the country will think is the right course, the Smethwick Conservatives – (*interruption*) – hon. members opposite will have to listen now – if, as I say, the right hon. gentleman takes what I am sure the country would regard as the right course, the Smethwick Conservatives can have the satisfaction of having topped the poll, and of having sent here as their member one who, until a further general election restores him to oblivion, will serve his term here as a parliamentary leper – (*Hon. members:* 'Shame').

Wilson's speech brought deafening cheers from the Labour benches. It was 'the clearest denunciation of the racialist policies and utterances of Smethwick's new MP'. It was also a calculated condemnation of Sir Alec, who sat speechless and motionless throughout the Prime Minister's speech. 'The Conservatives,' recalled one observer, 'shouted, shrieked and howled.'[297] Progress could be made only when the Speaker threatened to suspend the Commons unless the Conservatives behaved.

THIRTY-SEVEN

Best-laid Plans 1964–66

'Blown off course'

Wilson's new government faced stark challenges. Between 1951 and 1961 British indus-trial production rose by barely a third. In France it rose three times as fast and in Germany four times and in Japan ten times. UK inflation was higher than in all of them except France. Increased UK consumer consumption had led to steeply rising imports, while exports had failed to keep pace. This had led to balance of payments crises in 1955 and 1960. Now it meant Labour faced an £800 million trade deficit. The role of sterling as a 'world reserve currency' made Britain vulnerable to threats to its reserves through international currency speculation. The rate of the pound against the dollar had been declining steadily ever since the financial crisis of 1931. But the key triumvirate of Callaghan (Chancellor), Brown (Department of Economic Affairs) and Wilson (PM) were united in their determination not to repeat the devaluation that had been forced upon the last Labour government. Wilson, having been personally involved with the decision of 1949, felt this all the more strongly. They had said as much in the campaign, and knew that devaluation was not a panacea: it would require a measure of unemployment and deflation to make it a success. Roy Jenkins was almost alone in having publicly argued that sterling's world role was beyond the capacity of modern post-imperial Britain.

The decision not to devalue was reached at a meeting of Callaghan, Brown and Wilson on Saturday 17 October, the government's very first day in office. There was no official discussion of the issue until July 1966. Devaluation was to become the great unmentionable.

To sustain the rate of sterling, it was announced on 26 October 1964 that there would be a 15 per cent surcharge on all foreign imports. Britain's EFTA partners were under-standably livid at this flagrant breach of free trade and within months Britain was forced to agree to lift it.[298] Callaghan introduced an autumn Budget on 11 November 1964 increasing pensions, abolishing prescription charges, and increasing both National Insurance contributions and petrol duty. On November 23 interest rates were raised two points to 7 per cent. On November 25 a substantial loan negotiated from the US Federal Reserve was announced, increasing UK dependence on America, since it would of course, in time, have to be paid back. The Budget of April 1965 (much influenced by Callaghan's special adviser Nicky Kaldor) introduced capital gains tax and corporation tax, raised income tax and announced further rises in tobacco and alcohol duties. Additional savings were to be secured, it was announced, via the abandonment of the cutting-edge but highly expensive TSR2 military strike aircraft. Reaction was not uniformly enthusiastic: 'It was a revolution to achieve exactly the same results that they did with the guillotine in 1790 in the French Revolution,' claimed Major General Sir Edward Spears, Chairman of the Institute of Directors.[299] 'These were heady days,' recalled John Grant of the *Daily Express*. 'Labour's spanking new 1964-registered vehicle careered along, never entirely out of control but always threatening to run out of road.'[300]

While Callaghan was defending sterling, others in government were seeking to turn the rhetoric of a 'New Britain' into reality. Britain in 1963 was a country where some nine million people lived at or below the poverty line, of whom nearly four million were pensioners. Under the Conservatives an increasing proportion of the tax burden had shifted from the richest to the poorest sections of the community. While consumers now owned more televisions, cars and washing machines, public services had suffered from chronic under-investment. In 1963 there were about half a million people on hospital waiting lists and over ten thousand empty hospital beds through staff shortages, the Conservatives having cut the intake of medical schools by 10 per cent in 1957. Over a quarter of primary schools had no hot water. Nearly nine thousand schools had no staff room, over seventeen thousand schools had outside lavatories and nearly one and a half thousand schools had no flush lavatories at all. Eighty per cent of the houses being built were too expensive for 90 per cent of the population and over one million houses were classified as slums.[301] There was, in short, a lot of room for improvement.

Labour's leadership was convinced that better economic growth was central to creating the money to invest in improving society, and they believed that the way to do it was through planning. Wilson believed that the USSR 'plan their economic life in a purposeful and rational manner – however much we may detest their political framework'. Indeed planning was in vogue right across the political spectrum: it was the Conservatives, on the instigation of the CBI, who had set up the National Economic Development Corporation, modelled on the French Commissariat, to work out medium-term projections and advise on growth.[302] Labour, however, was convinced it could do it better. The aim was a 25 per cent growth in output over the next five years. This would facilitate, among other things, a record school building programme, the doubling of the numbers of teacher training places, and a 50 per cent increase in expenditure on further and higher education.

The Department of Economic Affairs (DEA) was, as George Brown's biographer has written, 'conjured into being by George Brown – shouting, cajoling, arguing, driving, sulking, cheering, scolding, drinking and hardly ever sleeping'. They were given offices on

Great George Street at the 'backside of the Treasury'. Brown himself recalled, 'when we got in there was only one office with a table, a chair and a telephone and that was the Secretary of State's room. The rest of the building was empty rooms and corridors. We had our first departmental meetings with me sitting in the chair and everybody else squatting on the floor or sitting on the desk!'[303]

Frank Cousins, newly installed at the Ministry of Technology, was even worse off: his office was initially the *entire* extent of the department. In the private sector, decades of under-investment, poor management and outdated working practices meant inadequate productivity and often inadequate product in the face of growing foreign competition. MinTech sought to improve the situation but it was an uphill struggle. Too often the mergers and reorganisations sponsored by Labour's new Industrial Reorganisation Corporation replaced small loss-making companies with larger loss-making companies.

The Declaration of Intent, a tripartite pledge to voluntary cooperation to conquer wage and price inflation and boost productivity, was published on 16 December 1964. Brown's appointment of former Tory minister Aubrey Jones to head the Prices and Incomes Board proved inspired. Under Jones it was perceived as 'fair, trustworthy and even-handed', recalled John Grant. It was, however, toothless and by the summer of 1965 wage rises were averaging 8 per cent. Brown and Callaghan were to become increasingly vexed at the inflationary consequences.

The relationship between the Treasury, the DEA and the Prime Minister was in fact never clearly resolved. Indeed, there were, argues Brown, 'too many of us advising and counter-advising each other'. Over the next two years the Treasury began to reassert itself and 'with its absolutely superb mastery of the governmental machine gradually either filched things back or – more to the point – made it rather difficult for us to effect the grand design we had in mind so that a coherent and continuous economic policy could emerge'.[304]

Brown's approach was to engage directly with union members and try to persuade them to confront the problem. He 'was born in the Labour movement', and for Wilson's former campaign manager George Wigg, not exactly an uncritical Brown admirer, 'no man is better able to maintain a dialogue with Labour's rank and file . . . [he is] extrovert, full of bonhomie and slap and tickle . . . generates enthusiasm and communicates it easily . . . has great generosity of spirit, rare courage, untiring energy and when his interest is captured, a quite brilliant capacity for mastering the details of any proposition or argument'.[305] The National Plan had captured that interest and Brown became 'the government's super-salesman', recalled John Grant of the *Daily Express*, 'ramming home his message at union conferences with passion and conviction'.[306] At the September 1965 congress he succeeded in persuading the TUC to support a statutory prices and incomes policy, though the giant TGWU remained uncompromisingly opposed to *any* interference in wage bargaining. On 16 September 1965 the National Plan was published, to a great fanfare of publicity. At Labour conference two weeks later Brown sought endorsement for his policy, including the planned prices and incomes bill, which provided for an 'early warning system' whereby prospective price, wage and dividend increases had to be announced in advance to the National Board for Prices and Incomes. 'I do not want to freeze wages and salaries,' he declared. Instead he wanted a system for the 'planned and the orderly growth of incomes related to the planned and orderly growth of production . . . ' rather than to 'bargaining power'. The status quo, free collective bargaining, was 'indefensibly unfair to . . . our own comrades who have not got that bargaining power . . . '

He won a standing ovation from the bulk of the delegates. Frank Cousins, however, 'pointedly joined the TGWU delegation in the hall and sat, stony-faced, while the applause rang out', John Grant of the *Daily Express* observed. The cameras popped and flashed, the journalists' questions flowed. Cousins' behaviour was 'a flagrant demonstration of dissent', and 'a public rejection of the doctrine of Cabinet collective responsibility'.[307] In other circumstances, and had he been anyone else, Cousins might have been sacked, as Brown told him in forthright terms the following evening.[308] But Wilson feared alienating Cousins further. The government needed him and his support (both as Minister of Technology and in terms of his leverage in the TGWU) for its central strategy to work. That it did not have his support even then was an uncomfortable fact that Wilson hoped not to have to confront. He still hoped to win Cousins over, and while he was still formally inside the Cabinet tent he hoped that ought to be easier.

The Prices and Incomes Bill that would facilitate a statutory incomes policy was delayed by the 1966 election and was not eventually published until 4 July 1966. Cousins would resign in protest the previous day, to be replaced by Tony Benn. Wilson again sought to persuade him to stay, but Cousins' conditions to do so were politically impossible.[309]

Callaghan's pre-election Budget on 1 March 1966 offered a populist combination of tax rebates for homebuyers' mortgages, a new tax on gambling and the announcement that in 1971 Britain would convert to decimal coinage. With the government's majority so tight, pressure for an election to secure a more workable majority remained strong. Shrugging off the resignation in February of Navy Minister Chris Mayhew in protest at the cancellation (essentially on the grounds of cost) of the navy's prospective new aircraft carrier, Wilson announced a general election on 31 March. He had been strongly influenced in his decision by the Hull North by-election of 28 January which Labour had held with a swing of 4 per cent from the Conservatives, giving them back a majority of three. Labour would fight the election on the slogan, 'You know that Labour government works.' The Conservatives had a new leader, Edward Heath. Like Wilson he was a grammar school meritocrat. Unlike Wilson, he appeared wooden and uncomfortable on television, and he appeared to have no convincing answer to Wilson's charge: 'If your new policies are so good, why did you not implement them when you were in power?' The election saw Labour win over thirteen million votes (47.9 per cent) giving them an overall majority of 97 on a slightly reduced turnout (75.8 per cent). Conservative support was down to 41.9 per cent and the Liberals lost nearly a third of their vote, but increased their seats to twelve.

Although Labour's enhanced majority enabled the government to press ahead with the nationalisation of steel, it did not, however, enhance the shape of the economy. The temporary 15 per cent import surcharge on goods excepting food and raw materials, imposed in preference to devaluation or import quotas, had caused indignant fury among the UK's EFTA trading partners. 'Uproar ensued and they accused the Labour government of every crime in the international calendar,'[310] recalled Callaghan. They had to be dropped. 'As the import controls were phased out, the current account once again plunged into deficit,' Peter Shore, another minister, would later write, adding, 'Moreover, in spite of the incomes policy, UK output was becoming increasingly uncompetitive as productivity failed to increase and as incomes rose.'[311] To deal with the deficit, Callaghan's post-election Budget of 4 May saw the introduction of a new Kaldor-inspired selective employment tax (SET) which imposed a flat-rate levy on employers for each of their employees, but discriminated in favour of manufacturing industry. It soon emerged, however, that the Treasury analysis on which SET had been based was flawed and it would simply not raise the £300 million of revenue that it had been supposed to. It was also highly unpopular among non-manufacturing and service industries. Worse: the markets reacted badly, and pressure on sterling rose once again.

A fresh blow to the economy was dealt by a seven-week seamen's strike from mid-May. Though it was fomented by hard-left 'plotters' (one of them was the industrial organiser of the Communist Party of Great Britain, Bert Ramelson), it was an oversimplification to believe that the entire dispute was a Communist plot. The strike leaders, whom Wilson famously denounced to the Commons on 20 June as 'a tightly knit group of politically motivated men', were only able to secure the necessary support from ordinary members to back and sustain the strike because of the existence of genuine and long-standing grievances which the members wanted resolved.

On 14 July it was revealed that the seaman's strike had doubled the trade deficit. Stock market prices tumbled and further pressure built up on the pound. Something had to be done. Callaghan favoured further defence cuts and the withdrawal of UK forces east of Suez. Brown now favoured devaluation, and advocated applying to join the European Economic Community (which would, insisted the French, necessitate a sterling devaluation). He was also desperate to save the remains of the National Plan and threatened resignation when it became clear how great were the cuts being proposed to defend the pound's current level. At Cabinet on 19 July a formal vote was taken: only Brown, Jenkins, Crosland, Crossman, Castle and Benn supported devaluation. Wilson, who remained personally opposed to devaluation, therefore proceeded with a package of detailed cuts, the 'July Measures', which he announced to the Commons on 20 July 1966, explaining that 'we were blown off course by the seven-week seamen's strike and when the bill for that strike was presented in terms of the gold and currency figures in June the foreign exchange market reacted adversely'. The measures themselves included increased interest rates, tougher hire-purchase and foreign exchange controls, increased petrol and alcohol duties, a rise in purchase tax, public expenditure cuts, and an imposed six-month wage standstill, with a further six months of severe restraint to follow.

This amounted, said *The Economist*, to 'perhaps the biggest deflationary package that any advanced industrialised nation has imposed on itself since Keynesian economics began', the equivalent of 1.5 per cent of national income.[312] 'Labour's authority was never the same,' Callaghan's biographer has written. Brown was absent, having sent Wilson a formal letter of resignation (though he was subsequently persuaded to reconsider). It was the death-knell of the National Plan. In 1965 the National Plan had forecast an increase of 25 per cent in economic growth, 27 per cent in public expenditure and 21 per cent in personal consumption; the results by 1970 were 14 per cent, 11 per cent and 13 per cent.[313] In August, Wilson would announce a job-swap between Brown and Foreign Secretary Michael Stewart. Brown would be charged with preparing Britain's application to join the EEC. Stewart was profoundly decent, able and worthy, but he lacked Brown's drive. The DEA never recovered its momentum.

With hindsight, had Labour devalued in the summer of 1966, rather than waiting until forced into it in October 1967, the deflationary measures necessary to make it work would have had time to take effect by the end of 1968, giving Wilson more of an opportunity to demonstrate that Labour had turned the economy round before an election. Moreover, the wage freeze imposed in 1966 to try and ward off devaluation made it all the more difficult to impose further wage freezes after devaluation. But Wilson felt he could not back out on a secret deal he had made with the USA in the summer of 1965 under which they had agreed to support sterling in exchange for no devaluation and the retention of UK overseas defence commitments. It was, argues Clive Ponting in his history of the 1964–70 government, *Breach of Promise*, 'the historic moment' when it took 'the wrong turning'.[314]

THIRTY-EIGHT

Liberalism and Internationalism 1965–67

*'We cannot just sit on these tiny little islands
and hope that our troubles will go away'*

Roy Jenkins had been appointed Minister of Aviation outside Cabinet in 1964. When in January 1965 Wilson was forced to replace Foreign Secretary Patrick Gordon Walker following his defeat at the Leyton by-election, a vacancy was created in Cabinet. Wilson had replaced Gordon Walker with Education Secretary Michael Stewart, and asked Jenkins if he would like to join the Cabinet at Education. Jenkins turned him down.

What Jenkins wanted was to be Home Secretary and to transform a society characterised by David Lipsey as being, 'like the governments that had ruled over it, pleasure-hating, penal-minded, mono-racial and homophobic'.[315] The incumbent Home Secretary, veteran Gaitskellite Sir Frank Soskice, Jenkins characterised as being 'a man of legal skill, very good manners, considerable charm . . . practically no political sense and an obsessive respect for legal precedent. In addition he was very indecisive.'[316] Clearly Soskice would not last. Jenkins had developed what he himself called 'an unauthorised programme for Home Office reform' in a chapter of *The Labour Case*, a Penguin Special written for the 1959 general election. In late 1965 it became clear that Soskice's retirement was imminent. Jenkins got his chance. As his biographer has written, 'few Home Secretaries have ever wanted that office more ardently than did Roy Jenkins in December 1965, or have come to it better prepared . . . Jenkins' two years at the Home Office are a classic example of the right man being in the right job at the right time.'[317]

Two of Jenkins' most significant achievements were to secure government support for Private Members' Bills that legalised abortion and homosexuality (divorce laws were liberalised in 1969, by which time Callaghan had succeeded Jenkins at the Home Office). Another was to introduce majority verdicts in jury trials, despite noisy opposition from the legal establishment, to prevent criminals escaping conviction by bribing a single juror. He ended corporal punishment in prisons, improved legal aid and outlawed the practice whereby a defendant could spring an alibi at the last minute in court, giving the prosecution no chance to refute it. His reorganisation of the police was more controversial and has given rise to considerable criticism in subsequent decades. Influenced by American experience, he combined a rationalisation of the police from over one hundred forces to fewer than fifty with a dramatic move away from traditional beat policing, towards an American-style radio-car approach. It was the end of the 'bobby on the beat'.

One of the most important areas that Jenkins sought to tackle was that of race relations. Frank Soskice's 1965 Race Relations Act had created a new Race Relations Board, which though lacking teeth and limited in scope was nevertheless a step forward. Jenkins however believed that more could and should be done. He used a meeting of the National Committee for Commonwealth Immigrants on Monday 23 May 1966 to deliver a speech which, as David Lipsey has written, 'defined the terms of the debate on race for a quarter of a century'[318] with its famous definition of integration: 'not as a flattening process of assimilation but as equal opportunity, accompanied by cultural diversity, in an atmosphere of mutual tolerance':

> Integration is perhaps rather a loose word. I do not regard it as meaning the loss, by immigrants, of their own national characteristics and culture. I do not think that we need in this country, a 'melting-pot', which will turn everybody out in a common mould, as one of a series of carbon copies of someone's misplaced vision of the stereotyped Englishman.
>
> It would be bad enough if that were to occur to the relatively few in the country who happen to have pure Anglo-Saxon blood in their veins. If it were to happen to the rest of us, to the Welsh (like myself), to the Scots, to the Irish, to the Jews, to the mid-European, and to still more recent arrivals, it would be little short of a national disaster. It would deprive us of most of the positive advantages of immigration, which as I shall develop in a moment, I believe to be very great indeed.
>
> I define integration, therefore, not as a flattening process of assimilation, but as equal opportunity, accompanied by cultural diversity, in an atmosphere of mutual tolerance. This is the goal . . . if we are to maintain any sort of world reputation for civilised living and social cohesion, we must get far nearer to its achievement than is the case today. In so far as this is something which can be brought about by government action, this is now a Home Office responsibility. I welcome this . . .
>
> In present circumstances we are bound, as almost everyone now recognises, to contain the flow of immigrants within the economic and social capacity of the country to absorb them – the social factor being for the moment, I believe, more restrictive than the economic. There are of course differing views about that absorptive capacity, but the government has a clear responsibility to see that it is not put so high as to create a widespread resistance to effective integration policies. Equally it must not be put so unreasonably low as to create an embittered sense of apartness in the immigrant community itself. But this will depend, in my view, not only on the numerical decisions but on the way these decisions are administered; and it is my firm intention to do so as sympathetically as I possibly can, especially when dealing with hard borderline cases.
>
> Furthermore, I look forward to the report of the committee under Sir Roy Wilson . . . which should give us a considered view of the possibility of an appeals procedure both for Commonwealth citizens and for aliens . . .

For centuries past this and every other country which has played a part in the mainstream of world events has benefited immensely from its immigrants . . . If anyone doubts this let them look at British business today, and at the phenomenal extent to which the more successful companies have been founded – or rejuvenated – by men whose origin was outside these islands.

But this is not merely a matter of business. Where in the world is there a university which could preserve its fame, or a cultural centre which would keep its eminence, or a metropolis which could hold its drawing power if it were to turn inwards and serve only its own hinterland and its own racial group? To live apart, for a person, a city, a country, is to lead a life of declining intellectual stimulation.

Nor should we underestimate the special contribution which has been made by the recent immigrants from the West Indies, from India and Pakistan, and from other Commonwealth countries . . . They work in our hospitals as doctors and nurses, they build houses and run transport services in urban areas, particularly in vital but undermanned public services which go with a full employment society . . . if only those who have come could find jobs back at home . . . our doctor shortage would become still more chronic . . . and our urban public transport systems would be reduced to skeleton services . . . There is therefore no overall rational basis for resentment of the coloured immigrant population in our midst . . .

In conclusion he highlighted challenges requiring further action, including 'racialist literature', and heralded his intention to commit the government to further race relations legislation. Before he left office in 1967, Jenkins was able to commit the government to what his successor, James Callaghan, would carry through Parliament as the 1968 Race Relations Act, containing further measures to tackle discrimination in housing, employment and the provision of services.

The other great issue with which Jenkins would become associated was support for the Common Market. Between 1950 and 1970 the evidence of Britain's relative decline compared to the countries of the Common Market grew and grew: in the numbers of cars, television sets, refrigerators, washing machines and telephones per 100 of population, the UK was being overtaken. Only in the bathrooms and lavatories per 1,000 people league table did Britain remain high up the chart.[319]

With the evident difficulties that the British economy was having outside the EEC, the Eurosceptics began to be more open-minded about the attractions of joining the Common Market. Some in the Labour Cabinet were not so much open for conversion as long-standing advocates. Jenkins was one, but at this stage he was still junior. The most senior pro-European figure was George Brown, and with his appointment as Foreign Secretary in August 1966, his mission was clear. For his biographer, 'More than any other individual [Brown] was responsible for Britain becoming a member of the European Economic Community . . . He battered on the door of Europe in an almost frenzied

263

attempt to break down the resistance of General De Gaulle . . . Edward Heath can claim the credit for Britain's adherence to the Treaty of Rome, but George Brown was his John the Baptist.'[320]

In January 1967 Wilson and Brown had an apparently cordial meeting with De Gaulle and in April a tense Cabinet meeting voted by thirteen to eight to endorse a bid to join. They did not get very far. De Gaulle made clear his profound scepticism on 16 May. Brown however persevered and Wilson smoothed the path with a government reshuffle in August that dropped the most determined opponent of EEC, Board of Trade president Douglas Jay, from the Cabinet. Labour's 1967 conference saw the issue thrown open, with an anti-EEC resolution proposed by Frank Cousins, newly reinstalled at the TGWU[321] and a rival pro-EEC resolution proposed by Fred Hayday of the General and Municipal Workers' Union. While Cousins denied the economic advantages of EEC membership, Hayday insisted that Britain would be better off inside rather than outside the EEC tariff wall, where, he pointed out, living standards and social security benefits had overtaken the UK. Moreover, declared Hayday, it was a myth that the Commonwealth provided some sort of alternative bloc. The debate that followed contained more rhetoric than substance. The ageing Manny Shinwell was shrilly 'agin it', characterising the decision to be made as being over whether Britain 'can solve our economic problems. You heard Hayday this morning telling us that we cannot' but he, Shinwell, believed it could, 'And damn the Common Market!' The equally anti-European Douglas Jay, always a staple for sketch writers with his 'stick-like body, cracked oboe voice, radar-screen ears and cautious Keynesianism',[322] declared that joining the EEC would mean abandoning the power to use exchange controls and regional policy. Jay was wrong to claim that there were 'no regional policies in the Common Market . . . ' insisted Eric Heffer, a self-consciously proletarian bibliophile and Liverpool MP whose pro-EEC views were exceptional among Labour left-wingers:[323]

> We are told about Europe being a capitalist organisation. Of course it is. I agree with this. So is EFTA. So is the Commonwealth. There are those who suggest that we ought then, if we reject the Common Market, to look towards the United States of America and have an Atlantic free trade area as a solution. I thought that the United States was the most capitalist country in the world . . .
>
> Is it not time that we created a third force in the world that is big enough and strong enough to stand up to the pressures of both the United States and of the Soviet Union? . . . we must . . . get into the European Economic Community, to fight for its expansion and to fight to turn it into a socialist economic community . . .

George Brown gave the concluding speech with passion and conviction:

> Nobody is being asked to declare for unconditional membership of the European Economic Community. Nobody is being asked today to decide that tomorrow we shall

be members of it. What we are asking you to do today is to decide that we shall negotiate to try to get in, and in the course of those negotiations, of course, we shall deal
with . . . the essential interests of this nation . . .

This little country – these islands have been magnificent, and still are, at discover-
ing, at inventing, at researching, and even at developing; but we are not that capable
by ourselves on our present size of then selling, because we have not got the base over
which to spread the research and development costs. We have not got the home market big enough to place the initial orders . . .

We can contribute technologically, inventively, in a united Europe, and then we
will have the market in that united Europe, the production resources of that united
Europe, in order to carry forward what we have invented and researched in.

Let me turn to the consequences of our not doing so . . . We cannot just sit on these
tiny little islands and hope that all the troubles will go away. I believe they will be very
considerable, and it will mean that policies that people were unhappy about in our
economic debate earlier in the week are likely to be a lot tougher if we try to go it alone
than they are now. I believe we can influence the development of Europe in the way
that we want it to develop . . .

'The vote for the government was rather bigger than we expected,' wrote Crossman,
'with a two to one mandate for its attitude to the Market.'[324] Nevertheless, on 27
November De Gaulle declared his formal veto of Britain's EEC application, claiming that
Britain's unstable economy would adversely impact on the rest of the EEC. George
Brown insisted that Britain's application remained on the table, but in March 1968 he
again resigned[325] (one estimate claims that he 'resigned' seventeen times during 1964–68).
And this time Wilson didn't appeal to him to reconsider. The reason was Wilson's failure
to inform Brown of an impromptu meeting of the Privy Council to accede to a US
request to close London's gold market for a day. Brown had not been informed. Wilson
said this was only because they had not been able to find him.[326] The incident itself on
one level was trivial, but for Brown it was emblematic of Wilson's personal style and
tendency to work through an inner clique of which Brown was not a part. Though he
remained deputy leader until he lost his seat at the next election, George Brown was never
to hold ministerial office again.

THIRTY-NINE

Defence, Deflation and Devaluation 1967

'Comrades, regretful though it is, ever since we left the Garden of Eden it has not been possible to have more than one bite at the apple'

The July measures of 1966 were not enough to save the pound. On 5 June 1967 the Arab–Israeli Six Day War led the defeated Egyptians to incite Iraq and Kuwait to impose an oil embargo on Britain in revenge for alleged British support for Israel. It was another nail in the coffin for the UK balance of payments, compounded by widespread unofficial dock strikes in September.

Meanwhile, the US government, fearing that a sterling devaluation would put pressure on the dollar and undermine world economic stability, put considerable pressure on Wilson not to devalue, as well as offering much-needed loans to help prop up the pound. Against this background, the sheer expense of UK defence commitments became all the more politically charged with the pressure for government cutbacks created by the decision to defend the level of sterling. Labour was again caught in the classic guns versus butter dilemma which had led to Bevan's resignation and torn the party apart during the 1950s. 'I came to the view, with my colleagues,' wrote George Brown in his memoir, 'that withdrawal from east of Suez and the dropping of a physical land presence in the Middle East was not only inevitable but essential.'[327] The issue was how quickly it could and should be done, a constraint being that America was against any British withdrawal. The Defence Secretary throughout the 1964–70 government was Denis Healey, who pushed through Britain's withdrawal from east of Suez and the cancellation of several expensive prestige projects, including the Royal Navy's projected new aircraft carrier and the famous TSR2 multi-role strike/reconnaissance plane for the RAF.[328] Nevertheless, activists felt frustrated that the government was not cutting deeper into defence expenditure before axing sensitive social programmes. The main reason, arguably, was the government's commitments to NATO and to defending the peace and security of the British people from the Soviet threat. It was this fear of Soviet and Communist expansionism which also lay behind US involvement in Vietnam, where Communist North Vietnam was supporting armed insurrection in non-Communist (but virtually fascist) South Vietnam. Labour's annual conference of October 1967 confronted the issue in open debate, with a resolution demanding the government disassociate itself from the US policy in Vietnam and support the unconditional cessation of bombing. The delegate from Cambridge Labour Party, which had proposed the resolution, branded US policy in Vietnam:

> ill-begotten, misdirected and wholly criminal [and attacked Harold Wilson for having] said that our objective is not to strike allegedly moral postures or to make unhelpful denunciatory declarations . . . I must say that no one ever told me the day when the Labour government ceased to follow courses of action from a moral starting line . . . [Moreover, he continued, given that] little has been achieved in changing United States policy as a result of *sub rosa* and *sotto voce* utterances behind the scenes, [should not Wilson try and] see whether a clear, loud declaration will achieve more than quiet murmurings down a private hot line . . .

The problem, he insisted, was that America misunderstood the Vietnam War, seeing it:

> as a means of combating the so-called menace of Communism [when it was instead, he believed,] a civil conflict on the part of the whole Vietnamese people seeking to shape their own future . . . If any moral posturing is unhelpful, it is this attitude still colouring American policy which has the United States posing as guardians of the Faith, as if in some holy war against the infidels. L. B. J.'s supporters may see him as the good Texan sheriff against the Red Badmen, but this attitude does not solve the war . . .

The strongest speech in defence of the government position came from Healey's PPS, London MP and former Welsh barrister Ivor Richard, who was frequently interrupted from the floor during his speech – a harbinger of conferences to come. Richard attacked the motion for its being 'totally unilateral in its condemnation'. It was not true that America was the only party at fault in Vietnam, insisted Richard, and:

> . . . since in my view the only conceivable outcome in the long run to this war is via a political settlement arrived at after negotiations, I have to ask myself why are the negotiations not taking place (*shouts from the floor*) . . . [It is] because the North Vietnamese government are not prepared to negotiate (*shouts from the floor*). I thought perhaps some people would not believe that so by an extraordinary coincidence, Mr Chairman, I brought along the speech which the President of the United States actually made and for those of our comrades who have not read it I think perhaps they should before they start howling. What he said was this: 'The heart of the matter is this, the United States is willing immediately to stop aerial and naval bombardment of North Vietnam when this will lead promptly to discussions. We would assume' – not 'we demand' but 'we would assume' – 'that while discussions proceed North Vietnam would not take advantage of the bombing cessation limitation.' That request has been rejected this morning by the North Vietnamese government. I must say I bitterly regret that decision.
>
> [Secondly, argued Richard,] a lot of people forget in this whole dispute . . . just how limited Britain's influence in the affair is. The one thing we do not have, as we had in

Korea, is the ability to apply the sanction of withdrawing troops, [for the simple fact that Britain had no troops in Vietnam to withdraw. Britain's influence was] persuasive only and . . . a policy of strident dissent such as the French government have been pursuing recently . . . would be a futile gesture on the part of the British government . . . the one line that we have got in an attempt to influence the situation is a line to Washington. I do not believe that this would be the time to cut that line . . .

Despite Richard's pleas, however, the conference voted to back the Cambridge Labour Party resolution, and, it being a matter on which the Prime Minister was not willing to change policy, it was one of several issues on which left-wing activists would accuse the Labour leadership of a failure to listen to the voice of the party.

The foremost of these issues was deflation. On 3 October, during that same conference, Clive Jenkins, leader of the small but growing white-collar ASSET union,[329] would seek to harness rank-and-file frustration with a resolution demanding the government abandon its deflationary stance: 'Unemployment is our bitterest enemy . . . We must not have a situation where men's work hangs on the unstable thin thread of the monthly trade figures,' he declared, calling for defence cuts, restrictions on capital exports, a re-examination of sterling's exchange rate and world reserve currency role. Instead of taking the soft options of cutting living standards here he urged instead that the government take the really tough decision to take the bankers on.

The government was not entirely lacking in allies. In the debate that followed, General and Municipal Workers' Union leader Lord Cooper appealed for:

This great party of ours . . . to pat the government on the back a little bit instead of trying to put in self-inflicting wounds [and attacked his trade union colleagues] who come here and mouth socialism but are not prepared to hold those who are doing damned well back for a little while, so those who are worse off can have a chance.

But it fell largely to the Chancellor, James Callaghan, to defend his and the government's record. He began by advising delegates against supporting:

A resolution which calls for a return to a free for all, because . . . a return to a free for all . . . would mean inflation, followed by balance of payments troubles, followed by deflation, followed by higher unemployment . . . [He then turned to confront Clive Jenkins directly:] I heard Clive Jenkins make one of the most remarkable statements in this conference. It is wrong, he said, it is wrong that a man's work should hang on the thread of the trade figures. Mr Chairman, what else does he think it hangs on? This is not a closed economy. This is not the USSR or the USA where foreign trade and exports and imports are, as it were, a small luxury by comparison with the strength and weight and size of the internal economy. If it was so he might well be able to make that speech, either in the USSR or the USA, but he lives in Britain (*cheers*). He lives in Britain and the simple truth is that this country, with 50-odd million people in it, depends on foreign trade, and it was a very experienced trade union leader who said the other day – indeed, the one who moved Composite Resolution No. 30 – 'If there is not any profit in these foreign orders there will not be any more orders,' and he was right. And unless – I do not have to state this do I? – our prices are competitive with the rest of the world in a situation in which foreign trade means so much to our own economy, Clive, there will be unemployment. It is daft to say that a man's job should not hang on trade figures. The trade figures are the measure of how well this country is doing in exporting commodities. That is what it is (*applause*) . . .

The complaint is made that wages have not risen. They did rise. They rose very fast between July 1965 and July 1966 . . . What the country did between July 1965 and July 1966 was to scoop the pool without having earned it . . . You will have stop–go again as sure as tomorrow's sun will rise if you once again go for an all-out scramble for higher wages without productivity rising at the same time . . .

Let me put one point to you that I do not think is ever generally recognised. The standard of life of the individual in this country could have gone up even in these days of economic pressure that we have had if we had not had the great advance in social benefits which you applauded yesterday (*applause*).

You cheered Barbara [Castle]'s new roads. You cheered Alice [Bacon]'s new schools. You cheered Tony [Greenwood]'s new houses. No doubt when we come to social benefits – and they are going up again on 30 October – you will cheer that, too, and rightly, because this is the choice that the people of this country made when this government was elected . . . (*applause*) . . .

If we had kept the Tory programmes where they left them, the average pay packet in this country could have been over 10s. a week higher now than it is . . . Yes, incomes would have been going up, but the social programme would have stayed still.

Comrades, regretful though it is, ever since we left the Garden of Eden it has not been possible to have more than one bite at the apple (*laughter*).

His speech was acknowledged as 'a triumph'[330] and 'the speech of the conference'[331] by Cabinet colleagues Castle and Crossman. The *Guardian* fêted Callaghan's speech as 'politically brilliant'; several unions, including Tom Jackson's post office workers, changed their votes as a result of the speech, ensuring the defeat of the resolutions critical of the government. *The Times* declared Callaghan's triumph 'as complete as it could be'; for the *Sunday Times*, Callaghan had displayed qualities of 'near-greatness'.[332] He also secured a major party power base: winning election as Labour Party Treasurer, defeating left-winger Michael Foot by 4,312,000 votes to 2,025,000.

For James Callaghan:

in all the offices I have held, I have never experienced anything more frustrating than sitting at the Chancellor's desk watching our currency reserves gurgling down the plughole day by day and knowing that the drain could not be stopped . . . The Gnomes of Zurich took advantage of every piece of bad economic news in order to take a gamble against sterling maintaining its parity. We could have ridden out these storms if our gold and dollar reserves had been adequate, but they were too exiguous to permit the Bank of England to ignore their raids.[333]

'Unfortunately,' recalled Peter Shore, the whole subject of devaluation

was taboo – even among Wilson's closest advisers and confidants – until further huge losses had been sustained in the summer and autumn of 1967. I remember all this vividly for I myself was appointed Secretary of State for the DEA in a further reshuffle in September 1967. The highly classified information to which I then had access, on the continuing loss of reserves and the uncompetitiveness of British industry – for example that British Leyland was losing money on every car it sold abroad! – led me to propose at once that we either devalue or impose tough import controls without delay.[334]

Everything was compounded by the confrontational culture of UK industrial relations so effectively caricatured in the seminal British cinematic extravaganza *I'm All Right, Jack*. The well-upholstered boss class had grown fat on the seed-corn it had eaten rather than invested during the 1950s. The workers wanted their share too and were often equally reluctant to embrace the modern technology that would have replaced workers' jobs in the short term but preserved the remaining jobs in the long term: containerisation at the ports was resisted by the dockers for just this reason. This meant that demands for better wages were often harnessed to a reluctance to improve productivity, making industry less competitive and potentially driving it to the wall.

October 1967 brought the worst trade deficit on record, heralding yet another run on sterling. Moreover, for the government, the past was catching up: the IMF loan of September 1965 would have to be repaid by the end of 1967, just a few months away. This time devaluation from $2.80 to $2.40 proved unavoidable and was formally announced in a Prime Ministerial broadcast on 18 November. Defending devaluation in the Commons debate on 22 November, an exhausted Callaghan seemed to summon up his last reserves of strength. He 'put party aside and spoke as though he was above the dust of battle', wrote Crossman.[335] Callaghan was 'completely in command of the House', speaking 'without flamboyancy, dealing meticulously with the different points that had been raised', in an 'astonishing speech', wrote Barbara Castle.[336] 'There was something in the sombreness and gravity in his manner that profoundly impressed the House,' wrote David Wood in *The Times*.

Devaluation was:

No substitute for greater efficiency or higher productivity [but] a breathing space – that is all. [He continued:] The dilemma that I think this country is faced with, and with which the House of Commons on both sides is faced, is that people will punish their governments if they cannot have both a perpetually rising standard of living and full employment and all the good things they need even though they are not earned.

We have seen the results of this in a number of elections and by-elections in many parts of the world and in many parts of the country.

The real question is this: we are going back now to a period of full employment and expansion in the economy and there is no doubt that, over the next year or two, there will be a rise in the real value of wages even though it is postponed for the next twelve months. Are we going to be able to hold ourselves in check when we have reached that position in order to ensure that we can maintain the momentum of growth? . . .

I want to see in this country the sense of self-discipline survive and grow which will enable us to combine those good things in life which the whole country wants . . . What we need is a country which is concerned not only with economic motivation but a nation that is both proud and self-reliant and compassionate. The British people have the qualities to achieve this. What we need and what I think we have been lacking is the self-confidence to take advantage of the changes that are ahead of us.

I believe that, if we make a united effort – every one of us, for everyone is needed for this purpose – then this country can recover from the slippage which has taken place in her standard of life and the way she has adjusted herself to the problems of the post-war years. If she does that, I have no doubt that we shall succeed. This government can succeed and when I look across the floor I recognise that there is no one there who can.

In an article headlined 'Bid by Callaghan for the Premiership', the next morning's *Daily Telegraph* carried an article from legendary political correspondent Harry Boyne suggesting that Callaghan's speech 'had struck many MPs as a declaration that he holds himself available as a future leader of the Labour Party . . . there was general agreement that Mr Callaghan's speech was on a much higher plane than the Prime Minister's a few hours earlier.'[337] It was an astonishing recovery. 'Like General MacArthur,' wrote Callaghan's biographer, 'he would return.'[338] It was, though, the end of Callaghan's Chancellorship. He would have been happy, indeed keen, to become Education Secretary, the job that Roy Jenkins had turned down two years earlier. Unlike Jenkins, Callaghan was genuinely and passionately interested in education policy and as Chancellor he had gone to great lengths to avoid having to impose cuts in that sphere.[339] Wilson, however, insisted that education was too lowly a portfolio for someone of Callaghan's seniority to occupy, which says something for the status of education policy at that time. On 30 November Wilson swapped Callaghan directly with Roy Jenkins, making him Home Secretary.

For the Labour government, the saga of cuts, devaluation and further cuts was searing. As Roy Jenkins put it, it was imperative that the next Labour government not become 'a prisoner of a rigid over-valued exchange rate, and a currency which was a national status symbol, and not an instrument of economic management'. Tony Crosland agreed.[340]

FORTY

The Agony of Liberal Internationalism 1967–68

'Our word of honour'

August 1967 saw racist measures imposed by the Kenyan government severely restricting access to work permits for the 200,000 Asians living in Kenya. Soon around five hundred Asians a week were leaving Kenya for Britain where, as UK colonial passport-holders, they were entitled to claim residence under the Kenya Independence Act passed by the previous Conservative government. Some seven thousand had come to Britain during 1966. By 1968, around 2,300 were coming to the UK every month.

Home Secretary Roy Jenkins brought the issue to the Cabinet's Home Affairs Committee in October 1967 and it was decided that the Home Office must draft a Bill in case it became necessary to take action to control the level of immigration. Within weeks, however, Jenkins had left the Home Office, swapping with James Callaghan at the Treasury in the wake of devaluation. It would thus fall to Callaghan to bring legislation through Parliament, while Jenkins would 'have the luxury of turning his nose up at it from the side-lines'.[341] Jenkins' biographer has acknowledged that 'Jenkins would have had to introduce very similar legislation had he still been Home Secretary.'[342] Indeed, writing in 1973, Jenkins was to concede that Gaitskell might also have had to soften his uncompromising opposition to all Commonwealth immigration controls: 'It was a position to which it is now difficult to believe that he [Gaitskell] could possibly have held. As a practical democrat he would have had to move. But he would have suffered great anguish in the process.'[343]

Uncomfortable as most of the government were with the idea of immigration control, they felt their hand forced by a cacophony of demands for action from senior Conservatives such as Enoch Powell and Duncan Sandys. Sandys was ironically the man responsible for the original Kenya Independence Act, which had given the Kenyan Asians, alongside all other holders of UK colonial passports resident in Kenya, the right of abode in Britain. He had anticipated the right of abode provision primarily being taken up by white colonists. Now that it was being used more widely he wanted it changed. His demands were echoed and amplified by Enoch Powell, whose increasingly strident speeches would reach a climax in April 1968 with the infamous 'rivers of blood' speech, for which he would be sacked by his leader, Ted Heath.

'If the government makes its decision now,' agonised Crossman on 11 February 1968, 'it will seem to be surrendering to the most reactionary forces in the country.'[344] To many, that was exactly what it did look like when days later the Cabinet decided that action was indeed necessary. It now fell to Jenkins' successor as Home Secretary, James Callaghan, to bring legislation through Parliament. On 22 February Callaghan announced that emergency legislation would be introduced to restrict the entry of Kenyan Asians to Britain to 1,500 heads of families per year, which, with dependants, would amount to some seven thousand people. The Bill was introduced in the Commons on 27 February. 'A few years ago everyone there [in Cabinet] would have regarded the denial of entry to British nationals with British passports as the most appalling violation of deepest principles. Now they were in favour of doing just that. Mainly because I'm an MP for a constituency in the West Midlands, where racialism is such a powerful force, I was on the side of Jim Callaghan.'[345]

Not everyone agreed with Crossman and 35 Labour backbenchers voted against their government (supported by a handful of Conservatives)[346] during the course of an all-night debate on 28 February. The opponents of the measure coalesced around an amendment designed to make the Bill more flexible. The arguments for the amendment were most passionately articulated by the young Scottish Labour backbencher John P. Mackintosh,[347] who had for several years worked as a professor in Nigeria. 'I have fluctuated since then on whether or not I voted in the correct division lobby that night,' wrote Mackintosh's friend, fellow Labour MP and future Foreign Secretary David Owen. 'I have felt particularly guilt-ridden because I believe that my vote helped make me a minister and that John Mackintosh's vote gravely damaged his chances.'[348]

> *Mackintosh:* ... [James Callaghan] has just said that we must not act in a manner which assumes that the Kenya government will legislate in a discriminatory fashion, but if they had not been legislating in that way, we should not be considering this measure now ...
>
> If ever I heard a good argument for writing these safeguards into the Bill, it was made by [Quintin Hogg].[349] He knows the Home Secretary, and he knows that he is an honest man, yet, sitting opposite him, he says, 'You are promising something which you may not be able to fulfil.' If the right hon. and learned gentleman believes that, how can the Asians of Kenya be expected to think anything else? If there is any possibility of the promise proving incapable of being kept, the only way to safeguard the position is to write it into the Bill.
>
> *Quintin Hogg:* In ten years' time, if it cannot be honoured, how does the hon. gentleman think that writing it into the Bill will do other than heap more obloquy on this unfortunate country?
>
> *Mackintosh:* I do not think that a position would arise where it could not be honoured. The numbers involved in this case are not beyond the capacity of a humane country to absorb. I deny the suggestion. I think that the whole situation is a

spurious, trumped-up one. I do not know who has put the wind up the Home Office and destroyed the reputation of the Labour Party for non-racialism by suggesting that we could not absorb 26,000 people this year into a humane and reasonable society. After this performance I will certainly not listen to any more speeches from either front bench advocating multi-racialism in other countries. I feel humiliated to have to stand here and make this speech.

We are asked why this safeguard for those deprived of their jobs should be written into the Bill. It is not because of any lack of confidence in the Home Secretary, because we know his character. But we have lost the confidence of certain people overseas. We have to restore their confidence in this House, in the British people and in our word of honour . . .

These people do not want to come to this country – they have built up businesses, homes and houses, their children are at school there . . . We are trying to restore security to those who thought they had earned it, people who thought that because they had a British passport they could come here . . . the words 'if you lose your job you will get into this country' actually written in would mean a fantastic amount to the British citizens in Kenya . . .

There is a particular sense of humiliation if we cannot do this, with decency and principle particularly for those of us who belong to families that over the years made their livelihood in parts of the empire, who have gone to India and Africa and earned our living and have come back here. This is one of our small, residual debts . . .

Despite the rebellion, the Bill was pushed through the Commons and Lords, receiving its Royal Assent on 1 March 1968. For Callaghan, who deeply resented the charge put about by the 'friends of Roy Jenkins' that he was less tolerant and liberal[350] than his predecessor, the achievement of the Bill was to 'reassure the country that the situation would not get out of hand'. In his memoir Callaghan argued that it had achieved its purpose: 'Thereafter, except for the zealots, there has been a growing acceptance that immigration is not out of control or "swamping" the country. Mrs Thatcher tried to revive that word and the charge several years later in a television interview, but she had no lasting success and she did not return to the matter.'[351]

While the consequences of Kenyan repression cast a shadow over the 'liberal hour' that in most other respects the 1964–70 Labour government represented, any hopes that the flowering of the so-called 'Prague Spring', Alexander Dubcek's 'socialism with a human face',[352] might precipitate a thawing of the Cold War and a new internationalism, were rudely shattered when Soviet tanks rolled into Czechoslovakia. The day it happened, 21 August 1968, the TUC General Council had been meeting in London. Electricians' Union leader Les Cannon knew the situation in Czechoslovakia well: in his youth he had been a Communist and had travelled there frequently. Indeed, it was there, in 1949, that he had married his Czech wife Olga. Olga had been in Czechoslovakia only ten days previously, on a trip to visit her elderly father. At the General Council meeting,

Cannon had suggested a motion be passed condemning the Soviet action and withdrawing the invitation to the Soviet equivalent of the TUC to be represented at the forthcoming TUC Centenary Congress in Blackpool the following month. He also suggested that UK unions should reconsider exchange visits with Soviet and other Warsaw Pact trade unions. Many left-wing members of the general council were reluctant, however, to break their links with Soviet sister unions. At the September 1968 TUC Congress, incensed at the reluctance of some other union leaders to take a stand against the Soviet invasion of Czechoslovakia, Cannon 'strode to the rostrum, and as he flung his notes on the speaker's stand, they scattered and floated down below him. Without pausing for a second he delivered a passionate speech – for once without interruptions from the so-called militants in the hall.'[353]

> Some people in the Labour movement find it difficult to understand this seemingly crazy act of aggression. I think the previous speaker has been shocked and seems to have failed to understand it as well. It is because many people still refuse to acknowledge the existence of such a thing as Soviet imperialism. The Soviet Union dominate the internal policies of Eastern Europe, they dominate their defence and foreign policies through the Warsaw Pact and their economic progress through Comecon. If that was done by America it would be regarded as imperialism, but according to the double-think in the case of the Soviet Union it is because of the leading role of the Soviet Union and the Communist Party of the Soviet Union. Soviet troops occupy Hungary and Poland and other countries in Eastern Europe. If this was done by America it would be a further example of imperialist aggression. The double-think in the case of the Soviet Union explains this as defending the socialist gains and security of the socialist countries.
>
> But this latest example knows no parallel . . . there is no case in history where a powerful – the most powerful military state in the world – makes an invasion of a friendly power, arrests its government, arrests the party leaders supported by the Communists of that country, hijacks them to Moscow, and compels an agreement under duress. That would be regarded as imperialism if done by America. What is it when it is done by the Soviet Union? It is a grave mistake based upon misinformation, and we ought not to make any more breaches but ought to establish friendly relations with the trade union leaders who are puppets of those governments of the countries invading Czechoslovakia now because it is in the interest of peace to do so . . .
>
> I do not know who are the friends of Czechoslovakia. I only know that many people have come to this rostrum and have defended what has been going on in the past 20 years in that country, all of which has now been exposed by the popular Communist leaders of Czechoslovakia – a history of 20 years of economic stagnation, of mass arrests of Communist leaders, of rigged trials and of a denial of their cultural heritage: years when Dvorak was not allowed to be played, years when Capek was not allowed to be published, and years when Kafka was an enemy of the people. Who were the friends of Czechoslovakia then? That was the Czechoslovakia that the Soviet

Union supported and that was the Czechoslovakia that Ralph Bond [a delegate who had just spoken] supported, just as in the same way he supports those trade union leaders who say 'Yes' to their governments which are raping Czechoslovakia at this moment.

I say that if the Czechoslovaks were allowed now, as they were just a few weeks ago, to make a request to this Congress, they would say to us, 'Until the troops of these nations leave our country and stop raping the people of Czechoslovakia have nothing to do with those trade union leaders who are supporting this massacre of our liberty.' If we were to agree to this amendment, then I reckon this Congress would be the Munich of the trade union movement. Each day and each hour that these troops remain in Czechoslovakia ought to put back for years the time when we can enter into any fruitful dialogue with the trade union leaders of these countries . . .

His speech received emotional endorsement from Norman Stagg of the Union of Post Office Workers:

When my country invaded Egypt in 1956 I protested, my trade union protested. On the Vietnam issue today American trade unions are protesting at the action of their government, but not one word of the protest has been uttered in the Soviet Union or the other countries which invaded Czechoslovakia, not one trade union voice of protest. I am entitled to expect that and until I get it I want no part of international contact with people who do not share my love of freedom, liberty and democracy.

At the TUC few delegates had actually overtly sought to defend the Soviet invasion, preferring instead to equate it with US behaviour in Vietnam or to say that past British imperialism made it unjustifiable for any British organisations to condemn Soviet behaviour. At the Labour Party conference on 3 October, Paddington North delegate Keith Dickinson[354] was more forthright on the Soviet behalf:

. . . this document which has been presented by the NEC is clearly lacking in any working-class content . . . the Czechoslovak invasion by Russia was one which result-ed from fear of the Russian leaders of the spread of liberalism. Of the spread of an independence of the working class in Czechoslovakia spreading to Russia. There were already complaints from the various secretaries of the communist parties in various states of this liberalism catching on in their states, and they did not want any of that. That is why they had to intervene in Czechoslovakia at that stage.

The position, then, is this . . . the Russians could walk through Europe in two weeks . . . This has been admitted by the American forces themselves, so what are the NATO forces in Europe for? As was demonstrated in the Belgian strike, these forces were so much needed to protect the West that the Belgian commitment was immedi-ately released in order to intervene and put down the Belgian workers. Likewise, if France had still been associated with NATO the situation would have been the same in the general strike in France, and elsewhere in the capitalist countries. Our allies, which are referred to in this document, it so happens are all the capitalist powers throughout the world. The working class has no say in the policies of this particular body.

Neath MP Donald Coleman, however, could find 'no justification at all' for Russia's action, calling in uncompromising terms for the conference to support the government and the NEC statement: 'If we fail to accept our responsibility today we shall never, never, be forgiven.' But though the vote saw Dickinson defeated, the margin of victory for the NEC statement was narrow, because the TGWU were unprepared to vote for the NEC statement calling for the breaking off of exchange visits with the Soviet bloc. Bevin and Deakin would have turned in their graves.

FORTY-ONE

Deflation and the Collapse of Pay Restraint 1967–68

'I see the Tiber foaming with much chaos'

The cuts that had been imposed by the government's desperation to avoid devaluation had been profoundly demoralising to Labour activists and voters. Now that devaluation had been found to be necessary, the new Chancellor, Roy Jenkins, argued that further cuts, and tax rises, were required to convince the international bankers and speculators that the new rate was sustainable. They included the levying of charges on NHS prescriptions, higher dental charges, reductions in road- and housebuilding,[355] further defence cuts and the two-year postponement of the raising of the school leaving age from fifteen to sixteen,[356] a decision that caused Lord Longford, Labour's leader in the House of Lords, to resign from the Cabinet in protest. Jennie Lee almost followed. Patrick Gordon Walker, back in Cabinet as Education Secretary, was supporting the delay in place of cuts to universities because, as he explained to the Cabinet on 5 January, 'universities represent such an influential body of opinion'. George Brown's reaction, according to Tony Benn, was vesuvian (though he did not, yet, resign): 'May God forgive you,' he exploded at Gordon Walker. 'You send your children to university and you would put the interests of the school kids below that of the universities.'[357] On 18 January 1968 26 Labour backbenchers abstained in the vote approving the cuts.

Labour's popularity declined still further. Labour had been behind in the polls since April 1967, when the party had been reduced to control of only three county councils. The February 1968 Gallup opinion poll showed a record 22 per cent Tory lead over Labour, a lead that increased to 28 per cent in May. 'The sad thing is that devaluation didn't do it,' mourned Crossman on 18 February, 'we had a real chance afterwards and our stock rallied a bit but in January came the announcement of the public expenditure cuts which sharply reduced Harold Wilson's prestige and the confidence in the government . . . for an ever-increasing number of Labour voters there is no difference between our government and a Tory government and the effect of prescription charges has greatly increased this feeling.'[358] In March Labour lost three seats to the Conservatives at by-elections[359] and in June it lost two more.[360]

April 3 saw the publication of a White Paper announcing the extension of the prices and incomes legislation for another year. Two days later Wilson announced that Barbara Castle would replace Ray Gunter at the Ministry of Labour (to be renamed the Department of Employment and Productivity). Castle had been a courageous transport minister who had imposed a 70 mph motorway speed limit, compulsory front seatbelts and breathalyser tests against noisy and vociferous protests from the motorist lobby. She would prove equally courageous in her new role. Gunter had set up a Royal Commission back in April 1965 to look at the reform of industrial relations, chaired by Lord Donovan, and had dearly wanted to be in a position to carry forward legislation on the basis of its findings. Instead the job had been given to Castle and he found himself moved to become Minister of Power. He was to resign, disillusioned, within months.[361]

Trade union loyalty was increasingly strained by Labour's incomes policy. Elections that year at the National Union of Mineworkers (NUM) saw the favourite, Joe Gormley, beaten for the general secretaryship by his left-wing rival Lawrence Daly. Gormley believed that his defeat had been due to his pro-government stance as a member of Labour's National Executive. It was the same story at the Amalgamated Engineering Union (AEU) where Scottish Salvation Army tuba player John Boyd, like Gormley a member of Labour's National Executive, had been favourite to succeed Bill Carron, the retiring president. Boyd was beaten by Communist-backed Hugh Scanlon. The mood at the September 1968 TUC Congress was sour. Frank Cousins was to secure an overwhelming vote of 7,746,000 to 1,022,000 for his resolution demanding the repeal of the government's incomes policy legislation. Electricians' Union leader Les Cannon attempted to convince the TUC that they should support incomes policy. His union was a lone voice. As that year's Labour Party chair, Jennie Lee made the fraternal address. 'It was a superb attempt,' wrote Geoffrey Goodman in the *Sun*. 'An artist's performance of skating round the cracks with masterly skill and at the same time injecting a revivalist message in old style to a congress which is traditionally reluctant to respond to "political" speeches.'[362] Instead of talking about incomes policy she focused on her role as Arts Minister, and the development of the Open University:

Which will be better than anything of its kind in the whole world. But you have got to wait for it; it will be two years before we are ready to start enrolling students, because I set my face against any 'Paddy the next best thing' and I said, 'We don't want the second best' . . . there need be no Jude the Obscures in the future, there need be no men and women old or young, whatever their colour, whatever their religion, who feel that by the circumstances of their life they have been excluded from so much that is best in life . . .

Now I hope you can somehow guard against the impression that the only thing you are concerned about is the wage packet, because you know perfectly well in this centenary year that the men and women who built our trade union movement would not have had the courage to stand up to the punishment they had to take if they had been fighting for material things alone. Do not insult the men of my family, do not insult my grandfather, who went from pit to pit, victimised, when the miners were establishing the eight-hour day for their industry. Of course he was concerned about a large family of hungry children in his home, of course he was concerned about wages and working conditions, but he was also concerned about dignity, he also had his dream, and education was so close to his heart. He was taught to read by my father, and nothing meant so much to him as the thought that one day the indignities as well as the physical hardships imposed on his friends and neighbours and the families around and all those who made his life would be removed.

My father, my grandfather, the man I married, all in the movement. And all of you in this hall, why are you here? You would not be here if you had not a long history of association with the labour and trade union movement. So I say in conclusion, do not let anyone dirty our dream, do not let anyone brainwash us with the idea that our democratic socialist ideas are out of date. If we argue with one another, if we agree or disagree, or even agree to disagree sometimes, until we find all the right solutions, but do it in that spirit, I am content that we have a very great deal that we can give to our fellow men and women in this country, and that we have also a healing message that we can give to other countries less fortunate than ourselves.

While many of her front-bench colleagues 'would have been howled off the platform', her biographer has written, she received polite applause. 'It was a triumph of sorts. No one could have done more.'[363]

Pay increases without productivity increases were potentially inflationary, and devaluation did not alter the fact that the tendency for consumer prosperity to suck in imports did nothing for the balance of payments situation. But pay restraint was difficult to achieve. For a start, between 1967 and 1970 the threshold for paying income tax at the standard rate was lowered by a third, squeezing take-home pay. Differentials in a number of industries were being eroded by technology: disputes could break out over relative pay rates and conditions between different trades within an industry. And militant union activists could and did tell the rank and file that more could be squeezed out of the bosses if only they squeezed hard enough.

At Labour's 1968 annual conference, a few weeks after Frank Cousins' triumph at the TUC, hostility against the prices and incomes policy exploded in a spectacular defeat for the National Executive when Frank Cousins' resolution demanding the total abandonment of the policy was carried by some five million votes to just over one million, despite a lucid exposition of the government's position from Chancellor Roy Jenkins. Cousins was 'sick of hearing some of our own people telling us about "the horrible workers"', and demanded the repeal of an incomes policy that was, he claimed, failing to deal with the issue of 'low-paid workers' and had, through its unpopularity, 'in my opinion, lost ten by-elections'.

Roy Jenkins began by explaining that since before 1964 Britain had been spending more abroad than it had been earning:

Other countries have temporarily subsidised us to this extent, [but would not do so indefinitely]: It is not some malevolent quirk of international bankers which makes a balance of payments surplus necessary for this country, it is the hard facts of life. Quite a lot of resolutions mention the need to get rid of the shackles of international finance. I think these shackles can be exaggerated. I am bound to say no international banker or any other banker has ever tried to lay down policy to me, but if you want to have less to do with bankers, if you want fewer IMF visits here, the answer is straightforward; help us to get out of debt (*applause*) . . .

I have long wanted to see some abatement of our reserve currency responsibilities. In this, as in other fields, I thought we were trying to do too much. But we cannot just pull out, as some resolutions suggest, without making any arrangements as to what is to follow. If that had happened the whole somewhat ramshackle house of the international monetary system might have come crashing down. A lot of other countries, some rich some poor, would have been badly hurt in the process. But it is we who would have been at the bottom of the pile of rubble.

Nor do I find particularly reassuring Mr Enoch Powell's suggestion the other day that if he were Chancellor of the Exchequer he would float the pound at 2.00 a.m. on the first morning - typical melodramatic touch that - without any prior arrangements about sterling balances. I think I see the Tiber foaming with much chaos (*applause*). But chaos, of course, is what dangerous and irresponsible demagogues always want, even if they are ex-professors of Greek (*applause*) . . .

The government cannot be faulted on the priority it has given to building up the social services . . . But . . . neither the growth of social services, nor the increase in real wages, unaccompanied as they seemed to be by a solution to our central economic problem, brought us electoral popularity. On the contrary, the very year in which we had this big unearned increase in real wages saw the collapse of our support . . .

Now, following devaluation . . . the major decision . . . was that to come out of east of Suez by the end of 1971, the earliest practicable date . . . for the first time since the war we shall be carrying no heavier a defence burden than our main competitors in Europe and a lesser one than some. It means that for the first time in the history of government in this country we shall be spending more on education than on defence (*applause*).

The new Engineering Union President Hughie Scanlon, whose union was threatening to unleash strikes in the motor and engineering industries, spoke up in support of Cousins' call for repeal and, with a swipe at Castle and Jenkins, attacked 'the so-called intelligentsia of our party', claiming 'an intellectual is one who is educated above his intelligence'. The temperature increased further as Bevanite firebrand Michael Foot chided the government for failing to heed his advice to devalue sterling and withdraw east of Suez four years earlier:

The best way, and the best socialist way to pay this country's debts, to make us independent, is to plan for full national production, and we are not doing that now . . . Of course, there are some people who are against full employment, against planning for full production, some people who openly say they want a large margin of unused resources. Those are the words of the Governor of the Bank of England, never repudiated by Jim Callaghan, never repudiated by the members of the government . . . The banks do not believe in full employment, and the people who have lent us the money do not believe in full employment as their policy. The remarkable fact is that those people who do not believe in the policy still give approval to the financial policy that the government is operating.

Governments must choose . . . between an old orthodox deflationary policy and an updated, full employment, socialist policy. This is what the government has to choose about, and so far it has made the wrong choice . . . the prescription charges, the cuts in school milk, the compulsory wages policy in defiance of all the pledges we were given – all these things derive from the government's apparent settled determination to pursue that old orthodox, conservative financial policy . . .

It was left to Barbara Castle, in a desperate speech, to try and turn the tide. She denied that it was the prices and incomes policy of the government that:

. . . has led to a wave of unpopularity. [The policy, she insisted, was necessary, because] we were consuming more of our national production – 66 per cent – than any of our major competitors . . . The result was that this country was lending long and borrowing short to give ourselves a standard of life that we had not earned. I really would say, you know, to those who hate our dependence on foreign bankers that there is one simple way out of it: we had better stop borrowing money from them . . .

I can understand those who say we should have devalued instead of deflating in 1966, but what I cannot understand is that they now refuse to face up to the consequences of the devaluation for which they asked. Now why is it so important to the success of the devaluation era? Because again, as the board points out, there is not any other way of acting directly on costs. [Cousins' alternative policy, namely a taxation increase, she dismissed] because no method of taxation or monetary management can restore export competitiveness; all it can do is create unemployment by reducing demand, and it is only by a direct influence on unit costs that we can retain the export competitiveness that we have endured devaluation to achieve . . . According to the figures published by the National Institute of Economic and Social Research wage costs per unit of output fell in France, Germany and Italy between April 1964, and April 1967, and in the United States they rose 5 per cent. In this country they rose 11 per cent, and this is the sort of basic industrial problem to which the government is facing up . . .

Turning to confront Michael Foot, she continued:

Recently I read a comment in *Tribune* which, frankly, Michael, made me want to weep. I quote: 'Productivity means the fewer the better', trying to suggest that productivity is intended to create unemployment. Michael quoted at the rostrum the philosophy of the pool of unemployment, which he said had been expounded by the Governor of the Bank of England, and that the Chancellor had not repudiated it. Well, I repudiate it (*applause*).

Do you think, Michael, that I would have left my job at the Ministry of Transport – where I occasionally got a very favourable byline in *Tribune* from time to time – to take on this job simply to create unemployment and to lower the standards of work-ing people? (*Shouts of Yes.*) All right, if you want to believe that you can, but I must have changed very radically in the last few months.

No, Michael, when I read that sentence in *Tribune* I wondered how Luddite you can get. I thought of the Rootes factory in Linwood from which I have drawn George Cattell, the head of my new productivity department. Linwood is in a development area of Scotland where we have been fighting to bring down the level of unemploy-ment, and I am glad to say beginning to succeed because unemployment fell 4,000 there last month, but of course unemployment there is still intolerably high. That is why the productivity deal they have negotiated at Linwood was so vital, because by increasing the production of cars by 350 a week with the same manpower it has enabled the company not only to continue its operations in Scotland but to hold out the prospect of expanding there so there are more jobs, not redundancies.

It is not a question of the fewer the better, Mike, but of the better the more . . .

Turning to 'the redistribution of income' she insisted that a prices and incomes policy was part of the solution, not the problem:

The real answer to the critics who say that the policy has done nothing for the lower-paid is that the opportunity is there, in our policy, if only the trade unions care to take advantage of it in any wage settlement . . . [The big wage gap, she continued, was between men and women, and that gap was] the product of years of free collective bargaining. [It was time, she believed, to begin the gradual, phased, introduction of a national minimum wage and she had] already started talks with both sides of industry . . .

In less than a year from now, we shall all have to face up to the decision: do we want the government to continue with the prices and incomes policy at all? And if so, in what form? . . . How many of you, I wonder, would really welcome the death of the Prices and Incomes Board?

As Nye Bevan used to quote, a man's reach must exceed his grasp, or what's a heav-en for? Clumsily, perhaps, inadequately no doubt, the government has been reaching for something better than crude industrial power politics, whether practised by indus-trial tycoons or trade unions. If you kill that without being clear what you put in its place, then you will share a very heavy responsibility.

But Castle's speech fell flat. It could have been worse – though only just. Labour's National Executive had almost voted to endorse Cousins' resolution itself: in the event the twelve-twelve tie was broken by Jennie Lee in the chair, who voted to back Castle against Cousins. It was Cousins' last Labour conference: he was retiring that year. 'The atmosphere between the ministers on the platform and the delegates in the body of the conference was as tense as it had been at any time since Scarborough in 1960,' recalled Geoffrey Goodman, then on the *Sun*.[364]

FORTY-TWO

Division and Defeat 1968–70

'In Place of Strife'

In the 1960s, there was no legal requirement for unions to hold a secret ballot before strike action. There was not even a legal requirement to hold a secret member ballot before electing a trade union's leader. Power rested with the activist shop stewards, a role that too easily could be hijacked by the militant minority. One of them, self-proclaimed Trotskyist and Morris Cowley TGWU deputy convenor Alan Thornett, proudly recalls in *Inside Cowley* that 'during the 1960s strikes in the assembly plant alone averaged over 300 a year and in 1969 rose to over 600'.[365] An opportunity for reform was created with the report of the Royal Commission that Ray Gunter had set up under the chairmanship of former Labour MP Lord Donovan. The report, when it was published in June 1968, emphasised that some 95 per cent of British strikes were 'unofficial' (without formal union backing) and 'unconstitutional' (in the sense that the strike had taken place before full use had been made of the available procedures for the resolution of disputes).[366] The Girling brakes strike that broke out in the autumn of 1968, dragging on for several months, was a prime example. It saw 22 machine-setters down tools without warning because they refused to accept instructions from a chargehand of another union.[367] Barbara Castle recalled,

> As they were key men producing a key component for the motor industry, their action led to some five thousand workers being laid off, some of whom protested publicly at the behaviour of the machine setters. As usual, we set up a court of enquiry, but the strikers refused to give evidence. I inspired one of our Labour MPs to put down a Private Notice Question to me in the hope that the adverse publicity would force Hugh Scanlon to act. It worked and eventually Scanlon persuaded his four shop stewards to get the strikers back to work. Ted Heath made great political capital out of all this and I began to feel that I would have to strengthen the Donovan Report.[368]

Castle's White Paper would be called *In Place of Strife*, after Bevan's book *In Place of Fear*, on the suggestion of Barbara Castle's husband Ted. 'My left-wing friends who considered themselves Bevanites and who were getting ready to smite me hip and thigh were furious,' wrote Castle in her memoirs. 'They considered my title a piece of *lèse-majesté*. In fact I was convinced that Nye would have been on my side.'[369] It was approved by

Cabinet on 14 January 1969 and contained three proposals not included in the Donovan recommendations. Firstly there was to be a power to enforce a 28-day 'conciliation pause' in the case of unofficial action, secondly it gave powers to the Secretary of State to impose a settlement in inter-union disputes and thirdly it gave power to the Secretary of State to order a strike ballot. It also gave new rights to trade unionists, such as protection from unfair dismissal, the statutory right to join a trade union and the encouragement of employers to cooperate with the check-off system of union due payments. Frank Cousins and Hugh Scanlon condemned it out of hand. In an oblique reference to the suppression of the Prague Spring, Wilson was soon forced to demand, 'Get your tanks off my lawn, Hughie.' TUC General Secretary George Woodcock was privately more sympathetic, but could do little against the big battalions. Moreover, he was retiring in March, ironically to head the newly established Industrial Relations Commission. His successor, Vic Feather, was unkindly disposed towards Barbara Castle, his animosity dating from shared childhood experiences in Bradford. It was a small world! Opinion polls showed backing for *In Place of Strife* from over 60 per cent of the public, but under pressure from sponsoring unions Labour MPs began to dissent heavily. On 3 March 55 MPs voted against it in the Commons and some 40 abstained. In an unprecedented move, an NEC meeting on 26 March voted 16 to 5 in favour of a trade union resolution rejecting *In Place of Strife*. One of those who opposed it was Home Secretary James Callaghan, who publicly cast his vote to help defeat a Cabinet policy. Other ministers Eireen White, Alice Bacon and Fred Mulley abstained. Callaghan's view, and in this he was backed by his mentor, PLP chair Douglas Houghton,[370] in addition to Cabinet ministers Tony Crosland, Fred Lee, Dick Marsh and Roy Mason, was that such was the degree of hostility to the government in general from union leaders and so firm was their opposition to legislative interference in industrial relations, that to press forward with *In Place of Strife* could lead only to a bloodbath within the Labour movement. On one level he was undoubtedly correct, and while some have painted his stance on the issue as being motivated by naked ambition, contrasting it with the more far-sighted approach of Roy Jenkins, who backed Castle virtually to the end, it is worth bearing in mind that Roy Jenkins's PPS Tom Bradley, who had succeeded Ray Gunter as TSSA president in 1965, took the same view as Callaghan.

Barbara Castle carried the arguments to the trade union conferences. On 18 April she addressed the Scottish TUC at Rothesay. 'I knew I would be up against a hostile atmosphere, and I was nervous,' she recalled. 'But as I stood up on the platform in a new scarlet dress, I said to them, "I am in my true colours here today," which raised a sympathetic laugh.'[371] Geoffrey Goodman remembers: 'She came in for a lot of stick, especially from the Scottish miners. She was fighting her corner in a typical Barbara way'.[372]

> . . . did we have to have legislation on trade union reform? Did we have to have the Donovan Report? My answer is an empathetic Yes. What the interim Bill will provide

is that where an employer refuses to recognise and negotiate realistically with a trade union, that shall go to the CIR. The CIR shall have complete freedom and discretion to judge the right of that union to be recognised. Not for us the mathematical strait-jacket the Tories advocate, that there should be no right to recognition unless there is first a majority membership.

Comrades, we know, don't we, that there are other types of problems arising from trade union recognition. We know there is a problem with inter-union rivalry that can lead, and has led, to damage in widespread disputes. Are we going to say it is part and parcel of a trade union philosophy where they cannot agree amongst themselves as to who should organise the workers in a particular factory or group they should have the right to conduct war to the death, particularly when the victim is the national economy? . . .

It is because we in your Labour government believe that that strike weapon is an integral and inalienable part of your armoury that we don't want to see it brought into disrepute when a group of workers here or a group of workers there in our modern highly complex, highly interdependent society can just say 'I don't care what my union negotiated, I don't like this bit,' or 'I don't like that and I am downing tools' – that has happened time and time again even in recent times – thus putting thousands of fellow trade unionists out of work . . .

Let us face up to something quite straightforward and fundamental. There are two schools of thought here. There are those who believe industrial conflict should be prosecuted wherever it can be prosecuted and whatever it needs and to whatever extent. That is their philosophy on working-class advance because their aim is to destroy that industry. But that is not our philosophy in the Labour movement. Our philosophy is that the changes in society, the changes in class structure in our society, have to be prosecuted through the trade unionists in their political wing in Parliament. So these conflicts of industry which are inevitable should be prosecuted in a way which, in the end, leaves the trade union movement stronger and leaves the people you represent with the higher standard of living, the higher status in society, that they created you to get for them, just as you created a Labour government.

So I challenge the trade union movement to abandon its defensive attitudes, to seize the opportunity we hold out here to you. I challenge the trade union movement to think as socialists, and if we think as socialists, we know we are interdependent one with another. We know it is no part of the socialist philosophy, in which I was brought up, that one section of workers should proceed to prosecute its interests in total dis-regard of interests elsewhere.

I remember too Nye Bevan once saying shortly after the 1959 election, when we lost our opportunity of power again, I remember him saying to some of our trade union colleagues on the National Executive: 'The trade unionist has voted at the polls against the consequences of his own anarchy.' . . . Your opportunity is here, the oppor-tunity of expanding membership, expanding negotiating rights, expanding authority, expanding status in society. Seize it and, in doing so, also strengthen your Labour government.

At a TUC Special Congress on 6 June Electricians' Union President Les Cannon was the only voice of dissent among a cacophony of condemnation directed against the government's proposals. Castle was at the time taking a holiday on a boat off the Italian coast. It was probably the safest place.[373] At Cabinet on 17 June, Chief Whip Bob Mellish made clear his view that there was now insufficient support among Labour MPs to get the Bill through, and most of Castle's remaining Cabinet supporters, including Peter Shore, Judith Hart and Roy Jenkins, abandoned her.[374] 'It was a sad story, from which [Wilson] and Barbara Castle emerged with more credit than the rest of us,' conceded Jenkins in his memoir.[375] Amid lurid press rumours suggesting multiple plots to overthrow Wilson and replace him with either Jenkins or Callaghan, Wilson raised the white flag on Castle's behalf. On 18 June a 'solemn and binding' undertaking was given to the government by the TUC that they would 'take energetic steps' in the case of unofficial disputes to encourage a settlement. 'The general public and the newspapers treated it with derision,' recalled Wilson's Press Secretary Joe Haines, 'the Cabinet, with the honourable exceptions of Wilson and Barbara Castle, treated it with relief. They hadn't fought; they had run away to live and lose another day.'[376]

In July 1969 Jack Jones took over the helm of the giant Transport and General Workers' Union from Frank Cousins. With more than 1.5 million members it was Britain's largest trade union and as its leader Jones had the biggest block vote at Labour Party conference. The president of Britain's second largest union, the 1.2 million-strong Amalgamated Union of Engineering Workers (AUEW), had since 1967 been the former Communist Hugh Scanlon. Scanlon had got swiftly to work in changing his union's political stance: his predecessor, Bill Carron, had been a notably loyal supporter of the Labour leadership. Dubbed the 'terrible twins' by the right-wing tabloids for their opposition to In Place of Strife and to incomes policy, Jones and Scanlon were powerful advocates of their members' aspirations for better wages and conditions.

By the end of 1969 the incomes policy had, in practice, collapsed. London busmen got a 16.5 per cent pay rise, dockers got 25 per cent and lorry drivers 45 per cent. During 1969, nearly seven million working days were lost to strike action – more than for a decade, while unemployment rose to 630,000, the highest level for two years.[377] During 1970 as a whole, wage earnings rose by some 15 per cent.[378]

While trade union leaders and shop stewards may have rejected In Place of Strife, both the wider electorate and union members themselves were more favourably disposed. With a general election imminent a Harris opinion poll found a two-to-one majority among rank-and-file trade union members for the proposals contained in In Place of Strife.[379] Labour clearly was incapable of bringing them in. The Conservatives, however, pledged to do so. For Callaghan's official biographer, 'the outcome of 1969 was an immense revulsion against trade union power. The public standing of men like Bevin and

Citrine in the past was no more. Union leaders like Jack Jones and Hugh Scanlon seemed entirely happy to defy the elected government and the law of the land. No reform of Mrs Thatcher's was electorally more popular, including amongst trade unionists and their families who were after all consumers as well as producers.'[380] Frank Cousins' biographer Geoffrey Goodman does not entirely dissent: 'In Place of Strife did contain the ingredients of a programme that, if it had been possible for it to succeed, then not only would the 1970 election result have been different, but we would not have had Thatcherism.'[381]

After the Conservative victory at the 1970 general election, Ted Heath's new government would bring in a modified version of In Place of Strife. Drafting errors created legal loopholes that in the end made it unfit for the purpose, and the incoming Labour government of 1974 would repeal it. In the meantime, the resistance to Heath's Industrial Relations Act would become a cause célèbre among trade unions. At Labour's 1970 annual conference Jack Jones rejected accusations that 'irresponsible' trade union wage claims were leading to wages rising faster than productivity. He attacked:

> . . . pampered, academic people, including a few journalists who dishonour the profession by their snide smears and downright lies (applause) and unfortunately by some politicians, the whole lot of whom, for the most part, have never been covered by a wage claim, because, frankly, they have never worked for a living (applause). Let them go down and work in the mines, or work in the racket and tension of a machine shop or try to keep pace with a fast-moving assembly line. Let them work in a dank, dirty hold of a ship, sweating one minute and shivering the next, with rats and insects lurking about, and then say their wage claims are irresponsible (applause).
>
> Spokesmen of the present government – wooden-faced and with a Victorian outlook – have moved into the attack in recent weeks and appear to be fanning the flames of industrial war . . . Organised labour is being made the scapegoat for inflation. Despite the fact that prices are rising all over the world, helped on by profiteers from all over the world, including British profiteers, we are being told that it is all the fault of wage pressure. In fact, prices and cost increases have been imposed on the consumer where there have been little or no wage increases and where unions are weak, including catering – and I can tell you a story abut that – or where labour costs are not even a major consideration.

The Tories, continued Jones, exaggerated the level of wage increases for the low-paid by citing percentages:

> Workers cannot spend percentages. They want wages to maintain a reasonable standard for themselves and their families . . . No sensible man or woman ever wants to strike for the fun of it. Indeed, the truth is that most potential strike situations are in our complex, industrial society avoided by the hard work and action of shop stewards and trade union officials. It is this work which should be encouraged, not legal intervention, which is no guarantee of either industrial justice or industrial peace . . .

Bringing the law into industrial relations would be like putting out a fire with a petrol pump. We have said: 'Let us find out why the people strike, and do something about the real problems. Let us try to remove the causes.' . . . Simply worded agreements, made by the workers themselves, democratically accepted and democratically operated, agreements which workers consider worth keeping.

It was 'a tremendous speech which moved [moderate Labour MP and USDAW president] Walter Padley to tears',[382] recalled Tony Benn.

On a hot June day in 1970, the UK went to the polls. The choice was characterised by the maverick Tory Enoch Powell as being between a man with a pipe and a man with a boat. The man with the pipe was Prime Minister Harold Wilson. Two times an election winner, he was confident of victory in a third. The man with the boat (or rather an ocean racing yacht) was Conservative leader Edward Heath. He had already been beaten by Wilson once, in 1966 when Labour had secured a landslide election victory and an over-all majority of 96 seats.

Many, if not most, Conservative MPs expected to be defeated again. Despite all the troubles that had beset the Labour government – enforced devaluation and consequent cuts, the abandonment of *In Place of Strife* and a fiasco over attempted Lords reform – Wilson's government seemed to have recovered. Heath seemed irredeemably wooden and did not appear to be able to catch the popular mood. And a considerable chunk of Conservative television and radio airtime was being hogged by Enoch Powell, who had for years nursed the grievance that he was not Tory leader.

Having trailed the Tories in the opinion polls since April 1967, sometimes during 1968 and 1969 by as much as 25 percentage points, Labour had regained several hundred seats at the local elections on 8 May 1970 with a swing large enough to re-elect a Labour government with a majority of 50. On 13 May Gallup gave Labour a lead of 7.5 per cent. By June, Gallup polls indicated only 13 per cent of people thought the Conservatives likely to win the election (down from 54 per cent in March) and 68 per cent expected Labour to win (up from 27 per cent in March). Labour MPs in marginal seats were confident. The £800 million balance of payments deficit that Labour had inherited from the Conservatives in 1964 had finally been turned round into a surplus of £606 million. Roy Jenkins, Chancellor of the Exchequer, seemed to have turned the economy round and the title of Labour's cautious and bland manifesto reflected a strategy designed to play upon this: 'Now Britain's strong, let's make it great to live in.' One unexpected announcement came from former Chief Whip Bob Mellish, recently appointed Minister for Housing and Local Government, who promised that a future Labour government would let local authorities build council houses for sale to owner-occupiers. Heath dismissed the plan as 'ridiculous and unnecessary'.[383] Ten years later, Margaret Thatcher would be less dismissive.

But it was not to be. Heath's three-pronged attack on 'Wilson's sham sunshine', claiming that prices, taxes and strikes would all increase under Labour seemed to resonate with voters. Heath's third prong, strikes, was given added piquancy by the SOGAT printworkers' strike which put the national newspapers off the streets for four crucial days of the election campaign (10–13 June). Election day, 18 June, saw a 72 per cent turnout, the lowest since 1935, and a uniform 5 per cent swing away from Labour across England (it was slightly less in Scotland and Wales), the largest since 1945. The swing to the Conservatives had been particularly strong among housewives, in Wolverhampton (where Enoch Powell was the candidate) and in Clapham, where but for the abnormally high 10.2 per cent swing against him, Dr David Pitt would have become Britain's first black MP. At the same time, there were clearly limits to Powellism's appeal: the rest of the West Midlands outside Wolverhampton itself had failed to swing Conservative to any greater extent than anywhere else and some seats with a higher ethnic minority population showed below average swings to the Conservatives. The parliamentary Liberal Party, now led by Jeremy Thorpe, was almost literally halved, from thirteen MPs to six, though its vote went down by only 1 per cent. The Conservatives, with 13.1 million votes (46.4 per cent) secured 330 seats and an overall majority of 32. Labour received 12.2 million votes (43 per cent) and 287 seats.

Some blamed Labour's defeat on England's ejection from the football World Cup four days before polling day. Others blamed the May balance of payments figures, published two days before polling, which showed a £30 million deficit caused predominantly by the purchase of two Boeing 747 'jumbo jets' for British Airways at a cost of £9 million each. Though the trade figures were a blip, they did not help inspire confidence, and having been through so much supposedly to sort out the balance of trade, the idea of going through it again did not exactly enthuse voters.

There were real achievements to the Labour government's credit. They included the Open University, the new polytechnics, an Equal Pay Act; a fourfold increase in comprehensive schools, most of the groundwork for the raising of the school leaving age to sixteen, the introduction of statutory redundancy pay, the creation of the Parliamentary Commissioner (Ombudsman), the two Race Relations Acts, and the introduction of rent tribunals. But the National Plan for 4 per cent annual GDP growth had been abandoned and with it the knock-on possibilities for extra investment. UK growth had lagged behind its main industrial competitors, and over the decade, Britain's share of world exports both as a whole and in manufactures had continued to decline. When Labour activists met for the 1970 annual conference the frustration of electoral defeat was tinged with anger that so many of the hopes of 1964 had been dashed. 'Blackpool weather excelled itself,' recalled shadow Chancellor Roy Jenkins, 'with an unrelenting muggy wind whipping up the rain-laden clouds and the coffee-coloured

Irish Sea.'[384] For the defeated government the reception inside the conference hall wasn't very warm either. Delegates spoke of 'the tragic reintroduction of prescription charges', the deflationary policies of a government elected on a 'pledge of higher economic growth', and the unpopularity of the wage freeze. 'Harold didn't like it very much,' observed Tony Benn.[385] New TGWU leader Jack Jones articulated a theme that was to underpin some of Labour's most fiercely fought internal battles over the fifteen years to come: the notion that Labour governments failed because Labour MPs were insufficiently committed to 'socialism'.

Calling for MPs to be required to consult with

community representatives [and] maybe . . . shop stewards in the streets, [he continued]: 'For too many [MPs] the constituency Labour Party is a bit of a nuisance, a device for giving him a free hand as the mood takes him. And when we are in power, with ministers the relationship is sometimes even more remote. Yet it is at that time that we need greater influence from below, not less.

For too long the idea has been about that an MP was just a representative, and not a delegate. That idea has been reinforced with such a snobbish view that decisions have been the exclusive prerogative of a few, and in so many cases the MP has not even been a representative. We need to open up those corridors of power, both for Parliament and local authorities. It is what group after group of people, whether it is Shelter, the Rents Campaign, motorway protesters or dozens of others, are trying to do . . . we should seize the leadership of protest – and, along with our fight for industrial democracy we must determine to build a people's democracy, for all the people . . .

Jones's speech was rooted in the age-old charge of 'leadership betrayal' which had bedevilled the Labour Party virtually since its inception. But the structural issue was new: the idea that the 'failure of will' by MPs could be overcome by making MPs direct delegates of the party rather than representatives. It was the bones of an idea that would be given flesh over the next decade by the Campaign for Labour Party Democracy (to be founded in 1973) and an article of faith which would find its high priest in Tony Benn.

The idea that Labour had lost the election because it had been insufficiently left-wing was still ringing in the ears of delegates as they left, having been drummed home in a powerful closing address from conference chair and veteran 'Keep Left' MP Ian Mikardo. Confronting 'the argument about whether we are a party of power or merely a party of protest', he declared:

I hope the protagonists on both sides of that argument will not mind my saying that I think their argument is a non-argument, I think they are posing an entirely false dichotomy. Power is not an alternative to protest, it is complementary to protest. Indeed, it is the instrument through which protest issues in action (*applause*).

We socialists do not seek power for its own sake, people who do that – and there are some – are merely masturbating their own egos. We socialists protest against the injustice, the ugliness, the inefficiency and the inhumanity of the selfishly acquisitive society, and we seek power precisely to remedy those evils (*applause*).

Some people seem to have been saying this week that radicalism and idealism are things that we would all like to have, but they are things which we cannot really afford, they are luxuries because the first job is to win an election, and they say that job is made more difficult by our being radical and idealist, aye, and socialist as well.

This was 'nonsense', he insisted, recalling his own speech to Labour's 1944 party conference that challenged the 'timid' NEC policy and successfully demanded that the 1945 Labour government be committed explicitly to nationalisation and Morrison's remark that:

> ... young man, you did very well, but you realise you have lost us the general election, don't you? [and that Labour] did not lose the general election of 1945 ... And in the next four succeeding elections ... in each one of them we had a more watered-down election manifesto than the previous one, and in each one of them we elected fewer MPs than in the previous one ... [Mikardo accused the] party leaders of failing to see that there might be a causal connection between the two. It was not until we got to 1964 when once again for the first time for a long time we had a manifesto with some guts in it that we achieved a victory once again. The whole history of our party goes to show that radicalism, idealism and socialism on our part freely expressed is not only decent, honest and right, it is also good business; it pays off (*applause*).
>
> So, comrades, my message to you as you start your party tasks next Monday is this: let us not be too timid to declare our convictions plainly. Let us not hide those convictions behind the cloak of an advertising agent's smart-aleck image building (*applause*). Let us win our elections not on the so-called respectability of 'me-too-ism', of the middle ground, but on the unashamed, nay, the proud propagation of our principles and our faith (*applause*). Let us not merely win the next election, let us do more: let us deserve to win it (*applause*) ...

Mikardo was memorably characterised by Harold Wilson's Press Secretary Joe Haines as 'a silver haired, black-browed, pot-bellied conspirator of the old (Tammany Hall) school, with a serpentine mind, a shuffling gait, and clothes which looked scruffy when new'.[386] His speech won a standing ovation from conference.

293

FORTY-THREE

Labour's Common Market Split 1970–72

'The language of Chaucer'

Among the Labour MPs who lost their seats in 1970 were deputy leader George Brown, Chief Secretary to the Treasury Jack Diamond, Woodrow Wyatt, future media mogul Robert Maxwell, Jennie Lee, Michael Foot's brother Dingle, and Britain's first husband and wife ministerial team: Gwyneth and John Dunwoody. George Brown's defeat necessitated his resignation as deputy leader. In the contest that followed, Roy Jenkins secured 133 votes to defeat Michael Foot, the candidate of the left (who got 67) and Fred Peart of the anti-EEC right (who got 48). 'The result implied,' wrote *The Times*, 'that the Labour Party has decided that it is going to continue in opposition to develop along the lines on which it was developing as a government . . . It means that the Labour Party has not swung emotionally against Europe in the way some people feared.'[387] Not for the last time the media were to be proved wrong.

Jenkins became shadow Chancellor, Callaghan shadow Home Secretary and most of the rest of the old Cabinet also continued to shadow their old jobs. The main changes were the promotion of Denis Healey to shadow Foreign Secretary, of Shirley Williams to cover Health, and of Michael Foot to shadow minister for Fuel and Power: Foot had for the first time stood for – and been elected to – the shadow Cabinet. George Thomson, who had been in charge of new negotiations to join the EEC that Wilson's government had opened shortly before it fell, became shadow Defence Secretary and was replaced on EEC matters by the equally pro-Market Harold Lever. Dick Crossman and Michael Stewart retired to the backbenches, as, temporarily, did Peter Shore, who wanted to spend more time campaigning against the EEC.

Heath's new government took over the Common Market negotiations that Wilson's government had opened. This time, moreover, the negotiations had a real chance of success (though Healey, apparently, was sceptical).[388] De Gaulle had retired and the new French President, Pompidou, was prepared to accept the possibility of a positive UK contribution to the EEC.

All the polls, however, showed a majority against EEC entry from May 1970 until June 1971. Although following the publication of Heath's White Paper there was a brief surge in support, polls once more swung against for the rest of 1971. Partly this can be attributed to the fact that Heath's government was so determinedly in favour: as David Owen recalls, 'in the early months of 1971, it became increasingly obvious that the high unemployment figures, the government's total inability to restrain prices and their determined commitment not to intervene in industry, were making them very unpopular . . . as the government's reputation fell, Labour leaders found it increasingly difficult to agree with them on anything and the European Community became another issue for instant opposition'.[389]

In Parliament an unofficial anti-EEC group of Labour MPs began to meet to coordinate tactics. It included Michael Foot and ex-ministers Douglas Jay, John Silkin, Fred Peart, Peter Shore and Barbara Castle. Labour's 1970 annual conference rejected a resolution from the TGWU opposing membership of the EEC. But while the 1967 annual conference had voted to back George Brown's attempt to lead Britain into the EEC by two to one, this time the pro-EEC majority was slim. In January 1971 the Tribune Group secured the signatures of 121 Labour MPs for an anti-EEC early day motion.[390]

The tectonic plates were shifting. Moreover Wilson was losing control of Labour's NEC. While the Labour left had won many if not most of the seats in the constituency section of the NEC since the Bevanite triumph of the early 1950s, the leadership had usually been able to count on a majority overall. Only occasionally, such as over *In Place of Strife*, had sufficient of the normally loyal members of the trade union and women's sections voted with the left to defeat the leadership. Times were changing. Disillusionment with the failure of the Wilson government to deliver on its promises helped ensure that old loyalists like Bessie Braddock, Alice Bacon and Peggy Herbison were being replaced in the NEC women's section by the left-wing MPs Judith Hart, Lena Jeger and Renee Short. By 1973 the left had three additional reinforcements. Hard-left Joan Maynard had joined Hart, Short and Jeger in the NEC women's section, leaving only Shirley Williams from the right. John Forrester of AEU-TASS had been elected to the trade union section and the creation of an additional place on the NEC for the Labour Party Young Socialists gave the left another supporter: Peter Doyle. And on the left, opposition to the EEC had become an article of faith.

One of the most sensitive to Labour's swings of mood was shadow Home Secretary James Callaghan. His attitude can perhaps best be characterised as that of a genuine 'eurosceptic' – not one in the post-1990s sense of actually being anti-European. He was not yet convinced of the economic advantages of EEC membership. He had written to the then Foreign Secretary, Michael Stewart, in 1969 suggesting that for him the most compelling attraction of the Common Market was the political dimension: the opportunity for Britain to take a political lead. His fear was that Britain might find itself playing second fiddle to France. It was this fear that came to the fore in a speech Callaghan delivered on 25 May 1971 at by-election meeting in the relatively humble location of Bitterne

Park School, Southampton. In recent media interviews, Pompidou had commented in passing on the desirability of having French as the first language of Europe and had dismissed English as being the language of the USA. His remarks fired up all Callaghan's populist instincts and his response was robust:

> . . . M. Pompidou is wholly opposed to any alteration in the fundamental character of the EEC. He intends that even after we join the outlook of the enlarged EEC on the world, its language, its relations with the United States, the Commonwealth, Africa and Asia shall be determined by a French Continental-European approach. He is no less clear that in so far as British history, our political ideas and our links with the world differ from those of the French-dominated EEC, then Britain must subordinate them to the extent of a complete rupture with our identity . . .
>
> M. Pompidou . . . said on *Panorama*: 'We (that is the EEC) are moving towards an economic and monetary union. I hope it is going to be a fact in the future. Is Britain ready to go ahead? For instance, in the monetary field?' [Callaghan doubted whether it would be] advantageous to the British people . . . if there is to be a successful economic and monetary union, then member states will have to subordinate their own fiscal, taxation and monetary policies to a central governing body and surrender their powers over these matters. Such a possibility is, in my view, a long way ahead, perhaps ten years from now, but I am quite clear that it cannot be achieved through a confederation of European states . . .
>
> Another difficulty I have is with the growing concept that it is not enough to be European but you must also actively desire to create a European Europe. This was illustrated by M. Pompidou's answer on the *Panorama* programme about the use of the English language. I doubt whether the French President realised how we bridled when he gave his answer about the need to regard French as the language of Europe. I suspect this has done more to confirm the doubts of many people than almost any argument about sterling, the Common Agricultural Policy or the economic and monetary union. Millions of people in Britain have been surprised to hear that the language of Chaucer, Shakespeare and Milton must in future be regarded as an American import from which we must protect ourselves if we are to build a new Europe. We can agree that the French own the supreme prose literature in Europe. But if we are to prove our Europeanism by accepting that French is the dominant language in the Community, then the answer is quite clear, and I will say it in French to prevent any misunderstanding: '*Non, merci beaucoup.*'

For pro-Europeans, Callaghan had 'played shamelessly to the gallery':[391] though 'it was not much worse, I suppose, than the "thousand years of history" argument of my hero Hugh Gaitskell in 1962', admitted Roy Jenkins, 'it filled me with a mixture of gloom and disapproval'.[392] As David Owen observed, 'the impact of the speech on Harold Wilson and its effect within the Labour Party was tremendous . . . as he had done with *In Place of Strife*, Jim was putting himself at the vanguard of mainstream Labour opinion . . . if

Wilson had any doubts about the way the wind was blowing the conduct of two other members of the shadow Cabinet, Denis Healey and Tony Crosland, would have convinced him.'[393] Jenkins was convinced that the main significance of the speech was that 'it filled Harold Wilson with fear. Tony Benn, a diarist writing from a very different point of view from mine, has testified that Wilson became "obsessed" that summer with the survival of his leadership and that what most frightened him was being outflanked on Europe by Callaghan.'[394]

Callaghan invented a formula that Wilson seized upon: that entry was unacceptable on the terms Heath had negotiated. Callaghan started talking about 'renegotiation', a term apparently suggested to him by his son-in-law Peter Jay, whose father Douglas was one of the most visceral anti-EEC campaigners in the Labour Party. It was this formula that enabled the next Labour government eventually to support remaining in the EEC. But it was not enough to prevent a split in the party: the pro-Europeans insisted that Heath's terms were as good as any that Labour would have been able to secure. Their argument was substantiated by the fact that it was advanced by the very people who had been conducting the negotiations: former Foreign Secretary Michael Stewart and Callaghan's friend George Thomson. For the pro-Europeans, to oppose membership on 'Tory terms' was inconsistent and intellectually dishonest.

Rival pro- and anti-EEC adverts signed by Labour MPs appeared in the press. Some MPs, like Tony Crosland, tried to keep out of the crossfire by playing down the importance of the issue. On 23 June Labour's NEC voted to hold a special conference on the EEC. It was held on 17 July, a beautiful hot day, in Central Hall, Westminster.

Jenkins himself, as deputy leader and a member of the NEC, was constrained from speaking on the NEC's behalf on account of the divergence of his view from its position. It also meant he was constrained from speaking against it. Others, however, were to do so with passionate conviction. The debate itself was unusually balanced: Ian Mikardo, that year's Labour Party chair and firmly anti-EEC himself, called pro- and anti-speakers alternately.

Shadow Defence Secretary George Thomson, who in the Labour government up until 1970 had been handling the negotiations for entry, made a strong speech in favour, declaring that:

> ... every trade unionist knows that if we go into the major negotiations, we do not expect perfect terms to emerge [and that] I would have recommended the Labour Cabinet to accept [the] terms [Heath had secured] ... most of those who had direct responsibility for those negotiations in the Labour government share my view ... my personal judgement is that if we had won the election ... these terms would have gone through a Labour Cabinet ...

ASSETT leader Clive Jenkins then responded for the antis, denouncing the EEC as:

a fraction of Europe, [with] France, strongly in the grip of a reactionary government, [brought] twice to the brink of civil war within a decade; Belgium, riven by problems of language and religion and in the hands of a tightly knit group of trusts; Italy, where there is a constant danger of a military coup. [He concluded:] Every supra-national company wants us in, and I suggest to you that if they have that motivation it might not be good for the ordinary citizens of this country.

Sir Fred Hayday of the General and Municipal Workers countered for the pros, emphasising the advantages of securing access to EEC markets:

The CBI have made a survey of the prospects on entry into the Common Market and the CBI are under no doubt as to what the prospects would be on entry. They decided to go in. We earn our livelihood in British industry, do we not? If British industry is in the hands of the CBI, it is the fault of the electorate of this country and not of mine . . . [Outside the EEC lay stagnation:] Our friends in OECD have told us that their estimates over the next five years are that our growth rate will be 2.8 per cent. as against 5.2 per cent in the Common Market.

It was then that the debate really heated up. Former Cabinet minister Peter Shore, 'a frail, bony man whose nose and front hair seemed to have made a *coup d'état* for the control of his face',[395] made a blazing attack on the EEC that 'made his political name in those five minutes',[396] recalled Douglas Jay. Shore's attack focused on the Common Agricultural Policy, which meant for Britain, 'the abandonment of the 120-year-old policy of cheap food for this country' and, he insisted, had since the beginning of 1970 been supported by a new system of contributions which, were they to be imposed on Britain, would be financially ruinous:

George Thomson, George Brown, the Labour government when it negotiated in 1967, did not negotiate against that background. It did not even exist (*applause*) . . . Do not be depressed by these feeble voices which convince you, or seek to convince you, first, that you have no capacity to solve your own problems; secondly, that the world of tomorrow is a world of vast aggregates, regional blocs from which it is death to be excluded, it is not; thirdly, do not fear, you have the power to stop this act of madness and to change the history of this country and to insist that we shall make arrangements for our future that are right – not for the CBI and for Edward Heath, but for the people of Britain.

Shore's reply came from East Lothian MP John Mackintosh, speaking from the gallery high above the conference floor. Jenkins judged it 'the outstanding speech'[397] of the conference, 'an amazing speech combining great passion and emotional force without demagogery'.[398] Benn acknowledged it 'brilliant'[399] while even Douglas Jay conceded it the best speech 'for the pro-Marketeers'.

Mackintosh refuted Shore's central charge, that the EEC had changed since the Labour government had negotiated to join. On the change to 'the organisation of payment for the common budget' that underpinned the funding of the Common Agricultural Policy, Mackintosh pointed out that it 'was fixed in December, 1969, and the Labour Cabinet reapplied to join in May, 1970'.

The Labour government's application to join the EEC was not:

> ... frivolous. This was serious, and when our leader said 'We mean business. We will not take no for an answer,' it was because we seriously wanted to join ... the Common Market ...
>
> What bothers me is when I look back at the experience of the last Labour government over six years. Peter Shore was Minister of Economic Affairs (*applause*). Does he remember – I wonder if he has been living in the same world as I have. Does he remember having to explain how we were blown off course? Does he remember a forced devaluation? Does he remember the cuts and the deflation which we had to explain all round the country? What is so desperately negative and insular about this situation is that we have to go back to that sort of situation with the next Labour government (*applause*).
>
> If there is another answer, it is no good producing slogans and talking about socialism. Our Labour Cabinet – did it not include socialists? Were not they trying within the limits? We are not going to turn on our own movement. We are going to have the same sort of leadership again. We cannot turn on our own movement and say, 'Let us destroy it,' or 'Let us turn it down.' If we had had one year of the growth which all the Common Market countries have had, we would still have been in power today, comrades (*applause*).
>
> I turn to this argument about our socialist colleagues in Europe. Let us be clear about this one. The fears we have heard today in this conference – every one of these fears was felt by our socialist comrades in Europe in 1957 and 1958 before they formed the Market ... What is the situation today? Not one of these fears has been realised – not one.
>
> If I heard one of our foreign socialist friends come and say, 'We were right. Stay out. We will not join a regional policy,' it would be different. But do they say that? On the contrary ... The most eloquent testimony of the lot that I heard was two weeks ago in Rome when I was speaking to one of the leaders of the Italian Communist Party – one of the most progressive and best organised Communist parties. He said that in the near future they hoped to support a coalition in Italy. I said, 'How can you possibly do that when you believe that the EEC is a capitalist bloc?' He shrugged his shoulders and simply said, 'That is what we used to think, but it has simply done too much for the Italian working class for us to turn against them now.'
>
> Comrades, I end with two points. Internationalism we have heard a lot about. I distrust people who are worldwide internationalists who do not risk their lives. The brotherhood of man begins with believing in, and cooperating with, the man sitting next to you. We must break down the barriers. We must build a new approach in this country. We must break the class system and carry our policies through to a conclusion. I believe that this is inside Europe (*applause*).

Mackintosh delivered a 'coruscating attack on the fainthearts who feared for national sovereignty and worried about economic growth', recalled Hugo Young. 'The speech was remembered in the annals for ever after. Reread, it sharpens a large truth about the history: that, of all those who contributed to it, none has been more eloquent, more completely and defiantly committed to Britain's European destiny than the Labour pro-Europeans of the Heath period.'[400] After Mackintosh, Chairman Mikardo called Michael Foot to respond:

> . . . I remember deflation. I remember 1966. I remember all the troubles the Labour government had. I remember some people who fought maybe a bit harder than John Mackintosh against some of those policies (*applause*). But I will tell him this. The major burden the Labour government had to fight was the crushing burden of our balance of payments. And he is proposing to add £500 million more to that burden (*applause*).
>
> As for the leaders of the Labour government, members of the Cabinet, I am sometimes surprised when one of them, like George Thomson, accepts that £500 million extra so easily. We would also have to accept the free movement of capital, and Labour governments – and not only the last one – have had trouble with that. We would have to accept the Common Agricultural Policy, which no Common Marketeer ever dares to defend . . . if the pro-Marketeers have their way, we shall have the value added tax, with no power of the British people to resist it. This is the constitutional issue. Of course the sovereignty of our Parliament is undermined if we accept provisions of that nature. This is only one example. John Hampden had a better chance to resist Ship Money than the British people will have had to resist the value added tax . . .
>
> We are not in this Market yet. We have got a right to determine the future of the British people. And if we decide against entry and there is a division between the major parties in the State, the Labour Party and the Tories – they having no mandate to enter – the only people to settle it between the major parties must be the British people. Everything else is a defiance of democracy (*applause*). That is what Hugh Gaitskell said at the conference in 1962 – and when Hugh Gaitskell and myself agree our unity is strong indeed! (*applause*).

Foot's fervour was echoed by a 29-year-old new Welsh MP, Neil Kinnock, though Kinnock's pragmatic Euroscepticism fell short of Foot's anti-Marketeering, because for Kinnock the real issue was Heath's government:

> . . . the burden of proof that we should enter the EEC . . . is not proved . . . For every single item that has been adduced in favour, there is an item against . . . In the short term the costs will be high, in the short term the going will be hard. But we are told to make a great act of faith, to take this historic opportunity because in the long term everybody will be all right . . . I will tell you what is the historic opportunity presented by the current EEC debate. The opportunity presented to us is the opportunity to lead the British people, and to kick the Tories out of power . . .

For 364 days out of the year on every issue – on school milk, the freeze on public employees, the lot – in Parliament and outside we stridently, without reservation, attack, attack, attack. We have called the Conservatives everything we can lay our tongue to. And then we are prepared to go before the British nation and say on the 365th day – not on a marginal issue, not on a minor non-contentious issue, but on the biggest issue of our generation – we are going to put our arms round him and say, 'After all, Ted, although we hate you for the rest of the time, we think you are right on this one.' It is not on (*applause*).

People talk about the continuity of ideas. People talk about the way that people will think of the apparent turn-round of this party on the Market. Well, if we want to maintain any kind of consistency at all, we cannot with one tongue be the enemies of this class-ridden government and with the other tongue embrace them and follow their policies. Because this is how it is seen in our nation which is at this time in a majority against going into Europe.

And it is because I am a member of the Labour Party, and because I am a trade unionist, and because I want to see the Tories beaten, and because I am willing to use any weapon to beat them, that I am against EEC entry on these terms at this time (*applause*).

One of the final speakers was veteran former Foreign Secretary Michael Stewart. He responded first to Shore, pointing out that outside the EEC:

It will be no good saying, 'Oh, we've got EFTA and we've got the Commonwealth.' The world will not stand still. If we do not go in through our own refusal, one Commonwealth country after another will do what a number have done already: make their own trading agreements with the Community. One EFTA country after another will do the same. [Turning then to Kinnock he declared,] it is a complete misreading of the Tory Party's will to survive and how things work in Parliament to imagine that by voting against the Community on this issue you will bring the government down. . . . People say Mr Heath is not the man to lead us in. No, and Mr Heath is not the man who can look after this country in the greatly difficult circumstances if we were out.

There was, of course, no vote, but the anti-EEC tone of Wilson's summing up made clear the way the wind was blowing. Two days later Roy Jenkins made an emotional speech to the Parliamentary Labour Party where he asserted that not only would a Labour government have accepted 'Tory terms' but that Heath's terms were as good as could be got. Moreover, he argued, to claim that they were unacceptable to Labour was to brand the entire approach of the previous Labour government a waste of time. 'Callaghan offered running the economy flat out for five years. That is not a policy: it is an aspiration. We were not lacking in aspirations in the early days of a Labour government. What we were lacking was results.' He then attacked the left: 'socialism in one country. That is always good for a cheer. Pull up the drawbridge and revolutionise the

301

fortress. That is not a policy either, it's just a slogan.' Rejection of the EEC would bring, he said, not 'rugged independence', but greater dependence on the USA. He concluded: 'I beg the party not to follow this recipe for disappointment and decline but to face problems realistically and to lift its eyes beyond the narrow short-term political considerations of the moment.'[401] His speech 'was interrupted by fierce applause; and at the end of it there was a sustained banging of desks', recalled Jenkins' lieutenant Bill Rodgers, 'the response was an entirely spontaneous expression of defiance and frustration from pro-Marketeers who felt they were being pushed into a corner by an inexorable process'.[402] Wilson, however, ever fearful of plots, suspected it represented an attempt by Jenkins to put himself at the head of a groundswell against his leadership.

Labour's annual conference voted on 4 October 1971 to reject the EEC. Given the decision of conference chair Ian Mikardo not to call anyone who had spoken at the special conference a few months previously, the debate itself was notably less sparkling. The vote, moreover, was not unexpected, being pretty much predetermined by the big trade union battalions.

After a marathon six-day debate, the decisive Commons vote came on 28 October 1971. The speakers ranged widely, but as they progressed, the *Daily Telegraph* reported: 'continuing a trend, MPs turned more and more to talking about the issue of sovereignty and tended to be rather brief on economic topics. It has now got through to a lot more MPs that sovereignty is a vital issue.'[403] For future Foreign Secretary David Owen, it was the 'most important debate in my time in the House of Commons'. He recalled in particular John Mackintosh's speech, 'at 6.30 a.m., and even at that unearthly hour it was a lucid demolition of the nineteenth-century concept of sovereignty'.[404] Citing 'the two most impressive anti-Market speeches that I have heard in the debate', from Edward du Cann and Michael Foot, Mackintosh denounced:

> . . . the nineteenth-century concept of sovereignty being put forward by those two speakers and the many others who agree with them. They have a purely legalistic concept of sovereignty, like an old lady with a basket of apples, who feels that each time she gives a bit of sovereignty in the form of an apple to someone else there is one less in her basket. What a very restricted and old-fashioned concept of sovereignty!
>
> The real point is that no nation has untrammelled sovereignty, no nation has complete power to do as it likes, and what matters to the public is not the legal power to act but whether the consequences may mean anything . . .
>
> We in this Parliament have the sovereign power to regulate many things in connection with sterling as a currency, its control and the rates of exchange at which we offer to trade in sterling. If other forces outside the country result in a serious run on our sterling reserves we cannot continue to operate the system; we do not have the sovereignty to carry out economic policies through to the conclusion that our people want. Then the politicians must find the bodies or individuals who have taken that

sovereignty away from us, and we turn and blame groups such as the gnomes of Zurich and international speculators. But if instead our legislators deliberately give sovereignty away and share it in an agreement at Basle with a number of other nations so as to regulate a reserve currency that Britain's trading objectives can be achieved, then they have conceded some sovereignty to the nations with which they have had to discuss the question. But out of this they can show that they are producing the achievement of solid trading results and stable employment, which was the objective of the sovereignty originally held by this country alone. So the decision to join with other powers was not in fact a derogation or loss of sovereignty; it was in reality an increase in the effective power of this House . . .

When my hon. friend the Member for Ebbw Vale[405] says that if we give away power over employment, regional policies, and wages and prices, people will condemn or look down on Parliament, he again has the wrong end of the stick. For years British politicians have told the public, 'We will do this for you and that for you. We will end stop-go. We will have full employment, and even cut prices at a stroke,' but they have never delivered the goods. That is why people look down on Parliament. That is why the public are less and less interested – because the politicians cannot achieve what they set out to do.

Why, over a period of time, have successive governments of both parties failed to achieve their economic objectives? Why have we counted for less in international affairs? Why have we depressed our public by a series of failures? I believe that it is because the context in which Britain is working is not adequate to the present circumstances . . .

There is, I regret to say, a type of 'conservative' with a small 'c' in the party to which I belong and when we approach change – radical change – in a radical attempt to grapple with the problems of this country, there is a negative response from the right-wing and left-wing forces of our society which wish to retain the status quo . . .

We are becoming, without joining, more European in defence and trade interests of all kinds. The act of joining the EEC . . . is more than just signing the Treaty of Rome; it is a broad change of direction. I deeply respect the views of the anti-Marketeers, but their speeches have shown no overall philosophy, only a discrete group of fears. They are fearful people, fearful that they cannot adopt a brand of socialism involving a wide extension of public ownership and physical controls. They fear that the regions will suffer and that it will not be possible to steer the extra growth engendered by a wider market in the right direction towards the regions. They fear contamination with what they regard as a less satisfactory attitude towards the Third World, and they fear that British industry will be incapable of taking advantage of the wider opportunities in the Common Market. And as each one of these fears is answered, they fall back on others because the fundamental point is that they are worried about change.

It was summed up for me in a sentence in the *New Statesman* which in a leading article said that the case for entering the Common Market was not proven because one could not prove that all the people in this country would benefit. But if one had to prove that every major change would produce a guaranteed benefit for all sections we should still be running round in the jungle as primitive tribesmen . . .

Offered a free vote by Heath, 41 Conservatives voted against Europe. The Parliamentary Labour Party voted by 140 to 111 to impose a three-line whip to vote against the EEC. Despite the slimness of this vote, a reported personal pledge by Wilson to Jenkins that there would not be a whip against entry,[406] and a pledge from Chief Whip Bob Mellish to both Bill Rodgers and Dick Taverne that an anti-EEC whip would be imposed 'over his dead body',[407] Wilson bowed to the will of the majority and the three-line whip was imposed by Mellish. Nevertheless, 69 Labour MPs voted with the Conservative government, including deputy leader Roy Jenkins, future deputy leader Roy Hattersley and future leader John Smith. Tony Crosland was among 20 more Labour MPs who abstained. Heath's proposal for EEC membership was carried by 356 votes to 244, giving a majority of 112.

The anti-Marketeers were furious at their defeat, and a wider swathe of Labour sup-porters felt that the pro-Marketeers, by putting principle above party, had let go a chance to bring down the Tory government. Whether that is the case, or whether Heath would simply have called and won a vote of confidence (which, given it was anyway a govern-ment free vote was all the more justifiable), we will never know. Harold Wilson, stung by press attacks on his lack of principle and consistency, felt that the coordinated activities of the pro-Marketeers were threatening the unity of the party and potentially his own leadership of it. He lashed out, sacking several from the front bench, including Bill Rodgers (who had been effectively the pro-Europeans' 'whip'), David Marquand and Cledwyn Hughes (though not David Owen or Roy Hattersley, who had been just as involved in the 'rebellion'). Some of the pro-Europeans were to pay an even higher price: deselection in their constituencies.

The bulk of the pro-Europeans, however, remained on the front bench, fortified by the re-election of Roy Jenkins as deputy leader. On 17 November 1971 Jenkins defeated Michael Foot by 140 to 126 on the second ballot (Tony Benn had secured 46 votes in the first ballot compared to 96 for Foot and 140 for Jenkins).

Roy Jenkins, son of a former Welsh miner who had gone to prison for his part in the 1926 miners lockout, was undoubtedly one of the great Labour figures of his time. His liberal reforms as Home Secretary and his relative success in holding the economy together as Chancellor had made him the darling of the liberal media and he was increas-ingly seen as Wilson's heir apparent. Nevertheless, Jenkins was already seen by some Labour MPs as aloof, as being more at home among the leather chesterfields of Brooks Club in St James Street than among the workers of, say, Chesterfield, or even among Labour MPs in the Commons Tea Room. His admirers, many of whom were increasingly frustrated with what they perceived as Wilson's failures, included earthy trade unionists of the calibre of Electricians' Union leader Frank Chapple and independent-minded maverick MPs such as John Mackintosh. But his social circle became increasingly a devoted band of invariably Oxford-educated and London-based intellectuals (dubbed the FORJ – Friends of Roy Jenkins). That the book of which as an author he was proudest was his elegant biography of the Liberal Prime Minister Herbert Asquith, rather than his biography of Clement Attlee, to whom his father had been PPS, was also a matter of suspicion to Labour MPs of socialist conviction. For Healey, Jenkins 'was not well suited to the politics of class and ideology which played so large a role in the Labour Party', though he 'had the same capacity as Nye Bevan and Hugh Gaitskell to inspire a deep and personal devotion among his disciples'.[408] It was not so much the impression that Jenkins was not 'one of us', but the feeling that he didn't quite want to be, that was his potential undoing among fellow Labour parliamentarians. When a fellow MP suggested to Nye Bevan that Roy Jenkins was lazy it is said that he replied: 'No boy from the valleys who has cultivated that accent could possibly be called lazy!'

Jenkins' supporters persuaded him that he should deliver a series of speeches to set out his vision. 'The intention behind the speeches was straightforward and political,' recalled David Owen, who with David and Judith Marquand assisted with the drafting. 'It was to be the "Unauthorised Programme". Just as Joseph Chamberlain, another Birmingham MP, had used this vehicle in 1885 to stamp his own distinctive mark on British politics, we hoped it would provide a rallying point for people who wanted to see Roy Jenkins succeed Harold Wilson as leader of the Labour Party.'[409] Moreover, recalled Jenkins, the speeches 'would also show that I had not become obsessed with Europe to the exclusion of all else'.

The first speech of the series of seven Jenkins delivered on Saturday 11 March 1972 to a Labour Party tea at Farnworth[410] in Lancashire. He denounced the Conservatives for having:

> helped to create a meaner, more selfish and more dangerously tense society [but continued, with a swipe at Wilson:] When the next election comes, we shall not be judged by the vehemence of our perorations, still less by the dexterity with which we follow the transient twists and turns of public opinion. We shall be judged by the quality of the programme we put before our fellow citizens, and by the consistency and courage with which we advocate it . . .
>
> Far too often, inequality is cumulative. The higher your income, the more likely it is that you possess inherited wealth – and that you, in your turn, will leave wealth to your heirs. The lower your earnings, the greater is your need for community services. But the more likely it is that you live in a poor locality which cannot afford to provide such services except on a niggardly basis. This is even more obviously true of the world beyond our shores . . .
>
> Although few Conservatives still advocate inequality as a positive idea, the

philosophy they espouse leads almost inevitably in that direction. At the heart of modern Conservatism lies a belief in the individual solution of economic problems . . . [which is] almost bound to benefit the strong at the expense of the weak. [Jenkins supported] individual freedom of choice if meaningful [and saw it as ironic that] many Conservative MPs who so strongly proclaim the virtues of individual freedom in the economic field, where it can do great harm to others, have bitterly resisted the growth of greater legal tolerance in the field of personal conduct, where individual behaviour rarely interferes with the rights of others. Many of them instinctively regard a young man with long hair as a greater enemy of society than a factory owner who pollutes a river.

But freedom of economic behaviour needs to be handled with far more care. If it is given primacy over all other values, and pursued without reference to social realities, the results are likely to be disastrous . . . Two hundred years ago, the pioneers of *laissez-faire* economics postulated a society composed of separate individuals, each pursuing his own individual wellbeing to the exclusion of all else, and each capable of making the choices that confronted him in the light of a rational calculation of advantage and disadvantage. In the real world . . . large numbers of our fellow citizens lack the knowledge to calculate the advantages and disadvantages of the choices they have to make. Many more lack the power to make the right choice at the right time.

To tell my deserted constituent in Birmingham – or, for that matter, an unemployed shipyard worker on the Tyne, or a coloured child in a dilapidated classroom in south London, or a low-paid worker in a Glasgow slum – that they have the freedom to choose a way of life for themselves, is, in a very real sense, to add insult to injury . . . The right to choose is meaningless without the power to choose; and in a society as riven by unfairness as ours still is, any approach to fairness, any approach to a real ability to choose, requires constant intervention by the state. In the real world, communal action is not the enemy of individual freedom, but its guarantor; the pursuit of individual economic freedom to the exclusion of all else may increase freedom for a few, but only by restricting the real freedom of the many . . .

Society is not, and never has been, simply a collection of individuals. Individuals belong to groups; and strong groups load the dice in favour of their members. Big firms take over their competitors; a child born into a rich family automatically starts life with an advantage; strong unions force up the price of their members' labour. In the same way the weak have the dice loaded against them . . . But the persistence of injustice is not an excuse for complacency or a reason for despair. It is a challenge to be overcome . . .

Over the past decade and a half there has been a great further social change. The world of deference has only a few traces left. But there has been no corresponding shift during this period in the pattern of rewards. The poor are still poor. Property speculators – and some others – are as relatively rich as were those who used to have an accepted position at the top of the old social structure. The result, quite inevitably, is increasing social strain . . .

Jenkins demanded:

a major attack on the unjustified disparities that still divide us from each other. Some levelling down will be required, but levelling up is far more important. *The next Labour government can be content with nothing less than the elimination of poverty as a social problem* . . . [This meant recognising that] Today the many are not poor. The many, while far from rich, have an approach to comfort and some free spending money. The poor are a minority, but a very sizeable minority. And the hard fact is that, if the social forces that sustain injustice are to be offset, then the comfortable majority will have to make their contribution. It is an illusion to imagine that the gap between rich and poor and the rest of us can be closed solely at the expense of the rich. The rich can and should make a disproportionate contribution, but it would be intellectually dishonest, and in the long run politically disastrous, to pretend that increased taxes on the rich can solve the problem altogether. Two years ago – all figures of this sort tend to be a little out of date – if the state had taken all incomes of more than £5,000 a year, the additional revenue at the Chancellor's disposal would have amounted to only about 1 per cent of Inland Revenue receipts . . .

The Labour movement was created to fight against a wealthy minority on behalf of a poor majority. Now it has a more complex and demanding task . . . We have to persuade men and women who are themselves reasonably well off that they have a duty to forgo some of the advantages they would otherwise enjoy for the sake of others who are much poorer than they are. We have to persuade motor car workers in my constituency that they have an obligation to low-paid workers in the public sector. We have to persuade the British people as a whole that they have an obligation to Africans and Asians whom they have never seen . . . We cannot hope to carry it out if we base our appeal on limited material self-interest . . . Our only hope is to appeal to the latent idealism of all men and women of goodwill – irrespective of their income brackets, irrespective of their class origins, irrespective in many cases of their past political affiliations.

The challenge of injustice, though centuries old in substance, has now taken on a new and more subtle form. To meet that new challenge we need a new kind of politics. Three centuries ago, the poet Andrew Marvell wrote of Cromwell:
> . . . *Casting the Kingdoms old*
> *Into another mould.*

That is our task too. We have to break the mould of custom, selfishness and apathy which condemns so many of our fellow countrymen to avoidable indignity and deprivation. In place of the politics of envy, we must put the politics of compassion; in place of the politics of cupidity, the politics of justice; in place of the politics of opportunism, the politics of principle. Only so can we hope to succeed. Only so will success be worth having.

The press had been briefed in advance and it splashed across the Sunday papers. The peroration, in which the pen of David Marquand had played an instrumental role, called for 'the politics of principle' to replace 'the politics of opportunism'. It was interpreted correctly in the media as being a direct swipe at Wilson. The headlines blazed: 'Jenkins opens his bid to oust Wilson.' This had been, indeed, the intention. So thought both David Owen and fellow Jenkinsite MP John Mackintosh. When he saw the headlines, however, Jenkins panicked and, 'much influenced by telephone advice from Roy Hattersley' he later claimed, Jenkins redid a BBC *World This Weekend* interview that he had already recorded the previous morning 'so as to make it more emollient'.[411] 'There was too much willingness to wound accompanied by fear to strike about my attitude,'[412] he later admitted. Mackintosh and Owen 'wanted [Wilson] out and would have preferred any of the likely alternatives – Roy [Jenkins], Jim [Callaghan] or Denis [Healey]. Roy of course had only one preference – to replace Wilson himself. Roy was always unsure as to whether he could use Wilson as the ladder to No. 10 or whether he had to destroy Wilson to achieve it.'[413]

Jenkins, in the end, succeeded in doing neither. In securing his victory in the deputy leadership election of 17 November 1971 Jenkins had given a pledge, in answer to a question at a PLP meeting from Glasgow MP Bruce Millan,[414] about his intentions regarding future votes on the EEC: that if he found it necessary again to vote against the party line he would resign as deputy leader. It was a fatal answer.

Tony Benn had begun a couple of years earlier to advance the case for a referendum on Britain's membership of the EEC. Initially he had attracted little support: in April 1971 he was unable to get a seconder when he put his proposal for a referendum to Labour's NEC. On 15 March 1972 the shadow Cabinet rejected Benn's proposal that the Labour Party support a referendum on the European Communities Bill by eight votes to four. With Wilson, Jenkins, Callaghan and Healey absent, however, Benn managed to convince the NEC to vote in favour of asking the shadow Cabinet to reconsider in the light of the news that there would be a referendum in France over EEC enlargement. This the shadow Cabinet duly did on 29 March, and with Wilson leading the switchers, despite having spoken against referenda during the 1970 election, it endorsed Benn's proposal. The prospect of having to vote in the Commons for a referendum was the final straw for Roy Jenkins.[415] On 11 April he resigned. He was followed out of the shadow Cabinet by George Thomson and Harold Lever and from the front bench by Dick Taverne, David Owen and Dickson Mabon.[416]

In the reshuffle that followed, Healey replaced Jenkins as shadow Chancellor and Callaghan replaced Healey as shadow Foreign Secretary. Signalling the new stance, Peter Shore returned as spokesman on Europe. In the election to replace Jenkins as deputy leader, former Education Secretary and Chief Whip Ted Short, a Geordie ex-headteacher of the solid centre of the party, came up through the middle to victory, defeating Michael Foot and Tony Crosland. Short became shadow Leader of the Commons. The Jenkinsites, angry at what they perceived to be a failure of fellow Gaitskellite pro-European Tony Crosland to back them up, mostly voted for Short.

The Jenkinsite resignation was 'a momentous event', recalled Bill Rodgers, 'but I did not foresee its full significance, which was that from now on Labour Europeans were to be outsiders in the party . . . The vote of 28 October 1971 and Roy [Jenkins]'s subsequent resignation had rearranged the pieces on a chessboard of the Labour Party, separating the European knights from the anti-European bishops of the right and centre.'[417] Some, indeed, of the chess pieces were never destined to return to the Labour game: George Thomson would go to Brussels as one of the UK's first pair of European Commissioners and Dick Taverne would be deselected by his constituency for his stand on the EEC. Taverne's revenge was to resign his seat and fight the consequent by-election on 1 March 1973 as 'Democratic Labour', comprehensively defeating the official Labour candidate.[418]

On 4 October 1972 the referendum policy was formally adopted at Labour's annual conference, in addition to a demand for withdrawal from the EEC unless terms could be 'renegotiated' to include the abandonment of the Common Agricultural Policy and VAT. Two days beforehand a Harris opinion poll in the *Daily Express* showed that 79 per cent of Labour supporters backed Wilson's leadership, while only 5 per cent said that they would prefer Jenkins. Judged against the yardstick of enhancing his future leadership prospects, Jenkins had resigned over the wrong issue. Wilson's biographer Ben Pimlott observed: 'Resented in the constituency parties in direct proportion to the praise he continued to receive in newspapers, Jenkins was no longer centre stage,'[419] and his credibility as a leadership challenger to Wilson was waning. Wilson had challenged Gaitskell overtly for the leadership. Jenkins never did, despite the urgings of MPs as disparate as David Owen, John P. Mackintosh, Tam Dalyell, Chris Mayhew and the famously republican MP for Fife Willie Hamilton. Partly this was because while Wilson believed that by challenging Gaitskell in the name of 'party unity' he would strengthen his position, Jenkins feared that by challenging Wilson he would diminish his position further by opening himself up even more to the charge of divisiveness.

FORTY-FOUR

The Rise of Tony Benn 1970–73

'A fundamental and irreversible shift in the balance of wealth and power in favour of working people and their families'

Tony Benn was 'an exceedingly bright, attractive, hail-fellow-well-met-chap with remarkable charisma, who carried people along with him in all his many enthusiasms', recalled John Golding, a fellow MP throughout the 1970s. 'Extremely plausible, he spoke clearly, movingly and persuasively. He had a magical talent with words.' It was as a young student during the 1950s that Golding had first met Benn, who had 'played table tennis with verve and spoke with greater enthusiasm'.[420] Benn was promoted by Gaitskell and indulged by Tony Crosland, his tutor at Oxford, who had helped Benn get a seat. When on his election to Parliament in 1950 Benn had publicly announced his intention 'to lose the stigma of being an intellectual', Crosland had joked: 'You'd better acquire the stigma before worrying about losing it.'[421] By the later 1950s Benn was transferring his affections to Wilson and was to indelibly associate himself with the Wilsonian 'white heat' of the early 1960s. It was Wilson who promoted Benn to Cabinet, where he served as Minister of Technology from 1966–70. There, Anthony Wedgwood Benn became 'Wedge Benn of MinTech', the 'quintessential whizz-kid, developing Concorde with the French, computerising industry, building up Britain's civilian nuclear energy programme as an enthusiast for fast-breeder reactors. Student audiences marvelled at this pullover-clad minister enthralled by his machines.'[422]

After the election Benn sought to use the defeat as an opportunity to reassess the approach of Labour in government. He convinced himself that he could succeed next time where last time he and his colleagues had failed. Susan Crosland recalled discussing with her husband Tony the impression she had after the 1970 election defeat that Benn seemed happier in opposition and increasingly saw himself as a populist guru of the left: 'the left-wing equivalent to Enoch Powell'. Her husband agreed: 'He is happier in opposition. There's no other time he can make his move [to become leader] . . . no one doubts his sincerity in seeing himself as the Messiah. The trouble with fanatics – why one should never underestimate them – is they're so assiduous.'[423] After the election, Benn had become the shadow Technology, Trade and Industry Minister, effectively a promotion. During 1971–72 he was able to combine this role with the annual chairmanship of the

Labour Party, which rotated on 'Buggins's turn'. It was a unique opportunity for Benn to push forward with a fresh policy agenda.

In December 1971 the NEC's Industrial Policy Committee had set up a Public Sectors Group chaired by ex-minister Judith Hart and assisted by a team of young researchers.[424] They confronted a situation where capitalism was ostensibly failing. Despite the attempts by Wilson, Benn and others in the 1960s to sponsor greater efficiency in private industry, too often Industrial Reorganisation Corporation (IRC)-sponsored mergers had replaced small loss-making companies with larger loss-making companies. The management blamed the unions, demarcation disputes and outdated working practices. Often they had a point. But they themselves were frequently guilty of incompetence, venality and greed. To avoid massive job losses both Wilson and Heath had been intervening to prop up ailing capitalist concerns and finding that the taxpayers' subsidies were all too often going into the pockets of the management and shareholders rather than being invested in productivity improvements. The shipyards were a case in point. What was needed was a means through which to tackle the reluctance of the private sector to invest. The NEC Public Sectors Group proposed a National Enterprise Board (replacing MinTech's IRC, which the Conservatives had abolished), which would be a state holding company, however, rather than simply a 'merger bureau' like the old IRC. They envisaged that at an early stage the NEB would take over some 25 of the largest UK manufacturers. They also planned a system of compulsory planning agreements with the hundred largest companies,[425] entailing the disclosure of future investment, product development, marketing, import/export and pricing plans, to enable them to be coordinated by government. Benn enthusiastically promoted their recommendations. Harold Lever, back in the shadow Cabinet since November 1972, regarded it as 'a naïve dream . . . of an omni-competent, all-seeing government, which can then act to inform, instruct, guide and persuade the hundred thousand different entrepreneurial components of private industry into one harmonious equivalent of the Russian Gosplan'.[426] He feared the NEB would be 'a dinosaur', too large to be controlled by any Labour Industry Secretary, that would follow its own bureaucratic agenda, irrespective of ministers' wishes.[427]

However, the idea that competitive public corporations had a constructive role to play was one accepted right across the Labour movement:

> The performance of our nationalised industries, especially in terms of productivity, has been outstandingly good by comparison with our other industries and also good by comparison with the corresponding industries in other countries [declared Roy Jenkins, in a speech on 5 May 1972.[428] He continued:] The remorseless pressures of a highly industrialised economy lead towards the need for greater public ownership. It was the complexities and cost of the RB 211 engine that forced this government to nationalise Rolls-Royce. It would be highly irresponsible for the government, now that

it has invested the taxpayers' money at high risk in rescuing Rolls-Royce, to carry out its doctrinaire promise of selling the company back to private ownership as soon as its economic prospects are fair enough to make investors believe that they could achieve a satisfactory return . . . The myth that only private ownership has the managerial ability, entrepreneurial flair and marketing skills to run modern industry dies hard in Britain. Yet experience abroad in the highly competitive motor car industry does not bear this out. [He went on to highlight the success of European government-owned car firms Renault, Alfa Romeo and Volkswagen (which had been government-owned during its crucial formative years).] Britain needs an investment stimulus, and especially a stimulus in the regions, that a major state holding company is ideally fitted to provide . . . Since the fulfilment of the 1945 government's programme of basic nationalisation, I have always believed that public ownership should be judged more by the results it will produce than by abstractions and preconceived views.

The new proposals were at the heart of the draft *Labour's Programme 1973*. On 14 May 1973 they were discussed at a special meeting of the shadow Cabinet and the proposal for the nationalisation of 25 companies was much criticised by Tony Crosland, Shirley Williams and Harold Lever, who argued that it would ruin Labour's election chances in every constituency in which the prospective companies were major employers. At a joint meeting between the shadow Cabinet and the NEC two days later, battle was rejoined. Whether it was Wilson, Healey or Crosland who asked 'Who's going to tell me that we should nationalise Marks & Spencer in the hope it will be as efficient as the Co-op?'[429] remains unclear, but they could all have agreed with the sentiment. Hart and Mikardo eventually accepted that a shopping list of 25 was not essential so long as the principle was preserved. Benn, however, did not. Perhaps most surprising for Benn was the sceptical reaction of TGWU chief Jack Jones, who told Benn on 12 June: 'we must deal with prices and pensions . . . we didn't want airy-fairy stuff. Nationalisation was unpopular; it failed.'[430] Benn, however, was never prepared to accept defeat. Ministerial colleague Joel Barnett had a sporting analogy for Benn: 'Imagine a brand-new squash ball: put a grand piano on top of it and when you release it the ball springs back to life.'[431]

The crunch came at a poorly attended special meeting of Labour's NEC on 31 May 1973; the issue was reopened during a gruelling eleven-hour discussion of the manifesto and to the surprise of many, a proposal by Healey to delete the reference to the 25 companies was defeated by seven[432] votes to six[433] with several abstentions. Wilson had incited Healey to call the vote. Much to Healey's surprise, he had decided as leader to abstain. Wilson had not, however, expected Healey's proposal to be defeated. The following day Wilson issued a statement to the press making clear that he planned to exercise his constitutional right as party leader to veto the inclusion in the manifesto of the 25 companies figure and the proposal to renationalise without compensation.

At Labour's 1973 conference, three 'composite resolutions' were debated, all of which urged the next Labour government to extend public ownership. Only one of them, how-ever, mentioned the specific figure of 25 companies that had been proposed by the NEC, and it demanded the nationalisation of not just that 25 but by means of 'an enabling act' a grand total of '250 major monopolies together with the land, finance houses, insurance companies and building societies . . . and the renationalisation of all hived-off sections of public owned industries without compensation'. This resolution, 'Composite 34', was proposed by Militant activist and Brighton delegate Ray Apps and fellow Militant sup-porter Edward Mooney from Liverpool Walton. Michael Crick argued, in his authorita-tive study of Militant, that

> Militant's demand to nationalise the top 200 monopolies is more than a radical form of the long-standing Tribunite demand to take the top 25 companies into public own-ership. Militant is committed to revolutionary change and believes that change cannot be achieved through parliamentary democracy: internally the [Militant] tendency is, after all, called the Revolutionary Socialist League . . . Tony Benn has defended Militant by arguing that Marxism has always been a 'legitimate strand of thought' within the Labour Party. He misses the point. Militant is not just Marxist but also Leninist and Troskyist; as a result it has a style of secretive and disciplined politics that is wholly alien from the democratic traditions of the Labour Party.[434]

It was Tony Benn who was to reply to the debate on behalf of the NEC, but not even the NEC left could support the demands contained in the Militant resolution. Moreover, both the TGWU and the AUEW were going to join the moderate unions in voting it down. Neither of the other two resolutions, both of which the conference would vote to endorse, mentioned a specific figure, 25 or otherwise. One urged 'the early nationalisation of important parts of the British economy', aiming, as its mover explained, 'to strike a bal-ance between on the one hand doing nothing and on the other starting a revolution'. The other, Composite 36, was still more moderate, suggesting that the manifesto should specifically reject 'the concept of shopping lists of industries and companies for social ownership', should commit to a programme that could actually be carried out within the lifetime of one Parliament and should take any decision to nationalise an industry on the basis of the likely impact of nationalisation on considerations such as investment policy, growth, unemployment and the national interest. This last resolution was proposed by the loyalist APEX trade union in the person of its president, Gaitskellite MP Denis Howell, and was seconded by a 26-year-old councillor from Sheffield Hallam called David Blunkett, who was perhaps the first blind delegate to address a Labour conference:

> We do not believe in public enterprise merely to improve the efficiency of the system. We believe in public enterprise because we believe in a philosophy of changing the power of this country and not merely in making a capitalist state controlled by the public. We do not believe in State capitalism. We believe in real social democracy . . .

We need to say to people that we are going to take control, 'we are going to use it for your benefit and we need your participation through democratic workers' control'.

It is up to me to say that my constituency included the words 'shopping list'. They did so not because they wished to restrict or to criticise the 25 companies but in fact because they wished to say that this should only be a minimum demand and not our full complement in this State . . .

The Howell–Blunkett resolution was also backed by a speech from ex-Chancellor Roy Jenkins:

It is not much good talking about fundamental and irreversible changes in our society and being content with a 38 per cent Labour voting intention, which is what we have in the polls at the present time, but which is less than we had at the last general election. Democracy means that you need a substantially stronger moral position than this to govern effectively at all, let alone effect a peaceful social revolution. Secondly, the programme we put forward must be capable of being carried out, carried out in what may well be extremely difficult economic circumstances. To do otherwise, to vote for things you do not believe in your hearts can and will be done, is a recipe for two highly undesirable things: first for embittered relations between conference and the government at just that stage in a government's life in which, if it is to get through, if it is to surmount the inevitable difficulties, if it is to fight off the attacks of its opponents, if it is to have a strong chance of winning the second election, harmonious relations between government and party are vital to both. But second, if one takes on what one cannot do, one will add to the dangerous public disillusionment with parties, with politics and with politicians. This country cannot afford a further letdown such as we have seen, particularly in the past three years . . . if it happens it will be the democratic process as a whole which will suffer and the beneficiaries from that will not be any of us, but some much more sinister forces.

This does not mean, in my view, excessive caution, or a 'do-nothing' government with a 'risk-nothing' programme. I agree with many of the criticisms, harsh, fundamental criticisms, levelled against the performance of private industry. I agree that the country needs a sharp change. I agree too that there is a case for a significant extension of public ownership. Indeed, I said so 18 months ago here in Blackpool at a meeting of the Lancashire miners. But it . . . is no good taking over a vast number of industries without a clear plan as to how and by whom they are going to be run. It is no good pretending a transfer of ownership in itself solves our problems . . .

Concluding the debate for the NEC, Tony Benn had no alternative but to endorse the resolution too, and the 'powerful speech from Sheffield Hallam':

The industrial policy which we put before the conference this year and which we have been debating today occupies a central place in meeting our central objectives of bringing about the fundamental and irreversible shift in the balance of wealth and power in favour of working people and their families. The changes in taxation that were discussed and agreed yesterday . . . cannot of itself achieve what we know has to be done unless we can bring about a great extension of public ownership . . . Those who talk about public ownership as if in some way it represented a threat had better realise the truth; which is that there are millions of workers, and I mean workers, right up to management level, who are much more frightened today of the possibility that Slater Walker will take them over and sell their assets and close them down than of anything we may do.

Moreover the violence of the attacks upon our public ownership plans and on us for defending them launched by big business and by the media confirm our judgement that these plans are a serious threat, as they are intended to be, to the unaccountable power they wield and the unacceptable privileges that they defend with that power.

Now in all this the mention of 25 companies has played an interesting part. In choosing those figures we were seeking to give some numerical significance to a better-known phrase 'the commanding heights of the economy', long accepted as the party's objectives in its extension of public ownership . . .

If those of us who have joined in this comradely debate have acted as a lightning conductor for the attacks of our opponents, I must tell the party that we have been getting a little battle practice for what will be happening over the whole range of our programme when people realise how radical it is. Our policy on public ownership is based upon a serious analysis of the developing power structure in our society: fewer, larger companies, many of them multinational, growing larger and more powerful, and we know, and we must say that if we do not control or own them, they will control and own us, and that is the challenge that we face . . . It is a matter of political power, for as Michael Meacher rightly said, if this political expression of unaccountable economic power is allowed to continue, our political democracy too will be reduced to a fiction, and that is what matters about the programme we bring forward.

Recommending acceptance of the two moderate resolutions, Benn had to oppose the Militant-supported Composite 34:

Nobody reading it can doubt that it is firmly based upon the ideas of Clause Four, and there is much with which we could all agree . . . but it calls for 250 companies . . . it is a composite that confuses strategy with tactics . . .

We are not, never have been and never will be, a party of confiscation . . . we will not over-compensate in the acquisition of profitable manufacturing industries, which we propose to bring into public ownership . . . but . . . we are not ready for Composite 34, and if conference takes its own decisions seriously we ask it not to pass that resolution. However, we are ready . . . to establish the National Enterprise Board, not to be an ambulance for lame ducks, but to move into the area of profitable manufacturing industry which is at the heart of the proposal . . .

Benn then turned to what would become a favourite theme: extra-parliamentary action:

Historically, all pressure for social change and improvement has begun outside Parliament . . . The trade unions, the Trades Union Congress, the Labour Representation Committee, got Labour members into Parliament and produced Labour governments. Acts of Parliament are the last, and never the first, stage in the process of political and economic reform. Therefore, we must now carry the debate we are having today out to the people of this country and we must begin with the workers in industry, and particularly in discussions with the workers in the firms that we shall need to acquire.

I cannot conceive of an extension of public ownership without the same active support and pressure from workers in the firms of which we are now speaking that we historically enjoyed from the miners, from the railwaymen, and from others who demanded public ownership and looked to us to give it to them . . .

We reject as a party and as a movement the idea that one worker on the board is industrial democracy (*applause*). We reject co-ownership. We reject the phoney works councils not rooted in strength and structure and traditions of the trade union movement (*applause*). All these are window dressing, designed to divert the demand for democratic control into utterly harmless channels . . . We have had enough experience now surely to know that nationalisation plus Lord Robens does not add up to socialism, and that is the message we are sending out (*applause*) . . .

One delegate said that we shall inherit a crisis when we come to power . . . We are saying, at this conference, that the crisis that we inherit when we come to power will be the occasion for fundamental change and not the excuse for postponing it . . .

Benn had failed to commit Labour to a nationalisation 'shopping list'. Nevertheless, Labour was committed to further nationalisation in principle. Benn claimed that nationalisation was popular. A confidential MORI opinion poll commissioned by the Labour Party during the weeks that followed to assess the popularity of its policies found otherwise. Labour's most popular commitment, with 74 per cent support, was its pledge to increase pensions. In contrast, nationalising shipbuilding, ports and aircraft industries attracted the support of only 7 per cent of the electorate and the proposed National Enterprise Board only 6 per cent. An NOP poll showed that 44 per cent of Labour supporters were against more nationalisation and only 37 per cent in favour.[435] The left claimed that it was because their proposals were complicated.

FORTY-FIVE

Deflating Heath 1973–74

*'The spectacle of a few fat men exhorting
the thin ones to tighten their belts'*

As the battling and bickering of his colleagues intensified, Wilson began to emerge once more above the fray. There was a growing recognition, among both MPs and the Fleet Street commentariat, of Wilson's achievement in holding his warring party together. Unlike Thatcher in later years, Wilson did not even face a 'stalking horse' leadership challenger. He used his speech at Labour's 1973 annual conference, what was to be last as leader of the opposition, to divert attention from the internal rows and towards the travails of Heath. There were allusions to Bevan, and his great assault upon the 'meretricious society' of 1959. And with a sideswipe at the resurgent Liberal Party, he also took aim at the Conservative-dominated media, deploying the Wilsonian wit to secure the prolonged applause of conference:

> If a century ago Palmerston, Gladstone and Disraeli could see that Britain's interest meant a breach with ancient empires and the support of national revolutionaries in Greece, Italy, Spain and Portugal, cannot the present rulers of this country see that not only the moral future of Britain but its real interests are bound up with the support of freedom movements in Southern Africa? There may be African freedom fighters who would appear incongruous in a Belgravian drawing room, but I guess Garibaldi and Kossuth did not bath twice a day either . . .
>
> For the first time in the history of this movement, the Labour Party – the National Executive Committee and the parliamentary party – and the Trades Union Congress – have reached agreement on a categorical programme for fighting inflation.
>
> We have set out measures which in our view must be taken as a minimum programme if we are to secure a policy for fighting rising prices and rising rents.
>
> Action to control prices, where it counts, where the housewife does her shopping.
>
> Direct action to deal with essential foods, using food subsidies.
>
> A freeze on all council house and new town rents.
>
> Action, such as I called for yesterday, to control the London capital market and freeze market interest rates.
>
> A crisis tax on land and property speculation.
>
> An adequate pension increase now.
>
> A declaration that in the next Budget provocative and divisive tax concessions to

317

the wealthy are to be reversed, and the proceeds to be used to help the less well off.

The country has rejected the government's excuses. And no wonder.

. . . month after month this year we have seen trade deficits of £150 million and above. In June they published the worst ever figure – a deficit of £209 million in a month; an average deficit for the proceeding three months of over £150 million. Where were the screaming headline writers of June 1970 (*applause*)? Perhaps it was the newsprint shortage (*laughter*). One great London evening paper printed a perfunctory statement in the bottom right-hand corner of the front page referring the reader to page 50 of the City section if he cared to read about it. In later editions it disappeared altogether from the front page.

After the trade figures had been published, the other great London evening news-paper produced an afternoon edition with a main headline across seven columns: 'EXCLUSIVE Soccer Star Marriage Shock' – (*laughter and applause*) – 'A London striker's "Wife goes home to Mum"'. This I can assert with confidence, recalling our experience of Mr Heath conducting a mighty press orchestra of June 1970, if there had been trade figures in that month such as those he achieved three years later, they would have been trumpeted abroad across all the columns there are. Even if the wives of every footballer in the First Division, the Second Division (*laughter*), the Third Division and the Fourth Division, the Scottish First Division, the Scottish Second Division, the Central League, the Lancashire Combination (*laughter*), the Isthmian League, the Spartan League, the Athenian League, indeed the entire Football Combination had all collectively gone home to their mums.

. . . the Conservative Party, at home and abroad, after all their boasts, has become tainted as the party of unsound finance and clipped money. And all the country is given is a repetitive speech about growth. Growth? A stretch of jungle, a foetid swamp, are certainly not deficient in growth; an unweeded garden, 'things rank and gross in nature possess it merely'. But Mr Heath has achieved a distorted growth by the unique prescription of applying fertilisers to the weeds and Paraquat to the fruit and flowers (*applause and laughter*).

. . . That is why when we look at these things in the public sector we find a mere-tricious vulgarity in Mr Heath's 'You've never had materialism so good' speech. There is little that is surprising in the fact that there now more colour television sets or dish washers than there were three years ago. Each decade sees an increase in the purchase of the products of technological advance. I should be very surprised if in 1933, when there were three million unemployed, there were not very many more radio sets than in 1930.

But we have to lift our eyes above the sales figures of an over-advertised society.

There are other values, and they are neglected by the kind of government Britain has got and the kind of people they exist to promote. Is the Admass profession capable of expressing – still less satisfying – the real desires of average parents, their hopes for themselves, their dreams for their children? . . . Are not working mothers more concerned to have adequate nursery facilities for looking after their children during working hours? Are not so many of our people concerned that they should not have to bring up their children in homes whose structure and amenities are a blot on our civilisation? . . . Would not our old people prefer to live the retirement they earned in better amenities than so many of them get, rather than hear on radios or TV about the material symbols of a society from which they are largely excluded? Would not all – young and old – yearn for greater access to green fields and open space in the countryside? Or when they go down to the sea or the river to have some confidence that their day or their week or their fortnight is not ruined by the pollution of modern society? . . .

A century ago Tennyson said 'We are not spinners all'. Today . . . we have got to ensure that our system of education is directed not to the creation of school-leavers who will be so involved in the rat race that they will never begin to live until they are too old to enjoy it. We have to end the artificial system under which education ceases for the majority of our people one day in July; their past school life and their continuing education must be part of the same process . . . That is why any programme for industrial democracy must provide for an obligation on the employer, public or private, to enable every employee to have continuing education, with compulsory facilities for day release not only in vocational training but in all forms of study which he wishes to follow so that he can play his full part in industry and in all the wide calls of citizenship . . .

The press build-up to our conference here this year is reminiscent of what happened exactly eight years ago [when] you would have thought from the build-up that one issue dominated any conference, namely what my response would be to Mr Grimond's offer to keep the Labour government in office as long as it dropped its programme in favour of whatever the Liberal programme happened to be about at any particular time (*laughter*). I rejected this out of hand . . . Now there are ancestral voices heralding a new alignment of political forces. With all the authority of a twice-defeated Conservative candidate, the editor[436] of *The Times* is thundering out his canonicals . . . he and his fellow manipulators dream of an election result in which the Liberal Party holds the balance in a newly elected Parliament. This, they pray, will lead to a situation which would mean a permanent majority for the Conservatives by the creation of a new Liberal Party out of the ashes of the Labour Party. They are wasting their time. This party is not for burning (*applause*).

Let this be clear: as long as I am leader of this Party, Labour will not enter into any coalition with any other party, Liberal or Conservative or anyone else (*prolonged applause*) . . .

If there is one thing some of our Fleet Street friends cannot stand, it is a successful and united conference. They are having a bad time . . . A front runner for the Aims of Industry prize for independent journalism . . . should you in fact have missed it . . . yesterday's *Daily Express* report of our conference . . . began like this:

'The scene, at first glance, in the Winter Gardens, Blackpool, might well have resembled Moscow's Palace of Congresses in Stalin's time' (*laughter*).

'All those massive crystal chandeliers under the gilded stucco ceiling, with its coats of arms and dancing cherubs, and below, those serried ranks of grim-looking delegates' – (*laughter*) 'in their square-cut lounge suits – not a smile between them – at the opening of the Labour conference.'

Then he goes on: 'Not forgetting the few women kept firmly in their place, so it seemed, well at the back' (*laughter*). 'And on the presidium – sorry, platform – the same grimness, the same authoritarian respect.

'Around was the colour red as the basic theme of the affair. Red plush seats. Red-draped platform. Red-backgrounded slogan, "Labour Leads to a Better Britain". And red costumes worn by MPs Mrs Barbara Castle, Miss Joan Lester and Mrs Lena Jeger.

'Small wonder the smile of expectancy on the face of the Tass man at the press table' (*laughter and applause*).

'Small wonder the approving clouds of Georgian tobacco smoke from certain sections of the diplomatic enclosure.'

This reference to red costumes – let us get it out of the way first, shall we? It is a very dated phrase of the fifties. I do not know who thought that one up. It really is a tribute to my lady colleagues' sartorial conservatism – they always wear red on conference Mondays! And then that smile of expectancy on the face of the Tass man on the press table. Has anyone ever seen a Tass man smile? And that egregious tobacco. What is it – 'Small wonder the approving clouds of Georgian tobacco smoke from certain sections of the diplomatic enclosure.' Speaking as one who is rapidly becoming an authority on tobacco, I have never learned how to make clouds of tobacco smoke approving. But if this is possible, I suppose next week in this hall it will be Rhodesian tobacco curling upwards in satisfaction (*laughter and applause*) . . .

But let us face it, in 28 years the Tories have not changed; 1945, Clem Attlee was the Gestapo; 1973, I am the KGB (*laughter*), and the ideals underlying this conference are to be disinterred from the archives of the Marx–Engels Institute. I thank them very much for that.

You, Mr Chairman, sought them in the words of Robert Blatchford. I could go back earlier to another impeccably democratic source, to the words of a statesman – who more than a century ago, fought for democracy and, indeed, died for democracy. And I want to sum up what I think this conference is about by quoting Abraham Lincoln, and this is what he said:

'In the early days of the world, the Almighty said to the first of our race "in the sweat of thy face shalt thou eat bread"; and since then, if we accept the light and the air of heaven, no good thing has been, or can be enjoyed by us, without having first cost labour. And, inasmuch as most good things are produced by labour, it follows that all such things of right belong to those whose labour has produced them. But it has so happened in all ages of the world, that some have laboured, and others have, without labour, enjoyed a large proportion of the fruits. This is wrong, and should not continue. To secure to each labourer the whole product of his labour, or as nearly as possible, is a most worthy object of any good government' (*prolonged applause*).

By the autumn of 1973 minds were turning towards the next general election and ranks were closing behind Wilson's leadership. The window of opportunity for a leadership challenge, if one there had been, had passed. Roy Jenkins let his friends persuade him to re-stand for the shadow Cabinet. He came a respectable fifth with 143 votes, behind Callaghan and Crosland. If he couldn't (yet) be leader, Jenkins still wanted to be Foreign Secretary. A fall-back position would be to be Chancellor again, though as neither Callaghan nor Healey wanted to relinquish their shadow portfolios, Jenkins had to make do with shadow Home Secretary, which Shirley Williams was persuaded to give up for him. Healey, whose great expertise was foreign affairs, was not however proving as effective at exposing the Conservatives' economic failures as Jenkins had done previously.

Edward Heath's government had since July been facing wage demands from the miners which, had they been conceded, would have breached the government's statutory incomes policy. Not conceding the demands led to escalating industrial action by the miners beginning on 12 November. In the context of the quadrupling of oil prices precipitated by the Yom Kippur War of October 1973, this led the government to declare a state of emergency from midnight on 13 November. On 26 November it was announced that petrol ration coupons would be issued from 29 November (though they were never used). From 12 December an overtime ban by the train drivers' union ASLEF restricted the movement of coal.

With negotiations failing to secure a settlement with the miners, on 13 December Heath explained in a televised broadcast to the nation that from 1 January a 'three-day week' would be imposed to conserve electricity and stave off total power-cuts, with dramatic restrictions on the use of electricity for heating and lighting shops, offices and street lighting.

On 19 December 1973 Jenkins returned to the economic fray. Healey had already spoken in a Commons debate that day on the economic crisis, but had failed to make an impact. Jenkins volunteered himself to wind up for the opposition. This he did 'with magisterial authority, not only virtually destroying the Tory Chancellor [Anthony Barber] single-handedly by the force of his oratory, but also raising the question of whether the right man was shadow Chancellor. Afterwards excited Labour members were heard to say that it was one of the most devastating attacks made in the Commons since the war, while, during Jenkins's speech, Tories remained silent, always a good indication of a really powerful Labour contribution.' In Giles Radice's 28 years in the Commons, 'only Sir Geoffrey Howe's 1990 resignation speech was comparable for power and impact':[437]

> ... The pattern of leadership which the government have chosen to present in the past couple of weeks has been fluctuating and confused. It was barely a few weeks ago that, long after the miners' overtime ban had started, the Secretary of State for Trade and Industry was still exuding the uncomprehending optimism of a professional salesman. It was only fourteen days ago that the Chancellor of the Exchequer was petulantly and publicly rebuking the Director General of NEDO for daring to suggest

that the 3¹/₂ per cent growth target for next year was no longer valid. It was only on Wednesday of last week that the Home Secretary was rejecting, with all the comfortable blanket indignation of a minister largely detached from central economic policy-making, my charge that the government were complacent rather than realistic.

Then on Thursday, without warning or consultation, the Prime Minister suddenly lurched into the announcement of the most serious crisis since the war, accompanied by the most drastic and damaging measures for a 40 per cent shut-down of industry and by the news that the Chancellor was to break his clearly given pledge of 27 July – repeated by the Leader of the House on 15 November – and introduce an autumn Budget. I do not accuse the Prime Minister (*interruption*). Yes it is just within time. Even phase three does not change the calendar! I do not accuse the Prime Minister of manufacturing an artificial crisis. I think it is a real crisis . . .

The Budget is trivial and wrong . . . The property development tax, which to be effective, should have dealt with unrealised gains – this is the real scandal – and, perhaps as a lesser issue, with unlet premises, has all the effectiveness of a feather duster fingered with the distaste which comes from a repugnance to pick it up at all. The total expected revenue is not enough to impose a deterrent upon even a single big property company . . . To continue in present monetary circumstances, as is now widely recognised, even in the City, with the relief against tax of personal borrowings is a mixture of economic lunacy and fiscal inequity.

Then there is the central issue of the Chancellor's decision to allow the public sector in a broadly, not wholly, undifferentiated way to bear almost all the brunt . . . it is the wrong way out. No one can look at Britain today without realising that for the majority it is not in private spending but in the public services where the weakness, the squalor and the pressures lie. It is not the shops and the restaurants that are breaking down but public transport, schools and parts of the Health Service.

Can it be right to make those areas bear the burden, particularly without singling out the big, prestige, money squanderers? Can it be right to talk piously, as we have done from both sides of the House, about the devastating problems of the cities and then make it overwhelmingly likely that a grinding shortage of money will be added to all the other difficulties? . . . The Chancellor has become a prisoner of his own tax hand-out past.

I read with amazement of the Chancellor's unctuous Monday-night statement that when he met his fellow Western Finance Ministers he felt a sense of shame for his country. Because of what? Because of two industrialised disputes leading to an overtime ban. That shows at once a remarkable personal brazenness and a national lack of proportion. Who does the right hon. gentleman think that he was meeting then? Was he meeting the Finance Minister of France, whose country went to the verge of civil war five years ago; the Finance Minister of Italy, who has had far worse industrial troubles with which to deal; or the United States Secretary of the Treasury, who came from a city sunk in political scandal?

The sense of shame that the Chancellor should have felt is far more personal. It is a sense of shame for having taken over an economy with a £1,000 million surplus and running it to a £2,000 million deficit. It is a sense of shame for having conducted our integral financial affairs with such profligacy that our public accounts are out of balance as never before. It is a sense of shame for having presided over the greatest depreciation of the currency, both at home and abroad, in our history. It is a sense of shame for having left us at a moment of test far weaker than most of our neighbours.

Whatever is the fate of the present government, I believe that the Chancellor ought now to go from his present office. He sits around in the wreckage of successive layers of his policy. I believe that by both temperament and outlook he is profoundly unsuited to the hard struggles which lie ahead. It is no longer a question of waiting for the old policies to come right. We need new policies to create hope out of dismay. The Chancellor had a last chance on Monday. He failed to take it. He showed himself tied to the past. He ought now to let a new man try.

On 1 January 1974 Britain began the 'three-day week' and though negotiations continued, Heath and his Chancellor did not believe private assurances from the TUC that if the government made an exception to the miners other unions would not use it as a precedent in their own pay negotiations. As January unfolded energy minister Patrick Jenkin attracted national ridicule by advising people to brush their teeth in the dark. Meanwhile the miners balloted overwhelmingly in favour of an all-out strike, announcing on 5 February that it would begin on 10 February. The Cabinet decided that they had little alternative to fight, and on 7 February Heath announced that Parliament would be dissolved the following day and a general election held on 28 February to resolve 'Who governs Britain?'

Wilson responded with an attack on Heath's handling of the coal dispute and called for a new 'social contract'. The idea had initially been floated by Callaghan at a joint meeting of the shadow Cabinet in May 1971, when he suggested that prices and incomes policies would be part of a social compact that 'would involve concessions from both politicians and trade unions'.[438] The elements of the social compact, or contract as it became known, were first revealed in a Labour NEC paper of February 1973. Essentially it envisaged the government introducing a wide-ranging system of price controls, including subsidies for 'essentials' such as food, an explicit commitment to the redistribution of wealth and income through taxation, improved pensions, NHS, housing and transport, and an extension of public ownership. Against that background, it was hoped that the unions would moderate wage claims.

As polling day approached the Conservative campaign was rocked by a speech from Enoch Powell urging people to vote Labour to secure a referendum in which they could vote for Britain to leave the EEC. Two days later, on 25 February, a record monthly trade deficit of £383 million was announced for January. If Labour had failed to build a New Britain in 1964-70 then the Conservatives hadn't sorted out the economy either. The election saw a high turnout (79 per cent) and while Conservative support fell to 38.2 per cent, Labour's fell to 37.2 per cent, its lowest since the war. Nevertheless Labour emerged with four more seats than the Conservatives, 301 as against 297. Though the Conservatives had clearly lost the election, Labour had not exactly won. Labour had done worse than when it had been defeated in 1970. Research suggests that Labour's more left-wing policies lacked resonance with the electorate. The British Election Study team at Essex University found that at the February 1974 election, among Labour identifiers, the proportion of voters favouring more nationalisation had fallen from 57 per cent in 1964 to only 50 per cent; those wanting more spending on social services had fallen from 89 per cent to 61 per cent; and those expressing general satisfaction with the power wielded by trade unions had fallen from 59 per cent to 44 per cent. The big gainers in the election were the Liberals, who secured just over six million votes, their highest ever, and their highest share of the vote, 19.3 per cent, since 1929. They won only fourteen seats, however, nevertheless their highest since 1935. The Nationalists also made record gains, winning seven seats in Scotland and two in Wales.

Heath did not immediately resign following the verdict of the electorate: having secured more votes than Labour, albeit fewer seats, he tried unsuccessfully to do a deal with Jeremy Thorpe's Liberal Party. Unable, however, to promise electoral reform, the Liberals turned him down. Wilson was back in Downing Street. The situation confronting the new Labour government was not pretty. There was still a state of emergency and an unfinished miners' strike. Wage settlements were nudging 20 per cent and the economy was reeling from the oil price shock.

'In terms of ability and experience the Cabinet appointed by Mr Wilson in February 1974 was perhaps the most impressive in Britain in this century,' wrote Wilson's former policy unit head Bernard Donoughue in later years, and he had a good case for saying so. The most experienced included James Callaghan (Foreign Secretary), Denis Healey (Chancellor), Roy Jenkins (a 'recidivist' Home Secretary), Barbara Castle (Secretary of State for Health and Social Services), Tony Crosland (Environment, incorporating Transport), Tony Benn (Industry), Fred Peart (Agriculture), Peter Shore (Trade), Willie Ross (Scotland) and Ted Short (Leader of the House of Commons), whose steady style as Labour's deputy leader contrasted sharply with George Brown. Among the newcomers to Cabinet office were Shirley Williams (Secretary of State for Prices and Consumer Protection), Roy Mason (Defence), Callaghan ally Merlyn Rees (Northern Ireland), financial wizard Harold Lever (Paymaster General)[440] and Wilson protégé Eric Varley (Energy). 'If such a formidable Cabinet were not to succeed it would be because of the force of events or the dead-weight of Labour's antique ideological commitments rather than deficiencies of human resources,' thought Donoughue.[441]

Perhaps the biggest immediate impact was made by the one member of the Cabinet without any previous ministerial experience. Since mid-1972 the shadow Employment

Secretary had been Reg Prentice, MP for East Ham North and a former TGWU official. Prentice had caused controversy among some of the union leaders by refusing to support strikers who broke the law. Jack Jones told Wilson that the unions wouldn't stand for Prentice as Employment Secretary and that they wanted Michael Foot. Wilson was easily persuaded. Foot became Employment Secretary and Prentice got Education. Foot, keeper of the Bevanite flame, was acknowledged even by Gaitskellites like former CDS secretary Bernard Donoughue as 'the best rhetorician of his generation'.[442] Foot got swiftly to work. Within days the miners' dispute had been resolved with a 29 per cent pay award. His first speech as a minister, on 18 March 1974, replying to Heath's shadow Chancellor Robert Carr, was a *tour de force* which brought Labour MPs 'to their feet in a storm of delighted applause'.[443] Carr was:

> . . . the father of the Industrial Relations Act. The Queen's Speech proposes to repeal that Act. Never was a father so impassive in the face of the prospective slaughter of his pride and joy. [Turning to the coal dispute, Foot denied Heath's accusation that he had] thrown out of the window [the relativities report:] as for throwing the relativities report out of the window, as far as I can recall I have not been guilty of a single act of defenestration since I have been in office . . . far from throwing the relativities report out of the window, I said that it must be in the hands of the negotiators so that they could start negotiations with the utmost speed . . . in my opinion it was a matter of supreme national interest that the strike should be settled as quickly as possible and that the country should be got back to work . . .
>
> There was no question of a blank cheque from the beginning of these negotiations until the end . . . We said that we would enable the people who really knew the industry to negotiate, and that is what they did, all the following day . . .
>
> It was very important to get a settlement speedily. If we had loitered, there might still be a strike on . . . we should still have been heading for the million or more unemployed which was the prospect if that dispute had continued for very long. As it is, on the last count, last Thursday, the number of people temporarily unemployed still as a result of the three-day week is down to 95,000 compared with 600,000 a week before. That is a good start, is it not? . . .
>
> Now let me come to the opposition amendment, or, if the leader of the opposition would rather, the 'repercussive effects' of the settlement. I have to eat this sort of phrase as a kind of porridge at breakfast now. It was a strange affair last week. At the beginning, in his first speech, apart from his reference to the mining dispute, first the leader of the opposition offered his good wishes to the government in language which was strangely tender, we thought. Then, within a day or two, we are confronted with this gruff and more characteristic amendment – the shortest and sharpest honeymoon since Lord Byron. He described his, however, as a 'treaclemoon' and perhaps that is what we have been engaged in for the last few days.

Accepting 'the gravity of the inflationary situation', Foot posited:

... a difficult choice to make. Of course we did not want all the settlements which we had made to be reopened ... On the other hand, we were committed, and are committed, to the abolition of the Pay Board. We are opposed – I am bitterly opposed – to the system of the statutory control of incomes ... But the position is this, governing the interim period. The government intend shortly to introduce legislation to give them power to abolish the Pay Board and the associated pay controls ... [Nevertheless it was] not possible for me to seduce the Chairman of the Pay Board from his statutory duties [and until he could secure the approval of Parliament, for which legislation would be prepared, it would continue to operate. Foot denied he had:] made some secret deal with the TUC ... I have something much more precious – that is, an honest understanding of our common objectives and a determination to pursue them in friendship and good faith ...

[The Conservatives were] in no position to say that we must observe the way that they dealt with pay policy, since their method of operating a statutory incomes policy, with all its defects and obstacles, led to the biggest industrial smash-up that this country has known since 1926 ...

Turning to 'the longer period', Foot continued:

I have always thought that one of the reasons why the discussion of incomes policy ... has been so difficult has been that, very often, the well-to-do or – even more offensively, perhaps – the truly wealthy have been inclined to threaten sanctions or preach sermons to people who have to fight every day of their lives to keep their heads above the inflationary flood. But the threat of sanctions in such cases does not work. It leads to clashes. The sermons prove boring and ineffective. That is what happens. Nothing can be more absurd than the spectacle of a few fat men exhorting all the thin ones to tighten their belts ...

There is also the question of relativities which has become a great favourite word ... relativities need not and must not be concerned only with the wages of miners, teachers, nurses and engineers. Relativities must be concerned with the whole question of the distribution of the national income. Relativities must be concerned with such matters as the East End and the West End, with rich and poor – with Disraeli's two nations, if one wishes to put it like that.

That is one of the purposes we have in mind for the Royal Commission on Incomes Distribution which we intend to set up. I am not saying that it is easy, but somehow or other, if we are to solve this problem ... we must take the hypocrisy out of the discussion of incomes.

Such is the fellowship and comradeship in this government that I am sure that my right hon. friend the Chancellor of the Exchequer will not mind even if I anticipate his Budget statement, at least if I do it in verse –

'Oh that in England, there might be
A duty on hypocrisy,
A tax on humbug, an excise

On solemn plausibilities.'

. . . I hope that our Royal Commission . . . will be a different kind . . . from those we have had in the past, and I think that one might almost rechristen it, call it a Roundhead Commission, and see how it goes . . .

So powerful was the impact of Foot's speech that the Conservatives actually withdrew their motion of no confidence in the government. The *Sunday Times* called it 'the most impressive ministerial debut in living memory . . . parliamentary sketch-writers reached for the word "magical" . . . the one-time Devonport reject has emerged as the superstar of the new Labour Cabinet . . . The extent of Foot's triumph is hard to overestimate.'[444] Not everyone approved of the substance of Foot's speech, however: 'Michael . . . was accepting the continuation of the Pay Board and the statutory pay policy, which is exactly what the whole establishment wants,'[445] wrote Tony Benn in his diary. Foot would also be driving through the repeal of Heath's Industrial Relations Act, which had tried and failed to achieve what *In Place of Strife* had intended to do. Additionally, he would establish a new Advisory Conciliation and Arbitration Service (ACAS), which prospers to this day, to mediate in disputes on a voluntary basis without recourse to the law.

Wilson's minority government struggled on through the summer of 1974, looking for a window of opportunity to call a general election to secure a working majority. On 18 September Wilson announced a general election for 10 October. For Wilson and Heath it was clear that whoever lost the next election, it was likely to be their last opportunity to fight an election as party leader. Labour's campaign concentrated on evoking memories of the 'three-day week' and claimed that the Conservatives would seek to create more unemployment to deal with inflation. Labour, insisted Wilson, would not resort to unemployment to cure inflation; instead, they hoped to do it through the 'social contract'. Healey pledged that Labour would get through 1975 with considerably fewer than a million unemployed. Moreover, Labour claimed, unconvincingly, they were bringing inflation under control. The Conservatives accused Labour of misleading the nation over the state of Britain's economic problems, attacked Labour's proposals for nationalisation and defence cuts and shadow Environment Secretary Margaret Thatcher promised cheap mortgages for first-time buyers. Heath also began to talk about the need for a 'government of national unity'. Wilson dismissed this as a Conservative 'con trick'.

When the results came in it became clear that Labour had made gains, though fewer than had been predicted by the opinion polls, which had shown Labour ahead through most of the campaign. On a reduced voter turnout, Wilson had got his overall majority, but one of only three! Labour's vote share, 39.2 per cent, meant that the governing party had won an overall Commons majority on less than 40 per cent of the vote for the first time since 1922. The Conservative vote share fell to 35.8 per cent, its lowest level in recorded electoral history. The Liberals, down to 18.3 per cent, were reduced from fourteen seats to thirteen. The nationalists made gains, securing eleven seats in Scotland and three in Wales.

One of the first issues to confront the government on its return to Parliament was an upsurge in IRA terrorist activity in mainland Britain. The situation was grim. Heath's attempt at power-sharing in Northern Ireland had been destroyed by the Protestant workers' strike incited by hard-liners led by Ian Paisley. Bombs were being planted in mainland Britain in increasing numbers and many were exploding. A series of pub bombings in Guildford and Woolwich preceded more in Birmingham on 21 November, killing 21 people and injuring over one hundred. Home Secretary Roy Jenkins, a Birmingham MP, brought in a Bill that outlawed the IRA, gave the police power to arrest and hold suspected terrorist suspects for five days without charge and gave the Home Secretary power to deport suspects to Northern Ireland and bar them from mainland Britain. Others wanted more drastic action. Conservative shadow Home Secretary Keith Joseph called for the restoration of the death penalty for convicted terrorists. The Bill came to the Commons on 11 December 1974 and Conservative MP Dame Jill Knight moved an amendment to restore the death penalty 'for acts of terrorism causing death'. The most powerful exposition of the case against restoration came from Brian Walden, the then Labour MP for Birmingham Ladywood and, with Enoch Powell and John P. Mackintosh, widely seen as one of the three ablest backbench debaters in the Commons:

> Terrorism has changed our attitudes, and we shall have to accept further change. Already this House has substantially curtailed civil liberties – in my view, an entirely justified decision, but undoubtedly a departure from our traditional values, and we shall have to accept without flinching the justifiable business of counter-terrorism and with good cause.
>
> Since I think deterrence will form a large part of our discussion today, let me give my view on that matter immediately. If I am asked what is the greatest deterrent that we can have against political terrorism, I answer thus: why, sir, the same deterrent as we have against any crime – the probability of apprehension . . . That is why the whole House welcomes the arrests that have been made in Birmingham and in Guildford. The police are alleging murder against some of those remanded. It is not for us to presume judgment on the likelihood of innocence or guilt, but we are entitled to say, and I shall say it, that in my view those widespread arrests will have done more to reassure the public than any scaffold that we might build . . . We cannot paint and varnish a judicial execution to make it appear anything other than what it is – the cold-blooded decision of the State to take a life, a wholly different matter, let me add, from killings by servants of the Crown in attempting to counter terrorism or in suppressing rebellious uprising. It is a completely different matter. Winston Churchill put it in context: 'Flowers grow soon over the battlefield, but over the scaffold – never.'
>
> I think the House should weigh those words.
>
> We are told that it must be done and we are given reasons . . .

The first argument that we are given is that the public demand the reintroduction of the death penalty for this crime. I concede that. I think the majority of them do. Any expression of public opinion must be a matter of grave concern to this House. It must form part of our judgement – part of our judgement, not the whole. Are we a House of delegates? Some of my hon. friends who support me today will know that never in any context have I succumbed to the constitutional heresy of seeing this House as other than what it is – a body ultimately responsible to the people but mandated by no one.

Against the strong arguments of my hon. friends, I have said, and will say now, that I shall never change that opinion. I shall ever hold on to it. When it does, parliamentary democracy will die with it and one may make one's peace with plebiscitary democracy, that friend of tyrants and demagogues . . . members opposite. No man should surrender what he owes most to his constituents, his judgement, simply because he fears that the expression of his convictions might prove unpopular outside this House. Our duty is to use reason, and to use it well.

The second argument we are given is that retribution is called for and that the only just retribution for this crime can be death. I do not know whether the Divinity exists, but if He does, retribution is certainly a matter for Him and not for us. If a word is to be used in the debased sense which had become current, then retribution is no different from revenge and there is no distinction between them. This House should have no business with revenge . . . The business of this House is justice, and justice is that punishment for the guilty that best preserves the lives and the values of the innocent.

The third argument that we are given is that we are not asked to discard our conscientious convictions; we are asked merely to bend them a little. It is not to capital punishment for all murder but only capital punishment for murder in furtherance of a terrorist act . . . I must remind this House that every attempt to give legislative effect to that distinction has proved an abject failure . . . Think what would be involved.

A women who hands explosives to a man knowing that those explosives are to be used to commit an act of murder may hang, but a man who commits multiple murder in furtherance of rape will not hang. How long do we think public opinion would be at ease with the moral standards implied in that judgment? In this case, it is doubly absurd, because I think that it is universally conceded that no man should suffer capital punishment without the benefit of trial by jury, which, as we are now situated, would produce the absurd situation that the terrorist murderer would hang in Great Britain but would not hang in Ulster.

I am told that this is a detail, that we could get round it and bring back trial by jury in Ulster – a fine disregard for the reasons why it was abolished in the first place. I wish hon. members joy of all the jurors they could empanel in Ulster who would convict a man on a capital charge . . .

Then we come to the very heart of the case for those who wish to reintroduce capital punishment, the claim that it will deter terrorist murderers. I should have thought that the whole of human history stood in disproof of that contention. But let us just consider the particular case of the IRA. Does anybody suppose that the self-appointed chiefs of staff of the Provisional IRA, men careful never to expose themselves to apprehension, are going to be deterred by the possibility that we might execute their convicted followers? . . .

We have seen it before, have we not? We solemnly shot the leaders of the 1916 Easter rebellion. I do not know whether that was just retribution or not, but much good it did us. It saved not a life, and it cost thousands. A population which had previously had no use for Sinn Fein was converted to it. That was the consequence of what we did then. Would it be different now? Can we never learn? . . .

Some hon. members will have seen the quite disgraceful interview which has been given by O'Connell in Bonn today, in which he threatens that for every convicted IRA terrorist we hang the IRA will take and hang two British soldiers . . . I will give my view on that. It is a considered one, and one which I give with grief and conviction. I would release no murderer to save any hostage. I think that that has to be done and that we should give no encouragement to them to suppose otherwise. But we should not deceive ourselves that they will not do it. They will do it . . .

In an earlier speech to this House I said that we may have to choose between victory or vengeance . . . Those who come into the lobby with me can have my assurance, after careful consideration of all the great pressures that have come from my constituency and my own town, that they will be prizing principle above popularity, they will be putting sense and reason above passion, they will be acting in the interests we seek to serve – the interests of victory. But it is a victory not purchased at an unacceptable price, a victory not simply for our policies but a victory for our values, without which those policies are meaningless.

After an impassioned debate, marked by an intervention from Conservative Willie Whitelaw, who declared that in the view of both himself and of Heath, the restoration of the death penalty for terrorists would be mistaken, the Commons voted by 369 to 217 against the Conservative amendment. Jenkins's Prevention of Terrorism Act entered the statute books.

FORTY-SIX

Britain Votes to Stay in Europe 1975

'If you believe "Workers of the world unite",
you cannot say that this stops at the Channel'

January 1975 found Wilson's Labour government facing both an extremely difficult eco-nomic situation and a referendum on Britain's continued membership of the EEC, on the basis of the terms 'renegotiated' by Foreign Secretary James Callaghan. Tony Benn, father of the referendum, was now Secretary of State for Industry. He was also, having been mildly pro-European in his MinTech days, noisily anti-EEC, although his convic-tions did not prevent him from giving the go-ahead to the Anglo-French Concorde: 'Beautiful and ruinous, a triumph over sense and arithmetic, the aeroplane would con-tinue to be built, providing,' as Edward Pearce observed, 'extensive employment in Benn's Bristol constituency.'[446]

Benn's enthusiasms were directed in particular towards worker cooperatives. But they lacked roots in economic realities. The three most famous worker cooperatives were the *Scottish Daily News,* based on the remaining personnel and plant of the *Scottish Daily Express,* KME at Kirby which made car radiators and orange juice and the great Norton Villiers Triumph motorbike plant at Meriden, which produced what were essentially 1950s technology motorbikes. Japanese rivals were cheaper to buy, cheaper to run, often easier to handle and maintain and more reliable. In consequence they were what con-sumers were buying. That was why the private firm was in financial difficulties. Healey claimed that Jack Jones had alarmed him with the view 'you didn't need research and development for motorbikes'.[447] On one level you didn't. But in a competitive market where overseas firms were producing better designs, you did. The alternative was the Soviet bloc model which culminated in the East Berlin of Wartburgs and Trabants so ridiculed in the West after the fall of the Berlin Wall. Norton Villiers Triumph's motor-cycles were not quite so backward, and many are prized by devoted enthusiasts, but the principle is the same, as it was with the British car industry. Given the choice between an Austin Maxi or a Morris Marina versus a BMW or a Honda, increasing numbers of Britons were buying the non-Leyland cars, because they were better. Import controls wouldn't change that.

Benn thought otherwise. On 16 January, he presented senior officials in his department with a draft paper outlining his 'Alternative Economic Strategy'. It had been prepared before Christmas and drafted largely by Benn's two special advisers: Francis Cripps (son of Sir Stafford) and Frances Morrell. 'The officials were riveted,' noted Benn in his diary, as he sent them away to add flesh to the bones.[448] The 'Alternative Economic Strategy', known sometimes as the AES and alternatively as 'the Alternative', envisaged import controls (quotas or tariffs on manufactured goods); rationing and allocation of certain imports and of fuel; work-sharing and employment subsidies; controls on capital outflows; tax increases; selective subsidies to industry; controls on banks and financial institutions to channel funds into the public sector; further defence cuts; and the wider development of Anglo-Soviet trading arrangements. Few of his Cabinet colleagues were enthused. 'It would produce a run on sterling', and 'a cut of 6 per cent on our living standards', declared Healey at the Ministerial Committee on Economic Strategy.[449] Callaghan was dismissive of import controls, arguing that in 1964 they had been a temporary sticking plaster over the country's economic ills rather than anything that addressed the fundamentals of the economy. Moreover, import controls were illegal under EEC rules.

The Commons debated the renegotiated EEC terms over three days during April 1975. The anti-Marketeers argued that the 'renegotiation' had changed little of substance and that therefore their objections to the EEC remained. They were, however, a diminished band. Several of those who had been vocal against Heath's accession to the Common Market now seemed to have little to say in criticism. Douglas Jay accused Education Secretary Reg Prentice and Welsh Secretary John Morris as having 'gone soft' and bemoaned Agriculture Minister Fred Peart as 'a lost cause'.[450] After a marathon two-day discussion over 17–18 March, Cabinet voted to accept the terms by sixteen votes to eight, the dissenters being Foot, Shore, Benn, Castle, John Silkin, Willie Ross and Eric Varley. A unique 'agreement to differ' was reached, under which ministers could speak and campaign on either side of the referendum debate so long as they did not speak against their own government in Parliament. In the Commons debate on the renegotiated terms, 144 Labour MPs voted against the government.

On 26 April a special Labour Party conference was held at the Sobel Sports Centre, Islington, to pass judgement on the renegotiated terms. Unlike the special conference of 1971 it was intended to have a vote. This it did, rejecting the terms, as expected (since the major trade unions had already decided their votes beforehand), by a two-to-one majority.[451]

Harold Wilson made the opening speech which was 'flat, dull', recalled Benn. Callaghan likewise played things down. 'The speeches that did make an impact,' wrote Tony Benn in his diary, 'were by Roy Jenkins who blustered and bullied but was passionately pro, and by John Mackintosh who made the only really good pro speech by lashing out all around him. He got a cheer as a result; if you are going to be in this game you've got to believe in it.'[452] Jenkins attacked the idea that EEC membership:

... would prevent any advance of public ownership. What happened to British Leyland during the past two days? In fact, the truth is almost exactly the reverse ... It is not the change of ownership which is threatened by staying in. The basic plan for the buttressing and rejuvenation of British Leyland and for saving the jobs which go with that would be fatally undermined by coming out. What is the essence of the plan? What is put forward in the plan for British Leyland is to increase our penetration of the European Community car market from 3 per cent to 4 per cent. Do you think you could do that over an 11 per cent tariff? Still more important, the plan is to increase our penetration of the truck market from 1 per cent to 5 per cent. Do you believe that that could be done over a 22 per cent tariff?

Some people say that we could get round all this difficulty, that we could come out and have a free trade area. We could not get a free trade area in 1958, and we would be very rash to assume that having just abrogated one treaty we could make another for a free trade area in the near future if we came out. But even if we got it, if the argument is 'Have a free trade area', be in no doubt that that argument undermines the case to do with our trade deficit. I know quite a lot about trade deficits. I spent two and a half years turning the biggest one we had then had into the biggest surplus we had ever had. I do not believe that this deficit is caused by our being in the EEC. It is caused by a combination of oil prices and the gross mismanagement of the economy in 1972 and 1973. But if you have a free trade area, whatever you believe about this, you cannot keep out the goods, you cannot deal with the deficit. The same thing applies to the sovereignty argument. Outside, Sweden and Norway have to accept the same industrial, trading and regional rules as we do inside, but the difference is that they have no say in how they are made.

In any event, I cannot regard the preservation of sovereignty as the ark of the covenant of socialism. You can argue about who you want to pool it with, although there are no available alternatives in the world, certainly not in the Commonwealth. But I do not believe that it is either socialist or realistic to think that you can cling to sovereignty in the world of today. We live in an integrated world, and our duty is to play our part in that, and to play our part with our neighbours. I distrust people who proclaim their love for humanity but illustrate it by being unable to get on with those who live around them. That is particularly true and particularly valid when nearly all the rest of humanity, including all the Commonwealth, the old Commonwealth and the poor countries, want us to stay in and help them from inside.

John Mackintosh picked up Jenkins's baton on sovereignty, pointing out that:

We have campaigned on the basis that social injustice is the same whether it is in Wales, England or Scotland. If you make that argument and believe in our old views of 'Workers of the world unite' you cannot say that this stops at the Channel. You cannot say that we are against national sovereignty in Scotland and yet talk of British national sovereignty. When was the Labour Party ever a nationalist party? When did we ever talk about national this, that or anything? We used to point at the Tories for having the Union Jack on their platform. We sang the Red Flag, not Land of Hope and Glory. That is not the tone for this party to adopt in the future.

I am delighted when Eric Heffer stands out of line with the government and appeals to people to support the Chilean workers. That is excellent. Why does he at the same time turn down the appeal of Chancellor Schmidt when he comes on behalf of the biggest Social Democratic Party in Europe and says to us, 'We, the German Socialist Party, want you in Europe?' Why does he do this when the Italian Communist Party says it, when the Italian Left Wing Socialist Party says it? The Italian Social Democrats say, 'Help us in Europe to build a positive socialist Europe.' Our left wing says, 'No. We won't touch it. It's a rich man's club.' Comrades, before we came to Westminster it was a rich man's club. We fought and we won. What did Nye Bevan say? Did he ever say to the Labour Party, 'If you see a lot of rich and powerful capitalists, ignore them. Leave them, do not trouble them?' He said that we have to take over the commanding heights.

If Europe is a centre of power and wealth, let us take it and use it for the good of the people. Let us take this power and wealth for the good of the people in Europe. Comrades, Europe has been the centre of the two most devastating world wars in history. The Common Market has knit these countries together so that this cannot happen again. This is a great step forward. Europe is a centre of great wealth and power. Who was it who said that the Common Market was the Magna Carta for the multinationals? When did we ever leave the barons to get on with it alone? If it is a Magna Carta for the multinationals let us win power there also . . .

Six out of nine countries of the Common Market are dominated by left-wing parties. Let us join them . . . If there is a butter mountain, let us redistribute it. If the CAP does not work, why not? What good is it standing aside and pretending that we are a little nationalist Britain on our own?

These arguments I hear about nationalisation and national sovereignty make me fear because they are the same arguments that the Scottish Nationalists use. They are the same little selfish, inward-looking 'keep for yourself', 'frightened of the foreigner', 'worried about the dangers' fears that have never led people inspired into victory . . . If our philosophy is worth anything, it is not just a British philosophy but a socialist one. We must fight for it at a world level and the first place to win is in Europe.

The anti-Marketeer's charge that the EEC meant the end of cheap food was redoutably rebutted by Post Office workers' leader Tom Jackson, who challenged Michael Foot to:

. . . tell us where the cheap food is coming from . . . I have talked to Bob Hawke, the General Secretary of the Australian TUC and Chairman of the Australian Labour Party, who said to me, 'Tom, I don't care whether you stay in or whether you come out, but don't come looking to Australia for cheap food.' There is cheap food all right. There is cheap tea from Ceylon – and what that means for the Tamils! There is cheap food, but do not go looking to what was the British West Indies for what was cheap sugar, because they will screw you, because they intend to give their people a better standard of life. [The economic issues were also emphasised by Bernard Bagnari of

APEX] . . . We used to talk about the advantages of our social system. We are now almost at the bottom of the league of social benefits . . . pensions inside the Community and family allowances and wages for the Italian, French and other workers far outweigh anything we have in this country.

Many of the anti-EEC speeches were a great deal more defensive than over the previous few years. It was as if the anti-Marketeers knew that they were on the back foot. Boilermakers' Union leader Danny McGarvey argued unconvincingly that Britain's trade deficit with the Common Market countries was due to being in the Common Market, and that, 'if we stay in Europe the Germans will want a finger on the nuclear trigger again. We could find ourselves, contrary to what Tom Jackson says, blasted off the face of the earth.' Barbara Castle, sitting in the front row of the conference platform between Harold Wilson and Ian Mikardo, felt 'gloomier as the day went on'. She blamed the chairman for calling 'a number of unattractive antis from the constituencies'. She was particularly infuriated by the power of John Mackintosh's 'unscrupulously brilliant speech'. She was reassured over the lunch break by Michael Foot's wife Jill: 'Don't worry, Mike is going to deal with [Mackintosh].' Given the lacklustre performance of some of the other antis, 'it was a terrifying responsibility', felt Castle.[453] Foot began:

> . . . John Mackintosh spoke most movingly of the fight to capture the commanding heights. I am very glad to join him in that battle. Or maybe he is joining us. I am not quite sure which way round it is. But you do not necessarily have to travel all the way from Scotland to Rome in order to capture the commanding heights. You might stop off at Westminster and have a try at doing it there. Of course, the phrase comes from Aneurin Bevan . . . I read this especially for the benefit of my comrade John Mackintosh:
>
> 'All the conception of a common market does is to elevate the marketplace to the status now enjoyed by the various European Parliaments. It is at this point that socialists become suspicious of what is intended. Is it the disenfranchisement of the people or the enfranchisement of market forces? The conception of the common market is the result of the failure of socialists to use the sovereign power of their Parliaments to plan their economic life. It is an escapist conception in which the play of market forces will take the place of political responsibility. Socialists cannot at one and the same time call for economic planning and accept the verdict of free competition, no matter how extensive the area it covers. The jungle is not made the more acceptable just because it is almost limitless.' This is what Aneurin Bevan had to say about the Common Market . . .
>
> Let me reply also to what John Mackintosh said about those who claim to be internationalists. I do not deride anybody who takes a different view from my own . . . but I shall not take a back place in the queue about international socialism. In these negotiations one of the things we can all be proud of is that Judith Hart on behalf of the government went to negotiate on the subject of how we were to assist with practical

measures the very people to whom Harold referred in his speech this morning, those who fight for subsistence and survival against desperate poverty conditions. Judith Hart went to the negotiations to fight for them. She did very well. She got a concession, but a concession which applied to only one-sixth of the population of the Commonwealth. Five-sixths of them – and they are the poorest members of the Commonwealth – were left out of that agreement. It was no fault of Judith Hart's, no fault of the Labour government's, no fault of our negotiators. It was the conception of the market that we were trying to change, and we did not succeed in changing.

I come to the question of food here at home . . . Talk of the Little Englanders! Some of the Little Europeans do not understand that food is produced in every hemisphere and on every continent . . . It is not common sense to say that we shall always have our food cheaper and easier if we go into the highly protectionist market of Little Europe . . .

Roy Jenkins said this morning that we cannot regard the preservation of sovereignty as the ark of the socialist covenant. I could subscribe to that doctrine, but supposing you change for the word 'sovereignty' – nobody knows quite what it means – the word 'democracy', which all of us should understand. If we said that you cannot regard the preservation of democracy as the ark of the socialist covenant, I would not agree . . .

For Foot, EEC membership risked the 'independent power' of Labour government:

. . . if we go into the Common Market for decades to come we shall be more enmeshed in various forms of coalition government than anything we have seen before . . . That is the way in which their institutions are devised. That is why maybe they have made arrangements whereby they do not have a democratic system of operating. The Brussels Commission is not a democratic system. The Council of Ministers is not a democratic system. It could only develop into a democratic system if you established full federal government with a federal parliament and all the rest, but nobody is saying that that is the issue to be put to the British people on 5 June . . .

Here in this country if you do not like a government – and this goes for the whole people, apart from our own movement – you can kick them out and start with another . . . But in the Common Market if the supreme powers are to be vested in those institutions, in the Council of Ministers, the Brussels Commission and the rest, as many supreme powers are under the Common Market Act, the British people can vote for a government to leave office, but they will still be left with the undemocratic authority of the institutions in Europe that are sustaining this. This issue goes deep into our history . . . When Hugh Gaitskell spoke in that famous debate in 1962 he talked of a thousand years of history . . . You do not need to go quite as far as that . . . I go back to Cromwell's armies, when the army was the most democratic institution in the country. I am not saying that the same goes now. Thomas Rainborowe said: 'I think it is clear that every man that is to live under a government ought first by his own consent to put himself under that government, and I do think that the poorest man in England is not at all bound in a strict sense to that government that he hath not had a voice to put himself under, in so much that I should doubt whether he was an Englishman or no that should doubt these things.'

. . . people say 'All these burdens, all these political disabilities, all these derogations from our sovereignty, all this dismemberment of our parliamentary institutions . . . all that must be done because of the economic circumstances that face us. We have no other choice.' I do not believe it . . . I say to our great country, 'Don't be afraid of those who tell us that we cannot run our own affairs, that we have not the ingenuity to mobilise our resources and overcome our economic problems.' Of course we have. We can do that and save the freedom of our country at the same time.

'Michael Foot wound up with a brilliant speech,' thought Benn, 'he really exceeded himself . . . we not only won the vote but we also won the argument.'[454] However, whether or not Benn and his allies won the argument to pull out of the EEC at the special conference, the British electorate proved considerably less receptive to their case. The referendum on 5 June saw Britain vote 'yes' to Europe by some 17 million to 8 million, a two-to-one majority. The 'yes' victory held right across Britain: the 'noes' won only in Shetland and the Western Isles. 'I have just been in receipt of a very big message from the British people. I read it loud and clear,' Benn conceded: 'By an overwhelming majority the British people have voted to stay in and I am sure that everyone would want to accept that.'[455]

When the shadow Cabinet had adopted Benn's referendum proposal in 1972, provoking the resignation of the Jenkinsites, Jim Callaghan had shrewdly observed: 'Tony Benn may have launched a little rubber dinghy into which one day we may all wish to climb.' As Phillip Whitehead put it, 'the cabin boy had found the dinghy, but it was his shipmates who were carried to safety'.[456]

In the ministerial reshuffle that followed the referendum, Wilson demoted Benn, swapping him with Energy Secretary Eric Varley. Benn's 'Alternative Economic Strategy' was on ice. Wilson then clipped both the political wings of his Cabinet. From the left wing, Judith Hart refused to move to become transport minister, outside the Cabinet, and was sacked. On the right wing, Reg Prentice, whose profile was growing as he became increasingly embattled by a left-wing attempt to deselect him in his constituency, was demoted to Overseas Development and replaced at Education by Fred Mulley, a less outspoken moderate.

FORTY-SEVEN

Wilson's Social Contract 1974–75

'We face an economic typhoon of unparalleled ferocity'

By the end of 1974 inflation was to hit 19 per cent and the rate of wage increases 29 per cent, while total industrial production fell by 3 per cent. Despite a mildly deflationary Budget in April 1975, the spring and summer of 1975 saw inflation continue to soar towards Latin American levels. While most countries had suffered high inflation in the immediate wake of the oil crisis, other countries were through it after a brief peak. In America, for example, it had peaked at 11 per cent and was already declining. Not so in Britain, where it was rising through 20 per cent. Much of this was caused by spiralling wages. The Social Contract, as originally conceived, was failing to deliver. Though the government had raised pensions and introduced food subsidies, the unions had proved unable to moderate wage claims. In the year to June 1975 wage rates for manual workers had risen by one third. Unemployment, meanwhile, had risen to 900,000, the point at which Heath had panicked and u-turned in 1971, and was continuing to rise at 30,000 a month.[457] By the end of the year it would exceed 1.1 million. The Prime Minister's Policy Unit had warned Wilson of approaching disaster back in November 1974 and again in the New Year. Wilson, however, 'did nothing',[458] being reluctant either to impose wage controls, which he had denounced under Heath, or to face record post-war unemployment.

But something had to be done. Healey was becoming increasingly worried about the wage–price spiral, a growing risk that sterling might collapse (it had been floating since 1971) and rising public borrowing. He was by now convinced of the necessity of some sort of incomes policy, fearing that unless inflation were brought under control, unemployment could spiral to two million.[459] In May 1975 Healey had proposed a £3 billion package of cuts, which the Cabinet decided to defer to July, after the EEC referendum campaign was out of the way. 'The smell of a bonfire of election promises was growing much stronger,' recalled Wilson's press secretary Joe Haines, 'and the high-bred nostrils at the Treasury were quivering in anticipation. Indeed, for months they had been drying the wood for the blaze.'[460]

Once the campaign was over, economic realities returned. The Treasury favoured a statutory incomes policy. Bernard Donoughue, Andrew Graham,[461] Gavyn Davies[462] and

David Piachaud in the Downing Street Policy Unit developed the idea of a voluntary flat-rate wage policy and convinced Wilson of its merits. Wilson persuaded the Cabinet, Jack Jones, and through Jones the rest of the TUC. The rate had to be settled too. Joe Haines had suggested a round £5. The unions preferred a higher figure. They settled on £6.

On 11 July 1975 the government published a White Paper announcing the universal pay rise limit of £6 (with zero increases for those on over £8,500) as from 1 August 1975 and a system of 'cash limits' for public expenditure programmes. When it came to be debated in the Commons on 22 July, 54 Labour MPs voted against the government, including Judith Hart, Eric Heffer and Ian Mikardo. Only through the support of the Liberals and the abstention of the Conservatives, who at that time supported incomes policy, was the government able to carry the day. Over the coming months ministers would be locked in negotiations with the Treasury to agree a programme of cuts. A package of £3.5 billion cuts was to be finally agreed in January 1976 and announced by Healey in March. In August 1975 inflation hit a new post-war record of 26.9 per cent, but fortunately for the government, that was to prove the peak. The incomes policy was to do its job. By July 1976 inflation would be down to 12.9 per cent.

On 29 September 1975 Labour's annual conference in Blackpool debated resolutions for and against the new social contract, incorporating the flat-rate pay policy. It was Michael Foot who had the job of winding up the debate for the NEC and defending the policy which he had helped create. 'Nerves had been shaken by the crisis in July [1975] and no one was confident that it would be the last. Thus Michael's speech to the conference was of greater political importance than any speech to parliament. If he failed to carry conviction and to offer inspiration, the government might forfeit the loyalty on which it depended':[463]

> I believe that this Labour government was saved by the negotiations that happened between the Labour government and the General Council of the TUC in those first days of July, and certainly I make no apologies for them . . . We could not continue in this country with . . . an inflation rate of 20 per cent or more . . .
>
> Now, of course, in taking that action we had to have some limitation – I think that is the fair way to describe it – on the way in which collective bargaining operated . . . We had to have some limitation, but nothing like the old statutory system. As the minister responsible for dismantling the whole of the Heath government's statutory system, I certainly was not prepared to be a party to re-establishing the whole of that system again. Of course not. Indeed, it was the consequences of that system itself which fed the inflation and contributed so much to many of our economic difficulties . . .
>
> People sometimes say: we will agree to some arrangements between the government and the trade unions about wages, but only when you have the full panoply of socialist measures actually put into full operation. I understand the argument, but I say it is unworkable. There is not a single government in the world aspiring to change

society that could work upon that system of transition, whether it is Communist, Maoist, Yugoslav, anything . . .

I am very glad that this conference, like the last two or three conferences, is going to be dominated also by the demand for new systems of investment in the National Enterprise Board and the planning agreements and all other matters that we have discussed and which we have had in our party programmes . . . But do not let anybody imagine that investment is a soft option. You can learn it from *Das Kapital* as well as from anywhere else, and I hope I will not be convicted for that . . . Investment means very often, almost always, forgoing present claims in order to have future benefits. And you can do it by not so many methods. You can do it by the brutal capitalist methods of the nineteenth century, or you can do it by the equally brutal, or maybe even more outrageous, methods of twentieth-century Stalinism, or you can do it by the politics of persuasion, by the social contract . . .

I am rather proud, if I can say it - not on my own behalf, but the Labour government's - of the progress we have made in industrial relations over the last year and a half. We had not only a miners' strike when we came in, but a threatened engineering stoppage, a threatened stoppage in the docks, very nearly a railway strike this year, very nearly - and utterly disastrous - a steel strike only a week or so ago. We have avoided those perils. I know the Tory newspapers will say that we avoided the perils by giving in, but we did not: we avoided the perils by intelligent collaboration with the trade union movement of this country. We avoided the perils by removing the Industrial Relations Act from the statute book. We avoided the perils by the future measures that are now coming into operation: the Employment Protection Bill, which carries much further the protections for trade unions in this country. We are going to take further steps in the next session; for example, in the docks, where we are fully committed and fully intend to carry out our commitment to ensure that our programme is fulfilled. We have also greatly assisted the industrial situation by the operation of the Advisory Conciliation and Arbitration Service, set up thanks to discussions which we had with the trade union movement as to how best we should go about the job. I believe that hundreds of millions of pounds for this country have been saved, because that body was set up on an independent basis, on the best basis on which we should have done it . . .

We must face the crisis, beat the inflation, start the regeneration of British industry, lift this scourge of unemployment from our people . . . We face an economic typhoon of unparalleled ferocity, the worst the world has seen since the 1930s. Joseph Conrad wrote a book called *Typhoon*, and at the end he told people how to deal with it. He said, 'Always facing it, Captain MacWhirr: that's the way to get through.' Always facing it, that is the way we have got to solve this problem. We do not want a Labour movement that tries to dodge it; we do not want people in a Labour Cabinet to try to dodge it. We want people who are prepared to show how they are going to face it, and we need the united support of the Labour movement to achieve it.

I am asking this movement to exert itself as it has never done before, to show the qualities which we have, the socialist imagination that exists in our movement, the readiness to reforge the alliance, stronger than ever, between the government and the trade unions, and above all to show the supreme quality in politics, the red flame of socialist courage . . .

For Barbara Castle, Foot 'triumphed by taking the challenge full on, giving all the emotional voltage he had got . . . I myself, sitting next to him, had been almost reduced to tears by his utter dedication and sincerity.'[464] A note from Geoffrey Goodman to Foot read: 'I have heard you many, many, many times. But none better than today. It was a superb performance: inspiring, courageous, outstanding by any standards. Even by the standards of Nye.'[465] Even Benn acknowledged it as a

> magnificent performance. There was this great figure with his white hair swept back, almost leonine, defending with a gale of oratory and eloquence the like of which I have not heard for a long time, a policy which is basically wrong and which I would like to say he doesn't believe in but he does . . . Jack Jones led the standing ovation and it reached Jim Callaghan at the far right of the platform but I didn't stand and neither did Frank Allaun and others to my left.[466]

After Foot's speech the votes were counted. Conference had backed the government and thrown out demands from the engineering union's foundry section and the firemen to return to a wages free-for-all.

At the *Tribune* rally in the Spanish Hall at the Blackpool Winter Gardens, on the Wednesday evening of conference, Ian Mikardo let fly a stinging attack on Foot and on the government and on the TUC for not demanding enough of it. Barbara Castle witnessed Mikardo 'piling selective statistic upon selective statistic to give a hostile distortion of the work of the government. Suddenly out of the crowded isle where he had been standing leapt Jack Jones, up on to the platform, jabbing an accusing finger at Mik like an Old Testament prophet pronouncing his doom. As Mik had the microphone, and Jack had not, all we could hear were a few snatches of what Jack said. "I detest these attacks on the trade union movement" was all I caught. But he stood there for a full minute, jab following jab with inarticulate shout after inarticulate shout. It was electrifying. The audience split into pro- and anti-Mik arguments and there was pandemonium,' eventually quelled by *Tribune* editor Dick Clements in the chair.[467]

On Tuesday 30 September, the morning after Foot's speech, the results of the annual NEC elections were announced. Barbara Castle had put fifty pence on Ian Mikardo's annual sweepstake on Denis Healey staying on, 'finding it difficult to believe that the party would be irresponsible enough to inflict this public humiliation on their Chancellor', but she lost her money: Healey was off, replaced by left-wing Liverpool Walton MP Eric Heffer. Later that morning came the debate on economic policy. It saw Healey challenged by another extreme motion from Militant-dominated Liverpool

Walton and Brighton Kemptown (though this time moved by Ted Mooney rather than Ray Apps) and another anti-government resolution from ASTMS boss Clive Jenkins, who demanded that:

parts of the British economy . . . now be put into an intensive care unit. [Import controls, he insisted, did not amount to] a siege economy . . . It is a phrase invented by those willing to surrender the fortress, and when others say that when we argue for protection against the dumping of textiles or electronics or shoes or motor cars, we provoke a trade war, have they not realised that the firing has been going on for a long time and we have suffered immense casualties? [The risk of retaliation, Jenkins insisted, was minimal:] I tell you this, if everyone were to attempt retaliation, if we go for highly selective import controls, we would still be better off . . . What about our motor-car workers? Foreign manufacturers now have 40 per cent of our market. Forty per cent, when we have four giant volume car manufacturers, 154,000 cars a year coming in and how many do we export a month? Two hundred and fifty-two.

Now I am not arguing for the establishment of massive bureaucracy to set and to administer quotas, but I think we could have a surcharge put on – 10 to 15 per cent at once . . . If the Australians can have car import quotas, if the Italians can have import deposit schemes, if the Japanese can have rigid, surreptitious controls, if the Finns can have import deposit schemes and the French can slap a levy on Italian wine, I think we can protect the heartland of our British industry.

Clive Jenkins's speech 'gave Denis the chance to make the speech of his life', recalled Castle. 'I couldn't help thinking that there is nothing like defeat for bringing out the best in one. He got a standing ovation and deserved it':[468]

You know, in a situation like I face today, I am always reminded of one of Frederick the Great's generals, who was ordered by his Imperial Majesty into a military action which was bound to lead to defeat. He sent the following message back; he said, 'Please tell his Majesty that after the battle my head is at his disposal. But during the battle, I propose to use it in his service' (*applause*).

Some of you have asked me today to turn my medals in. All right, I will. But I tell you I am going to go on fighting this battle, because it is your battle, and it is our battle, and I am not going to let up until together we have won a victory which is final and conclusive (*applause*). If, when that time comes, you can give me my medals back, so much the better . . .

Michael talked yesterday about this government having to face a typhoon . . . in the middle of this typhoon, we have also set ourselves the task of fitting a new engine to the ship, and making the crew's quarters more habitable. If some of you decide to throw the navigator overboard because you do not like being seasick, well, so be it.

The government had softened the cut in Britain's real income caused by the oil price shock by borrowing:

. . . but borrowing is all right at a time when the oil-producing countries cannot import goods to the value of the oil they export. It is all right when you have a world recession and countries are working far below capacity, most of them much further below capacity than we are in Britain. But when the oil producers are in a position to import goods to the value of the oil they sell they are not going to lend us the money to buy oil with.

That is beginning to happen already, and as the world recovers from recession, if we are going to find the money we need to re-equip our own industry we are going to have to reduce the amount of money we borrow as a government, as local authorities, as nationalised industries, so that the money we are now borrowing from the insurance companies and the pension funds will be available once again to re-equip our industry . . . there is no chance of regenerating British industry unless we can narrow drastically the gap between what we are spending in the public sector in this country and what we are raising in taxes.

That means something pretty unpleasant. That means either the government has got to spend less, or it has got to tax more, and I ask every one of you, particularly the trade unionists among us, to think very hard in the coming months about which you would prefer.

Public expenditure in Britain has been increasing over the last 25 years very much faster than our national wealth. The result is that tax has been shooting up in order to pay for it . . .

One of my major jobs as Chancellor in the last eighteen months has been to use the tax system to create a more equal distribution of wealth and income, so that the pensioners have seen their real standard of life go up 6 per cent in the last eighteen months, and . . . I have made the rich pay towards the nation's needs on a scale unprecedented in peacetime. Only this year – it has not been mentioned in the debate yet – we fought through the House of Commons against the most virulent and exhausting campaign the Tories have led against the government since Lloyd George 70 years ago. We have brought through the capital transfer tax which introduced the first tax on capital in this country and makes estate duty an unavoidable tax for the first time in eighty years.

But what I want to tell you straight is that there is no way on earth by which any government, Labour, Tory whatever you like, can have substantial increases in public expenditure without putting a substantial increase in tax burdens on the average working man and woman. I want you to face a few facts here as well, because general elections do not change the laws of arithmetic; nor, for that matter, do National Executive elections . . . if your government confiscated all incomes over £6,000 a year – and this is only just over twice average earnings now – that would bring in only . . . one twentieth of our present government public sector borrowing requirement, which is £9,000 million. And before you run away with very attractive new proposals on taxation, do really look at the sums, make sure they add up. In my first Budget in 1974 I took 1,400,000 of the lower-paid workers in this country out of tax altogether by raising the thresholds, but this year it cost me nearly as much money to take 400,000 people out of tax. I understand that many of you would have wished me to have raised tax thresholds to take full account of inflation. But if I had done that, I would have had to find an extra £1,400 million somewhere this year. If I had done it through income tax, that would have meant raising the standard rate, which is now paid by a family on only half average earnings, to 40 pence in the pound. Is that what you are really asking me to do? Because I should like to know. The only other way I could raise it would be by increasing indirect taxes and sending up the cost of living. Do you really think that would have made sense?'

Healey then turned on:

. . . my Conservative rival, Sir Geoffrey Howe . . . his only answer to the nation's problem is to cut the top rate of tax down to 50 per cent, and he says you would get just as much money as the people who had gone abroad to avoid taxes would come back to pay them. He has got a hope . . . If the top rate of income tax were 50 per cent, 50 pence in the pound, it would cost us £400 million. That would mean getting 8,000 pop stars earning £100,000 a year back to Britain (*applause*). Even if we could do it, the thought of 8,000 Bay City Rollers . . . (*laughter and applause*).

The fact is there is going to be a crushing burden of taxation on ordinary working people unless we can get better value for money spent in the public sector, and . . . look for savings . . . one area is subsidies on the nationalised industries . . .

Investment, as Michael said yesterday, is not a soft option. The most difficult thing in the world in a democracy is to persuade people to consume less now in order to be able to produce more and have more jobs in the future.

Unless we are prepared to do that, all we say about industrial regeneration is claptrap, and that is why I oppose the Liverpool Walton motion, and I hope the conference will. Apart from the fact that it flies in the face of the massive majority votes you passed yesterday, it is not an honest resolution. It suggests you can get 'summat for nowt', and Lancashire spreads far enough down to Merseyside for people in Merseyside to know it ain't true. If you have to find money for investment you have to find it from somewhere else, from the pockets of the workers or from other areas of public expenditure.

I now come to the ASTMS resolution, with its graceful and gentle criticism of the government; the resolution moved so gracefully and gently by Clive this morning that it was a pleasure to listen to him (*laughter*) . . .

The fact is, the American trade union movement has pressed in the United States for import controls. I spent weeks on end this year arguing with the American government not to keep Pilkington glass out of the United States, as Congress had voted they should. They have been compelled in the last few weeks to start an inquiry into the motor car imports, which is aimed directly at British Leyland. And, you know, do not turn round and ask us to do this and then, if we do it and we get retaliation, come to me and say, 'We did not know it was loaded.'

There are really difficult problems of judgement here, problems which your government takes very, very seriously; but I accept the gentle reproof that Clive gave us today and I appreciate very much the spirit in which he put his argument.

I will only say one thing: I do not want to be lectured by any member of our movement on the need for import controls when they ask their own trade union to provide them with a Volvo (*applause*).

There was just one thing in Clive's preamble which rather puzzled me: he talked about the fact that we were dangerously over-exposed in the international banking system; but I read the interesting pamphlet his union published only yesterday and, as far as I can make out, he wants me to borrow £9 billion from the international banking system. All I can say, Clive, is if you did that you would be so over-exposed you would be arrested! (*laughter and applause*). And do not imagine anybody is going to lend you the money if you do not support the government's counter-inflation policy, because there is not a cat in hell's chance of persuading people to lend you money with inflation running at 25 per cent a year . . .

The horrible truth is that in recent years for every unit of extra investment we have had in Britain we have only got half the return the Japanese have got and only 75 per cent the return that the French and Italians have got.

It is no good expecting people to put new plant in unless they know that full advantage will be taken of it. But it is equally true that you cannot expect working people in a recession to abandon practices which prevent full use being made of new equipment unless there is new investment providing new jobs for them to go to . . .

We would not be a Labour movement unless we had our heads in the stars, but we will never make a Labour government unless we keep our feet on the ground. It is this combination of idealism with practical efficiency, based on long experience, above all in the trade union movement, which alone can ensure that ordinary men and women will actually benefit from our ideals . . . (*standing ovation*).

It was, acknowledged Benn, who did not join Healey's standing ovation, a 'fighting speech', of which 'Clive Jenkins was his victim'.[469] Healey had a reputation for being blunt: 'at a meeting of the Parliamentary Labour Party I accused Ian Mikardo of being "out of his tiny Chinese mind" – a phrase of the comedienne, Hermione Gingold, with which I thought everyone was familiar. On the contrary, when he leaked it to the press, the Chinese Embassy took it as an insult to the People's Republic.'[470] Despite Healey's speech, the conference actually voted in favour of Jenkins's resolution. But Jenkins was an elephant who did not forget Healey's jokes at his expense. In leadership elections of the future Jenkins would be found doing his best to stick the knife into Healey, though he doubtless would have done that whether Healey had fought back or not.

FORTY-EIGHT

Callaghan Takes the Reins 1976–77

'I tell you in all candour'

As 1975 wore on, Harold Wilson was wearing out. Despite outward appearances, his health was not what it once had been. From December 1974 he would suffer recurrent bouts of 'racing heart'. The renewed economic crises and the grinding frustration of incomes policy took their toll. Bernard Donoughue remembers Wilson saying to him in the summer of 1975: 'Bernard, I have been round this course so often that I am too bored to face jumping any more hurdles.' On another occasion he said: 'The trouble with me now is that I only have the same old solutions for the same old problems.'[471] Through the autumn of 1975 Wilson talked to intimates about resignation, and informed the Queen of his intention shortly to do so on 9 December. He stayed on until the cuts package had been agreed and Healey had suffered the opprobrium of announcing them to the Commons. The following month, on 16 March 1976, he resigned. The race to succeed him was brief.

The left was split between Tony Benn and Michael Foot. The right was split even more. Callaghan was the leading candidate of the right, with the best-organised campaign (under Merlyn Rees and including Jack Cunningham and John Golding as key organisers) and the broadest political base. Tony Crosland, whose campaign team included Blair's future PPS Bruce Grocott and Bruce Douglas-Mann who later joined the SDP, was an outsider from the start. Roy Jenkins was well organised but had been damaged, even among pro-Europeans, by his resignation as deputy leader four years previously. Too many[472] who had been his supporters feared that he was now too divisive a figure, too aloof from the party, to be able to unite it under his leadership. Taking Roy Hattersley as an example, Roy Jenkins had been his mentor and had helped get him promoted, Crosland he admired, but it was to Callaghan that he gave his vote. Other pro-Europeans who swung to Callaghan included Cledwyn Hughes and the young John Smith. Healey had never really built a power base. His small campaign team consisted largely of his Treasury ministers. Moreover, the painful process of extracting cuts from departmental ministers and pushing them through the Commons had hardly won him new friends. On the first ballot the results were Foot (90); Callaghan (84); Jenkins (56); Benn (37); Healey (30); Crosland (17). Benn dropped out and backed Foot, while Jenkins and

Crosland dropped out and backed Callaghan. Healey, with pugnacious bloody-mindedness, fought on, dropping out after the next round where he received only 38 votes as compared to 133 for Foot and 141 for Callaghan. On the final ballot on 5 April, Callaghan beat Foot by 176 to 137. Callaghan was now Labour's leader and fourth Prime Minister.

In his first reshuffle Callaghan sacked Barbara Castle, with whom he did not get on, and Wilson's veteran Scottish Secretary Willie Ross. Other changes saw Chief Whip Bob Mellish and deputy leader Ted Short retire from government. Roy Jenkins desperately wanted the Foreign Office but Foot, with whom Callaghan consulted and was to form a strong partnership, made it clear that the left wouldn't wear it. Instead the Foreign Office went to Crosland, who actually wanted the Treasury, from where Healey, battling against economic crises, couldn't really be moved. Foot succeeded Short as Leader of the House of Commons, a job that Benn wanted, and secured the promotion to Cabinet of his Tribune Group allies Stan Orme at Social Security and Albert Booth at Employment, a job that Benn wanted as well. Peter Shore replaced Crosland at Environment, Edmund Dell was promoted to Cabinet to replace Shore at Trade and Callaghan's ally David Ennals replaced Castle at Health. Other 'Callaghan men' were new Scottish Secretary Bruce Millan and new Chief Whip Michael Cocks.

Benn remained at Energy (with a new Gaitskellite deputy, Dickson Mabon), and Jenkins, likewise disappointed, remained briefly at the Home Office, where he had recently brought in the Sex Discrimination Act and a further Race Relations Act to strengthen the previous two. Before the leadership election, Wilson had offered Jenkins the Presidency of the European Commission in Brussels. Jenkins had hesitated. Now Callaghan repeated the offer and Jenkins took it, leaving the government in September and precipitating a further reshuffle. John Silkin replaced Fred Peart at Agriculture. Peart took a peerage to become Leader of the Lords. Callaghan's campaign manager Merlyn Rees became Home Secretary, and was replaced at Northern Ireland by Roy Mason who in turn was replaced at Defence by Fred Mulley. He was replaced in his turn at Education by Shirley Williams, which enabled Roy Hattersley to join the Cabinet, succeeding Shirley Williams at the Department of Prices and Consumer Protection. Jenkins's lieutenant Bill Rodgers also joined the Cabinet as Transport Secretary. A few weeks later, on 21 October, the centrality of Michael Foot's role within the new Callaghan government would be confirmed by the result of the election to succeed Ted Short as deputy leader: 166 votes for Foot and 128 for Shirley Williams.

Through the spring and summer of 1976 Michael Foot had continued to work closely with Denis Healey on plans for a second year of wage restraint, fortified by the backing of Jack Jones. Nevertheless, September brought wildcat strikes at British Leyland and a national seamen's strike. Inflation was still around 14 per cent, overseas trade in deficit and interest rates up at 13 per cent. On 27 September, the Monday of Labour's annual conference in Blackpool, sterling collapsed to $1.63 and Healey warned Callaghan that worse could be expected. The Bank of England's reserves were depleting rapidly with unsuccessful attempts to stabilise sterling.

It was Bob Marshall-Andrews, a 32-year-old barrister and delegate from Richmond, Surrey,[473] who, speaking in the conference debate that afternoon, most powerfully expressed the frustration of Labour's rank and file over government cutbacks. The social contract, he argued, had entailed an agreement that the government would levy:

> ... an unprecedented, unparalleled contribution ... from those who had shown the ability time and again in the past to avoid entirely their share of the national sacrifice ... [while] those in our society consistently under the greatest peril from the capitalist system – the sick, the disabled, the handicapped, the poor and the mounting volume of unemployed – should be protected. There were many people who believed that this was not only a piece of economic management, but this in itself was the beginning of a genuine socialism ... [But while] working people ... stuck to the bargain ... in this movement there grew a horrified incredulity as we watched what happened in return ... the 'biggest ever run on the pound' despite massive public expenditure cuts [and the refusal of] ... those who believed that money is something to be manipulated and moved around the world in order to attract the biggest profit, irrespective of the human misery that it causes ... [to] give us credit for what we had done. We watched while the government imposed yet another £1,000 million [cut], and the horror and the incredulity reached a level which could only be matched by what we felt when we learnt of the news of the retiring Prime Minister's Honours List ... No more will we tolerate [this] ...
>
> But we must listen to the clever men, because we must not, in this conference, be irresponsible ... we should listen to the clever men in the Treasury who thought that it was economically viable to pour money into Slater Walker last year. We must listen to them – (*applause*) – when they say 'You cannot do it. You cannot reflate your economy. You cannot keep your public expenditure at these levels, which makes life decent for your people. You cannot do that because we owe £17 billion and because our creditors will not have it and because if you reflate the economy inflation will go through the roof and the balance of payments situation will worsen to an extent that the country cannot possibly tolerate, and also' – the most spurious argument of all – 'that by some law as yet unknown to God or man the £5,000 million that was buying cars and transport for handicapped children is going to find its way into the industries of this country, into the machine tool industry in the Midlands and the depressed areas where investment is desperately required' – because the lie to that argument was given by the Director of the CBI himself when he said, in answer to Labour's paper on banking and finance, 'We have never had a problem of finance. We have never wanted for investment.' So by what means do these clever men think that all of a sudden our employers will go out and use the surplus capacity that we have created for them to use? It is nonsense.

The second argument – which is the most prevailing argument of all – the argument which is barbaric in effect but is practically Neanderthal in concept – is the idea that if you have one and a half million of your productive workforce out of work that in some way will buy you out of a recession; that when you are paying £64.80 a week to a man who is out of work – £4,500 million a year for unproductive labour – that in some way will be a panacea for the ills of the country – this pre-Keynesian idea that the Treasury keep turning out to the eternal misery of our people, driving us further into a society where we are not allowed to spend our money to take up that surplus capacity we have. We know what the answers are . . . The answers are that we build a socialist economy in this country and . . . if we have to protect it by import controls in the short term, if we have to protect it in the longer terms by price controls . . . so that you force an investment-led boom so that spare capacity which we know there is in industry is taken up in capacity and not rising prices, it is simple economics . . . What we want is the government to do it (*applause*).

Judith Hart made clear in her speech winding up the debate for Labour's NEC that the only reason that the NEC could not support Marshall-Andrews was the statement in the resolution rejecting the economic analysis of the TUC/Labour Party liaison document they were debating. Hart ended with a direct challenge to the government:

> If Jim and Denis are worried, as they must be, about foreign confidence and about the run on the pound, then let them tell the IMF that we do not agree with the pre-Keynesian classical economics that dominate the IMF. Let them tell them that there are others with other solutions. Let us convince the international financial field that our answers are right. We cannot expect them to believe us unless we try to convince them.

Hart's speech ended proceedings for the Monday afternoon. The following morning conference opened at 9.30 with the announcement of the NEC ballot. The shock news was that Industry Secretary Eric Varley[474] had been heavily defeated by hard-left Tottenham MP Norman Atkinson in the election to succeed James Callaghan (who had stood down on his election as party leader) as Party Treasurer. The NEC had turned even further to the left. The first speech of the morning was Callaghan's big speech of conference, his first as Labour leader and Prime Minister. His speech, initially prepared in consultation with Bernard Donoughue and Gavyn Davies in the Policy Unit and Tom McNally in the Political Office, was altered at the last minute following telephone conversations with his son-in-law Peter Jay. It was this new passage that 'made the fur fly',[475] wrote Callaghan later:

> For too long, perhaps ever since the war, we postponed facing up to fundamental choices and fundamental changes in our society and in our economy. That is what I mean when I say we have been living on borrowed time. For too long this country – all of us, yes, this conference too – has been ready to settle for borrowing money abroad to maintain our standards of life, instead of grappling with the fundamental problems

of the British industry. Governments of both parties have failed to ignite the fires of industrial growth in the ways that countries with very different political and economic philosophies have done . . .

The cosy world we were told would go on for ever, where full employment would be guaranteed by a stroke of the Chancellor's pen, cutting taxes, deficit spending, that cosy world is gone. Yesterday delegates pointed to the first sorry fruits: a high rate of unemployment. The rate of unemployment today – there is no need for me to say this to you – cannot be justified on any grounds, least of all the human dignity of those involved. But Mr Chairmen and comrades, I did not become a member of our party, still less did I become leader of our party, to propound shallow analyses and false remedies for fundamental economic and social problems.

When we reject unemployment as an economic instrument – as we do – and when we reject also superficial remedies, as socialists must, then we must ask ourselves unflinchingly what is the cause of high unemployment. Quite simply and unequivocally, it is caused by paying ourselves more than the value of what we produce. There are no scapegoats. This is as true in a mixed economy under a Labour government as it is under capitalism or under Communism. It is an absolute fact of life which no government, be it left or right, can alter. Of course in Eastern Europe you cannot price yourself out of your job, because you cannot withdraw your labour. So those governments can at least guarantee the appearance of full employment. But that is not the democratic way.

We used to think that you could spend your way out of a recession, and increase employment by cutting taxes and boosting government spending. I tell you in all candour that that option no longer exists, and that in so far as it ever did exist, it only worked on each occasion since the war by injecting a bigger dose of inflation into the economy, followed by a higher level of unemployment as the next step. Higher inflation followed by higher unemployment. We have just escaped from the highest rate of inflation this country has known; we have not yet escaped from the consequences: high unemployment.

Now we must get back to fundamentals. First, overcoming unemployment now unambiguously depends on our labour costs being at least comparable with those of our major competitors. Second, we can only become competitive by having the right kind of investment at the right kind of level, and by significantly improving the productivity of both labour and capital. Third . . .[we cannot] buy our way out by printing what Denis Healey calls 'confetti money' to pay ourselves more than we produce . . .

Let me add one more thing about how to get a strong manufacturing sector of industry. Hold on to your seats. The willingness of industry to invest in new plants and machinery requires, of course, that we overcome inflation, but also that industry is left with sufficient funds and has sufficient confidence to make new investments. When I say they must have sufficient funds, I mean that they must be able to earn a surplus and that is a euphemism for saying they must be able to make a profit (*applause*).

Whether you call it a surplus or a profit, it is necessary for a healthy industrial system, whether it operates in a socialist economy, a mixed economy or a capitalist economy. If industry cannot retain and generate sufficient funds as a result of its operations, and replace old plant and machinery, then you will whistle in vain for the investment and we shall continue to slide downhill. These are elementary facts of life. They are known to every trade unionist. Who would they sooner go and negotiate with when they want an increase in pay: a firm that is bankrupt or a firm that is doing well and generating a good surplus?

We began as a party of protest. We must never lose that, never forget it. There are many ills and many evils in the condition of our society that have still to be remedied. But we are more; we are now a party of government, a party which has put many of the aspirations of the pioneers on the statute book, as the law of our land . . .

Tony Benn thought it a 'most patronising lecture about our economic problems . . . a reaction of horror came from the hall'.[476] But for Cledwyn Hughes, former Cabinet minister and now chairman of the Parliamentary Labour Party, it was 'a good, solid, honest speech and it was maddening to see NEC members, including some ministers on the platform, sitting on their hands when he had finished'.[477]

On 28 September, with the pound still on the slide, Healey and the Bank of England governor were at Heathrow Airport preparing to fly to the Commonwealth Finance Ministers' conference in Hong Kong. Things were so bad, however, that Healey felt it would be dangerous to be out of contact for the seventeen-hour duration of the flight and they decided to go back to the Treasury. On 29 September Ford car workers went on strike and it was announced formally that Britain was applying to the IMF for a loan of $3.9 billion, much the largest sum ever requested. It was, believed Healey, the only way to ensure that they could repay a six-month standby loan they had agreed with world banks that summer. Thursday 30 September was the economics debate at conference. Healey was in London, having been dissuaded by Callaghan from flying up to Blackpool to make his case. At 11.30 a.m. Healey received a message that Callaghan had changed his mind, and by way of an RAF flight from Northolt to Blackpool arrived in time to make a speech.

Speaking immediately before Healey was the hard-left MP Norman Atkinson, Labour's new Party Treasurer. Atkinson was speaking in support of an NEC motion which called for the government 'to resist any conditions of international loans which would be incompatible with the policies of the party and the TUC by imposing further cuts in public spending or increased unemployment'. Conference rules stipulated that since Healey was no longer a member of the NEC, having been defeated the previous year, he could make only a five-minute speech from the floor like any other delegate. 'The smell of 1931 is very strong in my nostrils,' wrote Benn in his diary, 'Denis had arrived during the banks and insurance debate with a flurry of cameras. There were hisses and boos when he came forward to speak . . . parts of the conference cheered him – the PLP, the Post Office Engineers, I think':[478]

Let me say, Mr Chairman, that about the only good thing about the events of this week is that it has given me a chance of coming again to conference, but I do not come with a Treasury view, I come from the battlefront.

Jim Callaghan said on Tuesday that the NEC is responsible for its statements and resolutions; the government is responsible for its actions (*cries of hear, hear*). But you must recognise, comrades, that statements and resolutions are not just words that die when the echoes fade in the Winter Gardens; they have their impact in the real world in which the government must act. An unwise resolution, an ill-judged statement, can knock £200 million off the reserves in a minute, or, if the rate goes down, it can add 20p to the price of the goods in your shopping bag in a minute – and that has happened before now.

And it is possible, you know – Mik[479] talked about kicking goals – sometimes people kick through their own goal (*laughter and applause*).

I have come here this morning, this afternoon – I left this morning and I have not had anything to eat since I left (*interruption*) – I have come here this afternoon to welcome the resolution put by the NEC. I did not really expect that, comrade chairman, when I left, but I have come here to welcome it because it asks conference to give overwhelming support to the government's fight to protect the value of our currency (*applause*). The government has decided, as Jim said it might on Tuesday, to ask the International Monetary Fund for more credit, not to finance more spending, public or private, but to protect our industrial strategy from speculative attacks on sterling and to give us time for our strategy to work, to get Britain standing on her own feet for good and all. That is an objective I hope we all share in common.

Norman [Atkinson] asked, 'What is the alternative?' There are some people who would like to stop the world and get off, and I do not blame them, it has not been an easy world for us in recent months. They say, 'Let's go to a siege economy', but a siege economy of a rather odd type, a siege in which we stop the imports coming in but we demand total freedom for the exports to go out. Now I have never heard of a siege in which you keep the enemy out of the castle, but the enemy allows you to go and come as you please through its ranks. And yet that is the sort of siege economy that some of our critics are asking for (*shouts from the floor*). Oh yes, you want the exports to go out, you want the jobs in the engineering factories to increase as the exports increase, but you want to stop other people having the advantage of selling their goods to us.

Now I tell you, comrades, the probability is that that would be a recipe for a world trade war and a return to the conditions of the thirties (*cries of dissent*) and I ask you to consider seriously, do you not believe there are trade unionists in Germany, in France, in the United States, who are considering exactly that type of siege economy for themselves? And do you think it would be of any advantage to any of us if we started off on that road again?

Even if it did not lead to a world trade war, general import controls – and do not kid yourselves that selective import controls is an alternative – means an immediate increase in the cost of living, an immediate increase in unemployment, and immediate problems throughout our economy (*shouts from the floor*). It is possible, theoreticians can argue, as the gurus of this particular proposal in Cambridge do argue, that in the long run, it will work providing you cut public expenditure four or five times more heavily than this government has had to cut it, but that is in the long run, and how long do you think this government would run under the sort of circumstances I have described?

The plain fact is that the strains, the tensions, the increase in inflation, the increase in unemployment would mean before many months were out a Tory government, and we know the Tory alternative – they have described it, they will be launching it again in detail next week – massive new cuts in public expenditure, unemployment in the low millions, and a return to the confrontation between a British government and the working people of this country. And if you do not want these alternatives, then we have got to stick to the policy we have got. I am going to negotiate with the IMF on the basis of our existing policies, not changes in policies, and I need your support to do it (*applause*). But when I say 'existing policies', I mean things we do not like as well as things we do like. It means sticking to the very painful cuts in public expenditure (*shouts from the floor*) on which the government has already decided. It means sticking to a pay policy which enables us, as the TUC resolved a week or two ago, to continue the attack on inflation (*shout of resign*). It means seeing that the increase in our output which has now begun goes not into public or private spending, but into exports or investment. That is what it means and that is what I am asking for. That is what I am going to negotiate for and I ask conference to support me in my task (*applause*).

It was a bravura performance, which Healey concluded with a defiant Muhammed Ali-style clasped salute. 'I couldn't even clap him,' wrote Benn, 'his speech was so vulgar and abusive.'[480] Others from the social-democratic wing of the party had a different view: 'I was one of those who applauded Healey's speech,' wrote Durham MP Giles Radice. 'At last there was someone who was prepared to tell conference the facts of life.'[481] But the day had not yet been saved (and indeed conference voted for Norman Atkinson's statement). On 7 October interest rates were raised yet again, to 15 per cent, but on 26 October, sterling was to reach $1.56, its lowest level yet against the dollar (though it was to fall to $1.09 under Thatcher). During November the IMF negotiators arrived in London and a battle raged within the Cabinet as to how best to deal with the crisis. Foreign Secretary Tony Crosland, supported by Harold Lever and Roy Hattersley, argued in Cabinet that there was no economic case for further substantial cuts, to which Healey, Trade Secretary Edmund Dell, Defence Secretary Roy Mason and Reg Prentice at Overseas Development replied that even if this were so the markets didn't believe it and unless the government's economic credibility were restored disaster could follow. Healey's bargaining position to the IMF was that in exchange for the loan the government would cut public borrowing by £3 billion and sell off £500 million of BP shares. Crosland argued that severe cuts, by increasing unemployment, would increase expenditure on unemployment benefits and cut tax revenues, leading to an increase in public borrowing, the reverse of what was intended. He suggested that they should call the IMF's bluff, offering £0.5 billion cuts and the share sell-off. Peter Shore and Tony Benn also argued against the Healey package, advocating instead import controls and in Benn's case the siege economy scenario entailed in the 'Alternative Economic Strategy'. Shore and Benn never managed to persuade Cabinet colleagues of the credibility of their proposals. The real battle was between Healey and Crosland. Eventually a compromise cuts package was agreed of £1.5 billion (including the sale of £500 million BP shares). Callaghan himself was reluctant to engage in further cuts. But Crosland failed to substantiate fully how his approach would work, which given that he was speaking without his departmental brief and therefore unable to rely on the support of official advisers in the same way as Healey, was not entirely surprising. Callaghan, therefore, ultimately had to back his Chancellor.

Ironically, Crosland, who was to die from a massive stroke on 19 February 1977, was in many ways correct. As Healey explains in his memoir, the Treasury's forecasts on public borrowing were wildly inaccurate, painting a far more pessimistic picture than was justified by reality, 'but it was all I had to go on and it was worrying the markets'.[482] Within a year the commentariat was praising Healey as the Chancellor who had turned the economy round. Unemployment peaked at 1.6 million in August 1977 and began to decline, interest rates were down to 5 per cent by October 1977, the pound had risen to reasonable levels and, benefiting from North Sea oil, the balance of payments situation improved. Part of the reason for this economic miracle was, however, that things had never really been as bad as the Treasury officials had claimed. For Healey's first Budget in 1974 the Treasury gave him a public borrowing forecast that was £4 billion too low, the equivalent of 5.4 per cent of GDP: 'The magnitude of that forecasting error was greater than that of any fiscal change made by any Chancellor in British history,' Healey later wrote. Two years later, the Treasury's public borrowing estimate was £2 billion too high, and in November 1976 its estimate of the loan required from the IMF 'turned out to be twice as high as it should have been'. Moreover, long before any of the IMF-linked cuts had any time to take effect the balance of payments moved into equilibrium: 'If I had been given accurate forecasts in 1976, I would never have had to go to the IMF at all.' Healey sensed a running theme and took action as early as 1974, when in his November Statement

> I decided to do to forecasters what the Boston strangler did for door-to-door salesmen – to make them distrusted for ever: 'Like long-term weather forecasts they are better than nothing . . . But their origin lies in the extrapolation from a partially known past, through an unknown present, to an unknowable future according to theories about the causal relationships between certain economic variables which are hotly disputed by academic economists, and may in fact change from country to country or from decade to decade.'[483]

But it was clearly not a problem the government was able to resolve. Previous Labour governments had sought to provide an alternative to the 'Treasury view', most notably with George Brown's ill-fated DEA. They had failed. But without some way of securing alternative expert advice what else had the government in general, and the Chancellor in particular, to go on? Gordon Brown's decision 20 years later to set up a Council of Economic Advisers within the Treasury directly appointed by the Chancellor and independent of the Civil Service-controlled chain of official advice is perhaps an attempt, in part, to learn this particular lesson from history.

As Prime Minister, James Callaghan faced daunting economic challenges. But he also had opportunities to make a positive impact and push the government agenda in new directions. Callaghan retained Wilson's Policy Unit head, Bernard Donoughue, and shortly after his new chief took over, Donoughue sent him a memorandum suggesting some areas of policy he might consider for special prime ministerial attention. One suggestion was education, and Callaghan, the only premier born in the twentieth century apart from John Major not to have attended university, seized it with both hands, asking the policy unit to draft a speech for him to deliver at the earliest opportunity. If there was one Cabinet role Callaghan had felt he had missed out on, it was Education Secretary. Now he would help the Education Secretary in his own Cabinet (Shirley Williams) steer her department in the direction he thought it ought to go. Wilson had once described the Department for Education and Science (DES) to Donoughue as being 'little more than a post-box between the teachers' unions and their local authority employers'. Indeed most politicians of the time seemed to discuss education entirely in terms of the structural battle between comprehensives and tripartism. 'Too few,' suggests Donoughue, 'were concerned with the daily experience of actual children in actual schools.'[484]

The final speech was written by Donoughue, the Policy Unit's education specialist Elizabeth Arnott, and by Callaghan himself. Before he could deliver it, recalled Callaghan,

> I tripped over some appalling educational snobbery – the Secretary of State's memorandum to me [on the issues Callaghan would raise in the speech] had been given to the *Times Educational Supplement* and they wrote an article that was both scornful and cynical about my intention. It complained that while I was a professional politician I was no more than an amateur educationalist and doubted the propriety of my raising questions of what should be taught and how it should be taught . . . the chalk dust flew.[485]

When on 16 October 1976 Callaghan finally arrived at Ruskin College, Oxford, to deliver his speech, it was disrupted 'by an outside group of boorish militant university students demanding more money for themselves at Oxford. Here were the privileged demanding even more privilege. Jim's speech was concerned with the educationally underprivileged. It received enormous coverage in the media and clearly touched a chord among the nation's parents':[486]

There have been one or two ripples of interest . . . in anticipation of this visit . . . I must thank all those who have inundated me with advice: some helpful and others telling me less politely to keep off the grass, to watch my language, and that they will be examining my speech with the care usually given by Hong Kong watchers to the China scene. It is almost as though some people wish that the subject matter and purpose of education should not have public attention focused on it; nor that profane hands should be allowed to touch it.

I cannot believe that this is a considered reaction. The Labour movement has always cherished education: free education, comprehensive education, adult education. Education for life. There is nothing wrong with non-educationalists, even a Prime Minister, talking about it again. Everyone is allowed to put his oar in on how to overcome our economic problems, how to put the balance of payments right, how to secure more exports and so on and so on. Very important, too. But, I venture to say, not as important in the long run as preparing future generations for life. R. H. Tawney, from whom I derived a great deal of my thinking years ago, wrote that the endowment of our children is the most precious of the natural resources of the community. So I do not hesitate to discuss how these endowments should be nurtured . . .

Let me answer the question 'What do we want from the education of our children and young people?' with Tawney's words once more. He said: 'What a wise parent should wish for their children, so the State must wish for all its children.' . . . Public interest is strong and legitimate and will be satisfied. We spend £6 billion a year on education, so there will be discussion . . .

First let me say . . . that I have been very impressed in the schools I have visited by the enthusiasm and dedication of the teaching profession, by the variety of courses that are offered in our comprehensive schools, especially in arts and crafts as well as in other subjects; and by the alertness and keenness of many pupils. Clearly, life at school is far more full and creative than it was many years ago . . . But I am concerned on my journeys to find complaints from industry that new recruits from the schools sometimes do not have the basic tools to do the job that is required.

I have been concerned to find that many of our best-trained students who have completed the higher levels of education at university or polytechnic have no desire to join industry. Their preferences are to stay in academic life or to find their way into the Civil Service. There seems to be a need for a more technological bias in science teaching that will lead towards practical applications in industry rather than towards academic studies. Or, to take other examples, why is it that such a high proportion of girls abandon science before leaving school? Then there is concern about the standards of numeracy of school leavers. Is there not a case for a professional review of the mathematics needed by industry at different levels? To what extent are these deficiencies the result of insufficient coordination between schools and industry? Indeed how much of the criticism about basic skills and attitudes is due to industry's own shortcomings rather than to the educational system? Why is it that 30,000 vacancies for students in science and engineering in our universities and polytechnics were not taken up last year while the humanities courses were full?

On another aspect there is the unease felt by parents and others about the new informal methods of teaching which seem to produce excellent results when they are in well-qualified hands but are much more dubious when they are not . . .

It is not my intention to become enmeshed in such problems as whether there should be a basic curriculum with universal standards – although I am inclined to think that there should be – nor about other issues on which there is a divided professional opinion such as the position and role of the inspectorate. What I am saying is that where there is legitimate public concern it will be to the advantage of all involved in the education field if these concerns are aired and shortcomings righted or fears put to rest . . .

There is no virtue in producing socially well-adjusted members of society who are unemployed because they do not have the skills. Nor at the other extreme must they be technically efficient robots. Both of the basic purposes of education require the same essential tools. These are basic literacy, basic numeracy, the understanding of how to live and work together, respect for others, respect for the individual . . . I do not join those who paint a lurid picture of educational decline because I do not believe it is generally true, although there are examples which give cause for concern. I am raising a further question. It is this. In today's world higher standards are demanded than were required yesterday and there are simply fewer jobs for those without skill. Therefore we demand more from our schools than did our grandparents . . .

Following his speech, Callaghan asked the Department of Education and Science (DES) to produce a 'Green' government discussion Paper to follow up on the themes he had raised. The DES officials, remembered Donoughue,

made it clear they were not enthusiastic. They moved slowly and when the draft Green Paper arrived in the summer of June 1977 it was sparse in content and deeply complacent in tone. Only three of its two hundred paragraphs were devoted to the criticisms and problems facing our schools; on a quick reading it was therefore possible to conclude there was nothing wrong with British education. There were three bland paragraphs on standards and discipline; and such important questions as the content of the curriculum and the role of the school in the community were ducked altogether. Parents were discussed only in terms of their being on the receiving end of information, rather than as participants with a personal interest in the education system. Finally, the draft Green Paper made only one hidden reference to the Ruskin speech and appeared to ignore the debate which had followed. The paper represented Whitehall at its self-satisfied, condescending and unimaginative worst.[487]

Even Callaghan's diplomatically written memoir described it as 'rather introverted', being addressed 'mainly to educationalists'. Shirley Williams, he recalled, had personally to redraft and 'liven up the turgid language.[488] Callaghan's government was to fall before the DES officials could be persuaded to do much to implement the new agenda. Nevertheless, his speech, and the 'Great Debate' it inaugurated, led to the National

Curriculum brought in under the Conservatives and the focus on literacy and numeracy, and overall standards in schools, that has been the hallmark of education policy under New Labour.

Although 1977 saw a general improvement in the economic situation, the issue of pay policy remained. On 8 July 1977 the CBI had told Callaghan that it was unable to stop its members paying over the odds to secure particular skilled employees. Indeed, it was said that companies were telling their workforces that they would like to pay them more but were prevented by the government's incomes policy. On the union side pressure was building up: though pay policy had helped reduce inflation to 7 per cent from its 27 per cent peak in 1975, prices were still outstripping wages and workers resented the undermining of their living standards. Callaghan recalled, 'neither employers nor unions were able to practise a form of self-discipline for a period long enough to have a lasting effect'.[489]

The rock upon which the success of the government's pay policy had rested was Jack Jones of the TGWU. Indeed, so central had Jack Jones's role become that a Gallup opinion poll suggested many people thought Jones the most powerful man in Britain. He had built up Bevin's mighty T&G into the largest trade union that either Britain or Europe had ever seen. But 1977 was his retirement year. The T&G's July 1977 biannual conference was to be his last as General Secretary. He planned to argue that the union should have priorities, to go for a shorter working week, for example, rather than for a wages free-for-all. 'But the conference would have none of that,' he later recalled, 'and before I went to the rostrum, I knew that the majority was against me.' It was a measure of his courage that he did not flinch from his determination to confront his conference with the consequences that could follow from rejection of the social contract, namely a Tory government:

> Everybody has been worried about returning to free collective bargaining. In fact one of the delegates, when he was coming over here, went to the railway station and said that he wanted a ticket to free collective bargaining, a return to free collective bargaining. The ticket clerk said, 'Do you want an orderly return or a disorderly return?' (*laughter*). Now we have all agreed on a return to voluntary collective bargaining. The question is how to get there . . . [Jones urged delegates to vote to] keep our agreements . . . until they run out and then we resume voluntary collective bargaining . . . in an orderly way, because settlements are phased . . . [It was] an illusion . . . to think that by removing all commitments and repudiating your Executive Council you will get real wages, real wage increases, for everybody all round at the same time . . .
>
> [Jones was] amazed . . . at the vicious criticism of the government and of the TUC, as though we were all enemies. Do you imagine that we from this platform and from the Executive Council would deliberately pursue a policy of low standards? I have devoted my life to trying to raise the standards of working people, not just in speeches but in action too . . .

We have had inflation caused by the oil crisis . . . and during this period, had we had free collective bargaining, it would not have maintained living standards.

[Rejecting the policy of the Executive would mean giving] the benefits of North Sea Oil and a stronger balance of payments . . . to the party of privilege. You will put back the mighty in their seat and kick the people of low degree in the teeth . . . The cry (and it has been made recently) 'Every man for himself' goes out when the ship is sinking. I say that we should not allow the ship to sink. Our policy is to keep it afloat and not to allow it to go down . . .

But his conference was not listening. As Postworkers' Union leader Tom Jackson remembered: 'It was a case of "when father turns we all turn". I mean, when Jack's conference turned, Jack turned, as he had no option . . . But when Jack turned a good many other people turned at the same time.'[490] The consequences of Jack Jones's defeat would prove 'devastating',[491] recalled Callaghan's Policy Unit head, and meant, as Employment Minister John Golding put it, 'quite simply the unions wanted to grab the benefit of any upturns themselves and to hell with the politicians and the general election'.[492]

FORTY-NINE

Division over Devolution 1966–79

*'The devolutionary coach, if this Bill is passed, will be on
a motorway without exit roads to a separate Scottish state'*

One of the greatest battles that split the Labour Party during the 1970s was over devolution for Scotland and Wales. Unusually, the fault-line within the party was not on conventional left–right lines. Nevertheless, it proved just as important as many that were, and the failure of Labour to be able to frame proposals which could secure sufficient support (at least 40 per cent) among the electorate to be carried through in the eventual devolution referendum of 1 March 1979 proved to be the final undoing of Callaghan's minority government in a confidence debate 27 days later. Labour had been committed to Home Rule for Scotland since the days of Keir Hardie and Ramsay MacDonald. But before 1945 it was never in a position to do anything about it and during 1945–51 it was felt that there was little public enthusiasm for radical constitutional upheaval. The priorities were thought to be bread and butter social reforms, such as the implementation of Beveridge and the creation of the NHS, and at that time it was believed that these would be easier to introduce on a UK-wide basis. There was a faith in national planning, in 'bigger means better' and in Whitehall expertise. If there was a Labour government in Westminster building the New Britain, why would Scots benefit from something different? During the 1950s the Scottish Labour Party establishment formally ditched Labour's long-standing commitment to Scottish devolution. One of the few, and arguably the most noisily determined, of those who stood out publicly against this development was John P. Mackintosh. In 1957, then a 28-year-old history lecturer and prospective parliamentary candidate for Edinburgh Pentlands, he spoke out in defence of Labour's commitment to Scottish Home Rule at Labour's Scottish annual conference. Over the next two decades, until his early death in July 1978, he maintained a vigorous and ultimately successful campaign to force Labour into a policy U-turn on the issue. In doing so he earned the undying enmity of Wilson's key Scottish ally, Ayrshire MP Willie Ross, who served as Scottish Secretary in Wilson's Cabinet and shadow Cabinet from 1964 until 1976. Wilson gave Ross, his 'old basso profundo', his full backing. Whatever Ross wanted he got. As Tam Dalyell observed, 'Not since Charles II placed total confidence in Lord Lauderdale or at least Pitt the younger in Dundas, has there been anything quite like it.'[493]

Elected an MP in 1966, Mackintosh's initial attempts to shift policy by full frontal assault proved less than successful. Ross regarded Mackintosh's kamikaze commitment to devolution as a personal challenge to his authority over the Scottish Labour Party. At its March 1968 conference Dick Crossman observed in his diary, 'the Scottish Labour Party under Willie Ross's leadership had crushingly rebutted John Mackintosh and the young Turks who were trying to get a motion put forward in favour of early considera- tion of Scottish self-government. This was obviously the work of Willie Ross.'[494] It was primarily through his friendship with Dick Crossman (who disliked Willie Ross) that Mackintosh was able to put devolution on the governmental agenda. Crossman was an intellectual magpie and Mackintosh sparkled. The Hamilton by-election of 2 November 1967 saw a shattering defeat for Labour at the hands of the SNP, then a fringe party with no other MPs. It crystallised in Crossman's mind the need at least to explore the devolu- tion proposals being advanced by Mackintosh and Cledwyn Hughes, then Secretary of State for Wales. Hughes had secured agreement within the Welsh Labour Party in favour of a nominated Council for Wales. Mackintosh urged the adoption of Hughes's blueprint in Scotland as a first step towards an elected assembly. Ross opposed its adoption in Wales for fear of its implications for Scotland. Crossman used his position in Cabinet as Leader of the House of Commons to force the government to confront the issue of devo- lution and convened a Cabinet committee to consider it.

Given the general inertia of the party and the dead-weight opposition to constitu- tional innovation of the government and Civil Service, progress was slow. The commit- tee was hampered by the frequent changes of personnel resulting from reshuffles and uninterested secretaries of state deputing different junior departmental colleagues to successive meetings who frequently contradicted the views of their predecessors. Crossman believed this forced the committee's paper 'down to the lowest common denominator of consensus', resulting by May 1968 in proposals which though 'they could have been effective two years ago are now totally inadequate to meet the tremen- dous tide of nationalist feeling in Scotland'.[495] Moreover, in April 1968 Wilson had moved Crossman over to run the new Department of Health and Social Services: his successor as Leader of the House, Fred Peart, was not interested in devolution.

The creation of a Royal Commission on the Constitution[496] was announced in the Queen's speech of 1968. Set up on the initiative of Home Secretary James Callaghan, it was the fruit of expensive lobbying by Callaghan's fellow Welsh MPs Cledwyn Hughes, John Morris and Elystan Morgan, and finally reported in October 1973. Taken together with the capture of Labour's Govan citadel by the SNP in November, the sevenfold increase in SNP seats at the February 1974 election (one gain being at the expense of Heath's Scottish Secretary, Gordon Campbell), and the fact the Wilson needed to minimise the hostility of nationalist parliamentarians in the context of minority government, it forced devolution firmly on to the political agenda, whatever Ross might protest. Recently elected Durham Labour MP Giles Radice correctly predicted: 'The Labour Party will obviously now have to change its policy on Kilbrandon if we are to get the support of the Scottish Nationalists in the new Parliament.'[497]

By now other Scottish Labour MPs were publicly supporting Mackintosh's position, including a left-wing group led by MPs Harry Ewing, Jim Sillars, John Robertson and Alex Eadie and backed by Scottish trade union heavyweight Alex Kitson. Even so, over-turning the entrenched fortifications of the anti-devolution establishment in the Scottish Labour Party proved too difficult for them, and at the annual Scottish Labour conference of March 1974 they were defeated. Eventually, as the late Donald Dewar recalled, London lost patience and 'hung the Scottish Executive out to dry'.[498] That August, a special conference of the Scottish Labour Party was summoned to Dalintober Street for the U-turn to be carried out. Mackintosh remained active too, scripting a Labour Party election broadcast of October 1974, presented by Jim Sillars, 31-year-old Edinburgh Councillor George Foulkes, 23-year-old Scottish TUC economist Helen Liddell and himself, which bounced the Scottish Labour Party into a commitment to give economic powers to the promised new Scottish Assembly. Dubbed 'Powerhouse Scotland', in practice this entailed promising control of the planned Scottish Development Agency to the Scottish Assembly. Ross was apoplectic, but it was too late. Moreover, that election of October 1974 saw the SNP gain over 30 per cent of the popu-lar vote in Scotland, pushing the Conservatives into third place. At Westminster, mean-while, Leader of the House of Commons Ted Short began work on a devolution White Paper, published in November 1975. It was an uphill battle against cautious colleagues such as Crosland, Jenkins and Healey. In November 1975, Short had to threaten resigna-tion unless the Cabinet agreed to the introduction of legislation in the next parliamen-tary session.[499]

When Callaghan became Prime Minister a few months later, one of his first acts was to retire Ross and replace him as Secretary of State for Scotland with the unflamboyant Bruce Millan who was nevertheless '110 per cent in favour of devolution', as his junior minister Harry Ewing remembered.[500] Michael Foot succeeded Short as Leader of the House and together with his deputy John Smith, and Millan and Ewing at the Scottish Office, they managed to accelerate progress. In late 1976 the Scotland and Wales Bill duly appeared. Unfortunately, by then the Labour government had lost its Commons majority. Neil Kinnock, a young Welsh opponent of devolution, attracted 76 signatures from fellow MPs to a Commons resolution calling for referenda, and claimed that 40 Labour MPs would vote against the Bill unless a referendum was granted. On 10 February 1977 Michael Foot's deputy John Smith announced that the government were giving in and there would be referenda in both Scotland and Wales before the Bill became law. It was not enough. On 22 February 1977, 22 Labour opponents of devolution led by West Lothian MP Tam Dalyell and Welsh MPs Leo Abse and Neil Kinnock, voted with the opposition against a crucial 'guillotine motion'. The Conservatives, having advocated, but failed to introduce, devolution under Heath, were in the process of a U-turn under Thatcher that had already brought about the resignation of her pro-devolution shadow Scottish Secretary Alick Buchanan-Smith and his deputy Malcolm Rifkind. The Liberals were unhappy at the government's refusal to countenance proportional representation for the assemblies (which had been recommended unanimously by Kilbrandon) or to accept any amendments to its Bill. Additionally the death of Tony Crosland, the loss of three by-elections and the defection of Roy Jenkins to Brussels meant that Labour had lost its overall majority. The crucial 'guillotine motion' was therefore lost and the Bill ran out of time. With opinion polls showing the SNP at 36 per cent the government could not simply abandon devolution even had it wanted to. But to carry it through would clearly require the agreed support of at least one of the opposition parties. In this lay the origins of the Lib–Lab Pact, agreed between Callaghan and new Liberal leader David Steel on 21 March. In November 1977 separate Scotland and Wales devolution Bills were reintroduced to the Commons, with Liberal support. The arguments against devolution were most famously marshalled by the West Lothian Labour MP Tam Dalyell,[501] whose speech on the second reading of the Scotland Bill, on 14 November 1977, set out the 'West Lothian Question' for which he became famous. For Dalyell:

> . . . the beneficiaries if the Bill is passed [would be] the SNP [because he feared the Bill was] a stepping stone to further changes. The West Lothian Question [was about MPs] being able to vote on the gut issue of politics in relation to Birmingham but not Bathgate. The fact is that the question with which I interrupted the Prime Minister on Thursday about my voting on issues affecting West Bromwich but not West Lothian, and his voting on issues affecting Carlisle but not Cardiff, is all too real and will not just go away . . .
>
> The truth is that the West Lothian–West Bromwich problem is not a minor hitch to be overcome by rearranging the seating in the devolutionary coach. On the contrary, the West Lothian–West Bromwich problem pinpoints a basic design fault in the steering of the devolutionary coach which will cause it to crash into the side of the road before it has gone a hundred miles.
>
> For how long will English constituencies and English hon. members tolerate not just 71 Scots, 36 Welsh and a number of Ulstermen but at least 119 hon. members from Scotland, Wales and Northern Ireland exercising an important, and probably often decisive, effect on English politics while they themselves have no say in the same matters in Scotland, Wales and Ireland? Such a situation cannot conceivably endure for long . . . [the] problem is that of having a subordinate Parliament in part, though only part, of a unitary State . . .

Dalyell feared the the SNP would use the Assembly as a bridgehead from which to demand the breakup of that unitary state:

> We are voting tonight to jump from the bank of the river on to a log raft which is bound to break up as we are carried downstream to a separate Scottish state . . . the devolutionary coach, if this Bill is passed, will be on a motorway without exit roads to a separate Scottish state – a journey on which my right hon. and hon. friends are unwilling to embark.

The answer to the 'West Lothian Question' came from Dalyell's friend, East Lothian's Labour MP John P. Mackintosh. Mackintosh contended that the 'West Lothian Question' was a red herring, underpinned by a 'complete myth about Parliament'. He argued that: 'The House of Commons does not sit down and make or devise educational policy for Bedford or for Liverpool. Policy is made by the government and the point of having MPs is to determine which party forms the government. Once this happens 99 per cent of the legislation is passed. The case that it is intolerable to have Scots MPs helping to decide which party is to form the government is a case against the continuation of the UK.'[502] From Mackintosh also came the most powerful intellectual case in favour of devolution, which, like Dalyell, he articulated in several of the parliamentary debates on the Bill, including on 22 February 1978 in what turned out to be one of his final Commons speeches.[503] It was firstly a case of taming the bureaucrats:

> . . . In Scotland we have 7,000 civil servants working for a single office which is the equivalent of nine English ministries. These civil servants are able and conscientious men, but they cannot themselves provide political decision making. For how long has it been part of British political philosophy that we are better governed by civil servants even if Scotland is an area set aside in administrative terms? The hon. Member for Aberdeen South says that the whole of the United Kingdom should be governed in the same way. That is not possible because we already have a separate Scottish Office which creates a separate situation which we have to improve.
>
> As the hon. member knows, one of the consequences of the situation is that every time a problem arises in Scotland a board, a bureau or a commission is set up to deal with it. A group of people is appointed and when the government worry about the democratic issue involved, an advisory committee is set up to watch over the body. That means that there are two appointed bodies – an executive board and an advisory board.
>
> I have tried to total the number of jobs that are in the gift of the Secretary of State. My arithmetic may not be accurate but I believe that they total 5,083. Of these, 90 are paid jobs. There are 204 ad hoc bodies in Scotland under the control of the Secretary of State. I do not include bodies that are appointed jointly with other ministries. Scotland is a different area of the country administered by a single Department – a competent and capable Department – surrounded by 204 ad hoc authorities,

appointed but not clearly responsible to anyone and not checked or debated in this House. This means that a preponderance of policies on health, education, housing and roads, for want of better things, emerge from this bureaucracy . . . Ideas emerge from these civil service and ad hoc bodies and from pressure groups which are never submitted to democratic scrutiny. That is the basic case for devolution. A greater say in their own government is what the Scottish people are demanding, as of today, from the government of the United Kingdom. We want to improve the situation by an effective democratic procedure . . . If the Bill were defeated here or lost on the referendum, the problem of Scottish government would not disappear . . .

Most people are bothered about their children's education, their jobs, their health and their welfare. What is disturbing is that underlying these concerns throughout Britain there is a certain gap between the governors and the governed, a certain suspicion of government and politicians, of those in authority and so on. The gap is worse in Scotland, where government is clear but the democratic control over it is not so evident . . .

It is no good for hon. members to ask 'How many people march into MPs' surgeries on a Saturday morning and say "Devolution is my big point"?' No one does that, because no one thinks of such things. Constitutional issues are not comparable with the National Health Service or with education . . .

Hon. members might think back to when the British colonies were demanding independence. The standard argument of every hon. member in those days was they used to say: 'It's a minority demand. I have visited Botswana – formerly Bechuanaland – India or wherever it may be. I found many loyal peasants who were worried only about where their next meal would come from. The people who were agitated about making the government more democratic were a little bunch of wretched "psychopaths", wearing curious dresses and chanting curious songs. Who would pay attention to them?' That is a caricature, but it is the kind of argument that the House in its complacency advanced again and again over Ireland and over various colonies.

I am not suggesting that Scotland is a colony – far from it. But it cannot be imagined that constitutional matters are uppermost in people's minds, for they are not. However, there is the nagging worry that the people running the country are not easily get-attable or controllable on major issues affecting the public . . .

It was said that an Assembly without the powers to tax is a disgrace, that it means representation without taxation. Then, when we moved to give the Assembly taxation powers, to provide a more coherent form of devolution, the Conservatives opposed it . . . I should have preferred taxing powers. I do not accept that it is impossible to devise them . . . Every other major State in the Western world except France devises methods by which taxation powers can be given to subordinate states or assemblies which govern certain areas.

I do not accept the argument of many people that it would be easier to set up a federal system. In my view it would have been more difficult, because in Scotland there is an existing administration on a regional basis that does not exist in large areas of England. It would have been a revolution in English administration, which is highly centralised, to have set up similar regional assemblies. To do something different for Scotland is a political reflection of the existing administrative structure. There is a certain coherence about it.

Similarly, it is true that to give powers of taxation to all sectors of a federal system creates power outside the federal government, but to give them to one area alone does not cause such a problem. Nobody imagines that decisions by the Scottish Assembly to increase or reduce its expenditure by 2 per cent or 3 per cent would affect United Kingdom Treasury demand management. That is well within the Treasury's present margin of error, so there is no problem there.

My hon. friend the Member for Liverpool, West Derby [Eric Ogden], to whom I apologise if I was brusque with him the other night in a debate, has often suggested that English regions are worried about the present situation. I do not see the force of his argument. If he is worried about a different matter – whether devolution is a sensible system of government – I should have thought it made sense to try it out in the Scottish region, where there is demand for it and an administrative framework to do it . . .

I cannot see that it is to anyone's advantage to say that, because England is not sure whether it wants this sort of thing in the regions, therefore an area such as Scotland, which wants devolution, and where there is an existing administration, should not have it. I am reminded of what happens sometimes when one of my children sits down at the table and is given a plate of pudding. When he says 'I don't want it' and I say 'Then pass it to your baby brother who likes pudding', the first child will say 'If he wants it, I will have the pudding, even if I don't like it.' There is a certain logic in that but it is not an admirable attitude . . .

When I first argued the case for devolution in this House many years ago, I was approached by Arthur Woodburn, an ex-Secretary of State for Scotland, who had been through these arguments. He said to me, 'John, you are crazy to make the case for devolution. Don't you understand that as a result of never totting up what Scotland gets and never treating Scotland as an area, we get more for housing, more for health, more for this and more for that?'

Surely it is better, in a democratic country such as ours, to see the block grant out in the open so that we understand what the Scots are getting. Then we can know whether it is a satisfactory method of doing it and whether it is fair to the English regions . . . I do not want more money for Scotland. I want a reasonable system of internal self-government . . .

I do not believe that the bulk of the Scottish people want independence. What I believe is that the Bill is a stepping-stone to a form of greater internal democracy which we, as a drastically over-centralised country, badly need.

The Bills received the Royal Assent and passed into law on 31 July 1978. The assemblies themselves, however, were never to be set up. On 28 January 1978 the Commons passed an amendment proposed by the Scots-born Labour MP for Islington South, George Cunningham, requiring at least 40 per cent of those entitled to vote to vote 'Yes' for the assemblies actually to be set up. When the referenda were held, on 1 March 1979, the Welsh were to vote 'No' by a decisive four-to-one. In Scotland the result was much closer. With the death of John Mackintosh in July 1978, the 'Yes' campaign had lost its trumpeter. Young pro-devolution campaigners Gordon Brown and George Foulkes were not yet MPs, while Jim Sillars, a charismatic pro-devolution MP from Labour's left, had resigned from the party and set up his own. Bruce Millan, who led the campaign for the government, was commonly perceived as a 'grey man who lacked the capacity to enthuse'.[504] The 'No' campaign, whose leading lights included Tam Dalyell and future ministers Robin Cook, Adam Ingram and Brian Wilson, did not actually win. The referendum result saw 1,230,937 vote 'Yes' and 1,153,502 vote 'No,' but as the 'Yes' vote totalled only 32.9 per cent of the registered electorate, some 7 percentage points fewer than the 40 per cent required, the 'No' campaign were declared the victors. It would have to wait until 1997 before a more united Labour Party was in a position to deliver on its 'unfinished business'.

FIFTY

Crime Concerns 1974–78

'Law and order is not the property of just one party'

If education had been the Cabinet job that James Callaghan had wanted but never held, another area in which he had maintained a consistent interest was home affairs. While Roy Jenkins preferred the liberal rhetoric of penal reform, Callaghan was more interested in the fight against crime. At the joint Cabinet–NEC meeting to discuss the manifesto for the October 1974 election, Callaghan had made clear his belief in the importance of tackling teenage hooliganism, to which Denis Healey gave a loud 'Hear, hear!' Callaghan would not have echoed Roy Jenkins's announcement to Cabinet that 'I do not like the phrase "law and order".'[505] Callaghan had criticised Labour's Benn-chaired NEC Home Policy Committee for its comparative neglect of violence, vandalism and what in the twenty-first century began to be called 'anti-social behaviour'.[506] Callaghan felt – and in this he had an ally on the left in the person of Eric Heffer – that such problems were most acute in working-class areas, that it was 'our people' who were suffering the consequences, and it was therefore all the more a Labour issue to confront them. Just such an opportunity came at Labour's 1978 annual conference, which saw a ferocious debate erupt over a resolution calling for 'bold and resolute action', to 'combat the menace of vandalism, wanton destruction and needless violence'. It was a call for the NEC to recommend measures that would be tough on crime, and also on 'the causes of the general increases in crime', prefiguring the agenda that Tony Blair, Jack Straw and David Blunkett would carry forward twenty years later. It also talked about the need to support the 'democratic community', and to 'shatter the sub-culture that is developing as a result of ineffective action', themes which David Blunkett and Hazel Blears would make their own as Labour ministers post-2001. The resolution itself was proposed by former Liverpool Councillor Andy Williams:

> . . . CLPs up and down the country have also discussed the problem and many trade unions have voiced their concern. So, indeed, have the Conservative Party, who are determined to use law and order as a main topic in their education campaign, laced with their usual platitudes and political gimmicks. They will lift people's hopes purely as a vote catcher. But at the end of the day they will not have prescribed the cure. That, comrades, is not the way that we in the Labour Party should do business.
>
> The general public, and that includes each and every one of us, have every right to

be worried about the growth of crime. Crimes of a serious nature are being blatantly pursued by the criminal fraternity on an ever-increasing basis. Murder and assassinations on our streets, British attacks on police officers, and so many more that time does not allow me to mention them. But I must mention what I term the doorstep crimes of mugging and vandalism.

Mugging is a crime that has introduced fear into the hearts and minds of many people, especially the aged and infirm. In certain areas up and down the country, old-age pensioners are afraid to leave their homes after dusk, and it goes without saying that they are not safe from some thugs in the sanctity of their own homes . . . Our streets must be made safe for every individual to walk freely and without fear at any hour of the night or the day (*applause*).

Allow me for a moment to turn to vandalism. This is a youthful amusement. It has reached intolerable proportions at the taxpayers' expense. It is not just broken glass in bus shelters. Schools are vandalised and set on fire, houses and whole blocks of flats are reduced to shells, there is damage to public property and buildings, and the funny thing is that nobody ever seems to see it happening. They are destruction jobs that would take demolition firms a fortnight to perform. These unlawful acts are damaging the fabric of our society. The situation has been deteriorating since the introduction of the Police Bill of the sixties, which, to my mind, was the first step towards a police state. If the Tories are given the opportunity, they will introduce a Bill that will give licence to the police to become a law unto themselves. I submit to conference that this will never be effective within a democratic country.

The local government reorganisation has made the police more remote from the local community. I do not blame the police – in fact, I am grateful for the way they perform their duties under very difficult circumstances – but I do question the system and the Police Acts under which they operate.

Television has been a scourge . . . Some parents are more conscious of the box than their children. Environment due to bad planning, wrong types of housing, the breaking up of communities, lack of facilities in new towns, and larger housing estates which in many cases have become concrete jungles. Have we become impressed with providing excuses? That is what the general public really believe.

He was echoed by Jack Smart, leader of the Labour Group on the Association of Metropolitan Authorities, who raised the:

. . . growing concern of the majority of society [with the] ever-increasing amount of vandalism and crime. [Citing] the ever-increasing number of crimes committed . . . particularly by young children and youths who resort to attacking the elderly and even the disabled, and robbing them in many cases, and causing them grievous bodily harm, [he declared,] law and order, and the concern with it, is not the property of just one party . . . The rise in crime is not simply within the experience of the rich. They do not have to live in vandalised communities. They do not have to drive the trams which have missiles thrown into the cabs . . . They do not have to take charge of the buses and deal with the rowdies . . .

For Jim Meakin of the National Union of Sheet Metal Workers:

... a lot of the present-day vandalism is an indictment of the education system. [He also demanded the repeal of the 1964 Police Act.] You have to have more police, but not in panda cars. Send them on the beat, because the system on the beat years ago kept my generation in order, and we respected law and order. If we repealed the 1964 Police Act, we could reorganise the police into smaller sections, instead of great big metropolitan areas where it is completely impersonal. Get the small police forces back where everybody knows one another and knows the policemen on the beat. This is part of the solution, and if it is going to cost more money to get police, get them, because the amount of money that is being wasted by vandalism would pay for them.

Opposition to the resolution was led by two young Labour activists from London, both of whom were to become Labour MPs and among the doughtiest opponents of the Blair/Straw/Blunkett approach: 29-year-old Haringey councillor Jeremy Corbyn and 34-year-old barrister Bob Marshall-Andrews from Richmond, Surrey. Corbyn declared the resolution more appropriate for a Conservative than for a Labour Party conference:

... and some of the sentiments in it would be more appropriate to the National Front than to the Labour Party...

Is it any wonder that some kids return to vandalism when they have no jobs to go to, when they live on an appalling council estate?...

The way to defeat vandalism is not by appeasing the reactionary forces that are calling for more and more law and order, and more and more money to be spent on it... No, it is a question of restoring the cuts in public spending and not allowing our economic policy, and thus our social policy, to be dictated by the IMF... There are social solutions to the problems and the solution is socialism at the end of the day...

Bob Marshall-Andrews branded the resolution:

... a wonderful motion for Rhodes Boyson[507] and William Whitelaw,[508] who would not disagree with a single word of it. The whole repugnance of this motion is that the central theme again – and it is not the first time it has come before a Labour Party conference – is punishment... It reads 'appropriate and consistent punishment... to shatter a sub-culture'... There is not one single criminal statistic to support the view that increased punishment cuts down crime... And I will tell you something about the people who commit acts of juvenile delinquency in this epidemic of destruction of public property in the country, which we all know exists. I will tell you why they do it ... It is that in this generation since the war we have destroyed their communities, we have blighted their environments, both in terms of scale and size and decay, we have thrown them into an educational experiment, a magnificent educational experiment, and then taken the funds that were necessary to make it a success. And those who get through that social assault course are told at the end of it, the least able and those in most need: 'You are not necessary. You are not wanted. You have no contribution to make, and for the rest of you life you are going to be regarded as a malingerer and a scrounger' (*applause*). It has nothing to do with punishment at all. And superimposed on that desolate life cycle, you have the twin great evils of a violent mass media culture supported by mass media advertising, which apply and attract the very worst aspects of human nature (*applause*).

I will tell you the cause of crime in this country . . . It is in eight words and it is this. It is the lack of values endemic in a capitalist society (*applause*). Of course, you can prop up that society for as long as you have a strong religious ethic to back it up, which tells you to love God and fear the boss. When that religious ethic begins to go – and it is going, and there are some of us who are not doing very much to put it back – you have got to have a new set of values. Those values are socialist values, and we must go on saying so (*applause*).

Despite the eloquence and passion of Corbyn and Marshall-Andrews, it was the arguments of Williams, Smart and Meakin that won the backing of the NEC and the conference vote, by 4,411,000 votes to 2,069,000. But in six months there would be no Labour government to take forward the NEC's recommendations. That opportunity would have to wait until 1997.

FIFTY-ONE

Revenge of the Radicals 1973–78

'MPs are people . . . If you cut us, we bleed'

Attempts to secure the automatic reselection of MPs were made by the hard left in successive years from 1973. They were rooted in the creation of the Campaign for Labour Party Democracy (CLPD) in June 1973. CLPD grew out of a meeting of some dozen Labour activists united in their frustration at Harold Wilson's ability as party leader to rule out the demand for the nationalisation of the top 25 companies from the next election manifesto. Its initial aims were to require the NEC to ensure that the manifesto 'accurately' reflected party conference decisions and to bind the Parliamentary Labour Party to implement them. This was, in effect, an attempt to reopen the battle between Keir Hardie and some of the delegates at the 1907 conference and change the relationship between MPs and party. It was underpinned by a suspicion that the failure of the previous Labour government to build the 'New Britain' had been partly a failure of will and partly an insufficient commitment to 'socialism' as defined by the activists in CLPD. Their suspicions seemed to be confirmed by Tony Benn, who had been there on the inside as a minister 1964–70 and seemed to be saying that there was indeed a failure of will and an insufficient commitment to socialism. If the former Minister of Technology, in 1973 a senior member of Labour's shadow Cabinet, who had just spent four years trying to sort out British industry, said that what we needed was to nationalise the top 25 companies, what possible reason could the rest of Labour's leadership have for blocking it other than an insufficient commitment to socialist values?

Newcastle-Under-Lyme MP John Golding recalled driving Benn to visit pickets in his constituency in January 1972, during the miners' strike: 'John, what shall I tell them that will please them?' Benn asked Golding. Golding was 'upset' by this: he thought that 'when the chips are down you owed your members the truth', while Benn 'just stuffed them up with what he believed, rightly, they wanted to hear'.[509] Barbara Castle, never a political soulmate of Golding's, later came to the same conclusion: 'I suddenly saw why I mistrust Wedgie [Benn] . . . he never spells out that responsibility involves choice and that the choices facing this country are by definition grim for everybody. He really cannot eat his seedcorn and sow it. But his whole popularity rests on the belief that he is spreading around: that he – and those that he seeks to lead – can do just that.'[510] And popularity he

372

was getting in spades. From 1965–73 Benn was usually elected to the NEC constituency section of the NEC second, third or fourth in the ballot with 52–72 per cent of the possible constituency Labour Party vote. Between 1974 and 1985 he topped the poll every year, with 72–91 per cent of the possible constituency Labour Party vote.

Coordinated largely by Vladimir Derer and his wife from their home in Golders Green, CLPD would make an impact greatly out of proportion to its numbers. Within months of its foundation CLPD decided that the best way to secure its objectives was to get rid of 'right-wing' Labour MPs who could and would ignore the wishes of Labour activists and the resolutions of Labour conferences and replace them with Labour MPs who would do what they were told. At that time, while this process was possible (as evidenced by the deselections of Dick Taverne in Lincoln and Reg Prentice in Newham), it was, believed CLPD, far too difficult. CLPD resolved to campaign for a requirement for MPs automatically to submit themselves to reselection conferences at least every parliament. For Golding, one of those 'right-wing' MPs who fought hardest against Benn, it was the creation of the Campaign for Labour Party Democracy in 1973 'that marked the beginning of Labour's civil war'.[511] For Joe Ashton, an MP who had served as Tony Benn's PPS and campaign manager during the leadership election of 1976, it was Benn's incitement of the CLPD 'compulsory reselection' agenda that drove a wedge between them. 'For Benn, reselection offered the prospect of replacing MPs who voted against his leadership bid in 1976 with left-wingers who would vote for him next time: an attractive prospect.'[512]

At Labour's 1974 annual conference a resolution proposed by Ken Coates,[513] demanding that every constituency party be required to hold a reselection conference at least once in every Parliament, was defeated. But the Campaign for Labour Party Democracy was not going to take no for an answer and using the device of model resolutions sent around the country to sympathetic activists, resolutions demanding automatic reselection were submitted by twelve constituencies in 1975, 40 in 1976 and 67 in 1977. The existence of a 'three-year rule' meant that having debated the issue in 1974, the conference couldn't debate the same thing for three more years. It was not until 1977, therefore, that the pressure cooker that CLPD was stoking exploded on to the conference agenda.

At the 1977 conference a composite CLPD resolution was proposed by Ray Apps, an active Militant supporter. CLPD's opponents were able to use another constitutional technicality to 'refer back' the resolution to the NEC for consideration by a working party over the coming year. The working party split between a compromise majority[514] report advocating reselection if local constituencies wanted it and a minority[515] report demanding automatic competitive reselection whether the constituency wanted it or not. Their recommendations came to Labour's conference in 1978 and on 3 October 1978 battle was again joined. One of the greatest ironies of the debate was provided by the speech of the delegate from Tottenham, Sheila Peacock, who demanded 'support for the 67 resolutions of last year'. Left-wing MPs like her own in Tottenham, Norman Atkinson, had 'nothing to fear from reselection'. Atkinson was to find the hollowness of her reassurance when he was deselected during the 1980s to make way for Haringey Council leader Bernie Grant. Two MPs spoke out in defence of their parliamentary colleagues. The first was Tony Benn's former PPS Joe Ashton, who began pugnaciously:

> I have four minutes to try to save three hundred jobs – because that is what you are talking about. Ah, the boot is on the other foot then when I talk like that. There are three hundred MPs who work in a non-union factory. We have ten minutes to try to put our side of the case. There are no shop stewards in our factory, like you have. We do not come under the Employment Protection Act. There is no unfair dismissal we can appeal to. There is no redundancy pay. There is no ACAS ballot (*background noise and disorder*). It is nice to have the sympathy of the workers. Well, I will tell you this. You got those benefits because three hundred MPs slogged it through the night, in a minority government, to give them to you (*applause*).
>
> A lot of them are not here today. In fact, eight died in the past year, some of them because they went to work when they were sick, working crazy hours to try to keep this party alive. All we are saying, and we are not asking for much, is that before you sack a man you give him the right to a defence (*hear, hear*).
>
> MPs are people. We have got wives, we have kids, we have mortgages, the same as you have. If you cut us, we bleed; we are people. What are you trying to do? You are asking us to try all the time to serve five masters – to do what conference tells us to do, to do what the constituency tells us to do, to do what our trade union tells us to do, to do what the government and the whips tell us. Then there is the electorate telling us what to do. We cannot win. If we vote for the 5 per cent, we get kicked up the backside by the constituency and the unions. If we do not vote for it and bring down the government, we get kicked up the backside by the electorate and lose our jobs that way.
>
> What I am saying is that we have the right to a defence, the normal right of any decent, humane, just society. Before you sack a man, you do not throw him straight to the wolves, you give him a night with a quarter of an hour for a speech and a quarter of an hour for questions. But if a man has given fifteen or 20 years to a constituency and you have fallen out with him, this sort of instant hire and fire, quickie divorce, call it what you like, will not do this party a lot of good. It will create the biggest Nights of the Long Knives and the biggest purges that you have seen for many a long time (*cheers, applause*).
>
> . . . All you are doing is creating a better system for the public relations men, the journalists, the lawyers, all the whizz kids, the ones who can use the media. All these sort of people will be able to come in, and I can tell the trade unionists this. It is the 55-year-old trade unionist who flogs himself on the Health and Safety at Work Bill who does not get anything in the *Guardian*, or who does not get on the telly, but who does a good job for his constituency, who will be chucked on the scrap-heap at the age of 55 without any compassion at all.

Why, I wonder, are places like Basingstoke and Woking getting worried about getting rid of MPs? They never had one. Some of them never even had Labour councillors. They had Labour candidates who would like to get into Parliament, and that is the sort of situation we are in danger of putting ourselves into. Don't think MPs are going to run away once they get sacked. A lot of them will stand and fight, and cause trouble – great, deep trouble. It could split the votes in 25 safe seats at the next election, and it would be disastrous.

The second was Labour's Chief Whip, Michael Cocks, who echoed Ashton:

Four years ago this month, the government was elected with a majority of three. I would remind you, comrades, that this is the same majority with which the Labour government went to the country in 1951. It has not been easy. It has put a great strain on members of Parliament. Joe Ashton mentioned the deaths. I have lost thirteen members by death since 1974, eight in the last year. Only two Conservatives have died in this time. The great majority of my members who have died have died of cardio-vascular disease, which is very much exacerbated by stress and strain. I am very much concerned about the effect of automatic reselection, and you must look at this . . . I have had members come to me and say: 'Mike, I know it's a critical vote tonight, but I must get away. I face a vote of censure in my party.' When I ask what on earth is the trouble and why they are being censured, some of my members reply: 'Because I supported the government last week – because I voted for the government.'

If that sort of pressure is going to be put on members, how can I justify bringing people in on stretchers or in ambulances to be nodded through, defying their doctors' orders, if other members are under pressure to abstain because their local party has taken umbrage about something which the government is doing?

CLPD had done its sums and was confident of victory: it had managed to get the support of both the TGWU and AUEW for its position. But it was the NEC majority report that had got the votes. AUEW President Hugh Scanlon had been persuaded by the arguments of Ashton and Cocks, and neglected to cast his union's block vote for the CLPD's amendment, rising afterwards on a point of order to claim he had been 'confused'. CLPD were furious and vowed revenge. Ian Mikardo, a veteran left-winger, was one of the first to feel the consequences of his decision to support the NEC compromise rather than the more radical CLPD proposals: he was knocked off the constituency section of the NEC on which he had sat for nearly 30 years.

FIFTY-TWO

The Turkeys Vote for Christmas 1978–79

*'If you now believe in the philosophy of the pig trough –
those with the biggest snout get the biggest share – I reject it'*

Of the debates that soured Labour's 1978 conference one more than all others was to have the most immediate impact. A resolution from Liverpool Wavertree demanded the government 'immediately cease interfering in wage negotiations'. It was carried overwhelmingly, as was a resolution from Clive Jenkins's ASTMS demanding 'a return to free collective bargaining', reflation and import controls. A further resolution was proposed by Alan Fisher of the National Union of Public Employees (NUPE).[516] NUPE members were at the lower ends of the pay scales and their resolution reflected the frustration of low-paid workers with an inflationary economic climate and the tendency for percentage-based incomes policies to keep them at the bottom of the wage pile. But it ignored the fact that they did even worse under free collective bargaining and it was low earners like themselves who had actually benefited most from the flat-rate £6 pay policy of the social contract:

> . . . the lower-paid workers in this country . . . are the men and women who work for an employer who is too mean to pay them a living wage, and forces them to live in the twilight between dignity and death, between poverty and the paradise that never comes, who fear the postman's knock because it brings another bill they cannot pay, who are denied many of those things that the rest of us take for granted and regard as the bare necessities of life . . .
>
> [For Fisher,] there are probably three major reasons why we still have low pay in this country. The first is that successive governments over the years have subsidised bad employers . . . we pay family income supplements, we pay rent and rate rebates, we give free school meals . . . And that all comes out of your pocket and out of mine, to subsidise the bad employer . . .
>
> There is a second reason for low pay, we must understand. It is the iniquity of percentages . . . You know what percentages do for the lower-paid? It gives least to those who need it most, and most to those who need it least (*applause*) . . . at the end of the day, 100 per cent of nothing is bugger all (*applause*) . . .
>
> The third reason is . . . many thousands of workers in our essential public services . . . because they are not willing to take industrial action if it is going to hurt the public and hurt the patient, we know what has happened. Their loyalty has been exploited. It is the exploitation of dedication and it is a disgrace (*applause*).

And the major point – the major point – the obscenity that there are thousands of workers in this country today who do a decent 40 hours' work each week and get paid less than if they were sitting at home doing nothing and drawing unemployment benefit . . .

What, then, is the solution? The composite sets . . . an objective on low pay which will give people at least two-thirds of the national average earnings figure . . . We want action on that resolution. That is why in the claims that are being made by my union and others for thousands of workers now in the public services – in the Health Service, the local authorities, in social service, the water industry, the ambulance services – between now and December, we are asking for what that two-thirds figure gives – for £60 a week. If that means breaking the 5 per cent incomes policy, so be it (*applause*) . . .

Fisher's call for a national minimum wage at a level that would have entailed 40 per cent wage increases for many NUPE members, clearly in breach of the 5 per cent pay policy, set out in a government White Paper of 23 July 1978, and would have also incited rival claims from better-paid skilled union members (like the car workers) who would want to avoid the erosion of differentials. Some of the big unions (such as the AUEW engineering union) opposed a national minimum wage for just this reason, and had overwhelmingly defeated Fisher's attempt at Labour's 1973 conference to commit Labour to a minimum wage set at 80 per cent of average earnings.

One of the few who spoke out against Fisher, Clive Jenkins and the Wavertree resolution[517] was Sid Weighell, General Secretary of the National Union of Railwaymen. 'In that highly charged atmosphere I managed to get to the rostrum. There is no point at all in mincing your words when you speak in the Labour movement . . . My speech at the 1978 party conference certainly raised the temperature but I was angry at hearing nonsense about the wages free-for-all when so much was at stake and as I walked to the rostrum I decided to make this plain':[518]

About 30 years ago, I listened in this very hall to Aneurin Bevan explaining the basis of his socialist faith. He said that socialism is the language of priorities. You have to learn to say 'No' to some things in order to say 'Yes' to the desirable things. And this week, as we did at the TUC, we wanted priority for the Health Service, more expenditure on social services, extension of public ownership, a solution to the one and a half million unemployment. And whether we like it or not, the trade union movement, and this movement, and the people responsible for carrying out those policies, will have to decide priorities. When they talk about it, whether they like it or not, whether it is in Downing Street or anywhere else, when they talk about Britain's economic strategy, they cannot exclude what we say ourselves. To argue like that is absolute nonsense, and Composite 37 [demanding total rejection of 'any wage restraint by whatever method'] is nothing more than an emotional spasm, based upon nothing (*applause*). If Alan Fisher wants to get out from under the bottom of the pile – Alan, you have got to support 38 [supporting government policy], because if you do not I will tell you what is going to happen. You say, 'Let's get 40 per cent.' That is what you want. Forty per cent in my industry will mean £320 million on the pay bill. You tell me that fares will not go up. Let me tell you this. If you get 40 per cent, Alan, in your world, I am going to get 40. And the difference between you and me: I have got some power to do it with (*applause*). And I tell you, Joe, if your members get 40 per cent, we are getting it, because you can produce as much coal as you like, you will not get it moved (*applause*). So let me tell you this as well. I do not come here on my knees to support a socialist strategy. I come because my union believes in it, and we are prepared to run a little slower in order that Alan can run a bit quicker (*applause*). Yes. And I will tell you something else. If Alan is on the TUC General Council, he says differentials do not mean a thing. You want to sit there, boy. Differentials do not create a problem? Wipe them away. Whatever problems today are British Rail in? What about the toolmakers? And I have got members who quibble about differentials. But I am prepared to say to them – 250,000 railwaymen – I am prepared to say we will hesitate, we will forgo the claims about maintaining high differentials, if we can get a socialist strategy which includes pay. I do not like the 5 per cent any more than you do. But the 5 per cent is there because the trade union movement . . . abdicated its responsibilities. Because I was in 10 Downing Street when the Prime Minister said: 'Can we reason this out together?' And he was told 'Leave it to us – and trust us.' Joe [Gormley] said that, and others. There are 112 General Secretaries on the Executive Committee. If they were left to determine the pay policy, they would not know what the hell to do (*laughter*). If you want to question the validity of that, look what is lining up now: 20 per cent, 35-hour week, a month's holiday for Fords. Alan wants 40 per cent. This is what they call responsible collective bargaining. Responsible. Really? When I entered this movement – and I am the third generation into it – my union helped to create this party. The union that sponsored the conference that created the Labour Party. I am not going to stand here and destroy it. But if you want the call to go out at this conference that the new philosophy in the Labour Party, that you now believe in the philosophy of the pig trough – those with the biggest snout get the biggest share – (*applause*) – I reject it. My union rejects it. And if I am the only one standing here saying it, I will reject it until I drop down dead (*applause*).

But it was to no avail. Labour's conference failed to heed Weighell's warnings and voted to support all the anti-government resolutions and reject wage restraint. The single resolution[519] in favour of the government's economic strategy, moved by Newcastle East MP Mike Thomas and Norman Stagg of the Union of Post Office Workers, was defeated. Thomas later joined the SDP in despair.

Callaghan's speech on the Tuesday morning of Labour's 1978 conference would be the last at a party conference by a serving Labour Prime Minister until 1997. He had discussed its main themes with No. 10 advisers, in particular his political secretary Tom McNally, his press secretary Tom McCaffrey, Bernard Donoughue and David Lipsey who had formerly been a special adviser to Tony Crosland. Much of the speech, in the event, comprised an off-the-cuff attempt to win the understanding of delegates in the hall, and those outside through their televisions, for the government's 5 per cent pay policy, even if the vote of the previous afternoon could not, of course, be reversed. In conclusion, Callaghan gave both a defence of the government's achievements and also a reassertion of traditional Labour values: the family, law and order, quality social provision, and an emphasis on both citizens' rights and responsibilities and their active participation in decision making that New Labour would take forward two decades later. Callaghan called for:

> ... greater participation by the citizen. We live in an age – and part of the debate yesterday showed this – where the old certainties are being challenged, where the experts, the bureaucrats, and even the politicians find their answers only partly acceptable or not wholly satisfying. We need a new basis for authority, and there will be no sounder guide than the words of R. H. Tawney, which Joan Lestor quoted in her Chairman's address yesterday – namely that authority 'must rest upon consent'. Joan, I picked it up as you said it – it is a good text. The informed, active agreement of the individual citizen will certainly be sounder than the notions of the gentlemen in Whitehall, or even – dare I say it? – of the editors in Fleet Street.
>
> One of the new phenomena of modern politics has been the rapid growth of what I call single-issue pressure groups, usually formed by concerned people, deeply devoted to a cause which they press vigorously. The devotion and effort that they expend reveals clearly to me that there is a source of democratic strength that we have not yet fully tapped, and to which we should respond. Our society will be healthier if we can find means of channelling this energy into new forms of participation. It will also ensure – and I think this is sometimes overlooked by these groups – that they are concerned not only with their own work, but with the consequences that their pressures have on other aspects of public policy. That is why I believe that in politics as a whole it is necessary to embrace all these individual issues. I would like to divert the energies of some of the single-issue pressure groups into the general political field. The Labour government is moving forward in this field. Let me give you five examples of increased participation, all of which are controversial, all of which we hope to carry forward in the coming session of Parliament.
>
> One, we intend to legislate to give employees in industry the right to more information about their firms' affairs, about their investment plans and other matters of importance. We want employees to have a bigger share in the taking of decisions that affect their well-being, and perhaps their very jobs ...
>
> Two, the referendum on devolution ...
>
> Three ... we shall legislate to give parents and teachers more influence in the way their schools are run.
>
> Four, we will legislate in the next session to give tenants living in council houses greater control over their own homes. We want to foster a greater sense of responsibility and a feeling of pride in them (*applause*).
>
> Five – controversial, but I know you will support it – subject to the recommendations of the Royal Commission on the Health Service, which we hope to receive during the next year, we intend to undo much of the damage caused by the Tory reorganisation (*applause*). We want to make the management of the Health Service more

responsive to the patients and to the dedicated people at all levels who work in the service.

Our aim in all these matters – and this is part of the kind of society towards which I want to see us moving – is a society in which everyone who wishes can feel that they can play a part, and do play a part, in the decisions that mould and shape their lives, that they do not feel that they are ciphers whose future is being decided for them by people who are supposed to know better.

Next, I hope we can give a deeper meaning to this participation by reasserting the traditional values of those who founded our movement. I do not wish to dramatise the changes that have taken place. There are countless examples of individual kindliness, selflessness and caring. We all know them. Yet we do seem to have lost – do we not? – a certain amount of consideration for one another. Modern society . . . is now so inter-dependent and organised that it is fatally easy to disrupt it. When there is a dispute, how often is it the innocent person caught in the middle who suffers most? That was not the attitude of the pioneers, nor is it the attitude of a society that calls itself car-ing and considerate. We have a responsibility, as a movement, to find a better way for resolving disputes than invoking anarchy to make our point.

Another issue of deep concern to our people, in which standards have slipped, is in the matter of crime, violence and vandalism . . . The nature of crime, the causes of crime, depend to a large extent upon the values that society lives by, and in determin-ing the attitudes of the young, the example of their parents is paramount (*applause*).

Next, let us place more emphasis on our belief that democratic socialism is about quality as well as equality. Let us take housing as an example of what I mean . . . There is much to be proud of in our post-war housing record, but if we are honest, we must admit in our eagerness to remove old evils, some new ones were created. We could all name developments built with pride two decades ago which are now themselves slums. In our eagerness for the grand design we should also remember that we are building for people, for families, for communities. In the old terraced streets there was a sense of warmth and community feeling, whatever their shortcomings. The daughter lived close to her elderly parents, the grandparents were around when the children came home from school, the neighbours were ready to assist in times of trouble. All this helped to create a real community. We have to get back to this. Too much of it was lost in the redevelopment schemes of the fifties and sixties (*applause*).

On the doorstep, every councillor and every canvasser hears the problems of coun-cil tenants: 'It's taken them six months to come round and fix the tap.' 'I want to move nearer my elderly mother, but I can't get a transfer.' 'The lift's gone wrong again.' Week after week we sit and we hear these complaints. Today we must stress that we are not just concerned about the number of houses that are built, but about the quality also, about the type of community we live in, to satisfy the needs of those who live in them. As democratic socialists we do care, we must care about these things, and we must do our best to get them right (*applause*). Quite apart from the position of the home-owner, which we have assisted, I believe that the Tenant's Charter is not only important in itself, but it also helps to raise the quality of living. We intend to introduce this new charter, which will extend the rights and freedoms of council tenants, the right of a council tenant to security, the freedom of a tenant to improve his own flat or home and to get improvement grants when he does it – like the owner-occupier (*applause*). Let the individual tenant decide if he wants a new kitchen. Let him have a choice of colour for his front door. Let the tenants be involved in running their estates, so that they suit their needs. These are for them, for their lives. They are not just there for the convenience of town hall officials. This is what we are about (*applause*) . . .

We do not want to win support as a Labour government that will be presenting itself to the people. We do not want to win support on the basis of fear. We are the party of hope. Yet I think we have every right to assert that Britain would be a cruder, a more unjust, a more selfish society if Tory values were to prevail (*applause*) . . . We deny, I repeat, that there is some choice to be made between an efficient Britain and a caring one. They go together.

Tony Benn was generous in his praise, writing in his diary that Callaghan had made 'the best speech I had ever heard from a party leader at conference'.[520] But his speech could not save the government's pay policy and within a couple of months the 'Winter of Discontent' left the government's economic strategy in ruins. Was the government mistaken to have sought to continue its pay policy for another year? Callaghan's critics have claimed that the 5 per cent norm he had announced in the summer of 1978 was unworkable and reflected the stubborn insensitivity of the Prime Minister to the known feelings of the trade union movement and his direct defiance of the rejection of pay policy by the Labour conference. That then raises the question of the alternative. No pay policy at all would have meant a return to galloping inflation and economic crisis. The country had been there in the summer of 1975 and was not keen to return. It would have been the low-paid, Alan Fisher's members, who would have suffered most. And the electorate would not have stood it. 'Despite the anomalies, and rigidities, thrown up by a succession of incomes policies,' wrote Callaghan's by then former Cabinet minister Joel Barnett in 1982, 'I believe a workable incomes policy is essential to the very maintenance of our democratic society; we have no alternative but to go on striving for its achievement.'[521] The other alternative might have been a slightly higher pay limit. One of those most involved at the time was the then Environment Secretary Peter Shore. He had actually advocated this, but he later wrote:

I myself – and one or two colleagues – thought in July [1978] that 5 per cent was too ambitious and had argued for a norm of 7 per cent. But one only has to recall the claims that were pressed in the late autumn and winter of that year to realise that 7 per cent would have been swept aside just as contemptuously as the 5 per cent originally on offer – or the later 5 per cent plus an additional increase for lower-paid workers that was swiftly adopted. The road haulage and oil tanker drivers were asking for 25 to 30 per cent, the manual workers in the health service 40 per cent. In my own department of the environment, the local authority manuals were demanding 40 per cent and the water workers 30 . . . Once the weakness of the government's powers to stop excessive pay awards in the private sector had been demonstrated both by Ford Motors' agreement to pay 17 per cent to their employees and the subsequent defeat in the House of Commons of the government's attempt to impose its puny sanctions on that company, public sector pay claims were pressed with the utmost vigour . . . It was a nightmare. No one, in their wildest dreams, could have predicted such collective barbarity in advance of the actual event.[522]

'Fisher was no natural militant,' recalled John Grant, then an Employment Minister and later to join the SDP, 'but Alan was a platform hothead who was increasingly influenced by the left within his own ranks, not least by his full-time officials.' Grant minuted ministerial colleagues that Fisher was anxious to avoid industrial action and had warned him of problems in some hospitals, 'with the Socialist Workers' Party and other fringe groups very active and awaiting their chance'.[523] But as the situation unravelled, recalled Tom Sawyer, then a young NUPE regional organiser in the north east of England, 'people just stopped talking to each other. Bernard Dix was behind the "Winter of Discontent". Reg Race, research officer at NUPE head office, thought it was the way to teach the government a lesson. I was looking for a deal and it just didn't happen.'[524] It was a disaster for the Labour movement, doing lasting damage to the reputation of trade unions in the public mind. A Gallup poll in January 1979 suggested that 51 per cent of the public believed that the trade unions were controlled by the Communists either 'considerably' or 'a great deal', up from 42 per cent in August 1978. In parallel, support had grown from 50 per cent to 61 per cent for legislation to ban unofficial strikes. A mere 29 per cent now opposed this, down from 35 per cent in August 1978.[525] A staggering 83.4 per cent of Labour voters now supported a legal ban on secondary picketing.[526]

'Soon we were identified with the even more offensive behaviour of an uncaring and malicious minority in the front line of the "dirty jobs" dispute,' recalled Electricians' Union chief Frank Chapple.

> Public service workers disrupted hospitals, refused to provide basic emergency services to the dangerously ill and even spited mourning relatives by impeding burials. There were ugly scenes on the picket lines. Whether the wildcat strikers in the vanguard were politically motivated, misled, sick-minded or just plain stupid, it was all as far removed from trade unionism as anything I could remember. Prime Minister Callaghan called them 'vandals' though he prepared to run up the white flag in the face of their demands. In all my years as a trade unionist I have never seen such hostility from the general public and from most trade union members . . . Someone had to show some concern and I minced no words. I said that some of the pickets were practising 'terrorism, not trade-unionism'. My sights were trained on that fairly small but very vocal minority who clearly gloried in their harmful and obnoxious antics. Most union leaders privately agreed with me.[527]

The Winter of Discontent knocked the stuffing out of the Callaghan government. 'We are prostrate before you – but don't ask us to put it in writing,' Electricians' Union chief Frank Chapple recalled Callaghan telling the TUC General Council at Downing Street shortly afterwards.[528] With the government by now short of an overall majority and lacking the formal backing of the Lib–Lab pact, which the Liberals had declined to renew the previous summer, defeat was at some point almost inevitable. To make things worse, with the trial of their former leader Jeremy Thorpe to begin in April, the Liberals were keen that an election be held before any damaging publicity could emerge. It was a tribute to the skill of Labour's whips and the stamina of Labour MPs that they managed to sustain the government for so long. Eventually, that stamina could be sustained no longer. For some Labour MPs, elderly and ill, the strain of the continual late-night votes was effectively fatal. Some MPs had actually been brought into Westminster from hospital to vote and then returned straight back again. Sir Arthur Irvine, Labour MP for Liverpool Edge Hill and a former Solicitor General, had already died and a by-election (that the Liberals were to win) was scheduled for 29 March. Another Labour MP, Tom Swain, had just been killed in a car crash. On 28 March 1978 the whips were told that Alfred 'Doc' Broughton was so ill that to leave hospital to attend the vote might kill him. They told him to rest. His doctors were right: he died but a few days later.

There was talk of deals with the minor parties. Indeed, Labour did get the support of Plaid Cymru and the two independent Scottish Labour members, John Sillars and John Robertson.[529] Callaghan ruled out bribing the Ulster Unionists with a promise of a gas pipeline across the Irish Sea between England and Northern Ireland. Two Ulster Unionists voted for the government anyhow. But eight voted to bring it down, alongside the Liberals, the SNP and the Conservatives. Alienated by Roy Mason's tough policies in Northern Ireland, Gerry Fitt of the SDLP and Frank Maguire, an 'Independent Republican', abstained.

The Conservatives were determined to bring down the government, but attempts to do so had failed when the smaller opposition parties had refused to back Conservative motions of no confidence. Thatcher needed a way of binding at least one of them into her stratagems. Eventually an opportunity arose. When the SNP, frustrated with the failure of the devolution referendum, put down a motion of censure, the Conservatives latched on to it. The SNP could hardly not back its own motion. The debate was scheduled for 28 March. It was tense and the result was in doubt to the end. Nobody could be sure which way Fitt and Maguire would vote, how the Unionists might split, or whether Broughton was coming. Callaghan spoke in reply to Thatcher with a last, dignified, speech in defence of his government:

> . . . our debate . . . follows directly from my proposal last week that in the light of the
> devolution referendums, and especially because of the result in Scotland, there should

be a limited period of discussion between the parties before Parliament debated the orders that would repeal the Scotland and Wales Acts once and for all.

The right hon. lady did not immediately reject that proposal. She waited for the well-advertised move by the Scottish National Party. Its members . . . tabled a motion censuring the government. For what? For not immediately bringing the Act into force.

The opposition, of course, want nothing like that. They want the very reverse. They want to get rid of the Act. But the SNP motion was enough for the opposition Chief Whip. I am glad to see that he is now securely perched on the front bench. I hope that he will not fall off. When the SNP tabled its motion, the right hon. gentleman went into action. He scurried round to the Liberal Party to find out if it would vote for a motion of censure – and he was not disappointed. The Liberals, spinning like a top, assured him they would be ready, indeed that they were anxious, to take part in talks with the government on the future of the Acts, but, equally, they were ready to vote for any motion that would prevent such talks from beginning.

Fortified by that display of Liberal logic, the opposition tabled their own vote of no confidence. We can truly say that once the leader of the opposition discovered what the Liberals and the SNP would do, she found the courage of their convictions.

So, tonight, the Conservative Party, which wants the Act repealed and opposes even devolution, will march through the lobby with the SNP, which wants independence for Scotland, and with the Liberals, who want to keep the Act. What a massive display of unsullied principle!

The minority parties have walked into a trap. If they win, there will be a general election. I am told that the current joke going around the House is that it is the first time in recorded history that turkeys have been known to vote for an early Christmas . . .

Callaghan defended his government's achievements:

We have given high priority to new investment in industrial plant and machinery, through tax reliefs and direct financial aid, and our industries have responded by investing more. We have made the restraint of inflation an overriding priority to keep our costs down. We have doubled our programme to train skilled men and women for new jobs and we have established the national enterprises like the Rolls-Royce aero-engines that will power the new American Boeing aircraft, and the microprocessor venture in which we must mark our place among the world leaders . . . If the Conservative Party were to get its hands on our affairs, it would be an act of vandalism . . .

I know that the opposition want to forget the years 1970–74 . . . What was the result when they were elected? Property speculators were given a free hand . . . credit control was abolished, and the money supply was increased to finance some pretty phoney finance companies. The Conservatives opened up one of the most discreditable periods in the history of the City of London . . . Now some of the speculators are emerging from their holes, rubbing their hands once again. I warn them not to count their chickens before their cheques bounce.

The Conservatives failed, when they were in government, to safeguard our greatest national asset – North Sea oil . . . They left gaping loopholes in the rules governing corporation tax paid by the oil companies. They did not even negotiate an arrangement to ensure that the United Kingdom, the home country, would ensure for itself a substantial proportion of the oil that was produced . . .

The right hon. lady calls for less government at local level. Does she really think we have forgotten the handiwork of the right hon. Members for Leeds North-East [Sir Keith Joseph] and for Worcester [Mr Walker]? Let her reflect, when she calls for less bureaucracy, that local authority manpower between 1970 and 1974 increased by nearly 300,000 – the biggest increase in bureaucracy ever in any comparable period.

In the Health Service the right hon. Member for Leeds North-East achieved the unenviable double of setting up a new form of organisation that was unsuited to the needs of the service and at the same time of dramatically increasing the numbers working in the administration. It does not lie in the mouths of the opposition to call for a reduction in bureaucracy, or for the right hon. lady to speak, as she did at Solihull, of Whitehall strangling local democracy.

The right hon. lady complains about inflation, and justifiably so. So do I, regularly. At 9.6 per cent it is higher than it should be, but we have brought it down from 25 per cent. What happened between 1970 and 1974? It more than doubled. Today, the figure that is complained of is lower than when the Conservative Party left office . . .

What about the pensioners? During the Conservatives' term of office, pensioners' living standards fell behind those of the population who were working. By contrast, this government . . . has improved the standard of life of the pensioner after he or she retires, by comparison with the wage earner . . .

Let need, not greed be our motto . . .

'The final scenes of the debate and vote were the most exciting anyone could remember. Mr Michael Foot, the Leader of the House, whooped and bawled his way through a magnificent, outlandish, winding up. He was in full Footage. If Mrs Thatcher is half as much a threat to socialism as he made out, the country is saved,' was the verdict of the *Telegraph* sketch:[530]

[Comparing the preparedness of SNP MPs to follow their leader into 'the lobby with those who are most bitterly opposed to the establishment of a Scottish Assembly', to 'the armies of ancient Rome' declaring to their General 'Hail Emperor, those who are about to die salute you,' Foot turned to] the leader of the Liberal Party. He knows that I would not like to miss him out. I am sure that I shall elicit the support and sympathy of [Mrs Thatcher] when I say that she and I have always shared a common interest in the development of this young man. If the right hon. lady has anything to say about the matter, I shall be happy to give way to her. I should very much like to know, as I am sure would everybody else, what exactly happened last Thursday night. I do not want to misconstrue anything, but did she send for him or did he send for her – or did they do it by billet-doux? Cupid has already been unmasked. This is the first time I have ever seen a Chief Whip who could blush. Anybody who was responsible for arranging this most grisly of assignations has a lot to answer for.

That brings me to the right hon. lady. I have never in this House or elsewhere, so far as I know, said anything discourteous to her, and I do not intend to do so. I do not believe that this is the way in which politics should be conducted. That does not mean that we cannot exchange occasional pleasantries. What the right hon. lady has done today is to lead her troops into battle snugly concealed behind a Scottish nationalist shield, with the boy David holding her hand.

I must say to the right hon. lady – and I should like to see her smile – that I am even more concerned about the fate of the right hon. gentleman than I am about her. She can look after herself. But the leader of the Liberal Party – and I say this with the utmost affection – has passed from rising hope to elder statesman without any inter-vening period whatsoever . . .

So what will happen? What will once again be the choice at the next election? It will not be so dissimilar from the choice that the country had to make in 1945, or even in 1940 when the Labour Party had to come to the rescue of the country – (*Hon. members:* 'Oh') . . .

Mr Foot: It was on a motion of the Labour Party that the House of Commons threw out the Chamberlain government in 1940. It was thanks to the Labour Party that Churchill had the chance to serve the country in the war years. Two-thirds of the Conservative Party at that time voted for the same reactionary policies as they will vote for tonight. It is sometimes in the most difficult and painful moments of our history that the country has turned to the Labour Party for salvation, and it has never turned in vain. We saved the country in 1940, and we did it again in 1945. We set out to res-cue the country – or what was left of it – in 1974. Here again in 1979 we shall do the same (*interruption*).

Mr Speaker: Order. The noise in the Chamber prevents me from hearing what the Lord President is saying.

Mr Foot: They are trying to stop me from getting your vote as well, Mr Speaker. (*Hon. members:* 'Shame'). I do not know why Conservative members are saying that this is shameful. I think that it is high time that the Tory Party recovered some sense of humour, even if it has lost everything else – (*interruption*). Conservative members real-ly ought to have had plenty of practice at laughing at themselves over these recent years, and they should make a better effort on this occasion . . .

Despite Foot's wit, Labour lost by one vote. After the announcement, Callaghan 'rose and the House fell silent', wrote *Telegraph* sketch writer Frank Johnson, 'smilingly, he announced a general election. Both leaders were cheered out of the chamber by their fol-lowers. Amid Tory jeers some Labour members, including Mr [Eric] Heffer of Walton, Mr [Bob] Cryer of Keighly and Mr [Chris] Price of Lewisham West, stayed behind and sang "The Red Flag", which must have been worth a few votes to the Tories in the marginals.'[531]

Some claim that Labour might have won had Callaghan called an election in October 1978, before the Winter of Discontent had so damaged the credibility of the government.

We will never know if that would have been the case, though it is, frankly, unlikely, though the Conservatives might have had a smaller majority. 'Those who believe that we could have won then in the autumn are the sort that make their judgements from reading the *Guardian*, rather than getting out on the streets,' was the typically pungent assessment of Employment Minister John Golding.[532] True, Labour had an opinion poll lead during October/November 1978, but it had been 7 per cent behind the Conservatives in September and it had spent most of the previous year marginally behind. Moreover, given that the Gallup opinion poll closest to the actual election overestimated Labour's support by 4 per cent, it is likely that the favourable polls of October/November 1978 also overstated Labour's support.

At the actual election, on a slightly higher turnout, Labour secured 11,532,148 votes, more than in October 1974, but a reduced share of the vote, 36.9 per cent. The Conservatives increased their vote by over three million on October 1974, securing 13,697,690 and 43.9 per cent. The Liberal vote fell by just over a million, giving them 13.8 per cent and eleven seats. The SNP reaped the whirlwind they had unleashed, being reduced from eleven seats to just two. Defeated MPs included Labour's Education Secretary Shirley Williams and former Liberal leader Jeremy Thorpe. For the first time, Labour support among manual workers fell to a bare 50 per cent (when Labour had lost in 1970 it had been 58 per cent).[533] Some 35 per cent of manual workers had voted Conservative, up from 24 per cent in 1974.[534]

Margaret Thatcher had led the Conservatives back to power. Labour was again tasting opposition, a flavour to which it would become all too accustomed over the next eighteen years. One of the most immediate consequences for Labour of the loss of office was the loss of Prime Ministerial patronage. As Prime Minister, Callaghan appointed all his ministers and whips. In opposition, twelve of his shadow Cabinet were elected by the full parliamentary party in an annual beauty contest. The first shadow Cabinet election came in June and saw the first head-to-head contest between the rival 'machines' of the two main factional groupings within the PLP: the left-wing Tribune Group and the moderate Manifesto Group.[535] The Tribune Group was largely the heir to the Keep Left Group/Bevanite flame. Indeed its 1965 'manifesto of aims' was entitled 'Keep Left'. It had been founded in the wake of Labour's 1964 general election victory by a small group of MPs meeting in the Commons office of Ian Mikardo, and by the late 1970s numbered some 80 MPs.[536]

The moderates had lacked any factional organisation since the Gaitskellite Campaign for Democratic Socialism had disbanded in 1965, and even that had been largely extra-parliamentary, established as it had been as a counterweight to CND and the *Tribune* 'Brains Trusts' in the constituencies. Though the left had thrown most of the moderates off the NEC constituency section by the early 1950s, it had never come near to doing the same in the shadow Cabinet elections of 1951-63 or early 1970s. The left candidates elected, Nye

Bevan, Tony Greenwood and, if he be counted as such, Wilson, in the 1950s, had been the exceptions. During 1951–64 'Bevanites' such as Dick Crossman and Barbara Castle had only ever been appointed, never elected, members of the front bench. Apart from Michael Foot, the left-wingers who were elected during 1970–73, such as Castle, Silkin, Shore and Benn, were all former Cabinet ministers with a far broader base of support than simply the Tribune Group (indeed Benn had always remained aloof from it). The election of a new generation of more left-wing backbenchers in February 1974 changed the balance of the parliamentary party and a split vote among several moderate candidates had enabled Ian Mikardo to win the election for chair of the Parliamentary Labour Party. The moderates were shocked into action and created the Manifesto Group as a counterweight to Tribune. Manifesto members were pro-NATO, supported multilateral nuclear disarmament, believed in a mixed economy, often supported incomes policy and were usually pro-EEC. Tribunites were invariably anti-EEC, often anti-American, pro-CND, wanted more nationalisation, import controls, and were sceptical of incomes policy. Both groups, during 1974–79, numbered some 70–80 MPs. After the October 1974 election the PLP chair was again up for the election. Battle was joined between 'Tribune' and 'Manifesto' and Mikardo was beaten by the 'Manifesto' champion, former Welsh Secretary Cledwyn Hughes. Manifesto also secured the vice-chair position for Tam Dalyell.

The 1979 shadow Cabinet elections saw an overwhelming success for the Manifesto Group. All but one of their 'slate' of nine were elected.[537] Denis Healey came top, followed by the anti-EEC duo of John Silkin and Peter Shore. Callaghan reshuffled his pack. Shore became shadow Foreign Secretary and former Foreign Secretary David Owen, who had done less well in the shadow Cabinet popularity poll, went to shadow Energy. Silkin, who had been Agriculture Minister, got Industry, Roy Hattersley, who wanted Industry, shadowed Environment and Bill Rodgers, who wanted something economic and rejected Education, got Defence. Eric Varley moved from Industry to Employment, while Albert Booth went from Employment to Transport, where he was to take on the young Peter Mandelson as his researcher. Education went to Neil Kinnock, who hadn't been elected to the shadow Cabinet but whose talents Callaghan was determined to harness. Kinnock had, with the hard-left Bolsover MP Dennis Skinner, been elected on to the constituency section of Labour's NEC the previous year, knocking off Tribune veteran Ian Mikardo and moderate Jack Ashley, who had defied political gravity to secure election in the first place.

One absence from the shadow Cabinet was Tony Benn, who had decided not to stand; he would instead be focusing his prodigious energies into converting Labour from the party it had been into the party he wanted it to become. 'From his base in the Home Policy Committee flowed the lava of new commitments,' wrote Derby Labour MP Phillip Whitehead. 'Each policy change pushed back the Labour right wing towards the beach.'[538]

FIFTY-THREE

Post-mortem 1979

' "Jim will fix it," they said. Ay, he fixed it.
He fixed all of us. He fixed it for me in particular'

'Nothing in the history of the Labour Party can be compared, in its sheer viciousness, with the Brighton conference of October 1979,' wrote Peter Shore, Labour's new shadow Foreign Secretary. It opened with 'a poisonous speech from the party's chairman for the year, Far-Left Frank Allaun,' alleging that 'the parliamentary leadership had defied, ignored and betrayed the wishes of the rank and file':[539]

The feeling was growing up at the grassroots about the parliamentary leaders: 'Whatever we say they take no notice at all.' That is a very serious feeling. A year ago the TUC conference almost unanimously rejected the rigid and inflexible 5 per cent wage ceiling. The Labour Party conference a month later voted equally solidly. But the Cabinet majority took no notice. Hence the troubles of January and February (*applause*). And this is why Mrs Thatcher is in Number Ten Downing Street at the moment (*applause*). This was not the first occasion by any means on which Labour spokesmen have ignored the grassroots. By the time last winter was upon us the Labour government had rejected the pleas of the Labour Party and of the trade unions for action to restore full employment and to reverse the cuts in public spending. This is the real issue behind all the reforms now before this conference.

How do we see that this does not recur? By insisting on greater respect for conference decisions by the parliamentary leaders . . .

This year there are pages of resolutions on our agenda seeking three changes . . . First, to see that every MP faces a re-election conference once between each election . .

Secondly, to see that the leader is elected by the whole party and not just part of it, that is by the Parliamentary Labour Party . . . Thirdly, there is the proposal that the manifesto should be drawn up by the NEC in consultation with the leader and deputy leader – who are already NEC members – and with Labour MPs. Indeed, the whole party would be involved by a programme brought for manifesto purposes before the party conference.

If this meant a more radical manifesto I would weep no tears. It was in the years when Labour had its most radical manifestos that it did best. I am thinking in particular of the 1945 manifesto . . . And in 1964 and in 1974 similarly we had really progressive election programmes, on which we won . . .

'When I think of that conference, held in Brighton, under the dreadful chairmanship of Frank Allaun, I only console myself that I am not back there in reality,' wrote former Employment Minister John Golding.[540] The great constitutional changes demanded by the Bennites outlined in Allaun's opening address were to dominate the conference.

Following Allaun's opening address came the general election post-mortem debate. Notably, Allaun failed to call one speaker who did not lay the blame on the government for having let the party down. Former Selly Oak MP Tom Litterick, described by sketch writer Edward Pearce as sounding 'like rancour and resentment made flesh and sent to a conference',[541] theatrically brandished a bundle of papers in his hand before hurling it to the conference floor as he reached the climax of his speech, for which, grasping at, but perhaps not quite reaching, populist metaphor, he invoked the analogy of Jimmy Savile:

> . . . Governments, and only governments, win or lose elections. Oppositions do not. It follows therefore that the Labour government lost the last election, and it is our business this week to understand how that election was lost . . . I have in my hand a sheaf of documents; each one is labelled 'Labour Party Campaign Handbook'. Each one on a separate topic – women's rights, the disabled, EEC, housing and so on, and each one drawn up by your NEC based on not one but many conference resolutions, based on not one NEC meeting but on hundreds of hours of committee and sub-committee work. It was these documents that your NEC sought to incorporate in our election manifesto this year. Then, one day in April of this year, Jim Callaghan turned up, and this is what he did to your policies. The end result was that fatuous, vacuous document called 'The Labour Party Election Manifesto 1979'. 'Jim will fix it,' they said. Ay, he fixed it. He fixed all of us. He fixed me in particular (*applause*).
>
> Our common sense tells us that Jim could not fix it. Our common sense tells us that Jim cannot fix it. And the evidence of history is that he certainly did not fix it. And we should not allow him to fix it. We should not expect him to fix it. At the very least it is too much to ask of one man – at the very least – and there are other interpretations . . .

For former Cabinet minister Roy Mason, 'If anyone these days complains about Tony Blair's stage management, they should remember the venomous shambles of the 1979 conference and those that followed. This was when decisions were taken which would keep Labour out of power for nearly a generation.'[542] 'The real attack on Mr Callaghan,' observed sketch writer Edward Pearce, 'came not from some lurking delinquent but from the party's machine-minder. Mr Ron Hayward, with a voice like curdled Cotswold cream,'[543] delivered 'a truly astonishing speech'[544] shadow Foreign Secretary Peter Shore remembered:

> . . . Is this debate to be a bit of Shakespeare? I come not to praise Callaghan but to bury him (*applause*). It was not a one-man Cabinet, was it? (*applause*). If we are going to start slinging labels about, let us get it around everybody's neck . . . We have got to be fair when we apportion blame . . . The divisions in this party start in the House of Commons . . .

Every single MP and every single defeated MP, when they were selected, signed a little bit of paper . . . They all signed the same: 'If elected we will stand by the constitution and the rules of the Parliamentary Labour Party.' That means the conference. I am very worried that they forget it once they get there. I still say that we did not – and you over there did not – select, raise the money, work to send an MP to the House of Commons to forget whence he came and whom he represents (*applause*). I read all the papers. One I read the other day – it cannot be true – said that one MP said, 'If I do not get my way this conference I will resign.' I have got some advice for them . . . I have got a queue a mile long that wants to go to the House of Commons (*laughter and applause*). It is a very short queue that wants to be Branch Secretary . . . I am sick of their being maligned as Trotskyists, Marxists, and every other label tied round their necks. I refer to them as activists . . . If that section of the hall departs tomorrow – what they represent – the people who do all the work year in, year out, the secretaries, the chairmen, the councillors – if that section departs, brothers in the trade union movement, you could not replace them for me over the next couple of years and you know it (*applause*) . . .

If it is to be said – and it has been said – that we lost the election because of the Winter of Discontent – it has been said that Alan Fisher's lads and lasses and Moss Evans lost us the election with the Winter of Discontent – if that is it, you have got to ask the first question: why was there a Winter of Discontent? The reason was that, for good or ill, the Cabinet, supported by MPs, ignored Congress and conference decisions. It is as simple as that (*applause*).

The Tories do it much better than we do. I wish our ministers and our Prime Minister would sometimes act in our interests like a Tory Prime Minister acts in their interests (*applause*). They make no bones about it . . . They say the haves are going to have more and the have-nots are going to have a little less. What we ought to be doing when we are in power, whether they term me a class warrior or not, we should be looking to our half of the nation that are the producers of wealth that put us there to do a job of work for them (*applause*) . . .

If you are going to say, or allow it to be said, that socialism failed, may I say this quite quietly and not in any way to raise applause, in my 46 years of membership of the party I have never seen it try socialism in any sense. You have nibbled at it. You pay tribute to Clause Four. I print it on your membership cards. People will make speeches from the rostrum and they will get a lot of applause for Clause Four. But you do not mean Clause Four. When we are in office we do not do anything about Clause Four. The last thing we want to do is to take things into public ownership, and when we do we appoint Tories to run them (*applause*). Fancy making a burglar the manager of the local bank . . .

'When it was over,' recalled Roy Hattersley, 'Jim Callaghan asked me for my opinion of what I had heard. I told him that I was undecided between "deplorable" and "despicable". He chose "despicable".'[545] Ron Hayward had been appointed as Labour's General Secretary in 1972. His rival, Assistant General Secretary Gwyn Morgan, had been backed by both Callaghan and Jenkins. Perhaps in consequence, Wilson had voted with the left to back Hayward producing a fourteen-fourteen tie on the NEC, broken by Tony Benn's casting vote in favour of Hayward. Hayward claimed personally to have burned the head-quarters files on left-wing extremists when he took office. As General Secretary over the next ten years, he would resolutely oppose attempts to tackle Labour's infiltration by Trotskyist groups such as Militant, do nothing to counter their takeover of the Labour Party Young Socialists (LYPS) and its seat on the NEC, and would appoint Militant supporter Andy Bevan to a staff job at Labour headquarters. He would also abolish the long-standing 'proscribed list' of organisations incompatible with Labour Party mem-bership. Hayward's benevolent indulgence of the extreme left, encouraged as it was by many on the NEC, was one reason why there were so many delegates at the conference baying for Callaghan's blood.

In the Moscow Show Trial that the conference had come to resemble, it was not until the following day, Tuesday morning, that anyone was given a chance to put the case for the defence. That person was Callaghan, whose 'Leader's Speech' was 'effective, to be candid', conceded Benn.[546] It was restrained, almost quiet in tone, but firm in its conviction nevertheless. Unusually for the speech of a Labour leader, it concluded with a quotation from a former Vice-President of the United States of America, one who might well have been the most progressive US President of the twentieth century, but was undone by the radical left wing of his own party, Hubert Humphrey:

> [Confronting] the charge that the Labour government and the Parliamentary Labour Party failed to carry out the manifesto or ignored the policies put forward by confer-ence and by the National Executive Committee, [Callaghan declared,] I wish to put the record straight ... You asked that North Sea oil should be brought under public own-ership and control: we did it ... You asked that the Price Commission should be set up: it was ... You asked that there should be a National Enterprise Board to stimulate British industry with new capital, new management and now the Tories are fettering it. You asked for Scottish and Welsh Development Agencies: they were set up ... They safeguarded old jobs, they developed new jobs, they built new factories and now the Tories are reducing the resources that were devoted to them.
>
> Reference has been made to the Employment Protection Act. Was that not worth-while, giving greater security to men and women in jobs and now the Tories are seri-ously weakening and undermining it. The aircraft industry, the shipbuilding industry, both nationalised and nationalised with a majority of one – and now the Tories are try-ing to sell them or shut them down ...
>
> Women's rights were established more firmly by legislation; legislation against discrimination against women in employment and in housing and now the Tories are undermining those rights. The improvement of the real standard of life for the pensioner by linking their pension increases to wage earners' pay increases – not worthwhile? Well, the Tories think it was; they are now abandoning it and every

pensioner will suffer as a result. Eighty-three per cent of children at the end of our period of office in comprehensive schools, and now the Tories are trying to reverse that.

And what about the other achievements? Legislation for a new Race Relations Act. The effective ending of the agricultural tied cottage. New benefits for the disabled. The highest number of doctors and nurses ever; 45,000 more nurses when we left office than when we came in; 5,800 more doctors. The largest number of teachers ever. Is that not socialism in action? And so I could go on (*applause*). The Devolution Bills, the mobility allowances for the disabled, the child allowances, invalid in-care, and I have left out a score of others . . .

How dare the government tell these groups – the children, the pensioners, the sick – come back in two generations; the money supply is more important than you (*applause*). [The] Conservative idea of values is to stick a price tag on everything. Some things and some values cannot be priced. People do expect community support. They do expect the government to bring forward programmes of action to protect our basic rights. The government is neglecting that responsibility today and it is our duty to take up the challenge . . .

The problems of the 1980s are before you . . . I sum up to you in six or seven words what they will be – employment, poverty, the use of resources – yes, the Ecology Party may not score many votes but they got to the root of the problem – (*applause*) – race and peace . . .

In the words of Hubert Humphrey, and I will end with this: 'Our strength is not to be measured by our military capacity alone, by our industry or by our technology. We will be remembered not for the power of our weapons, but for the power of our compassion and our dedication to human welfare.' Those were his words and that, Mr Chairman, should be the true face of socialism that this conference, and we ourselves, should present to our people – (*applause*) – and let me add, in this increasingly interdependent world, our compassion and our dedication which we should show in our own internal matters, every one of us, whenever we appear, not the arrogance of power . . .

It had been the suggestion of a constituency party to follow the leader's speech with a question and answer session and Callaghan had thought it a good idea. Unfortunately, instead of being an opportunity for him to explain the actions of the government, the antagonistic quality of the delegates called by Chairman Allaun to the rostrum and the barbed questions with which they sought to catch Callaghan out served only to reinforce the show trial atmosphere.

Of the three great constitutional battles Allaun had highlighted in his opening address, two were scheduled for debate on Tuesday afternoon. The first centred on whether to replace the existing system of electing the party leader and deputy by the MPs with an 'electoral college' composed of MPs, constituency party conference delegates and trade unions. Though on one level the debate was about democracy the sub-text was the issue of who might be most likely to do better or worse under any new system, and the fact that the existing system was perceived to have avoided the election of leaders from the left wing of the party.[547] Under the existing system, there were simply insufficient MPs prepared to vote for Tony Benn to make him leader. For his supporters it was therefore clear that the only way he could become leader would be to change the electoral system to one that gave power to trade union leaders and constituency activists. This was the case expounded that afternoon by Michael Meacher, who had become one of Benn's closest parliamentary lieutenants, so close, in fact, that he was nicknamed Benn's 'vicar on earth':

> The leader of the party is accountable, not just to the parliamentary party, but to the movement as a whole and he should, therefore, be elected by those to whom he is more broadly accountable . . . there is no single socialist or social democratic party in Western Europe that elects its leader solely through its parliamentary party. In Germany, in France, in Italy, in Austria and in many other countries too, the socialist and social democratic parties have all opted for an electoral college system . . . But changing the method of election, comrades, is not, by itself, enough. What we also need is a system of regular reselection and there is not anything particularly novel or remarkable about this either. The parliamentary party already annually reselects its full leadership each year it is in opposition. But there is one simple overriding reason why the wider electoral system, the wider electoral college and a system of reselection, is so important and it is this.
>
> What this debate on democracy is all about comes down in the end to one very simple thing. What is the point of having a carefully prepared and radical agenda in opposition if the heart of it is put into cold storage once the party is in power?

It was because they feared that ordinary Labour members lacked the enthusiasm for Benn of the hard-left activists and some of the trade union leaders that the Bennite left opposed the 'democratic nonsense'[548] of 'One Member One Vote' (OMOV) for all ordinary members of the party. Its pioneering advocates were the Electricians' Union, who had introduced OMOV postal ballots in their own union during the 1960s, following the Communist ballot-rigging scandal. They had found that though Communist members continued noisily to fight their corner at branch meetings, rank-and-file union members voted for the moderate anti-Communist candidates to run the union. While other moderates warned that constitutional change would be a leap in the dark and called for 'the most careful consideration'[549] before any precipitate action, it was only Electricians' Union chief Frank Chapple who spoke out in favour of OMOV in the debate that afternoon and struck at the heart of the issue:

> Ee, you do make a lad feel at home! Comrade Meacher has two single points for the solution of all our problems. I wish that it were so (*interruption*) . . .
>
> In so far as who the party leader is broadly responsible and accountable to, it has to be, if it is the next Prime Minister we are electing and not simply a leader of the party, to the whole of the British electorate . . .

This debate is not about democracy and accountability. It is not about extending the size of the NEC or broadening its composition. It is not about involving the mass of party members, or developing closer links with the grassroot views of Labour voters. It is not about giving a greater say to the constituency parties. If it were, the NEC could not have avoided questions and questioning the block vote system; nor could it tolerate allowing delegates to attend this conference on the patently untrue basis that they each represent one thousand party members. Nor could it allow the Militant Tendency to continue to act as a secret cabal within the party – (*applause*) – meeting before meetings, deciding resolutions in advance (*interruption*) . . . Why did the NEC not suggest a ballot vote of all party members to elect the leader? It is good enough to elect trade union General Secretaries, like Moss Evans and I. Why do they now suggest an electoral college, as unrepresentative as the present system?

No, this debate is not about democracy – it is about power and about policy . . . For 20 years this debate has been fudged and avoided. Instead of resolving it we have seen our membership fall, our electoral popularity sink and now it prevents us from effectively opposing the most doctrinaire government since the war. So, I do not agree with patching up this division any longer. I do not agree with suppressing our differences with talk of unity. There can be no lasting unity until political differences which divide us are settled one way or the other.

I am for another Labour government and a social democratic Britain. I am for a mixed economy and a free society and it is about time we fought it out with those who are not for these issues. Our movement has often been likened to a broad church. I accept this. I am not in favour of a narrow party which imitates the mistakes of the Marxist left and gleefully treats any dissident and disagreement as an excuse for an ideological purge of those who disagree. That is right. I know what democrats you are (*interruption*). Are you going to give me a fair hearing? . . . (*further interruption and Chairman's intervention*).

When the votes were counted it was the left who had been defeated. The AUEW engineering union's conference delegation had split on the issue, and with no mandate to vote in favour of changing the system for electing the party leader, they voted against. It was enough to carry the day against the electoral college. But it was also clear that with few backing the Electricians' Union's call for real democracy through an OMOV ballot of individual members, it was only a matter of time before, as Benn wrote in his diary that night, 'We'll come back next year and put it right.'[550] It was truly a 'heads I win, tails I come back and beat you next year' view of democracy.

The second great constitutional debate took place that same Tuesday afternoon. The NEC left had got the NEC to waive the 'three-year rule' and immediately following the debate on the system for electing the party leader, it was time yet again to debate the mandatory reselection of MPs, despite it having been defeated the previous year. Prominent among those calling for action was Liverpool Militant Derek Hatton,[551] 'as always dressed to kill', recalled Golding. 'As delegates applauded, MPs huddled in their seats in the hall, feeling more and more resentful at the total misrepresentation of their commitment to the cause.'[552] Hatton began his speech with a swipe at

> the carpet baggers like Brown, like Marsh, like Taverne, like Robens, like Mayhew (*applause*). And, of course, Prentice, [mandatory reselection, insisted Hatton, meant that] this treacherous rogues' gallery need never again be repeated . . . A crucial factor in the debate about the reselection of MPs . . . [is] that some right-wing MPs have memberships in their constituencies of less than two hundred. Members of previous Labour governments left the Labour movement for more lucrative fields, not only in Europe, and left Ron Hayward asking of one of them: how could he leave his constituency party in such a mess? I do not think comrades need reminding of Brian Walden, as it was covered in *Labour Weekly*, who left his constituency party with only 71 members.
>
> . . . In Liverpool recently we had a public meeting on the question of what Tory policies mean and how to fight them. This attracted an audience of almost 120 new members to the party. With all these attempts, the new members found the question of accountability of the Parliamentary Labour Party through the individual MPs totally unpalatable, particularly those workers who were used to working with accountable shop stewards' committees. It is only when the rank and file feel that their elected representatives are accountable with, of course, a socialist programme can the party really grow . . . It is only . . . with the correct socialist programme, that we will build a mass Labour Party . . .

One of the few who spoke up against Hatton and his allies was Post Office Engineering Union leader Bryan Stanley:

> . . . This is being done in the name of democracy, so some people say. Democracy, what crimes are committed in thy name. Because if this is democratic, can a constituency party who is totally satisfied with its Member of Parliament say 'No, we don't wish to carry out this mandatory reselection.' The word 'mandatory' seems to imply they cannot. How democratic is that? . . . [Instead Stanley advocated the compromise position previously advocated by the NEC:] The procedure that we adopted last year provides real democracy and I suggest that the campaign promoting this ought to now call themselves the campaign against Labour Party democracy because that is what they are doing. Since last year, when this was put to conference and accepted by conference, the Executive have done a turn-around and it was a turn-around that in my view was extremely weak and even cowardly, because there used to be a leader of this party that said, 'Fight, fight and fight again', but this Executive seems to say, 'Vote, vote and vote again until we get the result that the splinter group want' . . .

In conclusion, Stanley pointed out that the amendments to Labour's rules enabling the introduction of mandatory reselection were so badly drafted as to be in breach of Labour's constitution.

The left ignored his warning and the vote went against Stanley and in favour of introducing mandatory reselection. 'The right are furious at their defeat,' wrote an exultant Benn, 'Even if the election of the leader is left to the PLP, mandatory reselection changes the whole balance of power in the party.'[553] But it was a false dawn. Stanley was right. The NEC meeting following the conference received legal advice that the amendments that had been rushed through to enable the process of mandatory reselections to begin immediately had been botched and any MP deselected under them could mount a legal challenge.

The third great constitutional change demanded by the Bennite left was the removal of the power of the Cabinet or shadow Cabinet to influence (and the leader to veto) the content of the election manifesto. Instead, it was demanded, sole power of decision should rest with the NEC, and therefore, so the left believed, with them. The NEC elections the previous day confirmed them in this belief. With the election of hard-left Jo Richardson to replace Barbara Castle, who had stepped down to become leader of Labour's MEPs in Brussels, the NEC had just swung even more definitively to the left. If Castle had fought Callaghan on occasion out of bitterness at Callaghan's actions over *In Place of Strife*, Richardson, claimed Golding, 'needed no such motivation. She seemed genetically programmed to destroy.'[554] Stuart Weir, a young delegate from Hackney, proposed a resolution instructing the NEC to present the next year's conference in 1980 with constitutional amendments to vest control of the manifesto in the hands of the NEC. The issue on which he (and others who spoke in his support like Gavin Strang)[555] fastened was one that came to have almost totemic significance in the debate: Callaghan's decision to block a commitment to abolish the House of Lords:[556]

> ... the point of winning elections, and winning power, is to carry out agreed policies, to make fundamental changes in this country ... Comrades, we were clear on the policies on which we wanted to fight the last election. And what happened? When it came to the crunch, Mr Callaghan presented an entirely new draft from Ten Downing Street which became the basis for the manifesto. An official NEC report says that that draft ignored entire chapters of party policy ... He vetoed, for example, the pledge to abolish the House of Lords, and that pledge was not the only casualty. Scores of party political commitments were killed or maimed ...

Following an anguished appeal from Derby MP and former 'World at War' television producer Phillip Whitehead for the conference to look beyond the 'internal affairs' of the party and the 'ritual vilification' of the parliamentary party, a full-throated attack on the left from Sutton constituency delegate Geoff Guiness precipitated uproar:

> Mr Chairman ... Voters of this country do not want revolution or extreme left-wing socialism (*applause*). May's election proved that point. Mrs Thatcher's programme is as far away from pure socialism as you could get. Yet Mrs Thatcher won the election with

probably the biggest majority since the war, and to ram that home three months later after her first one hundred days, in spite of the cuts, in spite of the price increases, in spite of the rich man's Budget, a nationwide Gallup poll put her even further ahead. Why, you may ask? I will tell you why. Because the voters of this country are afraid that extreme left-wing socialism is the same as Communism and they do not want authoritarian Communism (*applause*).

Let us for a moment compare the voting appeal of three prominent left-wing socialists against three moderate to right-wing socialists. Am I entitled to name the people concerned?

The Chairman: No, no personal attacks.

Geoff Guiness: Right, well I tell you that these three prominent left-wingers received lower personal votes in the last election than they did previously, and the most prominent one, who was seen signing a book in Harrods the other week, had his majority reduced, from 9,388 in 1974 to 1,890 in 1979, whereas many prominent right-wingers actually increased their personal votes (*uproar and applause*). The NEC have failed to appreciate (*slow hand-clapping*) . . .

The Chairman: No, no. No slow claps.

Geoff Guiness: . . . that the voters in this country are not political and they are guided in their voting patterns by newspaper headlines. Let me tell you this: the great tragedy here is that while Hurricane Thatcher is devastating the country and the caring society that Labour built up over the years, you, the NEC and indeed the PLP are quarrelling as to who should lead the rescue team. May I say this, with enemies like you Mrs Thatcher does not need friends (*applause*).

Guiness was echoed by APEX General Secretary Roy Grantham:

Mr Chairman, comrades, the idea that we lost the election because the manifesto was not socialist enough is a myth. Last year I came to this rostrum and I denounced the 5 per cent norm; I denounced inflationary free collective bargaining. I appealed to both sides to get together and reach a compromise agreement, or be beaten by the Tories. When I left the rostrum, Moss[557] gave me the thumbs down. That was what cost us the election, the foolish belief that votes in this hall are more important than the votes of the ordinary people at the ballot box (*applause*). No decision by conference is worth anything to this party if it cannot deliver votes in the country. If our objective is to defeat each other, rather than to defeat Mrs Thatcher, then this party is wasting its time . . .

Has the NEC the authority, the confidence and the ability to be the final body to determine the manifesto? (*cries of:* 'Yes'). We saw them solely and exclusively determine one manifesto and run one election this year, the campaign for the European election. What a disaster, what incompetence, what a defeat . . . They were told by every union involved with members that their proposals were not sound. They reported back to this conference but ended up by saying they still preferred their original proposals to the advice given by all the unions concerned . . .

But the biggest tanks on the lawn were backing Weir's resolution: it passed. The next year would see the NEC bring forward the amendments.

The following morning, Wednesday 3 October, was the climax of the 1979 conference: the debate on 'future policy'. It was polarised between a moderate resolution moved by Newcastle MP Mike Thomas, a second resolution demanding 'the nationalisation of two hundred or so monopolies' moved by Brighton's hardy perennial Militant-supporting delegate Ray Apps, and a third which blamed Labour's election defeat on 'the failure of the Labour government to implement policies as agreed by successive party conferences'. The debate heard a blunt defence of the government and its leader from Denis Healey.

> Some of our delegates have been providing a field day for the Tory press by attacking our party leader who was our greatest asset in the last general election (*applause*), attacking our Labour Members of Parliament who have been working for the movement under appallingly difficult conditions up to 80 hours a week without overtime for the last five years . . .
>
> Now I hope, comrades, that next year, when you have got the bad blood after the election disappointment out of your system, we will concentrate on building a policy which will get back for our movement the millions of voters we have lost, not to the Communist Party, not to the Militant group, but to the Tories and the Liberals in recent years. We can only do that if we accept that conference resolutions do not change the laws of arithmetic, that if we try to run the country the way the National Executive runs the party finances, it will not be possible for the trade unions to bail us out . . .

A contrasting and somewhat millenarian note was struck by an appeal to support Apps's resolution from Keir Hardie's nonagenarian protégé Lord [Fenner] Brockway (who in his teens had, before converting to socialism, campaigned for the pre-Asquith Liberal Party):

> In 72 years' membership of this party I have become cautious about predicting the time when we shall achieve democratic socialism. In the first decade of this century we young socialists thought that it would come within ten years . . . But I believe we now have an opportunity for democratic socialism such as we have never had before . . . This government is the embodiment of capitalism as never before. Comrades, this government is going to fail . . . Within a year we will have more unemployment, higher prices, more destruction of our economy than we have ever known, and this government will be the most unpopular of this century. This gives us our opportunity: Mrs Thatcher – capitalism; Labour – democratic socialism . . .

Brockway was 'tremendously inspiring', wrote Benn, who made the concluding speech of the debate, but the NEC's position was to reject Apps's 'Composite 30' on the same grounds it had in 1973 (nationalising '200 or so monopolies' in one go is rather a lot). For Benn 'it was, I think, my best conference speech':[558]

> . . . We must campaign for the politics of hope against the politics of fear. But what is the basis of our hope? Twenty years ago – and many delegates here will have been at that conference as I was – after the 1959 election, we were offered a new policy

founded upon the belief that full employment was here to stay, that a successful mixed economy would always generate sufficient wealth for Labour governments to finance rising public expenditure that would pay for expanding public services that were needed to narrow the gap between rich and poor and to end poverty and inequality. We now know that that vision of the future was an illusion, for compassion in administering decaying capitalism does not make that system work. It was tried by a succession of governments, and I say to conference that that idea of socialism, presented to us then, was not undermined by party conferences; it was finally killed off by the IMF when they demanded large cuts in public expenditure from the Labour Cabinet in November and December 1976 (*applause*).

Comrades, that option is no longer open to the nation or to the party, because it cannot give us back full employment. This is the moment of truth, not only for the party, but for the nation; that is why we must re-examine our own experience in office, not to recriminate but to learn the lessons of those years, to help us build for the future. And the main lesson was that despite all our work as a movement – and this is our 78th conference – we have not yet really changed the structure of power in our society, and what we are allowed to do when we are in office is not sufficient. I do not think any Labour minister would deny that the City of London still has the power to dictate secretly to Labour Cabinets in such a way as to secure greater gains for themselves within 24 hours than the trade unions can gain by long weeks of industrial disputes; that the multinationals can tell Cabinets what they want; that the Civil Service has enormous political power, because it is always there; that the Common Market and the IMF and the media with their capacity to terrorise ministers or to secure reshuffles still have a great influence in the nature of our society.

Let me spell out, comrades, very simply, the policies which successive Labour Party conferences have discussed and endorsed. If capital will not put the nation's savings and the workers' surplus back into re-equipment, we will put it on public account, with public accountability and public ownership, to re-equip our industries and to finance smaller cooperative enterprises (*applause*). We must use the oil revenues not to pay for imports of manufactured goods to destroy our industry, but to re-equip that industry and to finance our public services. We must have a breathing space through import controls to rebuild our industry, and there is no reason why, if you can negotiate your money supply with the International Monetary Fund, you cannot negotiate your trading patterns with your major trading partners. That is what we have said.

We want expanded public services, in education, health and housing. We want an end to patronage in the public sector, in the nationalised industries and in the public services (*applause*). Comrades, it is not only the House of Lords that should have gone. The present appointments system under which our public industries are run leads to authoritarianism, to centralisation and to bureaucracy which have cheated us of the true social control which we intended by common ownership (*applause*). We said all this in 1973 and we put it in our 1974 manifesto, and we won two elections on it. People speak as if such a policy would frighten the electorate, but you know, our credibility in the campaigns that lie ahead depends on whether we are prepared to tackle the power structures and win the battles fought out in Whitehall.

We are a party of democratic, socialist reform. I know that for some people the term 'reform' is a term of abuse. That is not so. All our greatest historical successes have been the product of reform: the repeal of the Combination Acts, the victory of the Chartists, the women's suffrage, the campaign for the Health Service, the miners' campaign for public ownership of the pits. What is wrong is not that reform has failed but that we have not campaigned for reform with sufficient vigour. As socialist reformers we have the usual problem of the reformer: we have to run the economic system to protect our people who are now locked in it while we change the system. And if you run it without seeking to change it then you are locked in the decay of the system, but if you simply pass resolutions to change it without consulting those who are locked in the system that is decaying, then you become irrelevant to the people you seek to represent . . .

There will be a tremendous battle and . . . we shall win new members, as Fenner Brockway said, as young people learn that what their grandfathers told them about the 1930s is true, and that as the little pockets of socialism that we have built up in our comprehensive schools, or our elderly people's dwellings, or our centres for the disabled, or in our Health Service, that as pockets of socialism are attacked by the Conservative government they will turn to see the relevance of what we are saying to them . . .

And with Benn's words ringing in their ears, his supporters returned to their constituencies to mobilise the 'pockets of socialism' for the struggle to come.

FIFTY-FOUR

The Road from Abertillery 1979–80

'If the hard-line leaders of the left want a fight to the finish they can have it. But if as a result they should split the party, they should not suppose that the inheritance will be theirs'

Since 1977 Roy Jenkins had been in Brussels as President of the European Commission. January 1981 would see the end of his four-year term of office and he had begun to contemplate his political future. One option was to return to Labour politics. Denis Healey was keen to appoint him the Foreign Secretary of any future Healey-led Labour government. Frank Chapple of the Electricians' Union had offered to help him get a seat. But Labour politics no longer appealed. Jenkins had not, in fact, voted at the 1979 election and his wife Jennifer had voted Liberal. Roy Jenkins, in Edward Pearce's neat paraphrase of the former US President LBJ, 'would not seek and could not gain, the leadership of the Labour Party of which he was just about a member, in a parliament of which he was not'.[559] He had seriously considered following the example of Chris Mayhew[560] and joining the Liberals, but Liberal leader David Steel argued that he would make more impact by setting up his own party of Labour dissidents and working in alliance with the Liberals.

On 22 November Jenkins gave the BBC's annual Dimbleby Lecture and used the occasion to launch an 'experimental political plane'. He attacked the two-party system and the first-past-the-post electoral system that underpinned it, chastised Labour's trade union link, and in effect called for a new centre party to realign British politics.

It clearly signalled Jenkins's intention to return to British politics, something that had been in doubt. But most of Labour's moderates saw it as unhelpful, fearing that it would be used by the hard left to cast doubt on their loyalty to Labour, and that it would incite division between the pro- and anti-EEC right. One of them was shadow Energy Secretary David Owen: 'For someone in my position trying, with others, to mobilise the Manifesto Group of MPs in Parliament and the Campaign for Labour Victory to fight a desperate battle inside the Labour Party, Roy's speech was a diversion from the task in hand. Roy was out of British politics and was bound to see things differently.' The next evening, at a constituency Labour Party dinner in south-west Staffordshire, Owen declared that 'the centre of the Labour Party must now stand firm. We will not be tempted by siren voices from outside, from those who have given up the fight from within.'[561]

As the extra-parliamentary activity of the hard left increased, putting moderates under more and more pressure in the constituencies, the Manifesto Group of Labour MPs had agreed that they needed themselves to create an extra-parliamentary arm. They called it the Campaign for Labour Victory and, based in the Highbury office of the Electricians' Union, it was in effect an attempt to re-create the old Gaitskellite Campaign for Democratic Socialism (CDS). It was launched with a speech from Bill Rodgers on 20 February 1977 at Westminster Central Hall in which he sought to differentiate between the legitimate and the extreme left:

> The legitimate left is a different matter. The legitimate left has been an essential ele-ment in the coalition of the Labour movement from the earliest days. We may disagree with it but we respect its right to exist. But the legitimate left has an obligation. It must not be a Trojan horse for the wreckers. It would betray its own form of radical-ism if it provided a way in for those with whom we have nothing in common. The Labour Party is the party of Bevan as well as of Gaitskell. The heirs of Bevan – the legit-imate left – have a role to play in saving the party.[562]

While Roy Jenkins remained in Brussels, the Manifesto Group and the Campaign for Labour Victory continued the battle to save the Labour Party from plunging further to the left. It was their party, even if Jenkins considered that it was no longer his. More important therefore than the Dimbleby Lecture in terms of the future intentions of the moderates within the Labour Party was a speech delivered by Bill Rodgers a week later, on 30 November 1979, to the annual dinner of Abertillery constituency Labour Party.[563] He called for a fight to the finish, and he gave the party a year to save itself. Rodgers cir-culated it to the press and some 30 colleagues 24 hours beforehand: 'if I was going to ruf-fle a lot of feathers I might as well do so properly':[564]

> Our party has a year – not much longer – in which to save itself . . . A year in which to start proving that it is a credible alternative to the harsh and divisive government of Mrs Thatcher.
>
> But the omens are not good. The National Executive Committee remains ruth-lessly committed to a Commission of Enquiry rigged in favour of a single point of view. Its exponents want to clip the wings of Members of Parliament. They want to choose a leader who will do their bidding and conform to their requirements. They want to dominate the manifesto-making process at election time.
>
> But the issue goes much beyond a debate on the rights and duties of MPs. It is deeper than superficial slogans about accountability. The real argument is about power and policies and whether our party should remain a broad coalition of democratic socialists capable of winning an election and having a successful period in government.
>
> A party of the far left – in which Tribune members would be the moderates – would have little appeal to the millions of voters who reject doctrinaire and extreme

solutions . . . I do not believe that many of us would want to be a passenger on such a gravy train to disaster. Unity, yes – we all want unity. But on whose terms and at what price? Compromise, yes – it is often necessary. But where does it end and appeasement begin? If the hard-line leaders of the left want a fight to the finish, they can have it. But if as a result they should split the party, they should not suppose that the inheritance will be theirs.

It is not the long-standing loyalists on the right and centre of the party who are seeking to dragoon their colleagues into ideological conformity. It is not the vast majority of Labour voters, past and present, who ask that their Members of Parliament should become puppets on a string. From Keir Hardie to Jim Callaghan, our party has believed in a practical, humanitarian socialism – a creed of conscience and reform rather than of class hatred. It has owed its inspiration to British radicals, trade unionists, cooperators, nonconformists and Christian socialists – not to Marx or Lenin. Its enemies have been prejudice and tyranny everywhere and its objective the spread of social justice and the enlargement of human freedom. It has stood for the supremacy of Parliament, the rule of law and a Britain adequately defended. It has fought for an open democratic system which would improve the prospect of a more dynamic economy and a less class-ridden society . . .

I have been a member of the Labour Party for 33 years – and a member of no other party. I joined because it embodied these ideals and principles and was full of fellowship and generosity. Most of you joined in the same spirit and for similar reasons. If our party should abandon or betray these principles, it would be a tragedy. But they would not die. They would survive because there would be men and women prepared to carry on the fight. The enthusiasm and the vision would endure and the standard-bearers would not be lacking. It is for our party itself to choose. I hope deeply that it will stay true to its great tradition and continue to be the best means of building the good society.

On 26 March 1980 Labour's NEC agreed to a proposal from TGWU leader Moss Evans for a special conference to discuss industrial policy. In the event the policy agenda it debated became slightly wider than that, incorporating demands for the removal of US cruise missiles from Britain, import controls, an extension of public ownership, amendments to the European Communities Act and the abolition of the House of Lords. It was entitled 'Peace, Jobs, Freedom' and the special conference was held on 31 May. David Owen had arrived late to hear several speeches advocating unilateral nuclear disarmament. On being told by Peter Shore and Bill Rodgers, respectively shadow Foreign and Defence Secretaries, that neither was planning to speak, he decided that if nobody else was then he would. He began with a swipe at the Tories' 'candy-floss society' and then switched to defence, advocating a multilateral, rather than unilateral, approach to disarmament. Uproar ensued:

. . . I am telling you as someone who has dealt with these negotiations (*cries of protest from floor*). I will say it to you again. If you think you will enter into arms control negotiations with your hands tied behind your back, with no form of leverage, you are deluding yourselves.

Chairman: Order. The speaker has a right to be heard, comrades. Please be quiet.

David Owen: If we want to take arms control and disarmament seriously, it cannot be on the basis of already pre-empting decisions on a unilateral national basis. We want the removal of the SS 20 and the removal of cruise missiles in Europe. Don't pre-empt that choice before you have even entered into negotiations . . .

It was when he was almost shouted down by hecklers at this conference that David Owen became a convert to the possibility of a breakaway party, believes Bill Rodgers.[565] Owen may well have been encouraged by the uncompromising tone of the speaker who followed him to the rostrum, former Liverpool fire-fighter Terry Fields. Fields, whose trademark dark sunglasses were to grace a thousand television screens, would later be selected as a Labour candidate, endorsed by the NEC, elected an MP and finally expelled for his continued support for Militant:

. . . In the party, in the country and in the trade union movement our class as a whole has got to grasp this document one hundred per cent and give it one hundred per cent support . . .

Thatcher, under the capitalist system and ideology, will never be able to act in any other way than she is doing today. People are calling her lunatic, a bad, wicked woman. My kids sit and watch the television set. If they could get their hands on her, they would rip the throat out of her. But they do this because they are children and they are childish. We are adult . . . She will never be able to act any other way than she is now acting under this system, and a Labour government, working within the same capitalist framework, will fail also as sure as night follows day, as past Labour governments have shown us.

How do we maintain the expansion of our economy within the present crisis? . . . there will be a strike of capital on behalf of the capitalist class of this country . . . The major part of the economy will remain in the hands of big business, and given the degree of control the document talks about – whatever that might mean – there will be undoubtedly a retaliation by the uncontrolled elements against us who are trying to implement this programme . . .

We need coordinated action by the whole of our class to get the Tories out and the democracy that is being pumped out in the capitalist press is their democracy, not ours. We will found a new democracy when we have created a socialist state in this country . . .

To the weak-hearted, the traitors and cowards I say: 'Get out of our movement. There is no place in it for you. Cross the House of Commons, join Prentice and do the work that he is doing at the moment.'

Fields was followed by young Fabian Society General Secretary Dianne Hayter, who, despite heckling, reminded delegates of 'our obligations' to the Third World and the danger of 'hurting countries much worse off than ourselves by import controls'. Hayter also asked delegates to consider the popularity among 'Labour voters, particularly women voters, of cheap T-shirts and cheap jeans for their kids', which import controls would block.

Denis Healey, who spoke towards the end of the debate, was barracked by shouts of 'out' from the floor before he had even opened his mouth:

> Comrade Chairman and friends and those who shouted 'out' . . . we certainly will not win the next election if we follow the advice given by one delegate this morning and sit on our hands and let the Tories take over and stay in power unless every dot and comma of our own particular ideology is accepted by the National Executive and by the party in its next election manifesto . . . We will not do it if instead of meeting the real needs of people we go on ideological ego trips or accept the clapped-out dogmas which are now being trailed by the toytown Trotskyists of the Militant group . . .

In the weeks following the 'Peace, Jobs, Freedom' conference, shadow Cabinet member John Silkin had publicly declared himself in favour of Britain's withdrawal from the EEC without a referendum. This was in flagrant defiance of party policy and collective shadow Cabinet responsibility. Yet nothing was done to discipline him. David Owen was incensed and organised a joint letter from himself, Bill Rodgers and Shirley Williams to the *Guardian* condemning the idea. It was this letter that established in the public mind a 'Gang of Three'. For Rodgers, however, the prospect of Labour committing itself to withdrawal from the EEC and to unilateral nuclear disarmament were not a basis even to consider leaving the Labour Party. On both these issues Labour had changed its views over the years and the pro-EEC anti-CND position had always won through in the end. The issue for Rodgers was the prospect of constitutional changes to the party which might make it impossible for the moderates ever to bring Labour back towards a more social-democratic policy agenda. That was, indeed, the explicit objective of those pushing the constitutional changes, who had united, since 1979, under the banner of the 'Rank and File Mobilising Committee'.

Matters came to a head over the weekend of 14–15 June 1980 at a special meeting of Labour's post-election committee of enquiry at Clive Jenkins's ASTMS education college at Bishop's Stortford. The committee had been set up by the NEC in the wake of Labour's 1979 conference and its composition was heavily biased towards the left (10–4 in Benn's estimation).'The grandeur of the occasion may be judged from the fact that Clive had bought goldfish for the pond especially,' remarked John Golding.[566] After a brief attempt by Callaghan, Foot and engineering leader Terry Duffy to defend the status quo, the pass was sold and the principle of an electoral college as demanded by the left conceded. Other than walking out, Callaghan felt he had no alternative but to cave in.

The following week at the shadow Cabinet meeting, most of the senior moderates followed Callaghan and Hattersley in accepting the principle of an electoral college to elect Labour's leader, albeit one with 50 per cent of the vote reserved to Labour MPs. For Bill Rodgers, one of the few who wanted to stand and fight to defend the status quo of election by MPs, this was 'total capitulation on a central issue'. 'We had suffered a mortal blow,' thought David Owen, 'with this albatross of an electoral college, MPs had lost the last democratic safeguard of being able to mobilise the parliamentary party against the NEC and if need be the Labour conference.'[567] David Owen was almost alone among MPs in backing the system advocated by Electricians' Union leader Frank Chapple at party conference the previous year, of a One Member One Vote postal ballot of ordinary party members. On 22 September, in advance of Labour's 1980 annual conference, twelve Labour backbenchers (immediately dubbed the 'Dirty Dozen') wrote a joint letter to The Times advocating One Member One Vote. It had little impact but to raise their profile on the putative hit-list of the hard left. Of the twelve only George Robertson was to survive as a Labour MP beyond the next election; all the others either suffered deselection, retired in despair or joined the SDP.[568]

FIFTY-FIVE

The Rising Tide of Bennery – Labour's Conference 1980

'It is not a question of left and right.
It is a question of right and wrong'

Labour's October 1980 annual conference opened in Blackpool against a backdrop of the Conservative government pressing firmly forward with the most right-wing agenda in living memory. Unemployment had risen over two million, for the first time since 1935, and Mrs Thatcher was rumoured to be planning to purge her Cabinet of dissenters. Meanwhile the leading dissenter of the last Labour Cabinet was now using the freedom of the backbenches to the full: Blackpool 1980 was Tony Benn's conference.

The first morning, Monday 29 September, saw Benn wind up the economic debate with a call-to-arms for the left. The most moderate resolution, proposed by GMWU chief David Basnett, and seconded by the NUM, called for reflation assisted by reduced defence spending and import controls, more nationalisation, a wealth tax and a 35-hour week with no loss of pay. Much of the debate had been dominated by the hard left and based around several Militant-backed resolutions calling for redundancies to be banned and for any company threatening any redundancies to be nationalised.[569] Benn made clear in his speech that though the NEC would not support the most extreme motions, he himself shared the 'deep socialist conviction' on which they were based, 'and the British people will ignore their words at their peril, for what they are saying is highly relevant to the whole situation that we are confronting today'. It was as if he was saying, 'you are right, I agree, but they won't let me say so publicly'. The battle against 'they' was to burn Labour's credibility on a bonfire of Militant zeal. Benn concluded his speech with an announcement:

> Comrades . . . I believe that we shall require three major pieces of legislation within the first month of the election of another Labour government . . . First, an Industry Bill which will give us powers to extend common ownership as requested by the GMW, to control capital movements as requested by the GMW, to provide for industrial democracy as has been suggested and demanded by the GMW, and that Industry Bill must be on the statute book within a matter of days after the election of a Labour government (*applause*).

Secondly, the second Bill must transfer all the powers back from the Common Market Commission to the House of Commons, also within a matter of weeks. We kid ourselves, we absolutely mislead ourselves and our people in this country, if we tell them we will adopt the policy that David Basnett urged and do not also tell them that all that policy would be illegal under the Common Market unless we bring the powers back to Westminster. I might add that we will need a third Bill and I will tell you why we will need it, because neither the first Bill nor the second Bill would get through the House of Lords. Our third immediate Bill is to do what the movement has wanted to do for a hundred years, to get rid of the House of Lords and, if I may say so, we shall have to do it by creating a thousand peers and then abolishing the peerage as well at the time that the Bill goes through (*applause*). It is not possible for a Labour government to continue if it only has control of half a Parliament.

Finally, we must stand up to the pressure that these policies will bring about, because we must not be naïve. Even if we are not accepting some of the resolutions which I referred to, the pressure by the IMF, by the EEC, by the City – the bully boys in the City of London – that would be brought upon a Labour Cabinet committed to the GMW Composite alone will test us within hours as to whether we are serious or whether we are to be blown off course.

Comrades, this is the very least we must do . . .

The moderates were appalled. It was 'an extraordinary blast of demagoguery', recalled Giles Radice. Benn's pledges had not even been discussed by the NEC, never mind the shadow Cabinet.[570] At a Campaign for Labour Party Victory fringe meeting Shirley Williams repeated the three legislative commitments Benn had made in his speech and went on: 'And all this would be done in a couple of weeks. I wonder why Tony was so unambitious. After all it took God only six days to make the world.'[571] The newspaper headlines the following morning were 'pretty hysterical',[572] acknowledged Benn in his diary. For David Owen, Benn's speech was 'cloud-cuckoo-land . . . I could not believe that such flagrant nonsense could actually be taken seriously by a party which for all its faults had demonstrated over the years such deep moorings in the British way of life.'[573]

In addition to the constitutional battles there were two key policy areas that came to have almost totemic significance in the struggle between the moderates and the left: the EEC and defence. Labour's October 1980 conference saw swings in policy on both. Wednesday morning heard a debate on Europe over a resolution from the irrepressible Clive Jenkins's ASTMS union to commit Labour to withdrawal from the EEC without a referendum. Former Foreign Secretary David Owen spoke passionately against, attacking the idea of withdrawal and branding the proposition to do so without a referendum a 'constitutional outrage'. Peter Shore spoke as passionately in favour, declaring that he believed there was 'no necessity at all to resort to yet another referendum . . . so long as we state fairly and clearly in our next manifesto what our policy is'. The vote was just over five million to just over two million: below the two-thirds majority needed to require its inclusion in the manifesto, but, as Benn recognised, it was 'sensational, a fantastic victory'.[574] For the moderates, the writing was on the wall.

Thursday morning's defence debate saw the triumph of CND as Labour's conference voted for unilateral nuclear disarmament. With the development of new Soviet medium-range missiles during the 1970s and US counterparts, to be based in the UK, the debate over the Cold War had heated up. CND claimed that 80,000 people had joined their march on 22 June. Bill Rodgers, Labour's shadow Defence Secretary, made a fighting speech in defence of multilateral nuclear disarmament. It was not just the unilateralists who wanted peace:

> . . . We are all terrified of the horror of nuclear war . . . We all believe that Britain is spending too much on defence and I think that many of us for that very reason believe it is quite wrong to replace Polaris with the Trident missiles and submarines.
>
> But having said that we all want peace, I want to say this as well . . . We all want to retain our freedom. There is no point in debating democratic socialism and seeking to create it unless in the last resort we are prepared to defend it too . . .
>
> We in our movement have a very great respect for those of pacifist convictions, but go into the pubs, go into the clubs, go on to the shop floor, go on to the doorstep and you will find a great majority of people who deeply want peace and deeply want disarmament but who believe you cannot win the peace unless you are prepared to say you will defend yourselves. No trade union would go into negotiation and say beforehand it will not exercise the industrial power it possesses. You cannot win a negotiation if you give up in advance the authority and power that you possess . . .

But there were few voices raised in agreement. Perhaps the greatest impact of the speech was to confirm in his own mind the lack of potential allies alongside whom he could fight back as he had done successfully with Gaitskell after their defeat on this issue in 1960. Rodgers was attacked by the young MP for Edinburgh Central, Robin Cook:

> I will not bandy words with Bill Rodgers as to whether his position or my position will be the better electoral asset. I cannot think of a more frivolous position on which to make up our mind on the central issue facing mankind (*applause*).
>
> But I will say this to Bill. Bill, I do not believe we have a hope of convincing the people in the streets, in the factories, in the pubs so long as they see us hedging and fudging our opposition to nuclear arms (*applause*). That is why we need a clear position . . .
>
> We have been going on like this for decades and it has got to stop, not after we have got Trident, not after we have got cruise missiles in every lay-by. It has got to stop now (*applause*).
>
> Then we are told: 'Well, we don't really want you to agree to cruise missiles so we can have them; we want you to agree to cruise missiles so that we can talk to the Russians about how to get rid of them once again' (*laughter*) . . . I believe in multilateral

disarmament . . . but we have got to look at the record. We have had multilateral negotiations for 20 years and there has been no disarmament (*applause*) . . . they have the
nerve to say 'Give us one more bargaining chip and this time we will do it.'

Replying to the debate on behalf of the NEC, Joan Lestor[575] accused Rodgers of supporting Tory policies:

Comrades, the trouble is that Bill is dragging around with him the ball and chain of
Margaret Thatcher's policies (*applause*). They are not the policies of the Labour Party.
Bill, I appeal to you; I am sorry, the defence of missiles is not Labour Party policy, we
rejected it . . . we have to argue the case against the nuclear holocaust; argue the case
that the way to peace is to give up to our arms, and we will attract to our movement
thousands of young people with vision and idealism . . .

'Bill [Rodgers] argued passionately,' recalled John Golding,

It was bitterly upsetting to many of us that they were prepared to sacrifice the interests of the British working class for the sake of CND . . . The propositions which were
carried on a show of hands ensured that Labour lost the 1983 election and went into
the wilderness. They should be writ large on the tombstone of Old Labour. Jim
Callaghan went, the Social Democrats went and the policy landed the party with an un-
electable leader supporting a defence policy rejected by almost all the British public.[576]

As in the previous year, the conference was dominated by the left-led campaigns for
constitutional changes that would secure a fundamental and irreversible shift in the balance of power in the Labour Party into their hands. The previous year, the conference had
actually passed proposals to secure the mandatory selection of MPs, but they had been
so badly drafted that lawyers had warned the NEC that any MP deselected under the new
rules could sue the Labour Party. To rectify what MP Denis Howell delicately described
to the fully televised conference as 'an almighty cock-up', Wednesday afternoon began
with a debate on proposals to do what last year's proposals had done, except legally. Tony
Benn's former PPS Joe Ashton was, with Denis Howell, one of only two MPs given the
chance to speak against them. Ashton could see that if adopted and implemented with
the vigour the hard-left arditi clearly desired, then they would virtually force a breakaway
Social Democratic Party into being:

. . . Ask yourselves who outside the Labour Party wants mandatory reselection
[demanded Ashton]. The media cannot wait for mandatory reselection because they
will have Prentice sagas right through the country, right up to the next election
(*applause*). And Mrs Thatcher would vote for mandatory reselection . . .

I will tell you this. And I will tell my friend Tony Benn. When you were sacked,
Tony, from your seat by the House of Lords in a very unfair way you fought and fought
again to get that seat back, and you have never stopped fighting the House of Lords
since. And MPs who think they have been unfairly sacked will tend to react in the same

411

way. It is as simple as that. Because what a lot of the people who are shouting do not know is this. If an MP gets the sack and he walks away into the sunset and says noth-ing – he does not get a penny redundancy pay or anything – here comes the clincher. If he stands and fights he can pick up nearly twelve thousand quid. That is the differ-ence (*slow hand clap*) . . . If you look at the history of sacked MPS – Eddie Milne was sacked; he stood and he won. So did Taverne. So did S. O. Davies. They all won. And do not think that if 25 or so are sacked – if maybe the elderly Gaitskellite type of MP who you are wanting to get rid of who does not get a lot of publicity is sacked at the age of 58 what has he got to lose by standing? And do not forget this. That will hap-pen, not at the next election: it will happen before then. If Roy Jenkins wanted to form a party of 25 sacked MPs now in this Parliament, they could be in business in six months. And they would be backed by the media. They would get all the publicity. They would get all the cash. It would be the biggest push to the three-party system delivered by this conference that the political scene had ever seen. And if you want to look how it has worked in other places, look what has happened in America. For eight months it has been Carter fighting Kennedy; not Carter fighting Reagan. It has been Carter fight-ing Kennedy. And if you want to know why the political situation never changes in America and the poor never get any help at all, it is because the politicians are looking after their nominations and they are fighting each other for the nomination instead of doing something to change the system. And that is how it will be here (*applause*) . . .

The conference 'nearly went berserk',[577] wrote Benn in his diary. It was 'an uproar', recalled Ashton. 'The entire 2,000 delegates and visitors yelled, booed and slow-hand-clapped me off the rostrum. Sam McCluskie, the Seamen's Union Secretary who was [replying to the debate for the NEC] advised me to "go and join them", but later apolo-gised privately for his remarks. Actually I was wrong. When the SDP broke away three months later, led by Roy Jenkins, there turned out to be twenty-seven Labour MPs not twenty-five and one from the Tories too.'[578] Ashton's warning went unheeded. Conference voted to accept mandatory reselection by 3,798,000 votes to 3,341,000. It would have far-reaching consequences. Joe Ashton was one of those who realised that there was a good reason why the Trotskyist Militant Tendency was one of the strongest advocates of mandatory reselection: Militant

> thought that while ever there was a Labour government or even a large number of Labour MPs there could never be a revolution. They did not want capitalism to suc-ceed or even to be propped up. If Labour ever produced full employment, then who would storm the barricades? Sacking all the existing MPs and replacing them with Militant Tendency kamikaze pilots would be a good swap, they seriously suggested. Tony Benn, perhaps inadvertently, and with the best of democratic intentions, had opened the door to a wind of change which blew the party back twenty years.[579]

The second constitutional change the Bennites demanded was to remove the power of MPs, including the party leader, to influence the content of the manifesto and give sole control to the NEC. This had been agreed in principle the previous year and the Wednesday afternoon in 1980 saw the NEC put forward the constitutional amendment to secure the change. The debate was dominated by speeches demanding reform. Three in particular stood out. One was from the 31-year-old Australian-born delegate from St Pancras North, Patricia Hewitt. One of a new generation of young graduates coming into Labour politics from the world of pressure groups (she had been General Secretary of what is now Liberty since 1974), her speech reflected a frustration that it was easier for civil servants to influence the policies of Labour governments than ordinary Labour Party members:

> ... many of us in this conference are also angry about much of what the last Labour government did and a great deal of what the last Labour government failed to do (*applause*) ... Let me give you just one example. This Tory government has just published its proposals for a new Nationality Bill – a Bill that is racist, a Bill that will make people stateless, a Bill that would violate our international human rights commitments. But that Bill will be based on the proposals that were put forward by the last Labour government ...
>
> The policies on nationality of the Labour Party are very different indeed from the policies of the last Labour government. They represent a just and non-racist alternative to what the Tories are trying to do. And what we need and what we have the right to demand is a guarantee that the next Labour government will implement the policies which this Labour Party decided on, and not the policies of a handful of Cabinet ministers and a handful of civil servants ...
>
> That is what these constitutional issues are about. They are about getting rid of the divide between the policies that we as a party decide on, the policies on which we fight the election, and the policies which the Labour government implement in office ...

Coventry delegate Dave Nellist had a different agenda:

> In introducing some remarks on the manifesto, I should just like to attend to one remark made by Joe Ashton. If there are 25 Labour MPs supposedly supporting party policy who want to join Roy Jenkins and the so-called Centre Party, the sooner they do it and give us the chance to replace them with genuine Labour Party MPs, the better party we are going to have for it (*applause*) ...

Then a 28-year-old council building services worker, Nellist would in 1983 become one of two overtly Militant-supporting Labour MPs. Against Hewitt and Nellist spoke the lone voice of David Warburton of the GMWU, who was later to play a key role as an organiser of the moderates in the battle to bring Labour back from the political wilderness. For Warburton:

> ... the very idea that any single group possesses all the wisdom, the tact and all the

413

expertise to formulate an election manifesto for a socialist government is nonsense ... It is not a question of left and right. It is a question of right and wrong ...

There are three reasons why conference should reject the proposition. First of all, it is illogical. Does anyone seriously believe that the five-year programme of a majority Labour government can be determined by a short debate at a party confer-ence? Secondly, it is impracticable. No self-respecting decision maker, whether he is a trade union official or a branch secretary, would formulate a policy without liaising with others whose support he needs, particularly those who he is expecting to carry out those policies. And thirdly, it is undemocratic. We claim to be the most represen-tative democratic socialist party in the world. It would be a negation of that principle if we transferred this issue solely to the National Executive Committee ... It is the height of arrogance for the National Executive Committee to assume the mantle of having ultimate wisdom. It never has, it does not, and it never will, irrespective of the political composition of the NEC (*applause*) ...

After Warburton had spoken, it was for Benn to conclude the debate for the NEC:

... the manifesto is the buckle that links this conference with the policy of a Labour government ... I say this, having been at ... the Clause Five meeting that drew up the 1964, '66, '70, '74, '74 and '79 manifestos. First of all, when Labour is in power there is no parliamentary committee of the parliamentary party. When the manifesto in May of last year was drawn up not a single person there, except in the capacity of leader and deputy leader, had been elected by the parliamentary party. It was an appointed, hand-picked Cabinet who represented Labour Members of Parliament (*applause*) ... there was not a single Labour backbencher who saw that draft before it was approved by the Clause Five meeting. So do not think that the present provision provides for back-bench members to see the manifesto; they have never seen it ...

And last of all – and I do not want to make too much of it – there is a veto which has crept in where a succession of Parliamentary Labour Party leaders have said 'I will not have it. It must not appear.' ... If you have a veto, those who oppose policies do not bother to argue with conference, because they wait till the Clause Five meeting and kill it secretly, privately, without debate (*applause*). My resentment about the exclusion of the House of Lords – and you must not think I have any particular interest in that place – was not just that it was vetoed, but that when conference discussed it and decided it by an overwhelming majority, no voice was raised from the platform to persuade us to drop it. They let the conference pass it and it was vetoed secretly, late, quietly, before the party could discover what had happened. That is wrong, and it is out of that that the mistrust in our party grows ...

Is there anybody in this conference today who believes that, with our present par-liamentary Committee, there would in the next election be a commitment to withdraw from the Common Market in line with the two-thirds majority that was agreed this morning? It would not. It would be vetoed ...

Every one of the points that was moved by David Basnett on Monday was put by the National Executive at the Clause Five meeting and was ruled out, eighteen months ago. Immediate restriction of the export of capital – ruled out. Reflation of public sector service spending – ruled out. Substantial cuts in arms expenditure – ruled out. The immediate introduction of a wealth tax – ruled out (*applause*). The imposition of selected import controls – ruled out. I say there is no body of opinion at this conference that has a greater vested interest in carrying the Executive's constitutional amendment than the trade union leaders and the trade union movement (*applause*) . . .

'I must say,' wrote Benn in his diary that night, 'it was the best speech I have ever made in my life at a conference, probably the best speech I have ever made at a public meeting. It was followed by tumultuous applause from the CLPs and a standing ovation, while the trade union delegations sat looking very uncomfortable.'[580] Benn's former Cabinet colleague Roy Hattersley took a different view: 'Benn's speech was a long indictment of the defeated government's treachery. His list of broken promises was made up of policy commitments which had, in truth, either been kept or never been made.'[581] And when the votes came to be counted, conference, by a whisker, agreed with Warburton rather than Benn.[582]

On the Wednesday afternoon conference had voted on the third of the three great Bennite constitutional changes and by the flimsiest of majorities[583] it had agreed to change the system for future Labour leadership elections and accept the principle of the electoral college. But they had only been able to do so because of a backstairs intrigue in the Boilermakers' Union. Their delegation had voted by a majority to go against the Bennite proposals, and when the union's general secretary and his deputy had left the room after the vote the left members of the delegation engineered a 're-vote' which reversed the delegation's position.[584] When it came to the separate votes on the actual constitutional amendments that would create the electoral college and allocate shares of the vote between the three broad sections (MPs, unions and constituency party conference delegates) the left found, however, that they had not a majority to do it. Using their control of Labour's NEC, the left came back to conference the following morning and tried again, having cobbled together overnight a new proposal with different percentages. 'The National Executive met at 8 and it was clear that Frances,[585] Vladimir,[586] Jon Lansman, Peter Willsman, Victor Schonfield and Frances Prideaux have bullied the Executive into agreeing to the new CLPD alternative – 40 per cent for the unions and 30 per cent each for the MPs and constituencies. We kicked this around for a bit and eventually it was carried by 13 votes to 7 which was excellent.'[587] This formula Eric Heffer presented on behalf of the NEC to the conference, as he had the previous day, making clear his determination to push it through: 'If we do not get it out of the way, we can have another argument next year and that does not help in our fight against Thatcher . . .'

Heffer received a spirited reply from Postmen's Union leader Tom Jackson, who accused the NEC of: 'producing constitutional changes with the speed of a conjuror producing white rabbits from a top hat' and failing to give unions like his own adequate time to consult their members on hastily drafted proposals:

> Today we face a constitutional change which has had one hour's consideration by this lot up here between 8 o'clock and 9 o'clock this morning (*applause*). Look at paragraph four, if you want to see an abortion. He had to explain it to us. He said that when the general election was on and the party leader died, they would consult with the Parliamentary Labour Party, which is not even in existence at the time of a general election.

After Jackson came complete uproar as Warley East MP Andrew Faulds, an actor then famous for starring as Doone père in the film *Lorna Doone*, induced furious heckling from conference militants:

> I represent the true Labour Party in Smethwick, not the Workers' Revolutionary Party, nor the militant Trots (*applause*). They have infiltrated so many constituency parties, as you know (*applause*). Madam Chairman, the baying of the beast betrays its presence; you can hear them.
>
> I want to comment, if these 'democrats' will allow me, on the question of the election of the leader. We have had a great one in Jim (*applause*). He is the most popular political leader in Britain and we in the PLP chose him. But whatever way we set up an electoral college, however we balance the proportions, there is going to be a real quandary for all of us, responsible trade unionists, extreme leftists, reasonable constituency delegates and those of us who actually spend our lives working hours none of you would accept, putting into practical effect the manifesto of the party.
>
> Can I ask for the tolerance of the 'democrats'? There is a real quandary, we know where most of the leadership contenders stand: there is blunt, pugnacious Denis, there is forthright Peter Shore, there is outspoken John Silkin and we all know clearly where Shirley stands. None of them has welshed on the Labour government they have served in. But what of the Rt Hon. Anthony Wedgwood Benn? (*cheers*).
>
> *Chairman:* Andrew, I must ask for no personal attacks (*interruption*). No, Andrew no personal attacks. We are dealing with a National Executive statement.
>
> *Andrew Faulds, MP:* That is right. Madam Chairman, I am raising the matter because how we rig the proportions in this electoral college is very important. That is why I want to examine, if you will allow me – this is what conference is about – the record of some of the gentlemen involved.
>
> *Chairman:* No, that is not in order . . .

When the votes were counted it was clear that Heffer had failed again. The attempt simply to bulldoze through was not going to work. Basnett of the GMWU and Sir John Boyd of the Engineers made clear they needed time to consult their membership before supporting a particular formula. Heffer hadn't got the votes. The NEC therefore fell back on plan B: a suggestion from GMWU leader David Basnett to have another special conference in three months' time specifically to decide the formula of the electoral college.

This, argued Basnett, would enable delegations to consult their members properly before taking the plunge in favour of one option or another. It was overwhelmingly carried. Crucially, it meant that were Callaghan to resign before any change could be agreed at the forthcoming special conference, the leadership vacancy would be filled under the old system. Benn knew it, Callaghan knew it, they all knew it. The MPs would get one last chance to decide the party leader, and it wouldn't be Benn because most MPs would not vote for him. A year before, on 28 November 1979, Tony Benn took the future mineworkers' union president Arthur Scargill and his wife for dinner at the House of Commons. 'Arthur thought that, if there was an election in June and Denis was elected, there would be an opportunity to dislodge him after an electoral college had been established. That may be the best strategy.'[588]

FIFTY-SIX

Jenkins's Life Raft 1980–81

'Get out, we do not need you'

When Jim Callaghan resigned as leader of the Labour Party on 15 October 1980, GMWU General Secretary David Basnett, TGWU leader Moss Evans and ASTMS boss Clive Jenkins met 'at David's central London *pied-à-terre* office in Duke Street to talk it over. It was clear that the main contender was Denis Healey, whom none of us wanted because he was too aggressive and would split the party,' Jenkins's memoir recalls. 'I suggested Michael Foot and both Moss and David thought this was a good idea. Moss said, "You're an old mate of his – you go and ask him."'[589] After a great deal of effort Foot was finally persuaded. By then there were already three other declared candidates in the field: Healey, Peter Shore and John Silkin. Foot's candidature sealed the fate of Silkin and Shore. What was less clear before the final result was that it had also sealed Healey's. For all Healey's talents, there were simply too many MPs with whom at one time or another he had crossed swords or who feared retribution by the hard left in their constituencies. 'Even many of us who resisted that pressure feared that Denis's election would set off another explosion of hatred against the despised and detested parliamentary party,' wrote Hattersley in his memoir. 'Worse still, they knew that Tony Benn would declare Denis's election illegitimate and challenge him as soon as the rules were changed. Then all sorts of dangerous passions would again be unleashed in constituency managements through-out the country.'[590]

Moreover, while Healey was hit by serious flu for several key days of the campaign, Foot displayed his best form in a debate on unemployment on 29 October, the day before the first ballot of the leadership election. Healey had opened for the opposition. His speech was solid, but unremarkable. Foot's that evening had flashes of brilliance and it was this speech, with its dazzlingly witty destruction of the Secretary of State for Industry, Sir Keith Joseph, that was fresh in the minds of many of those voting the next day:

> . . . we face a more serious economic crisis than we have faced since 1945 . . . Those are not just my views. They are the views of the CBI. It says: 'We are now in a much more serious recession than that experienced in 1974–75. We would have to go back to before the war to find industry in comparable difficulties . . . Have we got to go through the next three or four years of destroying great tracts of British industry to convince the world that sterling is over-valued' . . .

I gather that the Prime Minister is not so much impressed by these events because she insists that the policy will not be changed. The lady is not for turning. (*Hon. members*: 'Burning.') No, let us not have any misquotations. The lady is not for turning. I suppose that we have to change the old adage – if mother does not turn, none of us will turn . . . I think that the Cabinet is in a slightly different mood from that.

We read in the newspapers that the Cabinet is to discuss these matters and possibly some aspects of public expenditure cuts tomorrow. I should like to intrude into that meeting, if I may, and offer my assistance to those sections of the Cabinet that deserve it.

The Secretary of State for Employment[591] is sometimes represented as a good man who fell among monetarists. I would not go as far as that. I shall come back to him in a moment. At any rate, I am chalking him up on my slate as one of the good ones . . .

The Secretary of State for Defence[592] . . . gets almost as big ovations at Tory conferences as the Prime Minister – and we know that is no accident. The right hon. gentleman has a powerful voice in the Cabinet. If he were to turn himself into the Field Marshal for the wets, that would cause quite an event, because some of the others might pluck up their courage, too. That is two of them.

Where is the Lord Privy Seal,[593] the philosopher Tory – as H. G. Wells said, like military intelligence, a contradiction in terms? His contempt for Tory policy is so determined that they all know it. That is three.

Now there is the Leader of the House.[594] We are told that at a fringe meeting at Brighton the Leader of the House came out in his true colours. We can imagine what a gaudy performance that would have been.

Now let us look at some of the others. Where is the Secretary of State for Scotland?[595] He must know what is going on, so we count him on that side. What about the Secretary of State for Wales?[596] Which side is he on? Maybe they do not count him.

Where is the Minister of Agriculture, Fisheries and Food?[597] We have always counted on him . . . The Minister of Agriculture takes the same precaution as his right hon. friend the Member for Sidcup [Mr Heath]: he does not turn up at these debates. He finds it easier to vote for them if he does not have to listen to them. The right hon. gentleman – (*An Hon. member*: 'Where is he?') . . . Tomorrow there will be a pious public relations office notice issued by the Ministry of Agriculture saying that, of course, the Minister of Agriculture was in the House of Commons but he was in his room working on his papers. I bet that is not what he is doing. The right hon. gentleman is upstairs saying that he does not believe in this monetarist malarkey any more than we do . . . he is one of us . . .

What about the others? . . . The Foreign Secretary[598] is an influential chap. I dare say that he is a bit persuaded by the Lord Privy Seal. In passing, there was a report the other day that one of the public expenditure cuts to be imposed tomorrow is a cut in the British Council. The greatest possession of this country – more valuable than North Sea oil – is the English language, which is becoming the language of the world. At such a moment this penny-pinching government are about to injure the processes whereby people throughout the world can acquire the right and capacity to speak English . . .

Whom does that leave? Where is the Home Secretary,[599] the long-playing vice-captain. I suppose that we can add him to the list . . . He may consider that these financial questions are a bit beyond him now. If he has to listen to the Chancellor of the Exchequer[600] at the peak of his form, as he was today, I am not surprised that he does. I have noted the right hon. and learned gentleman's words carefully. He says that the high rate of the pound is not an objective of policy. Can he tell us whether anything that is happening in the country at present is an objective of policy? Unemployment has not been created on purpose. What about inflation? The government are conquering inflation, but we should not know that if they did not tell us so. The right hon. lady will not answer this question tonight, but perhaps she can think up an answer for tomorrow. How long does she believe it will be before she gets the inflation rate down to what it was before she started putting it up? . . .

I sometimes feel that, when the right hon. lady stands on the burning deck all alone at the end, the only person who will be supporting her will be the Minister for Social Security.[601] I have warned the right hon. lady before. Does she not realise that we have put him here as an *agent provocateur* in order to test what damn fool statements can be made in Tory governments? . . .

I should not like to miss out the Secretary of State for Industry,[602] who has had a tremendous effect on the government and our politics generally. As I see the right hon. gentleman walking around the country, looking puzzled, forlorn and wondering what has happened, I try to remember what he reminds me of. The other day I hit on it.

In my youth, quite a long time ago, when I lived in Plymouth, every Saturday night I used to go to the Palace theatre. My favourite act was a magician-conjuror who used to have sitting at the back of the audience a man dressed as a prominent alderman. The magician-conjuror used to say that he wanted a beautiful watch from a member of the audience. He would go up to the alderman and eventually take from him a marvellous gold watch. He would bring it back to the stage, enfold it in a beautiful red handkerchief, place it on the table in front of us, take out his mallet, hit the watch and smash it to smithereens. Then on his countenance would come exactly the puzzled look of the Secretary of State for Industry. He would step to the front of the stage and say 'I am very sorry. I have forgotten the rest of the trick.' It does not work. Lest any objector should suggest that the act at the Palace theatre was only a trick, I should assure the House that the magician-conjuror used to come along at the end and say 'I am sorry. I have still forgotten the trick.' . . .

[And if Cabinet fail] to say that the lady must turn? . . . we shall organise the biggest protest campaign that this country has seen since the 1930s . . . Shall we call it a Midlothian campaign? It will be against the atrocities of unemployment this time instead of the other atrocities against which Mr Gladstone campaigned. I remind the House that when he embarked upon his Midlothian campaign Mr Gladstone was 68 years old. I must inform Conservative hon. members, who may not be aware of the facts, that Mr Gladstone lived thereafter to form three – or was it four? – separate administrations. So there is hope for all my hon. friends, including my right hon. friend the Member for Leeds East [Sir Keith Joseph].

Healey led on the first ballot of Labour's leadership election with 112 votes to 83 for Michael Foot, 38 for John Silkin and 32 for Peter Shore. On the second ballot, Silkin and Shore dropped out and endorsed Foot, most of their votes swinging with them, delivering Foot victory on 10 November by 139 votes to 129. Up to five MPs later to join the SDP voted deliberately for Foot in order to strengthen their own future case for departure. But most did not and while some of those who joined the SDP had been among Healey's greatest cheerleaders,[603] other Manifesto Group MPs who voted against Healey were among those who stayed.[604] The hard fact is that Foot won because Labour MPs chose him. Had Healey been elected leader, argues Hattersley, 'he might not have carried the party to victory in 1983. But we would have been beaten, not annihilated and during the following five years he would have led a convincing recovery. At the time when Michael Foot defeated him, Denis was comfortably the most popular politician in the country.'[605]

Healey succeeded Foot as deputy leader unopposed[606] and in the shadow Cabinet elections that followed it was Roy Hattersley who this time topped the poll, followed by Eric Varley and Gerald Kaufman, who was elected for the first time. Benn stood but came thirteenth with there being only twelve places. He would have to wait until Bill Rodgers' departure to rejoin, since it was he as runner-up who automatically filled the vacancy. Healey became shadow Foreign Secretary, swapping with Peter Shore who became shadow Chancellor. Hattersley was promoted to shadow Home Secretary, Gerald Kaufman to Environment and Foot's ally Stan Orme replaced Silkin at Industry who became shadow Leader of the House. David Owen, who following Healey's defeat in the leadership ballot had decided not to re-stand, was replaced at Energy by Merlyn Rees. Rodgers did re-stand, coming a respectable ninth out of twelve. But Foot's offer of a demotion (to Northern Ireland or Health minus Social Services which had always previously been combined) did not bode well for the future, and helped tip Rodgers to a decision to break with Labour. Owen had probably already reached it. Had Healey been elected leader it is possible, if not probable, that David Owen, Bill Rodgers and Shirley Williams would have remained in the Labour Party. Without them, Roy Jenkins's new party would have had no MPs of substantive national stature and consisted of little more than his core group of supporters around Dick Taverne and David Marquand, both of whom, like Jenkins and Shirley Williams, were now out of Parliament. They would have had difficulty establishing themselves and would soon have been absorbed into the Liberal Party. In the weeks that followed, some of the Manifesto Group[607] tried frantically to persuade Rodgers to stay. Owen, meanwhile, was meeting with other Manifesto Group MPs planning for a likely departure.

The Wembley special conference of 24 January 1981 was held finally to thrash out a

421

new system for electing Labour's leader. The left[608] wanted an electoral college which minimised the impact of the MPs. The right was split. They had all now abandoned the idea of defending the status quo. The majority of the shadow Cabinet backed a proposal from Roy Hattersley, advocating an electoral college formula which maximised the vote share for MPs (55 per cent). Others, led by David Owen and latterly by Bill Rodgers, advocated One Member One Vote for all party members. At a meeting of the Parliamentary Labour Party on 13 November Owen and Hattersley had battled it out. Owen lost and the proposal for One Member One Vote was defeated by 72 votes to 60 with over one hundred absentees. For Rodgers, the PLP 'had plainly lost the will to fight'.[609]

The conference, observed Healey, 'was an even bigger shambles than its predecessor'.[610] 'I slept through Heffer's boring opening speech proposing an electoral college,' recalled John Golding, 'I was, however, rudely awakened by the barracking of [Electricians' Union leader] Frank Chapple, advocating OMOV':[611]

> . . . The Labour movement has always fought for the principle of one person one vote. My union believes that we should uphold that principle today . . . We believe that One Member One Vote would encourage new membership and guarantee that the party retain close links with the millions of Labour supporters.
>
> Our commitment to One Member One Vote means that we are opposed to all those . . . who champion this alternative to One Member One Vote on the grounds of cost, administrative difficulty or that the rank and file cannot be trusted with a vote because of likely media interference. There is nothing new about these arguments . . . They were used by the Tory lords who fought against working men and women having the vote at all, and are regularly repeated in South Africa today . . .
>
> The trade union block votes exercised here are not the votes of real people. They represent the amount of money a trade union is prepared to put up to buy votes. Some trade unions buy more votes than they have members paying the political levy. Some would seem to buy more votes than they even have members. What a prospect of widening democracy, to have a future Prime Minister the subject of an auction by trade union leaders . . .
>
> The One Member One Vote proposal would give every trade unionist who was also a Labour Party member the chance of participating and voting. This would not happen in an electoral college scheme. Most trade unionists would be disenfranchised under this proposal . . . It is quite wrong that the leader of this party, and a possible Prime Minister of the country, should be appointed by a combination of a caucus vote in the constituencies and wheeling and dealing by trade union leaders and the say-so of people who are not even members of this party . . .

TGWU leader Moss Evans followed with a pedestrian speech for the electoral college. He was followed by Pat Wall, who made a fierce attack on Chapple's OMOV proposal. Wall, a clay-pigeon-shooting Militant supporter and former Liverpool councillor, would by the end of the year have deselected and replaced the moderate Labour MP for Bradford North, Ben Ford:[612]

I oppose in particular the so-called democratic idea of a One Member One Vote postal ballot ... What this conference is really about and what is more important that the system of voting which we decide is who controls the Labour Party. On the basis of the One Man One Vote sort of ballot, the most unrepresentative group of people in the country – the five multi-millionaires, soon to be four multi-millionaires, who control the media in this country, they will have the biggest influence in that ballot of anyone. And who elects them? ...

David Owen's reply to Wall was his last speech at a Labour Party conference:

My constituency supports the proposition of One Member One Vote. And there are 70 other constituency parties that have come to this conference believing that it is perfectly possible to arrange in their constituencies a postal ballot of individual members of the party, and they are prepared to pay the cost of such a new and important democratic innovation in this party. I have always supported – once it was clear that the party wanted constitutional changes – a radical overhaul of our constitution. I wanted One Member One Vote. I wanted a change in the National Executive ballots, and I was prepared to argue – when Michael Foot was arguing for the status quo in the shadow Cabinet and against the electoral college – for One Member One Vote ...

This party is known throughout the world for championing the widening of the franchise to one person one vote. In 1977 when a Labour government told Ian Smith [in Rhodesia] that he would never get independence without one person one vote, you all applauded it and stood by us as we held firm for that principle. Now in South Africa, as we argue for one person one vote, we all say that there cannot be A rolls or B rolls or property qualifications. Yes, Moss, you are quite right when you say that all the socialist parties in Western Europe and in Scandinavia consult all the members, but not one of them has a block vote ... If you want to ballot the individual trade unionists, members of the Labour Party, levy payers to the trade union, we would be totally content to have such a system, and balloting individual members of the party. But it was the trade unions themselves said they ... were not able to organise the system of involving individual trade unionists which I wanted, they were not able to do it technically. So we say trade unionists – and they should have the right to vote – should vote as members of the party in their constituency. That is the fair and democratic way.

I say to the conference – it, of course, will be passed, we all know. The votes have been cobbled up. The arrangements have been made. An electoral college is going to be done. But I say to the party this. The day this system is used to elect a Prime Minister, the whole of the country will be watching the procedures, and then these procedures will be shown to be totally undemocratic. They will be shown to be totally illegitimate as a way of electing a Prime Minister of the country. I beg the party, even at this late stage, to reconsider it. We have a leader who has been elected – fairly, openly. You know I did not vote for Michael, but he has been voted for and accepted. Why change for a system now which you know will split the party, which you know is unfair, which you know is undemocratic? Why not look at this again and produce a procedure which is practical, that we can finance, that trusts individual members of the party to make their judgement.

On the basis that OMOV, which he supported, would be defeated, National Union of Railwaymen General Secretary Sid Weighell spoke up for the Hattersley compromise, and attacked the behaviour of the left on the NEC:

> ... What my union objects to is the way the National Executive Committee manipulates the constitution of this movement. The '78 conference rejected it and asked for no change at all; '79 the same conference, your conference, rejected it. But this National Executive Committee, which spews out this claptrap that they say they support, about democracy in the unions and party conference being the sole arbiter of the policy of the movement, they mean that so long as conference conveys views the same as theirs. So in '78 it did not suit them and they bought it back. In '79 it did not suit them and they brought it back. In '80 it did not suit them, they brought it back and they scrambled it through with a wafer-thin majority. I am not arguing about it. One is enough. It is a majority. But what they also did was to propose something that was rejected at last year's conference – a third, a third, a third. I was there. A third, a third, a third was rejected. It is back again ...
>
> My union said to the Commission of Enquiry: all right, electing the leader is important, but there are other issues in this party that are equally important about grassroots voices in the movement. We said that the National Executive Committee is not representative of the movement. There is no grassroots representation on there. There is no parliamentary party as of right on there. We suggested, in our Commission of Enquiry recommendations, they should look at that. But that sort of democracy they are not interested in, because it destroys their majority and they do not want it disturbed ...

The final speakers included several who made clear their view of the social-democratic wing of the Labour Party in no uncertain terms. 'Of course we have our doubters; we have our gangs of three, opportunists of the worst kind,' declared Plymouth delegate Frank Clark. 'I will repeat Sam McCluskie's[613] demand at the Blackpool conference: get out, we do not need you . . . ' He was echoed by Blackburn delegate Dave Ryden:

> ... Those who argue in favour of 50 per cent are asking us to trust our MPs in the way they vote. Shortly before Reg Prentice left to join the Tory Party these MPs voted Reg Prentice top of the poll for the shadow Cabinet (*applause*). In the elections last time they showed their contempt for most of the people in the CLPs by not even voting Tony Benn into a seat on the shadow Cabinet. That is the attitude of the present PLP towards you and for those reasons I ask you not to vote for 50 per cent for the PLP . . . I am prepared to see people like Owen and Williams and Rodgers leave the party . . . the views of these people who are talking of leaving are so far removed from those of the rest of the party that they can play no part in our programme . . .

JENKINS'S LIFE RAFT 1980-81

Despite the passionate support of the Electricians' Union, OMOV simply didn't have enough backing to win the day. The voting came down to a battle between the union block votes who wanted to minimise the power of MPs and those who wanted to maximise it. Basnett's GMWU had proposed a formula, favoured by Foot, giving 50 per cent of the vote to the MPs; Heffer for the NEC, supported by Moss Evans's TGWU, backed 33 per cent; while USDAW, NUPE, Clive Jenkins's ASTMS and Benn backed 30 per cent for the MPs and 40 per cent for the unions. The other big battalion, the moderate-led Engineering Union, had been mandated not to vote for anything which gave less than 51 per cent of the vote to the MPs. This meant that they were compelled to abstain on the votes on the other options, ultimately giving the left a majority for the USDAW formula in a run-off with the GMWU formula. Had the engineers not been so hamstrung, it would have been the GMWU formula that would have carried, though it is possible that the proportions might have shifted in later years. As it was, the Bennites had triumphed. For Owen, Rodgers and Williams it was the end of the road.

The day after the conference, Sunday 25 January, Tony Benn had a 'victorious' group of supporters[614] round to his house to 'discuss the next stage', namely a campaign to get Benn elected deputy leader in place of Healey and 'the reselections'.[615] That same afternoon, Jenkins, Owen, Rodgers and Williams were also in conclave. They issued the Limehouse Declaration, calling for a realignment of British politics, with the support of eleven other Labour MPs. On 5 February the *Guardian* carried a list of one hundred founding supporters of the Council for Social Democracy and an appeal for support. On 9 February Shirley Williams resigned from Labour's NEC and on 2 March Owen, Rodgers and ten other Labour MPs resigned from the party and together with Williams and Jenkins announced their intention of creating the Social Democratic Party. Other MPs, peers and former Cabinet ministers Lord George-Brown, Lord (Hartley) Shawcross, Lord (Jack) Diamond, Lord (George) Thomson, Lord Aylestone[616] and Edmund Dell were to follow them. In July the SDP would contest the Warrington by-election, with Roy Jenkins as the candidate. It had been a rock-solid safe Labour seat. Jenkins came within 1,800 votes of victory. During August the new SDP–Liberal Alliance would exceed 32 per cent in the Gallup opinion poll.

The creation of the SDP split the Manifesto Group wide open and destroyed the CLV. It was this that led to the creation of a new moderate group, Labour Solidarity, based primarily in Parliament but with aspirations to establish a network of local groups. Co-chaired by Roy Hattersley and Peter Shore, it included most of the Manifesto MPs who had not joined the SDP and also soft-left MPs such as Frank Field and Martin O'Neill who had not been involved with Manifesto.

FIFTY-SEVEN

Healey Floats 1981

*'We sink or swim together, and for the sake of the party
and for the sake of this country let us do a bit more
swimming and a little less sinking'*

With the Social Democrats leaping overboard, the hard left pressed forward: having swept their enemy to the beach, those disinclined to opt for the SDP lifeboat could be driven into the sea. Denis Healey, as Labour's new deputy leader, was the figurehead for the remaining social democrats. Benn decided to use the machinery of the new electoral college to depose him. A gathering of Benn's political intimates at his Holland Park home on 29 March agreed to support his declaration of candidacy on 2 April. By 1 April news began to leak out and the Tribune Group, which Benn had finally joined in February, met to consider its position. Concerns were raised that they were going to be expected to support him when he had not discussed his candidature with them before deciding to run. Before they could decide to try and unload his starting pistol, Benn fired it, putting out a statement to the press announcing his candidature at 3 a.m. on 2 April. That day Benn wrote in his diary: 'People want to know what the Labour Party will do and I think the process is long overdue; the Labour Party are having a Turkish bath, and the sweat and the heat and the discomfort are very unpleasant.'[617] The year 1981 'could and should have been the [one] in which the Labour movement applied all its energies to concert united vengeance for the wounds inflicted upon our people and to destroy the Tory government', Michael Foot was later to write. 'Instead we turned it into a period of futility and shame and the responsibility for transmuting every controversy of the time into an internal Labour party dispute rested directly with Tony Benn.'[618]

Benn had already established himself as the *bête noire* of the moderates. Benn had 'done more than any other single individual to devastate the Labour Party, and to foster the atmosphere and to produce the policies that have divided it and driven decent social democrats away', believes Frank Chapple: 'I was once at a dinner party with him where he referred to the socialist commonwealth. "Do you mean Australia and New Zealand?" he was asked, since they had Labour governments at that time. Benn said: "No. I mean the Communist bloc." It is a clear illustration of his alignment and thinking.'[619] But Benn was now to succeed in alienating many on the left as well. His candidacy against Healey was to split the Tribune Group (which he had only just joined) and ultimately the entire Labour left. Some left-wingers gave their backing to Benn because they believed in him, others out of sectarian politics (he was the left candidate against the right-winger Healey and therefore they must support him) and still more (such as Heffer) out of fear of their Militant-dominated constituency parties. Others thought Benn had taken Tribune support for granted, resented his disloyalty to Foot and believing that the left had won on most of the policy battles within the Labour Party thought it the height of electoral madness to engage in unnecessary further battles with the depleted social-democratic wing of the Labour Party, particularly in view of the formation of the SDP. Those falling into this last group, among whom Neil Kinnock and Joan Lestor were to become perhaps the most prominent, were unable to bring themselves to vote for Healey, with whom they had disagreed over so much, and were instead to cluster round 'the alternative' candidature of the emollient Deptford MP and former Chief Whip John Silkin.

Silkin's backers included Foot's shadow Cabinet ally Stan Orme, younger MPs Frank Field, Jeff Rooker, Andrew Bennett and, from the unions, TGWU Deputy General Secretary Alex Kitson and Seaman's Union leader Sam McCluskie. Silkin announced his candidature on 24 May. In 1979, the ultimate leadership 'was thought to be a race between Shore and Silkin', recalled Healey's biographer Edward Pearce, 'but as shadow Minister of Industry facing Sir Keith Joseph [Silkin] became slightly liturgical. Conscientious but not passionate, he tended to put a spurt of shock and horror into the last paragraphs of speeches, as if the peroration had been marked out with four *f*s. But he is desperately unsuited to shouting at people or at punching dispatch boxes.'[620] Silkin was to prove the ideal 'abstention vote'. For some, such as Frank Field, a first vote for Silkin was also a staging post to a vote for Healey on the second ballot.

Healey's supporters too were put under tremendous pressure from the Bennites. Pro-Healey MPs were routinely threatened with deselection by Bennites in their constituencies and their unions. Foot has written of Labour rallies destroyed by 'indiscriminate scenes of sectarian shrieking' from pro-Benn campaigners, and 'the politics of the kindergarten'.[621] The fact that ordinary Labour voters and union members usually preferred Healey had little consequence. NUPE-sponsored MP Peter Hardy, for example, was told by his union leadership that unless he voted for Benn he would be stripped of his sponsorship. He stuck to his guns, voted for Healey and duly lost his sponsorship, despite the fact that the ordinary membership of NUPE had voted for the union to support Healey.[622]

It was not just ordinary NUPE members who backed Healey. In the minority of unions that actually consulted their members the pattern was repeated, including in both the left-led Fire Brigade's Union and the TGWU. In consequence NUPE and the FBU voted for Healey. The TGWU ignored their own consultation and backed Benn. Had they not done so, Healey would have won overwhelmingly. As it was, when the results were announced at a special Sunday session of Labour's annual conference on 27 September 1981, Healey had won by 50.43 per cent to 49.57 per cent. For the left, more bad news was to follow. Benn's campaign and the creation of the SDP had served to re-energise the moderates in the trade unions and with organisation and hard graft they had started to turn the tide on Labour's NEC. In February 1980 the main moderate union leaders had met secretly in the Charing Cross Hotel in London to discuss coordi-nating action.[623] If the Bennites were doing it why shouldn't they? In March 1981 they met again at the St Ermine's Hotel and would meet again, in secret, more regularly, known to each other as the St Ermine's Group.[624] The left had been organising within the unions for some years, their numbers man being Alan Meale at ASLEF, now an MP. A sig-nificant victory had been achieved in February when the right had regained control of the key delegations and committees within the Engineering Union. In consequence its President, Terry Duffy, was able to redeploy its vote. Labour's Treasurer Norman Atkinson was defeated by Eric Varley while left-wing MPs Renee Short and Margaret Beckett were knocked off the women's section by two Solidarity Group MPs Shirley Summerskill and Gwyneth Dunwoody. Also defeated was Bernard Dix of NUPE.

On Monday afternoon, Benn made his main speech of the conference, winding up for the NEC in the economic debate. He was as unashamedly populist as ever, proudly accepting on behalf of the NEC the demand 'to bring into public ownership the com-manding heights of the economy' from Brighton Kemptown's perennial Militant dele-gate Ray Apps, which, he declared, now meant that Clause Four 'must be more than just a vague constitutional aspiration':

> ... Comrades, what lies behind today's debate? ... First of all, the bankruptcy of those Social Democrats who believed that there was an alternative to socialism known as high public expenditure. That was to be the alternative – if you had high public expen-diture, you could iron out the inequalities of capitalism. And that view was not killed by people in bed-sitters, you know, but by the IMF, who came to the Labour govern-ment and killed our programmes of public expenditure (*applause*). And the fact that those bankrupt policies are now being repackaged and relabelled as the Social Democrats gives them no greater relevance to our situation. We are really the Labour Representation Committee. The Social Democrats are the Capital Representation Committee ...
>
> We have also had our view confirmed by Mrs Thatcher – do not think of her as an academic monetarist; she is using three political instruments – the dole queues, the statute book and the media – to crush the trade union movement and to dismantle the welfare state ... And instead of public expenditure in jobs and welfare, it is to go in riot shields and plastic bullets to deal with the consequences of her own neglect of human need ... we wish the next Labour government to represent our people as vigorously as Mrs Thatcher represents hers (*applause*) ...

We need the closest unity with the PLP. I may say to Michael: we do not want puppets, we want partners – nothing more, but nothing less (*applause*). We want partners
in the parliamentary party and we want the parliamentary party to have a better internal democracy, so that it is never again told that it is there by a dog licence issued by a
Prime Minister, but it is there as the spokesman of the working-class movement, put
there in Parliament (*applause*) . . .

Comrades, we shall have to have the courage to stand up to the extra-parliamentary
pressures that will assault the next government. They will come from the City, from
Brussels, from the IMF and from the media – not just the Tory press, but the *Guardian*,
which is now trying to persuade the Liberals they are marrying the SDP when actually
they are attending the funeral of all that is best in radical liberalism. And the *Daily
Mirror* – no friend of the working-class movement, but only says 'vote Labour' on eve of
poll . . . And if the press can pick our policy, they will pick our Cabinet and decide how
far we can go in implementing the policy that we put before you . . .

Benn 'reminded me more and more of Stafford Cripps (without the glasses)',
observed his former Cabinet colleague Lord Longford, who was in the hall for the speech.

Ice-cold manner, infallible capacity for striking the emotive notes, perfect control of
himself and of the effect to be produced. A standing ovation for him was attempted at
the end but did not come off – too many of us remained seated. Benn carries the young
with him because, apart from his great skill as a rhetorician, he alone seems to hold
out hope. He entertains a socialist vision of the kind that constituency activists want
to believe in. He tells them in effect that given the faith and the willpower it will all be
quite easy . . . Those who have served with him in two governments know all too well
that things are not remotely like that. They cannot believe that he is unaware of his
own oversimplifications. Hence the antagonism among the MPs is directed not only
against the policies but against the man.[625]

Thursday morning saw yet another attempt by the left to gain sole control of the
manifesto for the NEC. Manifesto Group chairman Giles Radice[626] spoke defiantly
against the demands for change, confronting Benn directly:

. . . Tony Benn told us last year that certain policies were ruled out of the manifesto.
That is not really true, Tony. If you had read the 1979 manifesto you would find that
it contained all those policies that you were talking about in your brilliant speech last
year – restrictions on capital going abroad, increases in public spending, cuts in arms
expenditure, the introduction of a wealth tax and selective import controls. They were
not ruled out at all. They were all in the 1979 manifesto (*applause*).

There is a deeper myth that needs to be exploded. It is simply not true that parliamentary leaders and MPs are, by definition, traitors who have only to get into
Parliament to betray those whom they represent . . . We must understand once and for
all that we sink or swim together, and for the sake of the party and for the sake of this
country let us do a bit more swimming and a little less sinking (*applause*).

Radice was echoed by party leader Michael Foot, who warned against the attempt by the left to bulldoze change, and insisted that the last manifesto had been drawn up in:

> . . . consultation with the parliamentary party. We had two meetings at which I was present and in which I reported back to the shadow Cabinet and to the meetings which drew up the manifesto. If anybody wants proof, I can provide it for them – because I have got the items in the manifesto which were raised at those two party meetings where I sat as the representative of the shadow Cabinet in order to give them a faithful report. That manifesto was drawn up by longer consultations of this character, not only with the parliamentary party but with the representative bodies of the NEC, than probably any other manifesto that we have had . . .
>
> There is no such thing in the constitution of the Labour Party – and I certainly make no claim or have no wish to exercise any such thing – as a personal veto. No leader of the party has a personal veto. No, he has not. He goes to that meeting and puts what he says and that meeting has to make up its mind whether to accept it or not. And at that moment, comrades, what you are doing is very often to seek how best you may devise the way in which you are going to win that general election that you face then, and if you think that any leader of any party, or the party itself, or the National Executive, is going to be able to escape from that responsibility, of course they are not. The National Executive ought to be giving all its time and all its energies to how best we are going to defeat the enemy at that election, and the enemy is not in this hall. The enemy is outside . . .

But despite their appeals, the conference voted narrowly, by 3,609,000 votes to 3,400,000, to suspend previous conference decisions and permit a debate and vote on amendments to secure the constitutional change. The Bennites were jubilant as, after the briefest discussion, the amendments were then put to the vote. 'Imagine the shock for us all then,' recalled Golding, 'when the result was announced that the moderates had won – defeating the plans by 3,791,000 to 3,254,000! At conference, everything was possible. In the interval a pivotal group of unions shifted their ground. Other delegates had simply returned to conference floor from the bar . . . Bill Whatley, USDAW's General Secretary, admitted to the *Guardian* that there had been "a spot of bother on his delegation", but that he had put the vote right second time round.'[627]

On the EEC vote, however, the left emerged triumphant. Having won the vote the previous year, but not by the requisite two-thirds majority to crow-bar it into the manifesto, the anti-EEC campaigners came back on Thursday 1 October 1981 to complete their victory. This time, with the creation of the SDP, the pro-Europeans were depleted. One of the few who remained with the courage to put his head above the parapet was Bill Sirs, leader of the ISTC steelworkers' union:

> . . . Tony Benn said of the referendum that he had done so much to achieve, that the British people had spoken and we must tremble before their voice. Well, the facts are

these. If the British people have spoken and if we have decided that they should make the decision – a decision of the greatest magnitude to the whole British nation – we should not, as a party, say that we are now going to deny them the same opportunity . . .

His reply came from Deptford MP John Silkin:

. . . There is only one referendum that we really ought to be having on the Common Market, and that is the referendum that we shall have at a general election . . . Let us just see what membership of the Common Market means. Import controls on the scale we want them, are forbidden under Article 12. Public subsidies to industry on the scale we want them, are forbidden under Articles 90–92. Exchange controls on the scale we want them are forbidden under Articles 67–73. How can you have an alternative economic strategy if you remain within the Market? (*applause*). And . . . God help us, there is the Common Agricultural Policy as well . . .

When the votes were counted that Thursday afternoon, the pro-Europeans had been annihilated by nearly six million votes to just over one million. Labour was now unequivocally committed to pulling out of the EEC without a referendum.

Foot's 'leader's speech' to Labour's 1981 conference included a plea for reconciliation, but it was also an uncompromising espousal of the convictions that he had long held, including his devotion to the cause of CND, convincing right-wingers like Golding that, 'we had kept the right of the leader effectively to control policy only to wake up to the fact that our leader supported policies on which we could not be elected'.[628] Foot began with a demolition of Thatcherite economic nostrums. Attacking the government's refusal to intervene to tackle spiralling unemployment Foot continued:

. . . what is missing is the money which will enable those people to be paid to do the work. It is this which the Tories have set their face against. They will restrict credit; they will not extend it to the private sector or the government. Yet it is the expansion of credit which enabled this and every other industrial country in the world to escape from peasant economies. They say that the funds available to finance government expansion or industrial expansion do not exist. They apply this principle, for example, to the gas-gathering pipeline in the North Sea. Here is something which would be of enormous benefit to the economy by harnessing North Sea gas cheaply and effectively, but to say that you are going to leave it, as the government does, to the individual operators, is like telling people that they must each be responsible for building the piece of road outside their own front door (*applause*). The government is in a unique position to organise the project, but the Tory obsession about finance, and about public sector finance in particular, blinds them to such opportunities. If they are so concerned about the shortage of money, why are they encouraging so much money to leave this country by the removal of exchange controls? (*applause*). Portfolio and other direct investment is now leaving the country at a rate of £6 billion a year, enough to finance a 50 per cent increase in government borrowing.

Or to turn to another project which illustrates the whole abject hopelessness of this government for our people. President Mitterrand paid a visit to London a few weeks ago . . . Falling momentarily under the influence of President Mitterrand, Mrs Thatcher agreed to go ahead with the Channel tunnel. Considering the number of jobs and the kind of jobs – steel and all the rest – the idea is certainly to be welcomed, but we must put to Mrs Thatcher the question she keeps putting so fatuously to us and the nation and, presumably, to her hand-picked, thick-skulled Cabinet: 'Where is the money to come from for the Channel tunnel?' Is she to print it? No, that would be wicked; she cannot do that. Is she to borrow it? No, that is wicked too. According to her theory, you cannot get it that way. So is she to raise it by more taxes? . . . Contrary to her election pledges, she happens to have raised taxes in this country higher than ever before in British history (*applause*). As far as I know, she is not proposing to raise the money from extra taxes. So is she to raise the money by cutting somewhere else? That would not help very much either, because wherever she cut, she would be cutting jobs, probably, and not increasing them. So on her theory, which she has told the country and preached to the country with such tireless reiteration, she cannot carry out the promise that she made to President Mitterrand.

I suggest she goes along and has another talk with President Mitterrand and asks him where he is going to get the money . . . He will say he is going to borrow it. And because he is a persuasive kind of chap, you know, he may add: 'Of course it always helps, you know, if you are able to give orders to the bankers instead of taking orders from the bankers' (*applause*). Of course the money can be borrowed; that is how every such great project in our economic history has been advanced.

And if it is sense to build the Channel tunnel that way – or the French tunnel, as some of them may call it – why is it also not sense for the reconstruction of our inner cities, for the improvement of our homes, for the rebuilding of all our shattered industries? . . .

After a plea for reconciliation with Benn and for 'partnership' between conference and Labour MPs, Foot delivered a 'Bevanite' homily and a plea for a new 'social contract':

We have at this conference been adding up a whole list of items which we are going to present to the nation: health, education, employment, our great industries that have got to be repaired, our housing policy and the rest. It is going to be a huge total, and quite right, because the pressures come from every quarter of our movement and they explode in conferences such as this with all the passion and feeling that we have seen at this conference too.

But we have to persuade the nation that we are capable of discriminating between the things we can do first, the things to which we give the highest priority. That is what Aneurin Bevan meant when he talked about the language of priorities being the religion of socialism. We have to choose. You have to choose all the time. Mendès-France says 'to govern is to choose'; of course that is correct. But we have to make a lot of the choices now, and one of the choices I say that we have got a long way to go on is to make a better agreement with the trade unions than we have ever had before. Certainly none of the things that we talk of can become credible in any sense unless we have that undertaking and understanding with the trade unions . . .

Lastly, Foot turned to the:

. . . subject even more important than anything else that we have been discussing . . . How we are to use the influence of the Labour Party, even before we get power, to stop the nuclear arms race (*applause*) . . .

I am . . . interested, as every sane man and woman on the face of the planet must be interested, in the possibilities of negotiations here and now. I think there could be a chance of getting some agreement between the superpowers. I think from what I heard in Moscow that they understand the impossibility of seeking nuclear superiority. I think they also understand the outrage of any ideas of so-called limited nuclear war in Europe. I think there certainly could be an agreement stopping the development of the neutron bomb. I think there could also be considerable advance towards all the ideas of nuclear-free zones . . . Nothing that I have seen persuades me that the CND campaign was wrong; indeed I think it was right (*applause*).

. . . Let me just say, if I may, one further word in conclusion. When I returned,[629] one of those Tory newspapers referred to me, and they referred to *Gulliver's Travels*. They made a bit of a mistake there, because I know more about *Gulliver's Travels* than the Foreign Office. . . Gulliver . . . when he came back from his travels . . . came back from his travels in a flaming state of anger, such as I am in now, about what he had seen of the infamies being done in the world. In one sense he saw those infamies expressed in imperialism, one nation trying to subdue another nation, but even beyond that he saw it in terms of war and the infamies of war itself.

. . . And you know, wonder of wonders, he also described how the brilliant scientists of those days or the generals of those days, getting together in some military, industrial complex, invented a weapon. A weapon of such power and strength and absurdity that it could only be used by the nation that invented it at the price of their total destruction.

. . . It is all in *Gulliver's Travels*. We should see that every member of the Foreign Office gets a copy (*applause*). We should see that we are not deterred by anything from the greatest crusade that our Labour movement ever set its hand to. The world is crying out for peace as it has never cried before. I tell you – I hope I am not boasting – that I am a peacemonger, an inveterate, incurable peacemonger (*applause*). I ask the support of this whole movement to translate that into action (*applause*).

But Foot's strategy for unity refused to work. Benn was not to be reconciled. As early as 10 November another row had broken out after Foot had let Benn wind up an energy debate in the Commons. Benn had used the occasion to expound his own interpretation of Labour policy, contradicting Labour's official energy spokesman Merlyn Rees who had spoken at the beginning of the debate. 'When I sat down Michael Foot was fuming and

Peter Shore was boiling like a kettle,'[630] noted Benn in his diary. The next day there was a furious row about it at the shadow Cabinet, compounded by Benn's refusal to repudiate an article in *London Labour Briefing* containing a deselection 'hit-list' of MPs who had not voted for Benn in the deputy leadership contest. And so it went on.

Benn's diary records discussion of leadership challenges to be mounted against Foot the following year, though they were to come to nothing. Significantly, with the failure of the Tribune Group to unite behind him in his bid to oust Healey, Benn formed a new group, the Campaign Group. 'Its distinguishing feature,' observed John Silkin, 'is its willingness to work with every group of entryists, including the Militant Tendency.'[631] Foot still hoped against hope that Benn would work with him. It was partly over the issue of Militant that he realised that the irreconcilable could not be reconciled.

FIFTY-EIGHT

Labour Torpedoed – The Falklands and Militant 1981–82

'They are allowing Thatcher to get away with murder'

While Labour tore itself apart, the policies of the Conservative government were ripping asunder the social fabric of the country. In January 1982 unemployment passed three million for the first time since 1933. Mrs Thatcher had by now purged her most dissident Cabinet 'wets' and pressed determinedly forward with her monetarist agenda. Meanwhile, the SDP–Liberal Alliance was soaring ahead in the polls. The Liberals won Tory Croydon North-West in a by-election in October and on 26 November Shirley Williams overturned a Tory majority of 20,000 to win Crosby for the SDP. By December 1981 the Alliance had reached over 50 per cent in the Gallup opinion polls, while Labour had slumped to 23 per cent. In March 1982 Roy Jenkins would return to Parliament after another SDP by-election victory as MP for Glasgow Hillhead.

A week later, on Friday 2 April, Argentina invaded a British colony, the Falklands, a small group of islands in the South Atlantic that had hitherto done little to establish themselves in the consciousness of the British populace. The Argentine government was a right-wing military junta led by General Galtieri that was thought to have been responsible for the 'disappearances' of six thousand democrats. Little wonder the Falkland islanders objected to the prospect of being ruled by them. The junta, seeking to boost their ailing domestic popularity, had thought the invasion a prospective easy victory. There were only a handful of UK troops present as an 'honour guard' for the governor and Mrs Thatcher had withdrawn the armed survey ship HMS *Endurance* to save money, despite protests from the islanders that it would give the wrong signal to Galtieri. Indeed, the negotiations that Thatcher's government had been conducting with Galtieri for a 'lease-back', whereby sovereignty would be conceded to Argentina in principle, in exchange for guarantees over English-language education and the like for the two thousand inhabitants, signalled to the Argentine government that the UK government wanted rid of them. Galtieri thought that they were taking the hint and that if they moved swiftly and avoided casualties then the British government would accept the Argentine victory.

Instead, it led to the first sitting of the House of Commons on a Saturday since Suez and Michael Foot's speech in reply to the Prime Minister was categorical in its sense of moral outrage, both at the invasion and the behaviour of the British government. At the time Labour was increasingly derided as 'weak' on defence, a situation compounded by the substitution of the unilateralist John Silkin for the multilateralist Brynmor John[632] as shadow Defence Secretary at the end of 1981. Foot's speech was reminiscent of his role in battling the 'Guilty Men' of appeasement during the 1930s:

> . . . I first wish to set on record as clearly as I possibly can what we believe to be the international rights and wrongs of this matter . . . There is no question in the Falkland Islands of any colonial dependence or anything of the sort. It is a question of people who wish to be associated with this country and who have built their whole lives on the basis of association with this country . . .
>
> The people of the Falkland Islands have the absolute right to look to us at this moment of their desperate plight, just as they have looked to us over the past 150 years. They are faced with an act of naked, unqualified aggression . . . Any guarantee from this invading force is utterly worthless – as worthless as any of the guarantees that are given by this same Argentine junta to its own people. We can hardly forget that thousands of innocent people fighting for their political rights in Argentine are in prison and have been tortured and debased . . .
>
> I believe that the government were right to take the matter to the United Nations . . .
>
> [But] what has happened to British diplomacy? . . . from what has happened it seems that the British government have been fooled by the way in which the Argentine junta has gone about its business . . .
>
> What about British communications and British intelligence? The *Guardian* states today in a leading article: 'This country devotes a greater proportion of its annual output to its armed forces than any other Western country, with the exception of the United States. It has extensive diplomatic and intelligence-gathering activities. And all of that gave Mrs Thatcher, Lord Carrington and Mr Nott precisely no effective cards when the Argentine navy moved' . . .

Foot then reminded the Commons that, as James Callaghan had helpfully flagged up 'only last Tuesday', the previous Labour government had been faced with just 'the same kind of threat' of Argentine invasion and had effectively deterred it with the judicious deployment of a submarine and a couple of frigates. Why, he asked, had Thatcher not taken the same sort of action?

> The right hon. lady has not answered that question. She has hardly attempted to answer it . . . The right hon. lady made some play, although not very effectively, with the time it takes to get warships into the area. We are talking about events several weeks ago . . .
>
> [The Falkland islanders] have been betrayed. The responsibility for the betrayal rests with the government. The government must now prove by deeds – they will never be able to do it by words – that they are not responsible for the betrayal and cannot be faced with that charge. That is the charge, I believe, that lies against them. Even

though the position and the circumstances of the people who live in the Falkland Islands are uppermost in our minds – it would be outrageous if that were not the case – there is the longer-term interest to ensure that foul and brutal aggression does not succeed in our world. If it does, there will be a danger not merely to the Falkland Islands, but to people all over this dangerous planet.

Thatcher's Foreign Secretary Lord Carrington would resign, the attempts to secure a negotiated solution would fail, the taskforce would sail, the invasion would be launched and to their shock and surprise the Argentine forces would be beaten. The junta never recovered its credibility and its collapse led to the flowering of a democratic Argentina. In the UK, Thatcher's triumph in the South Atlantic had a similarly destructive impact on the opposition's poll lead. It crowded the SDP out of the headlines and if Labour spokesmen were irresolute on the conflict then so was Roy Jenkins. It was David Owen whose stature grew. But it was Jenkins who was the SDP's leader. Labour was again embroiled in battles between the leadership and a dissenting Benn, whose motion to urge a cease-fire and the withdrawal of the taskforce was defeated in Labour's NEC by fifteen votes to eight. *Tribune*'s editor Dick Clements had meanwhile gone to work directly for his old friend Foot, and his successor, Chris Mullin, swung the paper overtly behind Benn's line. On 20 May 33 Labour MPs defied the Labour Whip to vote against the government (the official line was to abstain), further signalling Labour's divisions.

At the root of Labour's divisions was 'Militant'. Labour had always had to deal with the problem of Marxist 'entryism': at first it had been the Communist Party, but since the 1960s there had been a bewildering array of Trotskyist groups. For decades tough action, through the use of a 'proscribed list' of organisations of which membership was incompatible with membership of the Labour Party, had minimised the problem. But the authoritarian approach of the Bevin/Morrison/Gaitskell party right wing, who for decades controlled the party machine, alienated the dissenting Bevanite left, who resented being on the wrong end of it. In consequence, when in the Wilson years former Bevanites and others on the left began to take control of the party machine and disciplinary processes, they eagerly abolished the proscribed list. Some, moreover, naïvely hoped that the extreme Marxist left could be allies in the battles for the causes in which they both professed to believe. It was a dangerous misunderstanding. For Trotskist groups, 'policies' were merely transitional demands in the battle to overthrow capitalism by revolutionary means. They were not 'democratic' socialists. And that was a difference as fundamental as it can get in democratic politics.

The abolition of the proscribed list in the early 1970s followed the appointment of Ron Hayward as Labour's General Secretary, and enabled Militant, or the Revolutionary Socialist League as it was known to the initiated, to proliferate. By 1974, through their control of Labour Party Young Socialists, they had secured a place on Labour's NEC and access to its confidential papers. In 1976 Hayward picked the Militant supporter Andy Bevan as Labour's full-time Youth Officer, with a desk in Labour's headquarters.

In September 1975 Labour's National Agent, Reg Underhill, had secured NEC permission to prepare a report on Militant and other Trotskyist infiltration into the Labour Party. But when it was presented to the NEC Organisation Subcommittee, its chairman, the MP for Militant-dominated Liverpool Walton, Eric Heffer, successfully proposed that it not be published. Shirley Williams and Railwaymen's Union member Russell Tuck led an attempt to overturn the 'Org-Sub's' recommendation but was defeated by sixteen votes to twelve at the full NEC.[633] The report was suppressed, though much of its content leaked to the newspapers.

From its original base in Liverpool, meanwhile, the tentacles of Militant continued to spread. As early as 1976 Militant boasted internally that one third of the speeches from constituency delegates at conference came from Militant members, even though they had only forty constituency delegates out of nearly six hundred.[634] Leading Militant supporters seemed to have an unerring ability to catch the eye of the conference chair. At Labour's 1983 conference, one prominent Militant, Tony Mulhearn, managed to speak four times!

The Manifesto Group of MPs had been pressing for action for some years, but without success. The creation of the SDP added a new urgency to action: the fact that three out of the five Liverpool Labour MPs had defected, claiming that Militant had driven them out of the party, was not something to be ignored. Late in 1981, Foot came to agree that some action might be necessary and, overcoming the protestations of Benn, Foot, Neil Kinnock and John Golding secured NEC agreement to conduct another investigation. The new report was ready in June 1982, implicitly recognised the validity of Underhill's previous report and proposed the establishment of a register of non-affiliated groups. To be eligible to be included on the register, groups had to be open, democratic and whereas the likes of Manifesto, Tribune or Solidarity would comply, Militant, because it was not open and democratic, would not. Again Foot led a victorious charge against Benn's attempt to reject the report. The Tribune Group and CLPD both split on whether they should follow Foot or Benn.

The battle over these proposals was fought out at Labour's 1982 annual conference. APEX General Secretary Roy Grantham demanded action:

> . . . In the early seventies when conference voted to abolished the proscribed list, it was argued that there was no longer any need for it . . . That is only true if the rules are operated. Reg Underhill, the then national agent, produced evidence to the NEC which detailed the entryist tactics of the Militant Tendency. In his enquiry he had submitted to him documents produced by Militant entitled *British Perspectives and Tasks* in which they set out their intention of taking over the Labour Party. Militant, having no

defence, claimed that the documents were fakes. Today everybody knows that those documents were authentic . . . When Reg Underhill proved that the Militants were breaking the constitution, the NEC of that day locked away the report. That must never happen again.

This year Ron Hayward, Jim Mortimer and Michael Foot could have done the same . . . Their report does not open the way for a witch hunt; it opens the way to free this party of the cuckoos in our nest, to free us from those of a different species who wish to take us over (*interruption*). Yes, Militants are a different species. The Labour Party is a broad church of those who want socialism of varying kinds, but based on democracy and Parliament. Militant are opposed to democracy. They support a Trotskyist revolutionary philosophy and the creation of a Bolshevist leadership. It is to further those alien, undemocratic ideas that they have carried out their entryism.

The Militant Tendency argues against the NEC report, claiming that it is the beginning of a witch hunt against the left-wing groups within the party. They argue that this is the prelude to new bans and proscriptions, with the mass expulsion of people from our party. Well, as was said once during the Profumo scandal of 1963: 'They would, wouldn't they?' They want no witch hunts; we want no witch hunts, we want the rules upheld. Our motion supports the NEC and the register. When and if Militant fails to comply, we demand that the editorial board must go, that the paid sellers go and that the Militant prospective candidates be removed (*applause*).

Seconding his resolution was Electricians' Union political officer John Spellar,[635] who while conceding that:

> Militant have a perfectly legitimate right to organise a Trotskyist party in this country, [argued that what] they do not have the right to do is to live parasitically inside this democratic socialist party (*applause*). Parasites can live compatibly with some hosts, but some parasites kill the body they live in – and Militant is killing us with the electorate (*cheers, applause*). They are allowing Margaret Thatcher to get away with murder. She is murdering the economy, murdering the welfare state, and literally murdering many of those who have been thrown on the dole. But the electorate will not trust us unless we rid ourselves of this alien body . . . on the doorsteps . . . [we are] told: 'We won't vote for you as long as you have extremist groups inside the Labour Party' . . .

Militant's supporters did not take this challenge lying down. A counter-resolution was moved by Alan Sapper of the TV Technicians' Union, whose role in defence of Militant was a gift to sketch writers. Sapper, observed *Telegraph* sketch writer Edward Pearce, who 'looks as if a kiss from the right girl might turn him into a prince, snarls for the working class on behalf of a country club union whose typical member, at the expense of the TV licence, is on to his second Maserati'.[636] Sapper charged Militant's opponents with seeking 'the institutionalised elimination of those with whom we may disagree' which, he claimed, was an affront to democracy in the Labour Party. Brighton's delegate Ray Apps, a veteran Militant supporter, agreed, accusing :

... the right-wing of launching a witch hunt which will split the party from top to bottom (*applause*). The same right-wingers who are behind this witch hunt were in the same organisation that campaigned for victory with Owen, with Williams, with Rodgers ... Hattersley said the other day that he would like to welcome them back, at the same time as he wants to expel socialists from the party. The truth is this, he not only wants to bring them back, he wants to bring back their policies, the policies that lost us the general election ... This is not a constitutional issue; it is a political issue ...

Talking about organisations, I was at a Solidarity meeting yesterday. They admitted that they had a membership, that they had organisers. No one talked about expelling their gurus, Shore and Hattersley (*applause*). [His use of 'we' and 'our' as he concluded gave the game away.] Militant has no separate aims and policy. We have no aims and policy separate from the party as a whole. Our campaign for the nationalisation of the monopolies, the banks, the financial institutions, is on every one of our members' cards. That is what we are campaigning for ... We should be discussing how to implement Clause Four ... '

Several other Militant supporters, including Pat Wall,[637] spoke in the same vein. But this time Militant did not have it all their own way. Ricky Ormonde, a former steelworks fitter from James Callaghan's own Cardiff constituency, denounced Labour's failure to act earlier:

We have known the truth for many years and we have not had the guts to do anything about it. We have seen an uncontrollable Frankenstein of programmed robots nibbling away at the very foundations of this great labour movement ... The Militant Tendency has blatantly broken the rules of the constitution. Of course they will deny this, even in the face of irrefutable evidence ... they are dishonest. They deny that they are an offshoot of the Revolutionary Socialist League. They deny that they have secret meetings prior to the official Labour Party meetings ...

Lord Underhill, who had written the original report, was received with applause as he asked conference:

... Why does Militant deny the nature of its organisation? Why does it deny it has any organisation at all? Why is it trying to kid the whole country and the movement that all it is is a paper? ... Because they know that to admit them would amount to a breach of the constitution ...

Michael Foot, winding up the debate, confronted head-on Militant's claim to be nothing more than a group like the Bevanites:

When people say to me that Militant Tendency are just like Stafford Cripps or Aneurin Bevan, or the Salvation Army – as I am sometimes told – it is not like that at all. It is very different. There was no secret conspiracy with Stafford Cripps or Aneurin Bevan; they wanted everybody to know what they were doing (*applause*). There were no false colours about the way in which they were propagating their views. They were accused of trying to form a party within a party, but it was not true . . . but in this case it is true, and that is a big difference (*applause*).

The conference vote was an overwhelming defeat for Militant, but both Militant and the Labour Party received legal advice that yet again Labour's rule book was deficient and any expulsions on the basis of people belonging to groups incompatible with the new register could be challenged in the courts. It was back to the drawing board!

Meanwhile Militant could continue a systematic campaign to secure the deselection of sitting Labour MPs and their replacement by Militants. It was to secure them two Militant supporters in Parliament at the next election: Terry Fields in Liverpool and Dave Nellist in Coventry. Had Labour's vote not collapsed in so many seats they might have secured several more. They would also consolidate their control of Liverpool Council.

Meanwhile, both left and right had been organising furiously for the NEC elections. The hard left had drawn up a hit-list that set out to replace Joan Lestor and Neil Kinnock, who had failed to back Benn in the deputy leadership election, with Audrey Wise and defeated Treasurer Norman Atkinson. With Lestor they succeeded. With Kinnock they failed. The moderates were more successful. Foot's ally John Evans defeated the incumbent hard-left Les Huckfield in the socialist societies section, Eric Varley comfortably held off a challenge from Michael Meacher for Treasurer and Joan Maynard, nicknamed Stalin's Granny for her devotion to the Soviet cause, was defeated by a moderate: dark horse Anne Davis. Doug Hoyle of ASTMS and in a shock result NUM candidate Eric Clarke were also defeated. Clarke's defeat occurred because railwaymen's leader Sid Weighell broke the convention that the railwaymen would always vote for the candidates of the miners' union. When his vote was uncovered Weighell claimed that the NUM had never formally agreed the deal, which while technically true was subterfuge. It was a political decision to try and break the stranglehold of the hard left on the NEC. And it had worked, though Weighell was to pay the highest price for his vote when the left-wingers in his union managed to use it to precipitate his removal from office. Weighell's head on a plate was all the hard left were to get. When they demanded a re-ballot they were defeated. Basnett told NUPE that if they voted for a re-ballot he might not back their candidate next time. And the shift in personnel on the NEC, taken together with the changes the previous year, were profound in their significance. The hard left had now lost their controlling majority on the NEC and at the first meeting of the new committee John Golding was able to orchestrate the removal of Benn, Heffer and their allies from the key chairmanships and subcommittees that had been their power bases for so long. Golding himself succeeded Benn as chair of the Home Policy committee and Russell Tuck of the railwaymen succeeded Heffer as chair of the Organisation Committee that would be crucial to tackling Militant.

FIFTY-NINE

The Kiss of Life 1983–84

*'If Margaret Thatcher wins on Thursday, I warn you
not to be ordinary. I warn you not to be young.
I warn you not to fall ill. I warn you not to get old'*

By January 1983, unemployment had peaked at 3 million and over the next few months it gradually declined, to the still enormous figure of 2.98 million in June. The number of working days lost due to strike action had decreased to the lowest since 1976. The levelling off of unemployment, falling exchange rates which enabled British industry to raise wage rates and increase overtime payments and the tax-cutting budget of March 1982 helped prompt a Conservative recovery in the opinion polls, starting shortly before the Argentine invasion of the Falklands, which gave Tory poll ratings a further boost. After September 1981 Labour remained stuck below 35 per cent in the Gallup poll. However unpopular were the Tories, and they were down to 23 per cent in December 1981, too many people were simply not prepared to support Labour, whose popularity had plummeted in the wake of the creation of the SDP and Labour's policy shifts to the left. The Bennite proposition that a more 'left-wing' Labour Party would be more popular with the electorate was simply not being borne out in reality.

Labour's manifesto at the 1983 election was just what the hard left had always demanded. John Golding, strategist of the right on the NEC, had foreseen the obvious likelihood of electoral defeat and decided to play the left at their own game. Usually the moderates would try and sanitise the manifesto and be blamed by the left for diluting its socialist content. Not this time. As chair of the Home Policy Committee, Golding swung the right in support of what Benn and others demanded, a manifesto that included all the assorted demands that the hard left had got party conference to agree to. They put them all in the manifesto, which became rather long in consequence, hence the observation usually attributed to Gerald Kaufman that Labour's 1983 manifesto was 'the longest suicide note in history'.

The election itself saw a Conservative landslide majority of 144. Disturbingly for Labour, despite the fact that most of the record numbers of unemployed were, or had been, manual workers, the 1983 election saw, for the first time in post-1945 electoral history, a majority of the manual working classes not voting Labour: only 42 per cent voted

Labour, 35 per cent voted Conservative and most of the remainder voted SDP-Liberal Alliance. Among manual workers in the private sector, the workers Labour had originally been founded to represent, the picture was even worse: only 37 per cent voted Labour while 36 per cent voted Conservative and 27 per cent SDP-Liberal Alliance. And in the south of England, Labour's support among the manual working class was down to 26 per cent: 42 per cent voted Conservative and 32 per cent SDP-Liberal Alliance.[638]

Overall, though the Conservative vote share actually declined by 1 per cent on 1979, Labour's collapsed to 27.6 per cent. The 'first past the post' electoral system meant that Labour retained 209 MPs while the SDP-Liberal Alliance, with the highest 'Liberal' vote ever, nearly eight million (25.4 per cent), secured only 23 seats. Of over 30 SDP MPs before the 1983 election there were now only five (Roy Jenkins, David Owen Ian Wrigglesworth, John Cartwright and Robert Maclennan), with the addition of young newcomer Charles Kennedy. Shirley Williams, Bill Rodgers and Dickson Mabon were among those defeated. So were a host of Labour MPs and former ministers still in the Labour Party, including three former members of the Callaghan Cabinet: Albert Booth, David Ennals and Tony Benn. 'The next leadership election is going to be between Tony Benn and the man with the most chance of beating him,'[639] Edward Pearce had written in January 1983. It was not to be. Benn was *hors de combat* before battle could even be joined. The voters of Bristol had rejected him.

A depleted opposition faced another gruelling term of Thatcherism. On the eve of poll, shadow Education Secretary Neil Kinnock had described what might lie ahead in what was to become the most famous speech of the campaign. Hoarse with fatigue, he addressed a rally of the faithful in Bridgend, south Wales:

If Margaret Thatcher is re-elected as Prime Minister on Thursday, I warn you.

I warn you that you will have pain – when healing and relief depend upon payment.

I warn you that you will have ignorance – when talents are untended and wits are wasted, when learning is a privilege and not a right.

I warn you that you will have poverty – when pensions slip and benefits are whittled away by a government that won't pay in an economy that can't pay.

I warn you that you will be cold – when fuel charges are used as a tax system that the rich don't notice and the poor can't afford.

I warn you that you must not expect to work – when many cannot spend, more will not be able to earn. When they don't earn, they don't spend. When they don't spend, work dies.

I warn you not to go into the streets alone after dark or into the streets in large crowds of protest in the light.

I warn you that you will be quiet – when the curfew of fear and the gibbet of unemployment make you obedient.

I warn you that you will have defence of a sort – with a risk and at a price that passes all understanding.

I warn you that you will be homebound – when fares and transport bills kill leisure and lock you up.

I warn you that you will borrow less – when credit, loans, mortgages and easy payments are refused to people on your melting income.

If Margaret Thatcher wins on Thursday, I warn you not to be ordinary. I warn you not to be young. I warn you not to fall ill. I warn you not to get old.[640]

Though this speech is sometimes said to have won Kinnock the next leadership election, he had in reality won it long before. The new electoral college and the policies of the party meant that a candidate of the social-democratic right was doomed, while anyone tarred with complicity in the supposed betrayals of the last Labour government had less appeal among the constituencies than one such as Kinnock who had rebelled against it. As many expected, Foot announced his resignation as leader of the Labour Party shortly after the 1983 election. He was now 70 years old. Healey considered running again. But the fact that he himself would be nearly 70 by the following election led him to conclude that it was time to bow out gracefully for the next generation. He advised Peter Shore of this, but Shore did not heed his warning. The leadership election did become a battle between the next generation. Shore and the candidate of the hard left, Eric Heffer, were never seriously in the running. Shore would poll barely 3 per cent of the electoral college vote and Heffer just over 6 per cent. Kinnock, with Scots unilateralist Robin Cook as his campaign manager, was the standard-bearer of the Tribunite soft left and Roy Hattersley, with John Smith as his campaign manager, and the backing of Healey and Callaghan, was the candidate of the Solidarity right. Hattersley also stood for deputy, just in case he didn't win, where he faced Benn-backed Michael Meacher, Shore ally Gwyneth Dunwoody and Welsh anti-Marketeer Denzil Davies. Kinnock early on decided to back Hattersley as his deputy on a dream ticket that would unite the party and his campaign team worked strenuously to persuade the TGWU to back Hattersley for deputy rather than Meacher.

Though two-thirds of the shadow Cabinet voted for Hattersley,[641] it was Kinnock who secured victory in the electoral college. Moreover, Kinnock did not secure support just from the left. His backers included John Golding, whose constituency had an OMOV ballot of its members on its own initiative: they voted for Kinnock. Hattersley had never managed to translate the respect engendered among fellow MPs by his impressive performance in the Commons to widespread support among the union leaders, apart from David Basnett, even among those on the right. Moreover, all the unions who balloted their members found that they backed Kinnock for leader (and usually Hattersley for deputy). Kinnock became leader with over 71 per cent of the electoral college vote, to just over 19 per cent for Hattersley. Hattersley won just over 67 per cent of the vote for deputy, with Meacher on just less than 28 per cent. It would be a triumph for Michael Foot's protégé Neil Kinnock, and a disaster for the Bennites.

The TUC Congress of September 1983 took place while Labour's leadership election was still ongoing. It opened with the address from the year's retiring Chairman (the chair rotated annually among the General Council on 'Buggins's turn'). That year it was Frank Chapple of the Electricians' Union. The son of a cobbler, Chapple had grown up over his dad's one-man shop in a Hoxton slum. His early enthusiasms included racing pigeons and Communism, but after the Soviet invasion of Hungary in 1956 he changed his mind on one of them. Latterly among the most outspoken anti-Communists in the trade union movement, Chapple had been in the forefront of the battle for OMOV in the Labour Party. Physically, he bore an uncanny resemblance to 'the Godfather'. Sketch writer Edward Pearce described how Chapple's enemies, 'their passionate opposition to racialism briefly suspended, see in his Italianate handsomeness the features of a man as big in Chicago as in Palermo – Big Frank and the Capella mob. Mr Chapple, who is winning a lot of battles presently, responds to this like a slim-line rhinoceros.'[642] 'Chapple was a natural communicator, although his language was as garish as his neckties. He was one of life's self-educated successes,' recalled former Employment Minister John Grant.[643] 'If I chose my words with more than usual care,' Chapple remembers, 'I still left no room for doubt as to my meaning.'[644] He highlighted the challenges facing the movement:

> . . . Rising unemployment has also been accompanied by a further deterioration in our industrial structure . . . For the first time in our history, we now import more manufactured goods than we export, and there are no signs that this will be easily reversed . . .
>
> We have to campaign for shorter hours and be prepared to revise our attitudes to work, to education, to the importance of higher productivity and to the maximum use of capital equipment that shorter hours require.

Chapple then turned to the need to engage with those challenges, and took aim at those who preferred the governments of the Soviet bloc to an elected government in Britain:

> This government will eventually learn that free market extravaganzas are just as irrelevant as the inefficiencies of state planning bureaucracies, but in the meantime unemployment and its social problems will remain intolerably high.
>
> That is why our duty is clear. That is why we have to argue with the government and build a partnership that can revitalise Britain. We cannot contract out of this responsibility or behave like some obscure religious sect that insists on not talking to unbelievers.
>
> I am sure that the majority of our members are as baffled as I am that some trade union leaders will travel halfway across the world to sympathise with communist dictatorships yet seek to prevent the TUC from talking to the elected government of Britain.

Apart from being the voice of our movement, Congress also has to provide leadership. We have to be representative, brave enough to face difficult decisions, and far-sighted enough to see where our members have not even begun to look.

Crucial to these qualities is the willingness – indeed the determination – to look reality in the face: to confront the truth: to assess where we are. There is no doubt that our movement has suffered in the last few years. Membership has fallen from a high of 12 million in 1980 to 10 million by the latest count . . . For more than 20 years our public popularity has been sliding – at the same time, many of our members have been expressing their unease.

This unease has not all been simply whipped up by right-wing newspapers or man-ufactured by opinion pollsters. It has also reflected itself in the mass desertion of Labour votes and the support which this government's industrial relations legislation has attracted. It is crucially important that our movement recognises these criticisms. If we had listened earlier, we might not have suffered the [electoral] catastrophe of June 9 or the defeat of five years ago.

Accepting that we ourselves have to make necessary reforms will not only give us a fighting chance of regaining the trust we have allowed to wither; it would also blunt the attacks made upon us, put an end to some of the self-inflicted absurdities we stumble into, and strengthen our appeal in the final part of the twentieth century . . .

The working-class movement that is being fashioned by recession, new tech-nology, 40 years of a welfare state and ever-developing aspirations, is profoundly different from that in which most of us grew up.

In a few years' time women will constitute nearly half of the workforce; industry will be more concentrated in the south east; a larger number of our members will be home owners, new skills will have replaced the ones we know. If British trade union-ism is to avoid the mistakes which have weakened our colleagues in other countries, we have to adapt to these changes and provide the kind of movement that they imply.

We will have to stop wishing that the world was like it once was, and face up to what it is . . . to make special efforts to involve more women and members of ethnic communities in the policy making and leadership of our movement . . . we have to reassert in practice our greatest strength – the commitment to democracy . . .

Threats to destroy elected governments are not only infantile, but they are also a dangerous boomerang, alienating us from our members as well as threatening the only type of society that guarantees our own freedom.

Democracy is our cause and our protection. That is why our movement has always opposed fascism and curbs on liberty. We cannot remember Tolpuddle or condemn the murder of trade unionists in Chile whilst turning a blind eye to the fact that more trade unionists have been killed by the state in Poland since 1970 than in this country in a hundred years.

To its credit, Congress has never accepted Pinochet's men as part of the labour movement. Nor can we accept Jaruzelski's.

If we appear to equivocate between freedom and totalitarianism, we will injure ourselves and the values which founded our movement . . .

'The impact of his speech will certainly be felt in every debate at Blackpool this week,' wrote Geoffrey Goodman of the *Daily Mirror*: 'It was a courageous, controversial collection of home truths admired for its nerve if not for its content.'[645] 'Frank, your country NEEDS you!' echoed the *Sun*. Chapple's sentiments would be largely endorsed later in the Congress by TUC general secretary Len Murray, who would tell delegates: 'We cannot talk as if the trade union movement is an alternative government.' Chapple's condemnation of Polish Communist dictator Jaruzelski proved more timely then he had expected: later that week the Trotskyist newspaper *News Line* published a letter from new National Union of Mineworkers' leader Arthur Scargill which described banned Polish trade union Solidarity as 'an anti-socialist organisation which desires the overthrow of a socialist state'.

Chapple's speech was his swansong: he would retire as leader of his union the following year. It was also a clarion call for Labour's modernisation. The evening before his speech, Chapple had given a press conference where he had declared his support for Kinnock over Hattersley, even though as a fellow Labour 'right-winger' it was thought that Hattersley would be Chapple's natural choice. Kinnock he thought the man more likely to stand up to Militant. 'It is possible that Kinnock can put the party right,' he said. 'He's got balls.'[646] If Neil Kinnock was to be the father of Labour's modernisation, its Godfather was Frank Chapple.

Neil Kinnock's election as Labour's new leader was announced on 2 October 1983 at the annual conference in Blackpool. His youth, vitality and prodigious talents would restore to Labour hope where there had been only despair. At the same time, Kinnock would grapple the punctured Bennite balloon back to earth and release its adherents from the ideological basket in which they had become entrapped. 'Benn was the man who carried the torch,' recalled Tom Sawyer, newly elected on to the NEC.

> Benn embodied the hopes and aspirations of so many activists. But it was a blind alley. I had been a union officer up in the north east and had been influenced by reading about some of the same people he had, the suffragettes, the syndicalists. In 1981 I got the deputy general secretary and was put up for the NEC. In those days the top guy got the TUC General Council and the number two got the Labour NEC. We had never actually been able to get elected on to it before but people respected our new General Secretary, Rodney Bickerstaffe, and he got David Basnett of the GMB to vote for me, so I was on. I was a Bennitte. Benn saved a seat for me at the first meeting. At the Darlington by-election in March 1983 I was with Kinnock on the sleeper and we started to talk. He explained to me where he thought the Bennites were going wrong. In those days you were either hard-left or right-wing. He got me to focus on where the voters were. It was a lesson I'd known once but lost through being angry at what had been happening to low-paid workers under a Labour government.[647]

447

Kinnock's ability to reconnect idealism with realism, with the 'common sense of socialism', was not lost on the hard left. Sketch writer Edward Pearce observed:

> Miss Joan Maynard, one of Parliament's most notable admirers of the Soviet system, who, with her hair done up behind and her glinting glasses, irresistibly suggests one of those female Russian judges liable to send you down on a renewable sentence, once remarked of Mr Kinnock, 'I'm very worried about Neil. I'm afraid that he might do a Stan Orme.' It was a shrewd comment. Like the well-loved member for Salford East, Mr Kinnock has had his period of fervid, technicolor leftwingery, but like Stan Orme he is influenced by membership of the human race. He is also Welsh and intelligent, a combination which obliges anyone so endowed to start looking over his shoulder at Aneurin Bevan and Lloyd George. It also implies a facility which will be called wizardry and when it comes to words, a certain velocity of circulation.

As shadow Education Secretary his Commons performances were impressive, but as Pearce observed, not yet bomb-proof: 'Kinnock has a lovely gift of wit and fluency . . . but he tends to skate over boring difficulties and the horse work of getting his facts right . . . [Kinnock's] best speeches are a triumph of inspiration over absent homework.' When facing Education Secretary Mark Carlisle Kinnock would give the Commons 'the complete Welsh grandeur of the eloquent boyo bit – torrents coming down the Cader Idris, adjectives dancing in the stream like trout, a flood of glittering indignation cascading down in a way which should have carried the minister away'. Instead, Carlisle would ask, in for example a debate on the alleged shortage of textbooks, for Kinnock to tell him in which schools this was the case. Kinnock would then suffer what Pearce described as 'orator's block, a long pause accompanied by agitated movements. Mr Kinnock then muttered something about "well-known facts". And, as suddenly, Cader Idris was made to look a little like a stage set for *The Maid of the Mountains*. However, a reformed Kinnock if he can kick some of his gaudier habits and develop a modified passion for detail, would be something to keep the Tories awake at nights.'[648]

And Kinnock would reform, both himself and the party. In doing so he was to lead Labour back from the abyss. In both cases it was a reformation, not a transformation. He played to his strengths and sought to skate over his weaknesses, following the same strategy with the Labour Party.

In his acceptance speech, Kinnock quoted a maxim of Aneurin Bevan:

> My fellow countryman, my fellow townsman, my inspiration. Nye said, as a maxim for a political leader, and I commend it as a maxim for a political movement.
>
> 'He who would lead must articulate the wants, the frustrations and the aspirations of the majority. Their hearts must be moved by his word, and so his words must be attuned to their realities. If he speaks in the old false categories, they will listen and at first nod their heads, for they hear a familiar echo from the past; but if he persists, they

begin to appreciate that he is no longer with them. He must speak with the authentic accents of those who elected him. That means he should share their values, that is be in touch with their realities.'

That is not just my maxim, or Roy's maxim, or the maxim of any member of a shadow Cabinet or National Executive Committee or a trade union leader or a Member of Parliament. It is the maxim of the whole of this movement. We have to commend the common sense of socialism, the realism of socialism, for that is how we get the maxim of socialism – the most rational, reasonable, emancipating creed ever put on the agenda of humankind for the advancement of humankind. That is how we win. If anyone wants to know why we must conduct ourselves in this fashion, just remember at all times, with all temptations, how you, each and every one of you sitting in this hall, each and every Labour worker watching this conference, each and every Labour voter, yes, and some others as well, remember how you felt on that dreadful morning of 10 June. Just remember how you felt then, and think to yourselves: 'June the ninth, 1983; never ever again will we experience that' . . .

Kinnock's next task was to build a winning shadow Cabinet team. Most of his shadow Cabinet had backed Hattersley. An exception was Peter Shore, who had backed himself. Shore bitterly resented the implosion of his leadership aspirations, which so recently had tasted almost tangible. He was unconvinced that the 'politically unformed and immature' Kinnock, carrying a 'complete kit of then-fashionable left-wing viewpoints but . . . no settled convictions on any of them' and bereft of ministerial experience even at the most junior level, could be the credible leader that he believed Labour needed.[649] In his own mind he contrasted Kinnock unfavourably in stature with ex-Foreign Secretary David Owen, now leader of the SDP, and with himself, and he believed that the electorate would too. For Kinnock, Shore became 'so uncooperative that I decided to pile him with gifts – if he did well with two jobs [both shadow Leader of the Commons and shadow Trade and Industry] so much the better. If he didn't shine, politics would take its course and he'd be voted off the shadow Cabinet. That's what happened,' he told his biographer.[650] Kinnock wanted Peter Shore out, believing him too wedded to the economic strategy of 1979-83. He needed someone of Hattersley's stature within the party to replace him. Kinnock persuaded Hattersley to replace Shore as shadow Chancellor, technically a promotion, though Hattersley feared he was 'temperamentally unsuited'[651] to the role: he preferred to remain shadow Home Secretary, a role that he had grown into. Hattersley's job as shadow Home Secretary Kinnock gave to Harold Wilson's protégé Gerald Kaufman. Kaufman's role shadowing Environment went to Callaghan's former PPS Jack Cunningham, who was joined in the shadow Cabinet by another Manifesto Group ally, Giles Radice, who succeeded to Kinnock's old job of shadow Education Secretary. New faces from the left included Kinnock's campaign manager Robin Cook, who became spokesman on Europe; Benn-supporter Michael Meacher, who was given health; and John Prescott, once Peter Shore's PPS and in the days before Britain's MEPs were directly elected, the leader of the Labour group of MEPs. Prescott became shadow Transport Minister.

In the year following Labour's 1982 annual conference a battle royal had been fought out on the NEC between those, led by John Golding, Gwyneth Dunwoody and Michael Foot, who wanted action taken against Militant, and those, led by Benn, Heffer, Jo Richardson, Audrey Wise and Dennis Skinner, who did not. Militant's defenders were voted down and following legal advice on the best way forward the NEC decided to proceed.

One of the difficulties would be proving who among the array of Militant supporters was or was not a member of what was a secret organisation. The agreed first step was to take the straightforward approach: decapitation through the expulsion of the five named members of the *Militant* editorial board. This the NEC did in the spring of 1983. The five refused to accept expulsion and took up a right of appeal to the full plenary of Labour conference.

The five members of the *Militant* editorial board, Peter Taafe, Lynn Walsh, Keith Dickinson, Clare Doyle and Ted Grant, addressed conference in turn. Taafe declared: 'We will be rehabilitated into this party when those who are demanding our expulsion are in the rogues' gallery with the Browns and other traitors to the Labour movement.' Grant insisted: 'If we look at our history, we see that it was the traitors of the SDP – Rodgers, Owen, Williams – who first raised the question of a witchhunt in the Labour Party . . . one of the reasons they gave for leaving the Labour Party was that Militant was not expelled from the party . . . there is no way that Marxism can be separated from the Labour Party. There is no way you will succeed with these expulsions. We will be back.' They were not. Labour's left-wing General Secretary Jim Mortimer set out the case for their expulsion:

> There are many, including myself, who have been strongly influenced by Marxist ideas in bringing us to the Labour movement . . . the distinctive feature of the members of the Militant tendency is not that they are Marxists; it is not even that they are Trotskyists, because there are many Trotskyists who do not take their point of view. The distinctive feature of the Militant tendency is they are a Trotskyist entryist group.

The votes that followed on each of the five were decisive for expulsion in every case.

Militant's counterattack failed. Resolutions proposed by Militant supporters[652] demanded an 'immediate halt to all witchhunts', and deplored the ban on the sale of *Militant* at Labour Party meetings, but other speakers told a different story. For John Maxton:[653]

> . . . one thing we must stop in this party is the use of the term 'witchhunt'. Nobody in

this party is witchhunting. A witchhunt means one of two things. In its original sense it means hunting little old ladies for no reason except their mildly offensive behaviour (*shouts – interruptions*). In its modern sense it means persecuting people who have committed no offence, giving them no trial, no hearing and no ability to defend themselves . . . This party has given Militant every opportunity to defend itself . . . [For Jack Straw,[654]] people must make a choice . . . between Militant or the National Executive, between Militant and Neil Kinnock and Roy Hattersley (*interruption – shouts from the floor*). That is the choice and it will be the choice facing everybody on every doorstep at the next election . . . It is a choice between Militant and the Labour Party. A vote for these resolutions will deal this party a near mortal blow. Let us be serious about that (*interruption – slow hand clapping. Conference called to order by chair*). I am glad to have a practical demonstration of the tolerance that is practised by Militant members . . .

The pro-Militant resolutions were overwhelmingly defeated. The expulsions and the size of the votes against Militant were events of signal importance, recalled John Golding: 'It was the 1983 conference that crippled Militant.'[655]

Despite his retirement in 1983 as deputy leader, Denis Healey was to remain shadow Foreign Secretary and arguably the most heavyweight figure in Labour's shadow Cabinet, for another four years. No longer in the running to be leader, he remained, proudly, a 'good Labour man'. His continuing grievance was against, not the party that had failed sufficiently to appreciate his talents to elect him its leader, but against Margaret Thatcher, who having sacked most of her Cabinet dissenters was now in the full fire of her second term. 'Her speeches in Parliament became increasingly strident,' recalled Healey.

As I watched the numb rows of Tory backbenchers while she was speaking I was often reminded of Yeats' words:
'And now we stare astonished at the sea
And a miraculous strange bird shrieks at us.'
I always regretted that recent parliamentary convention forbids any opposition frontbencher except the Leader to take on the Prime Minister directly in the House of Commons . . . the best opportunity came in a speech on the Foreign Secretary [Sir Geoffrey Howe]'s announcement that members of GCHQ, the government's organisation for collecting signals intelligence, should no longer be members of trade unions.[656]

It was on the afternoon of 27 February 1984. Healey attacked the implied Tory accusation that trade unions lacked 'patriotism':

I remind the government of the last time when anything such as this happened. It was when Mr Chamberlain and his Home Secretary compared Ernie Bevin to Quisling. Within months they were out of office and Ernie Bevin was in office, helping to win the war for Britain.

I have not wasted time on the Foreign Secretary this afternoon, although I am

451

bound to say that I feel some of his colleagues must be a bit tired by now of his hobbling around from one of the doorsteps to another, with a bleeding hole in his foot and a smoking gun in his hand, telling them that he did not know it was loaded.

The Foreign Secretary, however, is not the real villain in this case; he is the fall guy. Those of us with long memories will feel that he is rather like poor van der Lubbe in the Reichstag fire trial. We are asking ourselves the question that was asked at the trial: who is the Mephistopheles behind this shabby Faust? The answer to that is clear. The handling of this decision by – and I quote her own backbenchers – the great she-elephant, she who must be obeyed, the Catherine the Great of Finchley, the Prime Minister herself, has drawn sympathetic trade unionists, such as Len Murray, into open revolt. Her pig-headed bigotry has prevented her closest colleagues and Sir Robert Armstrong from offering and accepting a compromise . . .

I put it to all Conservative members, but mainly to the government front bench, that to allow the right hon. lady to commit Britain to another four years of capricious autocracy would be to do fearful damage not just to the Conservative Party but to the state. She has faced them with the most damaging of all conflicts of loyalty. They must choose between the interests of their country, our nation's security and our cohesion as a people and the obstinacy of an individual. I hope that they resolve this conflict in the interests of the nation. If not, they will carry a heavy responsibility for the tragedies that are bound to follow.

Healey's biographer, at the time a parliamentary sketch writer, saw the speech from the gallery. He would 'hear nothing to compare with it for impact until the attack on Mrs Thatcher made in late 1990 by Sir Geoffrey Howe'[657] that was to precipitate the termination of her premiership. Within minutes of making his speech, Healey had to exit the Commons to make his way to Chesterfield where there was a by-election in a safe Labour seat. It had been precipitated by the decision of Healey's shadow Cabinet colleague, former Energy and Industry Secretary Eric Varley, to leave the Commons to accept the chairmanship of Coalite. Varley had concluded that such was the scale of Labour's electoral disaster in 1983 that it would be for a future generation to lead Labour back to government. The candidate selected for the by-election was one of the many recently defeated Labour MPs: Tony Benn.

SIXTY

Scargill and the Miners' Strike 1982–85

'Lions led by donkeys'

Uneconomic coal mines had been closing in Britain for decades. For some this was something to welcome. Labour MP Tam Dalyell had become an advocate of nuclear power when confronted by the harrowing respiratory diseases killing so many of his constituents in West Lothian who had worked down the coal mines. But for many miners and mining communities, coal was a way of life and the basis of local employment. If the mine closed, the pit villages in which miners had lived for generations risked economic collapse. It was all very well Norman Tebbit telling the unemployed, 'get on your bike', but who would want to move into the pit villages to replace those leaving?

The oil price shock of 1973–74 had given rise to a new approach. The Labour government of 1974–79 had drawn up a *Plan for Coal*, which, in recognising the new higher price of oil, anticipated replacing the contraction of coal mines with an expansion. But the plan did not work out. North Sea oil came on stream, energy efficiency improved, and the recession of Thatcher's first term further reduced the industrial demand for coal. Supply was exceeding demand and by 1983 the coal industry was losing £1 billion per annum. The Coal Board decided, therefore, on a programme of closing uneconomic pits. It was against this background that in April 1982 Arthur Scargill, a charismatic and determined former member of the Young Communist League, was elected to succeed the moderate Joe Gormley as President of the NUM. Scargill claimed credit for closing the Saltley Coke Depot with his 'flying pickets' during the successful 1972 miners' strike. His detractors said that the real victors of the 'Battle of Saltley Gate' had been TGWU-organised pickets who had persuaded TGWU lorry drivers to take solidarity action. Scargill made clear his determination to resist the closure of 'uneconomic' pits. But in October 1982 a ballot called on the pit closure programme went 61 per cent against a strike. Scargill tried again to get a vote for strike action in March 1983 and was again rejected. On 6 March 1984 the Coal Board announced the closure of Cortonwood colliery in south Yorkshire and stated that a further 20 pits would close over the coming year, with the loss of 20,000 jobs. A strike was called out locally and spread through Yorkshire and subsequently across Britain. Scargill's biographer Paul Routledge describes evidence to suggest that far from the strike action without a national ballot being spontaneous and unplanned, 'financial evasive action[658] that assumed a major dispute was under way was planned and executed by Scargill before the NUM executive even met to decide whether or not to back the Yorkshire strike call'. When the executive did meet, it overruled demands from the minority moderates for a national strike ballot, demands they continued to overrule throughout the strike. 'We will not be constitutionalised out of action,' NUM Vice-President Mick McGahey told the television news that evening.[659] At numerous junctures it looked as if a deal might be negotiated, but it always foundered on Scargill's refusal to compromise. Indeed, some NUM colleagues feared that whenever a deal hove into view Scargill became all the more intransigent, believing that it represented signs of weakness and therefore of impending defeat on the part of the Coal Board. When the Coal Board prepared to concede a rethink on the planned closure of the 20 pits in exchange for agreement on a formula by which agreement could be reached on when pits became uneconomic, Scargill made clear his belief that so long as there was coal left, pits were not uneconomic.

Public opinion was against Scargill from the start and moved overwhelmingly and decisively against him as the dispute progressed. In July 1984 Gallup opinion polls suggested that 40 per cent of the public backed the employers and only 33 per cent supported the miners. A full 79 per cent disapproved of the miners' militant approach (only 15 per cent approved). By November/December support for the employers had increased to 52 per cent as against between 26 per cent and 23 per cent for the miners, with as many as 92 per cent of the public disapproving of the 'methods being used by the miners'.[660] In parallel with the shift in public opinion against the miners came a swing against Labour in the opinion polls. On 28 September 1984 a MORI poll put the Conservatives on 42 per cent and Labour on only 36 per cent, the largest Conservative lead since December 1983. Over the next few months the Conservative lead grew.

Electricians' Union leader Eric Hammond had written privately to NUM General Secretary Peter Heathfield on 24 May 1984 offering to take solidarity action if ordinary miners were to vote for the strike in a national democratic ballot. But in his reply of 1 June, Heathfield made clear that not only had 'the NUM consistently recognised that legislation designed to weaken the trade union movement may have to be ignored' (i.e. they would break laws they didn't like) but 'I do not consider a ballot in such circumstances [i.e. where there was a likelihood that it might go against a strike) can be a part of the democratic process.'[661] At the TUC in September Hammond was virtually the only union leader to stand out against a statement giving pretty much unqualified endorsement to Scargill's approach. A few weeks later, at the Labour conference on Monday 1 October, Scargill moved a resolution pinning the entirety of the blame for the strike on the Conservative government and 'their determination to attack the National Union of Mineworkers and the whole trade union movement . . . unlawful actions by the police, organised violence against miners, their picket lines and their communities by means of an unconstitutional nationally controlled police force'.

For Scargill:

> ... The government's decision last year to appoint Ian MacGregor as Chairman of the National Coal Board was a blatant political decision designed to provoke the NUM . . . There are no uneconomic pits. There are only pits which have been deliberately starved of investment by successive governments . . .
>
> MacGregor says, 'Mr Scargill, what can we do with the coal?' I'll tell him what we can do with the millions of tons that we produce: we can begin to practise some compassion, and give it to the old-age pensioners in the twilight of their lives; that is what we could do with the coal (*cheers and applause*).
>
> We also have to remind this conference that in 1974 the Labour government signed an historic agreement called *Plan for Coal* . . . Nowhere in that updated version of *Plan for Coal* is there any reference to closing pits on the grounds of being uneconomic . . .
>
> The costs of closing pits and making miners redundant is twice as much as keeping those pits open and keeping jobs secure. And I am sick and tired of the balance-sheet mentality of this government, and the Coal Board talking about the fact that people will not be made compulsorily redundant. I want to make it clear to this conference we are not talking about a miner in work whose job may be made redundant. It is not his job to sell. It belongs to future generations (*cheers and applause*) . . .
>
> We have suffered attacks on the picket line from a state police force armed in full riot gear – state violence against miners (*cheers and applause*) . . . We have challenged this Conservative government's philosophy . . . As we go into the eighth month of this dispute, there is one thing coming through loud and clear: the miners' union is winning this fight and it is not only winning for miners, but for you and the entire labour and trade union movement (*standing ovation and prolonged applause and cheers*).

Almost everyone else called to the rostrum by conference chair Eric Heffer backed Scargill, including TGWU leader Ron Todd and ASLEF General Secretary Ray Buckton. Todd condemned:

> . . . the right of a scab to cross a picket line, the epidemic of ballotitis across the country, and, worst of all, the distortions of violence and intimidation . . . there is economic violence that destroys industry . . . judicial violence that orders sequestration . . . state violence that erodes the morale of a striking miner and uses the needs of his children to put pressure on his family. There is political violence . . . that brings in legislation to destroy our organisation.

Even GMB General Secretary David Basnett declared his support for Scargill's motion. When he pleaded plaintively against picket-line violence ('Arthur, it would help those who are striving to help you, if your members do not let themselves be provoked') he was heckled from the floor. Eventually, shouts from the floor to call someone against the motion managed successfully to appeal to Heffer's democratic streak and he looked around for a suitable victim: 'A request has been made that someone who is against should be called. I don't know who is for or against, do I? I would not dream of knowing. Eric Hammond.' Hammond then spoke against the motion:

> Chair and conference, the executive statement demonstrates what is wrong with policy-making in the party today. There is no attempt to analyse the real problems underlying the conduct of this dispute, no attempt to understand why the refusal to ballot the membership has split the NUM; no call for the TUC's guide for the conduct of disputes to be observed; and, most shamefully, no demand for the violence and hooliganism on the picket line to be stopped.
>
> After a powerful statement by Neil Kinnock at the TUC, this is a complete climb-down (*interruptions and order restored by conference chair*) . . . It seems some of the comrades are in favour of free speech everywhere in the world except this conference. After the powerful statement by Neil Kinnock at the TUC, this is a complete climb-down with no mention of hooliganism or violence in the statement. Conference can indulge itself with unthinking emotion today, but they will live to regret this charade at the next election. The British electorate does not trust appeasers at home or abroad. The cult of personality, the cult of violence, has been created and will haunt this movement for many years to come. Of course we want an honourable settlement to this dispute, a settlement acceptable to all miners. But an uncritical, unconditional undemanding statement like this does not help that end. It ignores, it undermines that prime responsibility of this party: the responsibility to gain power.
>
> Your approval of this statement will cheer the government and repel those supporters that Neil Kinnock almost alone has won back to Labour. We will be that much further away from power, and further away from the ability to deal with the pressing problems of our people. Our lack of success owes much to the gap we have allowed to develop between conference decisions and the conviction of our supporters . . . one prominent leader told me last week that I only argued for the ballot for electricity supply to support the NUM because I knew it would be opposed. He was more principled: he wanted action; the workers didn't – so they weren't going to have a ballot. Well, my union's power workers will vote, and we will abide by that decision. There is no other way in a party like ours. We trust our members and trust our people. If you don't, you end up rejected by the parliamentary process and look for answers in violence, intimidation and on the streets. Others have done that, let me illustrate with a quotation:
>
> 'We should not be passing resolutions and looking with confidence to elections two or three years hence. But we should realise the vital struggle of the age is upon us here and now, and we should sit down to the hard concrete work of devising measures for taking part in the struggle and driving the government from office and from power.' It is familiar: is it Scargill, is it Skinner, is it Benn? No it wasn't this year – it was taken from the 1926 conference report, and the speaker was Oswald Mosley . . . Beware the road you tread.

Among the block votes of Labour conference, the EETPU was in the minority. Conference backed Scargill, the strike continued, and the violence worsened. At a rally in Aberavon new TUC General Secretary Norman Willis stuck his neck out. He condemned unprovoked police aggression but went on:

> I could leave it there, but I will not; for I have to say that any miner, too, who resorts to violence wounds the miners' case far more than they damage their opponents' resolve. Violence creates more violence, and out of that is built not solidarity but despair and defeat. I have marched proudly before many miners' banners and I know there will never be one that praises the brick, the bolt or the petrol bomb. Such acts, if they are done by miners, are alien to our common tradition, however, not just because they are counter-productive but because they are wrong.[662]

Willis's reward for sticking his neck out was for striking miners to dangle a noose over his head in front of the crowd from atop the platform.

Amid great hardship, the strike dragged on for a year before petering out in a welter of mutual recrimination. Many miners lost their mortgaged homes. But as Paul Routledge observed, 'Scargill bought Treelands, the second-largest house in his native village, under the name of his daughter's fiancé. The so-called Great Strike destroyed the NUM.'[663] On 5 March 1985 a delegate conference voted by 98 to 91 for an organised return to work: the strike had collapsed. In his speech to the delegates that day, Scargill had declared 'The greatest achievement is the struggle itself . . . ' It was, as Scargill's biographer remarked, a 'strangely modified version of Marxism: "The means justifies the means." It's the struggle that counts not the winning.' Scargill's dream would cost some £6 billion, last almost a year, lead to 10,000 arrests of miners, 1,000 injuries, three dead, a hundred pits closed and 100,000 jobs lost.[664]

Against the recommendation of the TUC general council, the 1985 Blackpool TUC passed a resolution, on Arthur Scargill's instigation, calling for the next Labour government to undertake a complete review of all cases of miners gaoled as a result of the dispute, to reinstate all miners sacked for activities arising out of the dispute, and to reimburse the fines imposed on the NUM and all other unions during the strike. Nobody spoke against. 'I held fire, and everybody else did too,' recalled Electricians' leader Eric Hammond, who would otherwise have opposed it publicly. 'I thought I would get everybody's backs up, but it was a mistake not to speak.'[665] At the Labour conference a few weeks later Scargill planned a repeat performance. At the eve-of-conference meeting of Labour's NEC, Kinnock managed, by persuading Benn's now ex-ally Michael Meacher to change his vote, to defeat an attempt to get the NEC to back Scargill by fifteen votes to fourteen. 'Any residual links I had with [Meacher] are finished and done with,' wrote a furious Tony Benn in his diary, '[Meacher] came up afterwards and said he knew I was angry with him; I said he had to live with his own future.'[666] On the Wednesday morning came the debate. Scargill opened it:

I am moving the motion against a background of malicious hysteria whipped up by Fleet Street but, sadly, aided and abetted by sections even within our party ... I want to warn this conference that if, at today's debate, it fails to support this motion, it will make an absolute mockery of last year's standing ovations in support of miners, the women's support groups, and the historic struggle of miners for their jobs, pits and communities (*applause*) ... They concede that there is an overwhelming case for a review of all those cases of miners gaoled as a result of activities during the dispute ... [and] for the reinstatement of miners sacked by a vindictive National Coal Board supported by a Thatcher government determined to destroy British trade unionism.

When we meet the party leadership, we were told that the real issue – indeed, the only issue – was retrospective legislation and the reimbursement of funds confiscated by fines, sequestration and receivership ... in 1982 this party conference, by a majority of 6,000,000 to 66,000, passed a resolution accepting the principle of retrospective legislation to reimburse fines against trade unionists who were fined in this way. Surely if it was right in 1982 it is more than right in 1985 ...

There is nothing peculiar or strange about giving a commitment to the trade union movement, who find themselves at the wrong end of Tory legislation or at the wrong end of laws that are clearly designed to attack the basic democracy of unions ... (*applause*).

Among those who spoke in Scargill's support was a young delegate from Westminster North, the future MP Diane Abbott:

... We have heard a lot and we will hear a lot from the platform about the rule of law. Do not these people understand and appreciate how the law was actually used in the miners' strike? It was not some impartial abstraction out there dealing with people in an even-handed way. The law was used in the miners' strike as it has been used in Ireland, used against the black community, used in colonial struggles since time immemorial, as a weapon of the British state against working-class people (*applause*). How dare people who call themselves socialists pretend that the law was used against the miners in some kind of impartial way? ...

This time, Hammond intervened, in a speech that would hit the headlines with its description of the miners as being 'lions led by donkeys', German Field Marshal von Hindenburg's description of the British troops on the Somme. Hammond, whose father had fought in the trenches of the First World War, was acutely conscious that there had been many miners on the Somme and 'thought this description was not only apt, but would hit home where it hurt':[667]

Chair: I call Eric Hammond (*boos*) ...

Eric Hammond (EETPU): The NUM motion is dictated by the belief that the miners have been selected to be the victims of the full power of the state, judiciary and police. What it ignores is that the consequences the NUM seek to alleviate are wholly of their own making, a direct result of their strategy and their shortcomings.

The NUM were not financially crippled by the Tory industrial legislation. Miners seeking to enforce their own rules did that. Justice Nichols in the Derbyshire case stated: 'The rules are explicit. But for a period of over six months the officers of the Derby union and the NUM have chosen to disregard the constitution under which they hold office and to ride roughshod over their members by taking action which could be taken lawfully only with the support of a majority vote in a ballot.' The effect of this motion is to insulate and indemnify the NUM leadership from the law, to encourage them to ignore the genuine complaints of their members . . .

The Communist Party now maintains that to minimise the extent and reality of the setback does no service to the miners. *Tribune*: there should have been a ballot. Labour Co-ordinating Committee: failing to hold a ballot was bad politics. Violence weakened support for the strike. Where were they all at Blackpool and Brighton last year? They were the very elements urging the NUM leadership along the road to defeat. The miners were not defeated. How could they be? The miners did not choose to strike. The triumvirate did, and they were defeated. They were defeated because they did not trust the miners, because they refused to make the necessary industrial alliances. The miners were no more defeated than were their gallant forebears on the Somme. Lions led by donkeys. They should spend the rest of their lives atoning for that fault, not hawking their defeat from conference to conference (*applause and shouts of protest*) . . . Who wants the headline, 'Kinnock Defeated, Scargill Reigns Supreme?' Is it our friends or is it Thatcher and Owen who desperately want you to support this motion? This time use your hand and deny them (*applause and boos*).

Ron Todd, new leader of the TGWU, spoke too, backing Scargill: and attacking Hammond:

I want a Labour government . . . But I will not betray the National Union of Mineworkers to get it . . . I have heard reference this morning to lions being led by donkeys. Well, I am an animal lover. I tell you something. I prefer donkeys to jackals . . .

This time, however, Hammond was not alone. He would be supported by the AEU, the GMB, and by the party leader Neil Kinnock, who weighed in at the end of the debate with one of the most passionate speeches of his career, speaking from notes he had made that morning rather than from any prepared text:

Can I begin by saying that in this hall and in this movement, in all its unions, throughout the party, there are no donkeys, no jackals, only people (*applause*) . . .

The NEC is asking the National Union of Mineworkers to remit this resolution on the grounds that the NEC supports the first part, referring to a review, and supports the second part, referring to the reinstatement of victimised miners, and opposes the third part, calling for retrospective reimbursement . . .

The resolution cited by Scargill and passed so overwhelmingly at Labour's 1982 conference said that there would be legislation:

459

... to provide for reimbursement of any fines levied against trade unionists as a result of Tory legal measures ...

The first thing is, however, that that resolution was utterly irrelevant to the procedures that have inflicted such damage on the NUM. They have not been done under any Tory laws. They have been done under a common law that provides for an individual to take his union to court. Is anybody seriously suggesting we tear up common law and the protections for individual assertion? ...

The basic issue ... is helping the miners ... by the end of the dispute, they and their families were destitute and ... accepting redundancy to pay off debts that they ran up during the strike. It is pathetic, terrible, to see what they have been driven to. And all the time the question is asked, 'How did it come to that?' I will give you the answer of a lodge official in my constituency, a man who was on strike from the first day to the last, who picketed continuously, whose wife and family backed him to the hilt. He said to me, 'We knew about the Ridley plan. We knew we had a government of particular ruthlessness. We knew there was a build up of coal stocks, we knew that the refusal to strike had been registered in several ballots. We knew that the overtime ban had lost us shifts. We knew then that of all the times to call a coalmining strike, the end of winter is just about the point in the calendar least appropriate.' They are his words. 'The fact', he said, 'that it was called without a ballot denied to the miners unity and it denied to the miners the solidarity of so much of the rest of the trade union movement' (*applause*). 'On top of all that', he said, 'we were given continued, repeated promises that coal stocks were at the point of exhaustion, and it never was true. They never were at the point of exhaustion.'

The strike wore on. The violence built up because the single tactic chosen was that of mass picketing ... The court actions came, and by the attitude to the court actions, the NUM leadership ensured that they would face crippling damages as a consequence. To the question, 'How did this position arise?' the man from the lodge in my constituency said, 'It arose because nobody really thought it out' (*applause and shouts of protest*).

Now in those circumstances we ask how do we help miners ... By getting a Labour government that is committed to giving proper priority to the coalmining industry ... and if pits close through exhaustion alternatives to employment in coal ... (*applause*). It is a fact that if we were ever to endorse the idea of retrospective reimbursement we would harm our chances because people would be very confused about our attitude towards the rule of law and we would give heavy calibre ammunition to our enemies to misrepresent us, to defame us and to demolish the hope that miners have got of getting support from a Labour government.

But don't let the electoral consideration dictate your actions at all. Don't let a political party take any notice of electoral considerations. That would be class treachery, wouldn't it? (*applause*). Decide it on the basis of right and wrong. The wrong of it is that we would be making an entirely false promise to those who endure continual suffering and we would be giving the impression that we were prepared to extend a form of immunity regardless of the circumstances, and that we could never do. We know, Diane, what the state does, what the judicial system is. Do you think that you can make it better by copying the tactics of the Tories? Do you think you can make it better by having the same corrupt attitude towards the law of this land? (*applause*). That is not our Labour movement. That is not democratic socialism.

I say this in closing. Let us now go to the vote. I ask one thing in that vote, just one thing. That is that as you vote be sure that you can convincingly justify the way that you vote, not here in the tight circles, the comfortable, warm circles of the Labour Party conference, but in the street, to your neighbours, at work, wherever you go, in interviews. Justify it there (*applause*). I could not justify it. That is why I honestly say, if the NUM does not remit, please oppose the resolution so that we can really help the miners, the men who cut the coal (*applause and boos*).

Scargill's resolution was carried over the objections of the Labour leader, but not by enough to force its inclusion in the next manifesto, 'a comfort Kinnock will cling on to' wrote Benn.[668] It was a measure of how far Labour still had to go to rebuild itself as a party of government. But it was also an indication of Kinnock's preparedness to take it there. Like Gaitskell's decision to fight and fight again over unilateralism 25 years before, although it was Scargill who had won the vote, it was Kinnock who emerged looking the stronger for having stood and fought.

SIXTY-ONE

The Nemesis of Militant 1985–86

*'I'm telling you and you'll listen – you can't play politics with
people's jobs and with people's services or with their homes'*

The expulsions of the five members of the *Militant* editorial board in 1983 were a turning
point in the battle against Militant. But if Militant had been decapitated, it was still
twitching vigorously, like a multiple-brained invertebrate. One of its multiple brains was
in Liverpool, its founding base and stronghold for several decades. When Labour
regained control of Liverpool City Council in the municipal elections of 1983, only a
minority of its councillors were actually Militant members, but they were an organised,
disciplined and controlling minority. Liverpool's nominal leader was a nominally soft-
left councillor named John Hamilton. The power behind the throne was the Militant-
supporting council deputy leader Derek Hatton.

At Labour's annual conference in 1984 Hatton managed to get a vote in support of a
resolution to support 'any councils which are forced to break the law as a result of the
Tory government's policies'. Thus fortified, Hatton and his cohorts prepared for battle.
Some sixteen Labour councils, including Ken Livingstone's GLC, had been rate-capped
and considered setting an illegal rate rather than making the savage cuts to services
demanded by the government. All but Ted Knight's Lambeth eventually set a legal rate. It
was these councils that most Labour activists at the 1984 conference had in mind when
they had passed Hatton's motion on a show of hands. The irony was that Liverpool was
not actually rate-capped, and the government had even given £30 million in extra grants
to allow a balanced budget to be set for 1984–85. Militant was not prepared to be cheated
out of its confrontation. Kinnock had invited the leading Liverpool Labour councillors for
talks in Westminster at which he had urged them not to break the law. His reward was to
be treated to 'a tutorial in revolutionary strategy as the councillors explained to him how
"the time was ripe for revolution"'.[669] In June 1985 the council had set a budget that
created an illegal deficit, deliberately provoking a crisis in the city and confrontation with
the government. As with Scargill, the aim was 'the struggle'.

In August, council officers had warned Derek Hatton that the money for salaries
would run out by the end of the year. The council was obliged legally to issue redundancy
notices 90 days in advance of job cuts. The main council unions were understandably

furious that the livelihoods of their members was being put at such risk and refused to cooperate with Hatton in the distribution of redundancy notices. Without the unions to do it for him Hatton resorted to alternative means and on Friday 27 September, two days before Labour's 1985 annual conference began in Bournemouth, he hired a fleet of 30 taxis to deliver the redundancy notices to all 31,000 employees. It was an image that Neil Kinnock would etch in the memories of all who attended that conference, and many who did not, in perhaps the most dramatic Labour speech of the past forty years. It began with an attack on the Conservatives and set out Kinnock's vision of an 'enabling state'. But the part for which it is most remembered is the attack on Militant: ' . . . a Labour council, a Labour council, scuttling round the city in taxis handing out redundancy notices to its own members'.

Patricia Hewitt, now Health Secretary in Tony Blair's Cabinet, was at the time Kinnock's press secretary. She remembers:

Charles Clarke and I had been with him on the train to the TUC conference in Blackpool a few weeks earlier, when he started thinking out loud about what he want-ed to say, and that crucial section of the speech scarcely changed. Inevitably, however, we stayed up most of the night before his speech to conference, writing and rewriting the rest of the speech. We knew the attack on Derek Hatton and the Militant council-lors in Liverpool would have quite an impact and we were determined nothing should leak in advance. But we also had a commitment to the political editors of the region-al evening newspapers, who would miss the speech unless they got something in advance. So my usual pre-speech briefing was done in the conference hotel, rather than in the conference centre itself, with the journalists sworn not to approach anyone for reactions until the speech was delivered.

That was just as well, given what actually happened. When Neil got to the crucial words, to his and everyone's astonishment, Derek Hatton stood up, shouting, and then walked out, followed by (the late) Eric Heffer, MP and NEC member. There was mayhem in the hall. Sitting beside the main BBC news camera position on the balcony, I could also see from the monitor the live TV news coverage. I was terrified – I think we all were – that the whole thing would fall apart. But Neil just stood there, and drove the attack home: 'I tell you, you can't play politics with people's jobs, and people's lives.' People assumed he was ad-libbing, but the line had been there all along. It was a great speech – and the defining moment in Labour's long march back from the wilderness:[670]

. . . How does the party of enterprise preside over record bankruptcies? How does the party of tax cuts arrange that the British people now carry the biggest ever burden of taxation in British history? And how, above all, does the party that got the power by complaining that 'Labour isn't working' claim in the name of sanity that there is a recovery going on, when unemployment rises remorselessly to the point where this Thursday they will record 3.4 million British people registered unemployed even on their fiddled figures? That is an awful lot – 3.4 million – of 'Moaning Minnies', even for the most malevolent Maggie to try and explain away . . .

Change cannot be left to chance. If it is left to chance, it becomes malicious, it creates terrible victims. It has done so generation in, generation out. Change has to be organised. It has to be shaped to the benefit of a society, deliberately, by those who have democratic power in that society; and the democratic instrument of the people which exists for that purpose is the state – yes, the state. To us that means a particular kind of state – an opportunity state, which exists to assist in nourishing talent and rewarding merit; a productive state, which exists to encourage investment and to help expand output; an enabling state, which is at the disposal of the people instead of being dominant over the people. In a word, we want a servant state, which respects those who work for it and reminds them that they work for the people of the country, a state which will give support to the voluntary efforts of those who, in their own time and from their own inspiration, will help the old, the sick, the needy, the young, the ill-housed and the hopeless.

We are democratic socialists. We want to put the state where it belongs in a democracy – under the feet of the people, not over the heads of the people . . . It means the collective contribution of the community for the purpose of individual liberty throughout the community; of individual freedom which is not nominal but real; of freedom which can be exercised in practice because the school is good, because the hospital is there, because the training is accessible, because the alternative work is available, because the law is fair, because the streets are safe – real freedoms, real choices, real chances, and, going with them, the real opportunity to meet responsibilities. It is not a state doing things instead of people who could do those things better; it is not a state replacing families or usurping enterprise or displacing initiative or smothering individualism. It is the absolute opposite: it is a servant state doing things that institutions – big institutions, rich institutions, corporate institutions, rich, strong people – will not do, have not done, with anything like the speed or on anything like the scale that is necessary to bring change with consent in our society. That kind of state is the state that we seek under democratic control . . .

Comrades, 463 resolutions have been submitted to this conference on policy issues . . . Of those 463, three hundred refer to something called the next Labour government and . . . what they want that next Labour government to do . . . But there is of course a pre-condition to honouring those or any other undertaking that we give . . . It is the pre-condition that we win a general election . . . There are some who say, when I reach out . . . [to the electorate] in the course of seeking that objective, that I am prepared to compromise values. I say to them . . . there is no need to compromise values . . . But there is an implacable need to win and . . . to understand that we address an electorate which is sceptical . . . a British public who want to know that our idealism is not lunacy, our realism is not timidity, our eagerness is not extremism, a British public who want to know that our carefulness too is not nervousness . . .

We must not dogmatise or browbeat. We have got to reason with people; we have got to persuade people. That is their due . . . If our response . . . amounts to little more than slogans, if we give the impression to the British people that we believe that we can just make a loud noise and the Tory walls of Jericho will fall down, they are not going to treat us very seriously at all - and we won't deserve to be treated very seriously . . .

I shall tell you again what you know . . . implausible promises don't win victories. I'll tell you what happens with impossible promises. You start with far-fetched resolutions. They are then pickled into a rigid dogma, a code, and you go through the years sticking to that, outdated, misplaced, irrelevant to the real needs, and you end in the grotesque chaos of a Labour council - a *Labour* council - hiring taxis to scuttle round a city handing out redundancy notices to its own workers. I am telling you, no matter how entertaining, how fulfilling to short-term egos - I'm telling you, and you'll listen - you can't play politics with people's jobs and with people's services or with their homes. Comrades, the voice of the people - not the people here; the voice of the real people with real needs - is louder than all the boos that can be assembled. Understand that, please, comrades. In your socialism, in your commitment to those people, understand it. The people will not, cannot, abide posturing. They cannot respect the gesture-generals or the tendency-tacticians.

Comrades, it seems to me lately that some of our number have become like latter-day public school boys. It seems it matters not whether you won or lost, but how you played the game. We cannot take that inspiration from Rudyard Kipling. Those game players get isolated, hammered, blocked off. They might try to blame others - workers, trade unions, some other leadership, the people of the city - for not showing sufficient revolutionary consciousness, always somebody else, and then they claim a rampant victory. Whose victory? Not victory for the people, not victory for them. I see the casualties; we all see the casualties. They are not to be found amongst the leaders and some of the enthusiasts; they are to be found amongst the people whose jobs are destroyed, whose services are crushed, whose living standards are pushed down to deeper depths of insecurity and misery. Comrades, these are vile times under this Tory government for local democracy, and we have got to secure power to restore real local democracy.

But I look around this country and I see Labour councils, I see socialists, as good as any other socialists, who fought the good fight and who, at the point when they thought they might jeopardise people's jobs and people's services, had the intelligence, yes, and the courage to adopt a different course. They truly put jobs and services first before other considerations. They had to make hellish choices . . . but they did it . . . They used all their creativity to find ways that would best protect those whom they employed and those whom they were elected to defend. Those people . . . know life is real, life is earnest - too real, too earnest to mistake a conference resolution for an accomplished fact; too real, too earnest to mistake a slogan for a strategy; too real, too earnest to allow them to mistake their own individual enthusiasms for mass movement; too real, too earnest to mistake barking for biting. I hope that becomes universal too.

Comrades, I offer you this counsel. The victory of socialism, said a great socialist, does not have to be complete to be convincing. I have no time, he went on, for those who appear to threaten the whole of private property but who in practice would threaten nothing; they are purists and therefore barren. Not the words of some hypnotised moderate, not some petrified pragmatist, but Aneurin Bevan in 1950 at the height of his socialist vision and his radical power and conviction. There are some who will say that power and principle are somehow in conflict. Those people who think that power and principle are in conflict only demonstrate the superficiality, the shallowness, of their own socialist convictions; for whilst they are bold enough to preach those convictions in little coteries, they do not have the depth of conviction to subject those convictions, those beliefs, that analysis, to the real test of putting them into operation in power.

There is no collision between principle and power. For us as democratic socialists the two must go together, like a rich vein that passes through everything that we believe in, everything that we try to do, everything that we will implement. Principle and power, conviction and accomplishment, going together. We know that power without principle is ruthless and vicious, and hollow and sour. We know that principle without power is naïve, idle sterility . . .

I owe this party everything I have got . . . every life chance that I have had since the time I was a child: the life chance of a comfortable home, with working parents, people who had jobs; the life chance of moving out of a pest- and damp-infested set of rooms into a decent home, built by a Labour council under a Labour government; the life chance of an education that went on for as long as I wanted to take it. Me and millions of others of my generation got all their chances from this movement . . . That is why it is my duty to be honest and that is why it is our function, our mission, our duty – all of us – to see that those life chances exist and are enriched and extended to millions more, who without us will never get the chance of fulfilling themselves. That is why we have got to win . . .

It was not just Eric Heffer who walked out: 'Kinnock has released the hatred of the Tory press against his own people in the middle of a struggle,' wrote Tony Benn in his diary, 'I left because I couldn't bring myself to stay after that.'[671] But for Barbara Castle, it was 'the most courageous and effective speech I have ever heard a politician make'. Healey and Hattersley expressed similar sentiments.[672] Sketch writer Edward Pearce wrote:

They will talk about Bournemouth '85 as they talk about Scarborough '60, the last time a Labour leader, baited and abused by his left, turned round and baited them back. The story is told of how the young Neil, a few years back, had a punch thrown at him in the gents at conference (for voting against Benn as deputy leader) and how, being less meek than he looks, he 'beat the daylights out of him'. Bournemouth conference centre yesterday was converted yesterday into a vast political washroom with overtones of Agincourt . . . The Exocet qualities of the leader lie in the sheer, abrupt, brutal lucidity of his attack. One moment we were cruising on the affable lake waters of slogans and resolutions not being enough for victory, the next a viciously spinning disc had hit the hard left in a soft place . . . The immediate standing applause, the departure of Mr Eric Heffer in the stately waddle of an affronted Mandarin Duck, the frantic clapping of the left and the operatic boos of other people, created what the

THE NEMESIS OF MILITANT 1985–86

French call an *événement*, a happening . . . Mr Hatton, the flashily tailored representative of the authentic working class, gibbered like a sedentary King Kong . . . yesterday [Kinnock] offered the worst speech Mrs Thatcher and the Alliance could have hoped to hear.[673]

The day after Kinnock had denounced Militant, Hatton launched a counterattack, proposing a resolution demanding that legal charges and fines against councillors 'who have made a stand' be 'wiped out' by the next Labour government and that unions take industrial action in the councillors' defence:

I came to conference expecting this Labour Party conference to salute the stand and the achievements of the Liverpool City Council, of Liverpool local authority trade unions, of the wider trades union movement and of the public at large . . .

Neil Kinnock yesterday talked about the lowest number of housing starts since the war. Why did he fail to mention the fact that Liverpool City Council, by the end of next year, will have built 5,200 council houses, more than twice the number of every other city in the country added together? (*applause*). Neil, I am very happy that your parents were able to move out of slums into a house built by a Labour council. Don't you now turn your back on the thousands of Liverpool families who now have the chance for the first time of a decent council house built by a Labour council (*applause*) . . . Six nursery classes are being built in Liverpool which would not have been built had it not been for the fact that a Labour council was returned in 1983. Not a penny on the rates has happened since 1983 because a Labour council was returned then.

You see, Neil, in Liverpool we not only say what we mean, we not only mean what we say, but we do what we mean and we do what we say (*applause*). And in return for that the district auditor comes in as judge, as jury, as would-be executioner and tells us we have been breaking the law. He tells us we are criminals. He tells us we are going to be disqualified. And he tells us we are going bankrupt.

We made it clear last year after our victory with this Tory government that the fight would happen again and certainly it has. Over 30 Labour councils in May refused to set a rate. In Liverpool, we had a choice that was very simple. Do we make 5,000 local authority workers redundant and sack them? Do we put up the rates by 200 per cent and burden the people of Liverpool with the results of the government's cutbacks, or do we take a stand? After full consultation with the entire Labour movement in Liverpool, we decided we were going to take a stand. We understood that if the campaign was not successful in the first stage we would run out of money. Two weeks ago we were informed that that time was now. The Joint Shop Stewards Committee, to their credit, called an all-out indefinite strike. That might not have been supported by the majority of workers, but eight and a half thousand local authority workers said, 'Yes, we will go all out on indefinite strike action in support of our jobs' (*applause*). To them we take our hats off, and we also say to the NUPE and the NUT leadership, 'Why was it you failed to give our members even the chance to say whether they wanted to go out on strike or not? You failed even to do that'(*applause*).

As a result of that ballot, in order to buy three months, we decided that we were going to inform the workforce that by the end of December the money would run out. In other words, there would be a Tory lockout . . . And let us nail the lie that that was not done in full consultation with the trade union movement. We had full consultation with the Joint Shop Stewards Committee. In fact, it was at the Joint Shop Stewards Committee, moved by the TGWU, seconded by the G and M, [it was agreed] that we should adopt that particular tactic. I challenge you Neil Kinnock as well, to come to Liverpool, look through the books, and if you can show me any other option where all jobs are safe, then fine, we will do it . . .

But the debate did not go all Hatton's way. Jane Kennedy,[674] then the NUPE branch secretary in Liverpool, challenged him directly.

I am branch secretary of one of the Liverpool City Council branches of NUPE and an apparently redundant care assistant. NUPE members in Liverpool and NUPE nationally cannot accept that our members should be sacked in pursuit of a strategy which the council refused properly to discuss with national leaders of trade unions before issuing notices of dismissal to 31,000 workers (*applause*). Will those workers be reimbursed?

Councillor Hatton attacked the use of the district auditor in this issue. Yet his council has threatened their officers that failure to issue those notices will leave them vulnerable to the possibility of personal surcharge by the district auditor. Will they be reimbursed by the next Labour government? NUPE and the NUT do not need a lesson from Councillor Hatton in carrying out Tory Party policy on secret ballots before strike action (*applause*).

Here is my redundancy notice. What does it say? . . . that after 31 December, 1985 . . . I will not work at Caldway Manor Old People's Home in Netherleigh . . .

We say to Liverpool City Council . . . How can we possibly accept a strategy which sets out to save 4,000 jobs and ends up sacking 31,000 people? (*applause*) . . . There is no tactical justification for so seriously jeopardising vital services . . .

To boos and applause shadow Environment Secretary Jack Cunningham[675] accused the Liverpool Militants of betraying the trust of the electorate:

Is the organisation of a crisis atmosphere, week in and week out, the way to persuade people to trust us to manage their affairs? Is the political and physical intimidation of councillors, shop stewards, the black community, acceptable to a democratic socialist party?

Can we support the deliberate, the conscious fixing of a rate which ensures that income falls short of expenditure? . . . there is no bravery in knowingly leading the people who desperately need us and their jobs into a political confrontation with the government on grounds where the battle cannot be won. It is a strange socialist equation that says: we jeopardise 31,000 jobs to employ 2,000 or 3,000 more people . . .

The scene was set for a dramatic confrontation in the final vote. This time, Kinnock hoped to win. But Sheffield City Council leader David Blunkett, who was replying to the debate for the NEC, wanted to take a different approach. The spurious legitimacy claimed by Hatton for the action of Liverpool Council stemmed from their claim that they had been forced into taking it by government-imposed cuts. Blunkett was one of a number of council leaders who knew that the determination of the Tories to crack down on public investment programmes was all too real. His own Sheffield, like Ken Livingstone's GLC, had sought to invest in public transport and through a cheap fares policy make it a genuinely attractive alternative to the car. Hardly the stuff of revolution, but enough to put them in the Tory firing line. Liverpool claimed to be in the same boat. The suspicion was that they were not and had deliberately engineered the crisis. Blunkett sought to get the evidence:

> . . . I suppose I epitomise the conference by wearing red over my heart and a Fabian tie around my neck . . . Many Labour councillors have withstood the pressure to make cuts, to make redundancies, to attack their own communities. Those councillors deserve praise and they deserve our applause (*applause*) . . .
>
> We must not allow that achievement to be dissipated by our disagreements . . . We must not fudge, we must not pretend that the impossible is possible. We must not pretend that there are not major divisions . . . But how we deal with them and how we deal with other problems displays whether we are socialists or whether we are a rabble tearing each other's guts out (*applause*) . . .
>
> [The NEC statement, said Blunkett, committed the party] to seeking to prevent the disqualification and surcharge of the Lambeth and Liverpool councillors . . . because those councillors, up to 14 June in Liverpool and 3 July in Lambeth, carried out the non-compliance of last year by delaying the rate-making process – a very different issue to the question of Liverpool's deficit budget. I separate it because I wish to come to that in a minute.
>
> That non-compliance tactic of last year cannot, in my view, be repeated in the coming year. We cannot simply go over the same ground in order to fail again. We have to look at what non-compliance means in the new context. Non-compliance in cuts, in services and jobs and the destruction of our community is an overwhelmingly clear commitment from this and from previous conferences . . .
>
> I want to say about Liverpool that anyone who has a lapel badge that says, Support Liverpool, Support Militant, is doing a disservice to this movement (*applause*). Anyone who makes a speech that says, Support Liverpool, Support Militant, is doing a disservice, and anyone who suggests that supporting Liverpool is supporting Militant is also doing a disservice to this movement (*applause*). Because from 1974 at local government reorganisation until the present Liverpool councillors took over in 1983, for seven out of those nine years Liverpool was in the hands of the Liberal–Tory Alliance . . .
>
> I would like to propose that we open up the books not to Kenneth Baker, not to the district auditor, but to us and our colleagues (*applause*). I would like us, all of us,

every Labour council, every constituency, to place on record that they will commit themselves to helping, as we will with Lambeth and Liverpool over the surcharge, to find a way out. I would like us to have a commitment for our leader that if we can, by some means that does not involve cuts and the destruction of the housing pro-gramme, bridge that gap, he will give his support to ensuring that we save the city and the people of Liverpool in the future (*applause*). And because of the mention of the national local authority coordinating committee, the shop stewards' committee, based in Liverpool and its conflict with the trade unions, because of the contradiction that exists in [Hatton's resolution], which says that only the maximum unity of local authority unions and Labour councils can achieve the kind of victory they want, when we can clearly see in front of us the difficulties and disunity that potentially exists, because I believe, as the NEC believe, that that would not take us forward, I am not simply asking that you turn down [Hatton's resolution] – and we are certainly not ask-ing for remission – but I am asking the mover and seconder, in the interests of the city of Liverpool and the Labour movement to withdraw completely [Hatton's resolution] and allow us to go forward in unity. Will you do that? Will you do that, Derek? (*shouts of 'No' from floor*) . . .

Tony Benn recorded the scene that followed in his diary: 'There he was, this Christ-like bearded blind man, standing on the rostrum appealing to Derek Hatton to withdraw his Liverpool resolution. He stood there waving his hands into the darkness. So Hatton, who is a bit of a smart aleck, ran towards the rostrum in his neat suit, got up on the ros-trum and said, "Yes, in the interests of unity, Liverpool will withdraw its resolution." There was an explosion of applause.'[676]

Blunkett wrote later: 'I think that at the time, Neil Kinnock thought that . . . I had let Militant off the hook, whereas, as he generously acknowledged, the outcome helped to pull the Labour Party together. Never before had Militant Tendency been forced to open their books and allow us to see precisely what was going on. In due course, financial experts from local government examined the accounts and revealed that Militant had been pulling the wool over the eyes of the Labour Party as well as the people of Liverpool.'[677] The report led to the suspension of the Militant-controlled Liverpool District Labour Party and the establishment of a committee of enquiry to investigate allegations of malpractice, intimidation and Militant infiltration in Liverpool. Its key members included David Blunkett, Charlie Turnock of the NUR, who had taken over John Golding's role as coordinator of the NEC moderates, and NUPE's Tom Sawyer, who had been profoundly influenced by local NUPE secretary Jane Kennedy: 'We were the only union branch in Liverpool not supporting the Militant council strike for jobs. I spoke to Jane Kennedy and went up to see her. She was an independent woman and they were out to get her. I thought "why didn't anyone tell me this before". Militant had packed the branches of the other unions. I proposed the NEC enquiry into Militant in

Liverpool.'[678] The enquiry was a gruelling ordeal, and that was just for its members: 'One interview with Tony Mulhearn, Chairman of Liverpool District Labour Party, lasted sixteen hours. Derek Hatton, to the disappointment of a few, did not deign to attend when summoned before us and so was expelled in his absence.'[679]

The NEC meeting on 26 February 1986 to consider the final report was picketed by six hundred screaming Militant supporters. The commission had split and Margaret Beckett and Audrey Wise had dissented from the recommendation of the committee majority in favour of expulsions. It was the majority, however, who carried the day. Within weeks, Labour's notably moderate Nick Raynsford would win a stunning victory in the Fulham by-election, previously a Tory-held seat. Labour's 1986 annual conference would see Eric Heffer and Margaret Beckett voted off the NEC.

SIXTY-TWO

Defeat and Renewal 1987–89

'Why am I the first Kinnock in a thousand generations to be able to get to university?'

Labour's 1987 election campaign was an unqualified improvement on its ramshackle campaign in 1983. The incompetent organisation that had bedevilled the campaign four years previously was improved by its post-1985 Director of Communications, Peter Mandelson, and a new image was adopted, centring on the red rose. 'The brilliance of Peter [Mandelson]'s performance during the 1987 election campaign is beyond dispute,' Roy Hattersley remembers. 'So is (or should be) his performance in forcing Labour's pub- licity machine to face the realities of modern political life.'[680]

Labour anticipated that the Conservative campaign would be presidential in style and sought to project Kinnock as the alternative to Thatcher. Kinnock made nearly a dozen major speeches across the country between 19 May – the day when both Labour and Conservatives launched their manifestos – and the eve of poll on 10 June. His most significant speech, however, was made a few days before the campaign proper began, at the Welsh Labour Party conference at Llandudno on 15 May 1987. Kinnock's press secretary Patricia Hewitt recalls:

> Neil's economic adviser, John Eatwell, and I had worked with him on the speech
> through the night. (I'd developed the habit on these occasions of taking a short nap
> on the sofa at about 3 in the morning – followed by an early cooked breakfast at about
> 5, it left me irritatingly cheerful!) This time, we had no idea that part of the speech
> would be so memorable. His great line – 'Why am I the first Kinnock in a thousand
> generations to go to university?' was never in the written speech. He'd added it in the
> car while he and Glenys drove to the conference, and it came as a complete surprise to
> the rest of us. But [*Chariots of Fire* director] Hugh Hudson was there to film the
> moment, for the 'Chariots of Kinnock' broadcast that became famous in the 1987
> general election campaign, and as Neil added the line 'Because I had a platform on
> which to stand', Hugh's cameraman panned across the word 'Labour' behind him.[681]

Hudson's party election broadcast received unparalleled acclaim, lifting Kinnock's personal poll rating by 19 per cent overnight.[682] As Kinnock spoke, even the duty police were moved to tears:

Mrs Thatcher said this week that she was full of ideas for continuing in the direction they have been going. We know what she means: new ideas like privatising schools; new ideas like decontrolling rents; new ideas like paying for healthcare.

Wonderful new ideas. But anyone attracted by them had better ask themselves why every single one of these new ideas was abandoned 50 and more years ago . . .

The reason is simple: the system that existed before that – the system Margaret Thatcher wants to return to – was wrong and wretched, it was squalid and brutal. It was rotten with injustice and misery and division. This is why it was discarded. This is why it must never be restored . . . Britain has a Prime Minister who has allowed unemployment and poverty and waiting lists and closures and crime to go up and up and up. Britain cannot afford such a Prime Minister to go 'on and on and on'.

Britain has taken a beating in the last eight years from a government and its on-yer-bike employment policy, its stay-in-bed-to-keep-warm retirement policy, its flag-day health service policy and its jumble-sale education system . . .

Britain can't serve such a life sentence without it turning into a death sentence for more industries, more communities, more hopes. Not that it bothers the Prime Minister. She would have us think that we are in the middle of a great recovery . . .

Recovery is a funny word to use after eight years in which manufacturing production hasn't got back to the level of 1979. It's a very strange term to use to describe an economy in which there are two million more unemployed than there were in 1979 . . . Is it a recovery when you can hardly find a 'Made in Britain' label in the shops any more? . . .

Of course, there's been a little recent speeding up; there has been a little late thaw . . . And how has this little boomlet come about? Has it come because the policies are working? . . . The answer is not because they've been applying their policies, but because they've abandoned them as the prospects of an election came closer . . . Remember – it's only a few months ago – they couldn't afford to spend on roads, on nurses' pay, on the Airbus, on cancer screening, on hospital waiting lists. They couldn't afford to keep small schools open, they couldn't afford heating additions for the old. Now they can afford it all . . . The Tories knew that they couldn't face the country with Tory policies. They knew that they had to stimulate and soften and sweeten . . . because the election was coming . . . That is the total scope of Tory care. They only care because they are cornered.

That's the difference between us. We are democratic socialists. We care all the time. We don't think it's a soft sentiment, we don't think it's 'wet'. We think that care is the essence of strength. And we believe that because we know that strength without care is savage and brutal and selfish.

Strength is care with compassion – the practical action that is needed to help people lift themselves to their full stature. That's real care – it is not soft or weak. It is tough and strong. But where do we get the strength to provide that care? . . . We cooperate, we collect together, we coordinate so that everyone can contribute and everyone can benefit, everyone has responsibilities, everyone has rights . . . It is called collective strength, collective care. And its whole purpose is individual freedom.

When we speak of collective strength and collective freedom, collectively achieved, we are not fulfilling that nightmare that Mrs Thatcher tries to paint, and all her predecessors have tried to saddle us with. We're not talking about uniformity; we're not talking about regimentation; we're not talking about *conformity* – that's their creed. The uniformity of the dole queue; the regimentation of the unemployed young and their compulsory work schemes. The *conformity* of people who will work in conditions, and take orders, and accept pay *because* of mass unemployment that they would laugh at in a free society with full employment. That kind of freedom for the individual, that kind of liberty can't be secured by most of the people for most of the time if they're just left to themselves, isolated, stranded, with their whole life chances dependent upon luck!

Why am I the first Kinnock in a thousand generations to be able to get to university? Why is Glenys their first woman in her family in a thousand generations to be able to get to university? Was it because *all* our predecessors were 'thick'? Did they lack talent – those people who could sing and play, and recite and write poetry; those people who could make wonderful, beautiful things with their hands; those people who could dream dreams, see visions; those people who had such a sense of perception as to know in times so brutal, so oppressive, that they could win their way out of that by coming together? Were those people not university material? Couldn't they have knocked off all their 'A' levels in an afternoon? But why didn't they get it? Was it because they were weak? – those people who could work eight hours underground and then come up and play football? Weak? Those women who could survive eleven child-bearings, were they weak? Those people who could stand with their backs and legs straight and face the people who had control over their lives, the ones who owned their workplaces and tried to own them, tell them 'No. I won't take your orders.' Were they weak? Does anybody really think that they didn't get what we had because they didn't have the talent, or the strength, or the endurance, or the commitment?

Of course not. It was because there was no platform upon which they could stand; no arrangement for their neighbours to subscribe to their welfare; no method by which communities could translate their desires for those individuals into provision for those individuals. And now, Mrs Thatcher, by dint of privatisation, and means test, and deprivation, and division, wants to nudge us back into the situation where everybody can either stand on their own two feet, or live on their knees. That's what this election is all about as she parades her visions and values, and we chose to contest them as people with roots in this country, with a future only in this country, with pride in this country. People who know that if we are to have and sustain real individual liberty in this country it requires the collective effort of the whole community . . .

I think of the youngsters I meet. Three, four, five years out of school. Never had a job. And they say to me 'Do you think we'll ever work?' They live in a free country, but they do not feel free . . . And I think of the old couple who spend months of the winter afraid to turn up the heating . . . They live in a free country – indeed, they're of the generation that *fought* for a free country – but they do not feel free. How can they – and millions like them – have their individual freedom if there is not collective provision?

... They do not want feather-bedding, they want a foothold ... Freedom with fairness; that is our aim. And our means of fulfilling it is investment ...

Those resources are there ... in Nigel Lawson's 2p tax cut. The tuppeny Tories! Spent that way it will cost £2.5 billion and create 60,000 jobs in Britain and rather more abroad as the cash is spent mainly on imports. Targeted on construction and caring and manufacturing that same £2.5 billion would generate 300,000 jobs. That's the bargain for Britain ...

Though Labour's campaign was hailed as a success the electorate nevertheless judged it a failure. The votes hardly changed from 1983. Whereas Labour's 1983 débâcle had been the party's worst electoral disaster since 1931, 1987 was only the second worst, after 1983. In other words, had 1983 not happened, 1987 would have been the worst electoral disaster since 1931. Labour's only consolation was that by increasing the vote from 27.6 per cent in 1983 to 30.8 per cent in 1987, they opened up a gap with the Alliance, who fell back from 25.4 per cent in 1983 to 22.6 per cent in 1987. The Conservative vote share was diminished by a bare 0.1 per cent.

A BBC/Gallup poll in 1987 found that almost half the electorate thought that the nation's economic prospects had improved over the previous four years and only 28 per cent considered that over the same period their own financial position had deteriorated.[683] Moreover, though a clear majority of voters doubted that unemployment would fall under the Conservatives and feared a stagnation of welfare provision, more than two-thirds believed that Conservative government was the most likely to deliver low inflation and income tax cuts. Labour's manifesto priorities: an anti-poverty programme, a better NHS, and greater rights for women and ethnic minorities, did not address these areas. On other issues, in particular on tax, defence and 'the bomb', Labour's policies put off too many voters. Labour had stood up to Militant, and expelled Hatton, but other overt Militant supporters remained prominent in Labour's ranks and on the nation's television screens. Several of them were Labour MPs.

In Scotland the Conservatives were reduced from 21 MPs to ten and in Wales the Conservatives lost six seats. But in England their hegemony in the south remained stark. Even in London, once Herbert Morrison's great Labour redoubt, the Conservatives held a majority of seats. Outside London, in the south east, Labour held just one seat to the Conservatives' 107. South of a line from the Severn to the Wash, the Alliance won six seats, Labour 26 (almost all in London) and the Conservatives won 228.

That summer, Labour's leaders reflected upon defeat and contemplated the future. It was Tom Sawyer, NUPE Deputy General Secretary and chair of Labour's NEC Home Policy committee, who proposed what became a wholesale review of Labour's policies, in a paper presented to Labour's NEC that September. 'Our policy must be responsive to the concerns of voters – particularly those we want to win over,' it said. Sawyer proposed review groups comprising representatives from both the shadow Cabinet and NEC and coordinated from Kinnock's office. Sawyer's paper was approved without a vote, though Dennis Skinner argued against.

When delegates assembled in Brighton at the end of September for Labour's annual conference, 'Kinnock's wisest course might well have been to contract severe laryngitis and say nothing,' wrote journalist Peter Kellner.

> Were he to defend existing policies he could be mocked when they changed; were he to outline his ideas for new policies he would have been accused of pre-empting the process of review. His speech, therefore, was notable for its dearth of policy content. Commentators who looked (as I did) for a candid confession of past errors were disappointed. That summer Mikhail Gorbachev had regaled the Soviet Communist Party conference with a catalogue of its failings, and was widely praised for his frankness. Kinnock declined to follow his example.[684]

Instead he focused on the battle of ideas:

> . . . It appears, however, that there are still some who are timid about the idea of 'review'. They seem to have 'do not disturb' notices hung on their minds. The very activity of examination is described by some as a 'betrayal of fundamental principles'. I must say I have a very different opinion of 'review'. I believe that after losing three general elections any serious political party that did not undertake the assessment, the review, the examination – and do it honestly – that party would be betraying its principles and its policies and its people . . .
>
> The social realities that we face are the realities of increasing home ownership: the realities, too, of less housebuilding and of growing homelessness. We face the fortunate reality of earlier retirement and of longer life for an even larger proportion of the population; and we also face the grim reality of poverty and isolation that so frequently still accompany old age. We face the reality of many more people owning a few shares; and the reality alongside it of increasing poverty, of low pay and growing inequality and division. We face the reality of the change in the pattern of work from mass production manufacturing to high-tech custom production; and, alongside that, too, the reality of under-investment in science and in skills. They are just some of the mixed realities already here or in very firm prospect for the early 1990s – a time in which our economy can no longer rely on the bounty of oil, and there is nothing else left to privatise . . .
>
> Of course, again, not everyone appears to be willing to listen to that, to understand that. In the past few days I have heard such a recognition of the changing realities described as 'retreat', 'defeatism', 'pandering to yuppies'. It is not a retreat from anything, and it is not pandering to anybody. It is simply understanding the hopes and the doubts, expectations and reservations of people who are not necessarily young, not particularly mobile and who, in any event, did not vote Labour. They are frequently people – not yuppies – who live in the kind of places and work in the kind of jobs that

would qualify them for any certificate of working-class authenticity that any comrade wanted to award. And they did not vote Labour last time or the time before . . .

Ron Todd made the point with deadly accuracy just a couple of months ago when he asked: 'What do you say to a docker who earns £400 a week, owns his house, a new car, a microwave and a video, as well as a small place near Marbella? You do not say,' said Ron, '"Let me take you out of your misery, brother."' When he asked that question, Ron Todd . . . was facing a fundamental question for our party with admirable candour that I would recommend universally . . .

Of course, it is not really a very new question. I remember when I first faced it . . . after the 1959 election. I was seventeen and . . . I was devastated . . . not just by defeat but by the scale of our defeat. And I, like just about everyone else in the movement, was asking for explanations of the defeat because it had not felt as though it was going to happen. Amongst the most prominent of those explanations . . . was something called the Affluent Society. You could hear that everywhere. It was made to sound like a curse. Part of me actually wanted to believe that explanation – it was an easy explanation that had a certain appeal to someone who was convinced that socialism was fundamentally, primarily, a cause that existed to help the underdogs, the downtrodden.

. . . I was perplexed. I did what I always did on such occasions when I had these fundamental questions . . . I went to see an old socialist in Tredegar, Oliver Jones, and asked him whether there was a collision between affluence and socialism. He told me: 'There is no collision between affluence and socialism – I have been striving for both all my life.' And then he went on to say in words that were unforgettable: 'The point is, you see, that if socialism has got to wait for want, then socialism will wait for a very long time. And it will be right for socialism to wait for a very long time: because if it needs misery to give it majority, God forbid we have the misery.'

. . . Take the docker of whom Ron spoke, or many others like him earning a little more or a little less. Those kind of people are comfortable, secure, satisfied with decent conditions, and the best of British luck to them. But even with those wages, even with that security, even with that comfort, he is still not able to give the comprehensive care, the special housing, the sheltered accommodation, the support with transport, that his ageing mother and father might need. Even with those wages he is still not getting enough to enable him to meet the price of the schooling for his children, even more so if they wanted to continue into further education or go on to university. And still with those wages, he is not able to ensure that he and his family could meet their full medical needs without worry, especially if there happens to be in that family (as so frequently and tragically is the case) someone with a chronic or crippling illness or disease . . .

They are all assets which must be collectively supplied if they are to be there without fail, regardless of the changes of economic fortunes of an individual or the ability to pay . . .

The policy review process was approved by Labour's 1987 conference, though 'there was no enthusiasm among constituency activists, who made it plain that they believed the whole enterprise was a cloak for selling out', wrote Colin Hughes of the *Independent*

and Patrick Wintour of the *Guardian*: 'Equally they had no desire to be blamed for smash-
ing up the prototype on its launching pad.' There was clearly a long way to go before
tangible shifts in some of the more controversial policy areas could occur: the defence
debate that week merely confirmed Labour's unilateralist position. The policy review as
agreed by Labour's NEC at its post-conference meeting on 28 October 1987 would 'assess
policy issues and opportunities in the 1990s; make an assessment of the relevance and
credibility of existing party policy matched against the need and concerns of groups of
voters; and recommend broad themes of political strategy as well as policy areas in which
more detailed examination is required'. This meant the review would entail an appraisal
of policy options not in a vacuum but in the context of market research: the focus groups
of Philip Gould and Deborah Mattinson of Gould Mattinson Associates and Bob
Worcester's MORI polls among others.[685] It was all coordinated by Patricia Hewitt in
Kinnock's office and Labour's Communications Director Peter Mandelson.

The pollsters' findings were ominous: 78 per cent of voters thought Labour 'extrem-
ist' and at no stage in the previous five years had more than one-quarter of the electorate
felt that Labour's defence policies came closest to their own. The British Social Attitudes
Survey showed that nationalisation had not been supported by more than one third of
the electorate since 1964 and that 56 per cent of voters believed that an economic crisis
was more likely under Labour.[686] For Labour's left, it was a bitter pill.

As the policy review began the hard left discussed how best to organise a counter-
attack. Its figurehead, Tony Benn, 'began to issue a string of speeches as single sheet press
releases, with the most piquant attacks on the tenor of Kinnock's leadership picked out
in red ink', recalled two of the journalists who received them.[687] A speech in February
1988, listing 'The Ten Deficiencies of Mr Kinnock', recited 'a consistent failure to
support the socialist struggle outside Parliament, the abandonment or watering down of
basic policies, and an over-reliance on polls and pollsters and increasingly authoritarian
and intolerant behaviour within the party'.[688] The Campaign Group of Labour MPs
discussed the issue of mounting a leadership challenge to Kinnock and after several
meetings agreed to do so by a majority of two-to-one. Tony Benn was to be the candidate
against Kinnock and Eric Heffer his running mate for deputy against Hattersley. Though
few thought victory a possibility they did expect a sizeable vote, perhaps as much as a third
of the electoral college. That, they hoped, would help put the brakes on the Kinnockite
policy review and perhaps strengthen the hard left in the next round of NEC elections.

In fact it was to prove Benn's last hurrah. The decision to mount the challenge, the
first against a sitting Labour leader of the opposition since Wilson's challenge to
Gaitskell, led to a split within the Campaign Group just as Benn's challenge to Healey's
deputy leadership back in 1981 had split the Tribune Group and precipitated the
formation of the Campaign Group itself. Opponents to the Benn–Heffer challenge

included Tony Banks, Chris Mullin, Dawn Primarolo and a group of four who were to resign from the Campaign Group in protest: Margaret Beckett, Joan Ruddock, Clare Short and Jo Richardson.

Things became further complicated by the decision of John Prescott to throw his hat in the ring as a Labour Co-ordinating Committee-backed 'third force' candidate against Heffer and Hattersley. Prescott argued that the deputy leader role could and should be transformed into a campaigning post to build and motivate a truly mass party. He believed that he could fulfil that role better than Hattersley. Kinnock, however, could not allow the delicate left–right balance within the shadow Cabinet and on the NEC to be blown apart and he feared, probably correctly, that were Hattersley to be defeated that would be exactly what would happen.

Kinnock persuaded Robin Cook to act as campaign manager for a joint Kinnock–Hattersley re-election ticket. The Benn–Heffer campaign was organised by Jon Lansman, who had been Benn's campaign manager back in 1981. The campaign dragged on through the summer and the final vote of the complicated electoral college could not be revealed until the party conference. Benn's diary recorded a straw in the wind on 6 May: 'Had a word with Peter Heathfeld (Scargill's number two), who is crestfallen because the Yorkshire miners have decided to support Kinnock as leader.'[689] The result was announced at the Blackpool Winter Gardens on 2 October 1988. The electoral college gave Kinnock an overwhelming 88.64 per cent and Benn a mere 11.73 per cent. Benn had secured the support of a mere 38 MPs and none of the big unions. In the constituencies, where Benn did best, Benn won only 112, less than 19 per cent. Heffer later acknowledged he had been 'well beaten',[690] scoring only 9.5 per cent overall and 0.007 in the union section. Prescott scored better, securing 24 per cent. But Hattersley's position was comfortably confirmed by 67 per cent of the electoral college, which was essentially what he had got back in 1983. The NEC elections, announced the following day, saw Michael Meacher lose his seat to Kinnock's campaign manager Robin Cook. Benn and Heffer had suffered an electoral humiliation of the highest order and rather than providing a brake on the policy review, the leadership challenge gave a renewed mandate for the Kinnock–Hattersley reform agenda.

Kinnock's speech that week was an opportunity for him to articulate that mandate. Just before his early death in 1978, Labour MP John Mackintosh had in an article entitled 'Has Social Democracy Failed in Britain?' asserted that 'the building of a social atmosphere which regards profit as sordid and which suspects private enterprise has, over time, weakened and demoralised the private sector to the extent that it no longer provides the necessary growth to keep the whole economy moving'.[691] Ten years later, Kinnock's speech acknowledged the essential truth of this argument, striking out against the hard left's insistence on the moral superiority of the public sector in all circumstances. For the first time in a Labour leader's speech to conference Kinnock acknowledged the positive role of the market and of the private sector in a mixed economy.

Kinnock's new emphases included the importance of the environment and, in a crucial break with the past, of the European Union. A few weeks previously EU President Jacques Delors had addressed the TUC. He had spoken of a social Europe, an EU that could help restore to British workers the rights that Thatcher had taken away. It was the beginning of a process which would see Labour swing round to be the party of Europe as the Conservatives developed ever colder Eurosceptic feet. Most memorable, however, was Kinnock's attack on the values of Thatcher, on the idea that there could be no such thing as society:

> Now that everyone has had an opportunity to digest the results of Sunday night, I should like to thank you again for your support. You know that my feeling about the leadership election was that it was an unneccesary distraction from our work in the party. But the fact is, asked for or not, elections have results and results give mandates. That mandate was given democratically and it will be used democratically. It will be used very deliberately and very directly for the purpose for which I believe it was given to me by people right across the Labour movement. The purpose of unity. The purpose of change . . .

> We are socialists, we are rationalists. Our vision is insight, not a mirage. We have strong ideals, but our idealism is not naïveté. We do not pretend the world is as it is not. We have a dream, but we are not dreamers. We do not simply desire ends. We understand the necessity of committing means and it is precisely that which produces our commitment to social justice and to economic efficiency.

> There are those, of course, like the present government, who consider social justice to be an impediment to economic efficiency. There are some – including, from what they say, some in our movement – who consider economic efficiency to be a threat to social justice. Both are wrong. The simple fact is that sustained social justice depends upon a foundation of economic prosperity and economic success cannot be properly achieved without social justice. Justice and efficiency – the two go together.

> Of course, you can get some costs down, you can get some profits up, you can get some form of efficiency by ignoring social justice. You can say that you are slimming down, sharpening up, shaking out, and call it efficiency. But if in the process you shut down 30 per cent of your country's manufacturing capacity, if you refuse to modernise training or invest in science, if you have generated all the costs and losses of mass unemployment, if you have kept your interest rates and your currency at a level which helps importers and harms exporters, then the efficiency you get is going to be limited, fragile and temporary . . .

> For some people, judgement of the shape of the economy is very easy. There are those, like the government, who simply say 'private good, public bad'. There are those who say, in a mirror image, 'public good, private bad'. Neither of them are dealing with the realities. Neither of them are applying the real test, the real judgement of the shape

and performance of industry. Neither are asking the real question 'does it work?' . . . in Germany, in Japan, in Sweden, in France . . . they appreciated long ago that public and private sectors, government and market, had to work in combination if the strength of the economy was to be developed and the potential of the economy to be maximised . . .

But now we are facing the extra pressure and contests that arise from the completion of the European Community single market . . . This is the Prime Minister who whipped and guillotined the Single European Act through the House of Commons in 1985 specifically to spur the move to the single market. So it is no good her playing Boadicea now when she sold the pass three years ago . . . We want Europe to be a community as well as a market . . . In the TUC last month, Jacques Delors said: 'The European Community will be characterised by cooperation as well as competition. It will encourage individual initiative as well as solidarity. It would be unacceptable for Europe to become a source of social regression, while we are trying to rediscover together the road to prosperity and employment.' Of course, Delors was right.

If a single market is created that extends across half the continent of Europe and the requirements of social justice are not installed as a central component in that venture, then the fruits of economic efficiency will be scooped up by a few countries – indeed, a few regions in a few countries . . . Social Europe must mean getting the highest standards of working conditions and workers' rights right across that single market. It must mean raising pensions and benefits to European standards. British pensioners will know how far they lag behind their contemporaries in the rest of the European Community. It is a source of shame . . . social Europe must mean community action to safeguard, to protect and conserve the environment: land, sea and air . . . In her nine years of power the government has consistently weakened and blocked European moves to control industrial emissions and to improve the quality of water in the reservoirs, rivers and in the sea around our coasts . . .

If the Prime Minister really is serious about her commitment, she will have to respond to the repeated calls for urgent action and new legislation to control pesticides, to control the import of waste, to control and prevent dumping at sea and to reduce atmospheric pollution . . .

We want some answers to some questions as well: since the Prime Minister claims such zeal for the protection of the environment, is she going to introduce new regulations to stop the development sprawl into the green belt in the south east and elsewhere in Britain? Is she going to stop Ridley's raiders spraying concrete over this green and pleasant land? . . .

In Britain now nearly nine million men, women and children live on supplementary benefit. Another nine million live on low pay. That is one in three of the population . . . Our society is disfigured and endangered by such great poverty . . . a society with such great and growing differences in personal economic conditions is unlikely to be a society at peace with itself. It is an insecure society . . .

The expressions of insecurity take many forms. They include increasing family break-up, increasing neurotic stress and breakdown, poverty and homelessness, crimes of sexual abuse and robbery, drug and alcohol abuse, a huge rise in violence for criminal ends and – incredibly and terrifyingly – a spread in violence for entertainment, whether it is in football crowds or in quiet country towns on a Saturday night. Of course, no one could or would blame the government for all that. But it is impossible to accept that there is no connection between the fracturing of our society and the grabbing 'loadsamoney' ethic encouraged by a government that treats care as 'drooling', compassion as 'wet'. A government led by a Prime, Minister who says that: 'There is no such thing as society.'

'No such thing as society,' she says.

No obligation to the community.

No sense of solidarity.

No principles of sharing or caring.

'No such thing as society.'

No sisterhood, no brotherhood.

No neighbourhood.

No honouring other people's mothers and fathers.

No succouring other people's little children.

'No such thing as society.'

No number other than one.

No person other than me.

No time other than now.

No such thing as society, just 'me' and 'now'.

That is Margaret Thatcher's society.

I tell you, you cannot run a country on the basis of 'me' and 'now' . . .

The whole policy review process is a challenge that we have given ourselves. Many welcome it and participate in it as a means of refining and refreshing the ways of applying our values in practice. Others are not so bold . . .

When we speak . . . about individuals and consumers and competitiveness it is not long before we hear people in the movement saying that we are proposing 'to run the capitalist economy better than the Tories'. Comrades, the day may come when this conference, this movement, is faced with a choice of socialist economies. The debate will be fascinating as the Labour Party conference chooses between the two. But until that day comes, when that choice of socialist economies is actually presented, actually in existence, the fact is that the kind of economy that we will be faced with when we win the election will be a market economy . . .

Even after that has been the implemented programme of a Labour government for years, there will still be a market, still be a market economy. What will be different will be the condition of the people who have had the chance to train, who will have been engaged in the new industries, who will have benefited not just from the greater production but from the fairer distribution that it finances. That will be applying our values, our vision in practice instead of just talking about it . . .

The completed policy review was published in May 1989. The European elections the following month saw Thatcher lead the Conservatives to battle on a Eurosceptic platform, deploying posters around Britain threatening 'a diet of Brussels' for those who failed to vote Conservative. Labour, newly pro-European, won more votes than any other party for the first time in years. The recently merged Social and Liberal Democrats did disastrously: their credibility had been shattered by more than a year of internal wrangling over the merger of the SDP and Liberals and by a subsequent breakaway 'continuity SDP' led by David Owen. Their vote evaporated to Labour and the Green Party.

At Labour's 1989 annual conference the policy review documents, entitled *Meet the Challenge, Make the Change*, were passed. Labour's 1988 conference had voted yet again for unilateral nuclear disarmament. In May 1989, in tones reminiscent of Nye Bevan in 1957, Kinnock told Labour's NEC that he had, in effect, changed his mind:

> Many in this room have protested and marched in support of nuclear disarmament. I have done that. But I have done something else: I have gone to the White House, the Kremlin, the Elysée, and argued the line for unilateral nuclear disarmament. I knew they would disagree with the policy. But above that, they were totally uncomprehending that we should want to get rid of nuclear missile systems without getting elimination of nuclear weapons on other sides too – without getting anything for it in return. I argued the policy because of the integrity of the objective of eliminating nuclear weapons. But I have to tell you that I am not going to make that tactical argument for the unilateral abandonment of nuclear weapons without getting anything in return ever again. I will not do it. The majority of the party and the majority of the country don't expect me to do so.[692]

In public Kinnock still sought to side-step his change of approach rather than make a virtue of conviction, emphasising that the reorientation of defence policy was a consequence of changed international circumstances rather than a realisation that unilateralism had been a mistake. Nevertheless, the change in approach was sufficiently real to see Labour's 1989 conference vote through a new non-unilateralist defence policy by over a million votes, USDAW and Tom Sawyer's NUPE having abandoned their unilateralist policies and swung their block votes behind the leadership. The unilateralists still had the support of the TGWU and Tony Benn, but it was not enough. Kinnock concluded his speech of that year with a quotation from Shelley:

> A brighter dawn awaits the human day.
> When poverty and privilege,
> The fear of infamy
> Disease and woe,
> War with its million horrors and fierce hell shall live,
> But only in the memory of time.

SIXTY-THREE

Hopes Dashed 1989–92

'What else can we expect from an ex-Spam hoarder from Grantham, presiding over the social and economic decline of our country?'

Labour's 1989 conference also saw a debate on Labour's energy policy. Traditionally Labour had aimed to please the NUM with a policy that was pro-coal while seeking not to alienate either the other trade unions who represented the workers at nuclear power stations or the anti-nuclear pressure groups who wanted them closed. Under Scargill the NUM had sought to commit Labour to 'rid Britain of the evil of civil nuclear power' and replace it with coal. A rearguard action had been fought by Electricians' Union leader Eric Hammond on behalf of his members who worked in nuclear power stations and Labour MP Tam Dalyell who had seen enough of his constituents die of coal-induced respiratory diseases to convince him that if anything it was nuclear power that was safer.

The government's decision to privatise electricity gave energy policy an especially high profile. Labour fought hard in the Commons committees, forcing Energy Secretary Cecil Parkinson to abandon his original plan to include the older nuclear power stations in the sell-off: investors didn't want to take the potential safety risks. The resistance to the Bill was led by a young Durham MP and ex-barrister called Tony Blair, whom Kinnock had appointed shadow Energy Secretary on his election to the shadow Cabinet in November 1988. Blair's speech on 2 October 1989, his first to Labour's annual conference, offered both an uncompromising opposition to Tory privatisation plans and also a 'third way' through the Manichaean coal versus nuclear debate. At its core was the relationship between energy policy and the environment. The environment had been a key theme of Kinnock's speech to conference in 1988. But despite the success of the Green Party in securing 15 per cent at the June 1989 European elections, no senior politician in a potential party of government had tried to bring issues of energy efficiency and the utilisation of renewable energy sources to the heart of the policy debate. Blair was the first:

> On Friday, electricity privatisation finally descended into chaos. Yesterday we learnt that now even most Tory voters oppose it. Today, therefore, we speak for the country when we say we do not want our electricity service made into a plaything for City speculators, we do not want it bought and traded on the stock exchange. It is ours already and it should stay ours (*applause*).
>
> At the onset we said that [privatising] electricity would mean higher prices, and it

has done. We warned that the government would introduce a special nuclear tax for private nuclear power, and it has. We said that the government would be forced to admit there was no choice for consumers, and now they have. Born out of dogma, reared on deceit, this privatisation is now exposed for what it is and always has been, private prejudice masquerading as public policy.

Let us send this message to the government, we do not want it postponed, we do not want it delayed, we do not want it put off, we want it abandoned here, now and for ever (*applause*).

And in place of that tired Tory agenda for the eighties, privatisation, pollution, price rises, we give the country a new vision for the nineties where conserving energy is as important as producing it, where the consumer has rights to a decent standard of service and where, for the first time in our energy policy history, under Labour the environment will govern our energy policy not energy policy govern our environment. And yes, as part of that policy review, there will be no more nuclear power stations under Labour . . . we are committed to energy efficiency, not as an afterthought but as a centrepiece of strategy, to a major expansion of combined heat and power, to funding the fluidised bed combustion process at Grimethorpe, to providing our eleven million pensioners with a decent fuel poverty programme to see them through the winter months and why, most innovative of all, we are proposing for the first time that we attempt to meet a substantial part of our energy needs from alternative, benign, renewable sources of energy.

Private enterprise alone cannot do these things. It is our unique contribution, as socialists, that we recognise this simple truth, that energy policy is too important, too vital, too critical to our nation's future that we determine it according to the short-term whim of market forces . . .

In November 1989, the Conservatives took Blair's medicine and abandoned the proposed sale of Nuclear Electric altogether. Thatcher's government was coming apart. On 5 December 1989, 33 Conservative MPs voted for a 'stalking horse' leadership challenger, the long-serving backbencher Sir Anthony Meyer, over Thatcher.

By early 1990 Margaret Thatcher's government was mired in an ever deepening unpopularity. Ignoring Denis Healey's dictum (when in a hole, stop digging), Thatcher had pressed on with the poll tax, precipitating demonstrations of a million people, riots and widespread non-payment. At the same time, public services continued to suffer. Even the Royal Shakespeare Company was in financial crisis. In a Commons debate on 20 February 1990 Tory MPs such as Terry Dicks had argued that investment in Britain's cultural fabric was a waste of taxpayers' money. Labour MP Tony Banks hit back:

. . . My right hon. and hon. friends know that an economically efficient and socially just society will not only address the problems of homelessness, poverty and unemployment that the hon. Member for Hayes and Harlington [Mr Dicks] mentioned. Such a society will support also a thriving and burgeoning arts expenditure. It is a mark of a confident and strong society that it encourages and nurtures the arts. The Victorians did it in the past in this country, and the French, Germans and Italians do it today.

I am sorry that the hon. Member for Hayes and Harlington is not in his place, because listening to him opining on the arts is rather like listening to Vlad the Impaler presenting 'Blue Peter'. The hon. gentleman is undoubtedly living proof that a pig's bladder on a stick can be elected as a Member of Parliament.

(*Several hon. members rose.*)

Mr Speaker: Order. I know – but although the hon. gentleman's comments may not be very pleasant, they are not unparliamentary.

Mr Banks: They were artistic, Mr Speaker. I am just sorry that the hon. Member for Hayes and Harlington was not in his place to hear them. Still, I do not wish to offend you, Mr Speaker.

It is a comment on the depressing state of Britain today, with all its economic inefficiencies and social injustices, that a great cultural institution such as the Royal Shakespeare Company faces the crisis that it does. I speak of the theatre that bears and propagates the name of the greatest English playwright. However, the crisis that afflicts the RSC is not confined to that company. The English National Opera, Royal Opera House, South Bank Centre, London Festival Ballet and Royal National Theatre all face similar problems. Those problems extend to our museums and art galleries. We have heard complaints about the crumbling fabric of the Victoria and Albert Museum and of the British Museum that should shame us all. We are squandering a wonderful inheritance . . .

We are not just talking about high art or middle-class art . . . but all the provincial and municipal theatres in towns and cities throughout the country, which provide a lot of pleasure for working-class people and are also facing a crisis . . .

We face a depressing scenario in the arts, but one which is typical of the Prime Minister's philistinism and the unimaginative, shoddy, second-rate government that run the country. It is typical of a Prime Minister who goes to see *The Mousetrap* and rereads whodunits. Who has to read a whodunit, when she knew whodunit when she reads it again? It is typical of a Prime Minister who is happier getting in and out of tanks than in and out of museums or theatre seats, and who seems to derive more pleasure from admiring new missiles than great works of art. What else can we expect from an ex-Spam hoarder from Grantham, presiding over the social and economic decline of our country? . . .

Involvement in the arts, either as a creator or a consumer, is one of the finest forms of human activity that we can encourage. I remind Conservative members that there is very little crowd violence at the opera houses these days.

Secondly – this should appeal to the monetarists opposite – the economic significance of the arts is continually underestimated and undervalued. They have a £12 billion turnover; the industry employs some 450,000 people; it contributes £4 billion to the balance of payments . . .

People do not come to this country to see office blocks, Third World roads or crumbling transport infrastructure, or to learn how to control inflation or enjoy traffic jams. They come here to enjoy the enormously rich art legacy that we have inherited. They come for theatres, art galleries and museums. I remind Conservative members that that legacy is as important as North Sea oil, but unlike oil, it will not run out. However, it can be run down, and that is what is happening to the arts in this country today . . . It is interesting that we should have one of the highest defence budgets in western Europe, and one of the smallest arts budgets . . .

On 18 October 1990 the Conservatives suffered a stunning by-election defeat at the hands of the Liberal Democrats in a previously safe seat: Eastbourne. Thatcher had only weeks earlier dismissed the LibDems, who had over the previous two years somewhat languished in the polls, in her party conference speech as a 'dead parrot', a mocking reference, after the Monty Python sketch, to their new 'Bird of Liberty' logo which had been adopted in place of the SDP–Liberal Alliance-era diamond. The parrot had bitten back. Fatally. Conservative backbench panic hit fever pitch. They saw disastrous opinion poll results translating into their own electoral defeat unless Thatcher was persuaded at least to modify her most unpopular policies. The lady was not, however, for turning. Within weeks her deputy Prime Minister Sir Geoffrey Howe had resigned, driven to despair by his premier's increasingly strident anti-Europeanism, and a former Cabinet minister, Michael Heseltine, had announced that he would challenge Thatcher for the leadership.

To her great surprise, Margaret Thatcher failed to secure enough MPs' votes to win decisively on the first ballot: only 204 to 152 for Heseltine. It was the end. In the leadership election that followed, the relatively unknown Chancellor, John Major, came up through the middle to defeat Michael Heseltine and Foreign Secretary Douglas Hurd, an Old Etonian ex-diplomat, who had also now entered the frame. Major was thought to be the closest to a Thatcher-supported candidate – his meteoric rise to Cabinet had been largely based upon her patronage and he had little independent public standing – in stark contrast to Heseltine. In truth, however, no one was quite sure what his real agenda would be once he became Prime Minister and could be 'his own man'. This was to be, at least initially, his greatest strength. He was not Thatcher. Voters who had told the opinion pollsters that they would vote Labour to get 'her' out began to talk about giving 'the new man' a chance. People wanted to see what would be different. There was a feeling of liberation, even though Major's government was nearly identical to the one it had replaced. It took another by-election victory by the LibDems over the Conservatives at Ribble Valley, the fourteenth safest Conservative seat, in March 1991, to convince John Major's government to replace the hated poll tax. Indeed, from Major's election in November 1990 until then, the Conservatives had been ahead in the opinion polls.

For Labour, the resurgence of the LibDems should have given far greater pause for thought than it did. On one level it was positive: it meant that the Conservatives were again vulnerable to defeat in a number of rural Celtic seats that Labour could never hope to gain. But it indicated too an underlying failure of the policy review fully to convince the electorate that

Labour's convictions lay with its new social-democratic policy agenda. Had it not been, after all, the rejection by Labour of such policies that had driven the social democrats to defeat in 1981–82? Labour's opinion poll leads continued, but they were soft and overstated. On polling day on 9 April 1992 the exit polls suggested that Neil Kinnock was heading for Downing Street. But when the ballot boxes were emptied, sufficient voters in enough key marginals had plumped for the Conservatives to give Major a majority of 21. The Conservatives had secured the greatest number of votes ever achieved by a British political party. The high turnout meant that Labour, in percentage term, did worse than in 1979, securing only 35.2 per cent. The LibDems, with 18.3 per cent of the vote, claimed 20 seats, including the scalp of Conservative Party chairman Chris Patten, John Major's now ex-next Chancellor of the Exchequer.[693]

'Neil Kinnock was the only leader who was capable of pushing the party back into the mainstream of British politics,'[694] Roy Hattersley has written. It was because of the sincerity with which Neil Kinnock had held the policy positions which had underpinned his popularity and secured his election as party leader in 1983, his unilateralism, his distrust of the EEC and his commitment to nationalisation, that he was able to lead the party away from them as he became convinced that they no longer reflected the world as he saw it. But that same fact torpedoed his credibility as a potential Prime Minister. Older voters remembered, and younger voters were soon told by the other parties, that Kinnock had made his political reputation during the 1970s attacking members of the Callaghan government for supporting what were in many cases the very policies which post-policy review Labour now professed to support. Was Kinnock now really anti-unilateralist, pro-EEC, pro-devolution and against the sort of mass nationalisation as envisaged by Labour's Programme 1973? 'His conversion to collective security, Europe and the mixed economy was real – based as much on a changing world as an adjustment in his own principles,'[695] wrote Hattersley, whose defeat in the leadership contest owed something to the fact that he had believed in them all along. But the task of convincing a sceptical electorate was beyond Kinnock's human powers. To achieve the changes in policy Kinnock had successfully pursued a gradualist 'softly-softly' approach. 'Until as late as 1991,' Kinnock wrote in 1994, 'there was always a significant risk that any progressive lunge that was too big or too quick could have fractured the developing consensus and retarded the whole operation of reform and change.'[696] But to convince the public that Labour really had changed he would have had overtly to denounce the old policy positions, something which it was feared, probably correctly, would inflame many of the soft left who were unhappy enough at some of the policy shifts. And what, at any rate, did such profound changes of mind say about Kinnock's judgement? For his admirers it was precisely these changes of mind that showed his strength of judgement; but for his enemies in the Conservative press – and he had many – they showed either his lack of judgement to have held his original views or his opportunism in having abandoned them.

SIXTY-FOUR

Labour Rebuilt 1992–93

'Reclaiming the Ground'

Labour's election defeat in April 1992 precipitated the resignation of Neil Kinnock. The heir apparent had for several years been John Smith, the shadow Chancellor, and he immediately announced his candidacy. Smith was a Scots lawyer and university debating champion whose Gaitskellite pedigree extended back to his role as secretary of the local CDS while a student at Glasgow University. Like Hattersley, he had been a consistent pro-NATO, anti-CND, pro-EEC social democrat, and was one of the rebel 69 to follow Roy Jenkins in the great vote on the EEC in 1971. Moreover, with Hattersley's retirement from the front bench following the 1992 election, Smith was to become the only former Cabinet minister remaining in the shadow Cabinet (he had succeeded Edmund Dell as Callaghan's Trade Secretary in November 1978). With the party's policies having returned to what he had always believed in, Smith's popularity in the country made him the natural successor to Kinnock.

His one opponent in the leadership election was Bryan Gould, whose politics were of the 'soft left'. Gould, a New Zealander who had come to Oxford on a Rhodes scholarship, had served in the Foreign Office, as an Oxford don, and during 1974–79 as MP for Southampton Test, briefly becoming the PPS to Peter Shore, whose anti-EEC convictions he shared. Defeated at the 1979 election, he returned to the Commons in 1983, after a brief television career, as MP for rock-solid Dagenham. He rose quickly, despite backing Peter Shore's ill-fated leadership bid against Kinnock and Hattersley in 1983. He was, acknowledged Roy Hattersley, 'one of the cleverest men in politics',[697] and topped both the NEC and the shadow Cabinet poll in 1987 after his performance as election campaign coordinator. Appointed shadow DTI Secretary in 1987, he would soon clash with Smith, the shadow Chancellor, whose job Gould had wanted. Smith was steering Labour back towards a pro-EEC position and Gould tried to block him. One of them had to be moved and in 1989 Kinnock had shifted Gould, to Environment, replacing him with a talented young Scots MP called Gordon Brown. Gould now stood for both leader and deputy and was badly beaten in both. Smith was elected Labour leader with a record 91 per cent of the electoral college vote, more than Kinnock before and Blair after. Gould received just less than 9 per cent. Encouraged by the offer of funding for the purpose from the Electricians' Union, many of the individual constituency Labour parties held OMOV ballots of their members: they invariably voted for Smith. For deputy, Gould came third with just 14.5 per cent, behind Prescott on 28 per cent and Margaret Beckett, who, running on a right/left 'dream ticket' with Smith, secured 57.3 per cent.

John Smith was 'frequently described as the ablest man in the Labour Party', *Telegraph* sketch writer Edward Pearce had written as long ago as 1985:

> The connoisseurs take to him very much for his sheer intelligence and grasp ... Mildly overweight, beaming through black-frame spectacles, but able, I always feel, to stamp on the odd windpipe if required. He is more intelligent than Hattersley, actually knows more about the City and could give Nigel Lawson a terrible time ... he has a strong, amusing personality edgily respected by both sides.[698]

Now he was Labour's leader.

He set out his political philosophy most clearly in his R. H. Tawney Memorial Lecture of 20 March 1993, entitled 'Reclaiming the Ground':

> ... The fundamental flaw in the individualism of the classical writers, and their modern counterparts in today's Conservative Party is, I believe, their assumption that human beings conduct their lives on the basis of self-interested decisions taken in radical isolation from others. This thesis grotesquely ignores the intrinsically social nature of human beings and fails to recognise the capabilities that all people have to act in response to commitments and beliefs that clearly transcend any narrow calculation of personal advantage.
>
> Of course people have a natural and powerful regard for their own interests and that of their families ... As Archbishop Temple warned, 'a statesman who supposes that a mass of citizens can be governed without appeal to their self-interest is living in a dreamland and is a public menace' (adding the wise advice that 'the art of government in fact is the art of so ordering life that self-interest prompts what justice demands'). But although Temple accepted that 'man is self-centred', he also believed that 'this is not the real truth of his nature. He has to his credit both capabilities and achievements that could never be derived from self-interest.'

Smith agreed with R. H. Tawney that:

> ... meaningful freedom depended on real ability. That for millions of people citizenship was empty and valueless if squalor and deprivation were the reality of a society only theoretically free. What was needed was positive liberty – the freedom to achieve that is gained through education, health care, housing and employment. An infrastructure of freedom that would require collective provision of basic needs through an enabling state. It is this richer conception of freedom for the individual in society that is the moral basis of democratic socialism ...
>
> It is a sense of revulsion at denied opportunity, injustice and poverty, whether at home or abroad, which impels people to work for a better world, to become, as in our case,

democratic socialists. The powerful contribution of Christian socialists in all the denominations of the Church has always focused on the moral purpose of political action. How true it is that the Labour Party has owed more to Methodism than to Marx . . .

One of John Smith's first tasks was to reshuffle his shadow Cabinet pack. Margaret Beckett, his new deputy leader, became shadow Leader of the Commons: the old role occupied by deputy leaders Herbert Morrison, Ted Short and Michael Foot. Shadow Foreign Secretary, Harold Wilson's protégé Gerald Kaufman, retired to the backbenches and was replaced by Jack Cunningham, once PPS to Jim Callaghan. To fill his own shoes as shadow Chancellor Smith appointed Gordon Brown, who had topped the shadow Cabinet poll for the third time in four years. Brown had been a very impressive shadow Trade and Industry Secretary, making a particular name for himself in 1988 lacerating Tory Chancellor Nigel Lawson when standing in for John Smith, then the shadow Chancellor, who had been put temporarily out of action by a heart attack. Brown would be replaced as shadow DTI Secretary by one of the finest parliamentary debaters of his generation, Kinnock's former campaign manager Robin Cook.

Gordon Brown would in years to come become arguably Labour's, if not Britain's, most successful Chancellor of the Exchequer. In the summer of 1992, he was, with the rest of the Labour Party, still coming to terms with the shock of yet another general election defeat. One of the main reasons for that defeat was the ingrained folk memory among the electorate of Labour's approach to the economy during the early 1980s. It had meant, as John Major shrewdly observed in his memoir, that 'oddly the recession helped us. The electorate believed we could steer through it more effectively than Labour.'[699] It had been Nigel Lawson's unsustainable candy-floss boom, engineered to help win the 1987 election, that had overheated the economy and had led the Conservatives to slam on the brakes and create the recession. Nevertheless, the electors who had voted Conservative before were not swinging over to Labour. Although some of them did blame the Conservatives for mishandling the economy, they were simply unconvinced that Labour could or would do a better job, and feared they might make it worse. Brown was a historian, rooted in the values of the Scottish Labour Party. He had reworked his PhD thesis into a critically acclaimed biography of one of his heroes, Red Clydesider James Maxton, which had been published in 1986. As a historian, Brown knew that throughout its history Labour governments had inherited and ultimately been brought down by the economic disasters inherited from the Conservative governments they had replaced. The Conservatives had become adept at engineering pre-election tax-cutting booms, in effect electoral bribes, which had won votes in the short term but screwed up the economy in the long term, producing the stop-go pattern that so characterised the post-war years. In 1964 Labour had inherited the Maudling Boom, and in 1974 the Barber Boom. Post-1987, Lawson had inherited his own boom. And bust.

In one of his last speeches as shadow Trade and Industry Secretary, just days before Smith promoted him to be shadow Chancellor, Gordon Brown savaged the government's economic record in the Commons, focusing in particular on the failure of the 'President of the Board of Trade', as the new DTI Secretary Michael Heseltine had renamed himself, to get a grip of Britain's problems:

... This is the government and the Prime Minister who told us that they would create opportunities for all, yet, as unemployment, the biggest single destroyer of opportunity, has risen by one million, as fifty thousand businesses have closed, and as homes have been repossessed, they have done virtually nothing. This is the Prime Minister who promised during the general election campaign that he would create a classless society, a nation at ease with itself ...

During the campaign, the Prime Minister said: 'Britain is ready to move forward when others are sliding backwards. All that Britain is waiting for to achieve recovery is the confidence a Conservative government will bring.'

He also said: 'Vote Conservative on Thursday and the recovery will continue on Friday.'

Three months have now passed. What is industry saying about these promises? According to McAlpine Ewart Hill, one of the Tories' election backers, these are 'the most difficult trading conditions this company can recall'. Sir Anthony Pilkington said: 'I've not met a single industrialist who sees any sign of upturn.' The Burton Group said: 'The only pick up is not in consumer demand but in conversation about consumer demand.'

The Prime Minister who promised recovery last spring, last autumn, last Christmas and at the beginning of the year and was so explicit in his promises during the election campaign is responsible for a manifesto built on a fiction and has been guilty of misleading the country ...

Even the *Sun* tells the Chancellor of the Exchequer: 'For God's sake, wake up Norman. The economy is crumbling around you and yet you still do nothing.'

... The truth is that the only recovery that interested Tory members was the recovery of power, and the only unemployment that concerned them was fear of their own ...

Faced with all these problems – a recession, a trade deficit and Britain bottom of the league – what has been happening in government since 9 April? What has been achieved by the Trade Minister? His first action at the Department of Trade and Industry was not the much-needed change of policy, but the wholly unnecessary change of title – calling himself President. What has been achieved as the President approaches the end of his first one hundred days? ...

He has become President – but President of what? President of a Board of Trade which never meets, which has no active members, which must somehow spearhead a bold new industrial strategy for a new century and a new millennium, but which last met on 13 December 1850. The Board of Trade was wound up years ago, and there is no one there to notice should the President decide, on impulse and no doubt on a matter of principle, to walk out. The right hon. gentleman is not so much the emperor with no clothes as the President with no board and far too little trade . . .

How do we sum up the President's first one hundred days? After seven years of Kennedy-style build up and campaigning for the presidency and three months of Camelot hype, I can tell him what has happened. As President Kennedy would have put it, 'Ask not what you can do for the Cabinet; ask what the Cabinet has done to you.' The City responsibilities of the DTI have gone to the Chancellor, who is almost ten years younger. The film responsibilities for the DTI have gone to the rising star, the Secretary of State for National Heritage. Public spending directions are now at the behest of the youngest Cabinet minister, the Chief Secretary to the Treasury. As President Kennedy would have put it, 'The torch has passed to a new generation.'

The President . . . has full powers and unlimited responsibilities to reorganise the desks within his Department, but he cannot begin to contemplate the implementation of a genuine industrial strategy for Britain. Perhaps next week there will be an announcement on the dramatic reshuffle of the office furniture, and the week after that sweeping new recommendations on the colour of the curtains . . .

The Minister – the President – who spent years in exile working out his plans, who promised so much, who stormed the country with his new ideas for an industrial strategy, who was the darling of the Conservative associations, the hero of a thousand Conservative Party lunches, the interventionist tiger of the rubber chicken circuit, has been brought low, reduced to trophy status. The tiger that was once the king of the jungle is now just the fireside rug – decorative and ostentatious, but essentially there to be walked all over . . .

We need a government who will act in the public interest to end the recession, tackle the trade deficit and secure lasting recovery, preside over an investment decade for the British economy, and with the ambition to make our workforce the best trained and educated in Europe. We need a government who will take measures now to reduce unemployment, tackle poverty, and eliminate low pay . . .

We have instead a government who, three months after an election victory, have no strategy for recovery . . . We have a government who are creating not a classless society but a heartless society. It will be the job of the Labour opposition to attack Conservative failure, to expose the broken promises, and to point the way to a better future.

Kinnock's shadow Home Secretary had been the deputy leader, Roy Hattersley, who had now followed Kinnock to the backbenches. John Smith's new shadow Home Secretary would be Tony Blair, for the previous two years the shadow Employment Secretary, where he had successfully steered Labour towards acceptance of the illegality of the 'closed shop'. Since the early 1980s the public had tended to perceive Labour as soft on crime, as taking the side of the villain against the victim, indeed as seeing the villain as the victim of society and in so doing, failing to protect the innocent from the crimes of the guilty. All that was to change with Smith's appointment of Tony Blair as shadow Home Secretary.

In a speech at Wellingborough on 19 February 1993, Blair used the nation-wide horror at the child-murder of toddler Jamie Bulger as a spur to address wider social issues and their relationship with crime:

> . . . A solution to this disintegration doesn't simply lie in legislation. It must come from the rediscovery of a sense of direction as a country and most of all from being unafraid to start talking again about the values and principles we believe in and what they mean for us, not just as individuals but as a community. We cannot exist in a moral vacuum. If we do not learn and then teach the value of what is right and what is wrong, then the result is simply moral chaos which engulfs us all . . . The importance of the notion of community is that it defines the relationship not only between us as individuals but between people and the society in which they live, one that is based on responsibilities as well as rights, on obligations as well as entitlements. Self-respect is in part derived from respect for others.[700]

Within days Blair had followed up with a radio interview in which he first deployed what has been called 'probably the cleverest political slogan any Labour politician had hit upon in fourteen years of opposition':[701] 'tough on crime, tough on the causes of crime'. It was what Callaghan had been saying, and what Bob Marshall-Andrews and Jeremy Corbyn had objected to, back in 1978. But now it was said with a clarity which helped to transform political perceptions. As Andy McSmith, then of the *Observer*, shrewdly observed, 'it went straight to the heart of one of Labour's greatest political problems: that working-class voters, who are the most frequent victims of crime and anti-social behaviour, suspected that the Labour Party was a political home for liberals whose theories did not deter offenders and did not work'.[702] Blair would develop his theme in his speech to Labour conference on 30 September 1993:

> . . . for millions of our citizens the democratic freedom they value most is freedom from crime and fear of crime. We will put the victim at the heart of our criminal justice system . . . The hooligans who call themselves football supporters and inflict terror and violence on a neighbourhood on a Saturday afternoon; the muggers who beat up pensioners in their own homes; the perverted men who rape and molest women; the racist thugs who think a weekend sport is to beat up a defenceless black or Asian kid; the place for these people is out of society, until they learn to behave like human beings within our society . . .
>
> Labour is the party of strong communities. And that is why Labour now is the party of law and order in Britain today; tough on crime and tough on the causes of crime.
>
> . . . the Tory failure is not just one of policy, but of understanding and imagination. No one but a fool would excuse crime on the basis of social conditions. No one but a Tory could deny the impact of the conditions in which people live on the character which they develop. And when we allow a culture to grow outside society's

main stream, alienated from society's rules – a culture of people with no hope in that society and no stake in its future; a culture of broken homes, truancy, poor education, drugs, no jobs, or dead-end jobs – I say that when we sow the seeds of such a culture, we should not be surprised at the harvest we reap.

In making this speech Blair made use of a change in conference procedure that now enabled shadow Cabinet members to make set-piece speeches to conference. Tom Sawyer remembers:

Not until after 1990/91 did the shadow Cabinet get proper speaking slots at conference. Before that it was always the NEC who got the big speeches. When we had the policy review we agreed that when the policy commissions reported the commission chair, usually a trade unionist, would open the debate and the shadow Cabinet spokesman would reply. The hard left were very against it. Neil Kinnock asked me to look at other party conferences to see what lessons we could learn. We went to Italy, Germany, France and Sweden and talked to parties in other countries too. The most impressive we went to was Sweden, which had a rolling programme of policy making, with a conversational style at conference, rather than the semi-Leninist style we had at Labour conference. I do think that the Communist Party affected our speaking style. Or union leaders had to be able to toe-to-toe against the likes of Harry Pollitt and Tom Mann. It was great theatre but bad policy making. It does mean that there is less of an emphasis on rhetoric than there used to be. It used to be that people who wanted to make a name for themselves would make a good conference speech to get on the NEC. Tony Benn believed that in the end the NEC could control the PM. Bernard Donoughue once told me that in the Wilson years quite often the Cabinet would be stood down so that Harold could go to an NEC meeting. Quite often there would only be one vote in it.[703]

SIXTY-FIVE

The Brink of Victory 1993–94

'The opportunity to serve, that is all we ask'

One of the great battles of the 1992–97 parliament was over the EU. Thatcher's increasingly strident anti-Europeanism had helped terminate her premiership. John Major's public agnosticism helped secure him the succession. In office, but not quite in total control over his party, Major became prisoner of the feud between the anti-European Thatcherite right and the more traditional pro-Europeans led within his Cabinet by Michael Heseltine and Ken Clarke, and on the backbenches by Edward Heath and Sir Geoffrey Howe. As growing unpopularity cost his government by-election after by-election his parliamentary majority dwindled, increasing the power of the backbench 'bastards', as he famously dubbed them, to hold him to ransom. His determination to hold on to office was limpet-like in its intensity. Major had convinced himself that he was the best man to hold his party together and keep Labour out. His great achievement, as he saw it, was to negotiate an 'opt-out' from the Social Chapter of the Maastrict Treaty, which all the other eleven EU countries had signed up to in its entirety. Labour opposed the opt-out and insisted on a vote on the issue before the Act to incorporate the Maastricht Treaty into UK law could come into force. In the debate, on 22 July 1993, it was John Smith who led for the opposition:

> The other eleven states have agreed that there should be a modest extension of the Community's competence in social affairs – matters such as the protection of the health, safety and working conditions of people at work, workers' rights to information and consultation, and equality for men and women in relation to work opportunities and treatment at the workplace. The argument is all about those sectors where qualified majority voting applies . . . the government say that the proposals are a sinister threat to our economic future, a deadly plot by the Brussels bureaucrats to destroy jobs and economic growth from which, in the nick of time, our heroic Prime Minister has rescued us all. The irony of the Prime Minister posing as a job protector will not be lost on the millions of people who have been victims of the economic policies for which he has been responsible as Chancellor and Prime Minister. That self-styled saviour of jobs and growth has the worst record on jobs and growth of any British Prime Minister since the war . . .
>
> If the Conservative Party is so right on this subject, why is it that the only political party in the rest of the Community that supports it is Mr Le Pen's National Front? *(interruption)*. Why is it that even right-wing governments do not perceive the menaces

and the threats which the Prime Minister and his colleagues see on all sides? Can it really be true (*long and frequent interruptions*) . . .

The fundamental point is why, if the employers were so compelling in their arguments, they have not been able to persuade Chancellor Kohl, Mr Balladur and Mr Lubbers, the right-wing conservative figures in Europe, to listen to them. It passes belief that these people are involved in a nefarious plot to destroy their own prosperity. Are these right-wing conservative leaders so muddled and confused that they have become socialists by accident? . . .

Why is it that not one of the four countries seeking entry into the European Community wants to opt out of the Social Chapter? Fifteen countries in Europe – those in the Community and those wanting to join – are all of one opinion; only one party and one country is on the other side – all out of step except our John. The Prime Minister must believe that they are all deluded . . .

What kind of success is it to have engineered a situation in which, when social affairs are on the Community's agenda, British Ministers have to leave the room, bereft (*long and frequent interruptions*). Only in the Walter Mitty world that the Prime Minister increasingly inhabits could such nonsense be thought to be an achievement. Of course, we know that the Prime Minister wants the country to believe that, whatever the mess at home, he is really an ace negotiator abroad. Like the comic strip hero, Clark Kent, as soon as he leaves our shores behind, the Prime Minister is transformed into a diplomatic megastar. There he is, Britain's diplomatic megastar, his Superman shirt tucked neatly into his underpants; there he is, a very special kind of hero, shaping the very destiny of Europe, clutching his Maastricht opt-out as his colleagues gently take him to the door marked 'Sortie' (*long and frequent interruptions*) . . . their opt-out is Britain's lockout – a lockout from decisions . . .

The World Economic Forum recently published its world competitiveness report on the countries of the OECD, which showed that over the past five years the United Kingdom has fallen down the league. That is the sharpest deterioration in competitiveness of any EC country. The truth which must some day dawn on this government is that their policies simply have not worked. Even the expurgated version of the government's own Department of Trade and Industry report shows that Britain is still 25 per cent below France and Germany in terms of productivity.

The evidence shows that the member states which embraced the Social Chapter when Britain rejected it have more impressive records of competitiveness and productivity. The Conservatives fail to understand that low wages, inadequate skills and persistent under-investment are the real drag anchors on Britain's economic performance. We have no future as the sweatshop of Europe . . .

Warburg's briefing last week on competitiveness among the leading industrial countries stated: 'Despite having the lowest labour costs per working hour, Britain struggles with the highest unit labour costs.'

That is proof, surely, if it were needed, that having the lowest wages does not, as the opt-out merchants maintain, lead necessarily to competitive advantage. That is the answer to the question that I was asked at the beginning of this debate.

The Warburg study shows – sensible people know this – that improvement in productivity depends critically on capital investment, the pace of innovation and the quality of the labour force . . . not the bargain-basement techniques of wage cuts and skills depression . . .

The Nissan director of personnel gave evidence the other day to the Select Committee on Employment. He dismissed the Social Chapter as a significant factor in respect of inward investment.

It is also highly revealing that many Japanese firms in Britain bring with them much better working practices than are common in British firms and which far exceed anything that would be required by the Social Chapter . . .

It is now entirely clear that the whole of this argument about opting out of the social dimension of the treaty is not about Britain's national interest or our future prosperity. It is much more about the internal politics of the Conservative Party and increasingly about the tattered reputation of a discredited Prime Minister.

John Smith's speech caused serious damage to the Major government's public credibility. Although the votes on the opposition amendments were lost, the government was actually defeated on the substantive motion, precipitating a full-blown vote of confidence the next morning.

Only a few months later, Smith faced a vote of confidence of his own. Labour's 1993 annual conference has gone down in history as the scene of the final victorious battle for One Member One Vote (OMOV). The system proposed with John Smith's support for electing the leader and deputy was not actually OMOV in the original sense that it had been envisaged by Frank Chapple, the EETPU and the Manifesto Group back in 1981. They had advocated a postal ballot of individual party members with everyone's vote being equal. The Smith system of OMOV was, in fact, a rebalancing of the electoral college to equal thirds in which the constituent trade unions and constituency parties would be required to ballot their members and divide their votes accordingly. MPs, with one third of the votes of the electoral college, clearly had a greater value to their vote than ordinary party or trade union members. The other change was to replace the activists' vote of constituency 'General Committee' members with an OMOV ballot of members and trade union levy payers for selecting parliamentary candidates.

On the eve of the conference, it looked as if Smith had failed to secure the votes for change. The block votes of the four biggest unions were split: although the AEEU and UNISON backed reform, the TGWU and GMB opposed it. Over the lunch break before the debate the delegation from the fifth largest union, white-collar MSF, was closeted in a church hall debating its position. The composite containing the OMOV proposals also included a provision requiring half of all winnable seats with no sitting Labour MP to choose a candidate from an all-women shortlist. MSF opposed OMOV but supported all-women shortlists. After a great deal of argument the delegation voted by nineteen to seventeen that the unions' conflicting policy positions meant that it had to abstain. Their abstention would be crucial: MSF had 4.5 per cent of the block vote and Smith's eventual victory would be by a margin of only 3.1 per cent. The conference debate was opened by John Smith, who set out the case for change. In the general debate that followed, one of the most passionate interventions came from AEEU President Bill Jordan:[704]

> ... It is here, colleagues, at this conference in full view of every elector in the country, that the monstrous inequality of the block vote does the most damage ... They see just six men raise their block vote and outvote everybody else represented here at this conference. No wonder constituency delegates come to this rostrum every year and ask, 'Why do we bother coming?' John Smith is handing you real power ...

Against the reforms was the TGWU, whose leader Bill Morris declared:

> On the morning after the general election, I was very surprised to hear that trade unions were the problem and OMOV was in fact the answer. I said then and I say again, if OMOV really is the answer, it must have been a silly question in the first place.

The debate and the vote were on a knife edge. Smith had been warned that morning that support among the constituency parties was ebbing away. The doubters had to be won over. Margaret Beckett, Labour's deputy leader, would normally have wound up in such a debate, and the previous day she had indicated that OMOV had her less than wholehearted support in a BBC interview. What was Smith to do? He turned to John Prescott. So long as Margaret Beckett agreed to him doing so, Prescott said, he was prepared to make the speech. Beckett did agree, so over the lunch break, Prescott sat down with Smith and scribbled together the outlines for the speech. It was then that Smith told Prescott that if he lost he would resign. Prescott's speech, quickly scribbled over lunch with John Smith, was delivered largely off-the-cuff. He concluded:

> ... It may be felt, and it has been reflected in the movement of the debate today, that this issue really pales into insignificance compared with the issues of homelessness, of poverty, of pensioners trying to live on the incomes that they have - all these problems. Of course it does, but do not make any mistake: this debate is being watched throughout the country. The press are waiting to see what will happen. What are they waiting to see? They are waiting to see whether you want to support these proposals. That for you is just a normal matter, one way or another. Do you think the press are likely to take it one way or another? It is whether the proposals put and backed by the National Executive Committee in the name of the leader of the party are going to be supported today. That is the issue, and if it is not, that is what the press are making it.
> God knows I do not like the press setting the agenda, and you know I do not court publicity from the press! But there is a moment in time in the history of every movement when the issue does not look to be important, but what is important is the issue

as it is seen from outside, among the many millions of our people and the millions of trade unionists, and particularly among our enemies who have already started with their political propaganda. Last night the Tories reminded us of the connections between the trade unions and the Labour Party. There is no doubt that this man, our leader, put his head on the block by saying, basically: 'I fervently believe' – because that is what he believes – 'in the relationship, and a strong one, between the trade unions and the Labour Party.' He has put his head on the block. Now is our time to vote. Give us a bit of trust and let us vote to support him.

'If he does nothing else in his life, that speech had everything. No one can take that away,' John Prescott's wife Pauline told *Daily Mirror* political editor Alastair Campbell after-wards.[705] The vote that followed gave Smith and Prescott victory.

As John Major's government became mired in ever increasing unpopularity, rarely registering above 25 per cent in the Gallup opinion polls after May of that year, its attempts to relaunch itself became ever more desperate. One of the most infamous was the much-trumpeted 'back to basics' campaign, launched by means of John Major's speech to the October 1993 Conservative Party conference. 'It was a speech that was to be hung round my neck,' conceded a rueful Major in his memoir.[706] John Smith used his speech in reply to the Queen's Speech in November 1993 to do just that:

> . . . At the Conservative Party conference the Prime Minister launched his big idea – 'back to basics'. It is true that those magic words do not appear in the Gracious Speech itself. We should perhaps be grateful that Her Majesty was not obliged to repeat the mantra, but there is no doubt that that is the right hon. gentleman's chosen course. He could not have been clearer about it at Blackpool. The Conservative Party, he told us, is now going back to basics. Ever since then political commentators, some bewil-dered members of the Cabinet and millions of incredulous electors have been trying to work out what the Prime Minister means. The first thought that occurs to them, perhaps not surprisingly, is that the Conservatives have been in government for four-teen years. If now we have to go back to basics, what on earth has been happening over fourteen years of Conservative government? Or is this perhaps another coded attack on the glorious achievements of the former Tory leader – another oblique reference to 'the golden age that never was', to quote the Prime Minister's own revealing descrip-tion of his predecessor's achievements? I hope that there are still some loyal souls on the Tory benches who will be prepared, as a matter of honour, to rebut such a surrep-titious attack on the Thatcher Downing Street years.
>
> We know, of course, that the Prime Minister is haunted by those years and even more troubled by the recent flood of memoirs from former Cabinet ministers all bear-ing the same title, 'How I almost stood up to Mrs Thatcher'. Her memoirs rather stole the show at the Conservative Party conference. Even the Prime Minister's speech could not avoid them. At the start of his speech to the conference he said:
>
> Memoirs to the left of me

Memoirs to the right of me,
Memoirs in front of me
Volley'd and thundered.

He borrowed the quote from Tennyson's great poem, 'The Charge of the Light Brigade'. Perhaps he should have read on. The poem continues:

Boldly they rode and well,
Into the jaws of Death
Rode the six hundred.

I know why the Prime Minister did not finish the quote – there are only 332 Tory members facing obliteration at the next election. We all know that, after fourteen years of Conservative government, 'back to basics' is no more and no less than an appalling admission of failure. The Conservative Party and the Prime Minister have clearly reached the conclusion that they can no longer plausibly defend their record in office, so they are seeking to wipe from our consciousness the fact that they have been in power for the longest single period of any government since the Second World War and that they – and they alone – after all these years, are responsible for the state of Britain today.

Let us look at the record of failure from which the Conservatives seek to shy away. Since 1979, economic growth on average has been only 1.7 per cent per year – worse than the preceding decades of the 1960s and the 1970s. Now, after all those years, we have an economy weighed down by the burden of two massive deficits in our public finances and overseas trade. Worst of all, the fourteen Conservative years have seen the return of mass unemployment, with millions of our fellow citizens denied the opportunity, dignity and responsibility of work . . .

. . . We have been told that part of the intention of the 'back to basics' policy is to teach people the difference between right and wrong and the importance of the acceptance of responsibility. The problem for the government in that approach is their credibility as teachers and the example of responsibility that they have set. Surely it is wrong to break election promises as cavalierly as the government have done. Surely it is wrong to impose a tax on the heating of every household in Britain when such an action was expressly excluded before the 1992 election . . . Surely it is wrong to have deliberately widened the gap between the rich and poor in our society.

Those are actions of a government who purport to lecture others about getting 'back to basics'. I believe that 'back to basics' is easily exposed as a political sham, but there are basic needs and aspirations among our people. They want jobs for themselves and for their children. They want a truly national health service which is available to all and which provides the best possible health care proudly in line with the principles of the service's founders. They want well-equipped schools and well-trained and valued teachers to provide opportunities for their children to learn and to succeed. They want decent and affordable homes for their families. They want our industry to compete with the best and to win, for they know that that is the best security for their prosperity . . . instead of going 'back to basics', the government should be going back to the drawing board.

501

Labour went into the local election campaigns of April 1994 in optimistic mood. Gordon Brown had been campaigning vigorously on the issue of trust and tax, high-lighting the Conservatives' broken promises. In January a Conservative Treasury minis-ter had been forced to admit that a typical family would, from April 1994, be paying more in direct and indirect tax (35 per cent of their income) than under the last Labour Chancellor Denis Healey in 1979 (32.2 per cent). Opinion polls were beginning to show that voters trusted Labour more than the Conservatives on tax.[707] Over the previous months key policy shifts had entailed the abandonment of previous commitments to renationalisation and a new policy paper drawn up by shadow DTI Secretary Robin Cook and shadow Employment Secretary John Prescott envisaging an ambitious programme of investment in building new schools and hospitals, to be financed using public–private partnerships.

On the evening of 11 May, John Smith addressed a Labour fund-raising dinner at London's Park Lane Hotel. The following day, just after 8 a.m., John Smith suffered a massive heart attack in the bathroom of his Barbican flat. He was rushed to hospital, but desperate attempts to save his life were to no avail and he was pronounced dead at 9.15 a.m. The country was stunned; Labour activists grief-stricken. At 3.38 p.m. Margaret Beckett, now Labour's acting leader, paid tribute in the Commons to Labour's leader lost:

> . . . There are few people the announcement of whose death would bring tears to the eyes of everyone who knew them; John Smith was such a man. He was, as the Prime Minister said, a man of formidable intellect, of the highest ethics and of staunch integrity. Part of the conventional wisdom of British politics was that he looked like a bank manager – something that caused him amusement, and some bank managers some resentment. Perhaps in consequence, he was often labelled unduly sober or excessively cautious – especially by those who judge readily – and judged on the façade. But, although he certainly had a safe pair of hands, appearances were deceptive. John was no sobersides. He had a wicked sense of humour, often displayed – as the Prime Minister said – in the House. He loved a good gossip, and he liked nothing better than a convivial drink with friends, when he was excellent company.
>
> One of his favourite sayings was that to succeed in politics, you have to be pre-pared to take a risk. In fact, I used to joke with him that he was an ideal combination in a political leader: someone who looked the acme of sober judgement, but was per-fectly prepared to take a flier when he thought the occasion called for it.
>
> Some months ago, I saw a political profile of John which featured a photograph of him as a young boy. He had a wicked grin from ear to ear, his tie was around his ear and the text mentioned that his shirt tails were always hanging out. It was a kind of 'Just William' of a picture. Those who saw John Smith every day had no difficulty in detecting that boy in the statesman and the leader . . .
>
> He said to me recently, 'Why would anyone bother to go into politics, unless it was to speak up for people who cannot speak up for themselves?' That feeling for others,

along with his hatred of injustice, was the force which drove him – the service to which he gave his life.

Last night, he spoke at a gala dinner in London. He was in fine fettle and in high spirits. He spoke not from a text but from notes, and when he sat down I congratulated him especially on his final sentence – spoken, as it was, off the cuff and from the heart. They were almost the last words I heard him say. He looked at the assembled gathering, and he said: 'The opportunity to serve our country – that is all we ask.' Let it stand as his epitaph.

SIXTY-SIX

New Labour 1994–95

'It's time we defined our socialism for ourselves'

The political manoeuvring that followed John Smith's death has been the subject of unending speculation. Margaret Beckett had become acting leader, but it was Gordon Brown and Tony Blair who were the most likely successors to Smith. Both had their admirers. Many admired both. But only one could be leader, and were both to stand the closeness of their political positions would have created a campaign focused on personalities which could easily have descended into character assassination. It could only leave the victor weakened and risk creating divisions that the Conservatives could exploit. It was too great a risk for a party that had only just suffered its fourth election defeat. Although Brown had the greater political experience and as shadow Chancellor was the senior of the partnership, Blair's message on crime had helped him develop the more positive public profile of the two. Brown had set himself the task of rebuilding Labour's economic credibility. But he did so at a personal price. The strategy was 'prudence with a purpose'. The purpose was to get Labour re-elected, but the prudence required Brown to stand firm against the spending commitments popular with party activists. And it affected his speaking style. Whereas his speeches in the past were rich in warmth and humour, the new persona of future Chancellor imbued his oratory with a certain dourness of fiscal rectitude. In contrast, Blair's message on crime, and the soundbite 'tough on crime, tough on the causes of crime', ironically said to be the suggestion of Brown, touched a populist chord. At least in part, this is an explanation for the findings of several newspaper opinion polls[708] which suggested that Blair was more popular with the public, and forced Brown to stand aside and back Blair for the leadership. The exact nature of what deal was done remains publicly in doubt. But it was a deal that was ultimately to produce the longest-serving Labour government in history.

Blair would secure victory with an overall 57 per cent of the electoral college vote, compared to 24 per cent for John Prescott and 19 per cent for Margaret Beckett. Beckett, with Clare Short as her campaign manager, had announced her intention to contest the leadership and simultaneously to resign and re-contest the deputy leadership. It was a profound tactical mistake. As Tony Blair's biographer John Rentoul observed, by going for both jobs, she was 'gambling everything with the risk of winning nothing'.[709]

It enabled John Prescott to enter the race and to go on to defeat Beckett in the election for deputy by 56.5 per cent to 43.5 per cent, coming ahead in all three sections of the electoral college. Of the unions, Beckett defeated Prescott in only one, her own TGWU. Though Neil Kinnock, Gordon Brown, Harriet Harman and Donald Dewar had preferred Beckett, Blair's campaign team were split: Mo Mowlam and Peter Kilfoyle backed Prescott, Kilfoyle liaising with Prescott's campaigner Ian McCartney to promote an informal Blair–Prescott 'dream ticket'. Prescott was painted by his detractors as a man who 'shot from the hip and asked questions later',[710] while Beckett had shown herself an increasingly effective Commons performer, with an impressive grasp of detail and in government would prove one of the safest pairs of hands in Blair's Cabinet. But in the summer of 1994, memories were still fresh of the battle over OMOV at Labour's 1993 annual conference less than a year before. When John Smith had put his leadership on the line over OMOV, Beckett had failed to give him unequivocal public backing. It was therefore to Prescott that Smith had turned to make the great speech that saved the day at the conference. Others remembered Beckett's failure to support the expulsion of Derek Hatton and the Liverpool Militants during 1985–86, and her condemnation of Neil Kinnock's refusal to support Tony Benn's challenge to Healey in the deputy leadership contest of 1981. Alongside Robin Cook, Michael Meacher, Peter Mandelson and Gerald Kaufman, one of those who voted for Prescott was Roy Hattersley, against whom Prescott had campaigned so vigorously a few years before. Hattersley had become a convert to Prescott's conception of the deputy leadership as a campaigning platform to enthuse the party. 'I voted for John Prescott as deputy leader in 1994,' wrote Hattersley, 'and he has proved that the deputy's job is best done by a candidate who does not regard it as a consolation prize or is more interested in policy than in party management.'[711]

Hattersley was right. Prescott would come into his own as Labour's deputy leader. The loyalty and solidity with which Prescott has worked with Blair has resembled not the turbulent rivalry of Wilson and George Brown or the petty jealousies of Wilson and Jenkins or Attlee and Morrison, but instead the partnership of Foot with Callaghan and of Bevin with Attlee, who while never actually deputy leader, was nevertheless the rock of Attlee's premiership. The first test of the new leadership would come with an announcement trailed in Blair's first party conference speech as leader: that he intended to change Clause Four of Labour's constitution. Prescott was sceptical, fearing it would cause unnecessary and damaging splits, but having been persuaded of Blair's determination to push ahead with it, Prescott's loyalty was complete. Blair's 1994 conference speech, his first as leader, set out his vision for Labour and for Britain: 'New Labour, New Britain':

> Across the nation, across class, across political boundaries, the Labour Party is once again able to represent all the British people. We are the mainstream voice in politics today.

To parents wanting their children to be taught in classrooms that are not crumbling, to students with qualifications but no university place, let us say: the Tories have failed you. We are on your side. Your ambitions are our ambitions.

To men and women who get up in the morning and find the kitchen door smashed in again, the video gone again; to the pensioners who fear to go out of their homes, let us say: the Tories have abused your trust. We are on your side. Your concerns are our concerns.

To the small businesses, pushed to the wall by greedy banks, to employers burdened by government failure, to employees living in fear of the P45, to the thousands of others insecure in their jobs in every part of the country, let us say: the Tories have forgotten you, again. Labour is on your side. Your aspirations are our aspirations. We are back as the party of the majority in British politics, back to speak up for Britain, back as the people's party.

Look at Britain fifteen years after Mrs Thatcher first stood on the steps of Downing Street. Where there was discord, is there harmony? Where there was error, is there truth? Where there was doubt, is there faith? Where there was despair, is there hope?

Harmony? When crime has more than doubled? Truth? When they won an election on lies about us and what we would do? Faith? When politics is debased by their betrayal? Hope? When three million people are jobless, almost six million are on income support, and one in three children grow up in poverty?

They have brought us injustice and division, but these have not been the price of economic efficiency . . . Look at what they wasted on the way. Billions of pounds gifted by nature – the God-given blessing of North Sea oil. Billions we could have invested in our future. Billions they squandered. One hundred and eighteen billion pounds – £5,000 for every family in this country – gone, wasted, vanished.

And to hide the truth of the nation's problems they have sold our nation's capital assets, built up over many years, and have used the proceeds not to invest but to cover current spending. Seventy billion pounds gone for ever.

It's time to take these Tories apart for what they have done to our country. Not because they lack compassion – though they do – but because they are the most feckless, irresponsible group of incompetents ever let loose on the government of Britain.

And why are they incompetent? Not just because of the individuals. It is not this or that minister that is to blame: it is an entire set of political values that is wrong. The Tories fail because they fail to understand that a nation, like a community, must work together in order for individuals within it to succeed. It is such a simple failing, and yet it is fundamental.

Go and look at a company that is succeeding. It will treat its workforce not as servants but as partners. They will be motivated and trained and given a common purpose. Of course sweatshop conditions in the short term can make do. But in the end they fail. The quality and commitment aren't there.

It's the same with a country. It can be run on privilege and greed for a time; but in the end it fails.

This is not theory. We have living proof of it. At the end of fifteen years, we are tax-ing and spending more – not to invest in future success but to pay for past failure.

I don't mind paying taxes for education and health and the police. What I mind is paying them for unemployment, crime and social squalor . . .

The Tories' economics is based on a view of the market that is crude, out of date and inefficient. And their view of society is one of indifference – to shrug their shoulders and walk away. They think we choose between self-interest and the interests of society or the country as a whole. In reality self-interest demands that we work together to achieve what we cannot do on our own . . .

It is time we had a clear, up-to-date statement of the objects and objectives of our party. John Prescott and I will propose such a statement to the NEC. Let it then be open to debate. I want the whole party involved. I know the whole party will welcome that debate. And if it is accepted, then let it become the objects of our party at the next election and take its place in our constitution for the next century.

This is a modern party living in an age of change. It requires a modern constitution that says what we are in terms the public cannot misunderstand and the Tories cannot misrepresent. We are proud of our beliefs, so let's state them – and in terms that people will identify with in every workplace, every home, every family, every community in the country. And let this party's determination to change be the symbol of the trust they can place in us to change the country.

The reference in the final paragraph to changing Clause Four, contained as it was in opaque language, was central to Blair's conception of how Labour must explain its fitness to govern to a sceptical electorate. Labour's opinion poll lead, high under Smith, was stratospheric under Blair. But Labour had enjoyed poll leads before, only for them to crumble to dust in the cold metal of the ballot box. Blair knew that in the public mind Labour was still associated with the policies for which Benn had fought in the early 1980s and on which Labour had fought the elections of 1983 and 1987. Labour spokesmen had night after night gone on the television and advocated banning the bomb and defended the virtues of Militant and Arthur Scargill. The idea that many of these Labour spokesmen had not believed in such nostrums was not one which the public would understand unless it was made explicit; unless these old positions were overtly denounced. Nor would people believe that Labour had changed if the party kept to the insistence that it hadn't, just adapted to the changing world. Labour voters of the 1960s and 1970s, driven away by the Winter of Discontent and the Bennite policy agenda, did not accept that it was just that the world had changed when they themselves had regarded the Militant agenda as barmy throughout. Blair accepted that rather than demand that the people return to the people's party, the people's party must return to the people. To convince the public that New Labour really had renounced any residual affections voters might have thought it had for Militant and Scargill, Blair would create the 'Old Labour' Aunt Sally. Central to establishing the distinction between Labour 'Old' and 'New' was the reform of

Clause Four. Blair's speech had immediate effect: 'Arthur Scargill was livid and went upstairs to explode in front of the cameras.'[712] The public were more positive. On 15 December Labour would win a by-election in the Tory seat of Dudley West with a 29 per cent swing, the largest since 1933.

Tony Blair's conference speech on 4 October fired the starting gun for the Clause Four campaign. It would culminate in a special conference to vote on the new draft in April 1995. As Blair's biographer John Rentoul observed, Labour's special conferences, at Wembley on 24 January 1981 and in Westminster Central Hall on 29 April 1995, bracket 'Labour's wilderness years'.[713] Westminster Central Hall was somewhat appropriate for Labour's 1995 Clause Four conference: it was in the very same hall that the original Clause Four had been adopted at a Labour conference in 1918. The new text was unveiled on 13 March 1995. Early drafts had been written by Blair's policy unit but after several months of discussion with close aides a final version had not been agreed. 'In the end Blair wrote it himself,' one of those involved has written, 'with one line – "power, wealth and opportunity in the hands of the many not the few"[714] – surviving from the policy unit draft.'[715]

At the special conference, Blair's speech set the tone:

> This has been the widest consultation exercise ever undertaken by a British political party . . . Since last June almost 100,000 people more have joined the Labour Party. At this rate of growth, by the autumn conference we will have 350,000 members of the party. There are now three times as many members of Young Labour as there are in the Young Conservatives (*applause*). Almost half the party participated in membership ballots, and all but three constituencies that balloted showed overwhelming support for change. I asked you to be with me head and heart, and I believe that you are. Those ballots were the answer to the Tory charge that Labour's head is separate from Labour's body. This is a leader in step with his party and this is a party in step with the British people (*applause*).
>
> . . . New Labour means an economy based on partnership, not on state control or crude market dogma. It means not more benefits or cutting benefits, but moving people from welfare into work. It means being tough on crime and tough on the causes of crime. It means an education system that both supports our schools and puts pressure on them to achieve. It means rights and duties going together at work, in society. It will mean changing the traditional dividing lines between right and left, and I believe this party understands that, because the strongest impression of the consultation meetings on Clause Four was not the disagreement; it was the consensus. No one disputed the need for some public ownership. That's why we fought off privatisation of the Post Office. That is why we will fight to keep our railways as a proper public service, publicly owned, publicly accountable to the people (*applause*).
>
> But throughout all those meetings no one seriously argued the case, either, against the need for a thriving private sector. The new Clause Four expresses what we really

believe . . . Markets and enterprise are a necessary part of any developed economy, but markets alone are not enough . . . We need strength of partnership and cooperation and we need it at the workplace too. There is no future for Britain as a low-wage, low-skill, low-tech economy – none. That is the Tory way, and it will fail. Successful companies know that. Minimum standards at work achieve commitment to the enterprise. That is why part-time workers should not be treated as second-class. That is why we will sign the European Social Chapter and make this country part of its terms (*applause*). And that is why, sensibly and flexibly introduced, we will have a statutory minimum wage to protect our people at work (*applause*) and, with that, strong public services, as we say. Let me tell you this too. There is something that I will renationalise. I will renationalise the National Health Service to make it once more a service run for the whole nation (*applause*).

And we will make education the great liberator of our people. The goal of nursery education for all, raising school standards, broadening A-levels, bringing vocational and academic learning closer together, ensuring that no one is shut out of higher education through poverty, reforming our outdated methods of skills training to put education throughout life within the reach of all. What have the Tories done in education? First, classroom chaos under Patten,[716] now complacency under Shepherd. We need neither. What we need is David Blunkett's crusade for change and achievement in our schools. And I tell you this. When we say we will not tolerate failing schools, that is not right-wing; it is sticking up for the children of working-class people for whom education is the only way they can get a better future (*applause*). David may have taken some flak recently, but I believe he has shown great courage. But then that is typical of someone who was once told that he had three options in life: he could be a lathe operator, a piano tuner or a brilliant typist. Well, he won't be any of those things; he'll be a Cabinet Minister in a Labour government (*applause*).

Again, we say, the opportunity for all to work and prosper . . . A Labour government that did not strive for a high and stable level of employment would not be a government worthy of the name Labour . . .

Equality of opportunity too, which delivers people from the tyranny of prejudice and discrimination and the abuse of power, a healthy environment, for the first time a commitment in the party constitution by this generation to the generations that follow to cherish and enhance the environment for the future. And open democracy. I say it is time to end the quango state and put power back in the hands of the people, where it actually belongs (*applause*). Devolving power in Scotland and Wales, rebuilding local democracy, reforming Parliament, a Freedom of Information Act for government. Let no one say that radical politics is dead. In fact this statement is more radical than the original. Why? Because we intend to put it into practice (*applause*). Here's a pledge for you. I can be the first leader in our party's history to stand up and say that I will implement Clause Four of our party's constitution. Yes, it's radical, but it's also relevant, sensible, modern – definitely new, but definitely Labour . . .

I did not come into this Labour Party to join a pressure group. I didn't become leader of this party to lead a protest movement. Power without principle is barren, but principle without power is futile. This is a party of government or it is nothing, and I will lead it as a party of government (*applause*). Please let us not fall for this nonsense about stealing Tory clothes when we talk of crime or the family or of aspiration or of duty and responsibility. Let me quote to you from another woman I heard at one of our consultation meetings. She moved everyone with her account of her life trying to raise children and grandchildren on a run-down Glasgow estate, ruined by drugs, crime, vandalism and unemployment. 'Do something for us,' she pleaded. She's not a Tory, she's Labour, and it's high time we were back as the party speaking up for her and millions like her (*applause*).

We are reclaiming this ground, because it is rightfully ours. It is they, the Tories, who are the intruders. It's Labour that provides the real thing. We are reoccupying ground that we should never ever have vacated . . . We confused means with ends, allowing one economic prescription to eclipse the aims it was supposed to serve . . . We paid the penalty and we have learnt the lesson, and today we set our thinking free . . .

The ghosts of our history no longer rattle their chains, but they are there, with their spirit, to guide us and guide our country.

Let me say this to you. Never think that I lack pride in our past. Fifty years on from 1945 we can still say – I still say – no Tory government could ever have achieved the rebuilding of a nation as that Labour Party achieved in that government in 1945 (*applause*). What we need is that vision with its hope and its optimism, but achieved by today's means for today's world . . .

Today a new Labour Party is being born. Our task now is nothing less than the rebirth of our nation – a new Britain, national renewal, economic renewal, so that wealth may be in the hands of the many and not the few; democratic renewal, Labour in office, the people in power; social renewal, so that the evils of poverty and squalor are banished for good. New Labour, New Britain – not a slogan but where we are in British politics today. New Labour being born here in this hall today, the task of building new Britain now to come. Let us get on with it (*prolonged applause*).

The most powerful opponents of change were Blair's own union, the TGWU, and UNISON: ' . . . we do accept change, but we will not accept change at any price,' declared TGWU leader Bill Morris. Stan Newens[717] also spoke out against change: ' . . . the ditching of the fundamental ideas of which Clause Four is symbolic will be trumpeted by all those organs of the media which praised Thatcher as the rejection of the vision of a democratic and socialist society and the acceptance of a free market . . . '

But the tide was with Blair. Many unions, including the AEEU and the GMB, backed change. So, overwhelmingly, did the younger delegates who spoke, such as Young Labour[718] chair Rebecca Gray and Stephen Twigg, recently the President of the National Union of Students.[719] Twigg challenged Scargill directly:

Earlier on we heard Arthur Scargill tell us that this conference has no right to decide on this issue today. I say to you, Arthur, you are one member of this Labour Party.

More than 100,000 party members up and down the country have taken part in ballots on Clause Four. It is those members that give this conference the right to decide here today (*applause*).

We have just heard from a trade union voting for the old Clause Four. Many of us in the party would respect what we have just heard if it was based on a democratic ballot of the members of that trade union (*applause*). In fact the unions that have held a democratic ballot have voted overwhelming for a change, and 99 per cent of the constituencies that have balloted have voted overwhelmingly for change . . .

John Prescott was on easier ground this time as he wound up the debate for the platform than when he fought and won the battle for OMOV in 1993:

Bill Morris rightly reminded us that this debate is about winning the next election. Yes, but it is not only about that. It's about the policies that we present to the electorate to persuade them to vote for us, and that's what our statement of aims and values is about. They are relevant to the problems faced by the electorate today. It is relevant that we stand for a community in which power, wealth and opportunity are in the hands of the many and not the few. Isn't that a socialist principle that we always believed in and is now reflected in the new clause before you today? It is relevant that we believe that, by the strength of our common endeavour, we achieve more than we can achieve alone. Isn't that the principle of solidarity that our movement stands for, in which we believe that we are our brother's keeper, that we have a responsibility in society, and that's why it's expressed in our new clause in a way that it wasn't expressed in the old one (*applause*). That is the principle of solidarity behind trade unionism that brought me into the party . . .

I've heard it said that the new statement will attract outsiders to the Labour Party, that . . . Tories will vote for us. I might add that some of those Tories used to vote Labour before, and that's when we had Labour governments, and we should be asking that question when people say that to us . . .

You know, in changing Clause Four we do not reject our socialist values. We are simply restating them in the language of the present, and I believe that the new clause does that and more . . . for the first time we proudly state clearly that we are a democratic socialist party . . .

But unlike in 1993, it was Tony Blair who had the last word. Forty years before, Hugh Gaitskell had spoken off the cuff to Labour's conference about why he had become a socialist. Now Tony Blair spoke of why he had joined Labour:

I just want to say two things to you . . . if I can turn briefly to the name of the party, it's staying as it is (*applause*). Go on, admit it, I had you worried, didn't I? You know me, I don't spring surprises on you.

I just want to say something to you. I wasn't born into this party. I chose it. I have never joined any other political party. I believe in it, I am proud to be the leader of it and it's the party I'll always live and I'll die in (*applause*).

If sometimes I seem a little over-hasty and over-urgent, it's for one reason and one reason only: I can't stand these Tories being in government over our country. The people of Britain don't deserve this government, they deserve something better, and today we have shown that we can win their trust to provide something better, something our young people can look forward to, something we can bring up our children to be proud of, something that will go through generation and generation of people, that great spirit of principle that gave birth to our party and moves it still. Let today be a day of destiny for our party and our country, so that their futures are joined once again, as they should be, in Labour government for a better Britain (*prolonged applause*).

The vote for the new clause was 65 per cent. Over 90 per cent of the constituency parties had supported it.[720]

SIXTY-SEVEN

The Road to a Landslide 1996–97

'This is an arrogant government who have been in power too long to remember that they are accountable to the people'

By the time John Major's government finally fell in 1997, its reputation lay in tatters. Not only had Conservative economic credibility been shattered; a series of scandals cast a shadow across the probity of its ministers. Dangerously exposed by their attempt to occupy the high moral ground, the shrill cry of 'back to basics' became the much-mocked funeral dirge of Tory campaign hopes. The most prominent example of 'Tory sleaze' was the arms-to-Iraq affair, which came to light in November 1992. Former trade minister Alan Clark had been called to testify in a prosecution brought by Customs and Excise against executives of Matrix Churchill, a UK machine-tool company accused of breaking the arms embargo against Iraq. The defence lawyers argued that the government had in fact given Matrix Churchill the green light to export through the secret relaxation of the trade rules. Clark admitted that this had essentially been what had happened and after the judge overruled Public Interest Immunity Certificates preventing disclosures that would have helped the defence, the court case collapsed in uproar. The government had rejected a Commons motion condemning their behaviour, but had conceded a public enquiry, that was set up under a court of appeal judge, Sir Richard Scott.

Over three years later, on 15 February 1996, Scott's enquiry was published. Ministers received copies of the report eight days in advance of the publication date to give them time to digest it and prepare their response for the Commons debate. The government planned to give a copy to Robin Cook, who was to respond for the opposition,[721] only 30 minutes in advance of the debate. The intervention of the speaker secured Cook two hours. Two hours to digest a five-volume, two-thousand-page report, and to prepare his speech. Moreover, Cook was required to examine the report within the confines of a room in the DTI in which he was allowed only a pen and paper and was prohibited phone calls. The restrictions were, as Cook's biographer John Kampfner observed, 'a cross between Whitehall farce and the dying days of a one-party dictatorship'.[722] Cook's moral indignation and controlled anger would reinforce a flawless command of the minutiae. Ten days later, on 26 February, the Commons had a full debate on the issue. Cook's speech reduced the Conservative benches to silence:

... The first charge in the motion[723] was that the government had acted 'in clear breach of the Howe Guidelines of 1985'. Sir Richard returns a verdict of guilty. You can tell, Madam Speaker, the importance that he attaches to the conclusion, because, like all his key findings, it is expressed as a double negative: 'It is clear that policy and defence sales to Iraq did not remain unchanged.'

Indeed, Sir Richard reserves the most scathing passages in his report for those witnesses who tried to argue that the guidelines had not changed. The Chief Secretary submitted that the guidelines were not changed, but were only interpreted more flexibly. Sir Richard dismisses his view as one that 'does not seem to me to correspond with reality' ...

Upon reading the Scott report, I am unclear why an enquiry was needed to establish whether the guidelines were changed. In the week that the Prime Minister set up the enquiry, he was minuted by his private secretary, whose remarks appear in paragraph D4.51 of the report. He told him: 'as Chancellor of the Exchequer you knew that the government had decided to change the guidelines' ... why did the Prime Minister and others feel able to tell the House that the guidelines had not been changed when they had that evidence?

... our motion ...[724] said: 'British servicemen [in the Gulf War] may have been exposed to fire from shells and rockets made in munitions factories equipped by Britain.' Sir Richard's report reveals that, three years before the Gulf War, there were intelligence reports that Iraq had placed multi-million-pound orders with four British companies, including Matrix Churchill, to equip its armaments factories at Nassr. The same intelligence reports warned that annual production targets for Nassr were 10,000 missiles, 150,000 artillery shells, 100,000 mortar shells and 300,000 fin-stabilised shells ...

In February 1989, when he was in the very act of negotiating change in guidelines with his colleagues, the Chief Secretary was given a minute that told him: 'The Iraqis intended to use Matrix Churchill to supply machinery for the new armaments and munitions factories of the Nassr and Hutteen State Establishments.'

They knew what they were approving, and the knowledge went much higher than the Chief Secretary ... A year earlier, an intelligence digest warned the then Prime Minister that Matrix Churchill 'has been heavily involved [in the supply of equipment to Iraq for use in arms production]' ... Faced with that evidence, how dare ministers still claim that they did not arm Saddam Hussein?

The right hon. gentleman played the trade card and justified the decision to equip Saddam's armaments factories on the commercial grounds that it was good for business. Perhaps one of the Conservative members can help me. After all, they claim to be the party of business. Could one of them explain to me how it can be good for business to approve a contract for which one does not get paid?

That is what happened. Saddam did not pay for the machine tools that went into his factories – we did. The British taxpayer has been left with a bill for about £700 million for our total exports to Iraq. Incurring a bad debt of £700 million would surely be enough to get someone sacked from any organisation in Britain except the Conservative government ...

The last of those decisions was in September 1988, when export credits to Iraq were increased by £340 million, despite mounting evidence that Iraq did not have the cash to service existing credits. Sir Richard notes: 'The Chief Secretary endorsed the proposed new offer.' The Chief Secretary in question is, of course, the current Prime Minister . . .

I come to the third charge that we laid against ministers three years ago – that 'hon. members were persistently misled by assurances that the guidelines were being observed' . . . Sir Richard concluded that the failure to inform Parliament of the truth was deliberate, and was the inevitable result of the agreement among three junior ministers that no publicity would be given to the decision . . . Three years ago, the Prime Minister told the House: 'The suggestion that ministers misled the House is a serious and scurrilous charge and has no basis whatsoever in fact.'[725] I agree with the Prime Minister that it was a serious charge. Will he now accept that, far from being scurrilous, it was entirely accurate? (Hon. members: 'Answer'). Suddenly, we have a row of limpets stuck to the Treasury Bench.

Where does that leave the Chief Secretary? In the six months after the guidelines were changed, the Chief Secretary signed not one or two, but 30, letters to Members of Parliament denying any change in the guidelines . . . Sir Richard observed that the Chief Secretary 'knew, first hand, the facts that . . . rendered the "no change in policy" statement untrue' . . .

The desk officer for Iraq who drafted those letters for the Chief Secretary knew that they were untrue, and he said so to the Scott enquiry. That desk officer resigned from the foreign service, rather than be obliged to continue drafting them. Tonight, the House must judge whether he is the only person who should resign over the misleading of Parliament.

I come to the last of the four charges in our motion of three years ago. We said that the government were willing 'to see citizens put on trial for exports at which ministers had connived and to put their liberty at risk by attempting to prevent the disclosure of documents crucial to their defence'[726] . . . Sir Richard . . . concluded that the Matrix Churchill case should never have been brought to court, and that the claims of public interest immunity that were made in the course of it ought to have had no place in a criminal trial . . .

. . . Sir Richard Scott finds the Attorney General personally at fault for failing to convey to the court the reservations expressed by the Deputy Prime Minister . . . Yet . . . there are to be no regrets, no resignations. This is not just a government who do not know how to accept blame: they are a government who know no shame . . .

Though John Major's government won the vote it was by 320 to 319: a majority of only one. The end was in sight.

If New Labour was a coruscating critique of Conservative failure, it was also a positive vision of the future. Central to that vision was Gordon Brown, by far the most powerful Chancellor in recent times. Brown set out his political philosophy in early 1997 in a Fabian Society lecture marking the twentieth anniversary of the death of the Gaitskellite revisionist Anthony Crosland. Brown took as his theme the basic issue of equality, framing it in terms of 'life chances', a concept previously employed by Neil Kinnock in his most famous Labour conference speech in 1985:

> Today's world is of course quite different from the world of 1956 in which Crosland first formulated his policies for equality . . . in 1956 the UK economy was largely a closed economy subject to national controls – import controls, credit controls, demand management by the Treasury – effective within national boundaries. In 1956, under a Conservative government, exchange controls meant that an individual could take just £30 out of the country . . . When Crosland wrote, physical capital was more important to a firm than its employees . . . Finally, the most important change is the assumption of full employment . . . In 1956, just 1 per cent of people were unemployed . . . Today, nearly one in five of working-age families have nobody in employment. If Anthony Crosland had been writing today I believe it is to the issue of workplace-generated poverty and inequality that he would have turned his thoughts . . . Today we argue for equality not just because of our belief in social justice but also because of our view of what is required for economic success. The starting point is a fundamental belief in the equal worth of every human being. We all have an equal claim to social consideration by virtue of being human. And if every person is to be regarded as of equal worth, all deserve to be given an equal chance in life to fulfil the potential with which they are born . . . I believe that everyone should have the chance to bridge the gap between what they are and what they have it in themselves to become . . . Britain's economic weakness . . . has arisen because we have given insufficient attention in education and employment policies to the latent and diverse potential of the population as a whole . . . An unrealisable equality of outcome . . . decided irrespective of work, effort or contribution to the community, is not a socialist dream but other people's nightmare of socialism . . . A single chance to get your foot on a narrow ladder . . . is the equal opportunity only to become unequal . . . [Crosland] proposed what he called a democratic view of equality – one that sought to prevent the permanent entrenchment of privilege from whatever source it came . . .
>
> So what, in the 1990s, does this concept of democratic equality mean for me? First it demands employment opportunity for all, because work is central not just to economic prosperity for Britain but to individual fulfilment . . . Secondly we must as a society ensure not just a one-off educational opportunity in childhood, but continuing and lifelong educational opportunity for all . . . Thirdly, life-long opportunity must [involve] genuine access to culture – and most importantly, a redistribution of power that offers people real control over the decisions that affect their lives . . . So the issue for socialists is not so much about what the state can do for you but what the state can enable you to do for yourself.

Within months of this speech Gordon Brown would be putting his values into practice as Chancellor of the Exchequer, alongside new Deputy Prime Minister John Prescott,

Foreign Secretary Robin Cook, Home Secretary Jack Straw and Education and Employment Secretary David Blunkett. Labour's victory in the landslide election of May 1997 wiped out the Conservatives in Scotland and Wales for the first time in history: the party once known as the 'Unionists' was confined to England, and only bits of it at that. The scale of the Tory rout was compared to 1832. It was Labour's greatest ever electoral triumph: '1945 in spades,' as a beaming James Callaghan described it for the benefit of BBC television viewers on the brilliantly sunny morning of 2 May. Despite the poll leads, Labour campaigners had throughout the campaign been reluctant to accept the certainty of victory. Memories of 1992 were too strong, and of victory, untasted since 1974, too dim. Many feared Labour's opinion poll lead would encourage Conservative die-hards to come out and vote while Labour supporters stayed home on the assumption that their vote was unnecessary. Labour campaigners in Edinburgh Pentlands, seat of Foreign Secretary Malcolm Rifkind, had fretted at the high turnout in the traditionally Tory-voting areas of the seat. It was only at the count that it became clear that many of the voters in those areas had been won over to Labour. Rifkind was, with Michael Portillo and several other leading members of Major's Cabinet, to lose his seat.[727] With 419 seats and an overall majority of 179 it was a victory beyond Labour's wildest dreams.

AFTERWORD

New Labour: Old Values?

In May 1997 Tony Blair formed what became the first Labour government in history to be elected for more than one full term. In 2005 Blair became the longest-serving Labour Prime Minister and, securing re-election in June 2001 and May 2005 with very substantial majorities, he has arguably been Labour's most electorally successful leader to date. Like their predecessors, Blair's governments have had their ups and downs. But not until Blair had been drawn into war in Iraq post-2002 did they approach the levels of unpopularity sometimes achieved by Labour governments of the past[1] – and even then Labour maintained sufficient relative popularity *vis-à-vis* other parties to hold its own at the 2005 general election.

From the beginning of his leadership, Blair consciously sought to avoid 'over-promising', the mistake made by both Ramsay MacDonald and Harold Wilson. The famous pledge card carried round in every Labour Party member's back pocket during the 1997 election contained promises at once both radical and achievable. Not for New Labour the rhetoric of 'a fundamental shift in the balance of wealth and power in favour of working people and their families'. Yet the pledges contained promises that Labour had been making for decades and had failed in the past to keep. They included the historic demands for a minimum wage and for Scottish and Welsh devolution, to which Labour had been committed by Keir Hardie and had never managed to deliver – though the 1974–79 Labour government had spent a considerable amount of its parliamentary time trying and failing to get devolution on the statute book. Another pledge, to reduce class sizes to 30 or under in primary schools, was an old chestnut from the 1960s. Wilson went into the 1964 election pledged to reduce class sizes to 30 'at the earliest possible opportunity'. All of them. Thirty-three years later it remained to be done. Blair did not promise to do it all at one go, but he wanted to be able to make some progress at least.

Likewise, while Labour in the 1970s promised a wealth tax but never implemented it, New Labour pledged and implemented the more modest (but nevertheless substantial) windfall tax on the privatised utilities to pay for the New Deal, in itself emblematic of New Labour's commitment to Ernest Bevin's pledge on unemployment in 1944.

Perhaps the greatest contrast with previous Labour governments has been in the economic sphere. Gordon Brown, steeped in the history of the Labour Party himself,[2] has arguably done more to learn from the past than any of his predecessors. He has been unquestionably the most successful Labour Chancellor of the Exchequer in history, as well as being the longest-serving. Despite repeated predictions of impending recession from Conservatives and commentators (who now remembers the insistent 'downturn made in Downing Street' mantra of William Hague's Shadow Chancellor Francis Maude?) Gordon Brown has been the first Labour Chancellor not to have been embroiled in economic crisis. The fact that nobody accuses the government of stop-go (or boom and bust) economics is a tribute to his success.

In other areas there has been more continuity with previous Labour governments than some commentators recognise. The education standards agenda at the heart of New Labour policy making is rooted in the traditional Labour values expounded in James Callaghan's Ruskin speech of 1976. It was Callaghan who raised the question of literacy and numeracy standards in schools and it was David Blunkett's literacy and numeracy hours that sought to provide the answer. Likewise, New Labour's 'tough on crime, tough on the causes of crime' approach, including its focus on 'anti-social behaviour', bears a remarkable similarity to that which Labour's annual conference demanded of its government in 1978. Even its most eloquent critics, Jeremy Corbyn and Bob Marshall-Andrews, remain the same.[3] And Gordon Brown's famous 'Five Economic Tests' on the Euro bear a striking resemblance to the 'Five Conditions' which underpinned the basis of Labour's approach to membership of the Common Market from 1961.

Indeed, rhetorically the 'New Labour: New Britain' slogan of 1997 was much more traditional than contemporary observers perceived. As has been discussed, the New Britain metaphor was, on the advice of the young Tony Benn, central to Harold Wilson's 1964 campaign. It was also the oratorical device with which John Freeman sought to capture the hopes and aspirations of his generation in the first speech of the new 1945 Parliament. Perhaps Peter Mandelson was more self-consciously the grandson of Herbert Morrison than commonly thought.

There are areas where New Labour has been criticised as having nothing to say. 'The public schools offend not only against the "weak", let alone the strong ideal of equal opportunity; they offend even more against any ideal of social cohesion or democracy. This privileged stratum of education, the exclusive preserve of the wealthier classes, socially and physically segregated from the state educational system, is the greatest single cause of stratification and class-consciousness in Britain.'[4] So wrote Anthony Crosland in 1961. Previous Labour governments had failed to tackle this and as has been seen, Gaitskell had attacked the inadequacy of party policy on the issue from the floor of party conference in 1953. Crosland himself was to be in the privileged position, as Education Secretary in Wilson's Cabinet during 1965–67, to do something about it. He set up a Royal Commission, which, as they say, took minutes and wasted years. 'Of all the futile committees on which I have sat none equalled the Public Schools Commission,' recalled Noel Annan.[5] It reported in 1968. Nothing happened; such were the economic crises of the time, the Labour government felt it lacked the resources to take forward its recommendations. In many of the areas that New Labour can be most criticised for a lack of a fully thought-through solution to an ongoing conundrum, it is doing no worse than following in the good footsteps of 'Old Labour'.

Some of the more personal attacks have been similar too. Its detractors sought to brand New Labour's Blairite leadership an Islington elite. James Callaghan was attacked for his appointment of his son-in-law Peter Jay[6] to the Washington embassy. Harold Wilson was derided for his retirement 'lavender list'[7] of peerages for cronies, and for appointing a Cabinet full of Oxford dons and old public-school chums, one of whom, old-Etonian Lord Longford, had been Hugh Gaitskell's Tory flatmate at university. Gaitskell himself was mocked for consorting with his Frognal friends, while Nye Bevan braved barbed taunts for his 'Bollinger Bolshevism' and a friendship with Tory media mogul Lord Beaverbrook that he shared with Michael Foot. Ramsay MacDonald was accused of an undue fondness for marchionesses and even Keir Hardie had to face down accusations of putting his regard for certain suffragettes above the socialist crusade. Clement Attlee had an open bias towards promoting fellow alumni of his old public school, Haileybury, to senior government jobs, yet somehow managed to escape criticism. Hugh Dalton, who still mourned the death of his friend and idol Rupert Brooke,[8] who bore an alarming physical resemblance to actor Hugh Grant, urged the promotion of dashing floppy-haired young chaps who caught his eye.[9] The Bevanites backed other Bevanites, and the Bennites other Bennites. Ernest Bevin liked to promote people from the West Country, where he had been born. Herbert Morrison liked Londoners, and Scots. There was, perhaps, a grain of truth in many of these accusations of cronyism and human frailty.

It was the 'Islington elite' tag that the Scottish Labour MP and minister John Reid[10] sought to challenge in a series of speeches he made during 1999–2000 in which he drew a distinction between 'New Labour' and the media caricature he dubbed, after nouvelle cuisine, 'Nouvelle Labour'. In contrast, he insisted, New Labour was both substantial and rooted in Labour's traditional values:

> New Labour was . . . driven by the coalfields of Fife and the steel mills of Lanarkshire and the factory towns throughout Scotland and the rest of industrial Britain – because for twenty years we had to stand in impotent opposition while a government that didn't care and wouldn't act presided over such economic and social deprivation. We promised then that we would renew ourselves in order that we could renew our country . . . The biggest betrayal of all is lacking the courage to make the real choices to improve the lives of millions of ordinary people and to prefer the self-indulgence of standing carping on the sidelines as millions suffer.[11]

In his collection of Blair's speeches and articles, the former Fabian Society chair Paul

Richards has pointed out that as party leader and later as Prime Minister, 'all of Blair's pronouncements owe something to his advisers and civil servants, notably Alastair Campbell, and none can be credited solely to Blair . . . Major speeches . . . can be the result of scores of people's efforts.'[12] Richards is right, but this does not in principle make Blair different from either Harold Wilson, whose 1964 speeches had input from Tony Benn, or Hugh Gaitskell, whose 1959 conference speech was largely written by Tony Crosland. Blair's speaking style has had a mixed response from the 'commentariat'. He was of course famously criticised for dispensing with verbs. But his capacity to enthuse and inspire cannot be denied. Sometimes he is at his best when he departs from his script and speaks from the heart. At other times it has been when his back is to the wall.

One of those occasions was on 10 September 2002. September 11 2001 had been the day Blair was scheduled to address the annual TUC Congress. He never delivered the speech. During the year that followed a great deal was to happen in the trade union movement. The immediate impact of the September 11 tragedy included the collapse of the aviation market. Tourists, particularly American tourists, stopped flying. Airline revenue collapsed and orders for new aircraft, engines and other manufactures were axed. Massive job losses followed across the UK aviation and manufacturing industry. Despite the efforts of union leaders such as the Amicus–AEEU General Secretary Sir Ken Jackson to forge genuine industrial partnerships with management, the redundancy announcements often appeared high-handed. A further blow to employees was an accelerating trend within many firms to cut costs through the closure of final salary pension schemes for employees. The announcement by several large employers with Amicus partnership agreements of the closure of their pension schemes undoubtedly contributed to the defeat of Jackson, who was standing for re-election in the member ballot for Amicus–AEEU General Secretary in July 2002. Jackson, dubbed Blair's favourite union leader by the press, had been an outspoken supporter of both the Labour government and industrial partnership. His victorious left-wing challenger, a comparatively unknown regional officer named Derek Simpson, made clear that his approach would be different. Indeed, right across the union movement, more left-wing candidates, some of whom were openly Marxist, were being elected in place of moderates. Sir Ken Jackson, indeed, had been virtually the only moderate not tipped for defeat and, so close was the vote, the process had involved several agonising recounts. By the time Blair arrived in Blackpool for the 2002 TUC, he had lost his most powerful union supporter, and he was getting a great deal of opprobrium for his approach to the 'war on terror'. Any politician as overtly right-wing as George Bush could not fail to arouse the most profound distrust among trade union activists. Delegates wanted reassurance. The media were almost unanimous in their prediction that Blair would get a roasting such as no Labour leader had suffered since the days of imposed pay restraint.

But as Blair began to speak, it was clear that the mood in the hall was not of antipathy but of anticipation:

On September 11 last year, with the world still reeling from the shock of events, it came together to demand action. But suppose I had come last year on the same day as this year – September 10. Suppose I had said to you: there is a terrorist network called al-Qaida. It operates out of Afghanistan. It has carried out several attacks and we believe it is planning more. It has been condemned by the UN in the strongest terms. Unless it is stopped, the threat will grow. And so I want to take action to prevent that.

Your response and probably that of most people would have been very similar to the response of some of you yesterday on Iraq. There would have been few takers for dealing with it and probably none for taking military action of any description.

So let me tell you why I say Saddam Hussein is a threat that has to be dealt with.

He has twice before started wars of aggression. Over one million people died in them. When the weapons inspectors were evicted from Iraq in 1998 there were still enough chemical and biological weapons remaining to devastate the entire Gulf region.

I sometimes think that there is a kind of word fatigue about chemical and biological weapons. We're not talking about some mild variants of everyday chemicals, but anthrax, sarin and mustard gas – weapons that can cause hurt and agony on a mass scale beyond the comprehension of most decent people.

Uniquely Saddam has used these weapons against his own people, the Iraqi Kurds. Scores of towns and villages were attacked. Iraqi military officials dressed in full protection gear were used to witness the attacks and visited later to assess the damage. Wounded civilians were normally shot on the scene. In one attack alone, on the city of Halabja, it is estimated that 5,000 were murdered and 9,000 wounded in this way. All in all in the north around 100,000 Kurds died, according to Amnesty International. In the destruction of the marshlands in southern Iraq, around 200,000 people were forcibly removed. Many died.

Saddam has a nuclear weapons programme too, denied for years, that was only disrupted after inspectors went in to disrupt it. He is in breach of 23 outstanding UN obligations requiring him to admit inspectors and to disarm.

People say: but containment has worked. Only up to a point. In truth, sanctions are eroding. He now gets around $3 billion through illicit trading every year. It is unaccounted for, but almost certainly used for his weapons programmes.

Every day this year and for years, British and American pilots risk their lives to police the no-fly zones. But it can't go on for ever. For years when the weapons inspectors were in Iraq, Saddam lied, concealed, obstructed and harassed them. For the last four years there have been no inspections, no monitoring, despite constant pleas and months of negotiating with the UN. In July, Kofi Annan ended his personal involvement in talks because of Iraqi intransigence.

. . . to allow [Saddam] to use the weapons he has or get the weapons he wants, would be an act of gross irresponsibility and we should not countenance it . . .

I believe it is right to deal with Saddam through the UN. After all, it is the will of the UN he is flouting. He, not me or George Bush, is in breach of UN resolutions. If the challenge to us is to work with the UN, we will respond to it. But ... the challenge to all in the UN is this: the UN must be the way to resolve the threat from Saddam, not avoid it.

Let it be clear that he must be disarmed. Let it be clear that there can be no more conditions, no more games, no more prevaricating, no more undermining of the UN's authority. And let it be clear that should the will of the UN be ignored, action will follow. Diplomacy is vital. But when dealing with dictators – and none in the world is worse than Saddam – diplomacy has to be backed by the certain knowledge in the dictator's mind that behind the diplomacy is the possibility of force being used.

Because I say to you in all earnestness: if we do not deal with the threat from this international outlaw and his barbaric regime, it may not erupt and engulf us this month or next; perhaps not even this year or the next. But it will at some point. And I do not want it on my conscience that we knew the threat, saw it coming and did nothing ...

In conclusion, Blair turned to the home front:

My door is open to any union leader. There is no obligation, of course. But it's sensible to remember how very different things were just a few years ago. You suffered eighteen years of Conservative government in which union leaders couldn't get to discuss anything with the Prime Minister. Eighteen years of being kicked from pillar to post. Eighteen years of being ignored, derided and attacked as the 'enemy within', years of falling membership and zero influence. Eighteen years in which government never offered a partnership and employers were encouraged to decline one.

The trade union movement, however, didn't give up ... you worked hard to get a government in place that did believe in social partnership. It would be ironic if, just at the moment when trade unions are achieving such a partnership, some of you might decide to turn your back on it. It happened before: in 1948, in 1969, in 1979. The result then was the folding of the Labour government and the return of a Tory government ... Indulgence or influence. It's a very simple choice ...

Blair had faced a hard-bitten and sceptical audience, and as he finished they rose to him in a fifty-second standing ovation. It was a reaction of which Harold Wilson could only have dreamed. 'I would give him four out of ten for that speech,' RMT boss Bob Crow, one of Blair's fiercest critics, conceded to the *Guardian* – but those for whom he spoke, sitting pointedly in their chairs with their arms folded through the ovation, were conspicuously few. Even the notoriously sceptical GMB chief John Edmonds was tickled, remarking: 'There were no indications that he wants to start a new love affair with the unions, but perhaps there were signs that he might be prepared to start a subtle courtship.'[13]

Two months later, the House of Commons debated the Queen's Speech. The MP chosen to 'move the address' was George Foulkes, a political veteran[14] with a sense of Labour's history. It had begun, he reminded his colleagues, with Keir Hardie's campaigns in Ayrshire:

My constituency is the cradle of the Labour Party. Keir Hardie, the founder of our party, made it his home from 1880 until his death in 1915 and he returned there even when he represented West Ham and Merthyr here in the Commons. Keir Hardie's first manifesto included three key aims: home rule, a minimum wage and temperance. It has taken this Labour government to achieve two of those three – and, may I say it, the right two . . .

Less than two years later, on 30 September 2004, the Thursday night at the conclusion of Labour's annual conference, Blair announced to a stunned media his intention to fight one more election and no more. No previous British Prime Minister had ever taken such a step. Few, indeed, had ever voluntarily renounced the premiership, and those who had done so had rarely given advance warning to colleagues, never mind the nation.[15]

The achievements of Blair's premiership will need greater distance to assess fully in historical context. The electorate, meanwhile, has become less patient. 'Big Brother'-style reality TV shows have engaged millions in an 'electoral' extravaganza that produces a quality of instant gratification to the voter with which political democracy simply cannot compete: despite significant reforms to the electoral process, general election turnouts are now at a historic low, with turnout at its lowest among younger voters.[16]

In the general election of May 2005, Labour was re-elected for an unprecedented third term with a majority considerably more substantial than Clement Attlee's in 1950, Winston Churchill's in 1951, Anthony Eden's in 1955, Harold Wilson's in 1964, Ted Heath's in 1970, Wilson's in 1974, Margaret Thatcher's in 1979 or John Major's in 1992. But the electoral verdict was nevertheless markedly less ringing in its endorsement than in 2001. Labour's share of the vote had slumped to not quite 36 per cent. This was around the same proportion as in 1992, and less than at any election between 1929 and 1979 with the single exception of 1931. Although Conservative support remained at a historic low,[17] many Labour seats that had been won off the Conservatives in 1997 now had wafer-thin majorities. Other Labour seats, particularly those in 'university' areas, swung to the Liberal Democrats, who emerged with their largest tally of seats since pre-1929. The mood music had changed.

Why this had happened became a subject of great debate. On the domestic agenda, Labour's achievement since 1997 had been considerable, though substantial challenges remained. There was, in the oft-quoted New Labour mantra 'a lot done, a lot more to do'. It probably did not help that some of the extra investment in infrastructure and additional trained personnel for the public services would take several years to produce the results voters expected, and that some initiatives, such as those making up the considerable expansion in rehabilitative programmes for offenders in prisons, went unnoticed by the majority of the population. Despite real improvements, best efforts and substantial increases in investment, public services could still be over-bureaucratic and ill-integrated, a problem that had grown arguably ever since Sir Keith Joseph's McKinsey-directed reorganisation of the NHS in the early 1970s. The opaque jargon of managerialism, with its alphabet soup of acronyms, in which the language of polic mak-ing had so often become couched cannot have helped policy initiatives to catch the pop-ular mood. Indeed, for many political canvassers the response on the doorstep implied a failure by growing numbers of voters to perceive the differences to their lives that politics could make – a failure to connect the act of voting with, for example, the quality or pro-vision of national or local services experienced.

But the election had not only been fought on domestic issues. In the aftermath of September 11 2001, criticism of Blair's foreign policy had substantially increased, partic-ularly in relation to Britain's involvement in war in Iraq. Blair had previously faced criti-cism from some, most noisily over his advocacy of armed intervention in Kosovo. But during the 1997–2001 government, Blair's foreign policy critics had remained an essen-tially marginal force, and the bulk of the Labour Party and its voters had given Blair's approach their support. Indeed, many were enthusiastic at the contrast presented with the previous Conservative government's reluctance to countenance direct military inter-vention in Bosnia. It was the widespread antipathy among Labour activists to US President George W. Bush and to all that he represented that enabled the seeds of scep-ticism and distrust for Blair's support for armed US-led intervention in Iraq to take root and spread so swiftly. The more Blair emphasised the closeness of his relationship to Bush, the more profoundly Labour activists became worried. Unable to trust Bush on any other issue, they could not see the argument for trusting him on this one, and the more Blair appeared to say, 'trust me and therefore trust him', the more it undermined their trust in Blair. The decision to base the public case for intervention on the existence of 'weapons of mass destruction' which were not found gave Blair's critics a field day.

As Michael Foot has said in his Foreword to this volume, whether you agree with Blair or not, it is difficult to doubt the sincerity of his convictions or to substantiate an accu-sation that Blair intervened in Iraq merely to court domestic popularity. Moreover, the whole issue of interventionism versus isolationism, of the effectiveness of international institutions such as the United Nations and the question of alliances with right-wing leaders of democratic states against totalitarian dictators abroad brings us right back to the debates that wracked the Labour Party in the 1930s over Spain and rearmament. It was the memories of those debates that Anne Clwyd[18] evoked when she addressed Labour's 2003 annual conference:

> . . . I have believed in regime change for the last 20 years. I do not believe we should turn a blind eye to such atrocities. They have after all stirred this great Labour move-ment for over a century – in Spain, in Nazi Germany, Cambodia and Chile.
> Conference, the people of Iraq could not have toppled this evil regime on their

own. They tried and failed. They the victims needed our help. I believe, as do most of the Iraqi people, that for the sake of their human rights alone, Tony Blair did the moral and courageous thing in destroying the evil and terror of Saddam Hussein's regime.

For whoever succeeds Tony Blair – and Gordon Brown remains the clear front-runner – the challenge and the opportunity will be to revitalise their party for a fourth term. And for that an understanding of Labour's history cannot be anything but an asset.

Notes

Introduction notes

1   James Callaghan, Foreword to Roy Mason, *Paying the Price* (1999), p. 10.

2   Kenneth O. Morgan, *Labour People* (1992), p. 1.

3   Some speeches, especially those of Labour leaders, are increasingly the work of several hands. This is not entirely new. Certainly it is the case that as far back as Hugh Gaitskell and Harold Wilson, leaders would often have drafting assistance from colleagues or advisers. It was and is the case, however, that whether it be Wilson or Blair, the delivery style is unmistakable and integral to the speech. Moreover, no political leader would deliver a speech that he would not want to have written.

4   I have not sought to build an anthology of 'great speeches' though great speeches this does contain. Excerpts are included for their significance at the time, the effectiveness with which they present the arguments they deploy or the impact they had. Many speeches contain memorable lines that fill the pages of dictionaries of political quotations: soundbites are not new! But most speeches are more than just one soundbite, and those that are not (such as Harold Wilson's 'gnomes of Zurich' speech in 1956, and 'blown off course'/'tightly knit band of politically motivated men' speeches in 1966) are omitted. It was obviously impossible to draw on those of which there is no remaining transcript and those which do not really exist in the way that popular myth might have it: Denis Healey never actually promised to 'squeeze the rich till the pips squeaked' (although he did tell Labour's 1973 conference to applause that there would be 'howls of anguish from the 80,000 rich people' when Labour increased income tax on the better off to pay for reduced tax rates at the bottom of the ladder). Speeches are quoted verbatim as they were recorded, which means largely in the present tense, apart from some of the early speeches pre-*c*.1920, which were often written up in the past tense. Constraints of space have required judicious use of the editorial scalpel but the excerpts included do, I hope, preserve the flavour and content as much as possible. Deletions are indicated with an ellipsis (. . .).

5   Taking just one example, it is clear from the speeches and debates of the time, many of which are included here, that far from the issue of sovereignty never being discussed in the battles over Britain joining the EEC, it was central to the whole debate.

Chapter 1

1   The Fabian Society, founded in 1884, was then a small London-based and largely middle-class discussion group seeking to permeate the political parties of the time with progressive socialist ideas. Its leading members included Sidney and Beatrice Webb, playwright George Bernard Shaw, novelist H. G. Wells, Hubert Bland and his novelist wife Edith Nesbitt, and Besant. Though its strongest links were with Liberals such as R. B. Haldane, it would count among its members several 'collectivist Tory' politicians including the future Cabinet minister Leo Amery.

2   This included a donation of £50,000 from the Australian trade unions.

3   Many of whom, under the pre-1918 restricted male-only franchise, did not of course actually have a vote.

4   Hardie speech at Cambuslang, *Glasgow Herald* of 10 April 1888.

5   Kenneth O. Morgan, *Keir Hardie, Radical and Socialist* (1975), p. 51.

6   Dr Henry Pelling, *Origins of the Labour Party* (1965), p. 229.
7   Now part of Amicus.
8   Now part of the Rail Maritime and Transport (RMT) union.
9   Philip Snowden, *An Autobiography, Vol. 1* (1934), p. 88; Francis Williams, *Fifty Years March* (1950), p. 13.
10   Unfortunately the surviving report of the conference is insufficiently detailed to allow the reproduction of meaningful excerpts from the speeches.
11   Now part of the Transport and General Workers' Union (TGWU).
12   Now the Union of Shopworkers' Distributors and Allied Workers (USDAW). In 1924 Bondfield was to become the first woman Cabinet minister.
13   Seconded by the railwaymen and with the support of the Miners' and Gasworkers' Unions.
14   Unfortunately the surviving report of the conference is insufficiently detailed to allow the reproduction of more meaningful excerpts from the speeches.

Chapter 2
15   David Marquand, *Ramsay MacDonald* (1977), p. 4.
16   H. Hessell Tiliman, *Ramsay MacDonald* (1929), p. 49.
17   Formerly a leading Liberal, Chamberlain's refusal to support Home Rule for Ireland led him to break with Gladstone and create the Liberal Unionist Party in alliance with the Conservatives.

Chapter 3
18   Of the 29, one was in Wales (Hardie at Merthyr), two in Scotland (Glasgow Blackfriars and Dundee) and 26 in England. Of these, most were elected for northern industrial towns, preponderantly in Lancashire, with some in Yorkshire, two in the north east and additionally Leicester, Wolverhampton West and Norwich. The others were mainly dockers' seats, including Chatham, Barrow and all three elected in London (for Deptford, West Ham and Woolwich).
19   Keith Laybourn, 'Ramsay Macdonald', in *Dictionary of Labour Biography* (ed.) Greg Rosen (2001), p. 371.
20   16 February.
21   David Marquand, *Ramsay MacDonald* (1977), p. 60.
22   Believed to have been spinal tuberculosis.
23   Colin Cross, *Philip Snowden* (1966), p. 66.
24   Ibid., pp. 76, 79.

Chapter 4
25   Sixpence an hour.
26   Paul Richards, 'Ben Tillett', in *Dictionary of Labour Biography* (ed.) Greg Rosen (2001), p. 580.
27   Now part of the GMB.
28   Henderson was a former Newcastle ironfounder, Lib-Lab Mayor of Darlington and convert to temperance who had won the famous Barnard Castle by-election for Labour in 1903 and would more than once serve as Labour leader.
29   Kenneth O. Morgan, *Keir Hardie, Radical and Socialist* (1975), p. 169.
30   David Marquand, *Ramsay MacDonald* (1977), p. 102.
31   William Kent, *John Burns, Labour's Lost Leader* (1950), p. 174.
32   Marquand, *Ramsay MacDonald*, p. 103.
33   Ibid.

Chapter 5

34 *Labour Leader*, 24 March 1911, cited by John Shepherd, George Lansbury, *At the Heart of Old Labour* (2002), p. 105.

35 Hansard, 25 June 1912, cited in John Shepherd, *George Lansbury, at the Heart of Old Labour* (2002), pp. 111–13; Jonathan Schneer, *George Lansbury* (1990), pp. 99–100.

36 Women over thirty were eventually granted the vote under the 1918 Representation of the People Act, which also conceded a universal male franchise for the first time. It was not until the 1928 Equal Franchise Act, however, that women were granted the vote on the same basis as men (at the age of 21). University graduates and occupiers of business premises retained additional votes until the 1948 Representation of the People Act. In 1950 the first British general election was fought under the universal democratic principle of 'one person one vote'.

Chapter 6

37 Cited by Francis Williams, *Fifty Years' March* (1950), p. 223.

38 Albeit a few who included some of the ILP's best-known leaders such as Hardie, Snowden, Fred Jowett and the chair of the Scottish ILP Jimmy Maxton.

39 Emanuel Shinwell, *The Labour Story* (1963), p. 91.

40 Subsequently Labour MP for Preston and a Cabinet minister in both the 1924 and 1929–31 Labour governments.

Chapter 7

41 Emanuel Shinwell, *The Labour Story* (1963), p. 111.

42 Cited in Francis Williams, *Ernest Bevin* (1952), p. 75.

43 Cited in Alan Bullock, *The Life and Times of Ernest Bevin Vol. 1* (1960), p. 123.

44 Williams, *Ernest Bevin*, p. 77.

45 Ibid., p. 80.

46 Bullock, *The Life and Times of Ernest Bevin*, p. 128.

47 Williams, *Ernest Bevin*, p. 81.

Chapter 8

48 Keith Laybourn, 'Ramsay MacDonald', in *Dictionary of Labour Biography* (ed.) Greg Rosen (2001), p. 371.

49 Gordon Brown, *James Maxton* (1986), pp. 11–15.

50 Ibid., p. 125.

Chapter 9

51 Francis Williams, *Fifty Years' March* (1950), p. 278.

52 Gordon Brown, *James Maxton* (1986), pp. 14–15.

Chapter 10

53 David Marquand, *Ramsay MacDonald* (1977), pp. 479–80.

54 Ibid.,, p. 480.

Chapter 11

55 Patricia Hollis, *Jennie Lee* (1997), p. 35.

56 H. Hessell Tiltman, *James Ramsay MacDonald* (1930), p. 226.

57 Liberal MP and former Cabinet minister.

58 Emanuel Shinwell, *The Labour Story* (1963), p. 136.

59 David Marquand, *Ramsay MacDonald* (1977), p. 540.

60 Ibid.,, p. 568.

61 L. MacNeill Weir, *The Tragedy of Ramsay MacDonald* (1938), p. 237.

62 Of the seven other MPs who joined the New Party, one was Mosley's wife Cynthia, two (ex-Labour) changed their minds after only a day's membership and a third (ex-Labour) resigned after three months. After losing all its parliamentary seats at the general election later that year, it would eschew the democratic road to political change. Mosley visited Mussolini's Italy the following year, and returned to rename his party the British Union of Fascists. It advised its supporters to boycott the subsequent election of 1935, and in May 1940 was proscribed.

63 A. J. A. Morris, *C. P. Trevelyan, Portrait of a Radical* (1977), p. 183.

64 A preferential, not a proportional, system of voting similar to that introduced by the post-1997 Labour government for the Mayor of London.

65 They were joined by Baldwin.

66 On 21 September 1931.

67 Cited in Frank Owen, *Lloyd George, His Life and Times* (1954), p. 719.

Chapter 12

68 Henderson also continued his work as President of the World Disarmament Conference at Geneva, to which he had been appointed in May 1931 while still Foreign Secretary.

69 Graham was to die of pneumonia aged only 44 within weeks of the defeat. Some said that it was the shock of Labour's tragedy that had brought it on. Had he lived he was tipped to be Labour's next Chancellor of the Exchequer.

70 Twenty-five years earlier Attlee had visited London's East End with the vague intention of doing some charitable work and had been so affected by the conditions he found that he had given up the opportunity of a career at the bar for involvement in the ILP and local London politics. After teaching economics at LSE 1912–14 and serving in the army during the Great War, he had become Mayor of Stepney in 1920 and MP for Limehouse in 1922.

71 A. J. A. Morris, *C. P. Trevelyan, Portrait of a Radical* (1977), p. 191.

72 Hugh Dalton, *The Fateful Years* (1957), p. 31.

73 Francis Williams, *Ernest Bevin* (1952), p. 186.

Chapter 13

74 Hugh Dalton, *The Fateful Years* (1957), p. 41.

75 Emanuel Shinwell, *The Labour Story* (1963), p. 147.

76 Brian Brivati, 'Philip Noel-Baker', in Greg Rosen (ed.), *Dictionary of Labour Biography* (2001), p. 450.

77 *Democracy and Dictatorship*, cited in Alan Bullock, *Ernest Bevin, Vol. 1* (1960), p. 527.

78 TUC Report 1933, Appendix C, p. 434.

79 The Socialist League had been formed of former ILP members who had not wanted to follow James Maxton and 'Red Clydeside' in disaffiliation from Labour and into political obscurity in 1932.

80 Shinwell, *The Labour Story*, p. 148.

Chapter 14

81 Alan Bullock, *Ernest Bevin, Vol. 1* (1960), p. 550.

82 G. D. H. Cole, *A History of the Labour Party from 1914* (1948), p. 306.

83 Emanuel Shinwell, *The Labour Story* (1963), p. 150.

84 Francis Williams, *Ernest Bevin* (1952), p. 196.

85   Bernard Donoughue and George Jones, *Herbert Morrison* (1973), p. 236.
86   Ibid., p. 238.
87   Betty Vernon, *Ellen Wilkinson* (1982), p. 141.

Chapter 15
88   Michael Foot, *Aneurin Bevan Vol. 1* (1962), p. 229.
89   *Diary of Tom Jones* cited in ibid., p. 221.
90   Foot, *Aneurin Bevan*, p. 233.
91   Ibid.
92   G. D. H. Cole, *A History of the Labour Party from 1914* (1948), p. 328.

Chapter 16
93   Hugh Dalton, *The Fateful Years* (1957), p. 134.
94   Alan Bullock, *Ernest Bevin, Vol. 1* (1960), p. 593.
95   Cited in ibid., p. 592.

Chapter 17
96   Emanuel Shinwell, *The Labour Story* (1963), p. 161.
97   Herbert Morrison, *An Autobiography* (1960), p. 171.
98   Ibid., p. 172.
99   Hugh Dalton, *The Fateful Years* (1957), p. 306.

Chapter 18
100   Michael Foot, *Aneurin Bevan Vol. 1* (1962), p. 372.
101   Ibid., p. 378.
102   Ibid., pp. 386–87.

Chapter 19
103   He was then a young Royal Navy seaman.
104   James Callaghan, *Time and Chance* (1987), p. 61.
105   James Griffiths, *Pages from Memory* (1969), p. 71.
106   Michael Foot, *Aneurin Bevan Vol. 1* (1962), p. 409.
107   Kevin Jefferys (ed.), *Labour and the Wartime Coalition: The Diaries of James Chuter Ede* (1987), p. 121.
108   Although the Silverman amendment, which she was supporting, was defeated by 1,715,000 votes to 955,000, Betts's speech made enough of a stir for her photograph to feature on the front page of the next morning's *Daily Mirror* as 'The Voice of Youth'. The *Daily Mirror* night editor who had featured her was so inspired that he subsequently arranged to meet her. His name was Ted Castle. They were married on 28 July 1944 and Barbara Betts, or Barbara Castle as she now became, would be one of the leading figures in the Labour Party over the next half-century.
109   Lord Merlyn-Rees, letter to the author, 14 April 2004.

Chapter 20
110   Kenneth O. Morgan, *Callaghan, a Life* (1997), p. 53.
111   Bernard Donoughue and George Jones, *Herbert Morrison* (1973), p. 331.
112   Emanuel Shinwell, *The Labour Story* (1963), p. 173.
113   Cited by Alan Thompson, *The Day Before Yesterday* (1971), p. 14.
114   After Churchill, whom Denis's father had much admired.

115 Hugh Dalton, *The Fateful Years* (1957), p. 459.
116 Denis Healey, *The Time of My Life* (1989), p. 67.

Chapter 21
117 Denis Healey, *The Time of My Life* (1989), p. 67.
118 Emanuel Shinwell, *The Labour Story* (1963), p. 175.
119 Herbert Morrison, *An Autobiography* (1960), p. 251.
120 Cited by Alan Thompson, *The Day Before Yesterday* (1971), p. 17.
121 Hugh Dalton, *The Fateful Years* (1957), p. 481.
122 Ibid., p. 482.
123 Michael Foot, *Aneurin Bevan Vol. 2* (1973), p. 15.
124 During the late 1950s he left the Commons and would drift away from the Labour Party on a rightward trajectory, earning the soubriquet 'Sir Shortly Floorcross'.

Chapter 22
125 Patricia Hollis, *Jennie Lee* (1997), pp. 155-6.
126 Minister for Fuel and Power.
127 Minister of Food.

Chapter 23
128 *Daily Express*, 10 March 1951, cited in Bernard Donoughue and George Jones, *Herbert Morrison* (1973), p. 345.
129 Douglas Jay, *Change and Fortune* (1980), p. 161.
130 Denis Healey, *The Time of My Life* (1989), p. 87.

Chapter 24
131 John Campbell, *Nye Bevan* (1994), p. 157.
132 Ibid., p. 163.
133 Barbara Castle, *Fighting All The Way* (1993), p. 150.
134 Michael Foot, *Aneurin Bevan Vol. 2* (1973), p. 177.
135 Unfortunately there is no full surviving transcript of the speech. Quotations are drawn from press reports of 5 July including the *Daily Mail, Daily Express* and *Manchester Guardian*.
136 Cited in Foot, *Aneurin Bevan Vol. 2*, pp. 234-41.

Chapter 25
137 John Campbell, *Nye Bevan* (1994). p. 206.
138 Michael Foot, *Aneurin Bevan Vol. 2* (1973), p. 313.
139 Ibid., p. 267.
140 Campbell, *Nye Bevan*, p. 210.
141 J. P. W. Mallalieu in *Tribune*, 7 October 1949, cited in Foot, *Aneurin Bevan Vol. 2*, p. 272.

Chapter 26
142 Emanuel Shinwell, *The Labour Story* (1963), p. 186.
143 Hugh Dalton, *High Tide and After* (1962), p. 347.
144 Herbert Morrison, *An Autobiography* (1960), p. 270.
145 Alan Bullock, *Ernest Bevin, Foreign Secretary* (1983), pp. 815-16.
146 Tony Benn, *Years of Hope, Diaries 1940-1962* (1994), p. 142.
147 Philip Williams (ed.), *The Diary of Hugh Gaitskell* (1983), pp. 237-8.
148 Roy Jenkins, *A Life at the Centre* (1991), p. 87.

149 Michael Foot, *Aneurin Bevan Vol. 2* (1973), p. 313.
150 Benn, *Years of Hope,* p. 149.
151 Ibid.
152 Ben Pimlott, *Harold Wilson* (1992) p. 161.

Chapter 27
153 Cited by Alan Thompson, *The Day Before Yesterday* (1971), p. 148.
154 Ben Pimlott (ed.), *The Political Diary of Hugh Dalton, 1918–40 and 1945–60* (1986), pp. 598-9.
155 Douglas Jay, *Change and Fortune* (1980), p. 223.
156 Ibid.
157 Pimlott, *The Political Diary of Hugh Dalton,* p. 599.
158 Denis Healey, *The Time of My Life* (1989), p. 158.
159 Janet Morgan (ed.), *The Backbench Diaries of Richard Crossman* (1981), p. 150.
160 Pimlott, *The Political Diary of Hugh Dalton,* p. 599.
161 Michael Foot, *Aneurin Bevan Vol. 2* (1973), p. 378.
162 Denis Healey, *The Time of My Life* (1989), p. 152.
163 Cited by Thompson, *The Day Before Yesterday,* p. 150.
164 Cited in Kenneth Harris, *Attlee* (1982), p. 505.

Chapter 28
165 James Griffiths, *Pages from Memory* (1969), p. 135.
166 Denis Healey, *The Time of My Life* (1989), p. 153.
167 Ben Pimlott (ed.), *The Political Diary of Hugh Dalton, 1918–40 and 1945–60* (1986), p. 674.
168 Ibid.
169 Bernard Donoughue and George Jones, *Herbert Morrison* (1973), p. 537.
170 Leslie Hunter, *The Road to Brighton Pier* (1959) p. 143.
171 Robert Pearce (ed.), *Patrick Gordon Walker: Political Diaries 1932–71* (1991), p. 227.

Chapter 29
172 Michael Foot, *Aneurin Bevan Vol. 2* (1973), pp. 516-17.
173 Anthony Nutting interview, cited in Alan Thompson, *The Day Before Yesterday* (1971), p. 136.
174 *News Chronicle,* 5 November 1956, cited in John Campbell, *Nye Bevan* (1994), p. 322.
175 *Daily Express,* 5 November 1956, cited in Foot, *Aneurin Bevan Vol. 2,* pp. 524-5.
176 Herbert Morrison, *An Autobiography* (1960), p. 328.
177 Denis Healey, *The Time of My Life* (1989), p. 171.
178 Tony Benn, *Years of Hope, Diaries 1940–1962* (1994), p. 211.
179 Thompson, *The Day Before Yesterday,* p. 139.
180 Healey, *The Time of My Life,* p. 170.
181 Lord Boyle interview cited in Thompson, *The Day Before Yesterday,* p. 143.
182 Douglas Jay, *Change and Fortune* (1980), p. 260.
183 Foot, *Aneurin Bevan Vol. 2* (1973), p. 514.
184 Healey, *The Time of My Life,* p. 171.
185 Foot, *Aneurin Bevan Vol. 2,* p. 528.
186 Ibid., pp. 531-2.
187 Benn, *Years of Hope,* p. 217.

Chapter 30
188 Philip Williams, *Hugh Gaitskell* (1982), p. 297.
189 John Grant, *Blood Brothers* (1992), p. 18.

190 Lewis Minkin, *The Labour Party Annual Conference* (1978), p. 96, cited in Brian Brivati, *Hugh Gaitskell*, p. 353.
191 Janet Morgan (ed.), *The Backbench Diaries of Richard Crossman* (1981), p. 620.
192 John Campbell, *Nye Bevan* (1994), p. 338.
193 Ibid., p. 331.
194 Alan Thompson, *The Day Before Yesterday* (1971), p. 203.
195 Barbara Castle, *Fighting All the Way* (1992), pp. 256–7.

Chapter 31
196 Philip Williams, *Hugh Gaitskell* (1982) p. 294.
197 Janet Morgan (ed.), *The Backbench Diaries of Richard Crossman* (1981), p. 604.
198 Subsequently MP for Dagenham and during the 1980s a member of Neil Kinnock's shadow Cabinet.
199 Robert Pearce (ed.), *Patrick Gordon Walker, Political Diaries 1932–1971* (1991), p. 215.

Chapter 32
200 Tim Bale, 'Barbara Castle', in Kevin Jefferys (ed.), *Labour Forces* (2002), p. 176.
201 Andrew Roth, *Enoch Powell* (1970), p. 218.
202 Barbara Castle, *Fighting All the Way* (1993), p. 288.
203 One consequence was that after the 1959 election Macmillan would replace Lennox-Boyd by Iain Macleod, with a general brief to move towards de-colonisation, something that had been resisted by his predecessor.
204 Geoffrey Alderman, *Britain: A One Party State?* (1989), p. 8.
205 Robert Pearce (ed.), *Patrick Gordon Walker, Political Diaries 1932–1971* (1991), p. 257.
206 Gaitskell to John Beavan, 19 April 1961, cited in Philip Williams, *Hugh Gaitskell* (1982), p. 293.
207 Roy Jenkins, in W. T. Rodgers (ed.), *Hugh Gaitskell 1906–1963*, p. 127.
208 Tony Crosland interview, cited in Alan Thompson, *The Day Before Yesterday* (1971), p. 210.
209 Geoffrey Goodman, *The Awkward Warrior, Frank Cousins: His Life and Times* (1979), p. 241.
210 Michael Foot, *Aneurin Bevan Vol. 2* (1973), p. 636.
211 Janet Morgan (ed.), *The Backbench Diaries of Richard Crossman* (1981), p. 803.
212 Geoffrey McDermot, *Leader Lost* (1972), p. 179.
213 Dick Taverne, *The Future of the Left* (1974), p. 18.
214 Denis Healey, *The Time of My Life* (1989), p. 159.
215 Tony Benn, *Years of Hope, Diaries 1940–1962* (1994), p. 321.
216 Foot, *Aneurin Bevan Vol. 2*, p. 639.
217 Geoffrey Goodman, letter to author, 22 June 2003.
218 Healey, *The Time of My Life*, p. 155.
219 Gaitskell's Tory-supporting flatmate at Oxford University who later, as Lord Longford, would serve as a Labour Cabinet minister.

Chapter 33
220 Geoffrey McDermot, *Leader Lost* (1972), p. 186.
221 Cited in ibid., p. 195.
222 Such as Eireen White, Charlie Pannell, George Brown and Ray Gunter.
223 George Brown, *In My Way* (1972), p. 74.
224 Dick Taverne, *The Future of the Left* (1974), p. 18.
225 Interview with Rt Hon. Tom Clark MP, 25 October 2003.
226 Labour's Foreign Secretary 1965–66 and 1968–70.

227 Michael Stewart, *Life and Labour* (1980), p. 111.
228 Janet Morgan (ed.), *The Backbench Diaries of Richard Crossman* (1981), pp. 764, 766.
229 It demanded an end to all H-bomb tests; a pledge against first use; stopping production of H-bombs; and stopping nuclear-weapon-carrying aircraft using British bases.
230 Cited in Geoffrey Goodman, *The Awkward Warrior* (1979), p. 224.
231 Cited in Brian Brivati, *Hugh Gaitskell* (1997), p. 321.
232 Robert Pearce (ed.), *Patrick Gordon Walker, Political Diaries 1932-1971* (1991), p. 259.
233 A Labour Cabinet minister 1968-70 and 1974-79.
234 Roy Mason, *Paying the Price* (1999), pp. 70, 74.
235 Emanuel Shinwell, *The Labour Story* (1963), p. 207.
236 Tony Benn, *Years of Hope, Diaries 1940-1962* (1994), p. 347.
237 Shadow Secretary of State for War. Foreign Office minister 1946-50; appointed Navy Minister under Harold Wilson 1964-66.
238 Former TGWU official who became a minister 1964-69. Elected to the shadow Cabinet from 1971 he served in Cabinet 1974-76 as Education and then Overseas Development Secretary. He was deselected by his constituency party during 1975 and defected to the Conservatives in 1977.
239 At the time Foot was Labour's candidate for Ebbw Vale at the by-election caused by the death of his hero Aneurin Bevan.
240 Benn, *Years of Hope*, p. 348.
241 Brian Brivati, *Hugh Gaitskell* (1997), p. 374.
242 John Grant, *Blood Brothers* (1992), p. 19.
243 Patrick Gordon Walker interview, cited in Alan Thompson, *The Day Before Yesterday* (1971), p. 206. Those present included Christopher Mayhew, Austin Albu, Tony Crosland, Horace King, Gerry Reynolds, Reg Prentice and Jack Diamond.
244 Pearce, *Patrick Gordon Walker*, p. 270.
245 Morgan, *The Backbench Diaries of Richard Crossman*, p. 884.
246 McDermot, *Leader Lost*, p. 201.
247 Michael Crick, *The March of Militant* (1986), pp. 116, 120.
248 USDAW (shopworkers); NUR (railwaymen) and AEU (engineers).
249 Woodrow Wyatt, *What's Left of the Labour Party* (1977), p. 69. For a full account of the ETU controversy read C. H. Rolph, *All those in Favour? The ETU Trial* (1962).
250 McDermot, *Leader Lost*, p. 201.
251 Ben Pimlott, *Wilson* (1992), p. 238.
252 *Daily Telegraph*, 25 October 1960.
253 Morgan, *The Backbench Diaries of Richard Crossman*, p. 686.
254 Roy Jenkins interview, cited in Pimlott, *Wilson*, p. 243.
255 Letter, 2 November 1960, cited in Philip Ziegler, *Wilson* (1993), p. 128.

Chapter 34

256 The others were R. A. Butler (a Conservative) during 1951-64 and John Simon (first a Liberal and later a National Liberal) under Asquith and during the National governments of the 1930s.
257 K. O. Morgan, 'James Callaghan', in Kevin Jefferys (ed.), *Leading Labour* (1999), pp. 136-7.
258 Peter Kellner and Christopher Hitchens, *Callaghan – the Road to Number Ten* (1976), p. 34.
259 Cited in Kenneth O. Morgan, *Callaghan: A Life* (1997), p. 163.
260 Michael Foot, *Aneurin Bevan Vol. 2* (1973), p. 571.
261 Patricia Hollis, *Jennie Lee* (1997), p. 368.
262 Oswald Mosley had regrouped post-war, forming the neo-fascist Union Movement in 1948,

standing for North Kensington at the 1959 general election. He lost his deposit.

263 Roy Jenkins, *Nine Men of Power* (1974), p. 179.

264 Philip Williams, *Hugh Gaitskell* (1982), p. 385.

Chapter 35

265 Woodrow Wyatt, *What's Left of the Labour Party* (1977), p. 70.

266 France, West Germany, Italy and Benelux.

267 Austria, Denmark, Norway, Portugal, Sweden, Switzerland and the United Kingdom.

268 An Old Etonian ex-Communist who was by then the shadow Commonwealth Secretary and a firm Gaitskellite. But for his sudden death in July 1963 it is likely that he would have served in the next Labour Cabinet.

269 Philip Williams, *Hugh Gaitskell* (1982), p. 400.

270 Ibid.

271 George Brown, *In My Way* (1971), p. 212.

272 Brian Brivati, *Hugh Gaitskell* (1997), pp. 414-15.

273 Hugo Young, *This Blessed Plot* (1998), pp. 164-65.

274 Douglas Jay, *Change and Fortune* (1980), p. 286.

275 Philip Williams, *Hugh Gaitskell* (1982), p. 409.

276 Brown, *In My Way*, p. 213.

Chapter 36

277 Ben Pimlott, *Wilson* (1992,) p. 247.

278 George Thomson MP, cited in ibid., p. 249.

279 Pimlott, *Wilson*, p. 249.

280 Denis Howell, *Made in Birmingham* (1990), p. 110.

281 Bill Rodgers, *Fourth Among Equals* (2000), p. 73.

282 Brown's backers included James Griffiths, Roy Jenkins, Denis Howell, Bill Rodgers, Dick Taverne, Bob Mellish, Charlie Pannell, Desmond Donnelly and Patrick Gordon Walker while Callaghan's included Tony Crosland, Denis Healey, Douglas Jay, George Strauss, Michael Stewart and George Thomson. Crosland and Stewart both backed Brown on the second ballot while Healey backed Wilson.

283 James Callaghan, *Time and Chance* (1987), p. 150.

284 Denis Healey, *The Time of My Life* (1989), p. 297.

285 CDS witness seminar, cited in K. O. Morgan *Callaghan, A Life* (1997), p. 182.

286 Robens, a Mancunian former USDAW official, had served briefly in Attlee's Cabinet in succession to Bevan as Minister of Labour and thereafter in the shadow Cabinet 1951-60. George Brown argues convincingly in his memoirs that had Robens remained in Parliament it would have been he and not Brown who would have succeeded Bevan as deputy leader in 1960, and defeated Wilson in 1963 as the unopposed candidate of the centre and right: *In My Way* (1971), pp. 85-6.

287 Peter Paterson, *Tired and Emotional, the Life of Lord George Brown* (1993), p. 122.

288 Callaghan, *Time and Chance*, p. 151.

289 Philip Ziegler, *Wilson* (1993), p. 142.

290 Janet Morgan (ed.), *The Backbench Diaries of Richard Crossman* (1981), p. 1026.

291 Pimlott, *Wilson*, p. 305.

292 Austen Morgan, *Harold Wilson* (1992), p. 247.

293 Ziegler, *Wilson*, p. 143.

294 Tony Benn's wife.

295 Tony Benn, *Out of the Wilderness, Diaries 1963-1967* (1987), pp. 80, 83-4.

296 One now had to be found for him: it was, in Leyton, where the sitting MP was persuaded to accept a peerage. Gordon Walker fought the by-election on 21 January 1965: he lost and had to resign, though he would win it back at the 1966 general election. He was replaced as Foreign Secretary by Michael Stewart.

297 Dr D. R. Prem, *The Parliamentary Leper* (1965), p. 102.

Chapter 37

298 They were reduced to 10 per cent in April 1965 and abolished in November 1966. The fact that they were introduced as a necessary bulwark against devaluation, proved unsustainable, and were dropped but that the government never came up with anything to plug the hole they had left speaks volumes for the likelihood of staving off devaluation.

299 Cited in James Callaghan, *Time and Chance* (1987), p. 182.

300 John Grant, *Blood Brothers* (1992), p. 29.

301 DEMOS, *The Go-Ahead Year* (1966), pp. 15-17.

302 Ben Pimlott, *Wilson* (1992), pp. 276-7.

303 George Brown, *In My Way* (1971), p. 91.

304 Ibid., pp. 91, 92.

305 Lord Wigg, *George Wigg* (1972), p. 254.

306 John Grant, *Blood Brothers* (1992), p. 29.

307 Ibid., p. 31.

308 Geoffrey Goodman, *The Awkward Warrior* (1979), p. 471.

309 Cousins stipulated that he would stay only on condition the Bill was dropped and replaced by a price freeze, import quotas and productivity-linked wage increases.

310 Callaghan, *Time and Chance*, p. 171.

311 Peter Shore, *Leading the Left* (1993), p. 91.

312 Kenneth O. Morgan, *Callaghan: A Life* (1997), p. 246.

313 Mervyn Jones, *Michael Foot* (1995), p. 321.

314 Clive Ponting, *Breach of Promise* (1989), pp. 396-7.

Chapter 38

315 David Lipsey, 'Roy Jenkins', in Kevin Jefferys (ed.), *Labour Forces* (2002), p. 107.

316 Roy Jenkins, *A Life at the Centre* (1991), p. 175.

317 John Campbell, *Roy Jenkins* (1983), pp. 94-5.

318 Lipsey, 'Roy Jenkins', p. 107.

319 Brian Lapping, *The Labour Government 1964-70* (1970), p. 36.

320 Peter Paterson, *Tired and Emotional, the Life of Lord George Brown* (1993), p. 286.

321 Cousins' deputy Harry Nicholas had kept the seat warm as acting general secretary while Cousins had served in Cabinet.

322 Edward Pearce, *The Senate of Lilliput* (1983), p. 136.

323 During the 1970s Heffer would recant his 1960s EEC enthusiasms.

324 Dick Crossman, *The Diaries of a Cabinet Minister, Vol. II* (1976), p. 505.

325 He was again replaced by Michael Stewart, who by now shared Brown's pro-EEC views.

326 Joe Haines in his memoir *Glimmers of Twilight* suggests that the reason Brown was not to be found was that he was sleeping off the effects of alcoholic excess.

Chapter 39

327 George Brown, *In My Way* (1971), p. 133.

328 In place of these he ordered the world's first jump-jet, the Harrier, which would not need to be based on a traditional aircraft carrier, and the Invincible class of ships to carry them. He

also ordered the Nimrod anti-submarine patrol aircraft. But overall his policy was one of retrenchment.

329   Later MSF and now part of AMICUS.
330   Barbara Castle, *The Castle Diaries 1964–1970* (1984), p. 302.
331   Dick Crossman, *The Diaries of a Cabinet Minister, Vol. II* (1976), p. 503.
332   Kenneth O. Morgan, *Callaghan: A Life* (1997), p. 267.
333   James Callaghan, *Time and Chance* (1987), pp. 167, 172.
334   Peter Shore, *Leading the Left* (1993), p. 93.
335   Crossman, *The Diaries of a Cabinet Minister, Vol. II*, p. 588.
336   Castle, *The Castle Diaries*, p. 328.
337   Cited in Peter Kellner and Christopher Hitchens, *Callaghan – The Road to Number Ten* (1976), p. 70.
338   Morgan, *Callaghan: A Life*, p. 287.
339   He specifically sought to protect the planned Open University and the raising of the school leaving age.
340   Michael Hatfield, *The House the Left Built* (1978), pp. 62–3.

Chapter 40

341   David Lipsey, 'Roy Jenkins', in Kevin Jefferys (ed.), *Labour Forces* (2002), p. 107.
342   John Campbell, *Roy Jenkins* (1983), p. 93.
343   Roy Jenkins, *Nine Men of Power* (1974), pp. 179–80.
344   Dick Crossman, *The Diaries of a Cabinet Minister, Vol. II* (1976), p. 675.
345   Ibid., p. 679.
346   Including Ian Macleod, Edward Boyle, Michael Heseltine and Ian Gilmour.
347   Mackintosh was MP for Berwick and East Lothian 1966–February 1974 and again October 1974 until his death from a heart tumour in July 1978 at the age of only 48. One of the greatest parliamentary orators of his era, his determined public advocacy of the rights of the Kenyan Asians, British membership of the EEC, Scottish devolution, parliamentary select committees, and the leadership aspirations of Roy Jenkins helped confine his political talents to the Commons backbenches, television screens and newspaper columns.
348   David Owen, *Time to Declare* (1991), p. 113.
349   Shadow Home Secretary.
350   Despite his reputation for 'illiberality', Callaghan spent much of the next two years ensuring the final repeal of the death penalty. In December 1964 Sydney Silverman had introduced a private member's bill to fully abolish capital punishment. The Cabinet had agreed to provide parliamentary time for the bill to enable it to be passed and so it duly was in July 1965. The House of Lords then carried a Conservative amendment that the provisions of the Bill lapse automatically after five years unless both Commons and Lords passed motions for permanent abolition. With the death of the septuagenarian Silverman in 1968, Home Secretary James Callaghan took responsibility for seeing these motions through. He had always been a 'vehement and enlightened supporter of abolition', and indeed had declared that he would resign rather than order any executions (Kenneth O. Morgan, *Callaghan: A Life* [1997], p. 297). On a free vote the Commons voted for permanent abolition by 343 votes to 185. Labour's Lord Chancellor Gerald Gardiner then faced the tough task of winning over the traditionally more conservative House of Lords. This he did on 17 December 1969 when he succeeded by 220 votes to 174. It was to be a lasting achievement.
351   James Callaghan, *Time and Chance* (1987), pp. 266–7.
352   Dubcek had ended censorship and was dismantling the security apparatus. He had however pledged not to withdraw Czechoslovakia from the Warsaw Pact or Comecon.

353   Olga Cannon and J. R. L. Anderson, *The Road from Wigan Pier* (1973), p. 290.

354   A founder of Militant and one of the five key Militant figures expelled from the Labour Party in February 1983.

Chapter 41

355   Nullifying Wilson's pledge to build 500,000 homes by 1970.

356   This required a massive investment in new/expanded buildings and teacher training, all of which was ongoing.

357   Tony Benn, *Office without Power, Diaries 1968–72* (1988), p. 6.

358   Dick Crossman, *The Diaries of a Cabinet Minister, Vol. II* (1976), p. 686.

359   Acton, Meriden and Dudley.

360   Oldham West, Nelson and Colne.

361   It was a classic Wilsonian musical chairs reshuffle. Castle was replaced at Transport by Dick Marsh, whom Gunter replaced at Power. Ted Short replaced Patrick Gordon Walker (who was sacked) at Education. Dick Crossman moved to set up what would become the super-Ministry of the Department of Health and Social Services, replaced as Leader of the House of Commons by Fred Peart, who was replaced at Agriculture by Welsh Secretary Cledwyn Hughes who in turn was replaced by future Commons Speaker George Thomas.

362   *Sun*, 3 September 1968, cited in Patricia Hollis, *Jennie Lee* (1997), p. 369.

363   Hollis, *Jennie Lee*, p. 370.

364   Geoffrey Goodman, *The Awkward Warrior, Frank Cousins: His Life and Times* (1979), p. 569.

Chapter 42

365   He left the Communist Party for the socialist Labour League (later renamed the Workers' Revolutionary Party) as it was 'the biggest Trotskyist group in Britain'. Alan Thornett, *Inside Cowley* (1997), p. 4.

366   Hugh Clegg, *How to Run an Incomes Policy* (1971), p. 62.

367   The strikers were in the Amalgamated Engineering Union; the chargehand in Clive Jenkins's ASTMS, later renamed MSF. Nearly 35 years later, the merger of the AEEU and MSF would bring both groups into the Amicus super-union.

368   Barbara Castle, *Fighting All the Way* (1993), pp. 414–15.

369   Ibid., p. 418.

370   A former Cabinet minister and Inland Revenue Staff Federation leader.

371   Castle, *Fighting All the Way*, p. 422.

372   Geoffrey Goodman, interview with author, 21 June 2004.

373   An elaborate code had been constructed to enable her to communicate with Wilson by phone: 'Eagle' meant Wilson; 'Owl' meant Crossman; 'Starling' meant Jenkins; 'Bull' meant Cousins; 'Bear' meant Scanlon; and 'Rhino' meant Vic Feather. Castle was 'Peacock'. 'The Zoo' meant the General Council of the TUC. Barbara Castle, *The Castle Diaries 1964–1970* (1984), p. 659.

374   Those who backed Castle to the end are thought to have included Foreign Secretary Michael Stewart, Agriculture Minister Cledwyn Hughes and Welsh Secretary George Thomas. The position of Tony Benn, who had supported Castle's approach up until then, is less clear.

375   Roy Jenkins, *A Life at the Centre* (1991), p. 290.

376   Joe Haines, *Glimmers of Twilight* (2003), p. 17.

377   John Grant, *Blood Brothers* (1992), p. 43.

378   Clegg, *How to Run an Incomes Policy*, p. 59.

379   Grant, *Blood Brothers*, p. 44.

380   Kenneth O. Morgan, *Callaghan: A Life* (1997), p. 344.
381   Labour History Group Seminar, 12 November 2003.
382   Tony Benn, *Office without Power, Diaries 1968–72* (1988), p. 306.
383   *The Times Guide to the House of Commons 1970* (1970), p. 27.
384   Jenkins, *A Life at the Centre*, p. 312.
385   Benn, *Office without Power*, p. 306.
386   Haines, *Glimmers of Twilight*, p. 48.

Chapter 43

387   John Campbell, *Roy Jenkins* (1983), p. 135.
388   David Owen, *Time to Declare* (1991), p. 170.
389   Ibid., pp. 171–72.
390   Douglas Jay, *Change and Fortune* (1980), p. 451.
391   Owen, *Time to Declare*, p. 176.
392   Roy Jenkins, *A Life at the Centre* (1991), p. 319.
393   Owen, *Time to Declare*, p. 177.
394   Jenkins, *A Life at the Centre*, p. 319.
395   Edward Pearce, *The Senate of Lilliput* (1983), p. 38.
396   Douglas Jay, *Change and Fortune* (1980), p. 456.
397   Jenkins, *A Life at the Centre*, p. 320.
398   The late Lord Jenkins of Hillhead, interview with the author, 1996.
399   Tony Benn, *Office without Power, Diaries 1968–72* (1988), p. 356.
400   Hugo Young, *This Blessed Plot* (1998), p. 263.
401   *Times*, 20 July 1971, cited John Campbell, *Roy Jenkins* (1983), pp. 140–41.
402   Bill Rodgers, *Fourth Among Equals* (2000), p. 126.
403   Cited in ibid., p. 131.
404   Owen, *Time to Declare*, p. 184.
405   Michael Foot.
406   Jenkins, *A Life at the Centre*, p. 316.
407   Ibid., p. 329.
408   Denis Healey, *The Time of My Life* (1989), p. 329.
409   Owen, *Time to Declare*, p. 189.
410   The constituency of Jenkinsite MP John Roper.
411   Jenkins, *A Life at the Centre*, p. 340.
412   Ibid.
413   Owen, *Time to Declare*, p. 190.
414   In future years to serve as a European Commissioner.
415   In the vote itself the pro-referendum amendment was defeated by 49 votes after nearly a fifth of Labour MPs abstained.
416   Not all the leading pro-Europeans resigned: Shirley Williams and Roy Hattersley remained and both accepted promotion, Williams succeeding Callaghan as shadow Home Secretary and Hattersley replacing Thomson as shadow Defence Secretary. Hattersley always complained that he was subsequently accused of 'disloyalty' by his fellow pro-Europeans who had resigned while Williams somehow escaped opprobrium.
417   Rodgers, *Fourth Among Equals*, p. 134.
418   He again defeated the official Labour candidate, one Margaret Jackson, at the next general election of February 1974, only to lose to Jackson at the general election of October that year. Jackson subsequently married the local constituency chair, Leo Beckett, and went on to be deputy leader of the Labour Party and a long-serving member of Tony Blair's Cabinet.

Taverne later helped found the SDP and became a Liberal Democrat peer.

419   Ben Pimlott, *Wilson* (1992), p. 599.

Chapter 44

420   John Golding, *Hammer of the Left* (2003), pp. 17–18.
421   Susan Crosland, *Tony Crosland* (1982), p. 52.
422   Kenneth O. Morgan, *Labour People* (1987), pp. 304–5.
423   Crosland, *Tony Crosland*, p. 210.
424   Stuart Holland, who had briefly advised Wilson in Downing Street, AUEW Head of Research Tony Banks and Margaret Jackson (later Beckett) from Labour HQ's Research Department.
425   One wag was to ask how they could be agreements if they were compulsory. In the event only one was ever agreed, with Chrysler, which the firm then broke.
426   Phillip Whitehead, *The Writing on the Wall* (1985), p. 122.
427   Michael Hatfield, *The House the Left Built* (1978), p. 207.
428   Roy Jenkins, *What Matters Now* (1972), p. 31.
429   Tony Benn cites Wilson (Tony Benn, *Against the Tide, Diaries 1973–76* [1989], p. 34); Healey cites himself (Denis Healey, *The Time of My Life* [1989], p. 370.); Crosland's biographers suggest it was Crosland (Giles Radice, *Friends and Rivals* [2002], p. 213; Kevin Jefferys, *Crosland* [1999], p. 168).
430   Benn, *Against the Tide*, p. 46.
431   Cited in Edward Pearce, *Denis Healey* (2002), p. 420.
432   Benn, Judith Hart, Frank Allaun, Joan Lestor, Joan Maynard, Peter Doyle of the Young Socialists and John Cartwright, the representative of the Co-op who was infuriated by the suggestion that the Co-op was less efficient than Marks & Spencer.
433   Healey was supported by Callaghan, Shirley Williams, Michael Foot, Walter Padley of USDAW and Sid Weighell of the NUR.
434   Michael Crick, *Militant* (1984), p. 77.
435   Michael Hatfield, *The House the Left Built* (1978), pp. 228–9.

Chapter 45

436   William Rees-Mogg.
437   Giles Radice, *Friends and Rivals* (2002), p. 217.
438   Michael Hatfield, *The House the Left Built*, (1978), p. 55.
439   Bernard Donoughue, *Prime Minister* (1987), p. 48.
440   Harold Lever was a legendary bridge player who claimed to have made most of his wealth through share-dealing in his spare time. A stroke the previous year cost him the use of an arm but he remained both fully in possession of his mental faculties and, recalled Jack Diamond, 'as warm hearted personally as he was brilliant in his understanding of finance': Lord Diamond, 'Harold Lever', *Dictionary of Labour Biography*, Greg Rosen (ed.), (2001), p. 357.
441   Donoughue, *Prime Minister*, p. 50.
442   Ibid.
443   Mervyn Jones, *Michael Foot* (1995), p. 356.
444   Cited in ibid.
445   Tony Benn, *Against the Tide, Diaries 1973–76* (1989), p. 122.

Chapter 46

446   Edward Pearce, *Denis Healey* (2002), p. 419.
447   Phillip Whitehead, *The Writing on the Wall* (1985), p. 142.

448 Tony Benn, *Against the Tide, Diaries 1973–76* (1989), p. 302.

449 Ibid., p. 325.

450 Douglas Jay, *Change and Fortune* (1980), p. 479.

451 The bulk of the major unions voted to pull out of the EEC: TGWU transport workers, AUEW engineering union, Clive Jenkins's white-collar ASTMS, mineworkers, public employees and firemen. The GMWU general union, USDAW shopworkers, railwaymen (NUR), post-office workers (UPW) and Roy Grantham's white-collar APEX were pro-EEC.

452 Benn, *Against the Tide*, p. 369.

453 Barbara Castle, *The Castle Diaries 1974–76* (1980), p. 379.

454 Benn, *Against the Tide*, p. 369.

455 Castle, *The Castle Diaries*, p. 408.

456 Whitehead, *The Writing on the Wall*, p. 137.

Chapter 47

457 Edward Pearce, *Denis Healey* (2002), p. 430.

458 Bernard Donoughue, *The Heat of the Kitchen* (2003), p. 160.

459 Pearce, *Denis Healey*, p. 434.

460 Joe Haines, *The Politics of Power* (1977), p. 45.

461 Later Master of Balliol, Oxford.

462 Later Chairman of the BBC.

463 Mervyn Jones, *Michael Foot* (1995), p. 390.

464 Barbara Castle, *The Castle Diaries 1974–76* (1980), p. 510.

465 Jones, *Michael Foot*, p. 391.

466 Tony Benn, *Against the Tide, Diaries 1973–76* (1989), pp. 442–3.

467 Castle, *The Castle Diaries*, p. 512.

468 Ibid., p. 511.

469 Benn, *Against the Tide*, p. 443.

470 Denis Healey, *The Time of My Life* (1989), p. 444.

Chapter 48

471 Bernard Donoughue, *The Heat of the Kitchen* (2003), p. 178.

472 It is thought that Jenkins probably lost 15–30 essential first preference votes because of this: enough to have given him a chance of victory.

473 Since 1997, Bob Marshall-Andrews has been Labour MP for Medway.

474 A eurosceptic former PPS to Harold Wilson, close friend and ally of Gerald Kaufman and former Derbyshire mining electrician. MP for Chesterfield since 1964.

475 James Callaghan, *Time and Chance* (1987), p. 425.

476 Tony Benn, *Against the Tide, Diaries 1973–76* (1989), p. 615.

477 Cledwyn Hughes diary. Cited in Kenneth O. Morgan, *Callaghan: A Life* (1997), p. 536.

478 Benn, *Against the Tide*, p. 616.

479 Ian Mikardo.

480 Benn, *Against the Tide*, p. 616.

481 Giles Radice, *Friends and Rivals* (2002), p. 257.

482 Denis Healey, *The Time of My Life* (1989), p. 427.

483 Ibid., p. 381.

484 Donoughue, *The Heat of the Kitchen*, p. 241.

485 Callaghan, *Time and Chance*, pp. 409–10.

486 Donoughue, *The Heat of the Kitchen*, p. 242.

487 Bernard Donoughue, *Prime Minister* (1987), p. 112.

488   Callaghan, *Time and Chance*, p. 411.
489   Ibid., pp. 466–67.
490   Phillip Whitehead, *The Writing on the Wall* (1985), p. 267.
491   Donoughue, *Prime Minister*, p. 156.
492   John Golding, *Hammer of the Left* (2003), p. 64.

Chapter 49

493   Tam Dalyell, 'Willie Ross', in Greg Rosen (ed.), *Dictionary of Labour Biography* (2001), p. 495.
494   Dick Crossman, *The Diaries of a Cabinet Minister, Vol. II* (1976), p. 503.
495   Ibid., pp. 106, 82.
496   What was to become the Kilbrandon Committee.
497   Letter from Giles Radice to John P. Mackintosh, 5 March 1974, J. P. Mackintosh papers, Deposit 323/ file 73, in the National Library of Scotland.
498   Rt Hon. Donald Dewar MP, interview with the author, 5 June 1996.
499   Barbara Castle, *The Castle Diaries 1974–76* (1980), p. 538.
500   Lord Ewing of Kirkford, interview with the author, June 2 1996.
501   An Edinburgh-born Old Etonian and former schoolteacher, Dalyell had been President of Cambridge University Conservatives before joining Labour in the wake of Suez, where he became a staunch 'Gaitskellite'. MP for West Lothian since a by-election in 1962 and PPS to Dick Crossman during most of the latter's Cabinet career 1964–70, he was as passionate an advocate of Britain joining the EEC as he was an opponent of devolution and in later years, echoing his opposition to Suez, an opponent of Margaret Thatcher's approach to the Falklands War.
502   John P. Mackintosh, *Political Quarterly*, April 1978, p. 128.
503   He was to die of a heart tumour in July 1978, aged only 48.
504   Gerald O'Brien, interview with the author, May 23 1996.

Chapter 50

505   Barbara Castle, *The Castle Diaries 1974–76* (1980), p. 182.
506   Kenneth O. Morgan, *Callaghan: A Life* (1997), p. 504.
507   Former Inner London state-school headteacher, Conservative MP for Brent North since 1974 and a junior Conservative education spokesman/minister 1976–83. Famous for his Dickensian whiskers and right-wing views.
508   Conservative deputy leader, shadow Home Secretary and subsequently Home Secretary 1976–83.

Chapter 51

509   John Golding, *Hammer of the Left* (2003), p. 19.
510   Barbara Castle, *The Castle Diaries 1974–76* (1980), p. 393.
511   Golding, *Hammer of the Left*, p. 32.
512   Joe Ashton, *Red Rose Blues* (2000), p. 209.
513   A former Communist Party member, Ken Coates was one of the original leaders of the Trotskyist International Marxist Group which 'supplanted the Revolutionary Communist League as the United Secretariat of the Trotskyist Fourth International' (Blake Baker, *The Far Left* [1981], p. 77). During the 1960s had been expelled from the Labour Party. By the 1970s he had been readmitted. His son Laurence, a member of Militant, served as Young Socialist representative on Labour's NEC during 1981–83.
514   Backed by the right and also by Moss Evans of the TGWU and left-wing MPs Ian Mikardo and Eric Heffer.

515 Signed by Militant supporter Ray Apps and Tribune Group secretary Jo Richardson.

Chapter 52

516 Now part of UNISON.
517 Composite 37.
518 Sid Weighell, *On the Rails* (1983), pp. 40–41.
519 Composite 38.
520 Tony Benn, *Conflicts of Interest, Diaries 1977–80* (1990), p. 356.
521 Joel Barnett, *Inside the Treasury* (1982), p. 192.
522 Peter Shore, *Leading the Left* (1993), pp. 117–18.
523 John Grant, *Blood Brothers* (1992), pp. 86–7.
524 Lord Sawyer, interview with the author, 30 June 2004.
525 Gallup polls August 1978 and January 1979, Anthony King (ed.), *British Political Opinion 1937–2000: The Gallup Polls* (2001), p. 332.
526 Geoffrey Alderman, *Britain: A One Party State?* (1989), p. 38.
527 Frank Chapple, *Sparks Fly!* (1984), p. 150.
528 Ibid.
529 Both were elected as Labour MPs in 1974 but had broken away to create their own 'Scottish Labour Party' during 1976 in frustration at the failure of the government to push through its first devolution Bill.
530 Frank Johnson, *Out of Order* (1982), pp. 56–7.
531 Ibid.
532 John Golding, *Hammer of the Left* (2003), p. 65.
533 Alderman, *Britain: A One Party State?*, p. 8.
534 Ibid.
535 Manifesto's founding chair was former Scottish Office minister Dickson Mabon. Other key MPs included John Horam, John Cartwright, James Wellbeloved and Ian Wrigglesworth, who were all to join the SDP and Giles Radice, George Robertson, Phillip Whitehead, John Golding and Ken Weetch who were not. Its supporters included Gaitskellite elder statesmen such as former Foreign Secretaries Michael Stewart and Patrick Gordon Walker. A pamphlet entitled *What We Must Do* setting out their aims and values was published in 1977. It was written largely by John P. Mackintosh, David Marquand, Giles Radice, John Horam and Bryan Magee.
536 They included Norman Atkinson, Eric Heffer, Stan Orme, Stan Newens and Norman Buchan. Others who joined tham included TGWU chief Frank Cousins, legendary campaigner against capital punishment Sydney Silverman, future Cabinet members Michael Foot and Albert Booth, and past/present/future NEC members Frank Allaun, Tom Driberg, Lena Jeger, Renee Short, and Joan Lestor. Minutes were taken of their weekly meetings by Mikardo's secretary Jo Richardson, later an MP and left-wing member of Kinnock's shadow Cabinet.
537 The slate was Roy Hattersley, Denis Healey, Dickson Mabon, Roy Mason, David Owen, Merlyn Rees, Bill Rodgers, John Smith and Eric Varley. All but Mabon were elected. The only overtly Tribune-backed MPs elected were Albert Booth and Stan Orme. John Silkin and Peter Shore were by now regarded as anti-EEC centrists. Athough Silkin was pro-CND, Shore by now had become anti-.
538 Phillip Whitehead, *The Writing on the Wall* (1985), p. 350.

Chapter 53

539 Peter Shore, *Leading the Left* (1993), p. 128.
540 John Golding, *Hammer of the Left* (2003), p. 101.

541 Edward Pearce, *Looking Down on Mrs Thatcher* (1987), p. 4.
542 Roy Mason, *Paying the Price* (1999), p. 231.
543 Pearce, *Looking Down on Mrs Thatcher*, p. 4.
544 Shore, *Leading the Left*, p. 128.
545 Roy Hattersley, *Who Goes Home* (1995), p. 221.
546 Tony Benn, *Conflicts of Interest, Diaries 1977–80* (1990), p. 543.
547 It should not be forgotten that the existing system had elected Keir Hardie, Ramsay MacDonald, Clement Attlee and Harold Wilson, all of whom were candidates either of the left or having the support of the left against rival candidates of the party right whom they had defeated.
548 Joe Ashton, *Red Rose Blues* (2000), p. 209.
549 e.g. MP Jack Ashley, David Warburton of the GMWU and AUEW General Secretary John Boyd.
550 Benn, *Conflicts of Interest* (1990), p. 543.
551 A rising star of Liverpool City Council.
552 Golding, *Hammer of the Left*, pp. 107–8.
553 Benn, *Conflicts of Interest*, p. 545.
554 Golding, *Hammer of the Left*, p. 101.
555 MP for Edinburgh East and as Transport Minister 1997–98, one of the handful of members of Blair's first Cabinet with previous ministerial experience: he had been a junior minister at Energy and Agriculture 1974–79.
556 Callaghan had been persuaded by Chief Whip Michael Cocks that the procedure for doing so would be so complex that it would bog down the government's programme for a year. Callaghan himself had been Home Secretary during the 1966–70 Labour government's attempt to reform it which, despite a majority of nearly one hundred, had descended into chaos and had been abandoned. Nevertheless, Callaghan later conceded that it had been 'a mistake' to block it in 1979. Golding, *Hammer of the Left*, p. 88.
557 TGWU boss Moss Evans.
558 Benn, *Conflicts of Interest*, p. 545.

Chapter 54

559 Edward Pearce, *Denis Healey* (2002), p. 533.
560 Mayhew, a Gaitskellite ex-minister and MP for Woolwich, was unhappy at Labour's leftward drift and defected to the Liberals in July 1974. He unsuccessfully fought Bath for his new party at the two subsequent general elections and though created a Liberal Life Peer in 1981 he remained in relative political obscurity.
561 David Owen, *Time to Declare* (1991), p. 426.
562 Bill Rodgers, *Fourth Among Equals* (2000), p. 168.
563 It was drafted in consultation with his former special adviser, Roger Liddle, and MPs John Horam, Bob Maclennan, Ian Wrigglesworth, Giles Radice, Bob Mitchell and Ken Weetch. Of these, all were to join the SDP apart from Radice and Weetch.
564 Rodgers, *Fourth Among Equals*, p. 198.
565 Ibid., p. 197.
566 John Golding, *Hammer of the Left* (2003), p. 122.
567 Owen, *Time to Declare*, p. 441.
568 Of the other MPs Mike Thomas, John Cartwright, Tom Ellis, John Horam, Eric Ogden, John Roper and Ian Wrigglesworth joined the SDP. Alan Fitch, Willie Hamilton, Arthur Palmer and Tom Urwin did not.

Chapter 55

569 Birkenhead delegate Richard Venton, proposing Composite 31, was a Militant employee and its official Merseyside spokesman (Michael Crick, *Militant* [1984], p. 157). Tony Mulhearn, Militant-supporting ex-PPC for Crosby, also spoke.

570 Mervyn Jones, *Michael Foot* (1995), p. 447.

571 Giles Radice, *Friends and Rivals* (2003), p. 290.

572 Tony Benn, *The End of an Era: Diaries 1980–1990* (1992), p. 30.

573 David Owen, *Time to Declare* (1991), p. 450.

574 Benn, *The End of an Era*, p. 31.

575 MP for Eton and Slough 1966-83 and Eccles 1987-97, Lestor was a junior minister 1968-70 and 1974-76, later serving in the shadow Cabinet under Kinnock, Smith and Blair.

576 John Golding, *Hammer of the Left* (2003), pp. 128-9.

577 Benn, *The End of an Era*, p. 32.

578 Joe Ashton, *Red Rose Blues* (2000), p. 210.

579 Ibid., p. 211-12.

580 Benn, *The End of an Era*, p. 32.

581 Roy Hattersley, *Who Goes Home* (1995), p. 220.

582 3,625,000 to 3,508,000.

583 3,609,000 votes to 3,511,000.

584 Golding, *Hammer of the Left*, p. 138.

585 Morell – Benn's former Special Adviser.

586 Derer – organiser of CLPD.

587 Benn, *The End of an Era*, p. 33.

588 Tony Benn, *Conflicts of Interest, Diaries 1977–80* (1990), p. 560.

Chapter 56

589 Clive Jenkins, *All Against the Collar* (1990), p. 188.

590 Roy Hattersley, *Who Goes Home* (1995), pp. 225-6.

591 James Prior.

592 Francis Pym.

593 Sir Ian Gilmour.

594 Norman St John Stevas.

595 George Younger.

596 Nick Edwards.

597 Peter Walker.

598 Lord Carrington.

599 Willie Whitelaw.

600 Sir Geoffrey Howe.

601 Reg Prentice: formerly Foot's colleague in the Labour Cabinet who, having defected to the Conservatives, had become in 1979 Conservative MP for Daventry and Minister of State for Social Security.

602 Sir Keith Joseph.

603 Such as John Grant and Dickson Mabon.

604 Such as Phillip Whitehead.

605 Hattersley, *Who Goes Home*, p. 225.

606 Benn knew he couldn't win on the votes of MPs alone, and other candidates of the softer left were disinclined to challenge.

607 MPs Ken Weetch, Giles Radice, George Robertson and Phillip Whitehead.

608 Apart from the lone voice of Birkenhead MP Frank Field who was a pioneer advocate of

One Member One Vote (OMOV).

609 Bill Rodgers, *Fourth Among Equals* (2000), p. 204.
610 Denis Healey, *The Time of My Life* (1989), p. 479.
611 John Golding, *Hammer of the Left* (2003), p. 157.
612 Ford did exactly what Joe Ashton had predicted deselected long-serving MPs would do: he stood again at the next election (as Independent Labour) against the new official Labour candidate, Pat Wall. The split vote enabled the Conseravtives to win the seat on only 34.3 per cent of the vote.
613 General Secretary, National Union of Seamen.
614 Including Tony Banks, Ken Coates, Vladimir Derer, Stuart Holland, Frances Morell, Michael Meacher, Chris Mullin, Jo Richardson, Reg Race, Audrey and Valerie Wise and Benn's sons Hilary and Stephen.
615 Tony Benn, *The End of an Era: Diaries 1980–1990* (1992), pp. 70-71.
616 Formerly Herbert Bowden.

Chapter 57
617 Tony Benn, *The End of an Era: Diaries 1980–1990* (1992), p. 168.
618 Michael Foot, *Loyalists and Loners* (1986), p. 122.
619 Frank Chapple, *Sparks Fly!* (1984), pp. 144-5.
620 Edward Pearce, *The Senate of Lilliput* (1983), pp. 30-31.
621 Foot, *Loyalists and Loners*, pp. 122-3.
622 John Silkin, *Changing Battlefields* (1987), p. 48.
623 Terry Duffy of the Engineers, Sid Weighell of the Railwaymen, Bill Sirs of the Steelworkers, Bryan Stanley of the Telephone Engineers, Frank Chapple of the Electricians, Roy Grantham of white-collar APEX, Bill Whatley of the Shopworkers, Tom Jackson of the Postal Workers and Joe Gormley of the Miners.
624 Core organisers were Bryan Stanley and John Golding of the POEU, Denis Howell and Roger Godsiff of APEX, Charlie Turnock of the NUR, Sandy (son of former TUC General Secretary Victor) Feather of the ISTC and John Spellar of the EETPU.
625 Lord Longford, *Diary of a Year* (1982), p. 182.
626 Radice, a Wykehamist former head of the GMWU Research Department, and MP 1973-2001, would serve in the shadow Cabinet 1983-87 and play a key role in the intellectual battle to bring Labour back from the political wilderness during the 1990s.
627 John Golding, *Hammer of the Left* (2003), p. 204.
628 Ibid.
629 From a visit to Moscow.
630 Benn, *The End of an Era*, p. 70.
631 Silkin, *Changing Battlefields*, p. 80.

Chapter 58
632 Pontypridd MP 1970-88, John helped found the 'Labour First' group of MPs a bottom-up group of moderates which operated under the 'Solidarity' umbrella, on whose slate he was elected to the shadow Cabinet 1981-83. Having succeeded Rodgers as defence spokesman in December 1980, December 1981 saw Foot move him to shadow Social Security, where he remained until 1983. He had been junior RAF minister 1974-76, where he had robustly resisted calls for defence cuts, and Home Office Minister of State 1976-79.
633 Michael Crick, *Militant* (1984), p. 86.
634 Ibid., p. 207.
635 On 28 October 1982, Spellar would achieve a unique feat for a Labour Party candidate

during the period 1971–86: he would win a seat off the Conservatives at a parliamentary by-election. Not since Bromsgrove in 1971 had this been achieved and not until Nick Raynesford's victory at Fulham in 1986 was this feat to be repeated, and after that not until 1989 at the Vale of Glamorgan.

636 Edward Pearce, *Hummingbirds and Hyenas* (1985), p. 40.
637 By now Wall had succeeded in deselecting and supplanting as Labour candidate at Bradford North the sitting Labour MP Ben Ford.

Chapter 59

638 BBC/Gallup/Harris polls cited by Geoffrey Alderman, *Britain: A One Party State?* (1989), p. 15.
639 Edward Pearce, *The Senate of Lilliput* (1983), p. 40.
640 Cited in Robert Harris, *The Making of Neil Kinnock* (1984), p. 208.
641 Including Denis Healey; John Smith; Merlyn Rees; Gerald Kaufman; Eric Varley. Callaghan also voted for Hattersley.
642 Cited in Frank Chapple, *Sparks Fly!* (1984), p. 198.
643 John Grant, *Blood Brothers* (1992), pp. 126–7.
644 Chapple, *Sparks Fly!*, p. 194.
645 Cited in ibid., p. 198.
646 *Observer*, 4 September 1983, cited in Harris, *The Making of Neil Kinnock*, p. 226.
647 Lord Sawyer, interview with the author, 30 June 2004.
648 Pearce, *The Senate of Lilliput*, pp. 32–3.
649 Peter Shore, *Leading the Left* (1993), p. 155.
650 Martin Westlake, *Neil Kinnock* (2001), p. 254.
651 Roy Hattersley, *Who Goes Home* (1995), p. 260–1.
652 Including Liverpool's Tony Mulhearn and regular Brighton delegate Ray Apps.
653 MP for Glasgow Cathcart 1979–2001.
654 MP for Blackburn since 1979, formerly Special Adviser to Barbara Castle (1974–76) and Peter Shore (1976–79) and since 1997 a senior Cabinet minister under Tony Blair.
655 John Golding, *Hammer of the Left* (2003), p. 335.
656 Denis Healey, *The Time of My Life* (1989), p. 506.
657 Edward Pearce, *Denis Healey* (2002), p. 579.

Chapter 60

658 Instructing the union's trustees to consult with lawyers with a view to investing NUM funds in overseas locations from which it would be difficult for the courts to sequestrate the funds should the union be found to be in breach of the law.
659 Paul Routledge, *Arthur Scargill* (1993), pp. 142, 144.
660 Anthony King (ed.), *British Political Opinion 1937–2000: The Gallup Polls* (2001), p. 337.
661 Cited in Eric Hammond, *Maverick!* (1992), pp. 47–8.
662 Cited in Routledge, *Arthur Scargill*, p. 179.
663 Paul Routledge, 'Arthur Scargill', in Greg Rosen (ed.), *Dictionary of Labour Biography* (2001), p. 506.
664 Routledge, *Arthur Scargill*, pp. 183, 187, 145.
665 Hammond, *Maverick!*, p. 55.
666 Tony Benn, *The End of an Era: Diaries 1980–1990* (1992), p. 423.
667 Hammond, *Maverick!*, p. 43.
668 Benn, *The End of an Era*, p. 425.

Chapter 61
669 Martin Westlake, *Neil Kinnock* (2001), p. 321.
670 Rt Hon. Patricia Hewitt MP, letter to the author, 26 June 2003.
671 Tony Benn, *The End of an Era: Diaries 1980–1990* (1992), p. 424.
672 Westlake, *Neil Kinnock*, p. 326.
673 Edward Pearce, *Looking Down on Mrs Thatcher* (1987), pp. 129–30.
674 Since 1997 a Liverpool Labour MP.
675 Formerly James Callaghan's PPS and subsequently a Cabinet Minister under Tony Blair.
676 Benn, *The End of an Era*, p. 425.
677 David Blunkett, *On A Clear Day* (2002), p. 157.
678 Lord Sawyer, interview with the author, 30 June 2004.
679 Blunkett, *On A Clear Day*, p. 157.

Chapter 62
680 Roy Hattersley, *Who Goes Home* (1995), p. 293.
681 Rt Hon. Patricia Hewitt MP, letter to the author, 26 June 2003.
682 Colin Hughes and Patrick Wintour, *Labour Rebuilt* (1990), p. 26.
683 Cited in Geoffrey Alderman, *Britain: A One Party State?* (1989), pp. 21–22.
684 Peter Kellner, *Thorns and Roses* (1992), p. 124.
685 Other advisers included Roger Jowell of the British Social Attitudes Survey, Andrew Mackintosh, formerly Labour GLC leader and latterly of IFF Research Ltd, Andrew Shaw and John Curtice of Liverpool University, Paul Ormerod of the Henley Centre and Rex Osborn, Labour HQ's new Political Intelligence Officer.
686 Hughes and Wintour, *Labour Rebuilt*, p. 62.
687 Ibid., p. 79.
688 Ibid., pp. 79–80.
689 Tony Benn, *The End of an Era, Diaries 1980–90* (1994), p. 542.
690 Eric Heffer, *Never a Yes Man* (1991), p. 223.
691 John P. Mackintosh, 'Has Social Democracy Failed in Britain?', *Political Quarterly*, July–September 1978, pp. 266–7.
692 Martin Westlake, *Neil Kinnock* (2001), p. 444.

Chapter 63
693 John Major, *The Autobiography* (1999), pp. 307–8.
694 Roy Hattersley, *Who Goes Home* (1995), p. 305.
695 Ibid.
696 Neil Kinnock, 'Reforming the Labour Party', *Contemporary Record*, vol. 8, Winter 1994, pp. 537–45.

Chapter 64
697 Roy Hattersley, *Who Goes Home* (1995), p. 287.
698 Edward Pearce, *Hummingbirds and Hyenas* (1985), p. 91.
699 John Major, *The Autobiography* (1999), p. 303.
700 John Sopel, *Tony Blair* (1995), pp. 156–7; John Rentoul, *Tony Blair* (1995).
701 Andy McSmith, *Faces of Labour* (1996), p. 330.
702 Ibid.
703 Lord Sawyer, interview with the author, 30 June 2004.

Chapter 65

704 Jordan had succeeded his fellow Brummie moderate Terry Duffy as AEU President in 1985. With the merger of his AEU with the EETPU in 1992, Jordan had become President of the new AEEU.
705 Colin Brown, *Fighting Talk* (1997), p. 254.
706 John Major, *The Autobiography* (1999), p. 554.
707 Paul Routledge, *Gordon Brown* (1998), pp. 184–5.

Chapter 66

708 ICM for the *Sunday Express*, Gallup for the *Sunday Telegraph* and MORI for the *Sunday Times*, cited in Paul Routledge, *Gordon Brown* (1998), p. 197.
709 John Rentoul, *Tony Blair* (1995), p. 234.
710 Colin Brown, *Fighting Talk* (1997), p. 278.
711 Roy Hattersley, *Who Goes Home* (1995), p. 290.
712 Brown, *Fighting Talk*, p. 290.
713 Rentoul, *Tony Blair*, p. 425.
714 Far from being ahistorical, as its critics suggested, this was a phrase resonant of the Benthamite utilitarianism in which the early Fabian Society had been rooted.
715 Philip Gould, *The Unfinished Revolution* (1998), p. 229.
716 John Patten, former Conservative Education Secretary under John Major.
717 At the time MEP for London Central, Newens was a former chair of the Tribune Group of MPs, having been MP for both Epping (1964–70) and Harlow (1974–83).
718 The Militant-dominated shell of Labour Party Young Socialists had finally been shut down a few years previously and the new organisation, 'Young Labour', was thriving.
719 At the 1997 general election just over two years later, Twigg, by then General Secretary of the Fabian Society, would defeat Conservative Defence Secretary Michael Portillo at Enfield Southgate. His victory produced one of the iconic images of the election night.
720 Gould, *The Unfinished Revolution*, p. 230.

Chapter 67

721 Though Blair had made him shadow Foreign Secretary, Cook retained responsibility for dealing with the 'arms-to-Iraq' issue that he had carried under the shadow DTI portfolio he had had under John Smith.
722 John Kampfner, *Robin Cook* (1998), p. 109.
723 The motion that Labour had put down in the Commons on 26 November 1992, when the scandal had first come to light.
724 Of 26 November 1992.
725 Hansard, 17 November 1992; Vol. 214, c. 136.
726 Hansard, 23 November 1992; Vol. 214, c. 631.
727 Others included Trade and Industry Secretary Ian Lang, Leader of the House of Commons Tony Newton, Scottish Secretary Michael Forsyth and Treasury Chief Secretary William Waldegrave. Other defeated Conservative MPs included a host of ex-Cabinet members, including Major's former Chancellor Norman Lamont, Jonathan Aitken, Jeremy Hanley, David Hunt and David Mellor. Labour gains included Margaret Thatcher's old Finchley seat and Anthony Eden's old seat at Warwick. The Conservatives secured their lowest tally of seats (165) since 1906, their fewest votes (9.6m) since 1929 and their lowest vote share (30.7 per cent) since 1832.

Afterword

1 Gallup opinion poll ratings for previous Labour governments included 28 per cent for Harold Wilson's government in May/June 1968 and 30 per cent for James Callaghan's government in

November 1976. Attlee's government never descended below 38 per cent (November 1947) but it is likely that the less accurate opinion polls of that era exaggerated Labour's vote by several percentage points.

2   Brown, who published an acclaimed biography of James Maxton based on a reworking of his PhD, would have been in serious contention for a successful career as an academic historian had he not been tempted by Parliament.

3   See Chapter 50.

4   Anthony Crosland, *The Conservative Enemy* (1962), p. 174.

5   Noel Annan, *Our Age* (1990), p. 365.

6   Peter Jay, who married James Callaghan's daughter Margaret, who under Tony Blair was later to serve in Cabinet in her own right as Leader of the House of the Lords, was also the son of Callaghan's former Cabinet colleague Douglas Jay.

7   So called after the lavender-coloured notepaper on which it was drawn up by Wilson's political secretary and long-term associate Baroness (Marcia) Falkender. Infamously, one of the ennoblements it created, Lord Kagan, manufacturer of Wilson's trademark Gannex raincoat, would be imprisoned soon after for tax offences. One of the knighthoods went to James Goldsmith, a Falkender associate, who would later found the Referendum Party.

8   Fabian, poet and author of 'If I should die think only this of me: That there's some corner of a foreign field that is forever England . . . '

9   Both Dalton and others sometimes referred to his young protégés, who included Anthony Crosland, Roy Jenkins and Douglas Jay, as his 'poodles'. Stephen Howe, 'Hugh Dalton', in Kevin Jefferys, *Labour Forces* (2002), p. 45.

10   Born in Lanarkshire, the son of a postman and wartime factory worker, Reid was with John Prescott one of the few members of any post-1980s government not to have entered higher education directly from school. Like Prescott he was later a mature student, ultimately securing a PhD in economic history from Stirling University. Serving as the Scottish Labour Party's Research Officer 1979–83 he worked in Neil Kinnock's leader's office 1983–85 and became MP for Motherwell North in 1987. Appointed a junior defence minister in 1997 he won swift promotion to Cabinet, serving in several key portfolios including Scotland, Northern Ireland, Health and Defence.

11   Speech to Scottish Labour Party annual conference, 5 March 1999.

12   Paul Richards, *Tony Blair in His Own Words* (2004), p. xvi.

13   'Blair: we're better than the Tories' by Matthew Tempest, political correspondent, *Guardian*, Tuesday 10 September 2002.

14   A former Edinburgh University SRC president and city councillor, Foulkes had defeated Jim Sillars at Ayr in the 1979 election. One of the most articulate Commons debaters, his frontbench career culminated in a post of Minister of State for International Development. He retired from the Commons in 2005, becoming Lord Foulkes.

15   Harold Wilson was the only post-war PM to resign entirely voluntarily, and he gave warning to but a few intimates and senior Cabinet colleagues.

16   The 2005 turnout was marginally improved on 2001, which had the lowest turnout of any post-war general election.

17   Apart from in 1997 and 2001, not since the nineteenth century had the Conservative Party or its predecessors had a vote share as low as in 2005.

18   A left-wing Welsh Labour MP since 1984 and an MEP 1979–84, Clwyd was elected chair of the Parliamentary Labour Party in the new Parliament of May 2005. A former chair of the Tribune Group, she was a shadow Cabinet member under both Neil Kinnock and John Smith.

Index

Royal Shakespeare Company 485-6
Runciman, Walter 99
Russell, Bertrand 196, 222
Russia 62, 85-9, 110, 117, 161-2, *see also* Soviet
   Union
Ryden, Dave 424

Salisbury, Lord 28
Sandys, Duncan 272
Sankey, Lord 79
Sapper, Alan 439
Savoy Hotel 52
Sawyer, Tom 382, 447, 475-6, 495
selective employment tax (SET) 259
Sex Discrimination Act (1976) 347
Sexton, James 24-5
Scanlon, Hugh 279, 281, 285-6, 289, 375
Scargill, Arthur 417, 447, 453-5, 457-8, 484, 508,
   510-11
   speech to Labour Party conference
      (1984) 455
      (1985) 458
school leaving age 71, 78, 175, 177, 278, 291
schools 175-8
scientific revolution 221-2, 249-54
Scotland 360-7
   referendum (1979) 367
   and Wales Bill (1976) 362
   Devolution Bill 362-3, 376
Scottish Daily News 331
Scottish Labour Party 19, 24, 361-2
Scottish Miners' Federation 24
Scottish National Party 361, 363-4, 383-5, 387
Scott report, the 513-5
Scotsman 148
Shackleton, David 32, 34, 40
Shawcross, Sir Hartley 137, 163, 425
   speech to Commons (1945) 137-8
Shaw, George Bernard 24, 28, 59
Shaw, Tom 48-9, 60
Sheldon, Robert 202
Shelley, Percy Bysshe 483

Shinwell, Emanuel 48, 50, 54, 71, 83, 85, 91, 97, 98,
   112, 127-8, 135, 159-60, 162, 169, 171, 179, 184,
   202, 223, 227, 264
shipowners' 'model budget' 52-3
Shopworkers' Union 24
Shore, Peter 221, 239, 251, 259, 270, 288, 294, 298-
   301, 324, 354, 381, 388-90, 409, 418, 421, 425,
   434, 444, 449
   speech to Labour Party EEC conference (1971)
      298
Short, Renee 295
Short, Ted 324, 347, 362
Silkin, John 295, 347, 388, 406, 418, 421, 427, 431
Sillars, Jim 362, 367, 383
Silverman, Sydney 122-3, 140
Simon, Sir John 70, 79, 86
Simpson, Derek 521
Singapore 116
Sino-Japanese dispute 95
Sinn Fein 330
Sirs, Bill 430-1
   speech to Labour Party conference (1981) 430-1
Six Day War (1967) 266
Skinner, Dennis 388, 450
slum clearance 71
Smart, Jack 369
   speech to Labour Party conference (1978) 369
Smillie, Bob 24
Smith, Ian 423
Smith, John 304, 346, 362, 444, 489
   as leader of the Labour Party (1992-4) 489-91,
      496-503, 505
   R. H. Tawney Memorial Lecture (1993) 490-1
   speech to Commons (1993) 496-8, 500-1
Snowdon, Philip 35-6, 43, 48-50, 60, 66, 70-1, 75,
   78-9
speech to parliament (1906) 36-7
Social Democratic Federation (SDF) 25-6, 39, 41
Social Democrat Party (SDP) 412, 425-6, 430, 437-
   8, 442
   and Liberal alliance 435, 443, 475
   German 87-9, 110
social insurance 120